Perspectives on Language and Literacy

Beyond the Here and Now

SARAH W. BECK

and

LESLIE NABORS OLÁH

Editors

Harvard Educational Review

Reprint Series No. 35

Library of Congress Card Number 00-136366
ISBN 0-916690-39-3

Harvard Educational Review
8 Story Street
5th Floor
Cambridge, MA 02138

Cover Design: Alyssa Morris
Cover Photographs: Susie Fitzhugh and Dody Riggs
Editorial Production: Dody Riggs
Typography: Sheila Walsh

Dedication

*We dedicate this book
to our families,
and especially to our parents,
our first language teachers*

CONTENTS

INTRODUCTION

The subtitle of this volume, *Beyond the Here and Now*, was inspired by a concept commonly shared between the fields of language and literacy. "Beyond the here and now" refers to one of the most fundamental characteristics of language: it allows us to communicate the nonpresent. Only through language can we share information and ideas about last night's dinner, tomorrow's errands, or the hypothetical result of a hypothetical raise in salary. This phrase touches on a second significant feature of literacy, in that written text is necessarily decontextualized. In this way, literacy helps to preserve language so that it can be accessed at a future time. A third way in which the subtitle captures the spirit of this volume is more concrete. We have selected this collection of classic articles previously published in the *Harvard Educational Review* to represent a broad overview of research and theory concerning language and literacy. Our intention is both to provide a historical overview of trends in the fields of language and literacy research — with chapters such as Roger Brown and Ursula Bellugi's "Three Processes in the Child's Acquisition of Syntax" — and also to present articles that will have an impact on future research and practice — such as "Late Immersion and Language of Instruction in Hong Kong High Schools: Achievement Growth in Language and Nonlanguage Subjects" by Herbert Marsh, Kit-Tai Hau, and Chit-Kwong Kong. This collection also contains pieces that reevaluate classic works for new ideas, such as Penny Lee's "Language in Thinking and Learning: Pedagogy and the New Whorfian Framework." *Perspectives on Language and Literacy* represents the two fields' past accomplishments, as well as their contemporary concerns. Naturally, we hope that our book offers inspiration for future work in language and literacy as well.

The nature of the relationship between language and literacy has generated much discussion and debate. While some scholars view literacy as subsumed in language, others view language as one component of literacy. Of all the chapters in this volume, the former view is best represented by Charles Read's "Preschool Children's Knowledge of English Phonology," the latter view by Paulo Freire's "The Adult Literacy Process as Cultural Action for Freedom." Each of these two perspectives on the relationship between language and literacy entails a set of assumptions about the prerequisites for success at reading and writing, as well as what it means to be literate. As editors of this book we do not argue for one view or the other. Rather, our intention is to present language and literacy as two facets of the more general phenomenon of communication: making an imagined world known to an actual audience, or actual experience to an imagined audience. At the same time, we acknowledge that not all of the research reported in this collection is concerned to the same degree with the communicative nature of language. For example, several of the chapters in Part One, "Cognitive and Developmental Approaches to Language and Literacy Acquisition," take a more innatist view of human language. Read's "Preschool Children's Knowledge of English Phonology," Carol Chomsky's "Stages in Language Development and Reading Exposure," and Brown and Bellugi's "Three Processes in the Child's Acquisition of Syntax" reflect the influence at that time of the school of thought founded in the late 1950s by Noam Chomsky. Even though Brown and Bellugi's research would become instrumental in steering researchers toward a more sociocultural approach to observing language acquisition, they still postulate a latent structure that drives early syntactic development.

Given that language and literacy are linked in this way, it should come as no surprise that we observe parallel trends in the traditions of research in both fields. First, the trend toward conducting research in naturalistic environments — rather than clinical laboratory settings — reflects an emerging understanding that the phenomenon of communication is best studied in an authentic context. Furthermore, learner-centered research has now come into its own, especially where the fields of language and literacy and education overlap. For example, in "Late Immersion and Language of Instruction in Hong Kong High Schools: Achievement Growth in Language and Nonlanguage Subjects," Marsh and his colleagues designed their research on bilingual education in Hong Kong high schools to measure the students' second language exposure in a variety of settings, from traditional language instruction to the amount of the second language used in non-instructional activities. This approach more accurately reflects how students experience language learning in school than would a cursory review of language curriculum. Sofía Vernon and Emilia Ferreiro make a strong case for variation in the methods young children use to analyze speech, and advise that teachers take this variation into account when planning children's literacy instruction. Similarly, María de la Luz Reyes's chapter presents compelling evidence for the importance of adjusting or even departing from pedagogical approaches such as process writing and whole language when they do not meet the needs of linguistic-minority students. A final trend in both fields, noted by Kenji Hakuta and Herlinda Cancino in their review of trends in second language acquisition, is the prominence of discourse analysis as a research method. This method, represented in this volume by the interactions between Nathaniel and his mother in the second half of Catherine Snow's chapter, entails analyzing extended passages of written or oral text in order to study the features of these texts that support or hinder communication.

This volume is an updated version of the previous *HER* collection, *Language Issues in Literacy and Bilingual/Multicultural Education*, edited by Masahiko Minami and Bruce P. Kennedy in 1991. It almost goes without saying that the scholarly areas of language and literacy have changed substantially in the decade since publication of the previous compilation, and the content and organization of *Perspectives on Language and Literacy* reflects these changes. Not only have we added several recent articles to our assortment of classic works, but readers will find that we have changed the arrangement of articles as well. For example, Part Three, "Crosslinguistic and Bilingual Issues in Language and Literacy," is devoted to the growing field of bilingualism and to the still-evolving area of crosslinguistic studies. The fact that we now have an entire section, "Critical Perspectives on Language and Literacy Education," dedicated to the application of critical theory to language and literacy education is indicative of the influence that critical theory has continued to have on this field since the publication of Friere's "The Adult Literacy Process as Cultural Action for Freedom" in 1970.

Perspectives on Language and Literacy contains two features that will help to place the individual chapters in a larger context of scholarship. First, each section begins with an introduction in which we trace the development of each approach to language and literacy research and discuss how each chapter illustrates this approach. We have also provided editors' notes at the end of each section that recommend other *HER* resources, including book and essay reviews, on specific topics in language and literacy.

In this volume we have created four sections that in our view reflect the themes and theoretical perspectives that have been the most salient in language and literacy research over the past thirty years. In keeping with the title of this collection, we recognize that they may not continue to be the most salient themes. We have carefully chosen recent articles that we believe will have an impact on future research and practice, along with classic studies that, because of their significance, may continue to be mined for new ideas. We do recognize that we have not covered all major topics in the fields of language and literacy research. For example, we have not represented the large and significant corpus of clinical and diagnostic research on language deficits and reading impairments. While this strand of research has much to contribute to our understanding of the mental processes underlying language and literacy, we feel that this work speaks to a more particular audience than we aim to reach with this collection.

In Part One, "Cognitive and Developmental Approaches to Language and Literacy Acquisition," we have grouped together the cognitive and developmental studies because the earliest research into language acquisition and literacy development came from these traditions. Furthermore, the developmental studies in language use from this early era tended to look at *cognitive* development as reflected in the subjects' language and literacy use. The focus in this tradition was on the mind as an entity that operated upon and attempted to make sense of the environment, the environment of sounds and symbols. In keeping with the theoretical perspectives represented in this section, we have arranged the articles by the developmental age they represent, concluding with a theoretical piece that suggests new approaches to the relationship between language and thought. Penny Lee's provocative reexamination (ch. 4) of Benjamin Whorf's theory of the relationship between language and thought demonstrates the intellectual passion for revisiting classic scholarship that we hope this anthology will inspire in its readers. Although Whorf's work may be considered outdated by some researchers, albeit historically important, Lee suggests how some of Whorf's forgotten hypotheses might contribute to and even alter the course of future language research.

Part Two, "Sociocultural Approaches to Language and Literacy," differs markedly from Part One in its concern with language and literacy as used in naturalistic contexts, rather than as tested in clinical or laboratory settings. The sociocultural perspective has been widely adopted in the field of education and applied to a variety of disciplines such as math, science, and experiential education. In our field this perspective implies the assumption that individuals' language and literacy abilities are best studied in naturalistic settings that allow the researcher to document and analyze the role of social or cultural context in promoting the development of individuals' linguistic abilities. Several of the articles in this section also engage with the relationship between speech and writing at a cultural and individual level. David Olson's and Sylvia Scribner and Michael Cole's articles take opposing sides on the "ontogeny-phylogeny" argument that individual development from oral language proficiency to literacy mirrors a similar trajectory at the level of culture.

In Part Three of this volume, "Crosslinguistic and Bilingual Issues in Language and Literacy," we have grouped research that addresses these two topics because both raise important questions about universal and particular aspects of linguistic processes — for example, the extent to which knowledge of one language is transferable to a second language, or whether the relationship between literacy development and phonological knowledge is the same across all languages. Kenji Hakuta and Herlinda Cancino's 1977 essay on trends in second language research remains relevant to this day because it provides a concise and lucid overview of the major theoretical perspectives on and methodological approaches to second language acquisition. Building on the theoretical foundation laid out in this essay, Marsh, Hau, and Kong's recent study of achievement patterns in secondary students learning English as a foreign language provides compelling and statistically powerful evidence pertaining to the intellectual consequences of second language instruction. Reyes's chapter also explores important pedagogical issues in the instruction of bilingual students. Among the chapters in this section, hers is especially relevant to the focus of this book because it explicitly links second language instruction to literacy. Finally, Vernon and Ferreiro's recent research represents the cutting edge in research on language development.

The final section of the book, "Critical Perspectives on Language and Literacy Education," contains reprints of articles that reflect rapidly developing fields in language and literacy research. We lead this section with Paulo Freire's landmark essay on a radical method for teaching literacy to poor, disenfranchised adults. The subsequent chapters build on Freire's theory by critically examining the links among language use, literacy practices, and institutional power structures. The authors of these chapters question long-held assumptions about the cultural neutrality of school curricula and assessments, suggesting that in a multicultural society we need to consider carefully whose interests are served by which approaches to literacy and language teaching. These authors, then, are concerned with the role of communication in pedagogical institutions, where power structures and their impact on learning are especially salient.

We hope that *Perspectives on Language and Literacy* will appeal to a wide range of audiences. We believe that this book will be useful as an introduction to research and theory in the fields of language and literacy; we also believe that it may serve as a reference for landmark scholarship in these fields. Offering an abundance of insights and challenges, this collection is designed to guide both apprentice and veteran scholars beyond current paradigms and into the future of language and literacy research.

Sarah W. Beck
Leslie Nabors Oláh

PART ONE

Cognitive and
Developmental Approaches to
Language and Literacy Acquisition

PART ONE

Cognitive and Developmental Approaches to Language and Literacy Acquisition

This first part offers three classic studies in language and literacy acquisition as well as a contemporary reexamination of Benjamin Whorf's theories on the relationship between language and thought. In many ways, these four works speak to major themes that permeate many subfields in language and literacy. The chapters in this section, for example, address enduring issues such as the extent to which language reflects thought and the interwoven development of spoken and written language.

The first three chapters are arranged in order of the chronological development of the subjects under study. Roger Brown and Ursula Bellugi's chapter, "Three Processes in the Child's Acquisition of Syntax," addresses grammatical development in its earliest stage. This study emerged from a graduate seminar that Roger Brown held at Harvard University in the early 1960s. The research resulting from this seminar has had such a fundamental influence on the field of child language acquisition that Catherine Snow has claimed that the era of modern child language research began with the 1964 publication of Brown and Bellugi's original article in *HER* (Snow, 1994). In this chapter, Brown and Bellugi explore the nature of early grammar produced by two children who were just beginning to combine words to form sentences. Their first finding, which may be taken for granted today, was that "the dialogue between mother and child does not read like a transcribed dialogue between two adults" (p. 8). They also found, contrary to Noam Chomsky's claims at the time, that the language input to these young children was "perfectly grammatical." In other words, it seemed as though these children and their mothers were engaging in strategies that facilitated, or at least supported, the children's language development. Three processes were identified that specifically contribute to syntactic development: imitation and reduction, imitation and expansion, and induction of the latent structure. By demonstrating that children engage in this last process, induction of grammar, and that interlocutors help to "externalize the child's search for the regularities of English syntax" (p. 16), Brown and Bellugi again challenged Chomsky's view that language grammar is part of an innate mechanism.

Once children enter school, they are faced with an additional language-learning task: the development of literacy. The monumental challenge of learning how to read in English is further complicated by the opaque, or indirect, correspondence between English sounds and letters, more technically known as *phonemes* and *graphemes*. Charles Read's "Preschool Children's Knowledge of English Phonology" demonstrates that English-speaking children come to preschool with theories about English

3

sound-letter relationships. The evidence for this claim comes from Read's study of spontaneous spelling among 135 children, the youngest of whom was three and a half at the time of the study. These writings indicate that not only do children hold hypotheses concerning the English spelling system, but that "each child arrived at roughly the same system" (p. 25) for representing English phoneme-grapheme correspondences. Furthermore, these children's judgments reflect the phonetic properties of the English language, such as nasality, syllabicity, backness, height, and affrication. Read's message to preschool teachers is clear: "We can no longer assume that a child must approach reading and writing as an untrained animal approaches a maze — with no discernable prior conception of its structure" (p. 47).

This is not to say that the relationship between language acquisition and literacy development is unidirectional; in fact, in "Stages in Language Development and Reading Exposure," Carol Chomsky's study of thirty-six elementary schoolchildren aged five to ten, Chomsky indicates that some features of language development may benefit from increased reading exposure. She first identifies these children's "shared order of acquisition of structures" (p. 51) by using comprehension and production measures developed for this specific study. In the second part of her study, Chomsky investigates the relationship between the amount and complexity of reading and the rate of linguistic development, and finds positive correlations between reading and linguistic development and between IQ and linguistic development. Chomsky and Read agree on one final message — that children come to school with their "own internal organization" of language — but Chomsky's findings also point to the substantial linguistic development that occurs after children enter school.

The final chapter in this section helps to connect the empirical findings in chapters one through three with broader concerns about the relationship between language and thought. In "Language in Thinking and Learning: Pedagogy and the New Whorfian Framework," Penny Lee reports on her investigation of Benjamin Whorf's published texts and unpublished notes held in the Yale University archives. While Whorf (along with his mentor Edward Sapir) is best known for the linguistic relativity hypothesis, which posits that we can only think what our language allows us to represent, Lee argues that the scholarly attention given to this hypothesis has obscured the complexity of Whorf's original thinking. Lee proposes "twelve elements of theme and theory that interweave in Whorf's thinking" (p. 80), of which linguistic relativity is only one. We find Lee's chapter to be a refreshing reexamination of an oft-stereotyped theory of language and thought.

This section begins by presenting three classics in the field that are still relevant to the study of language development today. The authors of chapters one through three present their findings with an incredible attention to and respect for linguistic detail. In addition, Read's and Chomsky's studies are notable in their treatment of both language and literacy development. This section ends with a reminder of more global issues in language and thought — a perfect complement to the empirical detail presented in these chapters. We hope that Lee's work will have a similar effect on the study of Whorf's thinking in days to come.

REFERENCE

Snow, C. E. (1994). Introduction. In C. Gallaway & B. J. Richards (Eds.), *Input and interaction in language acquisition* (pp. 3–12). Cambridge, Eng.: Cambridge University Press.

EDITORS' NOTE: COGNITIVE AND DEVELOPMENTAL APPROACHES TO LANGUAGE AND LITERACY

For further reading about cognitive and developmental perspectives on language and literacy, we suggest these resources published in the Harvard Educational Review:

G. Omani Collison, "Concept Formation in a Second Language: A Study of Ghana School Children," August 1974, pp. 441–457.

Leslie Nabors Oláh, Editor's Review of *How Language Comes to Children: From Birth to Two Years* by Bénédicte de Boysson-Bardies and *How Children Learn the Meanings of Words* by Paul Bloom, Winter 2000, pp. 538–543.

Frank Smith, "Making Sense of Reading — and of Reading Instruction," August 1977, pp. 386–395.

Catherine E. Snow, "Literacy and Language: Relationships during the School Years," in this volume, pp. 161–186.

Sofía A. Vernon and Emilia Ferreiro, "Writing Development: A Neglected Variable in the Consideration of Phonological Awareness," in this volume, pp. 307–325.

Three Processes in the
Child's Acquisition of Syntax

ROGER BROWN
URSULA BELLUGI

Some time in the second six months of life, most children say a first intelligible word. A few months later most children are saying many words, and some children go about the house all day long naming things (*table, doggie, ball*, etc.) and actions (*play, see, drop*, etc.) and an occasional quality (*blue, broke, bad*, etc.). At about eighteen months children are likely to begin constructing two-word utterances; such a one, for instance, as *Push car*.

A construction such as *Push car* is not just two single-word utterances spoken in a certain order. As single-word utterances (they are sometimes called holophrases) both *push* and *car* would have primary stresses and terminal intonation contours. When they are two words programmed as a single utterance the primary stress would fall on *car* and so would the highest level of pitch. *Push* would be subordinated to *car* by a lesser stress and a lower pitch; the unity of the whole would appear in the absence of a terminal contour between words and the presence of such a contour at the end of the full sequence.

By the age of thirty-six months some children are so advanced in the construction process as to produce all of the major varieties of English simple sentences up to a length of ten or eleven words. For several years we have been studying the development of English syntax, of the sentence-constructing process, in children between eighteen and thirty-six months of age. Most recently we have made a longitudinal study of a boy and girl whom we shall call Adam and Eve. We began work with Adam and Eve in October of 1962 when Adam was twenty-seven months old and Eve eighteen months old. The two children were selected from some thirty whom we considered. They were selected primarily because their speech was exceptionally intelligible and because they talked a lot. We wanted to make it as easy as possible to transcribe accurately large quantities of child speech. Adam and Eve are the children of highly educated parents; the fathers were graduate students at Harvard and the mothers are both college graduates. Both Adam and Even were single children when we began the study. These facts must be remembered in generalizing the outcomes of the research.

Harvard Educational Review   Vol. 34   No. 2   Spring 1964, 133–151

While Adam is nine months older than Eve, his speech was only a little more advanced in October of 1962. The best single index of the level of speech development is the average length of utterance and in October 1962, Adam's average was 1.84 morphemes and Eve's was 1.40 morphemes. The two children stayed fairly close together in the year that followed; in the records for the thirty-eighth week Adam's average was 3.55 and Eve's, 3.27. The processes we shall describe appeared in both children.

Every second week we visited each child for at least two hours and made a tape recording of everything said by the child as well as of everything said to the child. The mother was always present and most of the speech to the child is hers. Both mother and child became very accustomed to our presence and learned to continue their usual routine with us as the observers.

One of us always made a written transcription, on the scene, of the speech of mother and child with notes about important actions and objects of attention. From this transcription and the tape a final transcription was made and these transcriptions constitute the primary data of the study. For many purposes we require a "distributional analysis" of the speech of the child. To this end the child's utterances in a given transcription were cross-classified and relisted under such headings as: "A + noun"; "Noun + verb"; "Verbs in the past"; "Utterances containing the pronoun *it*," etc. The categorized utterances expose the syntactic regularities of the child's speech.

Each week we met as a research seminar, with students of the psychology of language,[1] to discuss the state of the construction process in one of the two children as of that date. In these discussions small experiments were often suggested, experiments that had to be done within a few days if they were to be informative. At one time, for instance, we were uncertain whether Adam understood the semantic difference between putting a noun in subject position and putting it in object position. Consequently one of us paid an extra visit to Adam equipped with some toys. "Adam," we said, "show us the duck pushing the boat." And, when he had done so: "Now show us the boat pushing the duck."

Another week we noticed that Adam would sometimes pluralize nouns when they should have been pluralized and sometimes would not. We wondered if he could make grammatical judgments about the plural, if he could distinguish a correct form from an incorrect form. "Adam," we asked, "which is right, 'two shoes' or 'two shoe'?" His answer on that occasion, produced with explosive enthusiasm, was "Pop goes the weasel!" The two-year-old child does not make a perfectly docile experimental subject.

The dialogue between mother and child does not read like a transcribed dialogue between two adults. Table 1 offers a sample section from an early transcribed record. It has some interesting properties. The conversation is, in the first place, very much in the here and now. From the child there is no speech of the sort that Bloomfield called "displaced," speech about other times and other places. Adam's utterances in the early months were largely a coding of contemporaneous events and impulses. The mother's speech differs from the speech that adults use to one another in many ways. Her sentences are short and simple; for the most part they are the kinds of sentences that Adam will produce a year later.

TABLE 1

A Section from Adam's First Record

Adam	Mother
See truck, Mommy.	
See truck.	
	Did you see the truck?
No I see truck.	
	No, you didn't see it?
There goes one.	
There go one.	
	Yes, there goes one.
See a truck.	
See truck, Mommy.	
See truck.	
Truck.	
Put truck, Mommy.	
	Put the truck where?
Put truck window.	
	I think that one's too large to go in the window.

Perhaps because they are short, the sentences of the mother are perfectly grammatical. The sentences adults use to one another, perhaps because they are longer and more complex, are very often not grammatical, not well formed. Here, for instance, is a rather representative example produced at a conference of psychologists and linguists: "As far as I know, no one yet has done the in a way obviously now and interesting problem of doing in a sense a structural frequency study of the alternative syntactical in a given language, say, like English, the alternative possible structures, and how what their hierarchical probability of occurrence structure is."[2] It seems unlikely that a child could learn the patterns of English syntax from such speech. His introduction to English ordinarily comes in the form of a simplified, repetitive, and idealized dialect. It may be that such an introduction is necessary for the acquisition of syntax to be possible but we do not know that.

In the course of the brief interchange of Table 1 Adam imitates his mother in saying "There go one" immediately after she says "There goes one." The imitation is not perfect; Adam omits the inflection on the verb. His imitation is a reduction in that it omits something from the original. This kind of imitation with reduction is extremely common in the records of Adam and Eve and it is the first process we shall discuss.

IMITATION AND REDUCTION

Table 2 presents some model sentences spoken by the mothers and the imitations produced by Adam and Eve. These were selected from hundreds in the records in or-

TABLE 2

Some Imitations Produced by Adam and Eve

Model Utterance	Child's Imitation
Tank car	Tank car
Wait a minute	Wait a minute
Daddy's brief case	Daddy brief case
Fraser will be unhappy	Fraser unhappy
He's going out	He go out
That's an old time train	Old time train
It's not the same dog as Pepper	Dog Pepper
No, you can't write on Mr. Cromer's shoe	Write Cromer shoe

der to illustrate some general propositions. The first thing to notice is that the imitations preserve the word order of the model sentences. To be sure, words in the model are often missing from the imitation but the words preserved are in the order of the original. This is a fact that is so familiar and somehow reasonable that we did not at once recognize it as an empirical outcome rather than as a natural necessity. But of course it is not a necessity; the outcome could have been otherwise. For example, words could have been said back in the reverse of their original order, the most recent first. The preservation of order suggests that the model sentence is processed by the child as a total construction rather than as a list of words.

In English the order of words in a sentence is an important grammatical signal. Order is used to distinguish among subject, direct object, and indirect object and it is one of the marks of imperative and interrogative constructions. The fact that the child's first sentences preserve the word order of their models partially accounts for the ability of an adult to "understand" these sentences and so to feel that he is in communication with the child. It is conceivable that the child "intends" the meanings coded by his word orders and that, when he preserves the order of an adult sentence, he does so because he wants to say what the order says. It is also possible that he preserves word order just because his brain works that way and that he has no comprehension of the semantic contrasts involved. In some languages word order is not an important grammatical signal. In Latin, for instance, "Agricola amat puellam" has the same meaning as "Puellam amat agricola" and subject-object relations are signaled by case endings. We would be interested to know whether children who are exposed to languages that do not utilize word order as a major syntactic signal preserve order as reliably as do children exposed to English.

The second thing to notice in Table 2 is the fact that when the models increase in length there is not a corresponding increase in the imitation. The imitations stay in the range of two to four morphemes, which was the range characteristic of the children at this time. The children were operating under some constraint of length or span. This is not a limitation of vocabulary; the children knew hundreds of words. Neither is it a constraint of immediate memory. We infer this from the fact that the average length of utterances produced spontaneously, where immediate memory is not involved, is about the same as the average length of utterances produced as immediate imitations. The constraint is a limitation on the length of utterance the children are able to program or plan.[3] This kind of narrow span limitation in children is characteristic of most or all of their intellectual operations. The limitation grows less restrictive with age as a consequence, probably, of both neurological growth and of practice, but of course it is never lifted altogether.

A constraint on length compels the imitating child to omit some words or morphemes from the mother's longer sentences. Which forms are retained and which omitted? The selection is not random but highly systematic. Forms retained in the examples of Table 2 include: *Daddy, Fraser, Pepper,* and *Cromer; tank, car, minute, briefcase, train, dog,* and *shoe; wait, go,* and *write; unhappy* and *old time.* For the most part they are nouns, verbs, and adjectives, though there are exceptions, as witness the initial pronoun *He* and the preposition *out* and the indefinite article *a.* Forms omitted in the samples of Table 2 include: the possessive inflection *-s,* the modal auxiliary *will,* the contraction of the auxiliary verb *is,* the progressive inflection *-ing,* the preposition *on,* the articles *the* and *an,* and the modal auxiliary *can.* It is possible to make a general characterization of the forms likely to be retained that distinguishes them as a total class from the forms likely to be omitted.

Forms likely to be retained are nouns and verbs and, less often, adjectives, and these are the three large and "open" parts of speech in English. The number of forms in any one of these parts of speech is extremely large and always growing. Words belonging to these classes are sometimes called "contentives" because they have semantic content. Forms likely to be omitted are inflections, auxiliary verbs, articles, prepositions, and conjunctions. These forms belong to syntactic classes that are small and closed. Any one class has few members and new members are not readily added. The omitted forms are the ones that linguists sometimes call *functors,* their grammatical *functions* being more obvious than their semantic content.

Why should young children omit functors and retain contentives? There is more than one plausible answer. Nouns, verbs, and adjectives are words that make reference. One can conceive of teaching the meanings of these words by speaking them, one at a time, and pointing at things or actions or qualities. And of course parents do exactly that. These are the kinds of words that children have been encouraged to practice speaking one at a time. The child arrives at the age of sentence construction with a stock of well-practiced nouns, verbs, and adjectives. Is it not likely then that this prior practice causes him to retain the contentives from model sentences too long to be reproduced in full, that the child imitates those forms in the speech he hears that are already well developed in him as individual habits? There is probably some truth in this explanation but it is not the only determinant since children will often select for retention contentives that are relatively unfamiliar to them.

We adults sometimes operate under a constraint on length and the curious fact is that the English we produce in these circumstances bears a formal resemblance to the English produced by two-year-old children. When words cost money there is a premium on brevity or to put it otherwise, a constraint on length. The result is "telegraphic" English and telegraphic English is an English of nouns, verbs, and adjectives. One does not send a cable reading: "My car has broken down and I have lost my wallet; send money to me at the American Express in Paris" but rather "Car broken down; wallet lost; send money American Express Paris." The telegram omits: *my, has, and, I, have, my, to, me, at, the, in*. All of these are functors. We make the same kind of telegraphic reduction when time or fatigue constrains us to be brief, as witness any set of notes taken at a fast-moving lecture.

A telegraphic transformation of English generally communicates very well. It does so because it retains the high-information words and drops the low-information words. We are here using "information" in the sense of the mathematical theory of communication. The information carried by a word is inversely related to the chances of guessing it from context. From a given string of content words, missing functors can often be guessed but the message "my has and I have my to me at the in" will not serve to get money to Paris. Perhaps children are able to make a communication analysis of adult speech and so adapt in an optimal way to their limitation of span. There is, however, another way in which the adaptive outcome might be achieved.

If you say aloud the model sentences of Table 2 you will find that you place the heavier stresses, the primary and secondary stresses in the sentences, on contentives rather than on functors. In fact the heavier stresses fall, for the most part, on the words the child retains. We first realized that this was the case when we found that in transcribing tapes, the words of the mother that we could hear most clearly were usually the words that the child reproduced. We had trouble hearing the weakly stressed functors and, of course, the child usually failed to reproduce them. Differential stress may then be the cause of the child's differential retention. The outcome is a maximally informative reduction but the cause of this outcome need not be the making of an information analysis. The outcome may be an incidental consequence of the fact that English is a well-designed language that places its heavier stresses where they are needed, on contentives that cannot easily be guessed from context.

We are fairly sure that differential stress is one of the determinants of the child's telegraphic productions. For one thing, stress will also account for the way in which children reproduce polysyllabic words when the total is too much for them. Adam, for instance, gave us *'pression* for *expression* and Eve gave us *'raff* for *giraffe;* the more heavily stressed syllables were the ones retained. In addition we have tried the effect of placing heavy stresses on functors that do not ordinarily receive such stresses. To Adam we said: "You say what I say" and then, speaking in a normal way at first: "The doggie will bite." Adam gave back: "Doggie bite." Then we stressed the auxiliary: "The doggie *will* bite" and, after a few trials, Adam made attempts at reproducing that auxiliary. A science fiction experiment comes to mind. If there were parents who stressed functors rather than contentives, would they have children whose speech was a kind of "reciprocal telegraphic" made up of articles, prepositions, conjunctions, auxiliaries, and the like? Such children would be out of touch with the community as real children are not.

It may be that all the factors we have mentioned play some part in determining the child's selective imitations; the reference-making function of contentives, the fact that they are practiced as single words, the fact that they cannot be guessed from context, and the heavy stresses they receive. There are also other possible factors: for example, the left-to-right, earlier-to-later position of words in a sentence, but these make too long a story to tell here.[4] Whatever the causes, the first utterances produced as imitations of adult sentences are highly systematic reductions of their models. Furthermore, the telegraphic properties of these imitations appear also in the child's spontaneously produced utterances. When his speech is not modeled on an immediately prior adult sentence, it observes the same limitation on length and the same predilection for contentives as when it is modeled on an immediately prior sentence.

IMITATION WITH EXPANSION

In the course of the brief conversation set down in Table 1, Adam's mother at one point imitates Adam. The boy says: "There go one" and mother responds: "Yes, there goes one." She does not exactly reproduce the model sentence of the child but instead adds something to it or expands it. What she adds is a functor, the inflection for third-person on the verb, the very form that Adam had omitted when he imitated his mother.

One of the first things we noticed when we began to study child speech several years ago was the frequency with which adults imitated children. Indeed they seemed to imitate more often than did the children themselves. We later came to realize that adult imitations are seldom exact reproductions; they are usually expansions. The mothers of Adam and Eve responded to the speech of their children with expansions about 30 percent of the time. We did it ourselves when we talked with the children. Indeed we found it very difficult to withhold expansions. A reduced or incomplete English sentence seems to constrain the English-speaking adult to expand it into the nearest properly formed complete sentence. Table 3 lists a few sample expansions from the hundreds in the records.

The first thing worthy of attention in the expansions of Table 3 is the fact that the words spoken by the mother preserve the order of the words in the child's sentences. To be sure, words and inflections are added but they are fitted in — before, and after and between the words the child used; they are not generally permitted to disturb the order of the child's words. It is as if these latter were taken as constants by the mother, constants to which some sentence had to be fitted. She acts as if she were as-

TABLE 3

Expansions of Child Speech Produced by Mothers

Child	*Mother*
Baby highchair	Baby is in the highchair
Mommy eggnog	Mommy had her eggnog
Eve lunch	Eve is having lunch
Mommy sandwich	Mommy'll have a sandwich
Sat wall	He sat on the wall
Throw Daddy	Throw it to Daddy
Pick glove	Pick the glove up

suming that the child means everything he says, all the words and also their order, but as if he might also mean more than he says. From the mother's point of view an expansion is a kind of communication check; it says in effect: "Is this what you mean?"

The second thing to notice about Table 3 is the character of the forms added to the child's utterances. They include the auxiliaries *is* and *will*; the prepositions *in, on, to* and *up*; the verb forms *is, have, had,* and *having*; the articles *a* and *the*; the pronouns *her, he,* and *it*. For the most part, the words added are functors, and functors are of course the words that the child omits in his reductions.

The interaction between mother and child is, much of the time, a cycle of reductions and expansions. There are two transformations involved. The reduction transformation has an almost completely specifiable and so mechanical character. One could program a machine to do it with the following instructions: "Retain contentives (or stressed forms) in the order given up to some limit of length." The expansion accomplished by Adam's mother when she added the third-person inflection to the verb and said, "There goes one" is also a completely specifiable transformation. The instructions would read: "Retain the forms given in the order given and supply obligatory grammatical forms." To be sure, this mother-machine would have to be supplied with the obligatory rules of English grammar but that could be done. However, the sentence "There goes one" is atypical in that it only adds a compulsory and redundant inflection. The expansions of Table 3 all add forms that are not grammatically compulsory or redundant and these expansions cannot be mechanically generated by grammatical rules alone.

In Table 3 the topmost four utterances produced by the child are all of the same grammatical type; all four consist of a proper noun followed by a common noun. However, the four are expanded in quite different ways. In particular the form of the verb changes: it is in the first case in the simple present tense; in the second case the simple past; in the third case the present progressive; in the last case the simple future. All of these are perfectly grammatical but they are different. The second set of child utterances is formally uniform in that each one consists of a verb followed by a noun. The expansions are again all grammatical but quite unlike, especially with regard to the preposition supplied. In general, then, there are radical changes in the mother's expansions when there are no changes in the formal character of the utterances expanded. It follows that the expansions cannot be produced simply by making grammatically compulsory additions to the child's utterances.

How does a mother decide on the correct expansion of one of her child's utterances? Consider the utterance "Eve lunch." So far as grammar is concerned this utterance could be appropriately expanded in any of a number of ways: "Eve is having lunch"; "Eve had lunch"; "Eve will have lunch"; Eve's lunch," etc. On the occasion when Eve produced the utterance, however, one expansion seemed more appropriate than any other. It was then the noon hour, Eve was sitting at the table with a plate of food before her, and her spoon and fingers were busy. In these circumstances "Eve lunch" had to mean "Eve is having lunch." A little later, when the plate had been stacked in the sink and Eve was getting down from her chair, the utterance "Eve lunch" would have suggested the expansion "Eve has had her lunch." Most expansions are not only responsive to the child's words but also to the circumstances attending their utterance.

What kind of instructions will generate the mother's expansions? The following are approximately correct: "Retain the words given in the order given and add those functors that will result in a well-formed simple sentence that is appropriate to the circumstances." These are not instructions that any machine could follow. A machine could act on the instructions only if it were provided with detailed specifications for judging appropriateness and no such specifications can, at present, be written. They exist, however, in implicit form in the brains of mothers and in the brains of all English-speaking adults and so judgments of appropriateness can be made by such adults.

The expansion encodes aspects of reality that are not coded by the child's telegraphic utterance. Functors have meaning but it is meaning that accrues to them in context rather than in isolation. The meanings that are added by functors seem to be nothing less than the basic terms in which we construe reality: the time of an action, whether it is ongoing or completed, whether it is presently relevant or not; the concept of possession and such relational concepts as are coded by *in, on, up, down*, and the like; the difference between a particular instance of a class ("Has anybody seen *the* paper?") and any instance of a class ("Has anybody seen *a* paper?"); the difference between extended substances given shape and size by an "accidental" container (*sand, water, syrup*, etc.) and countable "things" having a characteristic fixed shape and size (*a cup, a man, a tree*, etc.). It seems to us that a mother in expanding speech may be teaching more than grammar; she may be teaching something like a worldview.

As yet it has not been demonstrated that expansions are *necessary* for learning either grammar or a construction of reality. It has not even been demonstrated that expansions contribute to such learning. All we know is that some parents do expand and their children do learn. It is perfectly possible, however, that children can and do learn simply from hearing their parents or others make well-formed sentences in connection with various nonverbal circumstances. It may not be necessary or even helpful for these sentences to be expansions of utterances of the child. Only experiments contrasting expansion training with simple exposure to English will settle the matter. We hope to do such experiments.

There are, of course, reasons for expecting the expansion transformation to be an effective tutorial technique. By adding something to the words the child has just produced one confirms his response insofar as it is appropriate. In addition one takes him somewhat beyond that response but not greatly beyond it. One encodes additional meanings at a moment when he is most likely to be attending to the cues that can teach that meaning.

INDUCTION OF THE LATENT STRUCTURE

Adam, in the course of the conversation with his mother set down in Table 1, produced one utterance for which no adult is likely ever to have provided an exact model: "No I see truck." His mother elects to expand it as "No, you didn't see it" and this ex-

TABLE 4

Utterances Not Likely to Be Imitations

My Cromer suitcase	You naughty are
Two foot	Why it can't turn off?
A bags	Put on it
A scissor	Cowboy did fighting me
A this truck	Put a gas in

pansion suggests that the child might have created the utterance by reducing an adult model containing the form *didn't*. However, the mother's expansion in this case does some violence to Adam's original version. He did not say *no* as his mother said it, with primary stress and final contour; Adam's *no* had secondary stress and no final contour. It is not easy to imagine an adult model for this utterance. It seems more likely that the utterance was created by Adam as part of a continuing effort to discover the general rules for constructing English negatives.

In Table 4 we have listed some utterances produced by Adam or Eve for which it is difficult to imagine any adult model. It is unlikely that any adult said any of these to Adam or Eve since they are very simple utterances and yet definitely ungrammatical. In addition it is difficult, by adding functors alone, to build any of them up to simple grammatical sentences. Consequently it does not seem likely that these utterances are reductions of adult originals. It is more likely that they are mistakes that externalize the child's search for the regularities of English syntax.

We have long realized that the occurrence of certain kinds of errors on the level of morphology (or word construction) reveals the child's effort to induce regularities from speech. So long as a child speaks correctly, or at any rate so long as he speaks as correctly as the adults he hears, there is no way to tell whether he is simply repeating what he has heard or whether he is actually constructing. However, when he says something like "I digged a hole" we can often be sure that he is constructing. We can be sure because it is unlikely that he would have heard *digged* from anyone and because we can see how, in processing words he has heard, he might have come by *digged*. It looks like an overgeneralization of the regular past inflection. The inductive operations of the child's mind are externalized in such a creation. Overgeneralizations on the level of syntax (or sentence construction) are more difficult to identify because there are so many ways of adding functors so as to build up conceivable models. But this is difficult to do for the examples of Table 4 and for several hundred other utterances in our records.

The processes of imitation and expansion are not sufficient to account for the degree of linguistic competence that children regularly acquire. These processes alone cannot teach more than the sum total of sentences that speakers of English have either modeled for a child to imitate or built up from a child's reductions. However, a child's linguistic competence extends far beyond this sum total of sentences. All children are able to understand and construct sentences they have never heard but that are nevertheless well formed, well formed in terms of general rules that are implicit in the sentences the child has heard. Somehow, then, every child processes the speech to which he is exposed so as to induce from it a latent structure. This latent rule structure is so general that a child can spin out its implications all his life long. It is both semantic and syntactic. The discovery of latent structure is the greatest of the processes involved in language acquisition and the most difficult to understand. We will provide an example of how the analysis can proceed by discussing the evolution in child speech of noun phrases.

A noun phrase in adult English includes a noun but also more than a noun. One variety consists of a noun with assorted modifiers: *The girl; The pretty girl; That pretty girl; My girl*, etc. All of these are constructions that have the same syntactic privileges as do nouns alone. One can use a noun phrase in isolation to name or request something; one can use it in sentences, in subject position or in object position or in predicate nominative position. All of these are slots that nouns alone can also fill. A larger construction having the same syntactic privileges as its "head" word is called in linguistics an "endocentric" construction, and noun phrases are endocentric constructions.

For both Adam and Eve, in the early records, noun phrases usually occur as total independent utterances rather than as components of sentences. Table 5 presents an assortment of such utterances at Time 1. They consist in each case of some sort of modifier, just one, preceding a noun. The modifiers, or as they are sometimes called the "pivot" words, are a much smaller class than the noun class. Three students of child speech have independently discovered that this kind of construction is extremely common when children first begin to combine words.[5,6,7]

It is possible to generalize the cases of Table 5 into a simple implicit rule. The rule symbolized in Table 5 reads: "In order to form a noun phrase of this type, select first one word from the small class of modifiers and select, second, one word from the large class of nouns." This is a "generative" rule by which we mean it is a program that would actually serve to build constructions of the type in question. It is offered as

TABLE 5

Noun Phrases in Isolation and Rule for Generating Noun Phrases at Time 1

A coat	More coffee
A celery*	More nut*
A Becky*	Two sock*
A hands*	Two shoes
The top	Two tinker-toy*
My Mommy	Big boot
That Adam	Poor man
My stool	Little top
That knee	Dirty knee

NP →   M + N
M   →   a, big, dirty, little, more, my, poor, that, the, two.
N   →   Adam, Becky, boot, coat, coffee, knee, man, Mommy, nut, sock, stool, tinker-toy, top, *and very many others.*

*Ungrammatical for an adult.

a model of the mental mechanism by which Adam and Eve generated such utterances. Furthermore, judging from our work with other children and from the reports of Braine and of Miller and Ervin, the model describes a mechanism present in many children when their average utterance is approximately two morphemes long.

We have found that even in our earliest records the M + N construction is sometimes used as a component of larger constructions. For instance, Eve said: "Fix a Lassie" and "Turn the page" and "A horsie stuck" and Adam even said: "Adam wear a shirt." There are, at first, only a handful of these larger constructions but there are very many constructions in which single nouns occur in subject or in object position.

Let us look again at the utterances of Table 5 and the rule generalizing them. The class M does not correspond with any syntactic class of adult English. In the class M are articles, a possessive pronoun, a cardinal number, a demonstrative adjective or pronoun, a quantifier, and some descriptive adjectives — a mixed bag indeed. For adult English these words cannot belong to the same syntactic class because they have very different privileges of occurrence in sentences. For the children the words do seem to function as one class having the common privilege of occurrence before nouns.

If the initial words of the utterances in Table 5 are treated as one class M then many utterances are generated that an adult speaker would judge to be ungrammatical. Consider the indefinite article *a*. Adults use it only to modify common count nouns in the singular such as *coat, dog, cup*, etc. We would not say *a celery*, or *a cereal*, or *a dirt; celery, cereal*, and *dirt* are mass nouns. We would not say *a Becky* or *a Jimmy; Becky* and *Jimmy* are proper nouns. We would not say *a hands* or *a shoes; hands* and *shoes* are plural nouns. Adam and Eve, at first, did form ungrammatical combinations such as these.

The numeral *two* we use only with count nouns in the plural. We would not say *two sock* since *sock* is singular, nor *two water* since *water* is a mass noun. The word *more* we use before count nouns in the plural (*more nuts*) or mass nouns in the singular (*more coffee*). Adam and Eve made a number of combinations involving *two* or *more* that we would not make.

Given the initial very undiscriminating use of words in the class M it follows that one dimension of development must be a progressive differentiation of privileges, which means the division of M into smaller classes. There must also be subdivision of the noun class (N) for the reason that the privileges of occurrence of various kinds of modifiers must be described in terms of such subvarieties of N as the common noun and proper noun, the count noun and mass noun. There must eventually emerge a distinction between nouns singular and nouns plural since this distinction figures in the privileges of occurrence of the several sorts of modifiers.

Sixteen weeks after our first records from Adam and Eve (Time 2), the differentiation process had begun. By this time there were distributional reasons for separating out articles (*a, the*) from demonstrative pronouns (*this, that*) and both of these from the residual class of modifiers. Some of the evidence for this conclusion appears in Table 6. In general one syntactic class is distinguished from another when the members of one class have combinational privileges not enjoyed by the members of the other. Consider, for example, the reasons for distinguishing articles (Art) from modi-

TABLE 6

Subdivision of the Modifier Class

(A) Privileges Peculiar to Articles

Obtained	*Not Obtained*
A blue flower	Blue a flower
A nice nap	Nice a nap
A your car	Your a car
A my pencil	My a pencil

(B) Privileges Peculiar to Demonstrative Pronouns

Obtained	*Not Obtained*
That my cup	My that cup
That a horse	A that horse
That a blue flower	A that blue flower
	Blue a that flower

---

fiers in general (M). Both articles and modifiers appeared in front of nouns in two-word utterances. However, in three-word utterances that were made up from the total pool of words and that had a noun in final position, the privileges of *a* and *the* were different from the privileges of all other modifiers. The articles occurred in initial position followed by a member of class M other than an article. No other modifier occurred in this first position; notice the "Not obtained" examples of Table 6A. If the children had produced utterances like those (for example, *blue a flower, your a car*) there would have been no difference in the privileges of occurrence of articles and modifiers and therefore no reason to separate out articles.

The record of Adam is especially instructive. He created such notably ungrammatical combinations as "a your car" and "a my pencil." It is very unlikely that adults provided models for these. They argue strongly that Adam regarded all the words in the residual M class as syntactic equivalents and so generated these very odd utterances in which possessive pronouns appear where descriptive adjectives would be more acceptable.

Table 6 also presents some of the evidence for distinguishing demonstrative pronouns (Dem) from articles and modifiers (Table 6B). The pronouns occurred first and ahead of articles in three-and-four-word utterances — a position that neither articles nor modifiers ever filled. The sentences with demonstrative pronouns are recognizable as reductions that omit the copular verb *is*. Such sentences are not noun phrases in adult English and ultimately they will not function as noun phrases in the speech of the children, but for the present they are not distinguishable distributionally from noun phrases.

Recall now the generative formula of Table 5, which constructs noun phrases by simply placing a modifier (M) before a noun (N). The differentiation of privileges illustrated in Table 6, and the syntactic classes this evidence motivates us to create, complicate the formula for generating noun phrases. In Table 7 we have written a single general formula for producing all noun phrases at Time 2 [NP → (Dem) + (Art) +

TABLE 7

Rules for Generating Noun Phrases at Time 2

$NP_1 \rightarrow$ Dem + Art + M + N	$NP \rightarrow$ (Dem) + (Art) + (M) + N
$NP_2 \rightarrow$ Art + M + N	
$NP_3 \rightarrow$ Dem + M + N	( ) means class within parentheses is optional
$NP_4 \rightarrow$ Art + N	
$NP_5 \rightarrow$ M + N	
$NP_6 \rightarrow$ Dem + N	
$NP_7 \rightarrow$ Dem + Art + N	

(M) + N] and also the numerous more specific rules that are summarized by the general formula.

By the time of the thirteenth transcription, twenty-six weeks after we began our study, privileges of occurrence were much more finely differentiated and syntactic classes were consequently more numerous. From the distributional evidence we judged that Adam had made five classes of his original class M: articles, descriptive adjectives, possessive pronouns, demonstrative pronouns, and a residual class of modifiers. The generative rules of Table 7 had become inadequate; there were no longer, for instance, any combinations like "A your car." Eve had the same set except that she used two residual classes of modifiers. In addition nouns had begun to subdivide for both children. The usage of proper nouns had become clearly distinct from the usage of count nouns. For Eve the evidence justified separating count nouns from mass nouns, but for Adam it still did not. Both children by this time were frequently pluralizing nouns but as yet their syntactic control of the singular-plural distinction was imperfect.

In summary, one major aspect of the development of general structure in child speech is a progressive differentiation in the usage of words and therefore a progressive differentiation of syntactic classes. At the same time, however, there is an integrative process at work. From the first, an occasional noun phrase occurred as a component of some larger construction. At first these noun phrases were just two words long and the range of positions in which they could occur was small. With time the noun phrases grew longer, were more frequently used, and were used in a greater

TABLE 8

Some Privileges of the Noun Phrase

Noun Positions	Noun Phrase Positions
That (flower)	That (a blue flower)
Where (ball) go?	Where (the puzzle) go?
Adam write (penguin)	Doggie eat (the breakfast)
(Horsie) stop	(A horsie) crying
Put (hat) on	Put (the red hat) on

range of positions. The noun phrase structure as a whole, in all the permissible combinations of modifiers and nouns, was assuming the combinational privileges enjoyed by nouns in isolation.

In Table 8 we have set down some of the sentence positions in which both nouns and noun phrases occurred in the speech of Adam and Eve. It is the close match between the positions of nouns alone and of nouns with modifiers in the speech of Adam and Eve that justifies us in calling the longer constructions noun phrases. These longer constructions are, as they should be, endocentric; the head word alone has the same syntactic privileges as the head word with its modifiers. The continuing failure to find in noun phrase positions whole constructions of the type "That a blue flower" signals the fact that these constructions are telegraphic versions of predicate nominative sentences omitting the verb form *is*. Examples of the kind of construction not obtained are: "That (that a blue flower)"; "Where (that a blue flower)?".

For adults the noun phrase is a subwhole of the sentence, what linguists call an "immediate constituent." The noun phrase has a kind of psychological unity. There are signs that the noun phrase was also an immediate constituent for Adam and Eve. Consider the sentence using the separable verb *put on*. The noun phrase in "Put the red hat on" is, as a whole, fitted in between the verb and the particle even as is the noun alone in "Put hat on." What is more, however, the location of pauses in the longer sentence, on several occasions, suggested the psychological organization: "Put . . . the red hat . . . on" rather than "Put the red . . . hat on" or "Put the . . . red hat on." In addition to this evidence the use of pronouns suggests that the noun phrase is a psychological unit.

The unity of noun phrases in adult English is evidenced, in the first place, by the syntactic equivalence between such phrases and nouns alone. It is evidenced, in the second place, by the fact that pronouns are able to substitute for total noun phrases. In our immediately preceding sentence the pronoun "It" stands for the rather involved construction from the first sentence of this paragraph: "The unity of noun

TABLE 9

Pronouns Replacing Nouns or Noun Phrases and Pronouns Produced Together with Nouns or Noun Phrases

Noun Phrases Replaced by Pronouns	*Pronouns and Noun Phrases in Same Utterances*
Hit ball	Mommy get it ladder
Get it	Mommy get it my ladder
Ball go?	Saw it ball
Go get it	Miss it garage
	I miss it cowboy boot
Made it	I Adam drive that
Made a ship	I Adam drive
	I Adam don't
Fix a tricycle	
Fix it	

phrases in adult English." The words called *pronouns* in English would more aptly be called *pro-noun-phrases* since it is the phrase rather than the noun which they usually replace. One does not replace "unity" with "it" and say, "The *it* of noun phrases in adult English." In the speech of Adam and Eve, too, the pronoun came to function as a replacement for the noun phrase. Some of the clearer cases appear in Table 9.

Adam characteristically externalizes more of his learning than does Eve and his record is especially instructive in connection with the learning of pronouns. In his first eight records, the first sixteen weeks of the study, Adam quite often produced sentences containing both the pronoun and the noun or noun phrase that the pronoun should have replaced. One can here see the equivalence in the process of establishment. First the substitute is produced and then, as if in explication, the form or forms that will eventually be replaced by the substitute. Adam spoke out his pronoun antecedents as chronological consequents. This is additional evidence of the unity of the noun phrase since the noun phrases *my ladder* and *cowboy boot* are linked with *it* in Adam's speech in just the same way as the nouns *ladder* and *ball*.

We have described three processes involved in the child's acquisition of syntax. It is clear that the last of these, the induction of latent structure, is by far the most complex. It looks as if this last process will put a serious strain on any learning theory thus far conceived by psychology. The very intricate simultaneous differentiation and integration that constitutes the evolution of the noun phrase is more reminiscent of the biological development of an embryo than it is of the acquisition of a conditional reflex.

NOTES

1. We are grateful for intellectual stimulation and lighthearted companionship to Dr. Jean Berko Gleason, Mr. Samuel Anderson, Mr. Colin Fraser, Dr. David McNeill, and Dr. Daniel Slobin.
2. H. Maclay and C. E. Osgood, "Hesitation Phenomena in Spontaneous English Speech," *Word*, 15 (1959), 19–44.
3. Additional evidence of the constraint on sentence length may be found in R. Brown and C. Fraser, "The Acquisition of Syntax," in *Verbal Behavior and Learning*, ed. C. N. Cofer and B. Musgrave (New York: McGraw Hill, 1963).
4. Brown and Fraser, "The Acquisition of Syntax."
5. M. D. S. Braine, "The Ontogeny of English Phrase Structure: The First Phrase," *Language*, 39 (1963), 1–13.
6. W. Miller and S. Ervin, "The Development of Grammar in Child Language," in *The Acquisition of Language, Child Development Monograph*, ed. U. Bellugi and R. Brown (Lafayette, IN: Society for Research in Child Development, 1964).
7. Brown and Fraser, "The Acquisition of Syntax."

Preschool Children's Knowledge
of English Phonology

CHARLES READ

The term *phonology* refers to the sound system of our language, a system of regular processes that determine the pronunciation of English. Part of what we acquire in learning a language is a mastery of these processes, so that when we encounter a new or unfamiliar word, we automatically (and for the most part, unconsciously) know some aspects of its pronunciation. In *telemorphic*, for instance, we know (without necessarily knowing what the word might mean) that stress falls on the third syllable and that the first and second vowels are not pronounced alike, despite the spelling. Linguists have shown that the processes determining these and many other details of English pronunciation are not simple "analogies" to familiar words (such as *telegraphic* in this case); they are a system of intricate but general rules of the language.[1] Exactly how and when we acquire our unconscious mastery of these rules remains largely a mystery; it is clear that we do not memorize individual pronunciations (since the rules extend to new words and sentences) and that we do not learn them directly from a study of English spelling.

In fact, a child must bring some knowledge of English phonology to his first encounter with reading and writing. Part of what he must have learned is that certain sounds are to be regarded as the same, despite differences in their pronunciation. For instance, the third segments ([n]) of *ten* and *tenth* are functionally the same in English, even though they are articulated differently; in another language, they might be as distinct as *tin* and *Tim* are to us. Variations in pronunciation take many forms; an example of a different sort is the contrast in timbre, pitch, and other qualities between the speech of a child and that of his father, even though they may be "saying the same thing." Such a contrast appears in all languages, of course, and perhaps need not be learned specifically for English; others must be learned as part of the particular language. For instance, in some languages the difference in aspiration between the [p] of *pit* and the [p] of *spit* would make them distinct sounds, while the difference in voicing between the first segments of *tin* and *din* might be entirely irrelevant; these would be two instances of the same word. As part of his knowledge of his language, a child must learn to attend to certain phonetic differences and to abstract from others in a specific and systematic way. Evidently, children possess some phonological

Harvard Educational Review   Vol. 41   No. 1   February 1971, 1–34

knowledge of this sort in their preschool years. Otherwise, they could not judge that two different speakers were saying the same thing; they could not understand a speaker of another dialect, however slightly different; ultimately, they could not understand English at all, for speech sounds can and do vary in a multitude of ways, many of which we must systematically disregard in understanding English.

Beyond the general observation that a preschool child's conception of English phonology is sufficiently abstract to permit him to understand and be understood under normal circumstances, however, we know few details of when and how this conception develops. Evidence about the nature of the development must come from children's judgments of phonetic similarities and differences, and these have proven elusive indeed. This chapter will present some evidence of such judgments, specifically about how children in their preschool and kindergarten years tacitly categorize the sounds of English. Which phonetic differences do they treat as important in relating one sound to another, which less important, and which ones do they regularly abstract away from? The evidence here suggests that the children's phonology is (necessarily) highly abstract, and that it differs in specific ways from that of adult speakers of English, including of course the children's parents and teachers.

In addition to its relation to the general question of how children learn a language, this evidence bears on a potentially more practical issue, namely, how a child's phonology compares to the abstract representation of speech that he learns in school — the standard English spelling system. It is obvious that any spelling system is highly abstract (again, necessarily so); in English, for example, all direct representation of pitch, stress, and intonation is entirely excluded. Further, as is well known, the standard alphabet does not provide enough characters to represent distinctly the forty-three or so autonomous "phonemes" that distinguish one word from another, and these phonemes are themselves classes of phonetically different sounds, as in the examples given for /p/ and /n/. A recent article in this journal[2] discussed and justified a class of still further abstractions, in which our spelling does not represent predictable phonetic variations in lexically related forms, as in the nonitalicized vowels of *extreme/extremity*, even though we have the alphabetic means to do so. We can compare such an analysis of the abstractions inherent in our spelling system with what we learn about the abstractness of the child's conception of English phonology. Differences between the two systems may define a large and central part of what a child must learn in order to read and write. In making this comparison, I will be assuming that what the child learns in mastering the spelling system is a representation related in complex, but generally systematic, ways to the phonology of English. The contrary assumption — that the child memorizes a long list of generally unpredictable spellings — fails to account for the abilities of mature readers and writers.

The evidence of phonological knowledge comes from preschool children who invented their own spelling system for English, influenced relatively little by the standard system. In each case, the child first learned the conventional names of the letters of the alphabet; then with blocks or some other movable-alphabet toy, began to spell words; and finally produced written messages of all kinds, including stories, letters, and poems. The writing began as early as age three and one half, usually before the child was able to read, and certain parts of the spelling system persisted well into the first grade, where they gradually gave way to standard spellings under the influence of formal instruction in reading and writing.

Such spontaneous spelling is relatively rare. Apparently, it depends on the coincidence of the child's interests and abilities with various other factors, such as the attitudes of the parents, particularly their tolerance for what appears to be bad spelling. In fact, the invented spellings sometimes look so little like English that parents and teachers may be unable to read them and may disregard or even suppress them. Hence, it is difficult to assess the actual (or potential) frequency of such early invented spelling. This report is based on twenty selected clear cases, together with some marginal ones.

What is significant, even from so few cases, is that each child arrived at roughly the same system, using certain spellings that seem implausible to his parents and teachers, but which can be explained in terms of hypotheses about the children's implicit organization of English sounds.

The structure of the argument, then, is this: to propose an explanation for invented spellings by showing that they follow from certain assertions about English phonology, independently justified, together with certain hypotheses about how the children perceive and organize the spoken forms; that is, what they know about English phonology. "Knowledge" and "organization" in this context refer to unconscious beliefs about English sounds and their structure, in the sense in which a reader or listener has notions of sound-structure that enable him to judge two sequences as similar, as in the recognition of rhyme, without his necessarily being aware of either the beliefs or the rhyme itself. This sense of "knowledge" has been explicated more fully and defended elsewhere.[3]

Even for one who accepts, at least tentatively, this line of argument from observed language behavior (performance) to hypothesized judgments and knowledge that underlie it (competence), each step of the argument is open to various questions. Although the statements about English phonology have independent linguistic justification, they are hardly so well established as to be beyond question. For certain fine phonetic details, one can even ask whether the accepted description is based on a physical or perceptual reality that is stable and independent of the linguistic beliefs of the perceiver. There are also questions about the spellings, of course. Children's printing frequently includes marks that are difficult to interpret. Children, like adults, commit apparently nonsystematic errors (even compared to the child's own spelling system), false starts, and inexplicable omissions. Sometimes conventional spellings occur; these may not reveal anything about the child's judgments, since one usually cannot know (certainly not from the written record alone) whether they are learned or created; they may have been copied or taken from dictation. Accordingly, I have usually left them out of this account.[4] It is also difficult to know about the children's language experience before they began to spell; none of the parents kept a systematic record of what their children heard or said, nor would such a record guarantee the accuracy of inferences from it about what the child knew. Some assumptions about the bases for the original spelling come from information provided by the parents, other investigations of children's language development, and the evidence of the early spellings themselves.

Consider the problem confronting the preschool child who wants to spell English messages. He knows the pronunciation of the words; that is, he recognizes the words when someone else says them, and he may pronounce them more or less as an adult does.[5] Without being aware of it, he knows certain syntactic and semantic relations among words, such as that -*er* is an agentive ending in a pair like *ride/rider* or that *eat-* is a verb stem in *eating*. He may have mastered certain regular phonetic alternations, such as the [s]—[z] forms for plurals. He recognizes the letters of the alphabet and knows their conventional names, or most of them.

The letter-names provide only partial help to such a child. Assume for the moment that he wises to represent English consonants at roughly an autonomous phonemic level of detail, and that he considers just those letters whose names contain consonantal segments, therefore leaving aside *a,e,i,o,u* and *y*, whose names contain only vowels and glides. He has fairly direct clues to the representation of [p,t,k,b,d,f,v,s,z,ǰ,m,n,r, and l] in the corresponding letter-names and [č] (as in *chin*) is the consonant in the name of *h*.[6] The names of *c,g,q,x*, and *w* provide no additional information, since they contain only consonants already accounted for. This leaves the child with no direct suggestion for representing [θ,ð,š,ž,g,ŋ and h].[7] The various English vowels are much less well provided for, but the children devise rather ingenious spellings for them, as we will see. Notice that to use even this information, the child must analyze the letter-names into their component segments and respect the consonantal or vocalic nature of each. There are indications in the invented spellings that the children can and do perform just such an analysis.

In addition, the children got information from their parents, but ordinarily only when they asked for specific help. Most of them apparently learned from adults the digraphic spellings of [θ], [ð], and [č], as in *thin*, *then*, and *church*. Certain common words, such as *the*, *day*, *Mommy*, *Daddy*, and the child's own name and those of his family were sometimes copied or dictated, but the evidence also includes invented spellings for each. In general, these preschool writers are remarkably independent; they create most of their own spellings by trying to represent the sounds as they relate them to the letter-names they know. Occasionally these efforts lead to a standard spelling, but most of the results are nonstandard, often extremely so, and they reveal aspects of the child's phonological system.

VOWELS

The children's representation of front[8] vowels presents a fairly clear system. The names of the letters *a, e,* and *i* correspond quite directly to the tense vowels in *bait*, *beet*, and *bite*. In the spontaneous spelling system these letters represent their own names in such words, usually without the standard devices, such as doubling the "silent" *e*, to show the tenseness of the vowel. So we have:

D*A*	(day)	L*A*DE	(lady)	T*I*GR	(tiger)
K*A*M	(came)	E*G*LE	(eagle)	L*I*K	(like)
TABIL	(table)	FEL	(feel)	M*I*	(my)

More interesting is the spelling of the lax vowels, as in *bit, bet, bat,* and *pot.* Altogether the children must extend the five vowel letters (or others, conceivably) to at least eight lax vowels, as well as some other tense ones. They choose a systematic phonological basis for making this extension.

Standard spelling accomplishes part of what is required by using the same letter to spell the distinct vowels italicized in the following pairs:

divine—divinity   extreme—extremity   phone—phonic

These pairs of vowels are related not only historically but lexically; that is, in the lexicon of an optimal grammar of English, the vowel segments of each pair will be represented in the same way. It is generally the case that standard spelling represents these lexical relationships; note that the relationships in meaning are thus embodied in spelling.[9]

Two general processes affect the actual pronunciation of the tense forms in contemporary English, however. The first combines them with a following [y]- or [w]-glide, converting them to diphthongs. The second, known as Vowel Shift, raises their place of articulation from that of the lax forms to the next highest position, lowering the highest to a low position. Other rules further modify their quality. Because all these rules affect only tense vowels, and because there was no corresponding change in spelling when Vowel Shift entered the language, the vocalic portion of a tense diphthong now differs phonetically in height and other qualities from the lax vowel that is usually spelled with the same letter. The phonetic correspondence is as follows:

	tense	lax	tense	lax	tense	lax
Symbol	[īy]	[i]	[ēy]	[e]	[āy]	[a]
Spelling	ser*e*ne—div*i*nity		c*a*me—extr*e*mity		l*i*ne—ph*o*nic	

With these correspondences in mind, consider the following typical invented spellings:

F*E*S	(fish)	ALRVATA	(elevator)
EGL*I*OW	(igloo)	SC*I*CHTAP	(Scotch tape)
FL*E*PR	(Flipper)	G*I*T	(got)
F*A*LL	(fell)	CL*I*K	(clock)
L*A*FFT	(left)		

Such examples could be multiplied many times, for among the children under five years, these representations of the lax vowels are extremely regular. The [i] of *fish* and *igloo* is represented as *E*, the [e] of *fell* as *A*, the [o] of *Scotch* as *I*. In other words, the children pair lax vowels with tense vowels on the basis of phonetic relationships. The resulting spellings seem odd to most adults, just because adults have long since learned that spelling represents the lexical level at which the first vowel of *penalty* is related to that of *penal*. To adults this relation has become a perceptual fact, and not always an easy one for beginning students of phonetics to displace.

What is surprising is that the children are able to recognize the phonetic relationships they represent in spelling. The children do not pair lax with tense vowels as if these were unanalyzable segments, as they seem to most adults, but rather on the basis of similarity in place of articulation, abstracting from differences in tenseness, diphthongization, and possibly length. The children organize the vowels according to an analysis of their phonetic features.

Further evidence that the children are employing such a tacit analysis appears much later in their careers as original spellers. After they have learned the standard spellings for the lax vowels, many of the children make a rather systematic mistake. They occasionally spell a high or mid tense vowel with the letter they have recently learned to use for the phonetically corresponding lax form.

SIKE	(seek)	CEME	(came)
AIRFILD	(airfield)	PLEY	(play)
FRONTIR	(frontier)	TEBL	(table)

It is as if, having learned that the spelling of lax vowels is not based on what they can hear in the letter-names, the children attempt to save the phonetic correspondence between lax and tense forms, even at the expense of ignoring the obvious congruence between letter-names and tense vowels that they began with. This error, as they are on the verge of learning the standard system, actually carries them away from it momentarily, overthrowing the best-practiced vowel spellings of all. This seems a plausible error only if general notions of phonetic correspondence, not memorized sequences, underlie the spellings. It suggests that the children's knowledge of such relationships may be a more important basis for their spelling than the establishment of "habits" through practice.

Note that the children analyze the articulation of the three tense diphthongs considered so far in the same way, despite the considerable differences among them. For example, the vowel and glide of [īy] are sufficiently close that the segment is not considered diphthongal by many linguists (e.g., Jespersen, Jones); they consider the vowel of *beet* to be a tense, slightly higher and more fronted version of the vowel of *bit*. On the other hand, [āy] combines a low back vowel with a high front glide. Not surprisingly, the latter spelling is the first to disappear as a child's analysis develops. Children who at first have all three of the above tense–lax relationships later may have only [e]—[ēy] and [i]—[īy], employing a new spelling for [a] — not *I*, but *O* or *A*. Some preliminary counting suggests that a common reflection of this early system among the "errors" of first graders who have, for the most part, learned the official spellings, is *A* for [e] as in KRAPT [crept].

Finally, in their analysis of front vowels all of the children seem to assume that the vowel of *bat* is to be spelled with an *A* — even at the same time that they are writing the "incorrect" forms just discussed. The vowel of *bat* is not a part of any letter-name, nor of any tense vowel in most northern U.S. dialects of English. Unless they learn the spelling of [æ] by asking their parents — and they clearly do not learn the spelling of any other lax vowel in that way — the children presumably choose the letter whose name is closest, in some sense, to it. In place of articulation, *A* [ēy] and *I* [āy] are the two possibilities. That the children always choose *A* may suggest that for them two vowels differing only in height of articulation ([æ—e]) are phonologically closer than two differing only in backness ([æ—a]); therefore they collapse the former pair in spelling. If the most fundamental phonological dimensions for the children are those along which contrasts are most likely to be preserved in spelling, this result contrasts with the suggestion of Jakobson, that height is the primary dimension for vowels.[10] On the same assumption, it is consistent with the hierarchy suggested by Chomsky and Halle, in which backness is the major dimension.[11] The entire discussion is highly tentative. At any rate, in the central and back vowels there is other evidence that backness is a more major determinant of the children's spelling than is height.

One result of the spelling of front vowels is that *bait, bet,* and *bat* all have the same spelling — BAT. Some homography is required by the lack of symbols, but the particular choices appear to reflect the children's own sense of phonological relations. The spellings are phonetic in the sense that they represent relations at a (broad) phonetic level of detail; they are abstract in that distinct segments are represented by a single symbol. The children evidently find this result acceptable enough that they do not introduce invented symbols, unlike those critics who reject standard English spelling for its lack of distinct representations for functionally distinct sounds.[12]

I will not discuss the invented spellings of back vowels in detail here. The phonetic relations are intricate, but the symbols available to the children from the standard alphabet are limited, so their spellings are highly abstract and reveal little internal structure. Also, there is a lack of clear evidence for some of the less frequent vowels. In general, the back rounded vowels of *boot, boat,* and *bought* are all spelled *O*. In this, the children disregard differences in height and tenseness, again choosing backness as the dimension to be represented. Typical examples at an early stage of development are:

SOWN	(soon)	WENDOWS	(windows)
EGLIOW	(igloo)	OL	(all)
SOWTKAC	(suitcase)	COLD	(called)
GOWT	(goat)	SMOLR	(smaller)
POWLEOW	(polio)		

As these suggest, vowels with back glides [w] as in *boot* [ūw] and *boat* [ōw], are often spelled *OW*. This remarkably accurate representation provides further evidence that the children can distinguish a vocalic segment from a glide, a distinction that is particularly notable for the vowel of *boat,* where *O* alone might have sufficed, had the children treated the letter-name as an unanalyzed whole.[13]

Further evidence that the children represent similarities in backness comes from their spelling of the lax, back, unrounded vowel [ʌ], the vowel of *hut.* The younger children (from three and a half to about four and a half years) spell this vowel *I*, indicating a relation to the other back, unrounded vowels [a] and [āy], not to [i].

LIV	(love)	BRITHR	(brother)
DIZ	(does)	SINDAS	(Sundays)
WIS	(was)	WINTS	(once)

Again the difference that the children abstract from is one of height and possibly tenseness. This fact, together with the treatment of back rounded vowels, is consistent with the system applied to front vowels.

The spelling of the "neutral" form to which unstressed lax vowels reduce is of some interest, because it illustrates both what the children know and what they do not yet know. Phonetically, this vowel is central, high or mid, and unrounded; the children pair it, accurately enough, with the vowel of *bit*, which they spell *E* at an early stage for the reasons mentioned above. This spelling appears in the italicized positions of:

PLEM*E*TH	(Plymouth)	SEP*E*KOL	(Cepacol)
AN*E*MEL	(animal)	RAJ*E*LASNS	([cong]ratulations)
B*E*NAN*E*	(banana)	PANS*E*L	(pencil)

Later, when the spelling of the vowel of *bit* develops to *I*, the reduced vowel also becomes *I:*

SIG*I*RAT	(cigarette)	KRISM*I*S	(Christmas)
OV*I*N	(oven)	CER*I*T	(carrot)
ROC*I*T	(rocket)	SRK*I*S	(circus)

In this detail again we see a system that abstracts from certain phonetic differences to relate one segment to another. Especially notable in this case is that the children give a consistent spelling to a segment that may be represented by various vowel letters in conventional spelling. Again, the reason is that standard spelling represents a lexical form that takes account of derivational relations like the one between *cigarette* and *cigar*, where the second vowel is not reduced. Preschool children have little or no knowledge of these relations and the lexical forms that preserve them, of course; in fact, it is just such information that they must eventually learn.

VOWEL ALTERNATIONS

As noted above, certain pairs of vowels alternate regularly in derivationally related forms in English. The following examples illustrate the major pairs:

	Vowel Alternation	*Spelling*
1.	[āy—i]	divine—divinity
		line—linear
2.	[īy—e]	please—pleasant
		serene—serenity
3.	[ēy—æ]	nation—national
		profane—profanity
4.	[ōw—a]	tone—tonic
		verbose—verbosity

5.   [āw—ʌ]   prof*ou*nd—prof*u*ndity
                                                      ab*ou*nd—ab*u*ndant

6.   [ūw—ʌ]   red*u*ce—red*u*ction
                                                       ind*u*ce—ind*u*ction

Chomsky and Halle have shown that these phonetic alternations can be derived from lexical forms in which both members of a pair have essentially the same vowel. The phonological rules that predict the difference in pronunciation are each independently required in the grammar of English. As a result, the fact that English spelling uses the same letter for both members of each pair (except for dropping the *o* in case 5) becomes simply another instance of the general practice in the language, of representing lexical forms in spelling.[14]

The question of how to relate such forms in spelling surely does not arise for children of the age we are discussing. As the examples suggest, the derivational processes involved are typical of the learned vocabulary that includes many polysyllabic forms of Romance origin. One suspects that within young children's vocabularies there is little generality to such relationships as these. As a result, if a preschool child had occasion to write *pleasant*, he would probably not try to display its relation to *please*. The following table contrasts the standard spellings for such pairs with the results of the children's own phonological system:

Phonetic Pair	Examples	Adult Spelling[15]	Child Spelling	
1. [āy—i]	divine—divinity	I	Different:	I—E
2. [īy—e]	serene—serenity	E	Different:	E—A
3. [ēy—ae]	nation—national	A	Same:	A
4. [ōw—a]	tone—tonic	O	Different:	O(W)—I
5. [āw—ʌ]	abound—abundant	(O)U	Different:	O(W)—I
				O—U later
6. [ūw—ʌ]	reduce—reduction	U	Different:	OW—I
				O—U later

In general, the children spell differently the pairs that are the same in standard spelling. On this basis one can suggest some empirical hypotheses: for example, that children find it easier to learn the relationship and the first vowel spelling of *nation/national* and similar forms than that of the derived forms in 1 and 2, and that the spelling of derived forms in 5 and 6 is easier to learn than that of their roots.

There are important questions yet to be answered, of course. We do not know what further development children's phonology may undergo before they begin to learn such words as these, nor do we know the exact role that the derivational relations play in the learning of spelling. Although these relations allow for a systematic account of English phonology and spelling, they may play little or no immediate role in learning. Furthermore, we do not know what individual differences there may be in preschoolers' conceptions of English phonology.

Nevertheless, one general insight seems clear: the children's created spellings, no less than the standard ones, are the results of a systematic categorization of English vowels according to certain articulatory properties. That children may tacitly recognize such phonological relationships spontaneously, even before their first formal encounter with reading and writing in the standard system, suggests that they need not approach the latter as a set of arbitrary sound-symbol correspondences — that is, as a long list of words to be memorized. Rather, the child's task is to master new principles that extend and deepen the already abstract conception of the sound system of English that he brings to school.

AFFRICATION

Turning now to consonants, we find other evidence of the preschoolers' phonological judgments embodied in their spelling. Consider the following:

AS CHRAY	(ash tray)	CWNCHRE	(country)
CHRIBLS	(troubles)	JRADL	(dreidel)
CHRIE	(try)	JRAGIN	(dragon)

The invented spelling of [t] and [d] before [r] is *CH* and *J*, respectively.

Again, these representations have a phonetic basis; the first segments of a pair like *truck* and *tuck* are not identical, in fact. Before [r] in English, [t] and [d] are affricated, i.e., released slowly with a resulting "shh" sound. They are articulated in the same place as the stops that we spell *t* and *d*, but in the manner of the palatal affricates [č] and [ǰ] that standard spelling represents as *ch* and *j* respectively. In that respect, they constitute a third possibility intermediate between the two phonological pairs that have distinct standard spellings. Because the affrication before [r] is predictable, standard spelling ignores it, using the lexical representations *tr* and *dr*. Evidently, the children perceive the affrication. Not knowing the lexical representations, they must choose between the known spellings *T/D* or *CH/J* for these intermediate cases. They consistently choose on the basis of affrication, abstracting from the difference in place-of-articulation. They always match affricate [t] and [d] with the affricates that correspond in voicing — [č] and [ǰ], respectively.

Sometimes this preference appears among first graders, even those who have done no original preschool spelling. A six-year-old, making average progress in reading and writing in first grade, wrote the following words for me when I asked what words begin with the same sound as *train*. (Note that *R* is usually omitted and *CH* is reversed):

HCEAN	(train)	HCRAK	(track)
HCEK	(check)	HCICN	(chicken)
HCIKMANCK	(chipmunk)	HCITO	(cheetah)
HCRP	(trip)	HCAFE	(traffic)

This boy's spelling is clearly different from that of the preschoolers — in the vowels, for instance — but he had no doubt that these words begin with the same sound. Similarly for [dr] sequences:

GIBOLL	(dribble)	(the word I asked about)
GIP	(Jeep)	
GIN	(Gene)	
GY	(draw)	(I attribute the *Y* to the [w] in the name of that letter.)

Another first-grade boy independently produced very similar answers; *cheat, traps,* and *chap* were all words with the same first sound as *train.* He spelled that sound *H* — remember that the name of the letter includes [č]. He suggested *drink* and *Jim* as having the same first sound as *dribble.* For these boys, [t] and [d] before a vowel were clearly another matter; after they had given me the above answers, I asked each about *toy, table, Dick,* and *dog.* Those are *t* and *d,* they told me, and they wrote them out with those letters.

I have conducted an experimental investigation with 135 children who had done no original spelling, seeking to determine their judgments of these affricates. The details of the test and its results are beyond the scope of this chapter,[16] but the general outcome provides some support for the inferences drawn from the invented spelling. For example, the children were asked to indicate which words in a set of examples like *train, turkey,* and *chicken* begin with the same sound as *truck.* The children supplied the words themselves, by naming pictures, so that I, as tester, rarely had to give my own pronunciation. There were at least eleven words in a set, so that the consistency of a child's judgment could be measured. Of the eighty kindergarten children, many could not make consistent judgments, but of those who could do so, fully half chose words like *train* and *chicken,* rejecting *turkey, tie,* and the like. The twenty-eight nursery-school children had even more difficulty making the required judgment consistently, a fact that suggests, not surprisingly, that the children who spelled spontaneously were better than most at becoming conscious of their phonological judgments. But again, most of the consistent nursery-school children chose the affricates and rejected the stops.

In a class of twenty-seven first-graders who had encountered *tr*-words in their early reading, most made the adult judgment. However, there were children even in this group who insisted on the similarity between [tr] and [č]. Furthermore, there were four who easily demonstrated their ability to read a set of words like *train, teddy bear,* and *chair,* and who asserted with equal confidence that it is the first and last that begin with the same sound, even while they looked at the printed forms. These children obviously distinguished standard spelling from their own phonetic judgments. Such results as these indicate at least that the spontaneous spellers are not unique in their phonological judgments, although they may be somewhat unusual in their ability to make them explicit, and that the affrication of stops before [r] in English may be an important phonetic fact for young children.

Just as there is no unaffricated [tr] cluster, there is no [čr] cluster within a syllable in English,[17] so, given the standard alphabet, either *tray* or *chray* would represent the word unambiguously. In a strictly taxonomic phonemic analysis, there is no relevant evidence for deciding whether the first segment of *tray* is to be classed with that of *toy* or that of *chin.* As usual, the standard spelling corresponds to the lexical representation from which the actual pronunciation is predictable by a general rule. That the children do not know this lexical representation is simply another instance of the general conclusion that it is such representations that they must learn in mastering standard spelling.

Perhaps the more remarkable fact is that knowing the usual uses of *T* and *CH*, the children are able to choose a consistent representation for this intermediate segment. They abstract from a difference in palatalization (so called because the tongue strikes the palate in the articulation of *chin*) in classifying the first segment of *tray* with that of *chin*, and they do so without parental guidance, obviously. Evidently affrication is for them a phonologically more influential feature than is palatalization, despite the otherwise general importance of place-of-articulation in their system. The children may represent palatalization if they have the alphabetic means to do so, as in SE (see) versus SHE, but they are capable of a more abstract spelling where it is needed, as in the [tr] and [dr] cases. In this, they are spontaneously employing one of the basic devices of spelling systems, namely consistent abstraction from phonetic variations.

The nature of this accomplishment is theoretically more important than the fact that they choose the wrong dimension, from the adult point of view. To learn standard (lexical) spelling, a child must acquire both the principle that spelling does not represent regular phonetic variation and a knowledge of just what is regular—affrication, in this case. The fact that children's spontaneous spelling is already systematically abstract suggests that it is chiefly the facts of English, rather than the principle of spelling, that they have yet to learn. We will examine other cases in which the original spelling is, or rapidly becomes, abstract in this sense. Teachers of primary reading and spelling should be aware of both the principle and the specific instances of it in English. In responding to children's first spelling, we should probably regard efforts that abstract in the wrong direction as misapplications of the right idea.

FLAPS

Another case that provides some information about the child's capacity for abstract representation is that of alveolar flaps, as in the following words:

LADR	(letter)	PREDE	(pretty)
WOODR	(water)	BEDR	(better)

Once again, the *D* in these words represents a phonetically correct perception. There is no contrast between [t] and [d] when they occur between vowels in English; both become a tap of the tongue against the alveolar ridge behind the upper teeth. Because this sound is voiced, it is closer to [d]. The same variation takes place across word boundaries, and the children do not fail to represent it:

AODOV	(out of)	GAD I CHANS	(get a chance)

In this case, the children represent a phonetic variation that the standard system does not. Presumably they have no basis for knowing that there is a lexical /t/ in such words. For the word-internal cases, they cannot receive any direct phonetic evidence, since [t] never occurs there.

Nevertheless, this is one of the earliest invented spellings to disappear. The child who wrote LADR and PREDE at age three and a half or four wrote LATR, SESTR (sister), and PRETE at age five. As these examples themselves show, other invented spellings, such as that of the lax vowels and the unigraphic representation of syllabic /r/ (see below), persisted longer, until age six in this case. Even children who at age six and later maintained some of the original spellings, such as CHR for [tr], stopped representing the flap even in internal positions, as in LETL (little).

How the children learn about the lexical /t/ in such words is not the issue. Most of these children were at least beginning to read at age five, and their parents say that they usually told their children the spelling of any word they asked about. Furthermore, at a boundary [t] alternates with the voiced flap, according to whether the following segment is a vowel, so that either may occur in the same word:

| [gɨD ə čæns] | [gɨt səm] |
| get a chance | get some |

More important than the source of evidence is the fact that the children learned to abstract away from this particular phonetic variation regularly. The relatively rapid development of this abstraction suggests that voicing contrasts may be less major determinants than others. Another section will present further evidence for this conclusion.

The extension of this abstract spelling to all appropriate instances despite deficient phonetic evidence supports the view that spelling is "rule-governed" behavior — that is, that spellings need not be learned one-by-one, but rather that what is learned is a principle. An important difference is that a principle extends to new instances. One cannot be sure what constitute "new instances" in children's writing, but the word-internal tongue flaps would seem to qualify, for phonetically they are always voiced, and the evidence that they are lexically (therefore graphically) /t/ is quite indirect. Yet once T appears in such a position, it appears consistently from then on, displacing *D* in words that the children have written previously. Accordingly, I suggest that the phonological relation between the voiced flap and the corresponding voiceless stop became a part of these children's knowledge of the language, and that they adopted the abstract form in their spelling as a result.

NASALS

Another interesting feature of the children's spelling is the treatment of the nasals [m], [n], and [ŋ],, as in *bumpy*, *end*, and *sing*, respectively. Initially within a syllable, only the first two occur in English, and in this position, the children spell them in the usual way:

| MARED | (married) | NIT | (night) |

These two nasals in final position also receive standard spelling:

POM   (palm)   WAN   (when)

But when any of the nasals occurs before a consonant, the children almost always omit it from spelling:

BOPY   (bumpy)   MOSTR   (monster)
NUBRS   (numbers)   WOTET   (want it)
THOPY   (thumpy)   DOT   (don't)
AD   (and)   PLAT   (plant)
ED   (end)

Velar nasals before phonetic consonants are slightly less common, but examples are:

HACC   (Hanks)
THEKCE   (think(s?))
AGRE   (angry)
SIC   (sink)   written three times in my presence,
                                along with a monologue on its nominal,
                                transitive, and intransitive meanings.
FAC   (Frank)   the [r] is also omitted
NOOIGLID   (New England)

This treatment of preconsonantal nasals is quite general and consistent; it is the usual (almost without exception) spelling for all the children up to about age five. Then most of them begin to represent the nasal, but still frequently omit it. In fact, on an informal spelling dictation given to forty-nine first graders, this spelling accounted for fifteen of the twenty-three erroneous spellings of *went* and *sent*. Unfortunately, these examples are ill-chosen, since *wet* and *set* also happen to be English words, and on that account may be more likely errors. Some first-grade teachers have indicated, however, that the omission of preconsonantal nasals is extraordinarily common.

What appears at first to be another and extremely common instance of this spelling is the use of *EG* and *IG* for *-ing* endings, the former being used by those children who write *E* for [i].

FEHEG   (fishing)   SKEEIG   (skiing)
SOWEMEG   (swimming)   CUMIG   (coming)
GOWEG   (going)   PLAYIG   (playing)
COLAKTGE   (collecting)   FILG   (feeling)

One cannot consider these as representing the *g* of conventional spelling and omitting the nasal, however, because the [g] is not realized phonetically in these forms in most dialects. The nasal is the final sound, and it seems plausible that the preschool spellings represent it, just as they do the other final nasals, but with *g*, since the alphabet provides no separate letter for [ŋ]. The stop [g] that the children otherwise spell *G* as in GEVS (gives) and EGLIOW (igloo) corresponds to [ŋ] in being velar. This suggests that place of articulation is a stronger determinant of the choice of symbol than is nasality, as indeed one would expect from the relative generality of these features in English. So when a nasal precedes a consonant (phonetically) it is not represented in the original spellings, but it is spelled (*M, N,* or *G*) when it does not precede a consonant. In the special case of the velar nasal, these rules give the same spelling for [ŋg] and [ŋ]: *G.* Words that include [ŋg] phonetically, such as *finger, longer,* or *linger,* the children spell FEGR, LOGR, etc., where the *G* evidently represents [g], and the nasal has been omitted.

When a nasal precedes a consonant in English, it must be articulated in the same place as the consonant; that is, within a syllable, only [m] precedes [p] and [b], only [n] precedes [d] and [t], and only [ŋ] precedes [g] and [k]. Thus, in the *-ing* of standard spelling, even when the *g* is not pronounced, we can regard it as corresponding to a lexical form, giving information as to where the nasal is articulated. In their original spellings the children are using *G* for a similar reason, apparently; when they learn standard spelling, they may find it natural in this respect.

The children do not often cooperate with direct requests to write particular words, but occasionally they provide some evidence that they distinguish the velar nasal and omit it before a consonant. One boy wrote FINGR for *finger* but then crossed it out, saying that that would spell [fingr]. He thought for a while, and then with a shrug, wrote FINGR anyway. He was older (6.2) and had begun to spell nasals before consonants in general. Another boy, who did not generally do so, wrote FIGR, sounding it out as [f-iŋ-g-r].

We could explain the children's treatment of nasals by assuming that they follow a strict segmentation principle under which a segment homorganic with and phonetically overlapping an adjacent one is not represented as a separate segment. There is no tongue-movement at all between a nasal and a following consonant, in fact. There is also support for the view that the children omit nasals on the basis of a systematic phonological abstraction.[18] Malécot has shown with spectrographic and kymographic evidence that preconsonantal nasals have the effect of nasalizing preceding lax vowels. In fact, the nasals constitute distinct phonetic segments only before voiced consonants, as in *amble, candor,* and *anger.* Before voiceless consonants, as in *ample, cantor,* and *anchor,* the nasal is phonetically realized (and perceptually recognized) through vowel nasalization alone.[19] This result holds in most dialects of English for [ʌ], [i], and [æ], especially the last. Given these phonetic facts, any uniform representation of preconsonantal nasals is an abstraction. We could regard the children as generalizing in the direction of nasalized vowels, contrary to standard spelling, and then abstracting from that nasalization in their spelling.

Finally, the children's judgments may be abstract in a slightly different sense. Nasals are partially redundant in English in just the position in which the children omit them from spelling — preconsonantally. "Partially" in this case means that, given that a nasal occurs before a known consonant, one can predict all its other features, notably its place of articulation. For this reason, English spelling would carry the same information if a single symbol, say *n,* represented any nasal before a consonant. *Bump* would be spelled *bunp; bunt* and *bunk* would be spelled just as they are, and no ambiguity would be introduced. The children's spelling ignores just this one piece of information, albeit a crucial one. In this respect, it is an over-abstraction.

Treating a partially redundant segment as wholly so is not unprecedented. In Old English, and Germanic languages in general, alliteration depends on the second segment of a word if and only if the first is an [s] and the second is a true consonant. That is, [sp] must alliterate with [sp], not with [st] or [sk]. In such a cluster [s] was (and is) partially redundant in almost the same sense as preconsonantal nasals are: given that a consonant occurs initially before a true consonant, it must be [s]. Similarly, in folk-rhymes generally and Faroese Kuæði rhyme particularly, imperfect rhymes are tolerated where rhyming words differ by only one phonetic feature.[20] At the lexical level, *wet* and *went* differ by a segment specified by just one feature.

These three proposed explanations are alike in that they involve abstraction — from articulatory overlap, vowel nasalization, or partial redundancy. They all imply that nasality is a relatively minor, and place of articulation a relatively major, feature in the children's phonological system. The problem is to show how these proposals are empirically different and to obtain evidence that distinguishes among them. Confirmation for any of them would raise the problem of explaining how the children acquired the relevant principle. What is clear from the present evidence is that the original spellings are abstracted from a perceived phonetic contrast, even in a case in which the spellers have the appropriate letters available and indeed use them in other contexts.

SYLLABIC SEGMENTS

When [r], [l], [m], or [n] occurs in an English word between two consonants or at the end of a word after a consonant, they become syllabic — that is, the segment constitutes a sonority peak (in effect, a loudness maximum) and is perceived as a separate syllable. Because they know that the peak of most syllables is a vowel, and possibly influenced by the conventional spelling, adults perceive a vowel before the liquid or nasal. This perceived vowel is usually spelled *e* and may be represented either before or after the syllabic segment. The children virtually never represent such a vowel.

TIGR	(tiger)	DIKTR	(doctor)
SOGR	(sugar)	OVR	(over)
AFTR	(after)	SMOLR	(smaller)
LITTL	(little)	CANDL	(candle)
WAGN	(wagon)	OPN	(open)

This spelling applies to medial syllabic consonants as well:

GRL	(girl)	SRKIS	(circus)
FRST	(first)	HRD	(heard)
BRD	(bird)	SODNLY	(suddenly)
ALRVATA	(elevator, pronounced [elərvēytə] in a dialect common in the Boston area)		

This spelling is particularly persistent; it frequently appears even in words for which a child has otherwise learned aspects of the conventional spelling, such as the two T's in LITTL or the LY in SODNLY. On a spelling-dictation exercise, out of forty-seven first graders, twenty-one (plus some who were inconsistent) produced:

BRATHR   (brother)   TABL   (table)   FETHR   (feather)

These same first graders produced other spellings consistent with the invented ones (e.g., the nasals discussed above), but none so frequently as this one. Among the spontaneous spellers, this representation persists even in common kinship terms that the children might have occasion to learn the spellings of, to the extent that they learn any spellings.

FOT(H)R   (father)   MUTHR   (mother)   SESTR (sister)

These spellings appear to be particularly independent of adult influence, and they occur quite consistently in every child's writing. Ultimately, we would like to explain both the occurrence of the spellings and their durability.

To adults these spellings seem to represent inadmissible consonant sequences — even whole words without a vowel — and on that account to violate an apparent principle of English, that each syllable contains a vowel. This principle is true, if at all, only of surface forms, however. A lexical representation that omits predictable detail need not specify the syllabicity — the apparent vocalic quality — of these liquid and nasal segments; it is an automatic effect of the rules of English phonology.[21]

The children's treatment of syllabic segments contrasts with that of syllables consisting of a reduced vowel and an obstruent (a non-nasal true consonant, restricted by definition from being syllabic). Where liquids and nasals are not involved, their general practice is to represent a vowel in each syllable, as in CERIT (carrot), the second syllable of SRKIS, and many other examples. It would be hard to argue that there is any consistent phonetic basis for this distinction, that is, a difference in vowel quality between the syllabic segments and [C] syllables (where C represents any obstruent). Rather, the basis appears to be that the vowel is redundant in the former cases but not in the latter, generally. In other words, the children represent only lexical (unpredictable) vowels in their spelling.

The explanation must involve one of two assumptions — that the children's knowledge of English phonology is sufficiently abstract to eliminate predictable vowels, or that at some level of the tacit phonological analysis reflected in spelling, syllabics (liquids and nasals) are distinguished from other consonants.[22]

The latter appears to be more nearly correct, for after about age five, when the children begin to represent the (predictable) reduced vowel in past tense endings after [d] or [t], as in STARTID and WONTID, they still do not do so with syllabics.[23] As in other cases, there is phonetic justification for distinguishing liquids and nasals from other consonants. The fact that the former can become syllabic is related to their similarity to vowels, namely that in their articulation there is a less radical obstruction of the flow of breath than in true consonants. This explanation suggests once again that an abstract classification of English segments may be part of the knowledge of the language that a child brings to school. Again the conclusion may apply both to spontaneous spellers and to first graders who have done no preschool writing.

The children's spellings would be the conventional ones if the rules of English spelling were to change so that syllabicity was not represented. Although it would be an overgeneralization, such a change would be appropriate to the lexical character of English spelling, since the syllabics are generally single segments at the lexical level. Perhaps it is just this property of these spellings that accounts for their slowness to change. In learning conventional spelling, the child is learning to represent his phonetic perceptions in a way that eliminates redundant variation. These representations of syllabic consonants are already of this sort, generally. In this case, as for preconsonantal nasals and certain others, all quite persistent, the child must learn to mark a phonetic detail.

An interesting footnote concerns the use of a letter to spell the syllable that is its name, as in

    STRT   (start)   GRDIN   (garden)

This phenomenon is not limited to liquids and nasals; occasionally the children use this rebus-device in other contexts. It is not typical of invented spelling, and in cases where I have been able to observe the writing firsthand, the child has been quite conscious of using it and somewhat amused at it. Frank, age five, wrote

    STṚT   (start)

When I asked him what the dot meant, he replied that it showed that the letter was spelling its own name. He applied this notation fairly regularly for a few months, but only where the syllable was exactly the letter-name, as in

    Ụ   (you)   QVR   (over)

    Ṛ   (are)   MẸ   (me)

This evidence suggests what I believe to be the general case: that the children distinguish the letter-names from the sounds that the letters represent. From the beginning of writing, they use a letter to spell only a certain segment of its name;[24] after some time, they may become conscious of this distinction and exploit it in rebus-fashion, but at no stage do they appear to be confused by the letter-names, as some have suggested in connection with proposals for teaching reading. This distinction is itself no trivial analytic accomplishment, especially for the vowels.

ALTERNATIONS

One effect of not representing predictable phonetic variation in English spelling is that the alternant forms of certain lexical items are spelled uniformly. The past tense ending is *ed*, whether it occurs in its voiceless variant as in *hopped* [hapt], voiced as in *hogged* [hɔgd], or with a vowel as in *wanted* [wantəd]. Exceptional spellings occur where some aspect of pronunciation is not predictable; for past tense, there are two main cases: (1) truly exceptional verb alternations, such as *go/went*, where presumably nothing in the past form is predictable, and (2) a tense-lax alternation in medial vowels, a subregularity of the language restricted to certain verbs and indicated by a final consonant cluster, as in *creep/crept*.

The same general principle carries over in part to the spellings of plurals, where the contrasts among the phonetic realizations [s], [z], and [əz] are completely predictable. [əz] occurs after coronal stridents as in *dishes*, [s] after voiceless consonants as in *cups*, and [z] everywhere else as in *bags*. English spelling marks the first as *-es*, noting its syllabicity, but uses *-s* for both of the others. For both inflections, the spelling system abstracts away from voiced/voiceless alternation. In general, only lexical contrasts are preserved in spelling.

With these facts in mind, we now consider how the children represent predictable contrasts. There are really two questions, although only rather indirect evidence could allow us to separate them: do the children recognize the various occurrences of past tense or plural as belonging to the same morphological item, and is there any evidence from their spelling that they perceive the predictability of the variation? Do they assign phonetic or morphophonemic spellings, and do they treat exceptional items in an exceptional manner?

The answer is that generally they assign phonetic spellings at age three or four, but that a dramatic change occurs around age five or six. For the younger children, the following are typical examples

MARED   (married)   LAFFT   (left)   HALPT   (helped)

all written at age four. The same child at age five, however, used *-d* fairly uniformly, as in

WALKD   (walked)   ARIVD   (arrived)
HAPPIND   (happened)   STARTID   (started)

But he treated irregular verbs differently, often with standard forms, as in *felt* and *slept*, but also:

KUT   (cut)   FOTE   (fought)   CGOT   (caught)

There are no exceptions to this general developmental sequence among the children for whom I have examples. For one child, Edith, there is a revealing month-by-month sequence from 5.10 to 6.3, during which time this change appears to have taken place. At 5.10 she began to mark past tense endings:

HOP-T   (hopped)
STOP-T   (stopped)

But she was unable to apply this diacritic orthography to past tense consistently:

HOPPED-T	(hopped, apparently with adult coaching for HOPPED, since the double consonant and -*ed* do not otherwise occur)
CAT-T	(cat)
WAT	(went)
WOCT	(walked)

The following month (5.11) showed more of the same; she had revised her notation slightly, and she treated an exceptional form as if it were regular.

THA'T	(that)
JUS'T	(just)
WAN'T	(went)

At 6.0 (really almost two months later) we have the first uniform treatment of regular past forms. The diacritics disappeared, along with any apparent confusion between verbal inflections and the inherent segments of other words.

PEKD	(peeked)
FILLD	(filled)

The -D of PEKD was the only morphophonemic spelling in this month; it was also the only phonetic [-t] as an inflection. Otherwise, [t] was spelled phonetically.

Two months later (6.2) there was more evidence that Edith could spell past tense endings uniformly; she had also, however, begun to learn that exceptions may be spelled more phonetically, an insight that she applies correctly in one case, fails to apply in another, and overgeneralizes in a third.

LAFT	(left)
WAND	(went)
WISPRT	(whispered)
RASTD	(rested)

Beginning the following month, and ever since, Edith treated regular and irregular forms correctly, except for the non-occurrence of the *e* in -*ed* endings.

WALKD	(walked)
SLAPT	(slept)

This girl's development in this detail is only a more fully illustrated and more explicit (with her diacritic innovation) version of what the other young spellers appear to have done.[25] Nevertheless, it would be hasty to base deep principles on so few cases. What does seem clear is that the invented spellings are phonetic in this detail until late in the preschool period. Then rather suddenly the children begin to abstract from the phonetic contrast toward a uniform spelling of past tense inflections. At the same time, they rapidly develop a correct distinction of regular and irregular cases, even when the irregularity involves a rather limited class like *wept—slept—crept*.

It would be incorrect, I think, to attribute all of this development to adult teaching. The girl who wrote the last class of examples attended a Montessori school, even in her sixth year, where the practice was to accept all the children's writing with a minimum of correction. Her mother, who had gone to a Montessori school herself, followed much the same practice at home; she told her children spellings only when they asked, and she rarely corrected what they offered. In fact, almost all of these children got correction from their parents only when they asked; that seems to have been a necessary condition for the spontaneous spelling to occur at all. Of course the child has used information from adults — by age six, most children have acquired information from reading as well as oral instruction — but this information apparently has been "filtered" through the child's own notions, which exert a powerful influence on what he writes.

Notice, furthermore, that almost all the spellings deviate from the standard, if not in the ending, then in the vowel, and they do so in regular ways. A uniform -*D* may appear for both [d] and [t] in regular past forms long before the standard -*ed*. These spellings are certainly not copied from adults in any simple sense. The development from phonetic to morphophonemic is not a direct move from phonetic to adult spelling; rather, there is a dramatic change in the type of (non-adult) spelling the child creates.

The treatment of plurals appears to be a special case of the general conclusion; from the first writings on, the children spell plurals -*s*, marking no distinction between the voiced and unvoiced variants. They do (sometimes) mark the vowel of the syllabic ending [əz], as adult spelling does. The following examples are typical:

WENDOWS	(windows)	RASIS	(races)
WANSAS	(Wednesdays)	CIDEJCHES	(sandwiches)
LADYS	(ladies [age five])	HOUESS	(houses)

The same children use -*s* for voiceless endings, too, of course.

SOKS	(socks)	STMPS	(stamps)	RABITS	(rabbits)

In fact, *s* stands for phonetic [z] and [s] in inherent segments as well as in inflections.

CLOWSD	(closed)	KUS	('cause)
WUS	(was)	SESTR	(sister)
BEECOS	(because)	SAND	(send)

In general, *z* occurs rarely and only in positions such as initial prevocalic segments, where the occurrence of voicing is not predictable, as in ZIP.

The phonetic difference between [s] and [z] is not as great in final position, at least for some speakers, as in other positions.[26] It may be important, then, to ask whether the children represent the difference medially, where the phonetic contrast is greater and where voicing is also sometimes predictable.[27] (Leaving aside many details, voicing is assimilative, so that [s] occurs in voiceless consonant clusters, but [z] occurs elsewhere.) Evidence is less plentiful, but what there is clearly supports the conclusion that the children ignore the phonetic contrast. Compare, for instance,

RASIS	(races)	SUSE	(Susie)
SESTR	(sister)	CLOWSD	(closed)
PANSEL	(pencil)	PRESINS	(presents)

That the children do not distinguish [s] and [z] in their spelling can be explained in three quite different ways. First, the children may not generally perceive the two sounds as distinct. This result would be a clear counter-instance to the general conclusion that the children perceive fine phonetic differences, including other voicing contrasts, as in the [t]-[d]-[D] alterations, for instance. However, children of even three and a half years can usually answer questions involving pairs that differ only in voicing, such as *sip/zip, racer/razor*, and *bus/buzz*.[28] Accordingly, I believe that this explanation is untenable.

Second, considering the reversals of letters in children's writing, it is conceivable that the visual distinction between *s* and *z* is too difficult for the children to make consistently; so they settle on one, the more common *s*, as the representation for both. This hypothesis does not deny that the children can make the phonetic discrimination. I am inclined to reject this view for a number of reasons: first, on this supposition one would expect the spelling distinction to reappear among children who make a very angular *z* but a curved *s*, or among children of European background who write a barred *ƶ*, or among children who learn to typewrite (as three of those discussed here did), and who therefore can rely on a positional as well as a shape difference. As far as I can judge, none of these expectations is correct. Furthermore, these children had no serious difficulty with other pairs of letters that are mirror-images or inversions, such as *b/d, w/m*, and *u/n*. There are occasional reversed letters, as in all children's printing, but not nearly enough to cause any of these other distinctions to collapse, nor is the reversal entirely in one direction.

A third interpretation is that the children distinguish [s] and [z] quite early and, perhaps even before beginning to write, conclude that their occurrence is predictable, so that spelling can be abstract from this difference without loss of information. This conclusion would be another overgeneralization, but not for plurals, the most common example. If this hypothesis is correct, we have another, and much earlier example of a typical process: the child has fairly narrow phonetic perceptions, but abstracts from these in systematic ways in spelling. In this case the abstraction is from a voicing contrast, just as in the case of the past-tense inflections and the rapid development of *T* for intervocalic flaps. Under this interpretation, the problem is to explain why this treatment of [s] and [z] emerges much earlier than these similar spellings for stops.

Adopting this view, we find evidence about a question raised by Berko in her classic study of children's acquisition of morphology. Having shown that preschool children can form the appropriate [s] or [z] plural of even nonsense forms, and thus that they have acquired knowledge of a rule that extends to new instances, Berko questions whether the rule is morphological or phonological in nature, and notes, "It would be interesting to find out what the child thinks he is saying — if we could in some way ask him the general question, 'How do you make the plural?'"[29] We might look upon the invented spellings as embodying an answer to this general question, namely that the children regard these plural alternants as a single form at the level relevant to spelling — just as adults do, in fact.

Accordingly, a pedagogical orthography, such as i.t.a., that employs distinct symbols for the voiced and voiceless plurals may be introducing phonetic detail that a pre-school child can readily, even spontaneously, learn to abstract away from. Considering the abstract nature of children's invented spellings, we find that phonemic accuracy in pedagogical spellings may be an inappropriate goal. The question is really deeper: which phonetic facts are relevant in the child's own phonological system as he begins to read and write?

CONCLUSION

We have seen evidence that children tacitly recognize certain phonetic contrasts and similarities, in that they represent these in their original spelling. For systematic reasons, standard English spelling does not reflect these same relationships. The contrasts, such as that between the first segments of *tuck* and *truck*, are predictable in context and therefore irrelevant to meaning and its representation in spelling. The similarities, such as that between tense and lax vowels, are not represented directly in standard spelling because of its abstract lexical character. Perhaps as a result of knowledge of this system, most adults do not recognize these phonetic relations; they have to learn, or relearn, them in order to understand the children's judgments. What the children do not know is the set of lexical representations and the system of phonological rules that account for much of standard spelling; what they do know is a system of phonetic relationships that they have not been taught by their parents and teachers.

We have seen that the children choose representations in terms of phonetic properties, such as nasality, syllabicity, backness, height, and affrication. These are some of the terms in which the rules of English phonology must be stated. The contrary result would have been entirely possible; the children might have recognized no relation between the "flap" in *water* and the [d] of *waddle*, or between the vowels of *bite* and *pot*, although these share the properties of voicing and backness, respectively. In fact, the children might not have judged the segmentation of English words as they did; for example, that DIKTR (doctor) has five segments that need to be represented.

Finally, we have seen that children treat certain relationships as more basic than others in their spelling. Backness is preserved in place of tenseness and height for the vowels; affrication and place-of-articulation predominate over nasality and voicing for the consonants. On these bases, the children's spelling is systematically abstract from perceived phonetic detail. This characteristic is particularly notable in the abstraction from nasality, syllabicity, and voicing in certain contexts. These choices are not required by any lack of symbols, since in other contexts the children use letters

(M,N,G,E,D, and Z) that represent these qualities. Evidently the children abstract on the basis of their tacit analysis of phonological features (as in distinguishing [r,l,m, and n] from other consonants in syllabic contexts) and possibly the predictability of certain details of pronunciation (such as the voicing of [t] between vowels). In general, the children treat sounds, not as unanalyzed wholes, but as items related by their constituent properties, and modified in regular, hence irrelevant, ways by their contexts. This result conflicts with the assumption that children are necessarily limited to matching spellings with phonemes defined on superficial taxonomic grounds. The children who created their own spellings arrived at a deeper analysis of English phonology a year or more before beginning school.

It would be easy but, I believe, incorrect to disregard the evidence presented here as having been produced by exceptional children. In that they began to spell and, often, to read early, these children were exceptional. Some, but not all, appeared to be independent and creative beyond the average, but their creativity was sometimes a result of their spelling accomplishments. Most of them came from relatively privileged middle-class families, with professional and academic parents, but this fact may have been a result of the informal procedure by which I located young spellers. Within this limitation, the families were quite diverse in beliefs and backgrounds. The one characteristic that all the parents had in common was a willingness to accept the child's own spelling efforts, to provide simple materials (first blocks and other elementary alphabet toys, then paper and pencil), and to answer questions. A cluster of unfortunate attitudes prevalent in our society may suppress this willingness in many parents: a fear that the child's own efforts will lead to "bad habits," a belief that English spelling is bizarre, and a corresponding reliance on the expertise of professional teachers or on sometimes complex educational devices that bear the stamp of expert approval. All of the parents provided just the information that any inexpert literate adult could provide: the names of the letters and answers to such questions as, "How do you spell 'chuh'?" They did not coax or expect their children to spell; most were surprised, in fact. There were no unusual educational devices relevant to spelling in any of the homes, and although the parents may have had inner qualms about "bad habits," their manner was relaxed and nondidactic. All of the children now in the primary grades and above have readily mastered standard spelling, with none of the laborious retraining that the notion of "habits" implies. Learning to spell need not be a process of acquiring habits, apparently.

In any case, to attribute the children's accomplishment a priori to exceptional general intelligence or an exceptional environment merely begs the important question. The children had tacitly acquired a knowledge of phonological relations of which their parents were themselves unaware. What the children had learned was not related in any obvious way to what they had heard or seen. The important theoretical question is how preschool children can learn abstract relations of this sort. Until we have serious evidence bearing on this question, we cannot assume that general intelligence must be the major factor in acquiring the knowledge that makes spelling possible. Even if it were true that all young spellers are exceptionally intelligent, the statistical observation by itself would not account for the occurrence of the spelling, nor, more important, for the specific and uniform character of what they all learned.

Whatever variations there may be in individual development, the crucial conclusion remains that children can (and to some degree, must) make abstract inferences about the sound system of their language before they learn to read and write.

The educational importance of this conclusion seems clear enough, at least in general. We can no longer assume that a child must approach reading and writing as an untrained animal approaches a maze with no discernible prior conception of its structure. We cannot assume, in the essentially digestive metaphor that Paulo Freire rightly ridicules,[30] that the child is an empty vessel, mentally inert although physically so dynamic, waiting to be filled with adult spellings. Evidently, a child may come to school with a knowledge of some phonological categories and relations; without conscious awareness, he may seek to relate English spelling to these in some generally systematic way. If this inference is correct, some long-neglected questions turn out to be crucial for understanding and facilitating the process of learning to read: what levels of phonological analysis do individual children tacitly control at various stages of development; how do these analyses relate to the lexical representations that generally correspond to standard spelling; and how can reading instruction build on this relationship, while encouraging children to extend and deepen their notion of the sound system of the language? Detailed answers to these questions are not at all obvious; in fact, it is difficult to devise means of acquiring some answers, since children's phonological judgments are rarely explicit, as they are in the invented spellings. So far, we have evidence that at least some children do not attend to statistical associations between spellings and autonomous phonemes, which have been the subject of much research in reading. Rather, the children pair spellings with segments abstractly categorized in terms of a hierarchy of articulatory features.

In the classroom, an informed teacher should expect that seemingly bizarre spellings may represent a system of abstract phonological relations of which adults are quite unaware. Until we understand this system better, we can at least respect it and attempt to work with it, if only intuitively. A child who wants to spell *truck* with a *ch-* will not be enlightened by being told that *ch-* spells "chuh," as in *chicken*. He already knows that; in fact, the relation between the first segments of *truck* and *chicken* is exactly what he wants to represent. Nor will exaggerated (or exasperated) pronunciation of *truck* help much, for monolingual adult speakers of English are usually limited to pronouncing the two possibilities that our phonology allows. We will either insert a false vowel after the [t], which does away with the affrication at the cost of distorting the word, or we will exaggerate that very quality that the child wishes to represent. Drill and memorization of words with *tr-* and *dr-* may help the child to learn such cases, but these techniques suggest that spelling is arbitrarily related to speech and can only be memorized. This suggestion is not true of either standard spelling or the child's own invention. Better, it would seem, to say something like, "Yes, *truck* sounds like *chicken* at the beginning, but it is also like the first sound of *toy*, and that's what we show by using a *t*." Similarly for the child who spells *pen* with an *a* (or *dent* without an *n*, *brother* without an *e*, *liked* with a *t*, or *butter* with a *d*). Such a child needs to be told, in effect, that his phonological judgments are not wrong (though they may seem so to most adults), and that it is reasonable, indeed necessary, to categorize abstractly what he hears.

However, he must also learn that standard spelling reflects a system somewhat different from his own. He will have acquired the basis for this adult system only when he has tacitly learned rules such as affrication and vowel shift that make the standard spellings systematically accurate.[31] Then he can learn to read and spell on the principle that the written form corresponds to an abstract (lexical) form, not directly to what he hears. He is on his way when he begins to abstract form phonetic variations, as the spontaneous spellers did in their preschool development. It may be particularly important to recognize when his own efforts are too abstract, or abstract in the wrong direction, and to suggest, at least implicitly, that he is using the right principle, even if in the wrong place. We cannot teach him this principle if we ourselves continue to believe that to learn to spell is to get in the "habit" of associating sounds with letters, or phonemes with graphemes. For at least some children, to learn standard spelling is to learn to broaden and deepen their preschool phonological analysis, which may already be abstract enough that phoneme-grapheme correspondences are indirect outcomes of an intricate system.

Our understanding of children's phonology is still shallow and fragmentary at best. The reasonable conclusion to be drawn from this work at this time is not that old dogmas should be replaced with new, but that we now have good reason to look more carefully at children's judgments of English phonology and spelling. In the meantime, we must assume that learning to read and write are matters of knowledge rather than habit, to use the terms of an old but honorable distinction.

NOTES

1. Noam Chomsky and Morris Halle, *The Sound Pattern of English* (New York: Harper & Row, 1968). The phonological analysis assumed in this chapter is largely that of this work.
2. Carol Chomsky, "Reading, Writing, and Phonology," *Harvard Educational Review*, 40 (Spring 1970), 287–309. This includes a helpful discussion of the lexicon. See also Noam Chomsky, "Phonology and Reading," in *Basic Studies on Reading*, ed. H. Levin and J. Williams (New York: Basic Books, 1970); Chomsky and Halle, *The Sound Pattern*, pp. 54–55 *et passim*; Wayne O'Neil, "The Spelling and Pronunciation of English," in *The American Heritage Dictionary of the English Language*, ed. William Morris (Boston: Houghton Mifflin, 1969), xxxv–xxxvii.
3. Noam Chomsky, *Aspects of the Theory of Syntax* (Cambridge, MA: MIT Press, 1965), ch. 1; Jerry A. Fodor, *Psychological Explanation* (New York: Random House, 1968).
4. I do not intend the term *conventional* to suggest that English spelling is conventional in the sense of "arbitrary." The references of footnote 2 discuss some bases of standard spelling.
5. Idiosyncrasies of a child's pronunciation do not always affect his spelling. Some of these children had well-known nonstandard articulations of sibilants, interdentals, and liquids; in some cases, they nevertheless spelled these sounds in the same way as other children. Nor was the parents' speech necessarily a model for spelling, in the case of parents with dialects different from their children's, especially a few non-native speakers of English. The evidence is too limited for any confidence, but it may be that children can abstract away from any one pronunciation in creating their spellings, at least for certain features.
6. (Broad) phonetic transcriptions will appear in square brackets; phonological representations, in slashes. The invented spellings will be entirely upper-case; standard spellings and individual letters will be italicized. Ages will be stated as, for example, 5.3 (five years, three months).
7. As in italicized positions in *th*in, *th*en, *sh*ip, mea*s*ure, *g*o, si*ng*, and *h*ave.

8. Vowels are described in terms of the position of the tongue during articulation — front or back, high, mid or low. Tenseness and laxness of vosels refer to a complex of articulatory properties. The vowel of *bite* is back, but unrounded.

9. See the references of footnote 2 for a further discussion of this issue.

10. Roman Jakobson, *Child Language, Aphasia, and Phonological Universals* (The Hague: Mouton, 1968), p. 75. First published in 1941, this is the seminal work in this field.

11. Chomsky and Halle, *The Sound Pattern*, p. 410.

12. In principle, the Initial Teaching Alphabet (i.t.a.) is based on this criticism. See chapter five of my "Children's Perceptions of the Sounds of English," Diss., Harvard University, 1970.

13. Further evidence that the children can analyze the letter-names occurs in the front vowels, not only for lax forms, but also in spellings like PLEYS (please), where the glide has been made explicit.

14. See Chomsky and Halle, *The Sound Pattern*, pp. 178–187, for a discussion of the rules relating these pairs. See Carol Chomsky, "Reading, Writing, and Phonology," for a less technical discussion of the alternations and their spelling.

15. The adult spelling includes a final "silent" *e* in some of the tense cases. This is not simply a discontinuous digraphic spelling but has an independent function in lexical representations. Chomsky and Halle, *The Sound Pattern*, pp. 147–150.

16. See chapter two of the dissertation referred to in footnote 12.

17. As there would be if words like *Christmas*, *chrome*, and *chronic* were pronounced with a first segment like that of *chop*, for instance.

18. There is no question, incidentally, that the children perceive the nasality that they do not represent — that they hear a distinctive difference between *wet* and *went*, for instance. An independent test with such pairs confirmed this point. The question is where they think the difference lies.

19. A. Malécot, "Vowel Nasality as a Distinctive Feature in American English," *Language*, 36 (1960), 222–229.

20. I am indebted to Wayne O'Neil for these observations about OE alliteration and folk-rhyme. They are reported in his paper, "The Reality of Grammars: Some Literary Evidence," unpublished manuscript.

21. See Chomsky and Halle, *The Sound Pattern*, pp. 85–89, for a discussion of such a rule and an independent justification of a lexical representation that omits syllabicity.

22. See Chomsky and Halle, *The Sound Pattern*, pp. 353–355, for a discussion of a classificatory framework that makes this distinction in terms of a feature called *syllabic*.

23. Furthermore, there is little evidence that the children distinguish between lexical and predictable vowels in syllabic positions. There are, however, the spellings MANTIN (mountain) and ANEMEL (animal) where the vowels explicitly represented must be lexical because they remain in nonsyllabic positions, as in *mountainous* and *animality*.

24. The children apply this principle even in the use of H [ēyč] to spell [č], as in the first grader's spelling of the initial sound of *try*, *train*, etc. A parallel example is the use of Y [wāy] to spell [w], as in YUTS (once). This came from a child, 4.6, whose parents often urged her to use the letter that seemed closest when she asked about spelling.

25. She was not the only child who marked inflections. Another girl, Pammie, went from LOOK, T (also NURS, T; CALL, D; NAME, D; etc.) at age seven to LOOK'D, etc., at age eight.

26. This was pointed out to me by Emmon Bach. Where it applies, it is perhaps a minor reflection in English of a general tendency toward de-voicing of final obstruents, as is the rule in German, for instance.

27. Some problems remain in the exact formulation. See Chomsky and Halle, *The Sound Pattern*, pp. 228–229 and 232–233.

28. See chapter three of the dissertation referred to in footnote 12.

29. Jean Berko, "The Child's Learning of English Morphology," in *Psycholinguistics*, ed. Sol Saporta (New York: Holt, Rinehart & Winston, 1961), p. 373.

30. Paulo Freire, "The Adult Literacy Process as Cultural Action for Freedom," *Harvard Educational Review*, 40 (Spring 1970), 205–225.

31. See Carol Chomsky, "Reading, Writing, and Phonology," for some suggestions as to how this process may be facilitated.

Stages in
Language Development and
Reading Exposure

CAROL CHOMSKY

This chapter summarizes a study of linguistic development in elementary school children. We investigated children's knowledge of specific aspects of the syntax of English by testing their comprehension of a number of complex structures. Thirty-six children between the ages of six and ten were in the experiment.

Because the study deals with only a few structures, it does not attempt a general description of children's grammar within the age group. Rather it traces the acquisition of specific structures, revealing interesting aspects of the children's construction of implicit grammatical rules. In addition, the results demonstrate a common order of acquisition of syntactic structures among the different children though there is considerable variation in age of acquisition. This shared order of acquisition of structures defines a developmental sequence of linguistic stages through which all of the children apparently pass. The ages at which different children reach the stages vary, but the sequence of stages appears to be the same for all.

A second aspect of the study investigated the children's exposure to the written language through independent reading and through listening to books read aloud. We examined the relation between rate of linguistic development and exposure to written materials as a source of complex language inputs. Our results show a strong correlation between a number of the reading exposure measures and language development. A description of the reading study is presented in the second half of this chapter, along with a discussion of the relations between language development, the reading measures, IQ, and socioeconomic status (SES).

This chapter is a brief and fairly condensed description of a detailed study of several years' duration, and it attempts to present only the highlights of the methods employed and the experimental results.

FRAMEWORK FOR THE LINGUISTIC STUDY

The approach and methods of the linguistic study, described in detail in an earlier work,[1] demonstrate the feasibility of dealing with the learning of complex syntactic

Harvard Educational Review Vol. 42 No. 1 February 1972, 1–33

structures in children beyond age five through psycholinguistic experimentation. This is the period of life when a major portion of the task of language acquisition has already been accomplished. The child of six exhibits competence with his* native language that appears to approach adult competence. Discrepancies between his grammar and adult grammar are rarely revealed in spontaneous speech.

Our purpose is to explore areas in which the six-year-old's knowledge of his language falls short of adult knowledge, and to gain information about the course of the acquisition of this knowledge as the child matures. In order to deal with these questions, we must first characterize what we mean by knowing one's language. In effect, we must answer the question, "What is the nature of the information that is acquired by the child?"

Clearly, speakers of a language do not draw from a memorized list of all possible sentences in their language each time they wish to say something. Rather, they can understand and produce sentences they have never before heard. Indeed, a major portion of language usage consists of sentences that have never been spoken or written before, for example, this sentence or the closing sentence of any article in today's *New York Times*.

Given any sequence of words we care to devise, speakers can recognize whether or not the sequence constitutes a sentence in their language. This creative aspect of language use rests on the fact that we have learned the system of rules for making sentences. This system is called the grammar of the language.

Our knowledge of these rules is implicit. We are not taught them, and we would be hard put to state even the smallest fraction of them. Yet they govern our speech.

Because these rules are implicit, they cannot be observed directly. While the linguist is interested in the speaker's *competence* (the underlying system of rules), he has access only to a speaker's *performance* (the way he uses the rules). Thus, various aspects of performance are used to reveal the nature of underlying competence.

What the child learns, then, as he acquires his language is a complex system of rules that enables him to understand and produce the sentences of his language. He internalizes these rules from what he hears by a process of active construction as yet little understood. His earliest utterances, even at the stage when he begins to put two words together to make sentences, are innovative and rule-governed. The evidence shows he is not just repeating fragments of sentences he has heard, but is creating his own sentences according to grammatical rules that he continually constructs and revises. The acquisition of syntax, then, means developing the rule system, restructuring it with increasing maturity as new evidence is added, and eventually producing an internalized grammar that accords with the facts of the language.

How do we employ this framework in studying knowledge of syntax in children between six and ten? The problem is that by age six, a child's grammar, as revealed in his spontaneous speech, does not appreciably differ from adult grammar. In order to identify areas in which child and adult grammar are different, we must actively probe the child's linguistic performance. We can do this by selecting complex grammatical structures — structures that we consider difficult and, therefore, likely to be acquired

---

*The masculine form of pronoun is used for convenience; children of both sexes were included in the study.

relatively late. Children's comprehension and interpretation of these complex structures yield evidence of the syntactic rules employed and the way in which these rules diverge from adult grammar. As we gain information about these child/adult discrepancies, we may contribute to existing notions about language complexity.

On the basis of current linguistic work we are able to select a variety of complex structures that appear to be likely candidates for late acquisition. Potential structures would include those "which deviate from a widely established pattern in the language, or whose surface structure is relatively inexplicit with respect to grammatical relationships, or even simply those which the linguist finds particularly difficult to incorporate into a thorough description."[2] Some candidate structures turn out to be difficult for the children; some do not.

In order to be useful in this study, a structure must also lend itself to testing with young children. We must be able to devise an operational test of comprehension that even six-year-olds can handle. This requirement sharply limits the selection. The structures and tests finally decided upon are the result of much planning and revision, a good bit of pilot testing, and many discards.

Altogether, we tested nine structures with the children. Of these, only the five that turned out to be relevant to an overall developmental sequence will be discussed here. The other four were either too easy (all the children knew them), too hard (known by only one or two of the children), or they elicited scattered responses not relevant to the sequence. Almost twice as many structures were tested as turned out to be relevant to the developmental sequence. Thus, we proceeded by collecting a range of structures, testing them all, and leaving it up to the experimental results to reveal a sequence, if any.

We did have some theoretical and practical guidelines to aid in selecting structures. For example, the relation between two structures, *promise* and *ask*, is such that a given order of acquisition is implied on theoretical grounds. *Promise* is simpler than *ask* along a particular scale of complexity, and ought therefore to be acquired first. And, in fact, evidence of this predicted order was found in an earlier experiment with *promise* and *ask*.[3] These two structures, then, were useful to include because of their strong potential for yielding developmental data. Another construction, *easy to see*, is recognized as a good indicator of grammatical development from the work of several different researchers[4] although no experimental work has yet suggested a relationship to other constructions in terms of order of acquisition. This construction was included because of its stability as a measure. Use of the measure led to identical conclusions in three separate experiments. Beyond considerations of this sort, there was little to go on. In fact, all of the constructions tested with children for the first time here resulted from a fortuitous intersection of complex structures and experimental techniques that could measure them.

Our experimental procedure elicited information from the children by direct interview. By age six, the children are willing to be questioned, play games, carry out tasks, manipulate toys, identify pictures, and engage in conversation. The interview was carried out informally and, for the children, was interesting play.

Our test group ranged in age from five years old, when many of the children gave evidence of not yet knowing the constructions, up to ten years old, when a number of the children exhibited an adult command of the structures. For some structures there was considerable variation in age of acquisition in different children. Of particular interest is that this variation in *age* of acquisition does not seem to affect *order* of acquisition of different structures. For the structures reported here, the evidence is that linguistic development, whether it occurs earlier or later, nevertheless proceeds along similar paths. This has been a basic and repeated finding of longitudinal studies with younger children at earlier stages of language development. It is encouraging that the same principle is demonstrable on the basis of cross-sectional studies with older children at much later stages of linguistic development.

We drew children from an elementary school in Cambridge, Massachusetts, which is predominantly middle-class, but has nevertheless some range in the socioeconomic background of the children. Thirty-six children from kindergarten through fourth grade were selected to ensure a representative sample in terms of age and reading level. The children were interviewed individually at school by the author and an assistant over a period of several months in the fall of 1969, with each interview lasting about a half hour.

THE TEST CONSTRUCTIONS

1.   The construction *Easy to See* in the sentence *"The doll is easy to see."*

In this interview we tested the child's ability to determine the grammatical relations that hold among the words in sentences of the form *The doll is easy to see*.

The complexity of this construction derives from the fact that the grammatical relations among its words are not expressed directly in its surface structure. Of the two constructions

(a)   The doll is eager to see.
(b)   The doll is easy to see.

which look alike on the surface, only (a) retains in its surface structure the relations of subject and verb that are implicit in the meaning of the sentence; i.e., not only is *doll* the subject of sentence (a), but it is also the implicit subject of the complement verb *see*. The surface structure of (a) expresses this by normal word order of subject precedes verb. In (b), however, the word order is misleading. *Doll* is actually the implicit *object* of the complement verb *see*, for in (b) it is easy for someone else to see the doll. The implicit subject of *see* is omitted in (b)'s surface structure, and the listener must fill it in for himself as "someone else." The child who has not yet learned to recognize the underlying difference in structure of these two superficially similar sentences will interpret them both according to surface structure, and report that in (b), as well as (a), it is the doll who is doing the seeing. Such a child would interpret (b) incorrectly to mean "It is easy for the doll to see," instead of "It is easy for someone else to see the doll."

The interview was opened by placing a doll, with eyes that close, lying down with eyes closed on a table in front of the child. The child was then asked to say whether the doll was easy to see or hard to see. After responding, he was asked the question "why?" Then he was asked to make the doll either easy to see or hard to see, depending on his response to the first question.

The child who interprets the sentence correctly will answer that the doll is easy to see and support this interpretation when asked by answering that the doll is right there in front of him. When asked to make the doll hard to see he will hide the doll under the table or cover his own eyes or make a similar meaningful response.

The child who misinterprets the sentence and answers that the doll is hard to see will support this interpretation by indicating that her eyes are closed so she can't see and when asked to make her easy to see will open the doll's eyes.

This construction was fairly easy for the children. Everyone over age 7.1[5] succeeded with it, and below this age there was mixed success and failure. Five of the children below 7.1 failed, approximately half of this age group. Our sample did not include children young enough for us to observe onset of acquisition. Below we will see that lack of competence in this construction constitutes Stage 1 in our developmental sequence.

2. The construction *Promise* as in *"Bozo promises Donald to stand on the book."*

Here we examined the child's knowledge of a particular syntactic structure associated with the word *promise*. His ability to identify the missing subject of a complement verb following *promise* was tested, a task that is relatively complex for the following reasons. Consider the sentences

    (a)   Bozo promised Donald to stand on the book.
    (b)   Bozo told Donald to stand on the book.

In these sentences the subject of the verb *stand* is not expressed, but must be filled in by the listener. Although the two sentences are superficially alike, differing only in their main verbs *promise* and *tell*, in (a) it is Bozo who is to stand on the book, and in (b) it is Donald who is to stand on the book. Since this information is not given anywhere in the surface structure of these sentences, the listener must, in order to interpret them differently, draw on his underlying knowledge of the verbs *promise* and *tell* and the structures associated with them.

Sentence (b) is a very common structure in English. The missing subject of a complement verb is almost always the first noun phrase preceding it. If Bozo tells Donald to stand on the book, it is Donald who is to do the standing. This is true for almost all verbs in English that can substitute for *tell* in this sentence, for example, *persuades, urges, expects, wants, orders, hires, likes,* etc. We learn this rule early and we learn it well. *Promise*, however, is an exception. With *promise* the missing subject is not the closest noun phrase, but a noun phrase farther away. This is a rare construction in English found with only a very few verbs. In order to interpret sentence (a) correctly, we must have learned in dealing with *promise* to discard the general rule and to substitute the special rule for *promise*.

Our expectation was that children who have not yet learned this exceptional feature of the verb *promise* will use their well-learned general principle and interpret sentence (a) according to the structure of (b). They will report that in (a) it is Donald who is to stand on the book; Bozo promises Donald that he, Donald, can stand on the book. In a previous experiment carried out by this writer, this was found to be the case; some children still misinterpreted the construction up to the age of eight and one-half, and uniform success was achieved only above this age.[6]

To test knowledge of this construction we had the child manipulate two toy figures to illustrate the action of a series of test sentences. The figures used were Bozo the Clown and Donald Duck, and a book was provided for them to stand on.

First it was determined that the child knew the meaning of the word *promise* by asking questions such as: Can you tell me what you would say to your friend if you promise him that you'll call him up this afternoon? What do you mean when you make somebody a promise? What's special about a promise?

Then the child was asked to name the two figures. Practice sentences were given to familiarize the child with the actions and with the "intentional" nature of the test sentences. The child has to illustrate how the stated intention of the sentence is carried out because in "Bozo promises Donald to stand on the book," the child shows who stands on the book. The practice sentences introduce this notion: Bozo wants to do a somersault — Make him do it. Bozo wants Donald to do a somersault — Have him do it. Donald decides to stand on the book — Make him do it.

This was followed by five test sentences of the form "Donald promises Bozo to hop up and down — Make him hop."

In general the children easily understood what they were to do, and appeared to enjoy the task. The sentences were repeated freely for those children who required repetitions or who seemed to hesitate.

The children who interpreted the sentences correctly selected the more distant noun phrase as subject of *stand*. For "Bozo promised Donald to stand on the book — Make him do it," they picked up Bozo and placed him on the book. The children who misinterpreted the construction selected the closest noun phrase as subject of *stand*. In response to this same sentence, they picked up Donald and placed him on the book.

We found the children to be highly consistent in their responses. The most common response was to assign the missing subject the same way in all five sentences, whether correct or incorrect, and to do so rapidly and with assurance. Only a very few children varied their responses, and generally these were the ones who hesitated and appeared confused.

Our results indicate that this construction was relatively easy for the children. Criterion for success was four correct out of five. Two-thirds of the thirty-six children succeeded with the construction. The failers, with one exception, were all under eight years old, with failure being the rule for the five-year-olds, as likely as success for the six-year-olds, and the exception for the seven-year-olds. Lack of competence in this construction with the verb *promise* distinguishes children in Stage 2 in our developmental sequence from those in Stage 3.

3.   The construction *Ask* as in *"The girl asked the boy what to paint."*

This interview examined the child's knowledge of a particular syntactic structure associated with the verb *ask*. This construction, or the child's handling of the verb *ask* in general, proves to be a particularly good indicator of syntactic development. The child must identify the missing subject of a verb following *ask* in a complement clause, introduced by a question word such as *when* or *what*, for example, the subject of *paint* in

The girl asked the boy what to paint.

The verb *ask* breaks a general structural rule of English as does *promise*. The nature of the complexity of this construction has been treated at length elsewhere,[7] and will be reviewed only briefly here.

Consider the sentences

(a)   The girl asked the boy what to paint.
(b)   The girl told the boy what to paint.

The missing subject of *paint* in (a) is *the girl*. The correct paraphrase of (a) is *The girl asked the boy what she should paint*. In (b), as in most other sentences of this form in English, the missing subject is *the boy*, that is, *the girl told the boy what he should paint*. Since the weight of evidence in the language as a whole favors the (b) interpretation, children who have not yet learned this exceptional feature of the verb *ask* will interpret sentence (a) according to the structure of (b). They will report that in (a) the girl is asking the boy what he is going to paint. This interpretation persists in some children until age ten or later.

The actual interview consisted of a conversational portion and a picture identification test. In the conversational portion, two children who knew each other well carried out a number of tasks according to instructions. Only one child was being tested, the second child serving as a conversational partner. The two children were seated at a table on which were placed toy food, and figures of Donald Duck, Pluto Pup, and Bozo. We explained to the child that he was going to play some games with the things on the table; he would feed the dog, for example, and so on.

The instructions themselves were then given. *Ask* instructions were interspersed with *tell* instructions, but the opening instruction was always *ask*. The interview proceeded as follows:

Interviewer: Ask Bruce what to feed the dog.
Child: THE HAMBURGER.
Interviewer: Tell Bruce what food to put back in the box.
Child: THE HOT DOG.
                   etc.

The interview was carried out in an informal conversational manner, with repetitions, extra instructions at the child's point of difficulty, discussion of confusions and inconsistencies, and with special attempts to draw the child's attention to his "errors." Maximum help was given the child to express what he knew.

Errors were of two kinds. Some children told their partner what to do in response to an *ask* instruction, rather than asking him. *The hamburger* above would be a correct response if the instruction had been "Tell Bruce what to feed the dog." Children who respond in this manner have failed to interpret *ask* as requiring a question response, and respond as if instructed to tell. This response error indicated the least competence with the verb *ask*.

When making the other error, children asked their partner a question, but assigned the wrong missing subject to the key verb, responding to "Ask Bruce what to feed the dog" with "What are you going to feed the dog?" The child who answers in this manner understands that he is to ask a question, but has not yet learned that *ask* signals an exception to his well-learned general rule of English for picking missing subjects. He picks his missing subject incorrectly, according to the general rule, which says to choose your partner rather than yourself. He may ask a variety of questions, all with the subject *you* following *ask;* for example,

> What do you want to feed the dog? or
> What are you going to feed the dog?

This response indicates greater competence with *ask* than the preceding response, but still reveals lack of knowledge of *ask* as signaling an exceptional structure.[8]

Only one-third of the children were able to give the correct response, asking a question and assigning the correct subject to the key verb, responding to "Ask Bruce what to feed the dog," with the question "What should I feed the dog?" This response indicates mastery of the construction, and was the only one accepted as correct for our purposes. Criterion for success was correct response to at least four-fifths of the instructions given.[9]

After the conversational portion of the interview was concluded, the partner left, and the subject was shown two pairs of pictures (Figures 1 and 2). For Pair 1 he was

FIGURE 1   *Test Pictures 1a and 1b.*

Test sentence: The girl asks the boy what to paint.
Subject is shown both pictures simultaneously and asked

1. *Which picture shows the girl asking the boy what to paint?*
2. *What is she saying to him?*

1a. Correct interpretation   *1b. Incorrect interpretation*

FIGURE 2   *Test Pictures 2a and 2b.*

Test sentence: The boy asks the girl which shoes to wear.
Subject is shown both pictures simultaneously and asked

1. *Which picture shows the boy asking the girl which shoes to wear?*
2. *What is he saying to her?*

2a. Correct interpretation   *2b. Incorrect interpretation*

asked: "Which picture shows the girl asking the boy what to paint?" and "What is she saying to him?"; for Pair 2 he was asked: "Which picture shows the boy asking the girl what shoes to wear?" and "What is he saying to her?" The child was instructed to look at both pictures of a pair before deciding on an answer. In each case, the correct choice is Picture a. For Picture 1a, the girl should be quoted as saying, "What should I paint?" and for Picture 2a, the boy should be quoted as saying, "What shoes should I wear?"

Here again, we find the same two kinds of error as with the conversational test of *ask*. Some children choose the wrong picture (b), giving a quote in which one child *tells* the other what to do, e.g., "Wear those shoes." This would be a correct response if the cue had been "Which picture shows the girl telling the boy what shoes to wear?" As before, children who respond in this manner have failed to interpret *ask* as requiring a question response. They respond as if instructed to tell. This response indicates the least competence with the verb *ask*.

The second error is to choose the wrong picture, quote the picture child as asking a question, but the wrong question: "What are you going to paint?"; "What shoes are you going to wear?" Again, the child who answers in this manner understands that he is to ask a question, but has not yet learned the exceptional nature of *ask*. He picks his missing subject incorrectly and proceeds to choose a picture and question consistent with his hypothesis. As before, this response indicates greater competence with *ask* than the preceding response, but falls short of total mastery.

In each of the above errors the picture choice and quoted command or question are consistent with each other. Given the way the child interprets the cue sentence, his response it logical and "correct." He is not confused nor is he guessing. This was true also for the conversational test, where the child's actions supported his words in almost all cases. He is operating successfully according to rule; it is just that his rule differs from the standard. This is a common observation in this type of linguistic testing, whether children are often confident when operating with well-entrenched, though inappropriate, rules. Indeed, confusion or hesitation, or recognition that a construction is problematic, may signal progress on the child's part, usually indicating that he has begun the process of restructuring his rule system.

An interesting feature of the results is that the picture test for *ask* was easier for some children than the conversational test. Five children succeeded with the pictures and failed the conversational test, and only one child reversed this pattern. The criterion for success with the *ask* construction as a whole was a success with both the pictures and the conversation test.[10]

An analysis of our results showed that this construction was considerably more difficult for the children than our preceding ones, and exhibited strong variability in age of acquisition. Only one-third of the children, ranging in age from 7.2 years to 10.0, succeeded at both the conversational interview and the picture test. The ages of those who failed ranged from 5.9 to 9.9. No child under 7.2 succeeded. From 7.2 up, we find the children fairly evenly divided among passers and failers. The mean age of the failers was six months under that of the passers, 8.2 as compared to 8.8.

The striking feature of these results is the high variability in age of acquisition of the structure, and the persistence of lack of knowledge right up to the top age in our sample. Clearly after age seven, individual rate of development is a stronger factor than is age in acquisition of the *ask* construction. Below we will see that knowledge of this construction distinguishes Stage 3 from Stage 4 in our developmental sequence.

It is interesting that the ability to assign a missing subject correctly following *ask* appears later in the child than the ability to carry out what appears to be the same task with the verb *promise*. Both verbs require that a general rule of subject assignment be broken and replaced with a rule specific to these two words. If the specific rule is the same for both *ask* and *promise*, why then does the child consistently learn to apply it first with *promise*?

The answer appears to lie in the great simplicity of the verb *promise* as compared to *ask*. *Promise* is a consistent verb, whereas *ask* evidences inconsistency when used in two different senses as follows. Consider (a) Seymour asked Gloria to leave, (b) Seymour asked Gloria when to leave. In (a) Gloria is to leave; *ask* behaves as the majority of verbs in English. In (b) Seymour is to leave; *ask* behaves according to the special rule. The child must learn conflicting rules for these two structures with *ask*, whereas no such problem exists with *promise*. *Promise* always requires the special rule — there is no structure such as (a) to complicate matters.

4.   Constructions following *And* and *Although*

Here we tested the children's ability to identify a missing verb differently in two sentences that differ only in the use of *and* and *although* as clause introducers. Consider the sentences:

(a)   Mother scolded Gloria for answering the phone, and I would have done the same.

(b)   Mother scolded Gloria for answering the phone, although I would have done the same.

These sentences do not say what I would have done; the listener must fill it in for himself. There are two candidate verbs preceding *done the same* that might serve as referent: *scolded* and *answered*. Following *and*, the referent is *scolded*; following *although*, the referent is *answered*; in (a) I would have scolded Gloria, and in (b) I would have answered the phone.[11]

No careful experimental technique was devised for testing these constructions. We simply read the sentences to the children and asked for each one: "What does this sentence say I would have done?" There was some question in our minds about the effectiveness of this direct approach, but it appears to have been adequate in this case. The results show interesting developmental patterns, and they fit in very well with the rest of our data.

The examples mentioned above were used as well as the sentences: "The cowboy scolded the horse for running away, and I would have done the same — What would I have done?" "The cowboy scolded the horse for running away, although I would have done the same — What would I have done?"

These sentences were usually read several times to the children, particularly the younger children, before they were able to formulate an answer. Those who could read were given the sentences typed on cards to follow as we read aloud.

We determined in an earlier portion of the interview that all of the children could correctly interpret the shorter sentence, "The cowboy scolded the horse for running away — Who ran away?" None of the children had any trouble assigning *horse* as subject of *running away*.

We also determined earlier in the interview session which children were competent in the use of *although* in simpler sentences where no deletions were involved. All but eight of the children performed successfully on an oral sentence-completion task with sentences such as "Although my favorite TV program was on, I . . ." and "I wore a heavy jacket although . . ." Those who failed were under seven years of age, and not among the passers of our *and* and *although* test.

This experiment turned out to be more interesting than anticipated. During the planning stage we considered the *although* sentences to be the difficult ones, and had included *and* sentences only for contrast. As it turned out, not only was the *although* construction very difficult for the children (only four children succeeded with it), but the *and* sentence, surprisingly enough, proved to be interesting in its own right. Unexpectedly, twenty-three children failed the *and* sentence. Whereas we had set out to test *although, and* itself proved to be a useful test construction as discussed below.

Scoring was as follows. In the *although* sentences the child had to choose the referent of *done the same* from two candidate verbs preceding it in the sentence: *scolded*, the far candidate, and *answering*, the near candidate. The correct choice is the near candidate, *answering*. Scoring, however, requires caution, for some children will choose the near candidate from lack of knowledge. As we have seen in the constructions of *promise* and *ask*, the child tends to always choose the *near* candidate to fill in a deletion when he works from general principles of English. In our test sentence the near candidate (*answering*) is the correct one, the one the child would choose also from specific knowledge of the *although* construction. Since both general principles and specific knowledge of *although* yield the same answer, how can we determine on what basis the child is choosing? Fortunately, our *and* sentence provides the means for distinguishing. It presents what appears to be the same construction differing only in the replacement of *although* by *and*, and requires the *far* candidate, *scolded*, as referent of *done the same*.

By correctly choosing the far candidate (*scolded*) for *and*, the child shows that he has learned to discard general principles in dealing with this surface structure. When this child then chooses the near candidate for *although* we can assume that he does so not from general principles but because he recognizes the different function of *although* in the sentence.

And indeed we find a pattern of development that supports this hypothesis. The younger children selected the near candidate for both *and* and *although;* apparently they worked from general principles for both words. As age increases children began to select the far candidate for both words; they have learned the exceptional nature of the surface structure, but not the specific *although* rule. In the most advanced stage, children have also learned the specific *although* rule and distinguish the two cases.

The criterion for success with *although*, then, was choosing the near candidate verb as referent of *done the same*, while at the same time choosing the far candidate verb for *and*. Children were scored correct only if all four test sentences were judged correctly. Only four children, ages 7.6, 8.3, 8.11, and 9.9. achieved this success. Clearly age is a poor predictor of success with this construction, and knowledge of it is strongly dependent on individual rate of development.

The relation between our simple use of *although* in the sentence completion task and its more complex use with verb deleted shows the expected course of development. There are children who know neither construction, children who know both, and many intermediate children who know the simple construction but not the complex one. No children reverse this order, and know the complex construction without knowing the simple one.

In summary, all children seven and older succeeded with *although* in its simple construction. The more complex *although* construction was very difficult for the children and only four succeeded at it. Knowledge of the simple construction precedes knowledge of the complex one.

This *although* construction was the most difficult of the constructions reported here, and we will see below that success at it constitutes the highest stage in our developmental sequence.

Considered separately, the *and* construction yielded interesting results. Above we pointed out that the youngest children dealt with *and* according to general principles of English and selected the near candidate to fill in the missing verb.

The parallel of these *and* results with our results for *ask* is remarkably close. Their main feature is the high variability in age of acquisition of the structure, and the fact that we find children up to the oldest failing. After age seven, age is less of a factor in acquisition of the construction than individual rate of development. We will see below that, with only minor exceptions, the same children succeeded with both *ask* and *and*. Accordingly, joint knowledge of *ask* and *and* serves to distinguish Stage 3 from 4 in our developmental sequence.

OVERALL DEVELOPMENTAL SEQUENCE

By measuring children's competence in dealing with individual grammatical constructions, we gain information about patterns of acquisition characteristic of the different constructions. If we are fortunate this information may shed some light on the nature of the constructions themselves. It is far more interesting, however, to deal with a number of related structures. With a variety of structures, we hope to observe developmental sequences in the acquisition of the different constructions.

Thus, for a set of related constructions, with the verb *ask*, for example, we find that an individual child's successes and failures on test questions always assume the same pattern. Consider for the moment two separate *ask* constructions, the one discussed earlier and another, simpler one: (a) Ask Harry what time it is; (b) Ask Harry what to feed the dog.

Sentence *a* is simpler than *b* in that there is no missing subject in the clause — all information is given and nothing has to be filled in by the listener. To interpret (a) or (b) correctly, the child must recognize that *ask* signals a question. To interpret (b) correctly, the child must, in addition, select the missing subject correctly. In effect, the child must carry out the following three tasks:

1. Recognize that *ask* signals a question before the simple construction (a);
2. Recognize that *ask* signals a question before the complex construction (b);
3. Assign a correct missing subject in the complex construction (b).

Now when we test children on these two structures, we find the following pattern of successes and failures: Task (3) implies (2), which in turn implies (1).[12]

Given this pattern, we conclude that the children attain competence on these tasks in the order listed. The grammatical development is observed to take place in an orderly fashion, from simple to complex, according to an invariant sequence.

That we can find such sequences when testing closely related structures is not very surprising. Sometimes, however, we find a stage we did not expect (such as the first two lines of Table 1). This is more interesting because we have learned something about how individual syntactic rules are adjusted in children's grammatical systems as their linguistic competence increases and they approach the adult linguistic system. This is the heart of the matter in linguistic work of this sort, for in this way we find out what the rules look like, how they change, what steps the child has to go through, what progress actually looks like step by step, what is hard and what is easy.

It is most interesting of all, of course, when structures that are related to each other only loosely reveal this same orderly developmental sequence. The five structures discussed exhibit this sequential relationship, in the order presented: *easy to see, promise, ask, and,* and *although.*

These structures appear to be quite divergent, and one would not ordinarily group them together as candidates for a developmental sequence, nor predict a specific order of acquisition. Yet our results show that they are acquired in the order listed. The children's performance on these constructions divides them into five stages as shown in Table 2.

TABLE 1

Stages in Acquisition of Ask *Constructions*

	Task 1	Task 2	Task 3
Stage A	–	–	–
Stage B	+	–	–
Stage C	+	+	–
Stage D	+	+	+

+ Success
– Failure

TABLE 2

Developmental Stages in Children's Acquisition of Five Test Structures

	Easy to See	Promise	Ask	And	Although
Stage 1: age 5.9–7.1 n = 4	–	–	–	–	–
Stage 2: age 5.9–9.5 n = 9	+	–	–	–	–
Stage 3: age 6.1–9.9 n = 12	+	+	–	–	–
Stage 4: age 7.2–10 n = 7	+	+	+	+	–
Stage 5: age 7.6–9.9 n = 4	+	+	+	+	+

+ Success
– Failure

Children who fail all five constructions are at Stage 1; Stage 2 children pass *easy to see* and fail the others; Stage 3 children pass *easy to see* and *promise* and fail the others; Stage 4 children pass all but *although*; Stage 5 children pass all five constructions.

What is interesting in the data is the uniformity of the results. The amount of divergence from this sequence of acquisition is extremely small, the children's individual responses deviating from the observed pattern at the rate of 4 responses per 100.[13]

How do we account for this striking orderliness in the children's acquisition of these seemingly diverse structures? A closer look at the structures themselves reveals that they do have one feature in common. They all require the listener to fill in a missing item in order to understand the sentence. The surface form of these sentences lacks either a noun phrase or a verb phrase that is crucial to its understanding, and the listener must know how to fill it in if he is to understand the sentence correctly. In each case it has to be filled in in a manner at variance with the general tendency of the language, which accounts for the difficulty. More technically, the listener, given only the surface structure of the sentence, must re-create its underlying form. To do this he has to know, among other things, the rules governing deletions from underlying to surface structure. If a child has not yet mastered the rules for these

TABLE 3

Correct and Incorrect Interpretations of Five Test Structures

	To Be Filled In	Near Candidate Incorrect	Other Candidate Correct
EASY TO SEE	subject of *see*	doll	somebody else
PROMISE	subject of *lie down*	Donald	Bozo
ASK	subject of *paint*	boy	girl
AND	referent of *done the same*	answered the phone	scolded
ALTHOUGH	referent of *done the same*	scolded*	answered the phone

* Likely candidate by analogy with AND sentence, once learned.

Structures: EASY TO SEE: The doll is easy to see.
PROMISE: Bozo promises Donald to lie down.
ASK: The girl asks the boy what to paint.
AND: Mother scolded Gloria for anwering the phone, and I would have done the same.
ALTHOUGH: Mother scolded Gloria for anwering the phone, although I would have done the same.

constructions, he will make mistakes in filling in the missing items, and end up with wrong interpretations.

The general rule in English for filling in deletions such as in the above constructions is to choose the nearest preceding candidate item in the sentence. The child has learned this as a general principle of the language very early on. These five constructions, although very different from each other, all require that this principle be abandoned. They require instead the rather unusual principle: don't choose the nearest preceding candidate items in the sentence, keep looking. In a sense the child has to be freed from a deeply entrenched constraint in order to interpret each one of these constructions. He has specifically to learn in each of the above cases that his general principle does not apply. Evidently the relative complexities of these five structures are such that children tend to master them in the order listed, with surprisingly little variation.

Table 3 summarizes our test constructions. It illustrates the five structures, with the correct and incorrect interpretations given. Children who do not know a construction respond with the incorrect interpretations (near candidate); those who know the construction respond with the "other" candidate.

Several interesting observations may be noted in connection with the sequence of acquisition outlined here.

First, *easy to see*, which was tested along with *promise* and *ask* by the author in an earlier experiment[14] did not precede *promise* in that experiment as it does in this one. The reason for this may be faulty experimental technique in the first experiment, which introduced extraneous cues and made the construction too difficult for the children. The current experiment, with improved technique, may reflect the children's competence more accurately.

Second, *promise* precedes *ask* in this experiment as in the 1969 experiment, confirming the earlier results. Only the final stage in the acquisition of *ask* (Table 1, Stage D) is relevant to this overall developmental sequence.

And finally, *and* and *ask* appear to "come in" together if *ask* is scored from both the conversational portion of the interview and the picture tests. Apparently the child learns the *and* construction at about the time he masters *ask*; if this result is borne out by future experimentation, it would suggest that the two constructions are of approximately the same degree of complexity.

In summary, the five constructions tested in this study can be ordered in a Guttman scale, indicating a developmental sequence in children's acquisition of these structures. The five structures, though quite diverse, all require that the child apply a specific principle of sentence analysis that is uncommon in English. Apparently, the child's ability to apply this principle progresses in a regular fashion from simple structures to more complex ones.

READING

A second portion of this study surveyed the children's reading background and current reading activity. We wished to consider the relation of the amount and complexity of what children read to rate of linguistic development, along with other factors such as IQ and SES. To do this we used the five linguistic stages outlined above as the measure of rate of linguistic development and a variety of information on reading and listening.

Reading information was gathered through questionnaires to both children and parents, and through daily records kept at home of all reading (and listening to books read aloud) engaged in by the child over a one-week period. We calculated amount and complexity of independent reading (and listening), background in children's literature, and recall and recognition of books read and heard. In order to judge the extent of the children's reading at different complexity levels, we applied our own formula for measuring syntactic complexity to the books and magazines reported by the children in their week's record of day-to-day reading.

Our records thus contain a variety of measures of each child's reading exposure that together yielded a general picture of some interest. We have information on books read over a week's time, books that the child named in the course of a half-hour interview, parent reports of reading aloud, and so on. By assessing how much and what is read to him, and how much and what he reads on his own, we attempted to characterize each child's independent reading and get a picture of how reading functions in his background and current life. As mentioned above, both the amount read and the complexity of the material were taken into consideration.

Our concern is not so much with the child's level of reading ability as it is with the reading that he actually engages in. That is, the mechanical skill that he has acquired is of interest for our purposes primarily in the way he puts it to use. The written language is potentially of a more complex nature than speech, both in vocabulary and syntax. The child who reads (or listens to) a variety of rich and complex materials benefits from a range of linguistic inputs that is unavailable to the nonliterary child. It is this exposure that we wish to examine for its relation to rate of linguistic development.[15]

TABLE 4

Average Scores at Each Linguistic Stage on a Variety of Reading and Other Measures

	Stage 1	Stage 2	Stage 3	Stage 4	Stage 5
Measures good at all stages					
1. Huck *Inventory of Literary Background*	23	31	38	39	43
2. Numerical scores from Child Interview	37	50	55	56	59
3. Numerical scores from Parent Interview	45	55	58	61	64
4. Weighted total books named—Parent Interview	21	30	42	47	49
5. Average level books named—Parent Interview	1.4	2.1	2.4	2.9	3.0
6. Master Book List—top level count	2.3	3.9	4.9	5.0	6.3
7. IQ (WPPSI, WISC) full scale	105	118	123	129	138
8. IQ—verbal	105	119	122	129	141
9. IQ—performance	104	114	120	123	129
	n = 4	n = 9	n = 13	n = 6	n = 4

In the following section we present some of our reading results and discuss their relation to linguistic development.

Relations of Reading Measures to Linguistic Stages

One excellent measure used in our reading survey was Huck's *Taking Inventory of Children's Literary Background*.[16] This multiple-choice quiz tests a child's knowledge of the content of sixty widely read books, poems, and stories from children's literature. Scores on the Huck inventory are positively related to linguistic stage. In other words, the higher the Huck score is, the higher, in general, is the child's linguistic stage in our data.

This can be seen from Table 4, line 1. Each of the Huck scores is the *average* for all children in the stage listed at the head of the column in Table 4.[17]

Other reading measures, developed by the author, also show a positive relation with linguistic stage. Like the Huck score, they appear as within-stage averages in Table 4. The data from which these measures were derived came from three sources:

1. *Master Book List*. This list contained the titles of some 400 children's books and was left in the home for the child and parent to complete jointly by checking off the titles of books with which the child was familiar. The number of books checked off that were at the top level of syntactic complexity was one positive measure and is presented in Table 4, line 6. The *total* number of books checked off on the Master Book List was also a good measure, though not quite as good as the top level count.

2. *Parent Interview*. One of the child's parents — in all but one case, the mother — was interviewed at home. Questions in the interview centered around the child's reading habits, library trips, reading aloud to the child, favorite books, time spent in independent reading, etc. Special attention was given to eliciting from the parent as

many titles as possible of books and magazines that the child had encountered over the years.

Three measures from this interview were found to relate positively to linguistic stage as shown in Table 4: (a) average complexity level of books named by the parent (line 5); (b) the total number of books named, weighted by complexity levels of the individual books (the raw total was not a distinguishing measure) (line 4); and (c) the total numerical score from the interview, calculated from questions with numerical answers such as time spent reading to the child during the early years, the amount of time the child spends reading now, frequency of public library visits, average number of books borrowed from the library each visit, and so on (line 3).

3. *Child Interview.* An interview was held with each child at school. Roughly the same information was sought as in the parent interview. The measure that correlated positively with linguistic stage from this interview was, as in the parent interview, numerical score. This score reflected the child's answers to questions concerning library trips (What books do you have out this week? How many of the books that you take out do you generally read?), favorite books and authors, books reread many times, time spent reading daily or weekly, TV watching (credit given inversely to amount of time spent watching TV), number of people at home who read to you, now or formerly, and so on. This numerical score measure for the child interview appears in Table 4 (line 2).

In addition to demonstrating a positive relation with linguistic stages displayed in Table 4, the five reading measures all relate positively to the Huck score. Four of the correlations were significant beyond the .001 level: Master Book List top level book count, average complexity level and weighted total of books from the parent interview, and the numerical score from the child interview. The Pearson product-moment correlations were .564, .577, .392, and .631 respectively. The numerical score from the parent interview was also positively correlated with the Huck score ($r = .462$, $p = .003$). With a sample of only thirty-six, these correlations indicate a high degree of association.

Given the positive relation of these five measures with linguistic stages in Table 4 (evidenced also by positive Kendall rank order correlations significant at least at the .013 level)[18] and the positive and significant Pearson correlations of these five measures with the Huck score, we conclude that the relation between reading exposure and linguistic stage is not due to a peculiarity of one of the reading measures. To assume otherwise, since the measures are largely non-overlapping, would lead us to claim that each measure has some unique peculiarity that causes it to produce a positive relation with linguistic stage that in fact has little or nothing to do with the child's reading exposure. Experience tells us that concentrating on six such unique measures is unlikely. Therefore, we conclude that a valid relation between reading exposure and linguistic stages exists.

It is worth noticing that the Huck Inventory, a direct and easily obtainable measure, apparently functions as an excellent single measure of reading exposure to which linguistic stages are related. We may speculate that the Inventory refines the notion of exposure to written materials by incorporating not just the amount read but internalization and retention of the material as well.

RELATIONSHIP OF OTHER MEASURES TO LINGUISTIC STAGES

One other measure, IQ, is positively related to linguistic development across all stages.

The Wechsler Preschool and Primary Scale of Intelligence (WPPSI) test was given to the six children in the study who were under 6.2 years of age at testing time. The remaining thirty children (ages 6.5 and over) were given the Wechsler Intelligence Scale for Children (WISC) test. IQ's ranged from 98 to 142 and the average scores within each linguistic stage are presented in Table 4, lines 7–9. Not only do the full scale IQ scores increase with linguistic stage but so do the verbal and performance subtests of the test.

The Kendall rank order correlations of linguistic stage with IQ, with each of the IQ subsets, with age, and with grade were all significant at the .001 level while the Pearson correlation of linguistic stage with the Census Bureau measure of SES, whose range is 01–99, was significant at the .02 level.

It is not surprising that SES was highly correlated with IQ but not with age or grade. However, the correlations of SES with reading vocabulary and with reading comprehension grade level scores from standardized tests were also nonsignificant while the correlation of SES with IQ was significant at the .001 level. Moreover, the Pearson correlations of SES with all measures of books from the parent interview, child interview, and Master Book List were significant at the .001 level.

What inferences can be drawn from this correlational information? First, if our five stages reflect an underlying developmental sequence, we would expect variables like age, grade, reading grade level scores, and IQ to be positively and significantly correlated with linguistic stage. They are.

Second, it is reasonable to speculate that the various IQ and reading exposure measures are not mere substitutes for the age measure; the exposure measures play an independent role in influencing linguistic stage. This follows because the IQ score and its components are age corrected[19] and are therefore uncorrelated with age. Also, the sample was stratified by age (young, medium, old) and by reading grade level score (low, medium, high). This stratification would lead at most to a negligible correlation between age and reading grade level score.

Third, given the pattern of significant and nonsignificant correlation of SES with various measures, *if* SES acts upon linguistic stage placement through any of the measures included in this study it is through general ability or the reading environment of the child. Statistical techniques for studying this question exist, but a new and large sample should be drawn.

Relationship of Listening Measures to Linguistic Stages

A calculation was made of the amount of time spent reading aloud to the children and the complexity of the books read to them at home during a one-week period. As might be expected, listening to books read aloud decreases sharply after first grade as the children's own reading begins to replace their listening. Even in the first grade independent reading is beginning to predominate for the more able readers.

Among the prereaders, listening to books read aloud is positively related to linguistic age. As the next section will show, those prereaders in higher linguistic stages are read to by more people and hear more books per week, at higher complexity levels than children at lower linguistic stages.

In summary, the measures that discriminate the whole linguistic range of stages include IQ, memory of content of books read (Huck), book counts weighted by complexity level, and questionnaire replies. In addition, certain measures work well at lower linguistic stages, and others at higher linguistic stages. Several of the book counts (number of books recalled and recognized) appear to discriminate best at the lower linguistic stages, and word counts (number of words read during the recorded week) discriminate best at the higher stages. Reading complex materials quite strikingly characterizes the top linguistic stage.

Mini-Comparisons: Uniform Age and IQ, Different Linguistic Stages

A natural question, given the type of data collected here, is, What factors differentiate children in different linguistic stages, who are of roughly the same age and IQ? If we control for age and IQ, do any of the various measures that we used serve to distinguish children in lower linguistic stages from those in higher stages?

The small number of children tested precludes a statistical answer to this question. At most we can compare individual children who meet the requirement of same age and IQ and different linguistic stage. The results are not uninteresting, however. We were able to select three such sets of children, one from among the youngest in the sample, one from the mid-age group, and one from the oldest. In each group there were three children of comparable age and IQ, who were nevertheless at different linguistic stages.

Such a procedure of "mini-comparisons" clearly has its limitations, but we are able in each age group to note a number of factors that vary as does linguistic stage. The overall picture shows that at each age, reading or hearing books read is a strong factor, with many different individual measures of reading exposure contributing to this trend. Interestingly enough, SES appears as a factor most strongly in the youngest group (5.9–6.1), where many of the reading measures vary directly with SES. It is hardly news that higher SES parents read to their young children more; what is interesting is that SES is less of a differentiating factor among the older children. In the middle and oldest group, the children share a relatively high SES. For these children (particularly the oldest group where SES varies least), it is their own activity, not SES differences, that varies with linguistic stage. This suggests the following speculation, which might be interesting to test further: given a high SES, once a child can read, he's on his own. His linguistic progress at this age may well turn out to reflect what he does with his time.

The accompanying tables (Mini-Comparisons 1, 2, 3) present the individual differentiating measures in each mini-comparison. Only the significant measures are included at each age, although all questions were asked of all children.

Notice that three items appear in all three age groups; the number of books named by the child in the course of his interview (child and parent in the youngest group), the average number of books taken out on regular visits to the public library, and interestingly, the number of books that the mother cited from her own childhood that

TABLE 5

Mini-Comparison 1

Measures That Vary as Linguistic Stage in Three Young Children
of Uniform Age and IQ

	Ling. Stage 1	Ling. Stage 2	Ling. Stage 3
age of child	5.9	5.9	6.1
grade in school	K	K	K
IQ (WISC)	118	120	118
SES (Census Bureau scale 01–99)	63	89	93
father's occupation score (Census Bureau scale 01–99)	80	80	99
father's years of education	12	16	20
WISC comprehension subtest	13	14	18
books named on parent and child questionnaires, weighted total	14	40	111
books named on parent and child questionnaires, average level	1	1	3
reading to child in experimental week, total number words read	0	6,700	17,500
reading to child in experimental week, number words read multiplied by complexity factor	0	17,700	62,500
Reported on parent questionnaire:			
books named by parent, weighted total	12	40	62
numerical score on parent's questionnaire	27	37	60
number of people at home who read to child	1	2	2
amount of time child is read to per week at home	½ hr.	½ hr.	>2hrs.
average level of books cited by parent as reread to child many times	1	1	2
does child visit public library?	no	no	yes
average number public library books taken out each visit	—	—	3
subscriptions to children's magazines	0	0	1
years nursery school attendance	0	0	1
number books from mother's own childhood cited as read to child	0	2	1

she has enjoyed reading to the child. This third item, though somewhat of a surprise at first, makes sense once its implications are considered. The mother who recalls certain books with pleasure from her own childhood may well transmit this enjoyment to her child very early on when she reads to him. We may speculate that this child learns to assign a special role to reading, for what his mother enjoys doing with him, he quite naturally comes to enjoy and recognize as a valued activity.

CONCLUSIONS

What status can we ascribe to the five linguistic stages observable in our data on the basis of the constructions tested? Given the small sample size and the fact that most of these relationships were observed for the first time here, they clearly should be considered as only suggestive. Further testing with larger groups of children, or at least replication with small groups, would be necessary if one wished to substantiate the order of emergence of the structures. My guess is that the distinction between Stages

TABLE 6

Mini-Comparison 2

Measures That Vary as Linguistic Stage in Three Mid-Age Children
of Uniform Age and IQ

	Ling. Stage 2	Ling. Stage 3	Ling. Stage 4
age of child	7.10	8.6	8.3
grade in school	2	3	2
reading grade score (school record)	voc: 5.2	voc: 7.1	voc: 4.8
	comp: 5.1	comp: 7.0	comp: 5.4
IQ (WISC)	138	136	136
SES (Census Bureau scale 01–99)	81	93	91
father's occupation score (Census Bureau scale 01–99)	68	94	92
child's reading in experimental week, total number words read	22,100	114,400	322,000
child's reading in experimental week, number words read multiplied by complexity factor	46,700	626,600	2,826,300
Reported on child's questionnaire:			
books named by child, weighted total	23	25	40
average number public library books taken out each visit	1	2	3
recent books read, number named	1	1	5
average level of books cited as recently read	2	2	5
average time TV watched each day	>1 hr.	1 hr.	< ½ hr.
Reported on parent's questionnaire:			
reads long books to child (now or formerly), continued from day to day	no	yes	yes
average level of long books named	—	3	4
rereads favorite books many times to child (now or formerly)	no	yes	yes
average level favorite books reread	—	3	4
frequency of child's visits to public library	irreg.	biweekly	> weekly
average number public library books taken out each visit	1	2	4
years nursery school attendance	1	2	2
number books from mother's own childhood cited as read to child	0	2	7

3 and 4 would hold up under additional testing, since it has a good theoretical base and was observed here for the second time. The other stages may or may not be borne out by future experimentation. This has been only a first trial, in no sense definitive. It is important to stress that the interest of results such as these lies not so much in the particular structures dealt with as in the confirmation of the continuing and orderly course of language acquisition among older children. The structures are more interesting as means to this end than in themselves.

In this vein, I would like to caution against considering these constructions relevant for practical purposes such as diagnostic procedures or for teaching to children. In interpreting results such as these it is important to recognize that the choice of structures is highly arbitrary as far as children are concerned. The selection reflects more the state of knowledge in the field of linguistics than the field of language acqui-

TABLE 7

Mini-Comparison 3
Measures That Vary as Linguistic Stage in Three Older Children
of Uniform Age and IQ

	Ling. Stage 3	Ling. Stage 4	Ling. Stage 5
age of child	9.4	10.0	9.9
grade in school	4	4	4
reading grade score (school record)	voc: 6.8	voc: 6.7	voc: 5.6
	comp: 6.6	comp: 6.5	comp: 6.3
IQ (WISC)	135	129	136
SES (Census Bureau scale 01–99)	93	96	96
father's occupation score (Census Bureau scale 01–99)	88	96	96
father's years education	16	16	20
Reported on child's questionnaire:			
books named by child, total number	6	10	14
books named by child, weighted total	14	32	39
numerical score on child's questionnaire	50	56	69
average number public library books taken out each visit	—	—	6
number library books out now	0	0	4
number favorite books named	1	2	3
are you in the middle of a book now?	no	yes	yes
child named last book read	no	yes	yes
level of last book read	—	2	3
do you ever read when you get home from school?	no	no	yes
average time spent reading	twice/wk.	daily< ½ hr.	daily > ½ hr.
average number books read per week	—	2	3
Reported on parent's questionnaire:			
average time child was read to when small	1 hr./wk.	daily<15min.	daily>15min.
average time child spends reading now	1 hr./wk.	15min./day	>15min./day
number books named by parent as read recently by child	1	1	7
average level of books recently read by child	2	2	3
number books from mother's own childhood cited as read to child	2	2	3

sition, for knowledge of child grammar is as yet far too rudimentary to guide such a choice. Further, our particular experimental requirements impose certain constraints. Thus our findings with regard to complexity of structure should not be interpreted to mean that because a child of eight does not know a particular construction, therefore we should attempt to teach it to him. All in all, our constructions may have little to do with what is important in children's knowledge and may tell virtually nothing about gaps that might be worth trying to fill in terms of enhancing development. Very likely they do reflect the extent of children's knowledge, but attempting to introduce these arbitrary structures artificially cannot be expected to have much effect on the total range of that knowledge.

What then are the practical implications of work of this sort, and what potential educational significance does it have? It seems to me that its relevance may lie in the continuing language acquisition that it reveals in school age children, and in the connections noted between this language development and reading. These results may have implications with regard to language programs in the elementary schools, and the philosophy underlying curriculum design and selection of materials.

We know very little about the actual processes by which children learn language, but there has been an increasing awareness over the past few years of just how much the child brings to the task by way of his own internal organization and innate human characteristics. He certainly is not "taught" language in any formal sense, but acquires it naturally, so to speak, in the course of maturing and developing in an environment where he is adequately exposed to it. Interestingly enough, we now see that this natural process of acquisition continues actively into the early school years, and perhaps beyond. The variety of linguistic material that the child is still learning on his own during the elementary school years must certainly be extensive, if our few, rather arbitrarily chosen examples (arbitrary from the point of view of language acquisition) uncovered this continuing acquisition so readily.

What results of this sort indicate is that the child enters the classroom equipped to learn language and able to do so by methods of his own. This suggests that perhaps the best thing that we might do for him in terms of encouraging his learning would be to make more of it possible, by exposing him to a rich variety of language inputs in interesting, stimulating situations. The question is how?

Our reading results indicate that exposure to the more complex language available from reading does seem to go hand in hand with increased knowledge of the language. This would imply that perhaps wider reading should find a place in the curriculum. The child could be read to, stimulated to read on his own, not restricted to material deemed "at his level" but permitted access to books well "above his level" to get out of them whatever he may. Perhaps he should be encouraged to skim when he reads, to skip uninteresting portions and get to the "good parts" instead of concentrating at length on controlled texts. In general it may be that the effort should be toward providing more and richer language exposure, rather than limiting the child with restrictive and carefully programmed materials. In this way the child would be permitted to derive what is accessible to him from a wide range of inputs, and put it to use in his own way. This approach would seem to be more closely in accord with the nature of language acquisition as we are coming to understand it.

These remarks are, of course, speculative. Their purpose is to emphasize that the potential relevance of work of this sort to language curricula will lie in its suggestiveness for effective use of classroom time, rather than in its relations to the specifics of grammar teaching.

NOTES

1. Carol Chomsky, *The Acquisition of Syntax in Children from 5 to 10* (Cambridge, MA: MIT Press, 1969).
2. Chomsky, *The Acquisition of Syntax*, p. 4.
3. Chomsky, *The Acquisition of Syntax*, p. 6.

4. Richard F. Cromer, "'Children are nice to understand': Surface Structure Clues for the Recovery of a Deep Structure," *British Journal of Psychology, 61* (1970), 397–408; Frank S. Kessel, "The Role of Syntax in Children's Comprehension from Ages Six to Twelve," *Monographs of the Society for Research in Child Development, Serial No. 139, 35,* No. 6 (September 1970); Chomsky, *The Acquisition of Syntax.*

5. 7.1 is used to indicate 7 years, 1 month.

6. Chomsky, *The Acquisition of Syntax.*

7. Chomsky, *The Acquisition of Syntax.*

8. The children's performance with *ask* in general reveals a number of levels of competence, which the present discussion only touches on. Since the various degrees of competence short of total mastery do not contribute to our developmental sequence, they are referred to only peripherally here.

9. The actual number of instructions given varied from child to child because of the informal nature of the interview.

10. This scoring procedure simplifies the stages of our developmental sequence, and was adopted for this reason. Separating the children who passed only the picture test would add one stage to the sequence, which might be useful for some purposes but seemed superfluous here.

11. This interesting and rather unusual aspect of the word *although* was brought to the author's attention by Adrian Akmajian.

12. Children who can do Task 3 can also do 2 and 1, and children who can do 2 can always do 1. There are no children who break this pattern, who can do 3, for example, and not 2 and 1; or who can do 2 without being able to do 1; or 1 and 3 without 2. On the other hand we do find children who can do 1 but not 2 or 3; and children who can do 1 and 2, but not 3. When our data are of this sort, when the operations can be arranged into a Guttman scale such that 3 presupposes 2 which in turn presupposes 1, then we have information about order of acquisition. Although we have not observed children over time as they progress from 1 to 2 to 3, we can nevertheless conclude that this is the order of acquisition and that we have an invariant developmental sequence.

13. When the stages are considered as a Guttman scale, the coefficient of reproducibility is .96.

14. Chomsky, *The Acquisition of Syntax.*

15. From the point of view of exposure to the written language, it may matter little whether the child has the book read to him, as would be the case with the younger children in our study, or reads it himself, as do the older children. It is possible, perhaps even likely, that in both situations the contents, style, and language usage of the book are made available to the child with little difference in effectiveness.

16. Charlotte S. Huck, *Taking Inventory of Children's Literary Background* (Glenview, IL: Scott, Foresman, 1966).

17. For example, 23 is the average Huck score for all children in Stage 1. The notation "n = 4" at the foot of the first column tells you that four children are at Stage 1.

18. Kendall rank-order correlations for these measures are:

Master Book List—top level count	.328	(.002)
Average Level books named—parent	.409	(.001)
Weighted total books named—parent	.274	(.009)
Numerical score—parent	.258	(.013)
Numerical score—child	.327	(.002)

19. $$IQ = \frac{Mental\ Age}{Chronological\ Age} \times 100$$

The work reported on here was performed under Office of Education Grant No. OEG-1-9-090055-0114 (010), Project No. 9-A-055, while the investigator was a Scholar at the Radcliffe Institute. This paper was prepared from the final report to the Office of Education. The full report, "Linguistic Development in Children from 6 to 10," is available through the Educational Resources Information Center (ERIC) Document Reproduction Service.

Language in Thinking and Learning: Pedagogy and the New Whorfian Framework

PENNY LEE

How does language relate to thought? Does learning to talk differently have implications for the way we think? Is our subjective experience and understanding of the world dependent in any way on the languages we know? Given the central role of language in teaching and learning, these questions are important ones for teachers and teacher educators. They were also fundamental for linguist Benjamin Lee Whorf (1897–1941), whose *linguistic relativity principle* (often referred to as the *Sapir-Whorf hypothesis*) continues to excite debate more than half a century after he formulated it.

Briefly characterized as the idea that the languages we know structure our understanding of the world in distinctive ways, the notion of linguistic relativity has long had, and still has, intuitive appeal for many bilinguals and multilinguals, who attest to its experiential validity in their own lives. Others too, who even from monolingually mediated worlds sense the infinitude of possibility beyond one's usual ways of making sense of experience, have been drawn to it and to Whorf's writing in general.[1] Although ideas about linguistic relativity have a long history dating back at least to the seventeenth century (Joseph, forthcoming; Koerner, 1995), relatively few people know that Whorf's theorizing was far more comprehensive than popular accounts suggest and that it has profound implications for our understanding of relationships between language, mind, and experience. As such, it must also have profound implications for the way we think about processes of teaching and learning. In this chapter I provide an overview of Whorf's theorizing as a whole, show how a framework for thinking about its applications can be extracted from the complex of ideas he explored, and suggest where further research might be undertaken for pedagogical benefit.

The account of Whorf's ideas presented here is an outcome of research conducted over the last ten years and fully detailed in *The Whorf Theory Complex: A Critical Reconstruction* (Lee, 1996). This book is part of a recent revival of interest in Whorf that is producing significantly different interpretations from those that predominated previously. For instance, in *Dialogue at the Margins*, Emily A. Schultz (1990) takes a

Harvard Educational Review   Vol. 67   No. 3   Fall 1997, 430–471

deconstructionist approach to Whorf's writings, arguing that he was successful both in capturing the *experience* of cross-cultural communication (of "dialogue at the margins") and in promoting "the experience of multilingual consciousness" (p. 98). Her willingness to look closely at what Whorf had actually written was a welcome departure from many of the brief (and often dismissive) accounts of his ideas found in introductory texts in the social and mind sciences. These texts frequently refer only to secondhand or unsourced accounts of Whorf's theories or to ideas expressed in one or two of his more popular papers and taken out of the context of the rest of his thinking. Although I believe there are some problems with Schultz's interpretation (see Lee, 1992, for a brief review), her work is thought-provoking and provides fresh insights, particularly into the value of what Whorf (1941/1956i) called "multilingual awareness" (p. 244).

John A. Lucy (1992a) makes another recent contribution to the new trend in Whorf studies with the most comprehensive review and evaluation to date of empirical investigations undertaken over the last fifty years in connection with Whorf's ideas. Although my interpretation of Whorf's reasoning about the linguistic relativity principle differs significantly from Lucy's,[2] his contribution, which includes new research on Yucatec Maya (Lucy, 1992b), is essential reading for anyone interested in Whorf. In *Grammatical Categories and Cognition,* Lucy (1992b) explains that Yucatec Maya and English organize a similar "semantico-referential domain" differently through the grammars of each language. Lucy's findings suggest that, in conceptual areas having to do with unitization, pluralization, and material form of objects, the cognitive operations of attending, classifying, judging similarity, and remembering items displayed during experiments may be linguistically structured to some degree.

The operational respect in which my work departs from all previous work, including Schultz's and Lucy's, is the breadth of the resource base I have used. Unlike most other researchers, I was fortunate to be able to draw on the entire corpus of published and unpublished material available to the public.[3] The latter includes a five-reel microfilm collection of unpublished letters, notes, drawings, drafts of papers, and miscellanea held in the Yale University archives (Whorf, 1979) and a few additional papers in other archival collections. Although Peter C. Rollins (1980) also had access to some of this material, his focus was mainly on Whorf's relation to what he (Rollins) called "lost generation America." His account is an interesting one, but unreliable when extended to interpretations of Whorf's later writings on linguistics. Here his remarks reveal only a sketchy understanding of the discipline in general, and Whorf's reasoning in particular.

A core theoretical respect in which my work differs from most previous work is the emphasis I place on the notion of *linguistic thinking,* or "thought insofar as it is linguistic," as Whorf (1937/1956b, pp. 67–68) put it. (He used the term *ling. thinking* in notes.) Whereas most previous investigators have focused on the idea that Whorf was interested in causal relations between two separate entities, *language* and *thought,* I argue that the evidence shows that Whorf was primarily interested in the phenomenon of *language in cognition* — in those cognitive processes that are linguistic in character, that appear initially during language acquisition, and that are modified, sustained, and extended throughout life in the course of social interaction. I believe that Whorf would have agreed with innatists such as Noam Chomsky who argue that humans are born with a predilection to become languaging beings and that language is a cognitive phenomenon. Whorf would also have had great sympathy for Lev Vygotsky's (1934/1986) argument that language, both in its intersubjective and intrasubjective manifestations — that is, in communication with others and also in thinking — is a social phenomenon. Language, from this perspective, becomes incorporated into cognition and mediates understanding of the world, advancing the development of certain kinds of cognitive processes that have their origins in particular ways of talking.

My work moves away from the notion that language and thought are essentially separate entities. Rather, I regard each as "inextricably interrelated," as Whorf's mentor Edward Sapir (1921, pp. 217–218) put it. My interpretation, I believe, is truer to Whorf's way of thinking than previous work and thus more useful in helping us understand what he might have meant by the term *linguistic relativity*. I also argue that when Whorf's thinking as a whole is taken into account, it becomes apparent that the linguistic relativity principle, as he formulated it, is merely a logical element of a larger *theory complex* that needs to be adequately understood before the validity of his reasoning can be assessed.

I developed the notion of a theory complex as it became evident to me that to understand any part of Whorf's theorizing, one needed to try to come to terms with those strands of thought that barely emerge from his writing, as well as those that achieve more explicit and definitive status. Some strands are explicit but have background thematic character, others are implicit rather than fully stated, others are more fully elaborated to the status of theoretical constructs (although Whorf himself may not have thought of them in this way), and yet others were still in the process of being developed when he died of cancer at the relatively young age of forty-four.

When I think of the Whorf theory complex, I think of a mass of interweaving elements of thought extricable from the whole only at the cost of oversimplification and loss of context. To understand Whorf, one needs to examine each strand without losing contact with the matrix from which it has been extracted and in which it has its being. As analytical beings, Westerners in particular seem to want to focus on one thing at a time, often out of context. I argue that this decontextualized and reductionist view hampers our understanding of human reasoning.

In the following section, I introduce each of twelve strands of theme or theory extractable from the Whorf complex. I use the terms *theme* and *theory* to acknowledge that some strands of the complex have pervasive thematic status in the whole, while others are more easily extracted as theoretical constructs. Isolated in this way, each strand may be regarded as part of a framework that can be used to guide thinking in specific areas of application, such as pedagogy. Like the theory complex itself, this new framework for thinking about relationships between language, mind, and experience works best when we are able to keep all its elements within mental reach, even as we focus on the significance of specific concepts.

Whorf's ideas are relevant to pedagogy because all learning has to do with the cognitive repercussions of experience. We are familiar with the idea that learning begins with experience at the level of simple conditioning (e.g., to avoid things that burn), but even the most complex development of judgment based on reasoning that involves high levels of conscious involvement and control also begins with experience. This is the case whether the experiences we start with are actual for the individuals concerned, hypothetical, or vicarious. And most human learning that goes beyond the immediate is mediated by language — language used both inter- and intrasubjectively, as I will show.

Certainly, nonverbal modeling, facilitating, and inhibiting acts are enormously important in the constellation of events that modulate learning experiences both within and beyond formally organized sites for inculcating culture. For instance, teachers model learning behaviors nonverbally when they reveal, through their own interest, attention, and knowledge-seeking actions, that they are genuinely curious beings who love to be engaged in learning. We facilitate others' learning nonverbally when we wait patiently for them to express their sometimes stumbling thoughts and when we provide a calm atmosphere for inquiry and classroom effort. We can inhibit learning nonverbally when our bodies are tense and our expressions disapproving or bored as we listen to learners (of any age). But language is nevertheless both pervasive and decisive in almost all teaching and learning. We model the language of inquiry, imagination, and reason, we praise, encourage, and explain, we condemn or denigrate — all through language. Therefore, activities that foster linguistic awareness, and that through such awareness bring relations between thinking, languaging, and being into focus, can have liberating potential in both our personal and professional lives and in the lives of our students. The final section of this chapter is devoted to exploring some applications of the framework to problems of teaching and learning. I also suggest areas where further research might be undertaken from Whorfian perspectives. My earlier work on Whorf has been largely theoretical and historical. My goal in this first attempt to show how the framework can be applied is to invite teachers and teacher educators everywhere to join me in exploring ways in which Whorf's ideas can help us reconceptualize our responsibilities and improve our practice.

AN OVERVIEW OF THE WHORF THEORY COMPLEX

In this section, the twelve elements of theme and theory that interweave in Whorf's thinking are extracted from the whole and introduced separately. Individually abstracted in this way, we can also regard each one as part of a framework for thinking about the role of language in teaching and learning.

1. Patternment

A pervasive and foundational element of the complex is the thematic use of notions of *pattern* and *configuration* throughout Whorf's writings (Lee, 1996). In this respect, he was very much a person of his time. His teacher, Sapir, for instance, was developing concepts of cultural and linguistic patterning and configuration prior to the publication of Ruth F. Benedict's classic anthropological text, *Patterns of Culture* (1934). What linguists and anthropologists were discovering is that even when we think we are behaving spontaneously and individualistically, what we do is in fact significantly structured by the patterns we have absorbed unconsciously during enculturation. From the way we walk or shape our lips (e.g., to make a "b" sound) to the way we talk to our babies, we are pattern driven whether we know it or not. Even behavior regarded as deviant from the norm is patterned differently in different cultures.

In addition to writing more generally about pattern and configuration, Whorf used terms such as *patternment, linkage,* and *rapport,* with specific application to cognitive organization. He also engaged in a far more explicit investigation of semantics and conceptual activity than did his contemporary behaviorists. For behaviorists in the 1940s, the "mental," being unobservable through external senses, was deemed out of bounds. But Whorf not only wrote about the complexity of observable patterns in language (sound, syntax, meaning, and discourse level patterns are just some of these); he also explicitly related this patterning to the mental domain (as we will see in the next two sections) and, indeed, to patternment in the universe at large. For instance, he declared that

> a noumenal world — a world of hyperspace, of higher dimensions, awaits discovery by all the sciences, which it will unite and unify, awaits discovery under its first aspect of a realm of PATTERNED RELATIONS, inconceivably manifold and yet bearing a recognizable affinity to the rich and systematic organization of LANGUAGE, including *au fond* mathematics and music, which are ultimately of the same kindred as language. (Whorf, 1942/1956j, pp. 247–248, original capitals)

He emphasized that linguistic "patterns are basic in a really cosmic sense, and that patterns form wholes, akin to the Gestalten of psychology, which are embraced in larger wholes in continual progression" (Whorf, 1942/1956j, pp. 247–248). Given this wholistic appreciation of patternment as the underpinning of everything we know, Whorf would undoubtedly have been comfortable with chaos theory had he lived to see it. James Gleick (1987) tells us that

> the first chaos theorists . . . shared certain sensibilities. They had an eye for pattern, especially pattern that appeared on different scales at the same time. . . . Believers in chaos . . . feel that they are turning back a trend in science toward reductionism, the analysis of systems in terms of their constituent parts: quarks, chromosomes, or neurons. They believe that they are looking for the whole. (p. 5)

I think Whorf would also have been comfortable with Mark Turner's (1991) assertion that "a human person is patterns of activity in a human brain." In other words, that when we look at the relation of "the body, culture, society, language, sex, table manners" to the human person, we are looking at "patterns of brain activity" (p. 30). Turner argues that we are used to thinking of a person from the outside, but that "we have been looking in the wrong places" (p. 31) to understand what it is to be human and what it is to make meaning. He asserts that we are better off imagining a person from the inside, specifically from inside the brain. Turner, like Whorf, sees that we are born into and continue to modify and elaborate systems of internal patterning all our lives. It is this dynamic continuity of patterning that make us who we are in the world, both in terms of our unique individuality and our cultural and social behavior.

2. Points in the pattern of the internalized linguistic system

Whorf went beyond general reference to patterns to develop a way of thinking about how culturally acquired patternment might be organized in the mind/brain. He took up an insight first explored by Sapir in his classic 1921 introduction to linguistics (a text still worth reading today for its lucidity and sophisticated grasp of basic linguistic concepts). In the paradigmatic use of what I call the *points in the pattern* construct, Sapir (1921) noted that the distinctive "speech sounds" of a language (which later became known as *phonemes*) are sustained as "points in the pattern" of a system of relationships in which their individual status as "entities" is as abstract and relativistic as the status of subatomic "particles" in physics. Their identification as entities is as much a function of the presence of an enculturated observer (a person familiar with the language concerned in this case) as is the identification of subatomic particles in physics. To people who cannot speak the language, the "points," or structurally meaningful sounds that speakers isolate unconsciously, are lost in what seems merely meaningless gabble. Their viability as speech sounds rather than random noises is thus a function of the systemic relationships in which they recur, and also, most importantly, of the hearer's knowledge of the system of those relationships. This point might be easier to understand if we think about our ability to identify a movement of the foot as a dance step rather than a random kick or twitch. Sapir (1925) pointed out that we know something is a dance step only if we know the sequence of movements that makes up the pattern as a whole, and within which this particular movement can be identified as an integral part of that pattern on the basis of its relationships to other movements.

This way of thinking about elements in systems is quite different from habits of thought that promote the notion that an entity, even when it is part of a set of relationships, is adequately described by its features and out of the environmental context in which it operates. It is also somewhat different from the notion of a system as a conglomerate of essentially independent entities that cooperate to create emergent order from the complexity of their organized interactions. Referring to the "psychological aloofness" of each element from all other points in the sound system of a language, Sapir (1925) stressed that the "relational gaps between the sounds of a language are just as necessary to the psychological definition of these sounds as the articulations and acoustic images which are customarily used to define them" (p. 35). Both Sapir and Whorf were also explicit about their insight that what the former referred to as "a vast network of associated localizations in the brain and lower nervous tracts" (Sapir, 1921, p. 10) and the latter a "matrix of relations" or a "state of linkage" or "rapport" (Whorf, 1937/1956b, p. 67) is physically entrenched in the human mind/brain when a person comes to know a language. What they meant is that the process of learning language physically changes the organization of the brain. They did not know then, as we do not yet know today, precisely what is involved in neurological terms. What is fascinating about their attempts to articulate their insights are the conceptual similarities generated by their wordings and the language modern cognitive scientists use when they talk about connectionism. In both cases the focus is on system and massive interconnectivity within systems and across systems. This is of particular interest to educators, as I will show in more detail below.

The logic of the points in the pattern theory of internalized systemic knowledge thus has clear affinities with the modern connectionist theory that is currently challenging traditional cognitivism in the mind sciences. For those unfamiliar with the literature, Bechtel and Abrahamsen (1991) and, for a rather more journalistic account, Allman (1989) provide introductions to connectionist research. To apply connectionist theory about brain processing to learning situations, we must regard learners as strengthening, creating, or eroding connections to established knowledge within and across their already internalized systems of understanding and behavior as they deal with new information. What we might miss in trying to comprehend what this means in cognitive terms is that with every input or modification (whether externally or internally generated), the whole system shifts and readjusts.

Points in the pattern or connectionist approaches to understanding cognition are essentially fluid, dynamic, and holistic, and therefore very different from the much more static metaphors educators usually use. The latter often require us to think of the mind as a container in which things are stored in various compartments. These more conventional ways of thinking about the mind downplay the massive connectivity that seems to characterize mental activity of all kinds.

Whorf went further than Sapir in trying to conceptualize the nature and mode of operation of internalized linguistic systems. Using concepts rather similar to those introduced more recently by the physicist David Bohm, who used holographic metaphor to explore ideas about the organization of the universe and human existence, Whorf (1942/1956j) suggested that any entity we are able to isolate from the matrix of experience in which it occurs can be thought of as being "emergent from a field of causes that is itself a manifold of pattern and order" (p. 269). He explained that "situations `actualize' it." In Bohm's (1980) terminology, elements of experience with which we can engage consciously are regarded as "manifest" or "unfolded" and part of the "explicate order." When "unmanifest" or "enfolded," they may be regarded as part of the "implicate order" of the universe — or of the mind, as the case may be. In the case of human knowledge, "everything is in there," as Charles F. Hockett, a student of Sapir and Whorf, once told me with respect to the internalized linguistic system about which he has written in terms of resonance theory (Hockett, 1987).

Hockett's resonance theory extends the points in the pattern notion and has interesting similarities with Bohm's theory. Hockett argues that every element of language within an internalized system operates on the basis of multiple resonances that reverberate throughout the system. When I asked him how he conceptualized the system in action, he talked of twinkling lights, points of light of varying intensities and duration flickering on and off without rest, a wonderfully intricate (and integrated) complexity of activity in constant change.

Using imagery no doubt drawn from his early training in the physical sciences (he was a chemical engineer by profession), Whorf (1942/1956j) also likened the human mind to a power plant or radio station, and in doing so experimented with an application of field theory to linguistics. In the case of the power plant, he pointed out that the use of mathematical formulas "make[s] possible the strategic arrangement of magnets and wires . . . so that, when the magnets (or rather the field of subtle forces, in and around the magnets) are set in motion, force is manifested in the way we call an electric current" (pp. 249–250). It was Whorf's opinion that language acquisition has a similar effect on the human mind/brain. While capacity to language may be inbuilt, it is linguistic enculturation, a quintessentially social matter, that brings potentiality into actuality and delivers our distinctive human heritage to us.

3. Linguistic thinking

That distinctive heritage is the capacity for *linguistic thinking,* a crucial element in the theory complex whose significance, like the points in the pattern theory, has not been fully appreciated previously. Whorf regarded language capacity as central to what is special about human cognition compared with that of other animals, not only because we can express, convey, or interpret our thoughts through use of language, and build new ideas dialogically in communication with other people, but also because the very process of incorporating linguistic activity into cognition during socialization changes the way the mind/brain functions, as we saw above. His concept of linguistic thinking is close to Vygotsky's (1934/1986) ideas about the operation of "verbal thought" in the cognitive interface of speech and thought. Whorf's explorations of the way we make meaning of experience were always investigations into the phenomenon of linguistic thinking, a complex of mental processes intimately associated with conceptual activity of a distinctively human and shareable kind. While other animals may think (and also communicate), it is not at all clear that they are able to share and intersubjectively elaborate or augment conceptual activity in the way we can. This does not mean, contrary to what has been asserted in some oversimplified accounts of his ideas, that Whorf believed that one could not think at all without language. On the contrary, he took it for granted (as Sapir had done) that certain nonlinguistic processes are foundational in human thinking. We will look at an example of these in the next section. It does mean, however, that simplistic accounts of language conceived as fundamentally different from thought miss much of what Whorf wanted to say about the operation of language in cognition and its relation to experience.

These points have not generally been fully appreciated even by scholars who have studied Whorf carefully. For instance, in spite of his understanding that Whorf was concerned "with fundamental problems of meaning, or . . . fundamental intellectual operations," John B. Carroll, in his influential 1956 introduction to Whorf's collected writings, used a dichotomy that may have partially distracted him from the revolutionary nature of Whorf's contribution. He differentiated, unnecessarily in my opinion, between "the content" or "substance" of thought and "the process of thought," associating the former with language and arguing that Whorf "appeared to believe" that the former influences the latter (Carroll, 1956b, p. 26). More recently, Lucy (1992a) has identified "content" with "concepts" and argued that Whorf rarely talked about thought processes and "probably had no well-formed view" of the "issues involved in the content-process dichotomy" (p. 43).

Whorf himself, however, argued that "every language is a vast pattern-system, different from others, in which are culturally ordained the forms and categories by which the personality not only communicates, but also analyzes nature, notices or neglects types of relationship and phenomena, channels his reasoning and builds the house of his consciousness" (1942/1956j, p. 252). Analyzing, reasoning, and building one's "house of consciousness" are all mental processes or activities, not "content." Although we might argue that a good deal of this kind of mental activity is nonlinguistic, it is hard to imagine how it can be communicated without the use of language in some form.

Some at least of the later developing processes seem to emerge only as the relevant linguistic patterns are internalized in the course of language acquisition. For instance, much of the reasoning that characterizes academic writing at advanced levels in English depends on writers' ability to manipulate words such as *whereas, however, alternatively,* and *consequently*. Competent writers also organize paragraphs and whole texts in characteristic ways that have to be learned and that facilitate the kinds of reasoning valued in academic environments. Extensive research on these phenomena is ongoing in the fields of tertiary literacy studies and English as a Second Language teaching. As Whorf (1940/1956f) argued, "Formulation of ideas is not an independent process, strictly rational in the old sense, but is part of a particular grammar and differs, from slightly to greatly, between different grammars" (pp. 212–213).

Both Carroll and Lucy, in spite of their valid intuitive responses to Whorf, were, in my opinion, impeded in explaining the nature of his theorizing as a whole by their acceptance of objectifying and dichotomizing paradigms that are endemic in Western psychology. Many others have also tried to interpret Whorf in these terms, failing in the process to give adequate attention to the theoretical significance of the wordings he himself used. For instance, since the 1950s, considerable empirical investigation into the linguistic relativity question has been conducted using psycholinguistic paradigms that require the operational separation of language and thought as independent entities. In defense of this procedure, Lucy (1992a) has argued that

> it is important that there be a clear analytic distinction between linguistic categories and cognitive categories so that the influence of the former on the latter (if any) can be detected and identified. If linguistic and cognitive categories are conflated in the research formulation, then the findings will be ambiguous: if they are directly equated with one another, then what is to be proven will, in effect, have been presupposed. (p. 264)

What I argue is that if we want to understand Whorf's insights, we need to put aside this dichotomy and the methodological problems it engenders and seriously explore what it means in cognitive terms to have domains of thought that are essentially or even significantly linguistic in character, in which what is conceptual is inextricable from the patterns of linkage and connection we think of as being primarily linguistic. At a commonsense level, for instance, it is hard to imagine general linguistic categories such as those of "noun" or "verb" existing independently of our thought processes. There are also many concepts that are hard to imagine developing and operating independently of language. How, for instance, should we think of the independent nonlinguistic existence of the concepts communicated in words like *however, therefore, consequently, if, wise, coherent, undoubtedly, alternatively, describe,* or the word *language* itself in both its nominal and verbal forms? But, you might respond, it is easy to imagine the independence from language of concepts communicated in words such as *arm, love, family, animal, blue, intelligent,* or *warm.* But is it?

To see how varied the reference domains of translation "equivalents" of ordinary words are from language to language, one only needs to reflect on one's own linguistic competence if one knows more than one language or spend a coffee break chatting with a bilingual person if one is monolingual. At what point is something no longer warm but hot? What does intelligence involve? Is love the same thing in my culture as yours? Children learn how words are used in social interaction with groups of speakers who unconsciously (and also consciously) demonstrate their use in natural conversation. As a word is acquired, the child develops a feel for its range of application. Learning its socially and culturally defined field of reference is part of knowing and being able to use a word appropriately. But range of application can vary sufficiently from language to language for it to be relevant to ask whether a word is *really* the same as its apparent counterpart in another language. A word and its conceptual ramifications are all part of the same phenomena, features of a person's internalized linguistic system, a system that cannot sensibly be imagined as existing independently of other cognitive systems that evolve over time in the course of physical, social, and intellectual maturation. Certainly some concepts are nonlinguistic in essence. The point is that conceptual activity is more varied in character than we might have imagined.

4. Isolates of experience and meaning

We come now to the fourth element of the theory complex and closer to the linguistic relativity principle itself. The fourth strand deals with the notion of nonlinguistic *isolates of experience* and their operationalization in language as *isolates of meaning* (Whorf, 1940/1956e, 1940/1956f). Isolates of experience are universally available to the species by virtue of the nature of the world we live in and its interface with our senses.

In line with early gestalt psychologists (Koffka, 1935; Köhler, 1929), Whorf (1940/ 1956f) argued that although we are confronted experientially with "a kaleidoscopic flux of impressions" (p. 213), these impressions are not unstructured, but, rather, organized perceptually on gestaltic principles of figure and ground in every sphere of perception or apperception.

Physiologically we are always isolating some "bits of experience" (Whorf & Trager, 1938, p. 8) for attention and backgrounding others in every sensory realm. The business of making meaning of experiential data is that of isolating or abstracting "essentials" out of situations and making sense of them, whether language is involved or not. The reason Whorf (1940/1956e) thought that the way our attention is organized has a lot to do with linguistic enculturation is that different languages encourage their speakers to draw "different essentials out of the same situation" (p. 162). He thought that because some "isolates from experience" are operationalized linguistically as "isolates of meaning" (Whorf, 1940/1956f, p. 208), those bits of experience tend to become more salient than others not reinforced in this way. Isolates of experience that are not taken up in a specific way in a language are harder to talk about when we notice them because we have to use more circumlocution to make our meaning clear.

For example, the Ḏätiwuy language of northern Australia is more efficient than English with respect to several body movements and types of event. One word picks out a particular isolate of movement or type of happening from the ongoing flow of experience, encouraging speakers to see it as a single unit of activity, whereas in English the same (equally observable) phenomenon requires us to put specific effort and more words into describing it. Merrkiyawuy Ganambarr (1994), a Ḏätiwuy speaker, gives the following examples: *barrwarryun*, to twist and turn (while sleeping, crying, or laughing); *marrnggatthun*, to look about from a sitting position, moving only the upper body; *watthun*, to look back over your shoulder; *mangutji-ngal'yun*, to stumble upon someone or something unexpectedly; *watjarryun*, to try and stop people from hurting each other; *mayali-wilkthun*, to not do what someone expects you to do (pp. 254–255). Of course every language has words that can only be translated into another language by circumlocution; Whorf's point was just that when we learn a specific name for something we are more likely to notice it as a separate phenomenon.

Whorf (1940/1956e) explained that isolates may be selected from both the "egoic" or internal field of perception (thoughts, feelings, pains, etc.) and the "external" field (primarily visual). He thought that isolates such as those of hearing and tasting fall into the egoic field, while the experience of seeing (not what is seen itself) seems to fall between the two fields. Although this isolate construct is an explicitly (albeit briefly) elaborated strand of the theory complex, it has not, to my knowledge, ever been previously recognized (or isolated!) as essential to understanding what Whorf said about linguistic relativity. He did, however, explore its application in a little known unpublished paper on the parts of speech in Hopi (Whorf, 1940) and in two of the articles (Whorf, 1940/1956e, 1940/1956f) included in the classic collection of his writings entitled *Language, Thought, and Reality* (Carroll, 1956a).

5. Abstractive processes in cognition

Before going on to look more closely at the way our ability to isolate aspects of experience and elaborate them in language provides the basis for linguistic relativity, let us briefly consider another element of the complex that, although it was not explicitly elaborated by Whorf, is implied in what he said about isolates of experience and meaning. The logic of Whorf's explorations suggests that we might find it useful (in cognitive science and education in particular) to consider the very activity of drawing gestalts or isolates out of the ongoing data of experience as the most fundamental cognitive process involved in learning.

In talking about abstraction in this way we focus on process rather than product. What we usually think about when we use the word *abstraction* is the outcome of the process of cognitive activity, not the process itself of drawing isolates of experience out of the undifferentiated input with which our sensory organs engage. I argue that it may be useful, particularly in pedagogy, to give more thought to the status of this generic process in cognition and learning. It seems to me that there is a valid argument for regarding abstraction in this process sense (because it is influenced by cultural factors and because it is trainable in each domain) as a general learning principle at the base of other learning and common to all sensory modes.

As pattern-processing beings, we are constantly and unconsciously noticing patternment in whatever we are involved in. Much teaching has the goal of facilitating the emergence of new habits of noticing in learners. What learners learn to notice and abstract from the matrix of their occurrence are isolates of experience. For instance, young children must learn to isolate and abstract away from the matrix of their occurrence such stimuli as letters, words, geometrical shapes, etc. Learners in different fields must be able to isolate and abstract such things as cancer cells, musical notes, specific sounds in the ongoing noise of a running motor, and so on in every field of expertise.

Perhaps it might be argued that the notion of "discrimination" in psychological and educational theory is the same as abstraction in the sense suggested here. I wonder, however, whether the act of discriminating in any field of perception might not have more to do with differentiating between similar features or things than isolating them in the first place. A dictionary definition, for instance, mentions "distinctions and differences." Discrimination occurs after the first acts of isolation and abstraction have taken place, it seems to me. The process of abstracting isolates out of sensory data is therefore primary when it comes to the task of learning to make sense of stimuli in any sensory domain.

Experiential data come in many forms, including the more easily conceptualized — auditory, visual, tactile, and so on. We isolate sounds, objects, colors, movements, sensations perceived through the skin, tastes, etc., when we separate them as entities from the ongoing background flux of data presented to us by the environing world, including the world of our body itself. In addition to the sensory domains that are most salient in conscious experience, there are probably other realms of perception in which we could become more competent too if our language elaborated these areas of experience in sufficient detail to draw our attention to what is involved in abstracting isolates within them.

For example, our proprioceptive abilities provide us with ongoing but generally unmonitored information about the states of our bodies. Athletes and gymnasts no doubt develop much more acute ability than other people to talk about, notice, and use isolates in this field of experience. We also have varying abilities to apprehend and monitor other people's emotional states, abilities that might, if the processes of abstracting isolates in this domain, and if the nature of the relevant isolates themselves were better understood and systematically trained, lead to greater mutual understanding of one another.

These ideas about the role of abstractive processes in cognition have emerged from the study of Whorf's ideas. It seems to me that there is a logical gap in the theory complex as a whole if the implicit strand relating to abstraction is not identified and elaborated in relation to the other strands. Whether or not the emphasis on abstraction as a process that I am suggesting here is taken up as a useful concept in relation to issues of teaching and learning, only time will tell. For the moment all I want to say is that the concept seems to be necessary to make sense of Whorf's thinking about relations between language, mind, and experience. As such, it is also relevant to pedagogy.

6. *The linguistic relativity principle*

The sixth element of the complex is the *linguistic relativity principle,* now associated with Whorf's name for over fifty years. Whorf (1940/1956f) considered that no one "is free to describe nature with absolute impartiality but is constrained to certain modes of interpretation even when" they think themselves "most free" (p. 214). We cannot be impartial or free of culture when we describe because describing is talking and the words we use, as discussed above, are often subtly different in meaning from language to language, even when they seem at first thought to be equivalent semantically. Whorf argued that through constant use of habitual patterns of speech, our patterns of attention themselves become linguistically conditioned. Defining linguistic relativity, he said, "We are thus introduced to a new principle of relativity, which holds that all observers are not led by the same physical evidence to the same picture of the universe, unless their linguistic backgrounds are similar, or can in some way be calibrated" (Whorf, 1940/1956f, p. 214). He is not claiming here that there is anything different about the physical world of speakers of different languages or about their processes of perception. These points have not always been appreciated in discussions about linguistic relativity. What varies has to do with which isolates are abstracted for attention and which are ignored. Whorf was not saying that it is impossible to understand the world in the same way as people who speak languages different from our own, but only that it doesn't happen automatically. By paying attention to the way our languages work, we can begin to identify the culturally specific patterns involved in drawing isolates from experience and understanding events.

Our predilection to segment and organize experience on the basis of unconscious linguistic influences that come to overlay universal perceptual principles during the process of language acquisition is not only a function of what is named in our culture (the specific things, attributes, actions, and events that our speech community labels), but is also, and with much more subtle and elusive implications, a function of logical relationships articulated by grammar. (The term *articulate* is used here in its structuring, organizing sense, as well as in the sense of expressing.) For instance, although time relationships can be communicated in all languages, it can be argued that a language like English (that ties obligatory time reference to verbs through its grammar) habituates its speakers to think differently about time, compared with speakers of other languages where time reference is optional or grammatical activity has a different effect.

For example, Whorf (1936/1956a) studied the grammar of Hopi, a North American language, and argued convincingly that it organizes an experiential reality different from that promoted by English. He demonstrated that whereas the English tense system provides a framework for conceptualizing experience in terms of a past, present, and future (ranged over the conventional European notion of the time line imported from our experience of physical space), Hopi understanding of the universe is facilitated by a tense-like system that articulates reality in terms of what is or has been manifest in experience in the relatively recent past contrasted with that which is inchoate, imagined, hoped for, or a function of events celebrated in myth or memory. In many respects, the traditional worldview Whorf ascribed to the Hopi language is similar to the Bohmian concept of the universe with its dialectically meshed implicate and explicate orders. Whorf's use of the terms "manifest" and "unmanifest" to describe what he discovered in Hopi makes this comparison even more striking. The subtlety of Whorf's reasoning in this regard has often been ignored.

For instance, although Ekkehart Malotki (1983) has argued at length that Whorf's claims about the Hopi worldview are not generally valid, there are some problems with Malotki's analysis. In the case of claims about a set of adverbial particles that Whorf called "tensors," I (Lee, 1991) have been able, by using Malotki's extensive database of examples and some of his own descriptions, to show that Whorf's arguments are sound if care is taken to understand his reasoning. Whorf argued that tensors automatically encourage Hopi speakers to isolate as experientially salient a sense of dynamism in events that, in conceptual terms, affirms the activity of "invisible intensity factors" (Whorf, 1941/1956h, p. 147). This dynamism is not as evident in English descriptions of the same events. Whorf considered that the Hopi experienced these factors as integral to the whole process by which what happens is continually manifesting out of the realm of the potential and unmanifest into the world we can experience. Malotki's analysis shows a sophisticated grasp of the semantics of tensors, but his agenda is devoted to showing that Hopi is not as different from English as Whorf thought. This agenda perhaps overlooks interesting ways in which Hopi grammar articulates experience differently from English, including what English speakers call the experience of time.

Conscious awareness of the logic of Hopi utterances is no more necessary to daily functioning within that worldview than is conscious awareness that the structure of English sentences requires that actors or doers be implicated in everything that happens for English speakers. As a concomitant of the way we talk, we unconsciously pick out or even artificially include an agent when we refer to an event. This is a distinctive feature of the way linguistic relativity operates to structure experience through English. In the statement "It is raining," the "it" here does not refer to any "thing" that does the raining; raining simply occurs. As Whorf (1941/1956i) pointed out, "We are constantly reading into nature fictional acting entities, simply because our verbs must have substantives in front of them" (p. 243). The fact that the Hopi language allows verbs without subjects suggested to him that it facilitates a logic subtly different from that of English, at least with respect to the way those particular verbs can be articulated in relation to experience.

7. The calibration of agreement

Whorf (1940/1956f) argued that "whenever agreement or assent is arrived at in human affairs, and whether or not mathematics or any other specialized symbolisms are made part of the procedure, THIS AGREEMENT IS REACHED BY LINGUISTIC PROCESSES, OR ELSE IT IS NOT REACHED" (p. 212, original capitals). Elsewhere, Whorf (1942/1956j) made it clear that he regarded "mathematics and music" as "ultimately of the same kindred as language" (p. 248). The implications of this strand of Whorf's theorizing for teaching and learning are as profound as any other part of the theory complex and flow naturally from the ideas we have been exploring in relation to the linguistic relativity principle.

Some readers may want to reject the notion that true agreement must involve language. Certainly we can empathize, experience fellow feeling, sympathize, understand, and even disagree without language. But can we really agree without using language? To know that agreement has really been reached, we must talk to each other or carefully note the words used, for instance, in a piece of writing. During this process we will frequently find it necessary to clarify what is meant. We can only achieve such clarification through careful and precise use of language, whether that use be internal (in thought) or externalized in speech or writing.

The process of coming to agreement requires that individuals calibrate the way they make meaning against the practice of other people. Just as we determine the accuracy of a measuring instrument by checking that the units or scale used on it conform with some socially agreed-upon reference, so we also calibrate our meanings with those of other people in order to facilitate agreement. *Calibration of agreement* often involves negotiation as people make adjustments to what they mean in the process of working toward mutual understanding.

There are three respects in which linguistic calibration facilitates agreement. The first is what I think of as ordinary agreement. In the most general sense we need to check that we and our interlocutors are talking about the same things before we decide whether we agree with them or not. In situations where disagreement threatens to bring disharmony or disruption, in classrooms for example, it is always worth stopping to check that the parties concerned are talking about the same situational parameters. Encouraging interlocutors to use clarifying phrases when they explain, accuse, or affirm, providing support for communication strategies that involve waiting for others to explain what they mean, and inviting participants to attempt such explanations are practices already integral to healthy interaction.

In intercultural situations, calibration of agreement also involves bringing to awareness which bits of experience count and which do not in terms of patterns of primary linguistic socialization and early training of attention. At the finest levels of subtlety, facilitating this second dimension of agreement involves studying morphological patterning within words, as well as investigating other grammatical processes at sentence and discourse levels in all the languages concerned.

The third sense in which agreement is a matter of linguistic adjustment has to do with the calibration of individual internalized linguistic systems against one another, even within single-speech communities. Even when we say we speak the "same" language, this is always only an approximation. As members of particular speech communities we do speak the same languages in a general sense, but no two internalized systems are exactly the same. The reason for this is that the complexity of the immense number of connections within each system and the specific configurations of those connections must vary from person to person because they are forged in different life circumstances. Every person's experience of a language is unique even within a family, because one's set of interlocutors is different, one's own place in the family communicative network has distinct characteristics, one's personal response to events and the language that articulates them is different from other people's, and so on. Add to this the dynamic nature of the internalized system that we discussed earlier and it is easy to see that an idiolect is just that — a unique version of the language of our speech community stamped irrevocably with our own personality and experi-ence and having to be continually calibrated against other people's internalized sys-tems to ensure that effective communication occurs.

In day-to-day experience, we are often in situations where the fact that words carry different constellations of connotation for different people comes to our attention. At such times we may marvel that we could have known someone for so long without appreciating that the aura of meaning carried by a particular word can differ so much from person to person. New insights into how our interlocutors make meaning with the words we share helps us adjust the way we understand and use the same words ourselves. For example, I tend to use the word *jargon* to refer in a connotationally neutral way to any specialized registers of talk or writing that are specific to particular groups, whether these be groups of physicists, political activists, or farmers. Many people feel uncomfortable with this usage, feeling that it is idiosyncratic because, in their experience, the word has had mostly negative connotations. I need to keep those connotations in mind when I use the word in the company of people who do not know me well. Our ability to adjust our internalized systems over time is enhanced when we train ourselves to notice and investigate patterns of meaning-making around us and learn to enjoy observing the workings of our own patterns of linguistic thinking.

8. Metalinguistic awareness and science

It should be evident by now that the eighth strand of the theory complex, language awareness, interpenetrates all the other strands. Whorf also stressed that more com-plex degrees of language awareness and the finer calibration of agreement that they make possible are crucial to the advance of science. The term *metalinguistic aware-ness* is used nowadays to draw attention to the degrees of sophistication that are pos-sible in language awareness. At its most basic level, language awareness is simply awareness of speech, our own and others. At more developed levels it involves the ability to attend to the stream of speech and break it up mentally into the various parts (sound, word, sentence, etc.) with which literate people in particular are famil-iar. Attention to the effects of variations in language — being aware, for example, of how different words impact on different speech partners in different situations — is also part of metalinguistic awareness.

When we as a global society train scientists or experts in any field, including edu-cation, close attention to the language professionals use is rarely high on our list of priorities, and yet Whorf (1940/1956g) argued that:

> The beasts may think, but they do not talk. "Talk" OUGHT TO BE a more noble and dignified word than "think." Also we must face the fact that science begins and ends in talk; this is the reverse of anything ignoble. Such words as "analyze, com-pare, deduce, reason, infer, postulate, theorize, test, demonstrate" mean that, when-ever [scientists do something they] talk about this thing that [they do]. As Leonard Bloomfield [1887–1949] has shown, scientific research begins with a set of sen-tences which point the way to certain observations and experiments, the results of which do not become fully scientific until they have been turned back into language,

yielding again a set of sentences which then become the basis of further exploration into the unknown. This scientific use of language is subject to the principles or the laws of the science that studies all speech — linguistics. (pp. 220–221, original capitals)

Whorf (1941/1956i) believed that if linguistics could evolve into a state where contrastive grammar is taught as a means of expanding awareness of different styles of logic and the "power[s] of thought" embodied in these logical styles, the "multilingual awareness" (p. 244) that would result would have the potential to expand conceptual range and flexibility even in monolinguals. This state of expertise is yet to be fully developed as an art and science within the broader field of linguistics and its applied branches. Whorf did not think it necessary to learn to speak additional languages in order to benefit from insights into the way they work; simply learning about alternative ways of relating to experience can itself have the liberating effect that he described and had himself experienced as a linguist familiar with different systems of grammatical patterning. The 1956 collection of Whorf's articles (Carroll, 1956a) abounds with interesting examples of the contrasts he noticed. Simply reading about them is enough to make us look at our own primary languages with new interest and attention. Just as acquiring new words and the concepts they embody can promote new ways of thinking, learning and teaching about alternative modes of logic manifest in grammatical patterning may also bring its rewards. Whorf's (1941/1956i) visionary goal in this regard was for "a new technology of language and thought" (p. 240) based on an advanced cognitive science of contrastive linguistics. This would require new approaches and emphases within linguistics and, by extension, within education as well.

9. A new technology of thought

Education can benefit from the development of a *new technology of thought* that focuses on relationships between language, mind, and experience. Whorf argued, with respect to science in general, that what is required is a "systematic view and classification of all known `linguistic species', i.e. individual human lgs [languages], in order that science may obtain a comprehensive view of the human linguistic faculty as one large whole, much as zoology classifies and studies all animal species, not merely a few preferred ones" (Whorf & Trager, 1938, p. 3). To this end he began serious work on a comprehensive scheme for cataloguing linguistic information (Whorf, 1938/1956d). He recognized that "long in advance of the ultimate possibility of such a linguistic world-picture it is desirable to compare many adequately comprehensive outlines and `trait-lists' of individual lgs to `see what we have got' world-wide and so make valid generalizations about the totality Language" (Whorf & Trager, 1938, p. 3).

Descriptive linguists make detailed analyses of languages as a matter of course, and many highly technical descriptions exist even for languages that have become extinct or are spoken by very small groups of people. What Whorf (1937/1956c) wanted to encourage was, first, a movement away from analyzing languages very different from European languages in terms of grammatical categories originally devised many centuries ago for the study of Greek and Latin. Second, as indicated in the quotations above, he wanted to see a world survey of languages attempted in order to better understand language as a cognitive resource. To this end, Whorf (1938/1956d) suggested a standard framework that linguists might use to organize the very complex task of analyzing languages into levels and fields within which comparisons could be made.

Although linguistic science has advanced considerably since Whorf died, contrastive linguistics as a subfield is relatively undeveloped, particularly with specific application of findings to education. Surveys of languages are often made, for instance, in the search for language universals or the semantics of a particular domain of meaning-making, but a comprehensive overview "to see what we have got," as Whorf put it, in terms of our total potential for linguistic thinking as a species has not been attempted. One problem is that it would certainly be an enormous task and impossible to complete in any definitive sense, because the world's languages are so numerous and because all languages still in use change constantly. Another problem with this goal is that relatively few linguists are trained to think of language as a cognitive resource with implications for the way people of different cultural backgrounds think. Educationists and psychologists can encourage professional linguists to give more attention to the role of language in cognition and to the educational significance of differences between languages in this respect. Such action will assist in realizing some part at least of Whorf's vision.

To summarize, this ninth strand of the theory complex, as I see it, is the notion that the only way that we can come to comprehend the full potential of the uniquely human phenomenon of language in cognition is by systematically cataloging the variety of linguistic thinking operations manifest in the thousands of languages spoken in the world. In plotting "the outstanding differences among tongues — in grammar, logic, and the general analysis of experience" (Whorf, 1941/1956i, p. 240), we also gain insights into the degree of variation that exists in the way we isolate, abstract, and variously segment experiential data to create the subjective realities we live in. In the course of so doing, we will develop a better understanding of what reality might be for the species as a whole. To argue that a technology of thought of this kind should be at the core of educational theory and practice at all levels is not inappropriate in the context of the global village evolving today. That so many small languages are being lost throughout the world each year as a consequence of the linguistic imperialism of a powerful few is tragic.

10. Intercultural understanding

The natural concomitant of all that has been said so far, and a matter that was dear to Whorf's heart, is the intercultural respect and understanding his ideas promote. This aspect of the theory complex has long been promoted by Whorf's admirers and is, indeed, a factor that has drawn many, including the present author, to closer study of his work. What is required for this understanding to grow is openness to the fact that each language reflects just one constellation of ways of relating to experience. There are many others. Learning about them is interesting and helps develop openness to other ways of thinking and being as we come to terms with the degree to which our own ways have been patterned during socialization.

It seems to be a fact of human existence that each person regards the worldview developed within her or his own culture as normal, seeing people from outside it as different. Criteria of normalcy are functions of human judgment, and human judgment is significantly developed through ways of talking and thinking learned in the course of maturation and enculturation. Misunderstandings are aggravated when we underestimate or are ignorant of the range of value systems and ways of understanding experience that have been developed over the centuries and that coexist in the world today. While we may not wish to change our own core values or systems for understanding the world, understanding those of other people gives us a better basis for working with them in an atmosphere of mutual respect. Such understanding also enables us to negotiate compromises that work for both parties.

Some people have argued that intercultural understanding would be increased if everyone spoke the same language. Such a state of affairs, however, would address only the most superficial of the three levels of agreement required for communicative precision. Although English is growing as an international language and in its most widely written forms tends to promote uniformity of expression, regional varieties of the language are also growing rapidly in all parts of the world and becoming the vehicles for artistic and political expression and first language communication for more and more people every day. Each of these dialects of English has features that articulate subtly different understandings of experience compared with the others. Rather than promoting intercultural understanding, the proliferation of dialects of a language can, paradoxically, create even more subtle misunderstandings in some cases than occurs in communication between speakers with totally different first languages.

11. Therapeutic value of language awareness

Whorf also touched on some further effects of metalinguistic awareness. He pointed out that "many neuroses are simply the compulsive working over and over of word systems, from which the patient can be freed by showing him the process and pattern" (1942/1956j, p. 269). It is not known what, specifically, Whorf had in mind in this brief reference to the therapeutic potential of language awareness. One possibility is the way we can let obsessive and unresolved preoccupations consume energy and constrain personal development. The central features of such preoccupations are often revealed by paying attention to the stream of silent "conversation" that goes on in our heads much of the time. Stopping to "listen" to internal talk may reveal that we are constantly (mentally) in argument with someone we feel has wronged or misunderstood us. This fantasy verbal engagement goes on in the background even when we are busy with other tasks. We may be shocked to find that instead of the silent interaction changing over time to a point where the conflict can be brought into the open and dealt with, the pattern of internal talk hardly changes over days, weeks, months, or years. Paying attention to the internal phenomenon instead of letting it go on unmonitored and unchallenged may help us break through to an improved frame of mind in which we feel more confident either to engage with the person in a real conversation or, alternatively, to let the obsession go altogether.

Noticing and attending to the way we explain things can also be useful. If we drop and break something, do we say "I dropped and broke it" or "It slipped out of my hand and broke"? In the first type of explanation (as a function of the grammatical pattern chosen for the sentence) we acknowledge our agency in both aspects of the event. In the second we attribute agency to the object that was broken, implying that the breakage was not our fault. By systematically considering whether to choose the first kind of statement over the second we can develop a more conscious sense of when we need to accept responsibility and when it is genuinely not warranted. If we find that we have a tendency to rely too exclusively on one pattern rather than the other, it may suggest to us that we either need to feel that we are controlling everything that happens around us or, alternatively, that we are helpless in a world in which everyone and everything has agency except ourselves.

The classic 1951 work, *Gestalt Therapy: Excitement and Growth in the Human Personality*, by Frederick S. Perls, Ralph F. Hefferline, and Paul Goodman, includes useful starting points for the personal work required to learn to attend to the way we use language to create and explain the world. Like Whorf, these authors also drew on gestaltism to develop their theories about the way humans experience the world. Their book, which offers a general course of personal awareness development dealing with many aspects of the self, also includes suggestions that focus on the way we use language.

Whorf also believed that developing enhanced language awareness skills helps us dissolve illusions about the nature of reality that arise when habitual patterns of naming and explaining are taken as constituting the only way in which the world can be understood. He believed that this experience too has personal therapeutic value. He went further, asserting that "study of languages and linguistic principles is at least a partial raising of the intellect" to achieve states of awareness characterized by "a tremendous expansion, brightening and clarifying of consciousness, in which the intellect functions with undreamed-of rapidity and sureness" (Whorf, 1942/1956j, p. 269). There are meditative traditions in many cultures where practices with such goals have been developed. For a modern introduction to some of the principles involved, see the fascinating 1991 work by Francisco J. Varela, Evan Thompson, and Eleanor Rosch, who bring cognitive science and Buddhist meditative psychology together, linking them with other traditions such as phenomenology and psychoanalysis. Their discussions about relations between science, mind, and experience are very compatible with Whorf's, although they do not highlight the role of language in cognition in the way he did.

What Varela, Thompson, and Rosch have to say has a direct bearing on the matter of dissolving illusions about the nature of reality, a traditional concern of mind sciences originating in Asia. Whorf's reasoning suggests that to embrace and even celebrate relativism is truer to the nature of the human condition than the obsessive grasping for certainty that trammels so many of us in so many dimensions of our daily lives. While near hysterical reaction to the relativist stance has prevented many otherwise thoughtful people from reading Whorf carefully, the disturbing rise of preoccupation with personal stress in Western society in recent years may be at least partly an outcome of socializing practices (including pedagogical practices) that flow from fear of relativism. In spite of modern rhetoric about coping with change, outrage when things are not as one expects or anticipates is currently endemic in Western culture and suggests that many of us have grown up with false and dysfunctional certainties about human nature and existence in general.

Life has never been certain from day to day, hour to hour, or minute to minute for individuals of this species (or any other for that matter), and the false security engendered by successes in modern medicine can keep the paradox of this single existential certainty from its rightful place in consciousness. Similarly, what we think we know one day can be undermined or radically transformed without notice through the agency of small amounts of new information. The mental adjustments that follow such information can send repercussions throughout entire belief systems, sometimes fracturing them. While it would be foolish to claim that giving more attention to language can on its own ensure emotional or psychological stability and improved resilience in the face of stress, it may be the case that using the new Whorfian framework as a basis for bringing linguistic science into greater prominence in educational contexts will provide teachers and learners with legitimate alternative avenues for exploring relativity and the human condition in general. Such a move would also encourage greater awareness of the centrality of linguistic thinking as a cognitive and social activity powerfully instrumental in creating the social realities in which we construct stress as a significant isolate of experience with daunting or even overwhelming influence in our lives.

12. Survival of the species

The sense of urgency Whorf felt about the importance of language awareness and its role in our lives was linked to his concern that not only is it language and our "great development of thinking" that distinguishes us from other animals, but that insofar as our future can be envisaged,

> we must envisage it in terms of mental growth. We cannot but suppose that future developments of thinking are of primary importance to the human species. They may even determine the duration of human existence on the planet earth or in the universe. The possibilities open to thinking are the possibilities of recognizing relationships and the discovery of techniques of operating with relationships on the mental or intellectual plane, such as will in turn lead to ever wider and more penetratingly significant systems of relationships. These possibilities are inescapably bound up with systems of linguistic expression. The story of their evolution . . . is the story of [human] linguistic development — of the long evolution of thousands of systems of discerning, selecting, organizing, and operating with relationships. (Whorf, 1937/1956b, pp. 83–84)

It does not seem to me that this reasoning can be faulted. While we can think without language and, indeed, destroy each other or reduce human existence to states of such abject misery that our cognitive inheritance as a species is seriously compromised without language, it cannot be disputed that our use of language takes such activities beyond the elementary struggle for survival of other species into increasingly

horrifying dimensions. As long as educators remain largely oblivious of the role of linguistic thinking in the way we structure our lives and our relations with other people,
generation after generation of learners will continue to talk and think about experience, beliefs, values, and understandings without giving adequate attention to the
possibility that the very talk they engage in provides all these with their structure and
logic.

I have now completed my introductory review of the twelve strands that make up
the Whorf theory complex. Some strands, like the emphasis on patternment in language, perception, and understanding of experience, and Whorf's concerns for improved intercultural relations and the growth of the human intellect, are thematic
throughout his work. Other strands involve new theoretical constructs that are yet to
be fully explored or developed. These include his gestaltic isolates of experience, his
elaboration of Sapir's insights about the points in the pattern organization of systems
of knowledge internalized in the course of socialization, and his ideas about the linguistic calibration of agreement.

What I have tried to show, both here and in more detail in my book (Lee, 1996), is
that it is futile to reject Whorf's ideas without first trying to understand them as a
whole. The outcomes of numerous attempts over the past fifty years to investigate his
ideas empirically (see Lucy, 1992a, for details) have disappointed many of his admirers, not because he was wrong, I believe, but because what he said was oversimplified
to make it fit experimental paradigms. Most problematic, perhaps, has been the failure to recognize that his theory is about the role of *language in cognition* and not
about the effect of one quite separate and noncognitive function (language) on a totally different cognitive phenomenon (thought). If we are to come to terms with the
implications of Whorf's thinking for our day-to-day lives, we need somehow to find
ways to take all strands of his theory complex into account.

In arguing that the various strands I have identified can provide us with a framework or set of starting points for reflecting on educational practice, I appreciate that
focusing too closely on any one strand to the neglect of the others could again encourage oversimplification of the theory as a whole and lead to distortion. There is a natural tension between the various elements of the complex and their status as parts of
whole that must be kept in mind as we work with his ideas.

APPLICATIONS OF THE NEW WHORFIAN FRAMEWORK

In this section I consider how instructional practice at all levels of education, including teacher education, might change in response to improved understanding of
Whorf's ideas about the role of language in thinking and learning. I begin by asking
what difference it makes to think of everything we learn as patterns in human brains
— to look at ourselves from the inside rather than the outside, as Turner (1991) ad-
vises and Whorf's reasoning suggests.

Children are pattern-processing beings from before birth, absorbing comfortable
rhythms with their mother's heartbeat and learning to cope with changes that may
disturb their equilibrium and set up new patterns of expectation. These new patterns
have to be fitted into the integrated whole that constitutes their relationship with

their embryonic world. By the time they come into formal schooling, their minds — those patterns in the brain that define their personalities and their understanding of the world — are already constituted as incredibly complex interpenetrative networks of systems within systems. Whether or not each system is modularized to some degree (an issue of some controversy in cognitive science), there can be no doubt that a huge amount of interconnection exists. Just think of the endocrinal repercussions we feel in response to certain words that have intense emotional impact for ourselves personally or for the group we associate with most closely. Or think of the complex patterns of association that flash through our minds when something reminds us of a whole set of related memories and aspects of knowledge.

While we share patterns of response with others of similar life experience, each person's particular constellation of responses is not only unique, but constantly changing. As learners, every experience life offers, whether subtle or gross, impacts on our internalized systems of knowledge. Existing points of potential resonance are activated, strengthened, weakened, or modified, and newly emergent points in the pattern ease into the system over time as relationships between existing points shift and change. We can think of each point as a center of more focused or intense energy within the general matrix of electrochemical activity that makes up the human mind/brain.

Each focal point is a potential anchor or attractant for new experiential input. Constellations of related points also represent, through their overall configuration, information accumulated over time. The old adage "Start where the learner is" translates into a responsibility to take time to find out what resonates for a particular learner in what you, as teacher, have to offer. In interpersonal terms it is about matching resonance points in my system with points in yours. In intercultural terms it is about recognizing that specific points that might resonate in harmony between individuals of different cultural backgrounds may nevertheless ramify very differently to constellations of linked points within each personal internalized system of world knowledge and understanding. Complex matchings of broader sets of linkage patterns are likely only when individuals have shared very similar life experiences. So even when we feel we are making contact, it is important to be prepared to notice indications that what is in contact in mental, intellectual, or emotional terms may be fairly narrowly focused, petering out as patterns of connection become more and more different with distance from the prime resonating point.

This approach to conceptualizing knowledge and learning differs dramatically from traditional accounts that take learning to be a matter of accumulating discrete items of knowledge — as though knowledge comes in concrete pieces that can be sorted, counted, stored in mental boxes or filing cabinets, valued or audited in quantity terms, hoarded as currency, or even given by one person to another. By contrast, this way of thinking makes learning a matter of accommodation, growth, and adjustment. We can perhaps think of knowledge as an organic function. One's personal (internal) body of knowledge grows, suffers invasive or disruptive influences, heals, becomes more intricately complex and highly tuned with attention and practice, and decays eventually with disuse or as its neurological substrate breaks down in old age or insult.

Although Sapir's and Whorf's points in the pattern theory and Hockett's resonance theory were developed with specific reference to internalized linguistic systems, we can talk and think in similar terms about all the learning, knowing, and understanding we do. Everything we are exposed to or expose ourselves to, both consciously and unconsciously, connects with resonance points in that internalized, dynamic state of linkage or rapport, that enormously complex set of systems within systems generated by our brain. New information resonates with established patterns of understanding and experience to strengthen or erode connections and restructure relationships between the points in the overall pattern. Domains of understanding and memory that have been enfolded into the implicate order of unconscious mental operation unfold into consciousness — into the explicate order of what is consciously accessible. As we notice them we send further waves of repatterning through our system as a whole, through all the interconnected domains of knowledge that together make us who we are in terms of personality and experience.

Using the points in the pattern model of the working mind/brain, teachers can conceptualize the particularities they present to students as merging into or meshing with knowledge already settled or beginning to settle into systemic configurations within learners' minds. Sharing the model with the students themselves may help them develop greater ability and confidence to notice, organize, and direct their own learning and actively shape their own growing knowledge base, taking pleasure in patterning its relational spaces and rhythms in personally satisfying ways. I make these suggestions on the basis of my own experience of working with this new approach to conceptualizing cognitive organization and knowledge building, but much more work needs to be done. It is also crucial to acknowledge that new ways of conceptualizing things we have always taken for granted and tended to leave unexamined require considerable time to become integrated into understanding.

The need to give ourselves time to think and grow and change in the cognitive domain can be undervalued in today's society, but it is essential. New ways of conceptualizing relations between language, mind, and experience take years to become fully integrated into one's existing worldview. For instance, in my own case the process began with my discovery in the late 1970s of the literature on similarities between modern physics and classical Eastern mind science (e.g., Bohm's work, and also Fritjof Capra's [1975] *The Tao of Physics*). This background allowed me, some six years later, to understand features of Whorf's work that also derived from his knowledge of physics and his interest in Asian philosophy. Since then, over more than a decade of actively working to explain Whorf's ideas and extend them, I know that my own concepts about the nature of thinking, learning, and knowledge have changed significantly. More conventional ideas persist, however, and can be revealed, for instance, in my unthinking use of container metaphors about the mind in casual or even professional discourse.

I have also experimented with the presentation of Whorf's ideas in graduate courses I teach. I introduce preservice and practicing teachers to the Whorf complex and to training in metalinguistic and metacognitive awareness. Many of these students have had little experience of metacognitive reflection in general and little awareness of how language operates in their personal and professional lives. Some find the experience of actively reflecting on their own patterns of linguistic thinking disconcerting at first. One of the first things many notice is that they talk to themselves (or to fantasized others) a lot more than they had ever imagined. Anxiety about this phenomenon usually passes in a few weeks, and most say that the experience of learning to notice language is helpful, both personally and professionally.

The task of conceptualizing their own knowledge building is also new for most students, and although most say that they find it interesting and illuminating, they, as do I, need time to find out whether the ideas I present can be integrated into their understanding of themselves and of their students as learners. Time to reflect, ponder, and consider tends to be undervalued in modern society, but it is a crucial part of being human. Just as many people prefer brewed to instant coffee, so brewed knowledge is often more fun and more interesting than instant. We need to give ourselves more time to think about new ideas instead of expecting that they can be accommodated or rejected at short notice. And we need more researchers who are interested in investigating the viability of these new ways of thinking about knowledge and learning and how they might be related to learning outcomes. Such investigations, for the reasons I have been trying to explain, cannot be done as quick and easy research projects, but, rather, require careful planning and long-term implementation if their results are to be truly useful.

Let us move on now from ideas about patternment and cognitive organization in a general sense to the role of language in cognition. As teachers, it is linguistic thinking that we are most usually in the business of nurturing and fostering through tutorial relationships with our students. Even in disciplines like mathematics we are teaching ways of talking that, once internalized and integrated as systems of understanding, foster distinctive ways of thinking. Vygotsky's insight that people mature cognitively in the course of dialogic engagement with others of greater life experience and language expertise has provided many teachers with a sound pedagogic rationale for the verbal environment they build with their students. His observation that young children first replay their interactions aloud and then subsequently interiorize the verbal behavior until it becomes cognitively entrenched as an integral part of their own internal system for reasoning and understanding is compatible with Whorf's (1937/1956b) ideas about the nature of linguistic activity in the cognitive domain, although Whorf did not deal with the dialogic dimension of the process of internalization.

Our potential to grow cognitively through exposure to other people's thinking (whether this contact occurs through dialogue or reading) does not diminish as we grow older. As learners ourselves, or, more properly, scholars with a focus on developing our distinctively human potential to the full, we are challenged to notice those linguistic operations that are isolable in consciousness, observing how they work and how they may be enhanced through deliberate practice, modification, and engagement with the thinking of others more skilled than ourselves. The most common instance of such learning is when, impressed with someone else's force of reasoning, we practice using some of their formulations ourselves, or in responding to intellectual challenges, bring into active use patterns of language we have only previously read. Although some may like to think that one's argument in some sense exists in nonlinguistic form in one's mind and that the mental work we do to find the best wording is a matter of finding the right garment for presenting the thoughts in public, this is not my experience. My own impression is usually that, as I experiment with different language patterns, I work my way into greater clarity of thought. My ideas seem relatively inchoate until the right words surface out of the implicate order of my unconscious mind into consciousness. The process of achieving greater precision of reasoning is significantly a process of sorting and selecting patterns of wordings.

It is all too easy for teachers necessarily focused on subject matter or occupationally appropriate skill development to sometimes forget that in teaching we are also (and always) promoting patterns, styles, skills, or inefficiencies of thinking in learners whether we are aware of it or not. Through the way we talk and through the kinds of talking we encourage, attack, or undermine, we model and teach thinking. Similarly, as learners focused on what we often metaphorically regard as "content," we may be unaware that what we actually embrace or resist intellectually are generally ways of thinking and understanding — ways of being, in fact — and that these come to us or are rejected by us on the whole as ways of talking. Even as we actively work to direct our intellectual growth either in congruence with or in opposition to the labors of our teachers, we are not always conscious that this, essentially, is the learning that makes us who we are and structures our understanding of the world.

I move now from linguistic thinking to the relevance for pedagogy of Whorf's linguistic relativity principle and the isolate construct Whorf introduced to explain it. In doing so, I also consider the fundamental nature of abstractive processes implied in Whorf's theorizing. In all learning contexts, the ability to isolate patterns of stimulation and discriminate between them provides us with the basis for noticing the kinds of variation we have to be able to attend to in order to learn from situations and apply that learning to new contexts. We have long been familiar with the fact that the ability to isolate and recombine specific phonemes and graphic forms plays a significant role in transition to fluent literacy. Similarly, the ability to differentiate the points in the sound pattern of a new language from the points in our own improves comprehension and often pronunciation. But learning is a matter of growing proficiency to isolate, abstract, combine, and recombine essentials in the same configurations as experts do in every area of knowledge or skill. In the case of divergent and creative thinking of all kinds, individuals either abstract perceptual isolates that are out of the ordinary from experiential flux, or connect commonplace isolates in novel configurations to generate new perspectives or understandings.

As noted in the previous section, Whorf divided the world of experience roughly into the "external" field of experiential data impinging on our bodies and consciousness from outside, and the internal or "egoic" field generated from within by physiological (including neurological) activity. Isolates are segregated out from the ongoing flux of sensation in both fields. Many of our feelings and sensations are isolated in culturally specific ways mediated by language. Indeed, this is one of the trickiest areas in which to attempt to match experience between people of different language backgrounds, not because the isolates in question cannot be pulled out for inspection or because they might not be available to be felt or noticed by everyone (they are, of course), but because the patterns in which they have been identified as separate feelings or sensations are culturally constructed and conditioned in the course of linguistic socialization.

We all tend to assume that those emotions or sensations named in our own culture are universally salient and are therefore named in other cultures as well. Translators can affirm that this is not the case. I remember my own surprise while working with the indigenous Yolngu people of North East Arnhemland, Australia, in the early 1980s when I realized that they labeled feelings of emotional involvement differently from the way I did in English. For instance, a friend in a nontraditional marriage that had been achieved only in defiance of indigenous social expectations and values told me that the English word *love,* although there was no exact counterpart for it in her own language, seemed the best word to use to explain why she and her husband had broken cultural norms to be together.[4] I left Arnhemland after only two years, still insufficiently proficient in the language to fully appreciate the range and depth of the indigenous concepts that she and her people normally used to structure their experience and understanding of deeply emotional relationships. These concepts, because they had no exact parallels in English, were too difficult to explain to me with my limited knowledge of the language in which they were an integral part.

One feels that differences in the way internal or egoic isolates are identified and labeled in different cultures must have pedagogical significance, especially with respect to cognitive constructs, yet very little work has been done in this area to date. Indications of how interesting such research might be are given in Michael J. Christie's (1985) pioneering work with the Yolngu. Based on observations taken over the course of more than twenty years of work in intercultural education, Christie reports that Yolngu "words for 'thinking', 'learning', and 'knowing' (*guyanga* is the main one) refer most often to unintentional activities like worrying, realizing, and recognizing, and less often to purposeful or creative cognitions" (p. 65). This phenomenon seems to be associated with a general "de-emphasis on purposefulness" that allows "for a high level of indirectness in everyday speech — something which facilitates harmonious relationships" (p. 65). Yolngu and English facilitate perspectives on intentionality that are thus quite different, making

> the individual creative knowledge-building process very difficult in the decontextualised learning setting of the classroom. Quite apart from the problems Aboriginal children experience dealing with the surface features of classroom English, their own distinctive world-view (which includes a particular view of what it means to know) inhibits the effective understanding of the English culture and language. English words which connote a wider range of intentional activity are unlikely to be understood by Aborigines in the same way [as by native English speakers]. Rather, the Aboriginal learners of English . . . will impose their Aboriginal semantic structure upon the new word. . . . For example, to a *yolngu* child the English classroom command "Try" means "Take a stab at it!" rather than "Think carefully"! This is because in Gupapuyngu [one of the Yolngu languages] *birrka'yun* means more commonly "try to do" rather than "try to work it out." (Christie, 1985, pp. 65–66)

Christie (1994) also contrasts the essentially atomistic and objectivist worldview of English speakers with that of the Yolngu, which he claims is structured through a "complex unbounded web of metaphors, drawn from the land, animals, and the body" (p. 30), where relatedness and connectedness constitute the core themes through which concepts of the self are constructed. In addition to "*integrated* fashions of speaking" (to use Whorf's 1941/1956h, p. 158, term) that are sustained by metaphor, aspects of grammatical organization also have implications for the way Yolngu relate to experiential input. For instance, like many other languages of the world, Yolngu languages do not require articles like *the* and *a*, which, Christie suggests, may play a role in English speakers' tendency to think of the world in terms of separate objects. As he points out, "Any language without articles like `the' or `a' must require quite some circumlocution to present a truly atomistic account of the world" (Christie, 1994, p. 27). He argues that the notions of cognitive development and eventual maturity on which Western education depends are "an artifact of western technological culture, a way of thinking that went hand in hand with our particular way of structuring political and economic realities" (p. 30). To think "like an objectivist requires an ontological commitment to an atomistic reality (complete with atomized subjecthood) in just the same way that Yolngu thinking requires a commitment to a radically different ontology which prioritises ancient webs of metaphors and meaning over individual attempts to make objective meaning through subjecthood" (p. 30). Aboriginal learners in Western educational contexts are being asked not only to acquire new knowledge along with their new language, but also ways of talking and thinking that fundamentally challenge the worldview they inherit from their own "knowledge makers," to use Christie's term.

Learners who are forced to learn through the cultural constructs of other peoples can benefit from improved understanding of key philosophical differences between the worldview in which they were socialized and the one in which they must now operate. Such understanding can be developed through systematic attention to semantic/conceptual contrasts revealed in the two languages. Christie's explications of Yolngu epistemology and ontology abound with examples of the kind of attention to detail required. His skill in this regard is the product of two decades of bilingualism in Yolngu languages and English informed by highly developed metalinguistic awareness. Investigations such as his can promote increased respect for traditional epistemologies, as well as having the pragmatic utility of revealing the normally nonexplicit cultural agenda of the foreign learning environment. In Arnhemland, the Yolngu themselves have reasserted the primacy and value of their own ancient understanding of reality by bringing it into Western classrooms in a serious way, using their own languages and the reality these articulate to teach complex abstract knowledge of the same order of sophistication as Western mathematics (Christie, 1995a, 1995b).

It is with respect to large-scale patterns of language use and their implications for understanding experience that the linguistic relativity principle operates most interestingly, and also most elusively, which is why its effects have so often been undervalued. We saw earlier how speakers of different languages are encouraged from childhood to attend (unconsciously) to different features of experience by the naming patterns and grammatical demands of their languages. Ganambarr's examples (1994), for instance, showed us how having a precise name for a movement can encourage us to isolate it as a specific unit of experience from ongoing events. With respect to overcoming the effect of linguistic relativity in naming, it is easy enough to learn new words and, with them, new ways of isolating elements of experience. People in the process of becoming skilled in any area of expertise do this all the time, as of course do learners of additional languages. Learning to notice contrasts in the way naming patterns work is relatively easy; it is more difficult to become aware of the effects of grammatical operations on the way we attend to things. Christie's example of the use of articles is an instance. Many monolingual native speakers of English find it difficult to imagine how languages work without them. Articles seem somehow natural and essential and very difficult to think about objectively from a monolingual perspective. By contrast, grammar-induced effects of contrasts between active and passive sentences may be easier for many teachers to appreciate, as these are frequently focused on in textbooks on the teaching of academic English and English as a Second Language.

Our worlds are broadened and deepened when new patterns for focusing attention are acquired through new ways of talking and thinking. And while it may be argued that expert discrimination (including isolation and abstraction) in such fields as music, eye surgery, interior decorating, or acupuncture, for example, is essentially nonverbal, there can be no doubt that language is significantly used to enculturate novices into expertise even in these domains. The process of learning specific terminology and ways of talking about phenomena helps learners direct their attention to subtle features of their art that they have to learn to isolate consistently. Expert and novice experience and understanding of the same phenomena can be so different that where language is a significant factor in mediating that difference, we are warranted in saying that the linguistic relativity principle is at work even within a single language. Insofar as that which we experience is the only reality we can actually *know,* experts and novices live in subtly different subjective realities. Similarly, persons socialized through totally different languages operate through "views of the world" (Whorf, 1940/1956g, p. 221) or "picture[s] of the universe" (Whorf, 1940/1956f, p. 214) in which different isolates and configurations of experience are salient.

Over the years, many research projects have tested Whorf's ideas about linguistic relativity, but more needs to be done to uncover interwoven "fashions of speaking" and their relationships to culturally distinctive patterns of behavior. Like other elements of the theory complex, the matter of linguistic relativity has important pedagogical implications, particularly for multicultural learning situations, but also in relation to teaching the languages of highly elaborated fields of expertise, as suggested above. In the case of cultural diversity, it is helpful to remember that students who speak more than one language often experience frustration in their least proficient mode of communication, not just because they know it less well, but also because their subjective experience may be that it doesn't have enough words to talk about some things properly. Their habitual patterns of attention and observation were originally formed as they acquired their first language, which, for many, remains the primary medium for thinking even after much daily discourse comes to be conducted in alternative languages. Learning a new language modifies, extends, and overlays patterns of attention and thought as it brings new ways of talking and thinking into the internalized linguistic system. If teachers and learners can conceptualize this process

as augmentational (with some inevitable, though preferably temporary, complica-
tions perhaps) rather than thinking of it as divisive or disruptive in a mental sense, it
is possible that transition to comfortable multilingualism may be easier and quicker
for those concerned.

These claims about the relevance of linguistic relativity to the realities of classroom life return us now to the matter of calibrating agreement. Those communicative strategies mentioned earlier — that allow time for people to reach agreement and
that foster tolerance of the need for that time to be built into interpersonal interaction
— are fundamental in teaching and learning and are already well established in many
classrooms where teachers care about the students with whom they work. Thinking
about calibration in terms of the three kinds of agreement mentioned earlier, however, may help teachers focus more clearly on exactly what is needed to achieve communicative precision and harmony in different situations.

To recall, achieving the first kind of agreement involves taking time to establish
that we and our interlocutors really are talking about the same things in general
terms. Exploring the second level of agreement in situations where speakers have different primary languages involves checking to see whether apparently equivalent
terms in different languages have the same semantic range. A speaker for whom English is a secondary language, for instance, could be using a word like *know* with the
semantic range of the apparent translation equivalent in her or his primary language.
Finally, even between speakers of the same language, it is often helpful to check
agreement at the idiolectal level. What we need to ask in this case is whether the resonances of a particular word or phrase within our own internalized system have similar configuration to those of our interlocutor. Talking to each other about what a
word means in terms of our personal experiences can help us find out whether we
share idiolectal congruity or are operating in a state of idiolectal dissonance.

In addition to attending to the achievement of ordinary agreement, therefore,
contrastive analysis of the language of instruction and home languages represented
among the learners may also be useful. We saw how relevant Christie's pioneering
contribution is in this respect. It seems that inter-translatability of language about
thinking and knowing may be more widely illusionary than we have wanted to think,
or for which our pedagogical practices have allowed. Until comprehensive contrastive
surveys of ways of talking about thinking, learning, and knowing have been made, we
cannot know whether our efforts in the cause of learning are well or poorly calibrated
with those of our students from different language backgrounds. Semantic noncon-
gruence (often of a very subtle kind) in this crucial conceptual arena can lie behind failure to provide effective instruction. Confusion at the very least, and burning resent-
ment or outright violence at the worst, can have its roots in our failure as educators to
attend closely to meanings and to calibrate linguistic agreement at its several levels.

To do the kind of work required, teachers will often need the help of linguists who
are interested both in contrastive linguistics itself and also in its pedagogical ramifications. Including more linguistics in professional education courses for teachers would
be immensely helpful, as would providing intending linguists with better access to instruction relating to the role of language in thinking and learning. Taking the time to
learn the languages students speak is also a rewarding experience for teachers. Even if

one never attains fluency, one often develops the beginnings of a sense of the ways in which thinking and being through another language may be different from one's own. The increased empathy for students and greater interest in their home cultures that arises naturally from such insights benefits all concerned.

Calibration of agreement is also important between educational theorists. While specialized terminology may seem at first thought to be highly precise, misunderstandings and fuzzy thinking about the nature of learning and teaching or knowledge are not only possible but prevalent. For instance, a thought-provoking metalinguistic investigation by Patricia A. Alexander, Diane L. Schallert, and Victoria C. Hare (1991) into the ways researchers in learning and literacy talk about knowledge reveals disconcerting disparities in the use of key terms such as "prior knowledge," "domain knowledge," "schema," and "metacognition." These authors point out that "terms used to designate knowledge constructs have proliferated in the literature and often seem to duplicate, subsume, or contradict one another" (p. 315). Conceding that "the labeling of knowledge constructs has fostered communication and stimulated activity within the research community," they also express concern that "the spawning of terms without thoughtful exploration of the assumptions underlying [them or their relationships] to existing terminology may have serious theoretical and practical consequences" (p. 315). On the basis of a survey of usage patterns displayed in the literature, they offer "a conceptual framework for organizing and relating terms that pertain to select knowledge constructs" and suggest definitions for twenty-seven terms. Urging greater precision in the way "researchers use the terminology of knowledge to identify their constructs, to state their objectives, and to direct their research activities," they point out that lack of consistency in this regard can lead "researchers to run the risk of misconceiving their studies, misjudging their results, and misinforming their readers" (p. 335). They remind us that the issues they raise have implications for instructional practice as well as research, and continue:

> For instance, the proliferation of terms we have attempted to organize in this review reflects the fact that prior knowledge in its many forms is a pervasive and potent variable in the educational process. Whereas the major task of schooling may well be fostering the acquisition of conceptual, or domain knowledge, it is important for educators to understand how the effectiveness of content-specific instruction is influenced by so many other aspects of prior knowledge. Thus, any attempt to impart new or complex information without careful consideration of the prior knowledge of students or without efforts to aid those students in integrating that information into their existing knowledge base, seems marked for failure. The many forms of knowledge referred to in the literature also suggest that the nature of schooling may be far more complex than many would like to believe. Perhaps, as the refinement in research of learning and research of literacy progresses, with regard to the knowledge constructs, educators may be better equipped to foster knowledge acquisition in students. (Alexander, Schallert, & Hare, 1991, pp. 336–337)

Research of the kind modeled by this team gives teachers as well as theoreticians starting points for systematically examining their own patterns of language use, for reflecting on the concomitant concepts and assumptions that inform their work, and, at the same time, for extending and rendering more precise their understanding of key constructs in their field. Such work has the potential to enhance day-to-day instructional practice.

Finally, all forms of calibration also involve agreement at the idiolectal level. Every time we take time to question whether words are being used in the same way by different people, our own internalized linguistic systems shift and adjust to accommodate new information. In this context, the question of whether multilinguals have more than one internalized system (a question that has been debated for many years by linguists and neurologists) may be of interest. Certainly internalized language systems are separable in some senses (we are capable of restricting ourselves to one language or another with only occasional confusion), but just how much fusion there is at the core of our knowledge of language as a whole remains a mystery. The very fact that knowledge of one language can interfere with production of another suggests partial meshing at least. Perhaps we have one extensive internalized system consisting of all the linguistic knowledge we have ever acquired. Perhaps this system can be switched into various modes according to the range of communicative situations in which we find ourselves. We can, after all, change from one register or dialect to another in order to speak appropriately in different situations, and we would not generally assume that we have totally different internalized systems for these variations within a single language. It may be helpful to think of different languages, too, as alternative manifestations or unfoldings of the one extensive, intricate, and convoluted internalized system.

Although earlier ways of talking and thinking may become deeply enfolded or overlaid when unused, they need not be regarded as lost or their influence completely suppressed. New modes of linguistic thinking are surely grafted onto established patterns, and even as they become more dominant they may retain some of the tonings of earlier modes of proficiency. Just as retaining a distinctive accent may assist some multilinguals in holding on to a sense of their origins, it is quite possible that some people may need to transfer non-native patterns of cognitive processing into their new languages in order to sustain the sense of who they are that developed as they grew up. This possibility requires considerable research, especially by fluent bilinguals and multilinguals themselves. The internalized linguistic system of a multilingual person, in this way of thinking, must be different from typical systems of monolinguals in any of the languages concerned because it would include selective fusion or merging of some patterns rather than the simple addition of the patterns of one system to another, with the two (or more) systems working quite separately from each other. In educational situations it is important to respect the complexity of the multilingual person's resources for linguistic thinking, supporting students where appropriate to focus on and develop those specific ways of talking and thinking that they decide they want to develop in order to achieve their learning objectives.

Some multilinguals and multidialectals, particularly in adolescence, may choose to restrict themselves to one mode of languaging for a while in order to give themselves time to consolidate their sense of themselves as effective agents in a complex or threatening world. When this happens, whether it is with respect to the way a particular dialect is used as an emblem of identity or whether it takes the form of complete rejection of a childhood language and avid embracing of a new one, the person's need to operate through this particular unfolding of their total internalized system must be respected. A teacher who can share the sort of conceptual tools for metalinguistic reflection that we have been considering can assist learners in accepting and celebrating their potential for linguistic flexibility and diversity and help them maximize its value in their lives, while at the same time respecting their need to hold some domains of their total linguistic proficiency in abeyance for the time being.

Even within a language, new ways of talking (as in situations where language mediates specific kinds of expertise) can be celebrated as new ways of thinking and being that diversify rather than undermine identity. Where for pragmatic reasons learners aspire to goals that are typically reached through the medium of distinctive ways of talking and thinking, teachers provide a service where they make this requirement explicit and attempt to demystify and actively teach the culturally specific patterns involved, or, alternatively, guide learners to find them for themselves. In doing these things, they are teaching metalinguistic awareness, whether it be of the language of science, of scholarly reasoning in the Western style, of art and design, of medicine, or, in the early years, those routines that are commonly used to express understandings expected at different developmental stages by the majority culture.

It is with the youngest children that teachers probably face the deepest dilemmas because, remembering Vygotsky again, it is at this age that new patterns of language probably make the most significant impact on cognitive development as they are internalized and absorbed into the child's growing linguistic/cognitive system. My own opinion in this respect is that communities and educators who care about nurturing and sustaining young children's minority culture identities need to ensure that a great deal of contact with highly competent speakers of children's home languages occurs throughout the school years and that students have ample opportunity to observe teachers showing respect for people from different linguistic/cultural backgrounds (see, for instance, Lee, 1993). All cultures include people who achieve cognitive sophistication and who can communicate it in culturally appropriate ways. Educators are sometimes confused because they may know so little about the home cultures of children that they cannot recognize cognitive sophistication in any other than the forms in which it appears in their own culture. The only way this can be overcome in the shorter term, in my opinion, is through extensive collaboration with community members and the students themselves.

Innovative examples of teacher-learner collaboration are described, for instance, in Shirley Brice Heath and Leslie Mangiola's (1991) monograph, *Children of Promise*. Their focus throughout is on the *potential* of learners in linguistically diverse classrooms, rather than on what are too often seen as their linguistic or cognitive limitations. In the various collaborative learning ventures described, the focus is strongly on students undertaking their own investigations of language. It is clear from the descriptions of each approach that both teachers and learners become highly metalinguistically aware as they work together, both groups growing in understanding not only of the requirements of schooling, but also of the richness of community and minority culture world knowledge.

It may be that the most helpful thing teachers can ever do is to help learners to conceptualize and notice their own cognitive activity and growth, and come to regard their capacity to actively nurture and expand their potential for cognitive flexibility and power as not only possible but also interesting and exciting. To develop the proficiency to accomplish this, teachers themselves need to become expert practitioners in what we can think of as the reflexive technology of the intellect, not only so that we can display evidence of our own metacognitive activity for others to observe, but also so that we can monitor our own thinking for its consistency and efficacy. If Whorf was right, it is *metalinguistic* awareness that provides essential (although not sole) access to that metacognitive awareness and its associated potential for cognitive self-direction and growth that is the most fascinating and challenging dimension of what it is to be a human learner.

Having reviewed some of the realities of teaching and learning and seen the relevance of language awareness to them, we can now appreciate why Whorf thought that multilingual awareness is essential for intercultural harmony and, in the last analysis, survival of the human species. In reviewing the range of ways in which calibration of agreement by both teachers and learners can improve classroom practice, I hope I have also given some indication of the reasons why Whorf thought language awareness can have therapeutic effects for individuals and foster social harmony. Survival of the species "on the planet earth or in the universe," as he put it, depends on individuals achieving greater personal insight, stability, and peace of mind, on groups of people achieving greater respect for each others' traditions and culturally generated ways of relating to experience, and on societies turning their scientific efforts from war and destruction to peace and life-enhancing pursuits.

As Christie (1994) emphasizes with respect to what he has learned from Aboriginal people in regard to influences from European pedagogies now dominant throughout the world:

> When we remember that every scientific statement carries with it a field of privilege and power for those who prosecute it, and at the same time renders all other possibilities absent, we perceive a need of great urgency to reshape the knowledge making business in western society so that everybody and everything is given a voice. We need to be asking the same questions as Aboriginal knowledge makers. Whose interests does this particular way of constituting reality serve? And what other possibilities may we be forgetting about? (p. 34)

Ben Whorf, as his family and colleagues called him, left a legacy of insights about relations between language, mind, and experience that have yet to be fully investigated and that have exciting potential to bring about critical changes of focus in the way we understand ourselves as individuals and as members of this planet's dominant species. In this chapter, I have attempted to show how the various strands of his theory complex can provide a framework of starting points that might be used to systematically investigate the pedagogical implications of what he had to say about relations between language, mind, and experience. The real work, involving changes in the way administrators and politicians understand the purpose of formal education, changes in the way linguists and educators are prepared for their professions, changes in classroom practice, and changes in the way cultural workers of all kinds see the role of language in their endeavors, has only just begun.

NOTES

1. *Language, Thought, and Reality: Selected Writings of Benjamin Lee Whorf*, edited by John B. Carroll (1956a), is the most accessible and well-known volume of Whorf's work, now in its twenty-second printing.
2. See Lee (1994) for a summary of my arguments in this respect.
3. I thank Louis Buchanan for his kindness in alerting me to the existence of the Whorf collection in the Yale archives.
4. I thank the woman I knew as Banunydji Marika for sharing this and other information with me. Our long conversations and her high level of bilingual proficiency and metalinguistic awareness were significantly instrumental in arousing my interest in language differences and later leading me to study Whorf.

REFERENCES

Alexander, P. A., Schallert, D. L., & Hare, V. C. (1991). Coming to terms: How researchers in learning and literacy talk about knowledge. *Review of Educational Research, 61*, 315–343.

Allman, W. F. (1989). *Apprentices of wonder: Inside the neural network revolution.* New York: Bantam Books.

Bechtel, W., & Abrahamsen, A. A. (1991). *Connectionism and the mind: An introduction to parallel processing in networks.* Cambridge, MA: Blackwell.

Benedict, R. F. (1934). *Patterns of culture.* New York: Mentor.

Bohm, D. (1980). *Wholeness and the implicate order.* London: Routledge & Kegan Paul.

Brice Heath, S., & Mangiola, L. (1991). *Children of promise: Literate activity in linguistically and culturally diverse classrooms.* Washington, DC: National Education Association.

Capra, F. (1975). *The Tao of physics.* Bungay, Eng.: Fontana/Collins.

Carroll, J. B. (Ed). (1956a). *Language, thought, and reality: Selected writings of Benjamin Lee Whorf.* Cambridge, MA: MIT Press.

Carroll, J. B. (1956b). Introduction. In J. B. Carroll, *Language, thought, and reality: Selected writings of Benjamin Lee Whorf* (pp. 1–34). Cambridge, MA: MIT Press.

Christie, M. J. (1985). *Aboriginal perspectives on experience and learning: The role of language in Aboriginal education.* Victoria, Australia: Deakin University Press.

Christie, M. J. (1994). Grounded and ex-centric knowledges: Exploring Aboriginal alternatives to western thinking. In J. Edwards (Ed.), *Thinking: International interdisciplinary perspectives* (pp. 23–34). Highett, Australia: Hawker Brownlow Education.

Christie, M. J. (1995a). Drawing the line: A history of Yolngu literacy. In D. Myers (Ed.), *Reinventing literacy: The multicultural imperative* (pp. 14–17). Rockhampton, Australia: Phaedrus Books.

Christie, M. J. (1995b, July). *The purloined pedagogy: Aboriginal epistemology and maths education.* Joint keynote address, Maths Education Research Group of Australia, presented at a conference of the Australian Association of Mathematics Teachers, Darwin, Australia. http://www.srl.rmit.edu.au/MERGA/christie.html

Ganambarr, M. (1994). Dätiwuy. In N. Thieberger & W. McGregor (Eds.), *Macquarie Aboriginal word: A dictionary of words from Australian Aboriginal and Torres Strait Islander languages* (pp. 234–265). Macquarie University, Australia: Macquarie Library.

Gleick, J. (1987). *Chaos: Making a new science.* New York: Penguin.

Heath, S. B., & Mangiola, L. (1991). *Children of promise.* Washington, DC: National Education Association.

Hockett, C. F. (1987). *Refurbishing our foundations; Elementary linguistics from an advanced point of view.* Amsterdam: John Benjamins.

Joseph, J. E. (forthcoming). The immediate sources of the Sapir-Whorf hypothesis. *Historiographia linguistica.*

Koerner, E. F. K. (1995). The Sapir-Whorf hypothesis: An historico-bibliographical essay. In E. F. K. Koerner (Ed.), *Linguistic historiography* (Amsterdam Studies in the Theory and History of Linguistic Science Series) (pp. 203–240). Amsterdam: John Benjamins.

Koffka, K. (1935). *Principles of Gestalt psychology.* New York: Harcourt Brace and Company.

Köhler, W (1929). *Gestalt psychology.* New York: Horace Liveright.

Lee, P. (1991). Whorf's Hopi tensors: Subtle articulators in the language/thought nexus? *Cognitive Linguistics, 2,* 123–147.

Lee, P. (1992). Review of *Dialogue at the margins: Whorf, Bakhtin, and linguistic relativity* by E. A. Schultz. *Language in Society, 21,* 317–319.

Lee, P. (1993). *Bilingual education in remote Aboriginal communities.* Broome, Australia: Jawa.

Lee, P. (1994). New work on the linguistic relativity question. *Historiographia Linguistica, 21*(1/2), 173–191.

Lee, P. (1996). *The Whorf theory complex: A critical reconstruction.* Amsterdam: John Benjamins.

Lucy, J. A. (1992a). *Language diversity and thought: A reformulation of the linguistic relativity hypothesis* (Studies in the Social and Cultural Foundations of Language Series, No. 12). Cambridge, Eng.: Cambridge University Press.

Lucy, J. A. (1992b). *Grammatical categories and cognition* (Studies in the Social and Cultural Foundations of Language Series, No. 13). Cambridge, Eng.: Cambridge University Press.

Malotki, E. (1983). *Hopi time: A linguistic analysis of the temporal concepts in the Hopi language.* Berlin: Mouton.

Perls, F. S., Hefferline, R. F., & Goodman, P. (1951). *Gestalt therapy: Excitement and growth in the human personality.* Harmondsworth, Eng.: Penguin.

Rollins, P. C. (1980). *Benjamin Lee Whorf: Lost generation theories of mind, language, and religion.* Ann Arbor, MI: University Microfilms International.

Sapir, E. (1921). *Language: An introduction to the study of speech.* New York: Harcourt Brace and Company.

Sapir, E. (1925). Sound patterns in a language. *Language, 1,* 37–51.

Schultz, E. A. (1990). *Dialogue at the margins: Whorf, Bakhtin, and linguistic relativity.* Madison: University of Wisconsin Press.

Turner, M. (1991). *Reading minds: The study of English in the age of cognitive science.* Princeton, NJ: Princeton University Press.

Varela, F. J., Thompson, E., & Rosch, E. (1991). *The embodied mind: Cognitive science and human experience.* Cambridge, MA: MIT Press.

Vygotsky, L. S. (1986). *Thought and language* (A. Kozulin, Ed. & Trans.). Cambridge, MA: MIT Press. (Original work published 1934)

Whorf, B. L. (1940). *The parts of speech in Hopi.* Unpublished manuscript (Whorf [1979] Series 2, Benjamin Lee Whorf Papers: Writings on linguistics. Microfilm reel 3, frames 497–537). New Haven, CT: Yale University Manuscripts and Archives.

Whorf, B. L. (1956a). An American Indian model of the universe. In J. B. Carroll (Ed.), *Language, thought, and reality: Selected writings of Benjamin Lee Whorf* (pp. 57–64). Cambridge, MA: MIT Press. (Original work written 1936)

Whorf, B. L. (1956b). A linguistic consideration of thinking in primitive communities. In J. B. Carroll (Ed.), *Language, thought, and reality: Selected writings of Benjamin Lee Whorf* (pp. 65–86). Cambridge, MA: MIT Press. (Original work written 1937)

Whorf, B. L. (1956c) Grammatical categories. In J. B. Carroll (Ed.), *Language, thought, and reality: Selected writings of Benjamin Lee Whorf* (pp. 87–101). Cambridge, MA: MIT Press. (Original work written 1937)

Whorf, B. L. (1956d). Language: Plan and conception of arrangement. In J. B. Carroll (Ed.), *Language, thought, and reality: Selected writings of Benjamin Lee Whorf* (pp. 125–133). Cambridge, MA: MIT Press. (Original work written 1938)

Whorf B. L. (1956e). Gestalt technique of stem composition in Shawnee. In J. B. Carroll (Ed.), *Language, thought, and reality: Selected writings of Benjamin Lee Whorf* (pp. 160–172). Cambridge, MA: MIT Press. (Original work written 1940)

Whorf, B. L. (1956f). Science and linguistics. In J. B. Carroll (Ed.), *Language, thought, and reality: Selected writings of Benjamin Lee Whorf* (pp. 207–219). Cambridge, MA: MIT Press. (Original work written 1940)

Whorf, B. L. (1956g). Linguistics as an exact science. In J. B. Carroll (Ed.), *Language, thought, and reality: Selected writings of Benjamin Lee Whorf* (pp. 220–232). Cambridge, MA: MIT Press. (Original work written 1940)

Whorf, B. L. (1956h). The relation of habitual thought and behavior to language. In J. B. Carroll (Ed.), *Language, thought, and reality: Selected writings of Benjamin Lee Whorf* (pp. 134–159). Cambridge, MA: MIT Press. (Original work written 1941)

Whorf, B. L. (1956i). Languages and logic. In J. B. Carroll (Ed.), *Language, thought, and reality: Selected writings of Benjamin Lee Whorf* (pp. 233–245). Cambridge, MA: MIT Press. (Original work written 1941)

Whorf, B. L. (1956j). Language, mind, and reality. In J. B. Carroll (Ed.), *Language, thought, and reality: Selected writings of Benjamin Lee Whorf* (pp. 246–270). Cambridge, MA: MIT Press. (Original work written 1942)

Whorf, B. L. (1979). *Benjamin Lee Whorf papers.* New Haven, CT: Yale University Manuscripts and Archives.

Whorf, B. L., & Trager, G. L. (1938). *Report on linguistic research in the Department of Anthropology of Yale University for the term September 1937 to June 1938.* Unpublished manuscript (Whorf [1979] Series 2, Benjamin Lee Whorf Papers: Writings on Linguistics. Microfilm reel 3, frames 385–419). New Haven: Yale University Manuscripts and Archives.

I wish to thank Jenny Barnett, Michael Christie, Tom O'Donoghue, Keith Punch, Judith Chapman, Susan Kaldor, and my *HER* editors for helpful feedback on this paper. One's writings always incorporate one's relationships with other people at some level, and it's nice to be able to acknowledge this formally when people take the time to read through draft papers and share their responses.

PART TWO

Sociocultural Approaches to Language and Literacy

PART TWO

Sociocultural Approaches to Language and Literacy

T he term *sociocultural* has been widely used in the field of education by scholars from diverse intellectual traditions. Although the term often invokes the work of educational psychologists following in the tradition of Lev Vygotsky and other Soviet psychologists, in this volume we use it in a broader sense to identify research that investigates language and literacy use in social and historical contexts. While the chapters in the previous section examined language and reading ability as they evolve within the mind, the following chapters are concerned with the reciprocal influence between mind and society. This difference in theoretical orientation has methodological implications as well. While the cognitive/developmental studies we presented earlier draw their empirical data primarily from laboratory or clinical settings, the studies in this section are based on data from historical documents, communicative interactions in the home, and ethnographic observations and personal narrative accounts of everyday literacy practices.

From a sociocultural perspective, spoken and written language is often viewed as part of a larger cultural system that involves nonverbal symbols (such as images and numbers) and powerful social institutions (such as schools, governments, and marketplaces). Another implication of a sociocultural approach to language is its resistance to narrow definitions of language use; it views all activities involving print as interrelated aspects of one system. For example, a sociocultural approach tends to favor the term *literacy* rather than *reading* to label activities that involve interaction with print.

This second part begins with Daniel and Lauren Resnick's now-classic comparison of different criteria for literate status across several different periods in history. "The Nature of Literacy: An Historical Explanation," originally published in 1977, is a call for us to recognize the historical uniqueness of contemporary standards for literacy. In this respect, it is interesting to note that the "contemporary" standards of the late 1970s, which were already high relative to what previous eras had asked of individuals, have since been surpassed. When the *Harvard Educational Review* first published this piece, to be literate was to be able to read a newspaper and other everyday texts for information. In the year 2000, as a result of widespread alarm over students' low test scores — not just in reading and writing but across subject areas — students are now expected to read and interpret complex literary and technical texts. The argument that we must acknowledge the unprecedented ambitiousness of our literacy goals for society is thus even more relevant today.

In "From Utterance to Text: The Bias of Language in Speech and Writing," David Olson also takes a historical perspective in his chapter on the differences between oral and written language use. Reviewing the debate about meaning in language — both oral and written — Olson observes that the debate is founded on different assumptions about the locus of meaning. Some theorists contend that meaning is in the language itself, others that it is shared between interlocutors and is constructed through their interaction. Olson aligns the concept of formal, written "texts" with the former view, and the concept of informal, spoken "utterances" with the latter. He argues that "there is a transition from utterance to text both culturally and developmentally and that this transition can be described as one of increasing explicitness, with language increasingly able to stand as unambiguous or autonomous representation of meaning" (p. 138). In this way, Olson links individuals' language development with broader cultural progress, suggesting that ontogeny replicates phylogeny. He further argues that the cultural development of the alphabetic writing system allowed for greater explicitness in writing than did pictographic or syllabic systems. The alphabetic system also made it possible for cultures to identify such explicitness as a developmental goal.

Catherine Snow, in "Literacy and Language: Relationships during the Preschool Years," illustrates such developmental progress through a review of research on the relationship between home and school literacy and empirical data from a case study of one child's interactions with his mother during book reading. At the same time, she discusses how oral language provides an important context for the development of reading skills. Snow disputes the claim that many children from low-income families suffer from poor reading performance in school due to a lack of literacy materials in the home. Instead, she finds an alternative explanation in the idea that children's proficiency in literacy in the elementary grades may have more to do with their ability to understand and produce what she calls "decontextualized" (and what Olson calls "autonomous") language. Regardless of the quantity of books and other printed materials in the home, Snow suggests, literacy before schooling is markedly different from school literacy in that the former is highly contextualized, drawing on knowledge that is shared between parent and child and on familiar printed materials. It is only in school that children must learn how to communicate in speech and writing *without* assuming prior knowledge on the part of the reader or listener. Snow illustrates the highly intertwined nature of language and literacy abilities, and suggests that children's failure to achieve in one area may be related to difficulties in the other.

While Snow contrasts literacy in the home with literacy in school, Sylvia Scribner and Michael Cole examine everyday literacy practices among the Vai people of Liberia, who acquire literacy independent of their schooling. In "Literacy without Schooling: Testing for Intellectual Effects," Scribner and Cole take issue with Olson's claim that the acquisition of literacy skills has general cognitive consequences, that is, that it endows literate individuals with higher capacities for logic and abstract thought. They reject Olson's argument that members of literate cultures are more advanced in their thinking than those of nonliterate ones and that individual intellectual development mirrors the historical development of cultures in which the progression has been from oral to literate traditions. Through ethnographic observation and naturalistic experiments, Scribner and Cole show that, for the Vai, proficiency in certain literacy practices are associated with greater ability in certain intellectual domains; however, this ability is highly specific to literacy and is not related to the general mental capacity of higher order thought. One of Scribner and Cole's most important contributions to the field of literacy research is the introduction of the metaphor of "literacy as practice." In their definition, literacy practice is a goal-directed sequence of activities that requires particular skills at each stage of the sequence. The learning of this practice, through practice, is highly influenced by the communicative context and by the tools available to the literate person. With this metaphor, Scribner and Cole were among the first to suggest that literacy has different consequences in different cultural contexts.

While Scribner and Cole are concerned with consequences, Deborah Brandt focuses on the conditions that enable the development of literacy in individuals in her chapter, "Literacy Learning and Economic Change." In this study of the literacy experiences of two women who lived during different eras in the United States, Brandt uses the concept of a "sponsor" to identify cultural agents who influence an individual's literacy growth. She also shows how economic forces shape the cultural contexts in which these two women acquire and use literacy skills, suggesting that learners may not all benefit to the same degree from higher and more complex standards for literacy achievement.

Because they are diverse in the populations they represent and in the research methods they employ, the chapters in this section aptly illustrate the sociocultural orientation to language and literacy research. As these chapters show, sociocultural researchers and theorists are concerned with understanding how individual language development relates to cultural norms. In doing so, they help to situate our understanding of individual learners' language practices against a larger backdrop of cultural progress.

EDITORS' NOTE: SOCIOCULTURAL APPROACHES TO LANGUAGE AND LITERACY

For further reading in sociocultural approaches to language and literacy research, we recommend these articles published in the Harvard Educational Review:

Eric Bredo, Mary Henry, and R. P. McDermott, "The Cultural Organization of Teaching and Learning," Essay Review of *Classroom Discourse* by Courtney Cazden, Spring 1990, pp. 247–258.

Kieran Egan, "Literacy and the Oral Foundations of Education," Fall 1987, pp. 445–472.

Nan Elsasser and Vera P. John-Steiner, "An Interactionist Approach to Advancing Literacy," Summer 1977, pp. 355–369.

Bernardo M. Ferdman, "Literacy and Cultural Identity," Spring 1990, pp. 181–204.

Kenneth Levine, "Functional Literacy: Fond Illusions and False Economies," Summer 1982, pp. 249–266.

The New London Group, "A Pedagogy of Multiliteracies: Designing Social Futures," Spring 1996, pp. 60–92.

The Nature of Literacy:
An Historical Exploration

DANIEL P. RESNICK

LAUREN B. RESNICK

R eports of low literacy achievement and widespread reading difficulties have lent strength to a still inchoate "back to basics" movement in education. The apparent suggestion is that methods of instruction that succeeded in the past can remedy many of our present problems. Looking backward for solutions, however, can succeed only when social conditions and educational goals remain relatively stable. Only by a serious examination of our history can we determine the extent to which older educational practices are likely to succeed in today's environment, for today's purposes. This chapter begins such an examination by exploring selected European and American historical models of literacy standards and training in order to access the degree to which the goals and practices of earlier times are relevant to our present needs.

Our research suggests that there has been a sharp shift over time in expectations concerning literacy. With changed standards come changed estimates of the adequacy of a population's literacy. To illustrate, if writing one's name were what was meant by literacy, we would not be worried that illiteracy was a national problem. Yet the signature was not always a demand easy to satisfy. Until well into the nineteenth century, the capacity to form the letters of one's signature was not a skill shared by the majority of the population, even in the more developed nations of Europe.[1] Even a somewhat more stringent literacy criterion would not force recognition of a major problem. If the ability to read aloud a simple and well-known passage were the measure, American would have a few "illiterates" but hardly a crisis. If we expected people to demonstrate after reading this simple passage, that they had registered its content at some low level, perhaps by saying who a story was about or what a named character did, we would probably find a low percentage of illiterates in our adult population.

But the number would start to rise, perhaps quite sharply, if unfamiliar texts were to be read and new information gleaned from them. And, if inferential rather than directly stated information were to be drawn from the text, we would probably announce a true crisis in literacy. If we used as a literacy criterion the ability to read a complex text with literacy allusions and metaphoric expression and not only to inter-

Harvard Educational Review Vol. 47 No. 3 August 1977, 370–385

pret this text but to relate it sensibly to other texts, many would claim that only a tiny fraction of our population is "truly literate," a charge not infrequently made in discussions about standards of literacy at the university level.

We think that this nation perceives itself as having an unacceptable literacy level because it is applying a criterion that requires, at a minimum, the reading of new material and the gleaning of new information from that material. We shall argue in this chapter that this high literacy standard is a relatively recent one as applied to the population at large and that much of our present difficulty in meeting the literacy standard we are setting for ourselves can be attributed to the relatively rapid extension to large populations of educational criteria that were once applied to only a limited elite. The result of this rapid extension is that instructional methods suitable to large and diverse populations rather than small and selected ones have not yet been fully developed or applied. Further, not all segments of our population have come to demand literacy skills of the kind that educators, members of Congress, and other government officials think necessary.

Our argument is that the standards currently applied to mass literacy have been with us for at most three generations. To examine the proposition that the current definition of literacy is a relatively new one, we have undertaken a selective review of published material on standards of literacy in various historical settings and on the social and political conditions under which these standards were applied. Some of the less commonly cited historical models seem especially instructive because of either the large size of the literate population, the high standards of literacy, or the democratic ideology. We will elaborate three major historical models for literacy development before the twentieth century: the Protestant-religious, the elite-technical, and the civic-national. To illustrate these models, we will describe literacy training and examinations in the seventeenth-century Swede, elite scientific and technical education in France since the eighteenth century, and schooling among the French peasants during the last century. In so doing, we shall try to relate particular kinds of literacy standards and instructional approaches to changing social needs and conditions. Finally, we will trace the changes in literacy standards that occurred in the first part of this century in the United States.

Having examined these historical cases, we will be in a position to consider the degree of fit between certain persisting traditions of education and present-day literacy standards. We shall also note a remarkable match between our conclusions and certain current theories of reading development that are based on observation of the stages through which individuals pass as they gain competence with the written word. In concluding we will consider various implications of our historical and theoretical analysis for current educational policy.

MODELS FROM THE HISTORICAL EXPERIENCE

Protestant-Religious Education

Historians have come to view the efforts of Protestant communities to bring their members into personal contact with biblical history and the Christian message as very important for the growth of literacy.[2] These efforts have also been recognized as significant in affecting social and economic development.[3] With respect to American development, Bernard Bailyn and Lawrence Cremin have described colonial literacy as so profoundly transforming that its development constituted a break with traditional attitudes.[4]

More recently, the connection between literacy and socioeconomic shifts has been called into question. Kenneth Lockridge has argued that literacy was of little significance for the shaping of modern social values in Protestant colonial New England.[5] The absence of such a relationship between schooling and economic development in Lancashire before the mid-nineteenth century has been one of the themes in the revisionist work of Michael Sanderson.[6] However, even for those who have been skeptical about its causal relationship to attitudes, the early modern Protestant experience with literacy has been seen as a watershed because of the great numbers of people who shared in that experience. In colonial New England, Lockridge estimates that male literacy, which was well above 60 percent for the generation born around 1700, became nearly universal by the end of the century;[7] in Scotland, Lawrence Stone found that the rate of literacy among adult males went from 33 percent around 1675 to almost 90 percent by 1800;[8] and in Sweden, Egil Johansson found that the number of males "able to read" in the parishes of Skelleftea went from half the population to 98 percent in the period from 1645 to 1714.[9]

The question of what kinds of knowledge defined literacy in these Protestant experiments has not been directly addressed by historians concerned with the relationship of literacy to economic and social development. We are able to respond to the question by considering the Swedish case, which represents the first instance of systematic record-keeping relative to reading. To cite one example, the oldest extant registers of Möklinta parish in central Sweden, for the years from 1656 to 1669, offer columns to note whether or not minimum competency had been met in each of five areas.[10] The first involved the actual words to the text of the *Little Catechism;* the second, Luther's explanations of the words of the text; the third, the Confession of Sin; the fourth, morning and evening prayers; the fifth, prayers said at the table.[11] Questions on Lutheran creed and practice were apparently posed by the pastor on each of these topics. The examination assumed the availability of a printed catechism and prayer book in every home and prior discussion of these materials at catechetical meetings, attendance at which was to be checked off in a final column of the register.

No formal column for the capacity to read, as such, is to be found in this register (although one would be introduced in its successor), but all the questions assume the capacity to read, review, memorize, and recall familiar material. A second register, used during the period from 1686 to 1705, includes a corroborating column for "literacy," which was understood as the ability to read to the satisfaction of the examiner. An analysis of this material indicates that, while only one-fourth of the parish residents born in the early part of the seventeenth century were described as literate, the percentage grew to three-fourths for those born at the end of the century.

From the standpoint of current expectations, the literacy criterion that yielded these figures is a limited one. No unfamiliar material was given to the examinee. No writing was expected. No application of knowledge to new contexts was demanded.

And no digressions from the text of the catechism and prayers were expected or permitted. The result was an exercise in the reading and memorizing of familiar material, to be recalled upon demand. Nevertheless, the Swedish experience, like the less controlled systems of early Protestant education in Scotland and the American colonies, represents more than simply a baseline of low literacy expectation. Instead, subsequent pedagogic efforts in literacy were heavily influenced by early religious activities.

The Elite-Technical Schools

A quite different tradition of literacy, one aimed at an elite, is represented by the growth of higher technical education in France. This system had its beginnings in the *collèges* and private academies of the Old Regime. The schools were run by such religious orders as the Oratorians and Jesuits, largely for sons of the aristocracy and bourgeoisie, although a few extremely able sons of the poor were accepted. Boys could enter at age seven and could stay until age seventeen or eighteen for an extended period of formal schooling. From these schools young men could enter a variety of state technical and professional schools that prepared their graduates for careers in civil and military public service.

By the eighteenth century, mathematics had become established as the touchstone of elite education. At all levels mathematics was stressed as the key to effective reasoning. For La Chalotais, in his *Plan d'education nationale* of 1673, it was "very possible and very common to reason badly in theology, or in politics; it is impossible in arithmetic and in geometry; if accuracy of mind is lacking, the rules will supply accuracy and intelligence for those who follow them." For Diderot, geometry was "the best and simplest of all logics, and it is the most suitable for fortifying the judgment and the reason."[12] But mathematics was deemed more than a better way to reason; it was central to the curriculum not only because of its alleged utility for developing young minds, but also because of its perceived usefulness to the state. It was essential for military purposes, civil engineering, and the monarchy's "civilizing" action in architecture, surveying, standard measures, and public finance.

In this context, literacy necessarily meant the acquisition of theoretical knowledge and the development of problem-solving capacities. But this criterion was thought to be applicable not to the whole population but only to a small elite. Competitive examinations restricted entry to the best state schools from the time of their establishment during the Old Regime; and the École Polytechnique, created during the Revolution, maintained the same standards of competitive entry.

The Revolution in no way challenged the definition or state support of this elite training at either the secondary or the graduate level. Established in 1795, the *écoles centrales* continued at the secondary level the scientific tradition of the collèges and academies of the Old Regime. The écoles centrales were succeeded by the *lycées*, which came to place greater emphasis on Latin than on mathematics. Despite this change in subject matter, a strong and visible place was maintained within secondary education for students who were preparing for the *grandes écoles*.[13]

Higher technical training was enshrined in the educational program of France and thus became — and continues to be — the distinguishing mark of the French graduate elite. Strong on theory and arrogant about their ability to apply knowledge to a variety of situations, these graduates have only recently found a world of technical literacy in which they feel comfortable despite the limits of their training. As Charles Kindleberger has argued, "Excessively deductive, Cartesian, geometric, mathematical, theoretical by nineteenth century standards, the system is coming into its own in a world of scientific sophistication."[14]

CIVIC-NATIONAL SCHOOLING

While elites continued to attend specialized academies, responsibility for mass education gradually shifted from religious communities to public bodies. We again consider France as an example. The French system of primary education has been credited with breaking new ground in secularizing education, universalizing schools, and fostering patriotism. From 1789 to 1914, this system of primary education increased the number of people with basic literacy from less than half to more than 90 percent of the French population.[15]

Primary education became a public commitment during the French Revolution. When the Revolutionary government introduced the first plan for national education in France in 1795, its major interest was military: the preservation of schools and training routes for those entering technical and military careers was considered essential. (Similarly, Napoleon's system of secondary education, the lycée, was focused on providing personnel for the nation's military and technical needs.) The 1795 plan contained only the outlines of a system for primary education. It neither provided funding for primary schools nor created a sufficient number to serve the predominantly rural public.[16]

Before legislation abolished the religious orders' endowments and their right to receive public and private contribution, these orders had played a major role in providing basic education. The restrictive measures of the Revolution, in combination with wartime activity, drove many of the clergy underground or abroad. This effectively dismantled the church system of primary education that had functioned at the village level.

However, even in those areas where public primary schools were established, it was difficult to separate primary education from religious instruction. The attempt to do so initially generated much hostility in conservative areas. For this and other reasons the separation between religious and public education was far from complete. Without public funding for school textbooks, religious materials continued to serve as beginning reading matter for children. The personnel of the old church primary schools also tended to reappear in the new secular ones.

Literacy levels appear to have remained fairly stable across the Revolutionary divide, despite the undermining of the church-run primary schools. There was no important growth in literacy, as measured by signatures on marriage contracts, in any department during the thirty years after the opening of the Revolution. Only one-quarter of the French departments had growth rates of more than 1 percent, in the male capacity to sign, and almost all of that growth was in the range of 1 to 2 percent.

Twelve departments showed declines in the male capacity to sign during this period, but all were of less than 1 percent.[17]

The literacy expectations in the primary schools that did function before the 1830s remained modest. This is hardly surprising since primary education was largely a catch-as-catch-can affair for the first two post-Revolutionary generations in rural France. Children usually attended school for only the winter months, since the demands of family and farm had priority, and even then they did so irregularly. Those who attended generally left between the ages of ten and twelve after confirmation in the Church. Communions were held rather early, to coincide roughly with the end of the primary-school course.[18]

In addition to irregular school attendance, poorly prepared teachers may also have contributed to low levels of literacy. Teachers were not professionally trained before the 1830s, even though efforts to impose professional standards for their certification were first made in 1816.[19] The minimum standard was a demonstrated ability to read, write, and use simple figures, yet even this standard was not always met. For example, even after 1830, teachers who hired themselves out by the season at fairs in eastern France reportedly placed one, two, or three feathers in their caps to indicate what subject or subjects they knew how to teach: the first stood for reading, the second for arithmetic, and the third for Latin. In arithmetic, moreover, those who could only add and subtract far outnumbered those who could multiply and divide as well. One teacher, Sister Gandilhon, who ran a school at Selins (Cantal) in the 1840s, taught "prayers, the catechism and the first two rules of arithmetic." According to a contemporary, "she had heard of a third but never learned it."[20] The teaching of arithmetic was further complicated by the use of regional units for weights and measures, like the *pouce* and the *toise,* which had no relationship to the metric system introduced by the Revolution.[21]

The methods of reading instruction were equally primitive. Before the 1840s, the teaching of reading was characterized by instruction in the names of the letters ("ah, bay, say, day . . ."), independent of any relationship to other vowels and consonants. From the pronunciation of letters, students moved directly to the pronunciation of words.[22] A study of a village in western France noted that one teacher, much respected, read aloud sentences from the children's readers and then had children repeat the sentences. According to a resident of the village:

> The children were not required to make any effort to understand the words or to attempt to associate the shapes with sounds and meanings. They merely repeated what had been said to them and gradually discovered . . . by the place on the page or the approximate shape of what they were being given to read the sounds they were required to emit to avoid being beaten.[23]

It is hardly surprising, given these methods, that many pupils did not learn how to read at all. Further, those who did manage to read generally worked only on religious books and simple readers.

Mastery may also have been rare because the language of instruction did not always match the vernacular of the region. Most of France was a nation of *patois,* and in many regions Provençal, German, Italian, or Catalan was the major language. Since the language of instruction during most of the nineteenth century was almost universally French, the result was predictable. Even when students were able to read the written language fluently, inspectors in Brittany noted, "No child can give account of what he has read or translate it into Breton; hence there is no proof that anything is understood."[24]

Persisting Limits of the Civic-National Model

School attendance rose sharply throughout France as a result of two major reforms of the primary system of public education, the first in 1833 and the second in 1881–1882.[25] Steps were taken under Ministers of Education Guizot and Ferry to democratize the system by increasing the number of primary schools, by reducing school fees, and by increasing the number of training colleges for teachers. These measures, in varying degrees, increased school attendance and contributed to the professionalization of teachers. However, despite these efforts toward democratization, primary schooling remained clearly distinct from the elite-secondary program.

Public schooling, moreover, did not for some time abandon its preoccupation with religious principles. Although in the field of education a civic religion of nationalism ultimately replaced traditional Catholic beliefs, schoolmasters remained dependent on local religious authorities for the nearly fifty years between the two reforms.[26] In 1833 the education minister attempted to make peace with the parish religious authorities in order to convince parents of the value of public primary schooling. "It is on the preponderant and united action of Church and State that I rely to establish primary instruction," Guizot told the legislature.[27] In practice this meant the responsibilities of the primary teacher included encouraging attendance at Mass, teaching prayers and biblical lore, and assisting the priest as needed. Reports from the 1840s and 1850s cite many examples of schools in which an alphabet book in Latin or a fifteenth-century *Life of Christ* served as the reading test.[28]

This educational alliance with the church was broken by the Ferry reforms of 1881–1882. The catechism was eliminated from the school reading program. Every *commune* was required to support a schoolmaster and a public school for girls as well as boys. A policy of free tuition, though not one of free books, replaced the earlier program of limited scholarships. For the first time school attendance was made compulsory, and the primary program was extended to age fourteen.[29] Finally, the national education ministry began a massive program of school construction.

Instruction was not designed to enlarge the skills of the literate or to encourage critical approaches to reading; rather, it was meant to cultivate a love of the familiar. History and geography texts were introduced to promote love of country.[30] The purpose of history instruction, for example, was unabashedly identified as patriotic. When questioned about the role of history in education, nearly 80 percent of the candidates for a *baccalauréat* in 1897 answered with statements about the "need to exalt patriotism."[31] Thus, despite the new curriculum, many of the criteria for literacy embedded in seventeenth- and eighteenth-century religious instruction were allowed to persist.

By the time of World War I, the successes of public primary schooling were clearly visible. Almost every child in the nation had relatively easy access to schools, and nearly all fourteen-year-olds by then had attended schools for seven years. Teachers were generally graduates of special training colleges located in each *département*. Attendance was increasingly regular for those enrolled in the schools, and students did not leave with the passing of winter. Inability to pay did not directly bar students' access to school. French was clearly the national language, and the metric system had triumphed over local measures. Statistics compiled by the Ministry of Education on years of schooling as well as the dramatic rise in the proportion of military recruits capable of signing their own names[32] are further evidence of these successes.

However, these facts do not inform us about the quality of education or the growth of individual capacity, and on these issues the evidence is mixed. Thabault observed that, while fewer than one-fifth of the inhabitants of his village knew how to form the letters of their names in 1833, more than half were able to do so thirty years later. Nevertheless, "the amount of knowledge that most of them had acquired did not make them very different from the completely illiterate."[33] By the eve of World War I, there had been considerable improvement in the knowledge of history, geography, and the French language. The inculcation of this knowledge took the form of a civic education, a new catechism based on patriotic devotion and civic duty. Eugen Weber has argued that this system, along with the army and improved transportation in the years from 1876 to 1914, contributed to the modernization of the attitudes and behavior of the French peasantry. But acculturation and adaptation do not necessarily produce generalized understanding, transferable learning, or reasoning skills.

TEACHING METHODS AND LITERACY CRITERIA IN AMERICA

American methods of teaching reading were influenced initially by approaches developed in Europe. The classic method, as we have seen in the French system, was alphabetic. Children were first drilled on the letter names and then on syllables. No attempt was made to select meaningful syllables or to emphasize comprehension; rather, accurate and fluent pronunciation was emphasized. The following description of reading instruction in the Sessional School in Edinburgh, Scotland, was reported to American educators in 1831. This account suggests the dominant goal of literacy instruction in the United States as well as in Scotland:

> English reading, according to the prevailing notion, consists of nothing more than the power of giving utterance to certain sounds, on the perception of certain figures; and the measure of progress and excellence is the facility and continuous fluency with which those sounds succeed each other from the mouth of the learner. If the child gather any knowledge from the book before him, beyond that of color, form and position of the letters, it is to his own sagacity he is indebted for it, and not to his teacher.[34]

Pedagogical reforms that had been introduced in Britain, Germany, and France during the eighteenth and nineteenth centuries later influenced instructional practice in the United States. The Prussian educator Friedrich Gedike[35] had introduced a "word method" of reading instruction, which used words as the starting point for teaching the alphabet and spelling. Other reformers substituted the use of sounds, or "powers," of the letters for their names in the initial teaching of the alphabet. Although these reforms improved the teaching of fluent oral reading, they did not imply any new or greater concern for students' ability to understand what was read.

In the United States many forward-looking educators recognized that a greater emphasis on meaning would enliven instruction and make it more palatable to children. Putnam, in 1836, stressed the need for comprehension while criticizing the dominant instructional practice:

> A leading object of this work is to enable the scholar, while learning to *read*, to *understand*, at the same time, the *meaning* of the words he is reading . . . if, for example, when the pupil is taught to read, he is enabled, at the same time, to discover the *meaning* of the words he repeats, he will readily make use of the proper inflections, and place the emphasis where the sense demands it. The monotonous sing-song mode of reading, which is common in schools and which is often retained in after life, is acquired from the exercise of reading what is not understood.[36]

Nearly fifty years later, Farnham voiced similar concern when proposing his sentence method of reading instruction:

> It is important that this two-fold function of reading should be fully recognized. The first, or silent reading, is the fundamental process. . . . The second, oral reading, or "reading aloud," is entirely subordinate to silent reading. While oral expression is subject to laws of its own, its excellence depends upon the success of the reader in comprehending the thought of the author.[37]

Although these educators laid the groundwork for new methods and standards in literacy, their ideas did not become common educational practice until much later. Fundamental change in the standards applied to reading instruction came early in the twentieth century with the advent of child-centered theories of pedagogy, which stressed the importance of intrinsic interest and meaningfulness in learning, and the introduction of standardized group testing during World War I.

The American entry into the war highlighted a national literacy problem. Under the leadership of Robert Yerkes, then president of the American Psychological Association, a group of psychologists prepared and validated group-administered forms of a general intelligence test.[38] This test had two forms — Army Alpha for literate recruits and Army Beta for recruits unable to take the Alpha form. The tests were administered in 1918 to 1.7 million men, and it was noted with dismay that nearly 30 percent could not understand the Alpha form because they could not read well enough. This discovery evoked the following comment by an American educator, May Ayres Burgess:

> [I]f those [men] examined were fairly representative of all, there must have been over one million of our soldiers and sailors who were not able to write a simple letter or read a newspaper with ease.
>
> [A]lthough one-fourth of the men could not read well enough to take tests based on reading, this deficiency was not caused by their never having learned to read. The fact is that an overwhelming majority of these soldiers had entered school, attended the primary grades where reading is taught, and had been taught to read. Yet, when

as adults they were examined, they were unable to read readily such simple material as that of a daily newspaper.[39]

After army intelligence tests had alerted people to defects in reading instruction, the growth in the 1920s of graded and standardized achievement testing gave educators tools for evaluating their efforts. The development of testing was stimulated in part by the successes of the army testing program and by the growing receptivity of school administrators to what they regarded as scientific tools of management.[40] The army program had demonstrated the practicality and validity of group-administered psychological tests. Because group-administered reading tests required silent reading rather than oral, the ability to answer questions or follow directions based upon a simple text became the most typical test of reading competence. This focus on deriving the meaning of a text fit well with what the most forward-looking educators had already been advocating. The ability to understand an unfamiliar text, rather than simply declaim a familiar one, became the accepted goal of reading instruction and the new standard of literacy.

This newer standard, previously applied only to the programs of elite institutions, required the ability to gain information from reading and use that information in new contexts. The 1920s marked the first time in history that such a rigorous standard had been applied in the United States. This emphasis on deriving meaning from text bolstered the cause of those educators advocating changes in reading instruction. With this change in the criterion of literacy, national aspirations also rose for the portion of the population expected to meet this new standard.

Patterns of school attendance in this century best illustrate these radical changes. Reviewing data from several American cities, Leonard Ayres reported in 1909 that of one hundred children who were in school at age seven, ninety would still be there at age thirteen, fifty at age fourteen, and only thirteen of the original one hundred would remain in school at age sixteen.[41] Equally important were the large numbers of students not promoted; attendance at school for six or seven years by no means assured passage into the sixth or seventh grade. In general, Ayres found that, from any given grade level, 20 percent would not be promoted — if they returned to school at all.[42] Ayres's statistics clearly demonstrate that only a limited percentage of the population completed elementary school in the early part of this century. Whatever the eighth-grade level of reading competence may have been, only half of those attending school ever completed that grade. The literacy level that came closer to being universal was the fifth-grade level, which was comparable to that attained at the completion of primary schooling in nineteenth-century France. Although we cannot estimate exactly the functioning level of literacy at the beginning of the century, it seems fair to conclude that it did not approach present standards.

THE GROWTH OF LITERACY EXPECTATIONS

This chapter documents changes in literacy standards and teaching methods in the United States and some European countries, chiefly France, during the past several centuries. Our evidence suggests a rough progression in literacy expectation and per-

FIGURE 1   *Schematic Representation of Shifts in Literacy Standards*

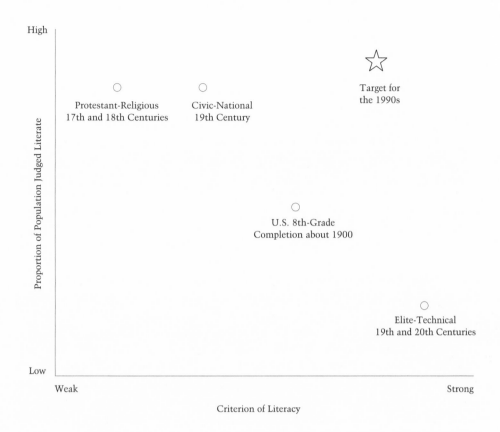

formance. Expectations for popular literacy appeared after a long period in which the general population could not read. The earliest mass-literacy effort, Protestant-religious instruction, was intended to develop not a generalized capacity to read but only the mastery of a very limited set of prescribed texts. Although civic-national public schooling introduced a slightly broadened set of texts, students were not expected to use their reading skills to acquire new information but only to become fluent oral readers. Nonetheless, some individuals did learn to read for information and even to engage in critical and inferential reading similar to that demanded by elite schools.

It is only during the present century that the goal of reading for the purpose of gaining information has been applied in ordinary elementary schools to the entire population of students. Today, the term *functional literacy* has come to mean the ability to read common texts such as newspapers and manuals and to use the information gained, usually to secure employment.[43] The objectives of functional literacy may seem limited, yet this mass-literacy criterion is stronger than that of any earlier period of history. Achieving universal literacy as it is now defined poses a challenge not previously faced. We estimate that literacy standards in the United States in the 1990s will be both more demanding and more widely applied than any previous standard. The accompanying Figure 1 permits a schematic comparison between the aspirations that we have projected for the United States and standards met by earlier literacy movements. Depending on how the figure is read we are either attempting to increase by a significant degree the quality of literacy competence in our population, or to increase, also very significantly, the portion of our population to which an already established criterion is to apply.

The historical development of ever more demanding criteria for literacy mirrors to some extent a model for individual development of reading competence that has recently been proposed by Jeanne Chall.[44] In this sense, social phylogeny seems to reflect ontogeny. Chall points out that at successive stages in reading development, "the reader is doing essentially 'different' things in relation to printed matter, although the term reading is used to describe each of these stages." Further, "the successive stages are characterized by growth in the ability to read language of greater complexity, rarity, technicality, and abstractness, and with a change in how such materials are viewed and used."

Chall proposes five stages of reading. After a prereading period the first stage is initial reading or decoding. The essential aspect here "is the learning of the arbitrary set of letters and associating these with the corresponding parts of spoken words. . . ." The second stage is confirmation and fluency: "Essentially reading at this stage is a consolidation. . . . By reading familiar stories, smoothness and fluency are gained." Chall points out that at one time the Bible and religious tracts were familiar texts. The congruence between Chall's earlier stages and the literacy standards of the religious and civic-national periods is striking. During these periods reading instruction centered on mastering print, associating letters with words, and reading aloud. Chall's stage of confirmation and fluency seems parallel to the practice, highly valued in the nineteenth century, of public reading of texts. Chall's third stage, "reading for learning the new," is the first point at which mastering the ideas conveyed comes to be the dominant goal. For a long time, reading for new information was not expected of many, and it is only now becoming a nearly universal standard.

IMPLICATIONS FOR POLICY

Our review of the Protestant-religious, civic-national, and elite-technical educational efforts has been very selective, but it nonetheless suggests the novelty of our present situation. Educational leaders often argue as if "real literacy" is compromised by an acceptance of functional-literacy standards tied to very practical demands of work and citizenship such as filing tax returns and reading technical manuals. On the contrary, our findings suggest that the serious application to the entire population of the contemporary standard of functional literacy would represent a real and important increase in literacy. This is not to deny the ultimate possibility and desirability of seeking a still higher literacy criterion, but forms of pedagogy will almost surely have to change to accommodate the changes in both the literacy criterion and target population.

This discussion of changes in literacy standards has implications for the growing "back to basics" movement. Although the claim is frequently made that a return to basics would improve our educational system, the consequences of such a program are not clear. Presumably, proponents of basic education want schools to stress skills of literacy and mathematics more than certain recent additions to the curriculum. This much is reasonable. But, unless we intend to relinquish the criterion of comprehension as the goal of reading instruction, there is little to go *back* to in terms of pedagogical method, curriculum, or school organization. The old tried and true approaches, which nostalgia prompts us to believe might solve current problems, were designed neither to achieve the literacy standard sought today nor to ensure successful literacy for everyone. Whatever the rhetoric of the common school, early dropping out and selective promotion were in fact used to escape problems that must now be addressed through a pedagogy adequate to today's aspirations. While we may be able to borrow important ideas and practices from earlier periods, there is no simple past to which we can return.

NOTES

1. For the use of signatures in public oaths and as a source on literacy in seventeenth- and eighteenth-century England, see Roger S. Schofield, "The Measurement of Literacy in Pre-Industrial England," in *Literacy in Traditional Societies*, ed. Jack R. Goody (Cambridge, Eng.: Cambridge University Press, 1968), pp. 311–325; and Richard T. Vann, "Literacy in Seventeenth-Century England: Some Hearth-Tax Evidence," *Journal of Interdisciplinary History, 5* (1974), 287–293. The uses of signatures for retrospective literacy assessment in France are discussed in François Furet and Vladimir Sachs, "La Croissance de l'alphabétisation en France (XVIIIe–XIXe siècles)," *Annales: Économies, Sociétés, Civilisations, 29* (1974), 714–737.
2. Lawrence Stone, "Literacy and Education in England, 1640–1900," *Past and Present, 42* (1969), esp. pp. 77–83, examines the relationship of Protestantism to the development of literacy.
3. For samples of current work exploring the effect of education on economic growth in different contexts, see Roger S. Schofield, "Dimensions of Illiteracy, 1750–1850," *Explorations in Economic History, 10* (1973), 437–454; and David McClelland, "Does Education Accelerate Economic Growth?" *Economic Development and Cultural Change, 14* (1966), 257–278. For the effect of education on personality change, see Howard Schuman, Alex Inkeles, and David Smith, "Some Social and Psychological Effects and Non-Effects of Literacy in a New Nation," *Economic Development and Cultural Change, 16* (1967), 1–14.
4. See Bernard Bailyn, *Education in the Forming of American Society: Needs and Opportunities for Study* (Chapel Hill: University of North Carolina Press, 1960), esp. pp. 48–49; and Lawrence Cremin, *American Education: The Colonial Experience, 1607–1783* (New York: Harper & Row, 1970), pp. 545–570. The counterargument by Kenneth Lockridge, *Literacy in Colonial New England: An Inquiry into the Social Context of Literacy in the Early Modern West* (New York: Norton, 1974), pp. 28–29 and nn., overstates Cremin's position but not the thrust of his argument.
5. On the failure of colonial wills to offer evidence of nontraditional social behavior, see Lockridge, *Literacy in Colonial New England*, pp. 33–35.
6. See Michael Sanderson, "Literacy and Social Mobility in the Industrial Revolution in England," *Past and Present, 56* (1972), esp. pp. 89–95, and the later exchange with Thomas Laqueur in "Debate," *Past and Present, 64* (1974), 96–112.
7. Lockridge, *Literacy in Colonial New England*, pp. 13, 87–88.

8. For Scotland, see Stone, "Literacy and Education in England," pp. 79–80, 82–83, 123–124, 126–127, 135–136.

9. Egil Johansson, "Literacy Studies in Sweden: Some Examples," in *Literacy and Society in a Historical Perspective: A Conference Report*, ed. E. Johansson, Educational Reports Umeå (Umeå, Sweden: Umeå University and School of Education, 1973), p. 49. We would like to thank Professor Kjell Härnqvist for his assistance in pursuing this investigation.

10. This discussion is based on Johansson, "Literacy Studies in Sweden," pp. 41–50, which includes reproductions of two pages from the registers.

11. The Little Catechism of Luther, translated into Swedish, with officially published "Explanations," functioned as did the Bible in Cromwellian England as a source of religious authority. One of the reasons for this was the failure of various projects to translate the Bible in its entirety into Swedish. The era of cheap Bibles opened in Sweden only at the beginning of the nineteenth century. See Michael Roberts, "The Swedish Church," in *Sweden's Age of Greatness*, ed. M. Roberts (New York: St. Martin's Press, 1973), pp. 138–140. Those who had not learned the Little Catechism were forbidden by law in 1686 to marry. See Claude Nordmann, *Grandeur et liberté de la Suède (1660–1792)* (Paris and Louvain: Béatrice-Nauwelaerts, 1971), p. 118.

12. See François de la Fontainerie, ed. and trans., *French Liberalism and Education in the Eighteenth Century: The Writings of La Chalotais, Turgot, Diderot and Condorcet on National Education* (New York and London: McGraw-Hill, 1932), pp. 95, 230, quoted in Frederick B. Artz, *The Development of Technical Education in France, 1500–1850* (Cambridge, MA: MIT Press, 1966), pp. 68, 71. The centrality of mathematics is also discussed in Roger Hahn, *The Anatomy of a Scientific Institution: The Paris Academy of Sciences, 1666–1803* (Berkeley: University of California Press, 1971), esp. pp. 95–97. For efforts to apply mathematics to social questions, see Keith Michael Baker, *Condorcet: From Natural Philosophy to Social Mathematics* (Chicago: University of Chicago Press, 1975), esp. pp. 332–342.

13. For the struggle between humanist classicists and scientists for direction of the secondary-school program, see Antoine Prost, *Histoire de l'enseignement en France, 1800–1967* (Paris: A. Colin, 1968), pp. 55–58.

14. Charles Kindleberger, "Technical Education and the French Entrepreneur," in *Enterprise and Entrepreneurs in Nineteenth- and Twentieth-Century France*, ed. Edward C. Carter II, Robert Forster, and Joseph N. Moody (Baltimore: Johns Hopkins University Press, 1976), pp. 26–27.

15. For eighteenth-century growth rates in literacy, as estimated by marriage-contract signatures, see Furet and Sachs, "La Croissance de l'alphabétisation," pp. 726–727.

16. For primary and secondary schooling during the Revolutionary and Napoleonic years, see Maurice Gontar, *L'Enseignement primaire en France de la Révolution à la loi Guizot (1789–1833)* (Paris: Belles Lettres, 1959); Louis Liard, *L'Enseignement supérieur en France, 1789–1893*, 2 vols. (Paris: A. Colin, 1888–1894); and Robert R. Palmer, ed. and trans., *The School of the French Revolution: A Documentary History of the Collège Louis-le-Grand . . . 1762–1814* (Princeton, NJ: Princeton University Press, 1975).

17. Furet and Sachs in "La Croissance de l'alphabétisation," pp. 722–737, argue that the Revolution accelerated trends in progress. The South continued to "catch up," the difference between male and female literacy rates narrowed, and the rate of literacy progress, within a narrow band, slowly moved forward. Evidence of some newly appreciated continuities in secondary education over the period from 1780 to 1836 are analyzed in the revisionist work of Dominique Julia and Paul Pressly, "La Population scolaire en 1789," *Annales: Économies, Sociétés, Civilisations*, 30 (1975), 1516–1561.

18. See Eugen Weber, *Peasants into Frenchmen: The Modernization of Rural France, 1870–1914* (Stanford, CA: Stanford University Press, 1976), p. 319, for an example of this relationship as late as the 1860s.

19. For a discussion of these standards in the context of the 1816 rulings, see Gontard, *L'Enseignement primaire*, pp. 300–306.

20. For the contemporary sources, see Weber, *Peasants into Frenchmen*, pp. 305–306.

21. On the metric system, made the only legal measure in 1840, see Weber, *Peasants into French-men*, pp. 30–35.

22. On the nineteenth-century pedagogy, see the observations of Prost, *Histoire de l'enseignement*, pp. 119–124, 276–282.

23. Roger Thabault, *Education and Change in a Village Community: Mazières-en-Gâtine 1848–1914* (New York: Schocken Books, 1971), p. 61.

24. Cited in Weber, *Peasants into Frenchmen*, p. 306.

25. A table of legislation affecting French education at all levels, 1794–1967, may be found in Prost, *Histoire de l'enseignement*, pp. 501–511.

26. For the preprofessional dependence of the French primary school teacher on local religious authority during the early nineteenth century, see Peter V. Meyers, "Professionalization and Societal Change: Rural Teachers in Nineteenth-Century France," *Journal of Social History*, 9 (1976), 542–546.

27. F. Guizot, *Mémoires*, III, 69-70, cited in Gontard, *L'Enseignement primaire*, pp. 495–496.

28. See Weber, *Peasants into Frenchmen*, pp. 305–306 and nn. In arguing the laicization of French education by the mid-nineteenth century, Michalina Clifford-Vaughn and Margaret Archer, *Social Conflict and Educational Change in England and France, 1789–1848* (Cambridge, Eng.: Cambridge University Press, 1971), p. 202, have not presented a convincing argument.

29. Prost, *Histoire de l'enseignement*, pp. 192–203. Legislation in 1886 was designed to eliminate the religious from a teaching role in public schools.

30. For an excellent discussion of the role of Ernest Lavisse in creating the "civic" and "national" history texts, see William R. Keylor, *Academy and Community: The Foundation of the French Historical Profession* (Cambridge, MA: Harvard University Press, 1975), pp. 92–100.

31. From Charles-Victor Langlois and Charles Seignobos, *Introduction aux études historiques* (Paris: Hachette et Compagnie, 1898), pp. 288–289, cited in Keylor, p. 99, and Weber, *Peasants into Frenchmen*, p. 333. On the relationship of this kind of instruction to nation-building, see Karl Deutsch, *Nationalism and Social Communication: An Inquiry into the Foundation of Nationality* (Cambridge, MA: MIT Press; and New York: Wiley, 1953), pp. 92–99, 155.

32. A graph showing the rise in literacy measured by the capacity to sign in the years from 1830 to 1910 is offered in Prost, *Histoire de l'enseignement*, p. 96. Also given (p. 98) is a graph showing the number and distribution of students in primary schooling from 1810 to 1890.

33. Thabault, *Education and Change*, p. 64. The relationship between capacity to sign and capacity to read is discussed by Schofield, "The Measurement of Literacy in Pre-Industrial England," p. 324; Furet and Sachs, "La Croissance de l'alphabétisation," esp. pp. 715–716, 720–721; and Stone, "Literacy and Education in England," pp. 98–99.

34. From Mitford Mathews, *Teaching to Read: Historically Considered* (Chicago: University of Chicago Press, 1966), p. 55.

35. For an assessment of Gedike's work, see Mathews, *Teaching to Read*, pp. 37–43.

36. Samuel Putnam, *The Analytical Reader* (Portland, ME: Wm. Hyde, 1836), cited in Charles C. Fries, *Linguistics and Reading* (New York: Holt, Rinehart & Winston, 1963), p. 10.

37. George Farnham, *The Sentence Method* (Syracuse, NY: C. W. Bardeen, 1881), cited in Fries, p. 11.

38. Clarence S. Yoakum and Robert M. Yerkes, *Army Mental Tests* (New York: Henry Holt, 1920), p. 2; and Lewis M. Terman, "Methods of Examining: History, Development and Preliminary Results," in *Psychological Examining in the United States Army*, ed. Robert M. Yerkes, Memoirs of the National Academy of Sciences, Vol. 15, Part 2 (Washington, DC: Government Printing Office, 1921), 299–546.

39. May Ayres Burgess, *The Measurement of Silent Reading* (New York: Russell Sage Foundation, 1921), pp. 11–12.

40. See Raymond E. Callahan, *Education and the Cult of Efficiency* (Chicago: University of Chicago Press, 1962); and David B. Tyack, *The One Best System: A History of American Education* (Cambridge, MA: Harvard University Press, 1974), pp. 198–216.

41. Leonard P. Ayres, *Laggards in Our Schools: A Study of Elimination and Retardation in City School Systems* (New York: Russell Sage Foundation, 1909). This book was prompted by concern with the large number of schoolchildren who were older than they should have been for their assigned grade level.

42. Ayres, *Laggards in Our Schools*, pp. 20, 38, 66.

43. On functional illiteracy, see David Harman, "Illiteracy: An Overview," *Harvard Educational Review, 40* (1970), 226–230. The United States Census Bureau, however, uses the completion of six years of schooling as the standard for literacy. For a review of the relationship of six years of schooling to selected measures of reading ability, see John R. Bormuth, "Reading Literacy: Its Definition and Assessment," in *Toward a Literate Society: The Report of the Committee on Reading of the National Academy of Education*, ed. John B. Carroll and Jeanne S. Chall (New York: McGraw-Hill, 1975), pp. 62–63.

44. Jeanne S. Chall, "The Great Debate: Ten Years Later, with a Modest Proposal for Reading Stages," in *Theory and Practice of Early Reading, I*, ed. Lauren B. Resnick and Phyllis A. Weaver (Hillsdale, NJ: Erlbaum Associates, 1979).

This paper was written during our stay at the Center for Advanced Study in the Behavioral Sciences at Stanford University. Lauren Resnick was supported there by a fellowship from the Spencer Foundation. The work was also supported in part by Contract #400-75-0049 of the National Institute of Education with the Learning Research and Development Center, University of Pittsburgh.

From Utterance to Text:
The Bias of Language in Speech and Writing

DAVID R. OLSON

The faculty of language stands at the center of our conception of mankind; speech makes us human and literacy makes us civilized. It is therefore both interesting and important to consider what, if anything, is distinctive about written language and to consider the consequences of literacy for the bias it may impart both to our culture and to people's psychological processes.

The framework for examining the consequences of literacy has already been laid out. Using cultural and historical evidence, Havelock (1973), Parry (1971), Goody and Watt (1968), Innis (1951), and McLuhan (1964) have argued that the invention of the alphabetic writing system altered the nature of the knowledge that is stored for reuse, the organization of that knowledge, and the cognitive processes of the people who use that written language. Some of the cognitive consequences of schooling and literacy in contemporary societies have been specified through anthropological and cross-cultural psychological research by Cole, Gay, Glick, and Sharp (1971), Scribner and Cole (1973), Greenfield (1972), Greenfield and Bruner (1969), Goodnow (1976), and others.

However, the more general consequences of the invention of writing systems for the structure of language, the concept of meaning, and the patterns of comprehension and reasoning processes remain largely unknown. The purpose of this chapter is to examine the consequences of literacy, particularly those consequences associated with mastery of the "schooled" language of written texts.

In the course of the discussion, I shall repeatedly contrast explicit, written prose statements, which I shall call *texts*, with more informal oral-language statements, which I shall call *utterances*. Utterances and texts may be contrasted at any one of several levels: the linguistic modes themselves — written language versus oral language; their usual usages — conversation, storytelling, verse, and song for the oral mode versus statements, arguments, and essays for the written mode; their summarizing forms — proverbs and aphorisms for the oral mode versus premises for the written mode; and finally, the cultural traditions built around these modes — an oral

Harvard Educational Review Vol. 47 No. 3 August 1977, 257–281

tradition versus a literate tradition. My argument will be that there is a transition from utterance to text both culturally and developmentally and that this transition can be described as one of increasing explicitness, with language increasingly able to stand as an unambiguous or autonomous representation of meaning.

This essay (a word I use here in its Old French sense: *essai* — to try) begins by showing that theoretical and empirical debates on various aspects of language — ranging from linguistic theories of meaning to the psychological theories of comprehension, reading, and reasoning — have remained unduly puzzling and polemical primarily because of different assumptions about the locus of meaning. One assumption is that meaning is in the shared intentions of the speaker and the hearer, while the opposite one is that meaning is conventionalized in a sentence itself, that "the meaning is in the text." This essay continues by tracing the assumption that the meaning is in the text from the invention of the alphabetic writing system to the rapid spread of literacy with the invention of printing. The consequences of that assumption, particularly of the attempts to make it true, are examined in terms of the development and exploitation of the "essayist technique." The essay then proceeds to reexamine the linguistic, logical, and psychological issues mentioned at the outset; it demonstrates that the controversies surrounding these issues stem largely from a failure to appreciate the differences between utterances and texts and to understand that the assumptions appropriate for one are not appropriate for the other.

THE LOCUS OF MEANING

The problem at hand is as well raised by a quotation from Martin Luther as by any more contemporary statement: scripture is *sui ipsius interpres* — scripture is its own interpreter (cited in Gadamer, 1975, p. 154). For Luther, then, the meaning of Scripture depended, not upon the dogmas of the church, but upon a deeper reading of the text. That is, the meaning of the text is in the text *itself*.[1] But is that claim true; is the meaning in the text? As we shall see, the answer offered to that question changed substantially about the time of Luther in regard not only to Scripture but also to philosophical and scientific statements. More important, the answers given to the question lie at the root of several contemporary linguistic and psychological controversies. Let us consider five of these.

In linguistic theory, an important controversy surrounds the status of invariant structures — structures suitable for linguistic, philosophical, and psychological analyses of language. Are these structures to be found in the deep syntactic structure of the sentence itself or in the interaction between the sentence and its user, in what may be called the understanding or interpretation? This argument may be focused in terms of the criterion for judging the well-formedness of a sentence. For Chomsky (1957, 1965) the well-formedness of a sentence —roughly, the judgment that the sentence is a permissible sentence of the language — is determined solely by the base syntactic structure of the sentence. Considerations of comprehensibility and effectiveness, like those of purpose and context, are irrelevant to the judgment. Similarly, the rules for operating upon well-formed base strings are purely formal. For Chomsky the meaning, or semantics, of a sentence is also specified in the base grammatical structure.

Each unambiguous or well-formed sentence has one and only one base structure, and this base structure specifies the meaning or semantic structure of that sentence. Hence the meaning of a sentence relies on no private referential or contextual knowledge; nothing is added by the listener. One is justified, therefore, in concluding that, for Chomsky, the meaning is in the sentence per se.[2]

The radical alternative to this view is associated with the general semanticists led by Korzybski (1933), Chase (1954), and Hayakawa (1952). They claim that sentences do not have fixed meanings but depend in every case on the context and purpose for which they were uttered. Chafe (1970) offers a more modest alternative to Chomsky's syntactic bias, asserting that the criterion for the well-formedness of a sentence is determined by the semantic structure; a sentence is well formed if it is understandable to a listener. This semantic structure is necessarily a part of language users' "knowledge of the world," and language can serve its functions precisely because such knowledge tends to be shared by speakers. Thus comprehension of a sentence involves, to some degree, the use of prior knowledge, contextual cues, and nonlinguistic cues.

In his philosophical discussion of meaning, Grice (1957) makes a distinction that mirrors the difference between the views of Chomsky and Chafe. Grice points out that one may analyze either "sentence meaning" or "speaker's meaning." The sentence per se may mean something other than what a speaker means by the sentence. For example, the speaker's meaning of "You're standing on my toe" may be "Move your foot." In these terms Chomsky provides a theory of sentence meaning in which the meaning of the sentence is independent of its function or context. Chafe, in contrast, offers a theory of intended meaning that encompasses both the intentions of the speaker and the interpretations the hearer constructs on the bases of the sentence, its perceived context, and its assumed function.

But these theories differ not only in the scope of the problems they attempt to solve. My suggestion is that these linguistic theories specify their central problems differently because of differing implicit assumptions about language; Chomsky's assumption is that language is best represented by written texts; Chafe's is that language is best represented by oral conversational utterances.

Psychological theories of language comprehension reflect these divergent linguistic assumptions. Psycholinguistic models of comprehension such as that of Clark (1974) follow Chomsky in the assumption that one's mental representation of a sentence depends on the recovery of the unique base syntactic structure underlying the sentence. Hence, a sentence is given the same underlying representation regardless of the context or purposes it is ultimately to serve. Similarly, Fodor, Bever, and Garrett (1974) have claimed that the semantic properties of a sentence are determined exclusively and automatically by the specification of the syntactic properties and the lexical items of the sentence. The assumption, once again, is that the meaning, at least the meaning worth psychological study, is in the text.

Conversely, a number of researchers (Anderson & Ortony, 1975; Barclay, 1973; Bransford, Barclay, & Franks, 1972; Bransford & Johnson, 1973; Paris & Carter, 1973) have demonstrated that sentence comprehension depends in large part on the context and on the prior knowledge of the listeners. In one now famous example, the sentence, "The notes were sour because the seams were split," becomes comprehensible only when the listener knows that the topic being discussed is bagpipes. Bransford and Johnson (1973) conclude, "What is understood and remembered about an input depends on the knowledge structures to which it is related" (p. 429).

Differing assumptions as to whether or not the meaning is in the text may also be found in studies of logical reasoning. Logical reasoning is concerned with the formulation and testing of the relations that hold between propositions. Such studies are based on models of formal reasoning in which it is assumed that the rules of inference apply to explicit premises to yield valid inferences. Subjects can be tested on their ability to consistently apply these formal rules to various semantic contents, and development can be charted in terms of the ability to apply the rules consistently to the meaning in the text (Neimark & Slotnick, 1970; Piaget, 1972; Suppes & Feldman, 1971).

Studies have shown, however, that formal propositional logic is a poor model for ordinary reasoning from linguistic propositions. Some researchers (Taplin & Staudenmayer, 1973) have suggested that logic and reasoning are discontinuous because "the interpreted meaning of a sentence is usually not entirely given by the denotative meaning in the linguistic structure of the sentence" (Staudenmayer, 1975, p. 56); factors such as prior knowledge and contextual presuppositions are also important. Analyzing the protocols of graduate students solving syllogisms, Henle (1962) found that errors resulted more often from an omission of a premise, a modification of a premise, or an importation of new evidence than from a violation of the rules of inference. If logic is considered to be the ability to draw valid conclusions from explicit premises — to operate upon the information in the text — then these students were reasoning somewhat illogically. However, if logic is considered to be the ability to operate on premises as they have been personally interpreted, then these students were completely logical in their operations. The critical issue, again, is whether or not the meaning is assumed to be fully explicit in the text.

Theories of language acquisition also reflect either the assumption that language is autonomous — that the meaning is in the text — or that it is dependent on nonlinguistic knowledge. Assuming that language is autonomous and independent of use or context, Chomsky (1965) and McNeill (1970) have argued that an innate, richly structured language-acquisition device must be postulated to account for the child's remarkable mastery of language. Hypothesized to be innate are structures that define the basic linguistic units (Chomsky, 1972) and the rules for transforming these units. Independent of a particular speaker or hearer, these transformations provide the interpretation given to linguistic forms. For example, at the grammatical level, "John hit Mary" is equivalent to "Mary was hit by John," and at the lexical level, "John" must be animate, human, male, and so on. These conclusions seem plausible, indeed inescapable, as long as it is assumed that language is autonomous and the meanings are in the sentences themselves.

Most recent research on language acquisition has proceeded from the alternative assumption that an utterance is but a fragmentary representation of the intention that lies behind it. Thus the meaning of the utterance comes from shared intentions based upon prior knowledge, the context of the utterance, and habitual patterns of interaction. The contextual dependence of child language was emphasized by de Laguna (1927/1970) and Buhler (1934). De Laguna (1927/1970) claimed, "Just because the terms of the child's language are in themselves so indefinite, it is left to the particular context to determine the specific meaning for each occasion. In order to understand what the baby is saying, you must see what the baby is doing" (pp. 90–91).

Recent studies extend this view. Bloom (1970) has shown, for example, that a young child may use the same surface structure, "Mommy sock," in two quite different contexts to represent quite different deep structures or meanings: in one case, the mother is putting the sock on the child; in the other, the child is picking up the mother's sock. The utterance, therefore, specifies only part of the meaning, the remainder being specified by the perceived context, accompanying gestures, and the like. Moreover, having established these nonlinguistic meanings, the child can use them as the basis for discovering the structure of language (Brown, 1973; Bruner, 1973; Macnamara, 1972; Nelson, 1974). In other words, linguistic structures are not autonomous but arise out of nonlinguistic structures. There is no need, then, to attribute their origins to innate structures. Language development is primarily a matter of mastering the conventions both for putting more and more of the meaning into the verbal utterance and for reconstructing the intended meaning of the sentence per se. In de Laguna's terms, "The evolution of language is characterized by a progressive freeing of speech from dependence upon the perceived conditions under which it is uttered and heard, and from the behavior that accompanies it. The extreme limit of this freedom is reached in language which is written (or printed) and read" (1927, 1970, p. 107). Thus the predominant view among language-acquisition theorists is that while the meaning initially is not in the language acquisition itself, it tends to become so with development.

Finally, theories of reading and learning to read can be seen as expressions of the rival assumptions about the locus of meaning. In one view the meaning is in the text and the student's problem is to find out how to decode that meaning (Carroll & Chall, 1975; Chall, 1967; Gibson & Levin, 1975). In fact, the majority of reading programs are based upon the gradual mastery of subskills such as letter recognition, sound blending, word recognition, and ultimately deciphering meaning. The alternative view is that readers bring the meaning to the text, which merely confirms or disconfirms their expectations (Goodman, 1967; Smith, 1975). Thus if children fail to recognize a particular word or sentence in a context, their expectations generate substitutions that are often semantically appropriate. Again, the basic assumption is that the meaning is — or is not — in the text.

To summarize, the controversial aspects of five issues — the structure of language, the nature of comprehension, the nature of logical reasoning, and the problems of learning to speak and learning to read — can be traced to differing assumptions regarding the autonomy of texts. Further, the distinction between utterances and texts, I suggest, reflects the different assumptions that meaning is or is not in the sentence per se.

THE BEGINNINGS OF A LITERATE TECHNOLOGY

Let us consider the origin of the assumption that the meaning is in the text and the implications of that assumption for language use. The assumption regarding the autonomy of texts is relatively recent and the language conforming to it is relatively specialized. Utterance, language that does not conform to this assumption, is best represented by children's early language, oral conversation, memorable oral sayings, and the like. Text, language that does conform to that assumption, is best represented by formal, written, expository prose statements. My central claim is that the evolution both culturally and developmentally is from utterance to text. While utterance is universal, text appears to have originated with Greek literacy and to have reached a most visible form with the British essayists. My argument, which rests heavily on the seminal works of Havelock (1963), McLuhan (1962), and Goody and Watt (1968), is that the invention of the alphabetic writing system gave to Western culture many of its predominant features, including an altered conception of language and an altered conception of rational man. These effects came about, in part, from the creation of explicit, autonomous statements — statements dependent upon an explicit writing system, the alphabet, and an explicit form of argument, the essay. In a word, these effects resulted from putting the meaning into the text.

Meaning in an Oral Language Tradition

Luther's statement, that the meaning of Scripture depended not upon the dogmas of the church, but upon a deeper reading of the text, seems a simple claim. It indicates, however, the profound change that occurred early in the sixteenth century in regard to the presumed autonomy of texts. Prior to the time of Luther, who in this argument represents one turning point in a roughly continuous change in orientation, it was generally assumed that meaning could not be stated explicitly. Statements required interpretation by either scribes or clerics. Luther's claim and the assumption that guided it cut both ways: they were a milestone in the developing awareness that text could explicitly state its meaning — that it did not depend on dogma or interpretive context; more importantly, they also indicated a milestone in the attempt to shape language to more explicitly represent its meanings. This shift in orientation, which I shall elaborate later in terms of the "essayist technique," was one of the high points in the long history of the attempt to make meaning completely explicit. Yet it was, relatively speaking, a mere refinement of the process that had begun with the Greek invention of the alphabet.

Although the Greek alphabet and the growth of Greek literacy may be at the base of Western science and philosophy, it is not to be assumed that preliterate people were primitive in any sense. Modern anthropology has provided many examples of theoretical, mythical, and technological systems of impressive sophistication and appropriateness. It has been established that a complex and extensive literature could exist in the absence of a writing system. In 1928, Milman Parry (1971) demonstrated that the *Iliad* and the *Odyssey*, usually attributed to a literate Homer, were in fact examples of oral composition composed over centuries by preliterate bards for audiences who did not read. In turn, it was recognized that large sections of the Bible possessed a similar oral structure. The books of Moses and the Prophets, for example, are recorded versions of statements that were shaped through oral methods as part of an oral culture.

To preserve verbal statements in the absence of a writing system, such statements would have to be biased both in form and content toward oral mnemonic devices such as "formalized patterns of speech, recital under ritual conditions, the use of drums and other musical instruments, and the employment of professional remembrances" (Goody & Watt, 1968, p. 31). Language is thus shaped or biased to fit the requirements of oral communication and auditory memory (see, for example, Havelock, 1973, and Frye, 1971). A variety of oral statements such as proverbs, adages, aphorisms, riddles, and verse are distinctive not only in that they preserve important cultural information but also in that they are memorable. They tend, however, *not* to be explicit or to say exactly what they mean; they require context and prior knowledge and wisdom for their interpretation. Solomon, for example, introduced the Book of Proverbs by saying: "To understand a proverb and the interpretations; the words of the wise and their dark sayings" (1:6). Maimonides, the twelfth-century rabbi, pointed out in his *Guide of the Perplexed* that when one interprets parables "according to their external meanings, he too is overtaken by great perplexity!" (1963, p. 6).

The invention of writing did not end the oral tradition. Some aspects of that tradition merely coexist with the more dominant literate traditions. Lord (1960) in his *Singer of Tales* showed that a remnant of such an oral culture persists in Yugoslavia. Even in a predominantly literate culture, aspects of the oral tradition remain. Gray (1973) suggested that Bob Dylan represents the creative end of such an oral tradition in Anglo-American culture; the less creative aspects of that tradition show up in the stock phrases and proverbial sayings that play so large a part in everyday conversational language.

With the introduction of writing, important parts of the oral tradition were written down and preserved in the available literate forms. The important cultural information, the information worth writing down, consisted in large part of statements shaped to fit the requirements of oral memory such as the epics, verse, song, orations, and since readers already knew, through the oral tradition, much of the content, writing served primarily for the storage and retrieval of information that had already been committed to memory, not for the expression of original ideas.

Scripture, at the time of Luther, had just such a status. It consisted in part of statements shaped to the requirements of oral comprehension and oral memory. Scripture had authority, but since the written statements were shorn of their oral contexts, they were assumed to require interpretation. The dogma of the church, the orally transmitted tradition, had the authority to say what the Scripture meant. In this context Luther's statement can be seen as profoundly radical. Luther claimed that the text supplied sufficient context internally to determine the meaning of the passage; the meaning was in the text. What would have led Luther to make such a radial claim? My suggestion is that his claim reflected a technological change — the invention of printing — one in a series of developments in the increasing explicitness of language, which we shall now examine.

Alphabetic Writing — Making Meanings Explicit

Significant oral-language statements, to be memorable, must be cast into some oral, poetic form. Consequently, as we have seen, these statements do not directly say what they mean. With the invention of writing, the limitations of oral memory became less critical. The written statement, constituting a more or less permanent artifact, no longer depended on its "poetized" form for its preservation.

However, whether or not a writing system can preserve the meanings of statements depends upon the characteristics of the system. An elliptical or nonexplicit writing system, like nonexplicit statements, tends to rely on prior knowledge and expectancies. An explicit writing system unambiguously represents meanings — the meaning is in the text. It has a minimum of homophones (seen/scene) and homographs (lead/lead) at the phonemic and graphemic levels, few ambiguities at the grammatical level, and few permissible interpretations at the semantic level.

The Greek alphabet was the first to approach such a degree of explicitness and yet to be simple enough to provide a base for mass literacy. Gelb (1952) differentiated four main stages in the development of writing systems. The first stage, which goes back to prehistory, involves the expression of ideas through pictures and pictographic writing. Such writing systems have been called ideographic in that they represent and communicate ideas directly without appeal to the structure of spoken language. While the signs are easily learned and recognized, there are problems associated with their use: any full system requires from four or five thousand characters for ordinary usage; their concreteness makes the representation of abstract terms difficult; they are difficult to arrange so as to produce statements (Gombrich, 1974); and they tend to limit the number of things that can be expressed.

The next stage was the invention of the principle of phonetization, the attempt to make writing reflect the sound structure of speech. In an attempt to capture the properties of speech, early phonetic systems — Sumerian, Egyptian, Hittite, and Chinese — all contained signs of three different types: word signs or logogens, syllabic signs, and auxiliary signs.

The third stage was the development of syllabaries, which did away both with word signs and with signs representing sounds having more than one consonant. Whereas earlier syllabaries had separate signs for such syllables as *ta* and *tam*, the West Semitic syllabaries reduced the syllable to a single consonant-vowel sequence, thereby reducing the number of signs. However, since these Semitic syllabaries did not have explicit representations for vowels, the script frequently resulted in ambiguities in pronunciation, particularly in cases of writing proper names and other words that could not be retrieved from context. Semitic writing systems thus introduced phonetic indicators called Matres Lectionis (literally: "mothers of reading") to differentiate the vowel sounds (Gelb, 1952, p. 166).

The final stage in the invention of the alphabet, a step taken only by the Greeks, was the invention of a phonemic alphabet (Gelb, 1952; Goody & Watt, 1963). The Greeks did so, Gelb suggests, by using consistently the Matres Lectionis that the Semites had used sporadically. They discovered that these indicators were not syllables but rather vowels. Consequently the sign that preceded the indicator also must not be a syllable but rather a consonant. Havelock (1973) comments: "At a stroke, by this analysis, the Greeks provided a table of elements of linguistic sound not only manageable because of its economy, but for the first time in the history of *homo sapiens*, also accurate" (p. 11).

The faithful transcription of the sound patterns of speech by a fully developed alphabet has freed writing from some of the ambiguities of oral language. Many sentences that are ambiguous when spoken are unambiguous when written — for example, "il vent toujours a sept heures" ("he always comes at seven o'clock") versus "il vient toujours a cette heure" ("he always comes at this hour") (Lyons, 1969, p. 51). However, a fully developed alphabet does not exhaust the possibilities for explicitness of a writing system. According to Bloomfield (1939) and Kneale and Kneale (1962), the remaining lack of explicitness necessitated the invention of the formal languages of logic and mathematics.

To summarize, we have considered the extent to which meaning is explicitly represented in a statement. Oral language statements must be poetized to be remembered, but in the process they lose some of their explicitness; they require interpretation by a wise man, scribe, or cleric. Written statements bypass the limitations of memory, but the extent to which a writing system can explicitly represent meaning depends upon the nature of the system. Systems such as syllabaries that represent several meanings with the same visual sign are somewhat ambiguous or nonexplicit. As a consequence, they again require interpretation by some authority. Statements can become relatively free from judgment or interpretation only with a highly explicit writing system such as the alphabet. The Greek alphabet, through its ability to record exactly what is said, provided a tool for the formulation and criticism of explicit meanings and was therefore critical to the evolution of Greek literacy and Greek culture.

Written Text as an Exploratory Device

Writing systems with a relatively lower degree of explicitness, such as the syllabaries, tended to serve a somewhat limited purpose, primarily that of providing an aid to memory. Havelock (1973) states:

> When it came to transcribing discursive speech, difficulties of interpretation would discourage the practice of using the script for novel or freely-invented discourse. The practice that would be encouraged would be to use the system as a reminder of something already familiar, so that recollection of its familiarity would aid the reader in getting the right interpretation. . . . It would in short tend to be something — tale, proverb, parable, fable and the like — which already existed in oral form and had been composed according to oral rules. The syllabic system in short provided techniques for recall of what was already familiar, not instruments for formulating novel statements which could further the exploration of new experience. (p. 238)

The alphabet had no such limits of interpretation. The decrease in ambiguity of symbols — for example, the decrease in the number of homographs — would permit a reader to assign the appropriate interpretation to a written statement even without highly tuned expectations as to what the text was likely to say. The decreased reliance upon prior knowledge or expectancies was therefore a significant step toward making meaning explicit in the conventionalized linguistic system. The technology was sufficiently explicit to permit one to analyze the sentence meaning apart from the speaker's meaning. Simultaneously, written language became an instrument for the formulation and preservation of original statements that could violate readers' expectancies and commonsense knowledge. Written language had come free from its base in the mother tongue; it had begun the transformation from utterance to text.

The availability of an explicit writing system, however, does not assure that the statements recorded in that language will be semantically explicit. As previously mentioned, the first statements written down tended to be those that had already been shaped to the requirements of oral production and oral memory, the Greek epics being a case in point. Over time, however, the Greeks came to fully exploit the powers of their alphabetic writing system. In fact, Havelock (1973) has argued that the Greeks' use of this invention was responsible for the development of the intellectual qualities found in classical Greece.

> And so, as the fifth century passes into the fourth, the full effect upon Greece of the alphabetic revolution begins to assert itself. The governing word ceases to be a vibration heard by the ear and nourished in the memory. It becomes a visible artifact. Storage of information for reuse, as a formula designed to explain the dynamics of western culture, ceases to be a metaphor. The documented statement persisting through time unchanged is to release the human brain from certain formidable burdens of memorization while increasing the energies available for conceptual thought. The results as they are to be observed in the intellectual history of Greece and Europe were profound. (p. 60)

Some of the efforts of the Greeks' utilization of the alphabetic writing system are worth reviewing. First, as Goody and Watt (1968) and a number of other scholars have shown, it permitted a differentiation of myth and history with a new regard for literal truth. When the Homeric epics were written down, they could be subjected to critical analysis and their inconsistencies became apparent. Indeed, Hecataeus, faced with writing a history of Greece, said: "What I write is the account I believe to be true. For the stories the Greeks tell are many and in my opinion ridiculous" (cited in Goody & Watt, 1968, p. 45). Second, the use of the alphabetic system altered the relative regard for poetry and for prose. Prose statements were neither subtle nor devious; they tended to mean what they said. Havelock (1963) has demonstrated that Plato's *Republic* diverged from the tradition of the oral Homeric poets and represented a growing reliance on prose statements.

Third, the emphasis on written prose, as in Aristotle's *Analytics* (see Goody & Watt, 1968, pp. 52–54), permitted the abstraction of logical procedures that could serve as the rules for thinking. Syllogisms could operate on prose premises but not on oral statements such as proverbs. Further, the use of written prose led to the development of abstract categories, the genus/species taxonomies so important not only to Greek science but also to the formation and division of various subject-matter areas. Much of Greek thought was concerned with satisfactorily explaining the meaning of terms. And formulating a definition is essentially a literate enterprise outside of the context of ongoing speech — an attempt to provide the explicit meaning of a word in terms of the other words in the system (see, for example, Bruner & Olson, in press; Goody & Watt, 1968; and Havelock, 1976).

The Greeks, thinking that they had discovered a method for determining objective truth, were in fact doing little more than detecting the properties implicit in their native tongue. Their rules for mind were not rules for thinking but rather rules for using language consistently; the abstract properties of their category system were not true or unbiased descriptions of reality but rather invariants in the structure of their language. Writing became an instrument for making explicit the knowledge that was already implicit in their habits of speech and, in the process, tidying up and ordering that knowledge. This important but clearly biased effort was the first dramatic impact of writing on knowledge.

The Greeks' concern with literacy was not without critics. Written statements could not be interrogated if a misunderstanding occurred, and they could not be altered to suit the requirements of listeners. Thus Socrates concluded in *Phaedrus:* "Anyone who leaves behind him a written manual, and likewise anyone who takes it over from him, on the supposition that such writing will provide something reliable and permanent, must be exceedingly simple minded" (*Phaedrus*, 277c, cited in Goody & Watt, 1968, p. 51). In the *Seventh Letter*, Plato says: "No intelligent man will ever be so bold as to put into language those things which his reason has contemplated, especially not into a form that is unalterable — which must be the case with what is expressed in written symbols" (*Seventh Letter*, 341 c–d, cited in Bluck, 1949, p. 176).

The Essayist Technique

Although the Greeks exploited the resources of written language, the invention of printing allowed an expanded and heterogeneous reading public to use those resources in a much more systematic way. The invention of printing prompted an intellectual revolution of similar magnitude to that of the Greek period (see McLuhan, 1962, and Ong, 1971, for fascinating accounts). However, the rise of print literacy did not merely preserve the analytic uses of writing developed by the Greeks; it involved as well, I suggest, further evolution in the explicitness of writing at the semantic level. That is, the increased explicitness of language was not so much a result of minimizing the ambiguity of words at the graphemic level but rather a result of minimizing the possible interpretations of statements. A sentence was written to have only one meaning. In addition, there was a further test of the adequacy of a statement's representation of presumed intention: the ability of that statement to stand up to analysis of its implications. To illustrate, if one assumes that statement X is true, then the implication Y should also be true. However, suppose that on further reflection Y is found to be indefensible. Then presumably statement X was not intended in the first place and would have to be revised.

This approach to texts as autonomous representations of meaning was reflected in the way texts were both read and written. A reader's task was to determine exactly what each sentence was asserting and to determine the presuppositions and implications of that statement. If one could assume that an author had actually intended what was written and that the statements were true, then the statements would stand up under scrutiny. Luther made just this assumption about Scripture early in the sixteenth century, shortly after the invention and wide utilization of printing. One of the more dramatic misapplications of the same assumption was Bishop Ussher's inference from biblical genealogies that the world was created in 4004 B.C.

The more fundamental effect of this approach to text was on the writer, whose task now was to create autonomous text — to write in such a manner that the sentence was an adequate, explicit representation of the meaning, relying on no implicit premises or personal interpretations. Moreover, the sentence had to withstand analysis of its presuppositions and implications. This fostered the use of prose as a form of extended statements from which a series of necessary implications could be drawn.

The British essayists were among the first to exploit writing for the purpose of formulating original theoretical knowledge. John Locke's *An Essay concerning Human Understanding* (1690/1961) well represents the intellectual bias that originated at that time and, to a large extent, characterizes our present use of language. Knowledge was taken to be the product of an extended logical essay — the output of the repeated application in a single coherent text of the technique of examining an assertion to determine all of its implications. It is interesting to note that when Locke began his criticism of human understanding he thought that he could write it on a sheet of paper in an evening. By the time he had exhausted the possibilities of both the subject and the new technology, the essay had taken twenty years and two volumes.

Locke's essayist technique differed notably from the predominant writing style of the time. Ellul (1964) says, "An uninitiated reader who opens a scientific treatise on law, economy, medicine or history published between the sixteenth and eighteenth centuries is struck most forcibly by the complete absence of logical order" (p. 39); and he notes, "It was more a question of personal exchange than of taking an objective position" (p. 41). In his introduction to *Some Thoughts concerning Education* (Locke, 1880), Quick reports that Locke himself made similar criticisms of the essays of Montaigne. For Locke and others writing as he did, the essay came to serve as an exploratory device for examining problems and in the course of that examination producing new knowledge. The essay could serve these functions, at least for the purposes of science and philosophy, only by adopting the language of explicit, written, logically connected prose.

This specialized form of language was adopted by the Royal Society of London, which, according to its historian Sprat (1667/1966), was concerned "with the advancement of science and with the improvement of the English language as a medium of prose" (p. 56). The society demanded a mathematical plainness of language and rejected all amplifications, digressions, and swellings of style. This use of language made writing a powerful intellectual tool, I have suggested, by rendering the logical implications of statements more detectable and by altering the statements themselves to make their implications both clear and true.

The process of formulating statements, deriving their implications, testing the truth of those implications, and using the results to revise or generalize from the original statement characterized not only empiricist philosophy but also the development of deductive empirical science. The result was the same, namely the formulation of a small set of connected statements of great generality that may occur as topic sentences of paragraphs or as premises of extended scientific or philosophical treatises. Such statements were notable not only in their novelty and abstractness but also in that they related to prior knowledge in an entirely new way. No longer did general premises necessarily rest on the data of common experience, that is, on commonsense intuition. Rather, as Bertrand Russell (1940) claimed for mathematics, a premise is believed because true implications follow from it, not because it is intuitively plausible. In fact, it is just this mode of using language — the deduction of counterintuitive models of reality — that distinguishes modern from ancient science (see Ong, 1958).

Moreover, not only did the language change, the picture of reality sustained by language changed as well; language and reality were reordered. Inhelder and Piaget (1958) describe this altered relationship between language and reality as a stage of mental development:

> The most distinctive property of formal thought is this reversal of direction between reality and possibility; instead of deriving a rudimentary theory from the empirical data as is done in concrete inferences, formal thought begins with a theoretical synthesis implying that certain relations are necessary and thus proceeds in the opposite direction. (p. 251)

The ability to make this "theoretical synthesis," I suggest, is tied to the analysis of the implications of the explicit theoretical statements permitted by writing.

Others have made the same point. Ricoeur (1973) has argued that language is not simply a reflection of reality but rather a means of investigating and enlarging reality. Hence, the text does not merely reflect readers' expectations; instead, the explicitness of text gives them a basis for constructing a meaning and then evaluating their own experiences in terms of it. Thus text *can* serve to realign language and reality. N. Goodman (1968), too, claims that "the world is as many ways as it can be truly described" (p. 6).

This property of language, according to Popper (1972), opens up the possibility of "objective knowledge." Popper claims that the acquisition of theoretical knowledge proceeds by offering an explicit theory (a statement), deriving and testing implications of the theory, and revising it in such a way that its implications are both productive and defensive. The result is a picture of the world derived from the repeated application of a particular literary technique: "science is a branch of literature" (Popper, 1972, p. 185).

Thus far I have summarized two of the major stages or steps in the creation of explicit, autonomous meanings. The first step toward making language explicit was at the graphemic level with the invention of an alphabetic writing system. Because it had a distinctive sign for each of the represented sounds and thereby reduced the ambiguity of the signs, an alphabetic system relied much less on readers' prior knowledge and expectancies than other writing systems. This explicitness permitted the preservation of meaning across space and time and the recovery of meaning by the more or less uninitiated. Even original ideas could be formulated in language and recovered by readers without recourse to some intermediary stage.

The second step involved the further development of explicitness at the semantic level by allowing a given sentence to have only one interpretation. Proverbial and poetic statements, for example, were not permissible because they admitted more than one interpretation, the appropriate one determined by the context of utterance. The attempt was to construct sentences for which the meaning was dictated by the lexical and syntactic features of the sentence itself. To this end, the meaning of terms had to be conventionalized by means of definitions, and the rules of implication had to be articulated and systematically applied.

The Greeks perfected the alphabetic system and began developing the writing style that, encouraged by the invention of printing and the form of extended texts it permitted, culminated in the essayist technique. The result was not an ordinary language, not a mother tongue, but rather a form of language specialized to serve the requirements of autonomous, written, formalized text. Indeed, children are progressively inducted into the use of this language during the school years. Thus formal schooling, in the process of teaching children to deal with prose texts, fosters the ability to "speak a written language" (Greenfield, 1972, p. 169).

THE EFFECTS OF CONSIDERATIONS OF LITERACY
ON ISSUES OF LANGUAGE

Let us return to the linguistic and psychological issues with which we began and reconsider them in the light of the cultural inventions that have served to make language explicit, to put the meaning into the text.

Linguistic Theory

The differences between oral language and written text may help to explain the current controversy between the syntactic approach represented by Chomsky and the semantic approach represented by Chafe. Several aspects of Chomsky's theory of grammar require attention in this regard. For Chomsky, the meaning of language is not tied to the speaker's knowledge of the world but is determined by the sentence or text itself. The meaning of a sentence is assigned formally or mechanically on the basis of the syntactic and lexical properties of the sentence per se and not on the basis of the expectancies or preferred interpretations of the listener (Chomsky, 1972, p. 24). Chomsky's theory is fundamentally designed to preserve the truth conditions of the sentence, and permissible transformations are ones that preserve truth. To illustrate, an active sentence can be related to a passive sentence by means of a set of transformations because they are assumed to share a common base or underlying structure. The equivalence between active and passive sentences is logical meaning: one sentence is true if and only if the other is true (see Harman, 1972; Lakoff, 1972).

My conjecture is that Chomsky's theory applies to a particular specialization of language, namely, the explicit written prose that serves as the primary tool of science and philosophy. It can serve as a theory of speech only when the sentence meaning is a fully adequate representation of the speaker's meaning. In ordinary conversational language this is rarely the case. The empirical studies mentioned earlier have provided strong evidence that experimental subjects rarely confine their interpretations to the information conventionalized in text. Rather, they treat a sentence as a cue to a more elaborate meaning.

As we have seen, other linguistic theories treat language as a means of representing and recovering the intentions of the speaker. The general semanticists and, to a lesser extent, Chafe, have argued that the linguistic system is not autonomous. The meaning of a sentence is not determined exclusively by the lexical and syntactic properties of the sentence itself; rather, the sentence is an indication of the speaker's meaning. While this assumption seems appropriate to the vast range of ordinary oral language, it overlooks the case in which the intended meaning is exactly represented by the sentence meaning as is ideally the case in explicit essayist prose.

We may conclude, then, that the controversy between the syntacticist and the semanticists is reducible to the alternative assumptions that language is appropriately represented in terms of sentence meanings or in terms of speaker's meanings. The latter assumption is entirely appropriate, I suggest, for the description of the ordinary oral conversational language, for what I have called utterances. On the other hand, I propose that Chomsky's theory is not a theory of language generally but a theory of a particular specialized form of language assumed by Luther, exploited by the British essayists, and formalized by the logical positivists. It is a model for the structure of autonomous written prose, for what I have called text.

On Comprehension

The comprehension of sentences involves several different processes. Ordinary conversational speech, especially children's speech, relies for its comprehension on a wide range of information beyond that explicitly marked in the language. To permit communication at all, there must be wide agreement among users of a language as to phonological, syntactic, and semantic conventions. A small set of language forms, however, maps onto an exceedingly wide range of referential events; hence, ambiguity is always possible if not inevitable. Speakers in face-to-face situations circumvent this ambiguity by means of such prosodic and paralinguistic cues as gesture, intonation, stress, quizzical looks, and restatement. Sentences in conversational contexts, then, are interpreted in terms of the following: agreed-upon lexical and syntactic conventions; a shared knowledge of events and a preferred way of interpreting them; a shared perceptual context; and agreed-upon prosodic features and paralinguistic conventions.

Written languages can have no recourse to shared context, prosodic features, or paralinguistic conventions since the preserved sentences have to be understood in contexts other than those in which they were written. The comprehension of such texts requires agreed-upon linguistic conventions, a shared knowledge of the world, and a preferred way of interpreting events. But Luther denied the dependence of text on a presupposed, commonsensical knowledge of the world, and I have tried to show that the linguistic style of the essayist has systematically attempted to minimize if not eliminate this dependence. This attempt has proceeded by assigning the information carried implicitly by nonlinguistic means into an enlarged set of explicit linguistic conventions. In this way written textual language can be richer and more explicit than its oral language counterpart. Within this genre of literature, if unconventionalized or nonlinguistic knowledge is permitted to intrude, we charge the writer with reasoning via unspecified inferences and assumptions or the reader with misreading the text.

Comprehension, therefore, may be represented by a set of procedures that involves selectively applying one's personal experiences or knowledge of the world to the surface structure of sentences to yield a meaning. In so doing, one elaborates, assimilates, or perhaps "imagines" the sentence. And these elaborative procedures are perfectly appropriate to the comprehension of ordinary conversational utterances. In turn, the sentence becomes more comprehensible and dramatically more memorable, as Anderson and Ortony (1975), Bransford and Johnson (1973), and Bransford, Barclay, and Franks (1972) have shown.

The price to be paid for such elaboration and assimilation is that the listener's or reader's meaning deviates to some degree from the meaning actually represented in the sentence. Such interpretation may alter the truth conditions specified by the statement. To illustrate, using Anderson and Ortony's sentence, if the statement "the apples are in the container" is interpreted as "the apples are in the basket," the interpretation specifies a different set of truth conditions than did the original statement. We could legitimately say that the statement had been misinterpreted. Yet that is what normally occurs in the process of understanding and remembering sentences; moreover, as we have shown in our laboratory, it is what preschool children regularly do (Olson & Nickerson, 1977; Pike & Olson, 1977; Hildyard & Olson, in preparation). If young children are given the statements, "John hit Mary" and "John has more than Mary," unlike adults, they are incapable of determining the direct logical implications that "Mary was hit by John" or "Mary has less than John." If the sentence is given out of context, they may inquire, "Who is Mary?" Given an appropriate story or pictorial context, children can assimilate the first statement to that context and then give a new description of what they now know. If the sentence cannot be assimilated to their knowledge base, they are helpless to arrive at its implications; children are unable to apply interpretive procedures to the sentence meaning, the meaning in the text. They can, however, use sentences as a cue to the speaker's meaning. if these sentences occur in an appropriate context. Literate adults are quite capable of treating sentences in either way. What they do presumably depends on whether the sentence is too long to be remembered verbatim, whether it is written and remains available for repeated consultation, or, perhaps, whether the sentence is regarded as utterance or text.

On Reasoning

Extending the argument to reasoning tasks, it is clear that solutions may be reached in either of two quite different ways. Relying on the processes usually involved in the comprehension of spoken language, one may interpret a premise in terms of previous knowledge of the world, operate on that resulting knowledge, and produce an answer other than that expected on a purely formal, logical basis. Such reasoning, based on an intrusion of unspecified knowledge, is not a logical argument but an enthymeme. Nevertheless, it is the most common form of ordinary reasoning (Cole, Gay, Glick, & Sharp, 1971; Wason & Johnson-Laird, 1972).

Logical reasoning, on the other hand, is the procedure of using conventionalized rules of language to draw necessary implications from statements treated as text. For such reasoning, the implications may run counter to expectancies or may be demonstrably false in their extension; however, it matters only that the conclusion follows directly from the sentence meaning, the conventionalized aspects of the statement itself. The fact that most people have difficulty with such operations indicates simply their inability or lack of experience in suspending prior knowledge and expectancies in order to honor the sentence meaning of statements. In fact, Henle (1962) has noted that in reasoning tasks subjects often have difficulty in distinguishing between a conclusion that is logically true, one that is factually true, and one with which they agree. According to the analysis offered here, in the first case the conclusion logically follows form the text — the meaning is restricted to that explicitly represented or conventionalized in the text and to the implications that necessarily follow; in the second case the conclusion follows from unstated but shared knowledge of the world; in the third case the conclusion follows from unspecified and unshared personal knowledge. I would argue that in neither of the latter cases are we justified in calling the reasoning logical.

Logical reasoning as defined here assumes that fully explicit, unambiguous statements can be created to serve as premises. This is a goal that consistently evades ordinary language use. It is extremely difficult if not impossible to create statements that specify all and only the necessary and sufficient information for drawing logical inferences.[3] Hence, formal reasoning has led to a reliance, where possible, on the use of symbols related by a logical calculus. To illustrate the difficulties, I will use three studies from our laboratory. Bracewell has shown that the simple propositional statement employed by Wason and Johnson-Laird (1970), "If p is on one side, then q is on the other," is ambiguous in at least two ways: "one side" may be interpreted as referring to "the showing side" or to "either the showing side or the hidden side"; "if . . . then" may be interpreted as a conditional relation or as a biconditional relation.[4] Differences in subjects' performance can be traced to different interpretations of the proposition. In a similar vein, Hidi has shown that if a simple proposition such as "if you go to Ottawa, you must travel by car" is understood as describing a temporal event, subjects draw quite different inferences than if it is treated purely as a logical statement.[5] In a developmental study, Ford (1976) has shown that, given a disjunctive statement, children (and adults in natural language contexts) treat "or" as posing a simple choice between mutually exclusive, disjoint alternatives (for example, "Do you want an apple *or* an orange?" "An apple"). When children of five or six years of age are presented with "or" commands involving disjoint events as well as overlapping and inclusive events — the latter being involved in Piaget's famous task "Are there more rabbits *or* animals?" — Ford found that children's logical competence breaks down only when the known structure of events runs counter to the presuppositions of the language. Rather than revise their conception of events — rabbits and animals are not disjoint classes — children misinterpret or reject the sentence. They say, for example, "There are more rabbits because there are only two ducks!"

There are, then, at least two aspects to the study of logical reasoning. The first stems from the fact that statements are often ambiguous, especially when they occur out of context. Thus failures in reasoning may reflect merely the assignment of an interpretation that, although it is consistent with the sentence meaning explicit in the text, is different from the one intended by the experimenter. Second, logical development in a literate culture involves learning to apply logical operations to the sentence meaning rather than to the assimilated or interpreted or assumed speaker's meaning.

Development consists of learning to confine interpretation to the meaning explicitly represented in the text and to draw inferences exclusively from that formal but restricted interpretation.

Whether or not all meaning can be made explicit in the text is perhaps less critical than the belief that it can and that making it so is a valid scientific enterprise. This was clearly the assumption of the essayists, and it continues in our use of language for science and philosophy. Explicitness of meaning, in other words, may be better thought of as a goal rather than an achievement. But it is a goal appropriate only for the particular, specialized use of language that I have called text.

On Learning a Language

The contrast between language as an autonomous system for representing meaning and language as a system dependent in every case upon nonlinguistic and paralinguistic cues for the sharing of intentions — the contrast between text and utterance — applies with equal force to the problem of language acquisition. A formal theory of sentence meaning, such as Chomsky's, provides a less appropriate description of early language than would a theory of intended meanings that admitted a variety of means for realizing those intentions. Such means include a shared view of reality, a shared perceptual context, and accompanying gestures, in addition to the speech signal. At early stages of language acquisition the meaning may be specified nonlinguistically, and this meaning may then be used to break the linguistic code (Macnamara, 1972; Nelson, 1974). Language acquisition, then, is primarily a matter of learning to conventionalize more and more of the meaning in the speech signal. This is not a sudden achievement. If an utterance specifies something different from what the child is entertaining, the sentence will often be misinterpreted (Clark, 1973; Donaldson & Lloyd, 1974). But language development is not simply a matter of progressively elaborating the oral mother tongue as a means of sharing intentions. The developmental hypothesis offered here is that the ability to assign a meaning to the sentence per se, independent of its nonlinguistic interpretive context, is achieved only well into the school years. It is a complex achievement to differentiate and operate upon either what is actually said, the sentence meaning, or what is meant, the speaker's meaning. Children are relatively quick to grasp a speaker's intentions but relatively slow, I suggest, to grasp the literal meaning of what is, in fact, said.

Several studies lend plausibility to these arguments. For example, Olson and Nickerson (1977) examined the role of story or pictorial context on the detection of sentence implications. Five-year-old children were given a statement and asked if a second statement, logically related to the first, was true. For instance, they were told, "John was hit by Mary," then asked, "Did Mary hit John?" The ability of these five-year-olds to answer such a question depended on how much they knew about the characters and context mentioned in the sentences. If they did not know who John and Mary were or why the experimenter was asking the question, they could not assign a full semantic interpretation to the sentence. This and other studies suggest that children, unlike adults, assign a speaker's meaning to a simple sentence if that sentence is contextually appropriate and directly assimilable to their prior knowledge, but they have difficulty assigning a meaning to the statement alone (Carpenter &

Just, 1975; Clark, 1974; Olson & Filby, 1972; Hildyard & Olson, in preparation). But by late childhood, at least among schooled children, meanings are assigned quite readily to the sentence per se. Children come to see that sentences have implications that are necessary by virtue of sentence meaning itself. They become progressively more able to exist in a purely linguistically specified, hypothetical world for both purposes of extracting logical implications of statements and of living in those worlds that, as Ricoeur (1973) notes, are opened up by texts. This, however, is the end point of development in a literate culture and not a description of how original meanings are acquired in early language learning.

On Reading

The relations between utterances and texts become acute when children are first confronted with printed books. As I have pointed out, children are familiar with using the spoken utterance as one cue among others. Children come to school with a level of oral competence in their mother tongue only to be confronted with an exemplar of written text, the reader, which is an autonomous representation of meaning. Ideally, the printed reader depends on no cues other than linguistic cues; it represents no intentions other than those represented in the text; it is addressed to no one in particular; its author is essentially anonymous; and its meaning is precisely that represented by the sentence meaning. As a result, when children are taught to read, they are learning both to read and to treat language as text. Children familiar with the use of textlike language through hearing printed stories obviously confront less of a hurdle than those for whom both reading and that form of language are novel.

The decoding approach to reading exploits both the explicit nature of the alphabet and the explicit nature of written prose text. Ideally, since the meaning is in the text, the programmatic analysis of letters, sounds, words, and grammar would specify sentence meaning. But, as I have indicated, it is precisely with sentence meaning that children have the most difficulty. Hence, the decoding of sentence meaning should be treated as the end point of development, not as the means of access to print as several writers have maintained (Reid, 1966; Richards, 1971).

ON LANGUAGE AND MEANING: SUMMARY AND CONCLUSIONS

Clearly some aspects of meaning must be sufficiently conventionalized in the language to permit children and adults to use it as an all-purpose instrument. Thus, children must learn grammatical rules and lexical structure to use language in different contexts for different purposes. However, the degree to which this linguistic knowledge is conventionalized and formalized need not be very great in oral contexts since the listener has access to a wide range of information with which to recover the speaker's intentions. Generally, nonlinguistic cues appear to predominate in that if the speaker is elliptical or even chooses the wrong word or grammatical form, we can successfully recover the speaker's intention.

To serve the requirements of written language, however, all of the information relevant to the communication of intention must be present in the text. Further, if the text is to permit or sustain certain conclusions, as in the essayist technique, then it must become an autonomous representation of meaning. But for this purpose the meanings of the terms and the logical relations holding between them must be brought to a much higher degree of conventionalization. Words must be defined in terms of other words in the linguistic system, and rules of grammar must be specialized to make them suitable indications of the text's underlying logical structure. Once this degree of conventionalization is achieved, children or adults have sufficient basis for constructing the meaning explicitly represented by the text. Written text, I am suggesting, is largely responsible for permitting people to entertain sentence meaning per se rather than merely using the sentence as a cue to the meaning entertained by the speaker.

The differences between utterances and texts may be summarized in terms of three underlying principles: the first pertains to meaning, the second to truth, and the third to function. First, in regard to meaning, utterance and text relate in different ways to background knowledge and to the criteria for successful performance. Conventional utterances appeal for their meaning to shared experiences and interpretations, that is, to a common intuition based on shared commonsense knowledge (Lonergan, 1957; Schutz & Luckmann, 1973). Utterances take for content, to use Pope's words, "What oft was tho't but ne'er so well expressed" (cited in Ong, 1971, p. 256). In most speech, as in poetry and literature, the usual reaction is assent — "How true." Statements match, in an often tantalizing way, the expectancies and experiences of the listener. Because of this appeal to expectancies, the criterion for a successful utterance is understanding on the part of the listener. The sentence is not appropriate if the listener does not comprehend. A well-formed sentence fits the requirements of the listener and, as long as this criterion is met, it does not really matter what the speaker says –- "A wink is as good as a nod."

Prose text, on the other hand, appeals to premises and rules of logic for deriving implications. Whether or not the premise corresponds to common sense is irrelevant. All that is critical is that the premises are explicit and the inferences correctly drawn. The appeal is formal rather than intuitive. As a consequence, the criterion for the success of a statement in explicit prose text is its formal structure; if the text is formally adequate and the reader fails to understand, that is the reader's problem. The meaning is in the text.

Second, utterance and text appeal to different conceptions of truth. Frye (1971) has termed these underlying assumptions "truth as wisdom" and "truth as correspondence." Truth in oral utterance has to do with truth as wisdom. A statement is true if it is reasonable, plausible, and, as we have seen, congruent with dogma or the wisdom of elders; truth is assimilability to common sense. Truth in prose text, however, has to do with the correspondence between statements and observations. Truth drops its ties to wisdom and to values, becoming the product of the disinterested search of the scientist. True statements in text may be counter to intuition, common sense, or authority. A statement is taken to be true not because the premises from which it follows are in agreement with common sense but rather because true implications follow from it, as Russell (1940) pointed out in regard to mathematics.

Third, conversational utterance and prose text involve different alignments of the functions of language. As Austin (1962) and Halliday (1970) argue, any utterance serves at least two functions simultaneously — the rhetorical or interpersonal function and the logical or ideational function. In oral speech, the interpersonal function is primary; if a sentence is inappropriate to a particular listener, the utterance is a failure. In written text, the logical or ideational functions become primary, presumably because of the indirect relation between writer and reader. The emphasis, therefore, can shift from simple communication to truth, to "getting it right" (Olson, 1977). It may be this realignment of functions in written language that brings about the greater demand for explicitness and the higher degree of conventionalization.

The bias of written language toward providing definitions, making all assumptions and premises explicit, and observing the formal rules of logic produces an instrument of considerable power for building an abstract and coherent theory of reality. The development of this explicit, formal system accounts, I have argued, for the predominant features of Western culture and for our distinctive ways of using language and our distinctive modes of thought. Yet the general theories of science and philosophy that are tied to the formal uses of text provide a poor fit to daily, ordinary, practical, and personally significant experience. Oral language with its depth of resources and its multitude of paths to the same goal, while an instrument of limited power for exploring abstract ideas, is a universal means of sharing our understanding of concrete situations and practical actions. Moreover, it is the language children bring to school. Schooling, particularly learning to read, is the critical process in the transformation of children's language from utterance to text.

NOTES

1. I am indebted to Frank Smith for pointing out that I use the phrase "the meaning is in the text" as a metaphor for describing language in which the meaning is fully conventionalized.
2. The hypothesis of autonomous meaning of sentences, that is, the assumption that the meaning is in the text, may simply reflect the presupposition that linguistics, as a discipline, is autonomous.
3. This question touches upon the important epistemological issue of the formal adequacy of the methods of science. The most common argument is that almost any important theory can be shown to be formally inadequate (see Gellner, 1975).
4. R. J. Bracewell, "Interpretation Factors in the Four-Card Selection Task," Paper presented at the Selection Task Conference, Trento, Italy, April 1974.
5. S. Hidi, "Effects of Temporal Considerations in Conditional Reasoning," Paper presented at the Selection Task Conference, Trento, Italy, April 1974.

REFERENCES

Anderson, R. C., & Ortony, A. (1975). On putting apples into bottles: A problem of polysemy. *Cognitive Psychology, 7,* 167–180.

Austin, J. L. (1962). *How to do things with words* (J. O. Urmson, Ed.). New York: Oxford University Press.

Barclay, J. R. (1973). The role of comprehension in remembering sentences. *Cognitive Psychology, 4,* 229–254.

Bloom, L. (1979). *Language development: Form and function in emerging grammars.* Cambridge, MA: MIT Press.

Bloomfield, L. (1939). *Linguistic aspects of science.* Chicago: University of Chicago Press.

Bluck, R. S. (1949). *Plato's life and thought.* London: Routledge & Kegan Paul.

Bransford, J. D., Barclay, J. R., & Franks, J. J. (1972). Sentence memory: A constructive versus interpretive approach. *Cognitive Psychology, 3,* 193–209.

Bransford, J. D., & Johnson, M. K. (1973). Consideration of some problems of comprehension. In W. Chase (Ed.), *Visual information processing.* New York: Academic Press.

Brown, R. (1973). *A first language: The early stages.* Cambridge, MA: Harvard University Press.

Bruner, J. S. (1973). From communication to language: A psychological perspective. *Cognition, 3,* 255–287.

Bruner, J. S., & Olson, D. R. (in press). Symbols and texts as the tools of intellect. In *The Psychology of the 20th Century, Vol. VII: Piaget's developmental and cognitive psychology within an extended context.* Zurich: Kindler.

Buhler, K. (1934). *Sprachtheorie.* Jena, Germany: Gustav Fischer Verlag.

Carpenter, P., & Just, M. (1975). Sentence comprehension: A psycholinguistic processing model of verification. *Psychological Review, 82,* 45–73.

Carroll, J. B., & Chall, J. S. (Eds.) (1975). *Toward a literate society.* New York: McGraw-Hill.

Chafe, W. (1970). *Meaning and the structure of language.* Chicago: University of Chicago Press.

Chall, J. S. (1967). *Learning to read: The great debate.* New York: McGraw-Hill.

Chase, S. (1954). *The power of words.* New York: Harcourt, Brace.

Chomsky, N. (1957). *Syntactic structures.* The Hague: Mouton.

Chomsky, N. (1965). *Aspects of a theory of syntax.* Cambridge, MA: MIT Press.

Chomsky, N. (1972). *Problems of knowledge and freedom.* London: Fontana.

Clark, E. (1973). Non-linguistic strategies and the acquisition of word meanings. *Cognition, 2,* 161–182.

Clark, H. H. (1974). Semantics and comprehension. In T. A. Sebeok (Ed.). *Current trends in linguistics. Vol. 12: Linguistic and adjacent arts and sciences.* The Hague: Mouton.

Cole, M., Gay, J., Glick, J., & Sharp, D. (1971). *The cultural context of learning and thinking.* New York: Basic Books.

de Laguna, G. (1970). *Speech: Its function and development.* College Park, MD: McGrath. (Original work published 1927)

Donaldson, M., & Lloyd, P. (1974). Sentences and situations: Children's judgments of match and mismatch. In F. Bresson (Ed.), *Current problems in psycholinguistics.* Paris: Editions du Centre National de la Recherche Scientifique.

Ellul, J. (1964). *The technological society.* New York: Vintage Books.

Fodor, J. A., Bever, T. G., & Garrett, M. F. (1974). *The psychology of language.* Toronto: McGraw-Hill.

Ford, W. G. (1976). *The language of disjunction.* Unpublished doctoral dissertation, University of Toronto.

Frye, N. (1971). *The critical path.* Bloomington: Indiana University Press.

Gadamer, H. G. (1975). *Truth and method.* New York: Seabury Press.

Gelb, I. J. (1952). *A study of writing.* Toronto: University of Toronto Press.

Gellner, E. (1975). Book review of *Against Method* by P. Feyerabend. *British Journal for the Philosophy of Science, 26,* 331–342.

Gibson, E. J., & Levin, H. (1975). *The psychology of reading.* Cambridge, MA: MIT Press.

Gombrich, E. (1974). The visual image. In D. R. Olson (Ed.), *Media and symbols: The forms of expression, communication and education* (The 73rd Yearbook of the National Society for the Study of Education). Chicago: University of Chicago Press.

Goodman, K. S. (1967). Reading: A psycholinguistic guessing game. *Journal of the Reading Specialist, 6,* 126–135.

Goodman, N. (1968). *Languages of art: An approach to a theory of symbols.* Indianapolis: Bobbs-Merrill.

Goodnow, J. (1976). The nature of intelligent behavior: Questions raised by cross-cultural studies. In L. Resnick (Ed.), *New approaches to intelligence*. Potomac, MD: Erlbaum and Associates.

Goody, J., & Watt, I. (1968). The consequences of literacy. In J. Goody (Ed.), *Literacy in traditional societies*. Cambridge, Eng.: Cambridge University Press.

Gray, M. (1973). *Song and dance man: The art of Bob Dylan*. London: Abacus.

Greenfield, P. (1972). Oral and written language: The consequences for cognitive development in Africa, the United States, and England. *Language and Speech, 15*, 169–178.

Greenfield, P., & Bruner, J. S. (1969). Culture and cognitive growth. In D. A. Goslin (Ed.), *Handbook of socialization: Theory and research*. Chicago: Rand-McNally.

Grice, H. P. (1957). Meaning. *Philosophical Review, 66*, 377–388.

Halliday, M. A. K. (1970). Language structure and language function. In J. Lyons (Ed.), *New horizons in linguistics*. New York: Penguin Books.

Harman, G. (1972). Deep structure as logical form. In D. Davidson & G. Harman (Eds.), *Semantics of natural language*. Dordrecht, Holland: Reidel.

Havelock, E. (1963). *Preface to Plato*. Cambridge, MA: Harvard University Press.

Havelock, E. (1973). Prologue to Greek literacy. *Lectures in memory of Louise Tatt Semple, second series, 1966–1971*. Cincinnati: University of Oklahoma Press for the University of Cincinnati Press.

Havelock, E. (1976). *Origins of Western literacy*. Toronto: Ontario Institute for Studies in Education.

Hayakawa, S. I. (1952). *Language in thought and action*. London: Allen and Unwin.

Henle, M. (1962). On the relation between logic and thinking. *Psychological Review, 63*, 366–378.

Hildyard, A., & Olson, D. R. (in preparation). *On the mental representation and matching operation of action and passive sentences by children and adults*.

Inhelder, B., & Piaget, J. (1958). *The growth of logical thinking*. New York: Basic Books.

Innis, H. (1951). *The bias of communication*. Toronto: University of Toronto Press.

Kneale, W., & Kneale, M. (1962). *The development of logic*. Oxford, Eng.: Clarendon Press.

Korzybski, A. (1933). *Science and sanity: An introduction to non-Aristotelian systems and general semantics*. Lancaster, PA: Science Press.

Lakoff, G. (1972). Linguistics and natural logic. In D. Davidson & G. Harman (Eds.), *Semantics of natural language*. Dordrecht, Holland: Reidel.

Locke, J. (1880). *Some thoughts concerning education* (Introduction and Notes by R. H. Quick). Cambridge, Eng.: Cambridge University Press.

Locke, J. (1961). *An essay concerning human understanding* (J. W. Yolton, Ed.). London: Dent. (Original work published 1690)

Lonergan, B. J. F. (1957). *Insight: A study of human understanding*. New York: Philosophical Library.

Lord, A. B. (1960). *The singer of tales* (Harvard Studies in Comparative Literature, 24). Cambridge, MA: Harvard University Press.

Lyons, J. (1969). *Introduction to theoretical linguistics*. Cambridge, Eng.: Cambridge University Press.

Macnamara, J. (1972). The cognitive basis of language learning in infants. *Psychological Review, 79*, 1–13.

Maimonides, M. (1963). *Guide of the perplexed* (S. Pines, Trans.). Chicago: University of Chicago Press.

McLuhan, M. (1962). *The Gutenberg galaxy*. Toronto: University of Toronto Press.

McLuhan, M. (1964). *Understanding media: The extensions of man*. Toronto: McGraw-Hill.

McNeill, D. (1970). *The acquisition of language*. New York: Harper & Row.

Neimark, E. D., & Slotnick, N. S. (1970). Development of the understanding of logical connectives. *Journal of Educational Psychology, 61*, 451–460.

Nelson, K. (1974). Concept, word, and sentence: Interrelations in acquisition and development. *Psychological Review, 81*, 267–285.

Olson, D. R. (1977). The languages of instruction. In R. Spiro (Ed.), *Schooling and the acquisition of knowledge*. Potomac, MD: Erlbaum and Associates.

Olson, D. R., & Filby, N. (1972). On the comprehension of active and passive sentences. *Cognitive Psychology, 3*, 361–381.

Olson, D. R., & Nickerson, N. (1977). The contexts of comprehension: Children's inability to draw implications from active and passive sentences. *Journal of Experimental Child Psychology, 23,* 402–414.

Ong, W. J. (1958). *Ramus, method and the decay of dialogue.* Cambridge, MA: Harvard University Press. (Reprinted by Octagon Books, 1974)

Ong, W. J. (1971). *Rhetoric, romance and technology: Studies in the interaction of expression and culture.* Ithaca: Cornell University Press.

Paris, S. G., & Carter, A. Y. (1973). Semantic and constructive aspects of sentence memory in children. *Developmental Psychology, 9,* 109–113.

Parry, M. (1971). The making of Homeric verse. In A. Parry (Ed.), *The collected papers of Milman Parry.* Oxford, Eng.: Clarendon Press.

Piaget, J. (1972). Intellectual evolution from adolescence to adulthood. *Human Development, 15,* 1–12.

Pike, R., & Olson, D. R. (1977). A question of *more* or *less. Child Development, 48,* 579–586.

Popper, K. (1972). *Objective knowledge: An evolutionary approach.* Oxford, Eng.: Clarendon Press.

Reid, J. F. (1966). Learning to think about reading. *Educational Research, 9,* 56–62.

Richards, I. A. (1971). Instructional engineering. In S. Baker, J. Barzun, & I. A. Richards (Eds.), *The written word.* Rowley, MA: Newbury House.

Ricoeur, P. (1973). Creativity in language: Word, polysemy and metaphor. *Philosophy Today, 17,* 97–111.

Russell, B. (1940). *An inquiry into meaning and truth.* London: Allen & Unwin.

Scribner, S., & Cole, M. (1973). Cognitive consequences of formal and informal education. *Science, 182,* 553–559.

Schutz, A., & Luckmann, T. (1973). *The structures of the life world* (R. Zaner & H. Engelhardt, Trans.). Evanston, IL: Northwestern University Press.

Smith, F. (1975). *Comprehension and learning.* Toronto: Holt, Rinehart & Winston.

Sprat, T. (1966). *History of the Royal Society of London for the improving of natural knowledge.* (J. I. Cope and H. W. Jones, Eds.). St. Louis: Washington University Press. (Original work published 1667)

Staudenmayer, H. (1975). Understanding conditional reasoning with meaningful propositions. In R. J. Falmagne (Ed.), *Reasoning, representation and process.* Hillsdale, NJ: Erlbaum and Associates.

Strawson, P. F. (1970). *Meaning and truth: An inaugural lecture delivered before the University of Oxford.* Oxford, Eng.: Clarendon Press.

Suppes, P., & Feldman, S. (1971). Young children's comprehension of logical connectives. *Journal of Experimental Child Psychology, 12,* 304–317.

Taplin, J. E., & Staudenmayer, H. (1973). Interpretation of abstract conditional sentences in deductive reasoning. *Journal of Verbal Learning and Verbal Behavior, 12,* 530–542.

Wason, P. C., & Johnson-Laird, P. N. (1970). A conflict between selecting and evaluating information in an inferential task. *British Journal of Psychology, 61,* 509–515.

Wason, P. C., & Johnson-Laird, P. N. (1972). *The psychology of reasoning.* London: B. T. Batsford.

An early version of this paper was presented to the Epistemics meeting at Vanderbilt University, Nashville, Tennessee, in February 1974, and published in R. Diez-Guerrero and H. Fisher, eds., *Logic and Language in Personality and Society* (New York: Academic Press, 1978).

I am extremely grateful to the Canada Council, the Spencer Foundation, and the Van Leer Jerusalem Foundation for their support at various stages of completing this paper. I am also indebted to the many colleagues who commented on the earlier draft, including Roy Pea, Nancy Nickerson, Angela Hildyard, Bob Bracewel, Edmund Sullivan, and Frank Smith. I would also like to thank Mary Macri who assisted with the clerical aspects of the manuscript and Isobel Gibb, Reference Librarian at OISE, who assisted with the reference editing.

Literacy and Language:
Relationships
during the Preschool Years

CATHERINE E. SNOW

T wenty years ago it was something of a commonplace to suggest that working-
class and minority children were deficient in language ability when compared
to middle-class, mainstream children. During the last two decades, however,
considerable effort has been expended to demonstrate that, although working-class
and minority children may use language differently from middle-class children, they
are not deficient in language ability. Their language is as complex and their mastery
of language as complete as it is for middle-class children (Dittmar, 1976; Edwards,
1976; Miller, 1982).

The conclusion that working-class children are different, not deficient, has not,
however, been extended from language ability to literacy. Social-class differences in
reading achievement are large and reliable (reviewed in Anastasiow, Hanes, & Hanes,
1982; Coleman, Campbell, Hobson, McPartland, Mood, Weinfeld, & York, 1966;
DeStefano, 1978; Stubbs, 1980). They have not been eliminated by *Sesame Street*,
Headstart, Follow Through, or other interventions aimed at poor and minority populations (Carnoy, 1976; Kennedy, 1978; Rivlin & Timpane, 1975; Stearns, 1971),
even though lasting effects of intervention on other aspects of school achievement
and school competence have been found (Lazar & Darlington, 1982).

The persistence of social-class differences in reading achievement is puzzling in
light of (1) the widespread assumption that language and literacy are closely related
skills (Cazden, in press; DeStefano, 1978; Loban, 1963; Simons, 1970; Shuy, 1981)
and (2) the evidence that there are no social-class differences in language skill.
Clearly, reading is a form of language use. Reading ability is highly correlated with
measures of language skill such as vocabulary (Davis, 1974; Farr, 1969; Spearitt,
1972; Thorndike, 1974-1975; Yap, 1979), tests of grammatical knowledge (Dale &
Chall, in press; Simons, 1970), and a metalinguistic awareness, the ability to reflect
upon and talk about linguistic forms (Menyuk & Flood, 1981; Salus, 1982). Why
then, if there are no social-class differences in language ability, do we find such differences in reading and other literacy skills?

Harvard Educational Review Vol. 53 No. 2 May 1983, 165–189

The answer to this question might be that literacy and language, though related, are in fact very different skills, and thus differently distributed in the population. If literacy is sufficiently different from language that its course of development is subject to a different set of influences, then a much greater degree of variation in literacy skill than in language skill could result.

This chapter first will argue that such an explanation is not correct and that, in fact, literacy and oral language are very similar and closely related skills that are acquired in much the same way. This argument rests on a demonstration of the many similarities between language and literacy during their acquisition. The second section will examine the major alternative explanation for social-class differences in reading achievement, that the level of literacy in the home predicts literacy skill, and will reject this argument as well. Finally, the third section will propose a reanalysis of the demands made on children during literacy activities, in an attempt to identify more exactly the nature of the failure of those children who do not progress in the acquisition of literacy.

LANGUAGE AND LITERACY DEFINED

The tendency in recent research on literacy (Olson, 1977; Scollon & Scollon, 1982; Tannen, 1982) is to emphasize the degree to which literacy is continuous with language, and to point out the ubiquity of literacy experiences in children's lives. Since this tendency has led to some blurring of the meaning of the terms *oral language* and *literacy*, it is important to define these terms precisely. By literacy, I mean the activities and skills associated directly with the use of print — primarily reading and writing, but also such derivative activities as playing Scrabble or Boggle, doing crossword puzzles, alphabetizing files, and copying or typing. Oral language refers simply to all oral forms of communication, speaking, and listening. Thus, I would reject such formulations as Scollon and Scollon's literate two-year-old (1982) to refer to a child who uses orally some of the conventions normally associated with written stories, or Tannen's description of literate conversational styles (1982). It seems to me that such uses of the term "literate" confuse frequently co-occurring but noncriterial characteristics of literate activities with the crucial defining feature of literacy, the use of print.

PARALLELS BETWEEN LANGUAGE AND LITERACY
IN DEVELOPMENT

Complexity of the System

Learning to read and learning to talk are both challenging tasks, in part because the systems that must be acquired are complex. Furthermore, both domains require a complex mapping of form onto meaning. Expert levels of performance in both domains require the knowledge and ability to honor, purely for the sake of correctness, conventions that are not derived from the semantic or communicative system. That learning language and learning literacy are complex tasks is evident in the length of time it takes children to master them and in the amount of concentrated effort, investment of energy, and frustration at failure both tasks occasion.

Maturational Limitations

No one could reasonably deny that the course of maturation plays a major role in the development of language and literacy. There is an age below which children have considerable difficulty learning to talk or to read — though for reading this age may be considerably lower than proponents of "reading readiness" are prepared to admit. The process of learning language is fairly slow and painful for the one-year-old and is considerably faster and easier for the older child (Snow & Hoefnagel-Höhle, 1978). Similarly, though it is clearly possible to teach a two-year-old to read, a six-year-old can be brought to the same level of reading skill in considerably less time. The finding that children with organic learning disabilities that slow the course of reading acquisition also show language disabilities (for example, Bannatyne, 1971) underlines the degree to which the state of the brain can influence the course of development of both language and literacy.

Centrality of Social Interaction and Communicative Needs to Development

Ten years ago, it was commonly assumed that syntactic development could be treated independently of pragmatic and semantic development. Today, however, no one would deny that language development can be understood only as an aspect of the development of communication in general, and only in the context of the child's interactions.

Learning to read has traditionally been seen as a cognitive problem — something children have to solve on their own, inside their own heads. Only recently has reading been treated as a social phenomenon — one that often occurs by and in groups (Bloome, 1981), and that is intrinsically embedded in the culture of its users (Heath, 1980). Many examples could be given to demonstrate that the social nature of the reading process is especially potent during the earliest stages of its acquisition. This chapter presents a few examples from one child, Nathaniel, in interaction with his mother, which demonstrate the relevance of three characteristics of social interaction in literacy acquisition and training — semantic, contingency, scaffolding, and accountability procedures.[1]

It is well demonstrated (Cross, 1978; Wells, 1980) that a major facilitator of language acquisition is *semantic contingency* in adult speech. Adult utterances are semantically contingent if they continue topics introduced by the child's preceding utterances. Semantically contingent utterances thus include: 1) expansions, which are limited to the content of the previous child utterance; 2) semantic extensions, which add new information to the topic; 3) clarifying questions, which demand clarification of the child utterance; and 4) answers to child questions. Topic initiations by adult speakers and attempts to switch the topic from the one introduced by the child constitute semantically noncontingent speech, and the frequency of such utterances in parents' speech correlates negatively with children's gains in language ability.

The notion of semantic contingency can be applied to the literacy domain as well. Examples of semantic contingency to literacy behaviors would include answering questions about letter and number names, answering questions about words, reading out loud on request, answering questions about pictures in books, carrying on coherent conversations with children about the pictures and text in books, and giving help with writing when requested. Semantic contingency to literacy-related behaviors seems to be associated with early acquisition of literacy. All of these literacy-contingent behaviors are typical of middle-class families, and they have been identified (Clark, 1976; Durkin, 1966; Söderbergh, 1971) as instrumental in producing preschool readers.

Parts of the lengthy exchange between Nathaniel at 31 months and his mother presented in Table 1 demonstrate many of these characteristics of semantic contingency (marked with a +). Nathaniel's mother had been proposing a trip to the playground but dropped that discussion when Nathaniel sat down at his playschool desk, picked up a magnetized plastic M, and said, "Put it on the board" (line 1). In the subsequent conversation his mother asked him to name the symbols he picked up (lines 6, 15, 18); repeated and confirmed his correct labels for symbols (lines 4, 22, 62, 80); corrected his errors (line 33); provided labels if he did not know them (lines 8, 33); and helped to accomplish tasks of finding letters (lines 42, 43, 44, 45, 47, 50, 52, 53, 54), finding number sequences (lines 72, 73, 75, 77, 78, 80), and creating letter sequences (lines 64-69). It is clear, though, that large chunks of Nathaniel's mother's speech in Table 1 are not semantically contingent. She introduced their major literacy task herself (spelling *Nathaniel*, line 34) and persisted with it rather than following his lead in other directions. In the conversation that continued from the one in Table 1 she twice even interrupted his concentration on the letters to clean out his ears!

Nathaniel's mother also demonstrates another commonly noted feature of language facilitation, *scaffolding*. Scaffolding (Bruner, 1978) refers to the steps taken to reduce the degrees of freedom in carrying out some task, so that the child can concentrate on the difficult skill he is in the process of acquiring. In interaction with younger children, for example, mothers may rearrange the pieces of a puzzle so they are right-side up or steady the bottom blocks in a tower so that the child can successfully continue the task. Nathaniel's mother extensively scaffolds the rather difficult task of spelling *Nathaniel* by reminding him of what they are doing, rejecting false starts (line 42), and guiding the letter search. She also rearranges the letters on the desk so he can find the required ones more easily.[2]

A more consistently semantically contingent interaction occurred between Nathaniel and his mother the evening of the same day (see Table 2), when he again sat down at his desk just after getting ready for bed. (At 31 months, Nathaniel was well aware that literacy activities were better bets for postponing bedtime than other types of play.) This time he introduced the task of spelling *Nathaniel* (line 87) after completing his other chosen task of spelling *Lia*. His mother did not respond immediately to his switch to *Nathaniel* because she was intent on holding him accountable for completion of the prior task, insisting that he repeat the spelling of *Lia* and "read" *Lia* before moving on. It is interesting to note that Nathaniel did not understand "you

TABLE 1

Semantic Contingency in a Literacy-Focused Interaction between
Nathaniel (31 Months) and His Mother

Line	Nathaniel	Mother
1	put it on the board	
2		*what's that
3	Mmmmm	
4		*Mmmmm
5		*put the M on the board
	(N picks up an 8)	
6		*what's that?
7	dat	
8		*eight
9	eight	
10		*that's a number
11	number	
12	rectangle	
13		+a rectangle
14		+that's a shape
	(N picks up a 2)	
15		*what's that?
16	that?	
17	is it?	
18		*what is it?
19	is it?	
20		*have you forgotten that one?
21	a two	
22		*two, that's right
	(N hiccups)	
23		+ you've got the hiccups
24	mommy have hiccups?	
25	stays up	
26		+stays up, yeah
27		+mommy gonna help, okay?
28	stays up	
29		+stay up
30	there's Nathaniel	
	(pointing to number sequence)	
31		*where's Nathaniel?
32	there's Nathaniel	
33		*that's not . . . this says # 1 2 3 4 5 6 7 8 9 10
34		*shall we make it say Nathaniel?
35		*do you want it to say Nathaniel?
36		*have to find the right letters
37		*find me an A
38	enne find a Z	
39	find a Z	
40		*is that a Z?
41		*you gonna put the Z up?
42		*okay, there's no Z in Nathaniel though let's see, here's an N and there's another N, Nathaniel, we need that
43		here's an l
44		here's a better l
45		we need an E
46	need E	

TABLE 1 *(continued)*

Line	Nathaniel	Mother
47		and we need a T and an H here's . . . here's an H
48	T	
49	H	
50		and . . . there's an L
51	L	
52		what else do we need?
53		can we put this in, pretend this is an A?
54		N A
55	this like that	
56		*you want to put that like that?
57		*okay
58		*that's not part of Nathaniel, you understand. Well, Nathaniel, I can't find all the letters we need
59		we need a T
60		where's the T?
61	here's the T	
62		*there's the T
63		oh, you found one
64		N A T H
65		we need another pretend A
66		here's another pretend A
67		A N I E L
68		spells Nathaniel
69		isn't that good?
70	enne do it	
71	enne do it 1 2 3	
72		*you can see where there's 1 2 3
73		*look, look, what does this say?
74	1 2 3	
75		*4 5 6
76	4 1 2 3 more	
77		*7 8 9 10
78		*right there it says that
79	enne do X	
80		*X

Note: + Semantically contingent response
* Semantically contingent response to a literacy-related behavior or utterance

read it" with reference to a word. He responded "(have to?) read de book te see Lia" and "read the book to Lia" (lines 89, 91), revealing his understanding of reading as an activity related to books, not to words.

Note in Table 2 the ambiguity in several cases about the status of maternal utterances as semantically contingent (marked with a ?). Many of the mother's comments fail to be semantically contingent to Nathaniel's immediately preceding remarks because she is persisting with the higher-order task of getting something spelled or read. The status of such deviations from utterance-by-utterance semantic contingency is unclear within Cross's (1978) or Wells's (1980) formulation of the semantic contingency hypothesis. However, Dore (in press) deals very well with such maternal behav-

TABLE 2

Semantic Contingency Limited by Accountability Procedures
(Nathaniel, 31 Months)

Line	Nathaniel	Mother
1	wanna spell Lia	
2		*you wanna what?
3	eh wanna spell Nathaniel	
4		*you wanna spell Nathaniel
5	eh wanna spell Lia	
6		*you wanna spell Lia
7		*okay
8		*what does Lia start with?
9	Lia starts with a N	
10		*no, Nathaniel starts with an N
11		*Lia starts with an L
12	Lia starts with a O	
13		*no, with an L
14		*not an O, an L
15	put the O up there de . . .	
16		*okay, we don't need an O
17		?have to find an L
18	de eh T I need a T either	
19		*don't need the T either, no
20	I need . . . I no moon	
21		*no, we don't need a moon either, no
22		?let's see
23		?let's put these things up here that we don't need
24		?cuz we don't need those, and maybe we'll find an L
25		?while we're looking
26	looking	
27		?see if you can find an L
28	eh . . . there's a T for to put it up there	
29		*no, we don't need a T
30	don't need the T	
31		*don't need the T
32	don't need to need that	
33		*what's that?
34	don't need that eiger	
35	don't need the big I	
36		*don't need the big I
37		*that's right
38	oh . . . dis doesn't work	
39		+that doesn't work?
40		+oh
41		+there
42	that doesn't work up there	
43		?are you looking for an L, Nathaniel?
44		?can you see an L?
45	I o . . . I don't know eh that Nathaniel is	
46		*you don't know what that is
47		*that's a number
48		*that says 4
49	I don't de dat spell Lia with a 4	
50		*no, you don't spell Lia with a 4, that's right

TABLE 2   *(continued)*

Line	Nathaniel	Mother
51		?why don't you see if you can find the L
52	iiii	
53	I find another 4	
54		*that's right, that is another 4
55		?see any L's yet?
56	this uh . . . this uh . . . this a O	
57		*that's an O
58	this uh . . . this uh . . . who's this?	
59	who de do like that(?)	
60	do dit on de dat	
61		?put your glasses on when you read, you can see better
62		?but we're looking for L's, Nathaniel
63		?we need the L's
64		?where are the L's
65	where's the L's?	
66		*see any L's?
67	this the L's	
68		*ooohh
69		*oh, there's an L
70		*put an L up, for spelling Lia
71		*very good
72	put the other L up spelling Lia with the other	
73		?now we need . . . we need an I, Nathaniel
74		?where's an I
75	eh enne need a other I	
76		*put the I over there
77		?I, I and now we need an A
78		*oh, you found it
79		*put it right next
80		*put it next to the I
81	that's an A	
82		*that's an A
83		?put it next to the I
84		?the other side
85		?oh, Lia
86		?that spells Lia
87	enne spells Nathaniel now	
88		listen, how do you spell Lia? you read it
89	(have to?) read de book te see Lia	
90		what does that say?
91	read the book to Lia	
92		it's just a letter, it's just a word
93		you spell it L I A
94		okay, Nathaniel, we're just going to spell Nathaniel, and then after that Nathaniel goes to bed
95	L O (?)	
96		?what do we need for Nathaniel?
97	enne need the S *(shaking head)*	
98		*you don't need the S for Nathaniel, no
99		?what do you need
100	eh put dit up dere	
101		*okay, what do you need for Nathaniel?

TABLE 2 *(continued)*

Line	Nathaniel	Mother
102		*what letter?
103	enne need de N	
104		*you do need the N, that's right
105		*put the N up
106		?what else do we need for Nathaniel?
107	need eh need de other I	
108		*that's right, we do
109		*you put that up there too
110		?what else do we need?
111	need the circle	
112		+no
113	put the circle right there	
114		?here, we need this L
115		?put that L over there
116	put the put the L right there	
117		*yeah, we put that L up there cuz we're gonna need that L
118	enne put the O right there	
119		?for spelling . . .
120		?but you don't need an O, Nathaniel
121		?don't need an O for spelling Nathaniel
122		?better take the O away
123		?okay, now we need an . . . here, we need this A
124		?and we need a T
125		?can you find a T?
126	enne find de other T	
127		*can you find a T?
128		*oh, very good
129		?you put that T right next to the A
130		?turn it upright . . . turn it right side up
131		?that's right
132		?and now we need an H
133		?can you find an H?
134	find de M	
135		?we don't need an M
136	that's an M	
137		*yeah, but we don't need an M
138		?no M in Nathaniel
	(puts down M)	
139		*that's right
140		?we need an H
141		?find an H
142	dere's de H dere's de H	
143		*there's an H
144		*can you put the H right next to the T?
	(does so)	
145		*very good
146		?now we need another A, and that's a problem cuz we don't have another A
147		?but you know what we always use for that
148	eh use de N eh de dat	
149		*no, we use a little triangle for an A
150		?okay, now we need another N
151		?see another?

TABLE 2   *(continued)*

Line	Nathaniel	Mother
152	see another N	
153		*see another N?
154		*look in your desk
155	see another N either	
156		*well I think there's one if you look around
157		*look in your desk
158	this uh there's another N	
159		*there's an N
160		?okay, you put that right next to the A over here
	(does so)	
161		*that's right
162		?then we have the I, and we need the E right there
163	I need the other E	
164		*oh, you've got the E right there
165		*stick it right up between the I and the I
166	there's the other E	
167		*yeah, there's an orange E
168		*put that right up there next to the I
169		*turn it around the right way
170	upside up	
171		+upside up
172		?there
173	enne enne need the P	
174		?no, we don't need the P
175		?look, what does that say?
176	that say Nathaniel	
177		*that says Nathaniel
178	enne put the put the M on it	
179		?no, if you put the end on the M *(sic)* it says Nathanielm and that's sort of silly
180		?okay, we just put these up, and then we close the desk and go to sleep

Note: + Semantically contingent response

* Semantically contingent response to a literacy-related behavior or utterance

? Utterance in which semantic contingency is unclear

iors within his two-by-two categorical split between positive/negative accountability/nonaccountability. In Dore's system, positive nonaccountability (or play) is the term given to the case where the mother follows the child's lead; and positive accountability (or teaching) refers to situations such as those in Table 2 where the mother demands that a task be completed. Such cases of positive accountability are also frequent in language-facilitating situations. Examples include a mother's refusing to answer her children's questions if she feels they know the answers, or demanding their most correct pronunciation of some word rather than a baby-talk form. Ninio and Bruner (1978) have referred to such behavior as "upping the ante," or requiring the most sophisticated behavior the child is capable of giving. Examples of such accountability procedures in Table 2 are the mother's insistence that Nathaniel find the

L (lines 10 through 70); her demand after they succeed in finding and placing the *L*, *I*, and *A* that he read the letters to spell *Lia* (lines 88, 90); and her general unwillingness to let Nathaniel divert from the tasks of spelling *Lia* and *Nathaniel*.

These examples demonstrate that the three characteristics of adult-child interaction that facilitate language development — semantic contingency, scaffolding, and accountability procedures — are also characteristic of interactions around literacy materials and activities. It is obvious that such characteristics can also contribute to the development of literacy skill.

Increasing Decontextualization

A well-documented aspect of language acquisition is children's initial limitation to talking about the concrete here-and-now, and the growth of their ability to discuss the remote and the abstract. Early utterances can be described as highly contextualized, both from the point of view of the child and from the point of view of the observer, who cannot make sense of the utterances without knowing the context in which they were uttered. Many different aspects of language development demonstrate increasing freedom from context; for example: 1) early words are used performatively (*brm-brm* while moving a car) or socially (*hi* and *bye-bye*), but later words can be used referentially as well, in order to talk about experience as well as to share experience (Nelson, 1981); 2) early utterances comment on physically present objects or current activities, and only later can children understand or make reference to absent objects or to past and future activities (Chapman, 1981); 3) early conversational competence relies on a familiar conversational partner who will ask the expected questions and give the expected answers, whereas older children can converse about familiar things with unfamiliar partners (Snow, 1978); and 4) young children often assume shared knowledge in their conversation, whereas later they can estimate what the listener is unlikely to know (Scollon & Scollon, 1982). All of these changes constitute decreasing reliance on the present or the historical context of interaction.

Full-blown adult literacy is the ultimate decontextualized skill. Even during the preschool years, children show a development from highly contextualized literacy skills to relatively decontextualized ones. For example, in addition to his own name the first words that Nathaniel could read were *Michigan* and *Go Blue* (printed on a football jersey that he wore frequently), *I Love NY* (printed on a T-shirt he was given as a present), and *Puerto Rico* (printed on a sweatshirt he wore). These words are not all phonetically simple or easily decodable, but their degree of contextualization supported their readability. Similarly, Nathaniel's early attempts to write or spell words all involved his own name or the names of good friends and favorite baby-sitters. Many examples are given in Mason's paper (1982) of the highly contextualized reading that young children do — *Stop and Shop* on the supermarket's sign, *Cheerios* on the cereal box, and *Gulf* at the gas station. Mason identifies contextualized print recognition as the first strand in prereading development. Moving from such highly contextualized reading (which many would deny is truly reading) to relatively decontextualized reading, such as reading words in isolation or reading sentences in a book where the pictures cannot be mapped easily to elements within the text, involves a real transition.

Context is usually thought of as physical context; for example, a particularly salient visual display or encountering a particular word always in the same place. For the very young child the physical context is no doubt the most important support for language or literacy skill. Another important aspect of context, though, and one that becomes very useful to the child as young as two years old, is the "historical" context. By this I mean children's previous experience with some event, place, word, or text, which can support their current interpretation or reaction. Nathaniel's hypothesis in Table 2 (line 9) that "Lia starts with N" is clearly a product of his previous experience in this same situation, spelling *Nathaniel*. Reading *Winnie-the-Pooh* cannot be a physically contextualized experience in the same sense that reading *Gulf* on the gas station sign can be, but it can be historically contextualized if the child has heard the book read aloud many times before trying to read it himself. Memory provides the context that the physical environment cannot.

Other books popular with children do provide a physical context that can, in combination with the experience of being read to, support word reading. The Dr. Seuss books, for example, often provide a few graphically salient displays (*so so so so* printed diagonally across the page in *The Cat in the Hat*, 1956; *Sam I am* printed on the sign carried by Sam in *Green Eggs and Ham*, 1960) that identify the word physically. The first picture-word books, with single words printed under easily identifiable pictures, have the same effect. In these cases, historical context is much less necessary to the reading of the words; for most books, though, even the ones designed for very young children, the historical context of words is probably of much more help than the physical context in supporting reading.

Clearly, the young child would prefer a world in which print was contextualized, predictable, and nonarbitrary. Table 3 presents an example of Nathaniel's presumption at 31 months that print would be both contextualized and nonarbitrary. He often played with a toy cargo truck on which was printed *KLM*. This toy was commonly referred to as the "airport truck." He recognized the print on the side of the truck as a word and could at this age read the letters *K, L,* and *M;* but he concluded nonetheless that the word on the truck could only be "airport truck." As his insistence reveals (see Table 3, lines 3, 5), he was firmly convinced that any writing on an object would be a label for that object — a conviction perhaps supported by his experience with cereal boxes and generic grocery labels, but one that probably emerged from a more general set of principles for dealing with the world.

An example of Nathaniel's increasing recognition of the existence of decontextualized text emerges from longitudinal analysis of his readings of one book (Scarry's *The Storybook Dictionary*, 1964) over the course of a year (Snow & Goldfield, 1982, in press). In the early sessions, Nathaniel and his mother discussed the pictures and, through their conversations, jointly developed complex information structures about the characters and events. At 40 months Nathaniel started to resist conversing about the pictures. Rather than selecting a picture by pointing to it and asking a question about it, he pointed to the text and said, "Read this one." Although it was still possible to get him involved in a conversation about the pictures at 40 months, shortly thereafter he became quite insistent that he be read to out of this book and all others. He would still occasionally discuss the pictures but only after hearing the text.

TABLE 3

Nathaniel's Presumption That Literacy Is Contextualized (31 Months)

Line	Nathaniel	Mother
	(pointing to KLM on toy truck)	
1	that say airport truck	
2		no, that says KLM
	(insistently)	
3	that says de airport truck	
4		KLM cargo
	(more insistently)	
5	that says airport truck	
		(patiently)
6		In the airport the trucks have to carry the cargo from the planes to other planes, or into the city and that's what this truck does
	(pointing to KLM)	
7	who's this	
8		where . . .
9	that says . . . de airport . . .	
		(interrupting)
10		KLM, Nathaniel, this says KLM

The Role of Routines

Although responsiveness and semantic contingency are the aspects of parent-child interaction that are recognized facilitators of language development, another aspect of interaction that also contributes to language acquisition is parental use of routines (see Peters, in press; Snow, in press; Snow, deBiauw, & Dubber, 1982). Bruner refers to such routines as *formats* (in press, 1981), emphasizing the fact that they are neither rigid nor unexpandable, but are highly predictable and thus constitute ideal contexts for language acquisition.

Such routinized or formatted contexts could also contribute to literacy acquisition; in fact, the most studied format for language learning is book reading (Ninio, 1980a, 1980b; Ninio & Bruner, 1978; Snow & Goldfield, 1982, in press), which can be seen to contribute to language and to literacy simultaneously. Book reading routines constitute occasions for vocabulary acquisition (Ninio, 1980b), for the acquisition of book-handling skills (Mason, 1982), for the discovery of print, for the recognition of words, and for the development of a story scheme that could ultimately contribute to reading comprehension (Snow & Goldfield, 1982).

A prime example of the exploitation of a format is given by traditional ABC books, with their standard, "A is for a— B is for b— form; their use of simple pictures corresponding to the least predictable item in the format; and their reliance on such a well-learned sequence as the alphabet. Tables 4 and 5 present excerpts from two sessions, two weeks apart, using two ABC books with Nathaniel. Comparisons of these conversations reveal how much he had learned about the format of ABC books in this short time, even though the particular book used at the later reading was unfamiliar to him. At 32 months, 4 days (Table 4) he treated the first ABC book much like any other

TABLE 4

Nathaniel (32 Months, 4 Days) and His Mother Reading an ABC Book

Line	Nathaniel	Mother
1	wanna read dat . . . dat book dis book	
2		wanna read that book?
3		okay
4	read dis dat book	
5		this is a Christmas book
6	ABC book	
7		that's an ABC book
		how did you know that?
8	dat's a present	
9		where's it say ABC?
10	dis eh A	
11	dat's a present	
12		yeah, it was a present a long time ago
13	as a present day	
14		this says A is for angel
15		B is for bell
16		C is for candle and carol as well
17		D is for
18	donkey	
19		E is for elf
20		F is for fun
21		filling Christmas itself
22		G is for gifts
23		what's a gift?
24	dat's a gift	
25		gifts are the same thing as presents, Nathaniel
26	gifts are the same thing as present	
27		right, gifts and presents are the same thing
28		H is for holly
29		I is for . . . ice cream
30	eh dis a I	
31	I for ice cream	
32		which is the I?
33	dis is de I	
34		I
35	E	
36		no that's an I
37	dat's a I	
38		and that's a little I
39	dat's a little I	
40	dis is E . . . dis is de little I	
41		no this is a big I a big I

book, identifying a picture or a letter when he could and talking about the pictures with his mother. By 32 months, 20 days (Table 5), Nathaniel had learned the "X is for X-word" format, as indicated even more clearly by his errors (lines 22, 27, 94) than by his correct use of the format.

Another effective exploitation of formats is exemplified by the Dr. Seuss books, which use rhyme, rhythm, and nonsense words in ways that facilitate rote memoriza-

TABLE 5

Nathaniel (32 Months, 20 Days) and His Mother Reading an ABC Book

Line	Nathaniel	Mother
1	how 'bout dis book?	
2		how "bout this book?
3	how 'bout de banana	
4	wanna read dat . . . wanna read . . .	
5	how 'bout dat book?	
6		how 'bout that book?
7		this is an ABC book
8	eh eh dis eh banana	
9		that's right
10		and what's this?
11	das da dat's banana peels	
12		that's the B for . . .
13	dat's a banana	
14		B for banana
15	B for banana	
16		A for apple
17	A for apple	
18		C for cup
19	C for cup	
20		what's that say?
21	det	
22	C for plate	
23		(*laughing*) no it's P for plate
24	P for plate	
25	C	
26		C for . . .
27	A for plate	
28		A for apple
29	A for apple	
30	dis eh banana	
31		that's right
32		B for banana
33	B for banana	
34		what else begins with B?
35	b . . . B for . . .	
36		bagel
37	B for bagel	
38	where's eh bagel?	
39		we don't have a picture of a bagel
40		C for cup
41		C for coffee
42	c for de . . . C C for coffee	
43		E for egg
44	E for egg	
45		G for . . .
46	G for . . . uh	
47		those what are those?
48	grapes	
49		grapes, right
50	four	
51		F for four
52		that's right

TABLE 5   *(continued)*

Line	Nathaniel	Mother
53	hamburger	
54		hamburger, right
55	ice cream	
56		ice cream
57		what's this?
58	wha deh?	
59		I think that's lollipop
60	one two three	
61		three
62	dese are light en put up deh	
63	who dat?	
64		that's a kettle for the tea
65		to make tea
66	what dat?	
67		what's that?
68	milk	
69		milk, yes
70		M for milk
71	M for milk	
72		N for
73	dis eh nut en walnut	
74		a walnut, right
75		O for
76	O for	
77	ah ah	
78		orange
79	orange	
80		P for
81	P for plate	
82		right
83		Q for
84	for	
85		quince
86	quince	
87		R for
88	for	
89		raspberry
90	raspberry	
91		S for
92	S for spoon	
93		T for
94	T for . . . apple	
95		tomato
96	tomato	
97	dis eh dis?	
98		that's a cake
99		that's an upside down cake
100	upside down	
101	eh book upside down	
		(laughing)
102		oh no it doesn't mean
103		you don't have to turn the book upside down
104		well never mind

tion. Rote learning of a text, with subsequent matching of the role-learned sequences to the visual display, is an effective way to learn to read — a method discovered spontaneously by some children in this society and used as the major pedagogical method in the Koranic schools of the Arab world (Wagner & Lofti, 1979). Table 6 exemplifies the relatively early stages of such rote learning and the changes over a short time, as revealed in Nathaniel's reading of *Hop on Pop* (Seuss, 1963) at 37 months, 6 days and 37 months, 26 days. During the earliest readings of this book, Nathaniel's contribution had been primarily imitative. At 37 months, 6 days he mixed imitation and memorized bits. Twenty days later, his contributions suggested that he had memorized a rather large portion of the book.

At the age of 5 years, 7 months, Nathaniel, who by this time had developed considerable decoding skills, was observed to read books of nursery rhymes and poems by scanning the pictures until he found a rhyme he knew by heart then reading those rhymes by sounding them out. He was quite capable of sounding out unfamiliar rhymes or of reciting the memorized ones fluently without any decoding, but chose to apply his decoding skills to familiar texts instead.

Summary

The acquisition of language and of literacy can be seen to be very similar to one another on a number of points: the complexity of the learning involved, the centrality of communicative needs to the early stages of acquisition, the nature of the social interactive factors that contribute to acquisition, and the child's increasing ability to perform the tasks required without the support of social, physical, or historical context.

DISSIMILARITIES IN THE DEVELOPMENT OF LANGUAGE AND LITERACY

Whereas the similarities between language and literacy acquisition are impressive, there are several points of dissimilarity as well. These will be discussed in this section and analyzed to determine if they constitute true or apparent differences.

Teaching versus Learning

The most striking difference between the acquisition of language and the acquisition of reading is that the first occurs naturally whereas the second relies on formal instruction. This difference holds for the vast majority of children but constitutes a statistical rather than an absolute difference. Some children learn to read more or less on their own (for example, Durkin, 1966), at least without formal school instruction. I have argued that language acquisition, seemingly natural, is supported by patterns of interaction with adults that, if analyzed carefully, tend to be quite pedagogical. Thus, although most children are taught to read, the fact that some learn without formal instruction from precisely the same kinds of interactions that support language acquisition suggests a greater similarity than dissimilarity between the processes on this point.

TABLE 6

Nathaniel's Development of Knowledge about a Single Text

Printed Text	Conversation at 37 months, 6 days	Conversation at 37 months, 26 days
	M: what is this book called?	
	N: steppin' an on . . .	
	dis one	
	step onnn	
	step on	
	M: it's called hop on . . .	
	N: hop on . . . top	N: eh I wanna read hop on top
Hop on Pop	M: hop on pop	
	by . . .	M: hop on pop
	N: by . . .	by . . .
by Dr. Seuss	M: Doctor	N: Doctor Seuss
	N: Seuss	
	. . . .	
PAT PAT	M: Pat pat	M: Pat pat
They call him Pat.	they call him . . .	they call him pat
	N: Pat	
PAT SAT	M: Pat sat	Pat sat
Pat sat on hat.	Pat sat on a . . .	Pat sat on . . .
	N: hat	N: the hat
	M: this is a . . .	
	N: hat	
PAT CAT	M: Pat cat	M: Pat cat
Pat sat on cat.	Pat sat on a . . .	Pat sat on . . .
	N: cat	N: a cat
PAT BAT	M: Pat bat	M: Pat bat
Pat sat on bat.	Pat sat on a . . .	Pat sat on
	N: cat	
	M: bat	N: a bat
	N: bat	
NO PAT NO	M: no Pat no	M: no Pat no
	don't . . .	N: he sayin' no?
		M: that's right
		he's saying no Pat no, don't . . .
Don't sit on that.	N: sit on that	N: sit on that
THING THING	M: thing	M: thing thing
	N: thing	
What is that thing?	M: what is that . . .	what is that thing?
	N: thing	
THING SING	M: thing sing	thing sing
That thing can sing!	that thing can . . .	that thing can sing
	N: sing	
SONG LONG	M: song	song long
	N: song	
	M: long	
	N: long	
A long, long song.	M: A long long song	a long long song
	N: song long song	
Good-by, Thing.	M: good-by Thing	good-by Thing
You sing too long.	you sing too . . .	
	N: too long	N: you sing too long
	. . . .	

TABLE 6   *(continued)*

Printed Text	Conversation at 37 months, 6 days	Conversation at 37 months, 26 days
FATHER MOTHER	M: father mother sister . . .	
SISTER BROTHER	N: brother	M: father mother sister brother
That one is	M: that one is . . .	that one . . .
my other brother.	N: my other brother	N: my other brother
My brothers read	M: my brothers read a little bit	M: my brothers read a little bit
a little bit.	little words like	little words like . . .
Little words like	N: it	N: bit and it
if and it.	M: and	
	N: hit	
My father can read	M: my father can read big words too	M: my father can read big words too
big words, too	like . . .	
Like . . .	N: like . . .	N: like Consandople and Timbuctoo
CONSTANTINOPLE	M: Constantinople	
and	N: Constantinople	
TIMBUKTU	M: and	
	N: and	
	M: Tim . . .	
	N: Tim . . .	
	M: buk . . .	
	N: too	

Note: M = mother; N = Nathaniel.

Universal Success versus High Risk for Failure

All children, barring extreme deprivation or organic damage, learn to talk; but a significant number of children, even those whose intelligence is in the normal or above-average range, fail at or have great difficulty in learning to read. The universal success of language acquisition is, of course, related to the fact that language need not be taught whereas literacy acquisition, a riskier venture, requires instruction. One explanation given for this difference is that literacy skills rely on higher metalinguistic functions than do language. The status of this distinction between literacy and language will be discussed further; here I will only outline the problem by making the distinction in this way: while it is true to say that most children learn to talk without explicit instruction, the language skills achieved naturally by children constitute the highly contextualized skills of communication, not the decontextualized uses of language such as presenting monologues, doing abstract verbal reasoning, and giving metalinguistic judgments.[3]

Reading and writing as normally used in school are two examples of decontextualized language use, and we might therefore expect considerable variability in the speed and ease with which they are acquired. An example of decontextualized language in the purely oral mode is giving metalinguistic judgments; for example, judging sentences as grammatical or ungrammatical, identifying ambiguity, and giving definitions. This is also an area in which enormous individual differences in ability are found, differences that correlate furthermore with educational level (Gleitman &

Gleitman, 1970). This finding supports the suggestion (Scribner, 1977) that the process of education consists largely of training in decontextualized language use.

I would argue that the existence of individual differences in literacy skills does not differentiate literacy from language. Rather, any skill that must be acquired or plied in a decontextualized way — whether that be reading, writing, talking, or listening — will be difficult, require some instruction, and show individual differences. By their very nature, most literacy experiences are somewhat decontextualized. By the nature of Western schooling, most of our children's literacy experiences are highly decontextualized. If we were to compare moderately decontextualized literacy skills with equally decontextualized language skills, I predict we would find them to be of the same level of difficulty.

Role of Practice in Acquisition

Basic tenets of reading and writing curricula are that practice makes perfect and that achieving higher levels of skill, especially for reading, requires having achieved a minimum speed and fluency at earlier levels through practice. Practice has never been suggested as a major factor influencing the speed of first language acquisition, though it certainly can be demonstrated to have a positive effect on second language learning. Recent evidence, however, suggests that, at least at the level of articulatory skill and sentence production planning, children get better partly as a product of practice with talking. Here again, then, an apparent difference may be illusory.

Imposition of Conventionality

Conventions, the "right way to do it," are important both in oral and in literate exchanges. Violations of conventions, such as using nonstandard speech forms or making spelling errors, reflect badly on the user, at least in some circumstances. Observing conventions in print is, however, more important to successful communication than in oral exchanges, partly because of print's greater decontextualization. Following the conventions helps to ensure effective communication even in situations where communicative repair is not possible. Face-to-face exchanges do not break down if an unconventional form is used because a speaker's meaning can be questioned and clarified. Defying convention in written communication is much riskier because one's communicative partner is at a distance and unavailable for checks and confirmation.

Purely conventional forms are infrequently required of young speakers though "May I please be excused?" and other such formulas are certainly not absent from their repertoires (see Gleason, Perlmann, & Greif, 1980), despite the fact that children seem to have an expectation that rote-learned utterances will be appropriate ways of dealing with certain communicative situations (see Snow, in press). Reading and writing require conventional forms from the very start though children who do spontaneous spelling are freed from even this demand. Interestingly, children who are more advanced in their understanding of the nature of literacy may well resist nonconventional spelling — they know that "there is a right way to spell it" and do not want to produce their own, incorrect forms (Giacobbe, 1982). For example, though Nathaniel at four years could be forced to provide his own spellings, he preferred to copy or be told how to spell things and asked after each letter in a spontane-ously spelled word if it were correct. Part of his unwillingness to do spontaneous spell-ing derived from his knowledge of the arbitrariness of English spelling — he knew that he could not be sure, for example, if a *C* or an *S* spelled an /s/, if *C* or *K* was needed for /k/, or if *EA, EE,* or *IE* was appropriate for /i/.

Nathaniel's interpretation of literacy tasks as ones where the conventions must be followed was also evident in the development of his book-reading routine with his mother. Although at 30 to 35 months he gladly discussed the pictures in the books be-ing read, at about three years he discovered the text and reinterpreted "reading books" as "being read to." He became increasingly insistent on this as the correct book-reading activity and impatient with his mother's attempts to discuss the pictures.

It may thus be the case that the power of the convention is first discovered by many children in the context of literacy tasks rather than for oral language, though this difference between language and literacy acquisition is one of degree. The degree of difficulty most children have when asked to call a cow "ink" (Piaget, 1954) demon-strates their natural commitment to the notion that words are conventional. It would be surprising, then, if they had any particular difficulty with understanding this fact about written language.

Summary

The differences between language and literacy are differences more of degree than of absolutes. Reading requires more explicit teaching, is more susceptible to failure, may be more dependent on practice, and may be more limited by conventions. Neverthe-less, none of these characteristics is entirely untrue of language during the early stages of its acquisition. Indeed, the more decontextualized the oral language task, the more these characteristics apply.

LITERACY IN THE HOME

This review of the similarities and differences between language and literacy in the early stages of their development provides a picture of enormous similarity on several points and differences of degree rather than of kind. We are left, then, with the trou-blesome questions with which we began. Why do some children have so much trouble learning to read? If learning to read is supported by the same sorts of interactions that support language development and if all children learn to talk, we should expect that all will learn to read as well.

One answer that has been offered to this question is to invoke the degree of "liter-acy" of children's home cultures as a determining variable in their acquisition of school literacy. Middle-class homes in which books are present familiarize children with the purpose of books and ways to use them, thus providing school-relevant skills very directly. However, recent studies of low-income preschool children (Heath, 1982; Miller, 1982) suggest that some of these children have considerable access to and experience with books. In fact, very low-income children studied in South Balti-more were socialized for school in quite direct and explicit ways by their mothers

(Miller, Nemoianu, & DeJong, 1981). Thus, simple access to literacy materials probably does not explain the large differences between middle-class and working-class children in reading achievement. It has been argued, though, that in addition to experience with books, middle-class homes prepare children for written forms of literacy by providing literate features in oral discourse: that is, by telling or reading stories in which the author is impersonal, the setting is distanced, deictic contrasts have to be understood from the writer's or speaker's point of view, and relatively complex language forms are used. Such features show up in very young middle-class children's own oral stories (Scollon & Scollon, 1982) long before they learn to read or write.

Another feature of literate interaction in middle-class homes is the use of conversation to build "shared histories" between mother and child. The mother asks the child questions about past, shared events, thus providing the child with help in recounting and in building internal representations of those events (Schieffelin & Eisenberg, in press). Such establishment of shared, permanent histories is characteristic of the "literate" approach to information as stable and enduring, rather than the "oral" approach in which shared representations are reconstructed as needed. Since information is not made permanent by being written down in oral cultures, it does not endure except as synopsized by epigrams and proverbs.

Even classroom teachers have been described as giving children an "oral preparation for literacy" in the form of sharing time (Michaels & Cook-Gumperz, 1979). Children are expected, during their sharing turns, to present information in much the same way it would be presented in a well-written paragraph: assume no prior knowledge on the part of the listener, present the topic in a topic sentence, include only information relevant to that topic in subsequent sentences, and be explicit. Children's difficulty in following these rules demonstrates how foreign the rules are in normal conversational exchange in which the listener and the speaker share considerable knowledge. High levels of explicitness in face-to-face interactions often constitute redundancy with information available from the nonverbal context.

THE ORAL AND THE LITERATE: SEPARATE DOMAINS

The argument that some homes prepare children for literacy by giving them experience with "literate" oral discourse flirts with terminological confusion and obscures the nature of the experiences that are crucial to preparing children for literacy. The characteristics of oral discourse that have been identified as potentially facilitative for literacy are distance between sender and receiver, explicitness of reference, fictionalization of sender and of receiver, complexity of syntactic structures, permanency of information, autonomous rather than interactive establishment of truth, and high degree of cohesion (Tannen, 1982). These are the characteristics of decontextualized language use. Literacy is normally decontextualized, and literate activities normally show these features. But if oral discourse can have these characteristics and be used in a decontextualized way, so too can literate activities be context-bound. Prime examples of contextualized literacy are given by Scribner and Cole (1981) from their study of Vai literacy.[4] Vaiscript literates use their literacy skills primarily for two activities: writing letters intended for one reader and keeping personal diaries. Both of these uses of literacy are relatively contextualized because they rely on shared information between writer and reader.

Consider the literacy of the preschool child. The first part of this chapter presented many examples of highly contextualized literacy skills — reading the words on shirts and cereal boxes, reading one's own name, reading well-memorized rhythmes in a book. Somewhat older children's abilities to deal with tasks such as reading a note taped on the refrigerator, finding favorite programs listed in *TV Guide*, or selecting lunch from the menu at Burger King (see Bloome, 1981) similarly constitute positive evidence of children's ability to deal with literacy but no evidence about their ability to deal with decontextualized information.

Perhaps most children are not failing at reading and writing but at comprehending and producing decontextualized information. Cox and Sulzby (1982) have found a relationship between skills at producing monologues (one-person narratives and descriptions) and reading ability in kindergarteners and have hypothesized a direct connection between monologue skills and literacy skills. I suggest that they found this relationship because the reading tasks they used as an outcome measure conflate two sets of abilities — the strictly literate abilities involved in decoding and comprehending print and the decontextualization skills involved in using language without the support of conversational context.

By about fourth grade, many school literacy activities are highly decontextualized. Children are no longer asked just to fill in worksheets or read from books with pictures but are expected to read from textbooks and write clear paragraphs. Thus, the basic reason for children's failure in the middle grades may not be the difficulty of literacy but the problems associated with decontextualizing language use. It is clear that the academically successful twelve- or thirteen-year-old must have mastered skills of literacy and of decontextualization. These skills are at least theoretically separable, and Scribner and Cole's finding that literacy and schooling have differential effects on cognitive skills suggest that they are practically separable as well. Further, success at either set of skills can be related to experiences during the preschool years. It seems likely, though, that different sets of preschool experiences contribute to literacy skill and to skill in decontextualized language use.

Much research remains to be done in order to test the hypothesis that the development of literacy skills and of skills at decontextualized language use emerge from different ontogenetic roots. As difficult as these skills are to distinguish from one another in testing or in school performance, the interactive situations that facilitate their acquisition may be even more difficult to separate.

It is clear, though, that many of the experiences identified as contributing to preschool children's literacy development (such as being told stories, being read to, receiving help in constructing descriptions of past events, being asked tutorial questions) contribute more to their ability to use language in a decontextualized, and even noncommunicative, way than to their literacy skills per se. The teaching built into *Sesame Street, The Electric Company*, and many prereading curricula, in contrast, provides hardly at all for skills of decontextualized language use. Children need both literacy and decontextualized language skills to succeed in school; but it may be that literacy skills are simple enough to be acquired at school, whereas developing the skill of using language in a decontextualized way relies more heavily on experiences only home can provide.

NOTES

1. Nathaniel, the first-born child of academic parents, was tape-recorded at home during everyday activities such as meals, dressing, undressing, and playtimes, between the ages of 18 and 36 months. Recordings were made approximately every other week, in one-half to 3-hour sessions. Reading books was among Nathaniel's favorite activities during this time, and many of his book-reading interactions were recorded.
2. Farr (1982) discusses how a teacher uses comments on a student's journal to scaffold the writing process for the child.
3. A related point has been made in the domain of second language learning by Cummins (1979a, 1979b), who distinguishes between Basic Interpersonal Communicative Skill, acquired relatively quickly by most second language learners, and Cognitive-Academic Linguistic Potential, required for academic success and acquired much more slowly.
4. See Patricia Marks Greenfield, "Review of *The Psychology of Literacy,*" *Harvard Educational Review, 53* (1983), 216–220.

REFERENCES

Anastasiow, N., Hanes, M. L., & Hanes, M. (1982). *Language and reading strategies for poverty children.* Baltimore: University Park Press.

Bannatyne, A. D. (1971). *Language, reading and learning disabilities.* Springfield, IL: Thomas.

Bloome, D. (1981). *An ethnographic approach to the study of reading activities among black junior high school students: A socio-linguistic ethnography.* Unpublished thesis, Kent State University.

Bruner, J. S. (1978). Learning how to do things with words. In J. S. Bruner and R. A. Garton (Eds.), *Human growth and development.* Oxford, Eng.: Oxford University Press.

Bruner, J. S. (1981, October). *The social context of language acquisition.* Keynote address, Sixth Annual Boston University Conference on Language Development.

Bruner, J. S. (in press). The acquisition of pragmatic commitments. In R. Golinkoff (Ed.), *The transition from prelinguistic to linguistic communication.* Hillsdale, NJ: Erlbaum.

Carnoy, M. (1972). Is compensatory education possible? In M. Carnoy (Ed.), *Schooling in a corporate society: The political economy of education in America.* New York: McKay.

Cazden, C. (in press). Literacy in school contexts. In *Proceedings of the International symposium on New Perspectives on the Process of Reading and Writing.* Mexico City: Editorial, Siglo XXI.

Chapman, R. (1981). Cognitive development and language: Comprehension in 10- to 21-month-olds. In R. Stark (Ed.), *Language behavior in infancy to early childhood.* New York: Elsevier.

Clark, M. (1976). *Young fluent readers.* London: Heinemann.

Coleman, J., Campbell, F., Hobson, C., McPartland, J., Mood, A., Weinfield, F., & York, R. (1966). *Equality of educational opportunity.* Washington, DC: U.S. Government Printing Office.

Cox, B., & Sulzby, E. (1982). *Evidence of planning in dialogue and monologue by five-year-old emergent readers.* Unpublished manuscript, Northwestern University.

Cross, T. G. (1978). Mother's speech and its association with rate of linguistic development in young children. In N. Waterson & C. Snow (Eds.), *The development of communication.* London: Wiley.

Cummins, J. (1979a, November). *Cognitive academic language proficiency, linguistic interdependence, the optimum age question, and some other matters* (Working Papers in Bilingualism, No. 19). Toronto: Ontario Institute for Studies in Education.

Cummins, J. (1979b). Linguistic interdependence and the educational development of bilingual children. *Review of Educational Research, 49,* 222–251.

Dale, E., & Chall, J. (in press). *Readability*. New York: McGraw-Hill.

Davis, F. B. (1974). Fundamental factors of comprehension in reading. *Psychometrika, 9,* 185–197.

DeStefano, J. (1978). *Language: The learner and the school.* New York: Wiley.

Dittmar, N. (1976). *Sociolinguistics.* London: Edward Arnold.

Dore, J. (in press). Intentionality, accountability, and play: The intersubjective basis for language development. In R. Golinkoff (Ed.), *The transition from prelinguistic to linguistic communication.* Hillsdale, NJ: Erlbaum.

Durkin, D. (1966). *Children who read early.* New York: Teachers College Press.

Edwards, A. E. (1976). *Language in culture and class.* London: Heinemann.

Farr, M. (1982, March). *Learning to write English.* Paper presented at the meeting of the American Educational Research Associaton, New York.

Farr, R. (1969). *Reading — What can be measured.* Newark, DE: International Reading Association.

Giacobbe, M. E. (1982, December). Personal communication.

Gleason, J. Berko, Perlmann, R., & Greif, E. (1980, April). *What's the magic word? Learning language through politeness routines.* Paper presented at the meeting of the Southeast Regional Conference on Human Development, Alexandria, VA.

Gleitman, L., & Gleitman, H. (1979). *Phrase and paraphrase.* New York: Norton.

Heath, S. B. (1980). The functions and uses of literacy: Literacy in a media world. *Journal of Communication, 30,* 123–133.

Heath, S. B. (1982). What no bedtime story means: Narratives at home and school. *Language in Society, 11,* 49–78.

Kennedy, M. (1978). Findings from the Follow Through planned variation study. *Educational Researcher, 7,* 3–11.

Lazar, I., & Darlington, R. (1982). Lasting effects of early education: A report from the consortium for longitudinal studies. *Monographs of the Society for Research in Child Development, 47,* (2–3, Serial No. 195).

Loban, W. (1963). *The language of elementary school children* (Research Report No. 1). Urbana, IL: National Council of Teachers of English.

Mason, J. (1982, March). *The acquisition of knowledge about reading: The preschool period.* Paper presented at the meeting of the American Educational Research Association, New York.

Menyuk, P., & Flood, J. (1981). Language development, reading/writing problems, and remediation. *Orton Society Bulletin, 31,* 13–28.

Michaels, S., & Cook-Gumperz, J. (1979). A study of sharing time with first grade students: Discourse narrative in the classroom. *Proceedings of the Fifth Annual Meeting of the Berkeley Linguistics Society, 5,* 647–660.

Miller, P. (1982). *Amy, Wendy and Beth: Learning language in South Baltimore.* Austin: University of Texas Press.

Miller, P., Nemoianu, A., & DeJong, J. (1981, March). *Early socialization for schooling in a working-class community.* Paper presented at the Ethnography in Education Research Forum, University of Pennsylvania.

Nelson, K. (1981). Acquisition of words by first-language learners. In H. Winitz (Ed.), *Native language and foreign language acquisition.* New York: New York Academy of Sciences.

Ninio, A. (1980a). Picture book reading in mother-infant dyads belonging to two subgroups in Israel. *Child Development, 51,* 587–590.

Ninio, A. (1980b). The ostensive definition in vocabulary teaching. *Journal of Child Language, 7,* 563–575.

Ninio, A., & Bruner, J. (1978). The achievement and antecedents of labelling. *Journal of Child Language, 5,* 1–15.

Olson, D. (1977). From utterance to text: The bias of language in speech and writing. *Harvard Educational Review, 47,* 257–281.

Peters, A. (in press). *The units of language acquisition.* New York: Cambridge University Press.

Piaget, J. (1954). *The construction of reality in the child.* New York: Basic Books.

Rivlin, A. M., & Timpane, P. M. (Eds.). (1975). *Planned variation in education: Should we give up or try harder?* Washington, DC: Brookings Institution.

Salus, M. (1982). *The syntax and metalinguistic skills of children who read early.* Unpublished doctoral dissertation, Boston University.

Scarry, R. (1964). *The storybook dictionary.* London: Hamlyn.

Schieffelin, B., & Eisenberg, A. (in press). Cultural variation in dialogue. In R. Schiefelbusch (Ed.), *Communicative competence: Acquisition and intervention.* Baltimore: University Park Press.

Scollon, R., & Scollon, S. (1982). *Narrative, literacy and face in interethnic communications.* Norwood, NJ: Ablex.

Scribner, S. (1977). Modes of thinking and ways of speaking: Culture and logic reconsidered. In P. Johnson-Laird & P. Wason (Eds.), *Thinking: Readings in cognitive science.* New York and Cambridge, Eng.: Cambridge University Press.

Scribner, S., & Cole, M. (1981). *The psychology of literacy.* Cambridge, MA: Harvard University Press.

Seuss, Dr. [T. Geisel]. (1956). *The cat in the hat.* New York: Random House Beginner Books.

Seuss, Dr. [T. Geisel]. (1960). *Green eggs and ham.* New York: Random House Beginner Books.

Seuss, Dr. [T. Geisel]. (1963). *Hop on pop.* New York: Random House Beginner Books.

Shuy, R. W. (1981, April). *Relating research on oral language function to research on written discourse.* Paper presented at the annual meeting of the American Educational Research Association, Los Angeles.

Simons, H. D. (1979). *The relationship between aspects of linguistic performance and reading comprehension.* Unpublished doctoral dissertation, Harvard University.

Snow, C. (1978). The conversational context of language acquisition. In R. Campbell & P. Smith (Eds.), *Recent advances in the psychology of language: Social and interactional factors* (vol. 2). New York: Plenum.

Snow, C. (in press). Saying it again: The role of expanded and deferred imitations in language acquisition. In K. E. Nelson (Ed.), *Children's language* (vol. 4). New York: Gardner Press.

Snow, C., deBlauw, A., & Dubber, C. (1982). Routines in parent-child interaction. In L. Feagans & D. Farran (Eds.), *The language of children reared in poverty.* New York: Academic Press.

Snow, C., & Goldfield, B. (1982). Building stories: The emergence of information structure from conversation and narrative. In D. Tannen (Ed.), *Analyzing discourse: Text and talk.* Washington, DC: Georgetown University Press.

Snow, C., & Goldfield, B. (in press). Turn the page please: Situation specific language acquisition. *Journal of Child Language.*

Snow, C., & Hoefnagel-Höhle. (1978). The critical period for language acquisition: Evidence from second language learning. *Child Development, 49,* 1114–1128.

Söderbergh, R. (1971). *Reading in early childhood: A linguistic study of a Swedish pre-school child's gradual acquisition of reading ability.* Stockholm: Morssedt.

Spearitt, D. (1972). Identification of subskills of reading comprehension by maximum likelihood factor analysis. *Reading Research Quarterly, 8,* 92–111.

Stearns, M. S. (1971). *Report on preschool programs: The effects of preschool programs on disadvantaged children and their parents.* Washington, DC: U.S. Government Printing Office.

Stubbs, M. (1980). *Language and literacy: The sociolinguistics of reading and writing.* London: Routledge & Kegan Paul.

Tannen, D. (Ed.). (1982). *Spoken and written language: Exploring orality and literacy.* Norwood, NJ: Ablex.

Thorndike, R. (1974–1975). Reading as reasoning. *Reading Research Quarterly, 10,* 135–147.

Wagner, D., & Lofti, A. (1979). *Traditional Quranic education in contemporary Morocco.* Unpublished manuscript, University of Pennsylvania.

Wells, G. (1980). *Some antecedents of early educational achievement.* Edinburgh: British Psychological Society.

Yap, K. O. (1979). Vocabulary — Building blocks of comprehension. *Journal of Reading Behavior, 11,* 49–59.

Literacy without Schooling:
Testing for Intellectual Effects

SYLVIA SCRIBNER

MICHAEL COLE

In most discussions of schooling and literacy, the two are so closely intertwined that they are virtually indistinguishable. Yet intellectual consequences have been claimed for each as though they were clearly independent of one another. For several years we have been studying the relation between schooling and literacy, particularly the psychological consequences of each and the extent to which they substitute for each other. Our research among the Vai, a West African people for whom schooling and the acquisition of literacy are separate activities, has led us to reconsider the nature of literacy and its intellectual effects.

Over the centuries and across disciplines, there has been remarkable agreement that the written word has its own peculiar psychological properties. Its relationship to memory and thinking is claimed to be different from that of the spoken word, but conceptions of this relationship are as diverse as the perspectives brought to bear on the question.

Plato considered the issue within the context of basic educational goals and values, suggesting that the relationship of writing to intellect be considered problematic, rather than taken at face value. To the claim that letters would give men better memories and make them wise, Socrates replied that, on the contrary, letters would create forgetfulness. Learners would not use their memories but rely instead on external aids for "reminiscence." Disciples of the written word would "have the show of wisdom without the reality" (Plato, p. 323). Plato, on the other hand, was suspicious of education that relied solely on the oral mode of the Homeric tradition. Oral thinking in this context was considered the enemy of logic (Havelock, 1963).

The view that the relationship between writing and mental abilities is problematic has given way to the dominant belief that literacy leads inevitably to higher forms of thought. Oral and literate thought are often contrasted in a modern version of the old dichotomy of primitive and civilized thought. Increasingly, literacy instruction is justified not only as a means to material advancement for the individual and society but also as a means of transforming minds. The UNESCO Secretary-General has recently

Harvard Educational Review   Vol. 48   No. 4   November 1978, 448–461

urged the acceleration of worldwide literacy programs to overcome the deep psychological differences between oral and literate thought (UNESCO, 1965). Similar arguments are made in pedagogical discussions here in the United States (Farrell, 1977).

Debates about the cognitive consequences of literacy play a role in determining priorities for national investments in education and in defining outcomes of schooling. Moreover, the claims for consequences themselves have consequences. If, for example, we believe that literacy is a precondition for abstract thinking, how do we evaluate the intellectual skills of nonliterate people? Do we consider them incapable of participating in modern society because they are limited to the particularistic and concrete? If we believe that writing and logical thinking are always mutually dependent, what do we conclude about the reasoning abilities of a college student who writes an incoherent essay? Is this an automatic sign of defective logic? Answers to these questions have implications for social and educational policies that are at least as profound as those questions that concerned Plato.

To examine some of these implications, we will consider recent works in experimental psychology that brings an empirical perspective to these questions. We will analyze how different investigators specify the relationships between literacy and intellectual skills. Oversimplifying, we will contrast two perspectives: one represented by the metaphor of literacy as development, and the other, by literacy as practice. The developmental framework is an established theoretical tradition. Its presuppositions implicitly or explicitly inform the great majority of literacy and instructional writing programs. The framework of practice, or function, is our own attempt at systematizing the knowledge we gained while investigating literacy without schooling among the Vai. Although the two perspectives start from similar questions, we will intentionally sharpen their contrasting features to bring out their different implications for research and educational policy. The differences lie both in the nature of the evidence considered crucial for developing hypotheses about literacy and in the procedures for relating evidence to theory. Our purpose is not to pose them as entirely antagonistic or to argue for the one best model. Rather we advocate an approach to literacy that moves beyond generalities to a consideration of the organization and use of literacy in different social contexts.

LITERACY AS DEVELOPMENT

In the 1960s Greenfield and Bruner (1966) put forward the thesis that writing promotes cognitive development. This was derived largely from Greenfield's (1966) studies in Senegal, comparing the performance of schooled and unschooled Wolof children on experimental cognitive tasks. In one task, children were required to sort pictures of objects into groups of things that belonged together and to explain the basis of their sorting. The items could be exhaustively grouped by form, function, or color. Three aspects of performance were considered especially indicative of levels of abstract thinking. First, schoolchildren more often shifted the basis of their grouping from one attribute to another over trials. For example, if they sorted by color on the first trial, on the second trial they might sort by function or form. Second, when asked to explain the basis of their sorting, schoolchildren tended to state their reasons in sentences with predication, saying, for example, "these *are* red," instead of using a label "red" or a phrase "this red," such as unschooled children tended to do. Finally, schoolchildren could easily answer questions about why they thought items were alike whereas unschooled children had difficulty doing this. Greenfield interpreted these performance characteristics as measures of a general ability for context-independent, abstract thinking that only schoolchildren displayed.

Greenfield (1972) suggested that oral language relies on context for the communication of messages and is, therefore, a context-dependent language. In contrast, written language requires that meaning be made clear, independent of the immediate reference. If one assumes that context-dependent speech is linked with context-dependent thought, and context-dependent thought is the opposite of abstract thought, it follows that abstract thought fails to develop in an oral culture. Put the other way around, societies with written language provide the means for decontextualized abstract thinking; and since schooling relies primarily on written language, those attending school get a greater push toward abstract thought than those not going to school (Bruner, Olver, Greenfield, Hornsby, Kemey, Maccoby, Modiano, Mosher, Olson, Potter, Reisch, & Sonstroem, 1966, p. 318).

Bruner has presented the most general form of this argument — namely that technologies available in a given culture determine the level and range of abilities in its members. Environments with such symbolic technologies as a written language "push cognitive growth better, earlier and longer than others" (Greenfield & Bruner, 1966, p. 654).

Olson also believes that literacy and education push cognitive growth. In recent essays (1975, 1977, 1977) he contends that a unique form of logical competency is linked to literacy. This competency involves the mastery of the logical functions of language apart from its interpersonal functions. According to Olson, literate individuals come to regard meaning as residing in the text. An example is the ability to derive from the sentence "John hit Mary" the logical implication that "Mary was hit by John." Another is drawing logical conclusions from propositions solely from their linguistic evidence and without considering their factual status. Such logical abilities are not universal, Olson (1977) maintains, but are the endpoint of development in literate cultures. To secure evidence for literacy-related logical processes, Olson and his colleagues (for example, Olson & Filby, 1972) have conducted experimental studies of sentence comprehension and reasoning, comparing the performance of preliterate, preschool youngsters with schoolchildren of varying ages and with educated literate adults. Olson's speculations about how literacy develops these abilities come from historical analyses of the cultural changes accompanying the invention of the alphabet and the printing press. Both these inventions, Olson says, increase the explicitness of language, biasing cultures toward the development of explicit formal systems and accounting for distinctive modes of thought in Western societies.

This brief summary fails to do justice to the full argument of these psychologists but it does permit us to focus on what we conceive to be certain limitations and difficulties of the developmental perspective. This work is important and innovative, but we wish to caution against the notion that this evidence of the effects of literacy can provide a foundation for educational programs and that it offers a model strategy for future research.

A defining characteristic of the developmental perspective is that it specifies literacy's effects as the emergence of general mental capacities — abstract thinking, for example, or logical operations — rather than specific skills. These abilities are presumed to characterize the individual's intellectual functioning across a wide range of tasks. Thus, based on a limited sample of performance in experimental contexts, the conclusion has been drawn that there is a great divide between the intellectual competencies of people living in oral cultures and those in literate cultures.

From this perspective the capacities generated by literacy are seen not merely as different, but as higher-order capacities because they resemble the abilities that psychological theories attribute to later stages in development. For decades, developmental inquiry has been organized around the notion that children's thinking progresses from the concrete to the abstract. Olson specifically links literacy-related logical operations to Piaget's final stage of formal operational thought. It is within this framework that statements are made about arrested mental growth in cultures without literacy. Since this research compares children of different ages as well as children and adults, a developmental interpretation seems to have some validity. Can it be extrapolated, without further evidence, to characterize changes in the intellectual operations of adolescents and adults? Whether or not these changes are developmental, in a transformational sense, should at the very least be considered an open question.

Perhaps the most serious problem with this work is its vagueness about the mechanisms by which literacy promotes new intellectual capacities. Both Greenfield and Olson present plausible hypotheses about how literacy achieves its effects, but they offer a multitude of possibilities and no systematic theory for selecting the most fruitful for further exploration. Greenfield (1972) variously attributes the effects of literacy to the structure of the written language, to the school-based uses of language, or to growing up in a literate culture and speaking a written language. Olson (1977) stresses the effects on mental skills of the properties of an alphabetic script, of the exposure to the school language of written text, or of the acquisition of bodies of written knowledge. The ways in which these alleged antecedents exert their effects, however, are neither specified nor linked to the observed behaviors. Piaget (1976) has recently pointed out the limitations of this perspective: "To explain a psychological reaction or a cognitive mechanism . . . is not simply to describe it, but to comprehend the process by which it is formed. Failing that, one can but note results without grasping their meaning" (p. vi).

These empirical studies do not clarify the specific contribution of any of these experiences. None tested literacy as such. In all research, literacy was confounded with schooling; yet students are engaged in many learning experiences in school besides learning how to read and write. And we are all aware today that some children spend many years in school without learning how to read and write. There is little guidance here for educational policies and programs. To set educational goals and to plan curricula, research is needed that relates particular kinds of experiences with written language to the development of particular skills.

A final observation is that the developmental perspective supports an "inevitability" interpretation of literacy. It assumes that various components of literacy — say, an alphabetic script or an essayist text — are likely to have the same psychological consequences in all cultures irrespective of the contexts of use or the social institutions in which literacy is embedded. In reality, however, the developmental model has been elaborated in terms of institutions and technologies specific to our own society. It has been restricted to literacy as practiced in the schools. In addition, confusion stems from failure to differentiate the consequences of literacy over the course of human history from its consequences for the individual in present-day societies. It is a big jump from intellectual and cultural history to a theory of ontogenetic development in any present-day society.

A FUNCTIONAL APPROACH TO SCHOOLING AND LITERACY

We have long been interested in cultural influences on the development of thought, particularly the influence of literacy (Scribner, 1968) and formal schooling (Scribner & Cole, 1973); however, we have been skeptical about the usefulness of applying current developmental theory to these problems. Some of our doubts arose from the observation of unschooled nonliterate adults in other societies, some from experiments comparing schooled and unschooled individuals on cognitive tasks. We concluded from these data that the tendency of schooled populations to generalize across a wide range of problems occurred because schooling provides people with a great deal of practice in treating individual learning problems as instances of general classes of problems. Moreover, we did not assume that the skills promoted by schooling would necessarily be applied in contexts unrelated to school experience. This orientation led us to concentrate on the actual practices of literacy that hypothetically produced behavioral changes, looking for likely causal mechanisms. We needed a way to examine the consequences of literacy apart from schooling under conditions that made literate practices most accessible to observation.

The Vai are a traditional society on the northwest coast of Liberia who are well known in that area for their invention of a syllabic writing system to represent their own language. Preliminary reports (for example, Stewart, 1967) and our own observations indicated that between 20 and 25 percent of Vai men could read and write using their own script, which was invented approximately 150 years ago and transmitted from one generation to another without schooling or professional teachers. The mere existence of an indigenous writing system was enough to arouse our curiosity, but we were interested in the Vai for two additional reasons. First, except that they are predominantly Muslim, the Vai, according to ethnographies of Liberia, are virtually indistinguishable from their neighbors in terms of ecology, social organization, economic activities, and material culture. Second, their writing and reading are not activities separate from other daily pursuits, nor does learning to read and write require a person to master a large body of knowledge that is unavailable from oral sources. These two characteristics of Vai literacy provided an extremely interesting, if not unique, opportunity to investigate the effects of becoming literate separately from the effects of attending school or becoming educated, an inquiry that had heretofore eluded social science.

A detailed description of this work is beyond the scope of this chapter; however, we will briefly describe its major phases to explain what we mean by a functional approach to the study of literacy and thinking. To begin with, we gave questionnaires and tests to more than 700 Vai adults. Our survey included a variety of tasks based on previous research showing the effects of formal schooling among tribal Liberians. These tasks were included to determine if cognitive performance that was improved by schooling was similarly influenced by indigenous Vai literacy. The test battery also contained sorting and verbal reasoning tasks similar to those used by Greenfield and Olson as the basis for speculations about literacy effects. Results were clear-cut. As in previous research, improved performance was associated with years of formal schooling, but literacy in the Vai script did not substitute for schooling. Vai literates were not significantly different from nonliterates on any of these cognitive measures, including the sorting and reasoning tasks that had been suggested as especially sensitive to experience with a written language.[1]

In the next phase of our work we moved down one level of generality in the kinds of hypotheses we tested. Instead of looking for improvements in general cognitive performance associated with literacy, we concentrated on the hypothesis that literacy promotes metalinguistic skills — the idea that in acquiring literacy skills an individual acquires the ability to analyze language (Goody, 1977). One task tested nominal realism, the identification of name and object; other items tested the ability to specify the nature of grammatical rules, to reason from evidence provided by a syllogism, and to define words.

This series of studies showed that Vai literacy was associated with small increments in performance for some of the tasks (for example, increased ability to specify the nature of a grammatical error in spoken Vai) but there was no across-the-board evidence of enhanced performance associated with this unschooled literacy. Furthermore, and most damaging to the metalinguistic hypothesis, our results showed virtually no correlations among performances on the various probes of metalinguistic ability.

At the end of our first year of fieldwork, we had not made much progress in illuminating literacy skills among the Vai by administering standard laboratory tasks whose theoretical status with respect to literacy was uncertain. We decided to take a different approach. Instead of working down from developmental theories, we began to work up from actual observations of how literacy was socially organized and used by the Vai. We decided to base our experimental activities on our ethnographic observations — to let our fieldwork generate specific hypotheses and suggest appropriate tasks.

Reading and writing are not prominent activities in the villages; still, the knowledge and use of the script by Vai literates are manifest in many ways. For one thing, the arrival of a taxi often brings letters, written in Vai, from relatives and business associates in other areas of Vai country and other parts of Liberia. We found that Vai literates write and receive between one and forty letters a month, depending upon a number of factors, including the kinds of economic enterprises in which they are involved and the location of the town in which they live. Funerals are a ubiquitous feature of life in a Vai village, where the infant mortality rate exceeds 50 percent and life expectancy is low. Funerals attract relatives and acquaintances from many parts of the country, each of whom is obligated to bring gifts in money or kind that must be reciprocated. Consequently, recording the names of donors and their gifts at funerals, as well as a variety of other administrative activities such as listing political contributions, are features of Vai life in which literacy plays a central and visible role. Some religious and fraternal organizations maintain records in Vai script, and we have documented at least one case in which a Muslim association was governed by a constitution and by-laws written in Vai script (Goody, Cole, & Scribner, 1977). Farmers and craftsmen use the script for business ledgers and technical plans. A few who might qualify as Vai scholars write family and clan histories, keep diaries, and record maxims and traditional tales in copybooks.

Despite test results, we know that Vai literacy functions in the society and that Vai people seem to feel that it functions well since literates are accorded high status. We began to look carefully at the specific skills these literacy activities seemed to involve: what did it require to write a letter, record contributions to a funeral feast, or list contributions to a religious society? We made functional analyses of the skills involved in these activities. Then, on the basis of these analyses, we designed tasks with different content but hypothetically similar skills to determine if prior practice in learning and use of the script enhanced performance.

Since letter-writing is the most common use of the Vai script, we closely studied the cognitive consequences of letter-writing. In the psychological literature, written communication is said to impose cognitive demands not encountered in face-to-face oral communication. In writing, meaning is supposed to be carried entirely by the test; thus, effective written communication requires sensitivity to the informational needs of the reader and skill in the use of elaborative linguistic techniques. We speculated that Vai literates' experience in writing and reading letters would contribute to the development of these skills, especially because the ability to communicate in writing with people from different places signifies successful completion of the study of the script.

To test this proposition, we adapted a communication task used in previous research (Flavell, Botkin, Fry, Wright, & Jarvis, 1968). Individuals were taught to play a simple board game with little verbal explanation; they were then asked to explain the game, without the materials of the game present, to a listener unfamiliar with it. In addition, we asked subjects to dictate a letter explaining the game to someone far away who had never seen it before.

The game involves two players taking turns racing their counters on a board of eight colored stripes. A counter's movements are governed by the color of the chip selected from a cup on each turn (Flavell et al., 1968). Board games are familiar to the Vai, who play a game called "ludo," which has a similar racing format.

We coded the transcribed protocols for the amount of game-related information they contained and for the presence of statements describing the materials of the game. On both of these measures of quality of communication, we found that men literate in the Vai script were far superior to nonliterates, and that this pattern was apparent in both the face-to-face explanation and the dictated letter. We also analyzed the protocols to see whether they reflected characteristics of Vai literates' style of communication in their day-to-day letter writing practices.

Over the years, Vai letters have evolved certain stylized formats. Here is a sample:

17/7/1964
Vaitown

This letter belongs to Pa Lamii in Vonzuan. My greeting to you, and my greeting to Mother.

This is your information. I am asking you to do me a favor. The people I called to saw my timber charged me $160.00. I paid them $120.00 and $40.00 still needed, but business is hard this time. I am therefore sending your child to you to please credit me amount of $40.00 to pay these people. Please do not let me down.

I stopped so far.

I am Moley Doma
Vaitown

The statements "This is your information" and "I am asking you to do me a favor" are examples of what we call the contextualization of the communication. They tell the recipient what the communication is all about and what information to expect. This aspect of an affective communication was well understood by Vai literates and clearly explained to us in some of our interviews. In one discussion on what makes a good letter, a middle-aged farmer told us, "You must first make the person to understand that you are informing him through words. Then he will give his attention there. It is the correct way of writing the Vai script." When we examined game instructions for this characteristic we found that Vai literates almost always contextualized their communication by giving some general characterization of the game — for example, "This is a game I am coming to tell you about where two people take a race and one of them wins."

A second set of studies tested for the transfer of skills needed to read Vai text. Our observations of Vai literates deciphering letters from friends and coping with mundane reading indicated that decoding the script is extraordinarily difficult because of special properties of the Vai writing system. Vai script characters map the consonant-vowel syllabic structure of the language in a systematic manner; however, this does not produce a direct one-to-one correspondence between the visual symbols and the units of sound. Vowel tone, a phonological feature that is semantically crucial in the spoken language, is not marked in the script. In addition, because the script is not standardized, the representation of vowel length, another semantically distinctive feature of the language, varies considerably from one script-writer to another. Finally, the script is written without division into words or other language units; a string of syllabic characters runs across the page without spacing or segmentation. Each character, depending on its semantic function, may represent a single-syllable word, one of several such words differentiated by tone, or a component unit of a polysyllabic word.

How does a literate Vai resolve these ambiguities? From observations of men reading letters we found that a common technique is what we have called experimentation in pronunciation — saying strings of syllables aloud recursively, varying vowel tones

and lengths until they click into meaningful units. Readers must keep separate syllables in mind until they can be integrated into words or phrases. We supposed that this
experience might foster skills in language analysis and integration and that these skills
might apply in language contexts that did not involve the script. To test this idea we
devised a listening task. Each person listened to tape recordings in which a native
speaker of Vai slowly read meaningful Vai sentences. Sentences were segmented either
into word units or syllable units. The listener was simply asked to repeat the sentence
and answer a comprehension question about it. On sentences containing word units,
there was no superiority for individuals with experience in Vai script; but, on sentences composed of syllable units, Vai literates with advanced reading skills outdis-
tanced all others, including those with fewer years of practice in reading.

These two tasks, and the remainder of our research, demonstrate that skills involved in literacy behaviors are indeed transferable to behaviors unrelated to literacy.
The effects reported — analyzing oral speech and giving clearer instructions — are
neither self-evident nor trivial. Speech perception and instruction have real utility.
These studies provide the first direct evidence that what an individual does with text,
or with pencil and paper, can promote specific skills that are available to support
other behaviors. In terms of the concerns with which the research began, we believe it
is important that these skills are associated with literacy, not with schooling — they
are not by-products of general learning experiences in the classroom. Although our
demonstration of literacy-related skills is limited by the range of literacy practices in
Vai society, it stands as the first clear-cut evidence in a present-day society that personal engagement in reading and writing does have psychological consequences.
These consequences, however, are all highly specific to activities with the Vai script.

The metaphor of literacy as a practice will help us put the Vai research in a more
general framework. By combining several dictionary definitions, we can state what we
mean by "a practice." A practice may be considered to be the carrying out of a goal-
directed sequence of activities, using particular technologies and applying particular
systems of knowledge. It is a usual mode or method of doing something — playing the
piano, sewing trousers, writing letters. This definition shares certain features with the
notion of practice in educational psychology — repeated performance of an act in order
to acquire proficiency or skill. How does this apply to literacy? Consider a goal-
directed sequence of activities such as letter-writing. This involves a technology — a
particular script and particular writing materials. It also requires knowledge of how to
represent oral language in script and of the conventional rules of representation. One
must know the form and style suitable for writing personal letters as well as what the
intended reader knows about the subject of the message and how the new information
will fit into the old. A variety of skills at different levels is required to perform this
complex act. As one writes more letters, these skills should become more efficiently
organized, less dependent on content, and more transferable to new contents and contexts. We did indeed find transfer of these skills in our game-instruction task but the
range of transfer was narrow. In summary, our results show that certain literacy practices among the Vai produced intellectual outcomes closely tied to those practices.

Our negative findings are an equally important part of the story. We did not find
that literacy in the Vai script was associated in any way with generalized competen-

cies such as abstraction, verbal reasoning, or metalinguistic skills. The tasks used in North American research as alternative measures of these capacities simply did not show consistency of performance in any group except the schooled group. Furthermore, we did not find that either literacy or schooling had an all-or-none effect; on all experimental tasks, including those showing the strongest effects of Vai literacy, some nonliterates achieved high scores and displayed the same skills as literates.

The results of our research among the Vai present us with two apparently contrasting conclusions about the effects of literacy. The literacy as development view would have us believe that literacy, in combination with schooling, produces generalized changes in the way people think. Our functional perspective suggests that the effects of literacy, and perhaps schooling as well, are restricted — perhaps to the practice actually engaged in or generalized only to closely related practices. These extreme alternatives echo an educational debate that began at the turn of the century. Thorndike and Woodworth (1901) suggested that learning is specific and transfer from one task to another will occur only when both tasks shared identical elements. Their antagonists believed that education, through mental discipline, strengthens the mind in general. (For a summary of the arguments at that time, see Thorndike, 1969, p. 357.) However, no theory guided the search for identical elements and no theory gave substance to the mental discipline position. After seventy-five years of debate and data accumulation, the issue of the effects of practice has not been resolved. We have no illusions that our skimpy data with respect to literacy will resolve the discrepancies between these two viewpoints, but our framework may help us think about literacy and its effects in a way that does not get us lost in unsupported generalities or insignificant particulars.

The specific outcomes that we observed in our studies of Vai literacy confirm earlier observations that certain cognitive skills show little generalizability across experimental tasks among traditional adults. The situation with respect to Vai writing and reading is similar to that of other skilled practices — such as weaving (Childs & Greenfield, in press) or pottery-making (Bunzel, 1953) — in nontechnological societies, in which highly organized, complex skills are applied to a limited set of problems. Previously, we argued that generalized skills might not arise when common operations are applied to a limited set of tasks (Scribner & Cole, 1973). If the uses of writing are few and limited, skills should be applied to each use in a more or less original way. As the repertoire of functions expands, the operations necessary for each may be applied across a range of tasks and contexts. For example, an individual might write a letter to distribute proceeds from a funeral feast — two functions that are usually separate. This example represents the upper limit of typical Vai writing practices because each individual's practices are restricted.

As the technology of any society becomes more complex, the number and variety of tasks to which literacy skills must be applied increases as well. A task might include some mix of a common core of skills like decoding, for example, with new skills or more complicated versions of old skills, as when Vai tradesmen begin to write to people they have never met before because business practice makes this necessary. If our argument that specific uses promote specific skills is valid, we might expect to find the outcomes that Olson or others predict, but only under conditions evoking these skills. Carrying out critical analyses of text, for example, might promote certain analytic operations with language, whereas rote learning from the same text, or reading it for some other purpose, is not likely to do so. Writing poetry is likely to have different consequences for language skills than preparing a letter to a department store requesting a refund for damaged goods.

As practice in any activity continues, we would expect that skills would extend to a wide range of tasks and materials and when the skill systems involved in literacy are many, varied, complex, and widely applicable, the functional and general ability perspectives will converge in their predictions of intellectual outcomes. Whether we choose to interpret these acquired functional skill systems developmentally is a matter of theoretical predilection, the discussion of which lies outside the argument of this chapter.

Although we do not advocate a single approach to the complex issues of the psychology of literacy, we believe that the strategy of functional analysis emerging from the Vai research may have particularly useful implications for educational research in our own society. It suggests that different literacy activities need to be analyzed independently. If, as we have demonstrated, particular skills are promoted by particular kinds of literacy practices, we need to know a great deal more about just how literacy is practiced. Studies of the range of reading and writing activities carried out in school, including those outside the official curriculum, would be a useful extension of work such as that done by Martin, D'Arcy, Newton, and Parker (1976). We have far fewer precedents, however, for an equally important research task: finding out what people in various communities and walks of life do with literacy — how they use their knowledge of reading and writing, to what tasks they apply it, and how they accomplish these tasks. Such analyses should help us understand the differences between school-based literacy practices and literacy practices unrelated to schooling as well as their possibly different implications for intellectual outcomes. Although attempts to arrive at some overall measures of literacy competencies may be useful for certain comparative purposes, the conceptualization of literacy as a fixed inventory of skills that can be assessed out of the contexts of application has little utility for educational policies.

We need to acknowledge, however, that we are a long way from having the methods, techniques, and theories required to make a systematic analysis of the component skills involved in reading and writing. Considerable progress has been made in identifying components in decoding activities and, more recently, in the higher-level intellectual skills involved in controlled reading tasks under laboratory-like or highly constrained classroom conditions. (See especially the reports of The Center for the Study of Reading, 1975–1978). Sticht, Fox, Hauke, and Zapf (1977) have used the skills-analysis approach to reading activities outside the classroom and have distinguished between reading-to-do and reading-to-learn activities. The long-range objective is to devise methods for an adequate description and analysis of skills in out-of-school literacy practices that can be coordinated with the microlevel analyses of laboratory studies.

Both educational practice and research might benefit from a recognition of the complex interrelationships between mental skills and literacy activities. Terms that refer to oral and literate modes of thought, although historically significant, are not useful characterizations of the mental abilities of nonliterate and literate adults in American society; in fact, most research with adults in traditional societies confirms their inappropriateness for any contemporaneous culture. Thus research does not support designing adult literacy programs on the assumption that nonliterates do not think abstractly, do not reason logically, or lack other basic mental processes. In each case, the skills available for learning how to read and write or for improving rudimentary literacy abilities need to be assessed with respect to the accomplishments nonliterates display in other activities — for example, disputation, hypothetical reasoning, or oral narrative. To the question posed at the beginning of this chapter — "Is a college student's incoherent essay symptomatic of faulty reasoning?" — our answer would be, "No, it is not a symptom; it is a sign to be evaluated."

If different literacy activities are linked to different intellectual outcomes, a second implication of our research is that reading and writing activities need to be tailored to desired achievements. These outcomes can be defined in terms of the literacy competencies required for participation in our highly technological society, but they need not be defined in narrowly pragmatic terms, reflecting merely the current demand for job security or advance. A skills approach might make it possible to identify a common core of skills that will enable an individual to master more intellectually demanding reading and writing tasks after completing the school curriculum or literacy program. If the educational objective is to foster analytic logical reasoning, that objective should guide the choice of instructional program. It should not be assumed that these skills will follow inevitably from practice in writing essays. Writing essays may be helpful, as may oral practices. This is undoubtedly the common wisdom of the classroom and the educational planner. But it would be helpful to ally this wisdom with the psychological literature on literacy so that the broad conceptual framework informs teaching practice and practice informs the theory.

We realize that the kind of program implied by our discussion may seem difficult to attain. The comments of the Soviet psychologist Vygotsky (1934/1978) some fifty years ago on the status of the specific-skill versus mental-development argument of his day offer useful guidance for our research choices today: "Such a matter cannot be dealt with by a single formula of some kind, but rather suggests how great is the scope for extensive and varied experimental research" (p. 34).

NOTE

1. Any effects reported as significant refer to regression analyses in which the variable in question entered the equation at the .05 level of significance or better.

REFERENCES

Bruner, J., Olver, R., Greenfield, P., Hornsby, J., Kemey, H., Maccoby, M., Modiano, N., Mosher, F., Olson, D., Potter, M., Reisch, L., & Sonstroem, A. (1966). *Studies in cognitive growth*. New York: Wiley.

Bunzel, R. (1953). Psychology of the Pueblo potter. In M. Mead & N. Calas (Eds.), *Primitive heritage*. New York: Random House.

Center for the Study of Reading. (1975–1978). *Technical reports 1–102.* Champaign: University of Illinois at Champaign-Urbana.

Childs, C., & Greenfield, P. (in press). Informal modes of learning and teaching: The case of Zinacanteco weaving. In N. Warren (Ed.), *Advances in cross-cultural psychology* (vol. 2). London: Academic Press.

Farrell, T. (1977). Literacy, the basics, and all that jazz. *College English, 38,* 443–459.

Flavell, J., Botkin, P., Fry, C., Wright, J., & Jarvis, P. (1968). *The development of role-taking and communication skills in children.* New York: Wiley.

Goody, J. (1977). *The domestication of the savage mind.* Cambridge, Eng.: Cambridge University Press.

Goody, J., Cole, M., & Scribner, S. (1977). Writing and formal operations: A case study among the Vai. *Africa, 47,* 289–304.

Greene, W. (1951). The spoken and the written word. *Harvard Studies in Classical Philology, 60,* 23–59.

Greenfield, P. (1966). On culture and equivalence. In J. Bruner et al. (Eds.), *Studies in cognitive growth.* New York: Wiley.

Greenfield, P. (1972). Oral or written language: The consequences for cognitive development in Africa, the United States and England. *Language and Speech, 15,* 169–178.

Greenfield, P., & Bruner, J. (1966). Culture and cognitive growth. *International Journal of Psychology, 1,* 89–107.

Havelock, E. *Preface to Plato.* (1963). Cambridge, MA: Harvard University Press.

Martin, N., D'Arcy, P., Newton, B., & Parker, R. (1966). *Writing and learning across the curriculum 11–16.* London: Ward Lock Educational.

Olson, D. (1975). Review of *Toward a literate society,* ed. J. Carroll & J. Chall. In *Proceedings of the National Academy of Education, 2,* 109–178.

Olson, D. (1977). From utterance to text: The bias of language in speech and writing. *Harvard Educational Review, 47,* 257–281.

Olson, D. (1977). The language of instruction. In R. Anderson, R. Spiro, & W. Montague (Eds.), *Schooling and the acquisition of knowledge.* Hillsdale, NJ: Erlbaum and Associates.

Olson, D., & Filby, N. (1972). On the comprehension of active and passive sentences. *Cognitive Psychology, 3,* 361–381.

Piaget, J. (1976). Foreword. In J. Piaget, B. Inhelder, & H. Chipman (Eds.), *Piaget and his school.* New York: Springer-Verlag.

Plato. Phaedrus. (1928). In I. Edman (Ed.), *The works of Plato.* New York: Modern Library.

Scribner, S. (1968). *The cognitive consequences of literacy.* Unpublished manuscript, Albert Einstein College of Medicine.

Scribner, S., & Cole, M. (1973). Cognitive consequences of formal and informal education. *Science, 182,* 553–559.

Stewart, G. (1976). Notes on the present-day usage of the Vai script in Liberia. *African Language Review, 6,* 71–74.

Sticht, T., Fox, L., Hauke, R., & Zapf, D. (1977). *The role of reading in the navy* (NPRDC TR 77–40). San Diego: Navy Personnel Research and Training Center.

Thorndike, E. (1969). *Educational psychology* (vol. 2). New York: Arno Press.

Thorndike, E., & Woodworth, R. (1901). The influence of improvement in one mental function upon the efficiency of other functions. *Psychological Review, 8,* 247–261.

UNESCO: World Congress of Ministers of Education on the Eradication of Illiteracy, Teheran. (1965, September 8–19). Inaugural speeches, messages, closing speeches. Paris: Author.

Vygotsky, L. (1963). Learning and mental development at school age. In B. Simon & T. Simon (Eds.), *Educational psychology in the USSR.* London: Routledge & Kegan Paul. See also Vygotsky, L. (1978). Learning and development. In M. Cole, V. John-Steiner, S. Scribner, & E. Souberman (Eds.), *Mind in society: The development of higher psychological processes.* Cambridge, MA: Harvard University Press.

The preparation of this paper was made possible by support from the Ford Foundation.

Literacy Learning and
Economic Change

DEBORAH BRANDT

The foundation of national wealth is really people — the human capital represented by their knowledge, skills, organizations, and motivations. Just as the primary assets of a modern corporation leave the workplace each night to go home for dinner, so the income-generating assets of a nation are the knowledge and skills of its workers — not its industrial plants or natural resources. As the economies of developed nations move further into the post-industrial era, human capital plays an ever more important role in their progress. As the society becomes more complex, the amount of education and knowledge needed to make a productive contribution to the economy becomes greater. (Johnston & Packer, 1987, p. 116)

With this policy blueprint, the U.S. Department of Labor exposes the processes by which individual literate ability and corporate profitability have become entangled. Where once U.S. workers had value for a capacity to transform raw materials into consumable goods, by the end of the twentieth century they have become the raw material itself. In an information economy, reading and writing serve as both instruments and products by which surplus wealth gets produced and competitive advantage gets won. If the ability to read and write was once regarded as a duty to God or democracy (Soltow & Stevens, 1981), it is now, according to the government, a duty to productivity, and one with increasingly sharp consequences for those not in compliance. Unrelenting economic change has become the key motivator for schools, students, parents, states, and communities to raise expectations for literacy achievement. It also is considered the key reason for widening gaps in income between skilled and unskilled workers (Reich, 1992).

However, for all of the attention paid to a demand for literacy that seems chronically to outstrip supply, little concern has been paid to how economic change itself affects people's ability to become and stay literate. How does broad-based economic restructuring — especially the kind that this country has seen over the last several decades — affect the contexts in which people learn to read and write? As we shall see below, the shifts that move us "further into the postindustrial era" do not merely apply the pressure for a more highly literate workforce; they also, more profoundly, constitute the turbulent conditions in which individuals, families, and entire regions

Harvard Educational Review   Vol. 69   No. 4   Winter 1999, 373–394

must collect resources for literacy learning. Fierce economic competition, including the changes in communication it stimulates, can destabilize the public meanings and social worth of people's literate skills. It also can ruthlessly reconfigure the social and material foundations upon which people must pursue literacy and pass it along to others (Brandt, 1995, 1998, in press; Gowen, 1992; Purcell-Gates, 1995; Stuckey, 1991; Taylor, 1996).

Over the last several years, I have been tracking the changing conditions of literacy learning as they have been experienced by ordinary people living through them. My aim is to understand especially what sharply rising standards for literacy have meant to successive generations of Americans and how people have responded to the steady changes in the meanings and methods of literacy learning. How do people experience what too many pundits call the literacy crisis: the relentless demand for more and more people to do more and more things with reading and writing? Throughout the early 1990s, I interviewed more than eighty people born between 1895 and 1985, all of whom were living at the time of the interviews in south-central Wisconsin. In wide-ranging discussions lasting from one to three hours, I asked people to remember everything they could about how they learned to write and read across their lifetimes, focusing particularly on the institutions, materials, people, and motivations involved in the process. What counted as literacy in these discussions was anything that people thought significant. No threshold was set for what counted as literacy learning, and nothing that was mentioned was excluded. The aim was to gather a chronicle of literacy learning set within the economic and cultural movements that changed this area of the country from an overwhelmingly agrarian society at the turn of the twentieth century into a principally information and service society at the turn of the twenty-first century. Taken together, the accounts link literacy learning to regional transformation over a period of more than eighty years.[1]

The project is grounded in principles of oral history and life history research developed by Bertaux (1981; Bertaux & Thompson, 1993, 1997), Thompson (1975, 1988, 1990), Lummis (1987), and others who emphasize the dynamic relationship between individual and collective practices and sociohistorical change. In this approach, the history of a period is apprehended through the life span, which sets the material and cultural boundaries within which people live out social and economic relationships with others. Of key significance in this approach are similarities and differences in the lives of people who have experienced similar social structures or have lived through the same historical events. This method is useful for gathering information about changes in the material and social networks through which people have learned and practiced literacy across time. It also exposes dynamic changes in definitions and expectations for literacy and the ways they are experienced at different times by different groups and generations (see also Conger & Elder, 1994; Elder, 1974, 1994; Elder & Liker, 1982; Ryder, 1965).

In analyzing the interviews, I sought frameworks that would be particularly sensitive to the presence of economic forces at the scenes of literacy learning. What was the relationship, I kept bluntly asking of the data, between the way that surplus wealth gets made and the way that literacy gets made? The analysis needed to capture both the value of literacy for individual learners and the value that literate individuals had in wider arenas of economic competition into which their skills were recruited. These two sides of literacy are not necessarily easy to separate, yet they are both key, I believe, to understanding the increasing demands on reading and writing skill in the twentieth century. For purposes of the analysis, then, I approached literate skills as a resource, which, like wealth or education or trade skill or social connections, is pursued for the opportunities and protections that it potentially grants its seekers. As a resource, literacy has potential value for gaining power or pleasure, and accruing information, civil rights, education, spirituality, status, or money (see Bourdieu, 1990; Bourdieu & Wacquant, 1992; Grubb, 1990, 1992; Murray, 1997). To treat literacy as a resource is to appreciate the lengths that families and individuals will go to secure (or resecure) literacy for themselves or their children. But it also takes into account how individuals' literate skills are exploited in competitions for profit or advantage that go on within the larger communities in which they live and work, and in which their literacy learning takes place. Like other public and private resources, literacy is valuable — often volatile — property. And like other resources, it is grounds for potential exploitation, injustice, and struggle, as well as potential hope, satisfaction, and reward. Wherever literacy is learned and practiced, these competing interests will be present.

Using grounded theory (Strauss, 1987; Strauss & Corbin, 1990), I developed an analytical concept that was most sensitive to these competing forces, a concept that I came to call "sponsors" of literacy. Sponsors are any agents, local or distant, concrete or abstract, who provide, enhance, or deny opportunities for literacy learning and gain advantage by it in some way. Sponsors appeared all over people's memories of how they learned to write and read, in their memories of people, commercial products, public facilities, religious organizations, and other institutional and work settings. As we will see below, sponsors are an especially tangible way to track connections between literacy as an individual development and literacy as an economic development because of how closely literacy in this century grows integral to the interests of capitalism. Sponsors, then, as I came to understand them, embody the resource management systems of literacy, particularly avenues to access and reward. Sponsors also introduce the instability in the worth of people's literacy. As various sponsors of literacy emerge and recede, and as their prospects rise and fall as part of economic and political competition, so go the prospects of those they sponsor, both in terms of opportunity for literacy learning and the worth of particular literate skills.[2]

The following discussion looks through the lens of sponsorship at the literacy learning memories of two women who were both raised on family-owned dairy farms in the Midwest — one who was born at the beginning of the century and one near the end. Because of the similarities of these two women's upbringing and their shared interest in writing, their accounts provide a stark and immediately accessible illustration of a relationship between literacy learning and economic change. Their cases are also useful because changes to rural life in the United States are both dramatic and familiar to the society. Born two generations apart, these two individuals witnessed from different points in time the steady decline of independent dairy farming and its transformation by the forces of mechanization, vertical integration of food processes, and consolidation of land, capital, and information under corporate control. They

also witnessed, from different positions, the effects on their communities of competing social and political arrangements as other forms of work encroached on former
farmland and altered the status of rural societies. A close analysis of their accounts of
literacy learning will uncover the cumulative effects of radical economic and regional
change on opportunities for literacy learning. My aim is to extract from their experience lessons that can be applied to literacy learning in other economic configurations
— not in order to predict particular outcomes, but to understand better the struggles
that economic transformations bring to the pursuit of literacy. With this knowledge,
educators might be in a better position to find ways to compensate for tears in social
fabrics that these transformations leave behind, tears that can make the pursuit of literacy feel so unfair and at times so harrowing for so many.

Consider then the parallel lives of two European American women, Martha Day
and Barbara Hunt.[3] Both were raised on eighty-acre, low-income dairy farms that their
fathers had inherited, Martha Day in northern Indiana and Barbara Hunt in southern
Wisconsin. Both grew up in sparse, rural settlements of five hundred or fewer families
that were some distance from stores and schools. Both were the middle child of three
children. Both found much of their academic writing less memorable and satisfying
than their extracurricular writing: Martha Day with the high school yearbook and
Barbara Hunt with her State Forensic Association. Both read often for pleasure, and
both kept journals. Neither had much money nor family encouragement for schooling
beyond the twelfth grade, and both left home and went to work shortly after high
school graduation. For all these striking similarities in background, however, the differences in their life circumstances are pronounced. For one thing, they were born
sixty-eight years apart, Martha Day in 1903 and Barbara Hunt in 1971. Further, while
Martha Day found her way in her early twenties into a journalism career, eventually
becoming a columnist and women's editor for a farm magazine, *The Mid-Plains
Farmer*, Barbara Hunt, in her early twenties, was cashiering at the *Mid-Plains* Mobil
Station, doing child care on the side and taking an occasional course in the human services program at a two-year technical college twenty-five miles from her home.

The contrast in their birth dates and the work they were doing after high school
speaks directly, of course, to the rising standard for literacy and school achievement
across a sixty-year span (Resnick & Resnick, 1977). Martha Day's high school graduation in 1920 made her among the best-educated members of her community, while
the only thing guaranteed to high school graduates in the 1980s was that they were
likely to earn several hundred thousand dollars less over their lifetimes than college
graduates ("Income, Poverty Rate," 1990). But these accounts also point out subtler
cultural changes that affect literacy development. Martha Day came of age when the
small family farm economy in the Midwest was worth more, both literally in terms
of dollars and jobs, and culturally and socially. At the beginning of the twentieth century, Martha Day belonged to the 40 percent of the U.S. population engaged in the
agricultural sector. By the time of Barbara Hunt's birth in 1971, farm kids belonged
to the 2 percent of the population still in agriculture. Martha Day's residence on an
eighty-acre farm and her attendance at a two-room country school made her background typical of European Americans in her predominantly rural state. Sixty years
later, rural schools had joined urban schools in being chronically underfinanced in

comparison with suburban districts, and family-owned dairy farms were disappearing from the Wisconsin landscape at a rate of a thousand farms a year (*Census of Agriculture*, 1992; also see Saupe & Majchrowicz, 1996). Although Martha Day and Barbara Hunt were both affected by profound transformations in rural life, Martha Day was able to trade more effortlessly on the status of her farm girl background to make the transition from physical to mental labor. For Barbara Hunt, similar features of the farm girl background found little value within the economy in which she was competing.

The following discussion will look systematically at sponsorship patterns in the literacy learning of these two women across their lifetimes. Of special significance are the webs of social relationship in their lives, the gendered divisions of labor, the media they used, the relative health of the institutions that supported and exploited their literacy learning, as well as the broader economic and cultural contexts in which their communities were competing.

"THE TYPICAL LITTLE VILLAGE OF THAT DAY":
THE CASE OF MARTHA DAY

Martha Day's childhood coincided with the "golden age of agriculture," a twenty-year period at the turn of the century when average farm incomes were doubling, the value of farmland was more than tripling, and profits and tax revenues were invested in local improvements (Danbom, 1995). Martha Day's early literacy memories are set within an emerging infrastructure of electric lights, paved roads, rural mail delivery, rising farm prices, farm journalism, and expanding schooling that developed as part of an unprecedented boom time in midwestern rural areas.[4] Like many people I interviewed who were children during this period, Martha Day proudly recalled a progressive family identity that seemed to be delivered into many rural households along with the local newspaper. Periodical reading was linked to forward-looking thinking, intelligent farming, and political participation among people like Martha Day's parents, who typically ended their schooling by seventh or eighth grade. Here is Martha Day's recollection of the presence of newspapers in her home:

> Dad always subscribed to [the nearest daily] and took it by the year. My Dad was smart and a good scholar and a most interested man in politics and everything that was going on. I don't remember reading it much, but I remember when my father came in from working in the fields, the first thing he'd do is, if the paper, if the mail had come, he would sit down and read the newspaper. He was very sharp on that kind of thing. For that day.

Martha Day attended grade school about one mile from her farm in one of the many two-story brick schoolhouses that had been scattered around her county in the late nineteenth century.[5] Because her community did not provide public education beyond tenth grade, she and her brother finished high school in a larger town, carpooling with neighbors to make the ten-mile drive. It was in high school that Martha Day discovered her love of writing, primarily through work on the yearbook and through the school library. Current books also arrived to her home by mail, sent at birthdays and holidays by a favorite aunt who was a librarian in Washington, DC. "I got the feeling of emotions coming through words on paper," Martha Day recalled. "I think reading makes people want to write."

At the time of our interview in 1992, Martha Day was still stinging from what she considered the gender discrimination that sent her brother away to college while she stayed in the area to care for her invalid mother. "[My brother's] teachers encouraged him," she explained. "They got a rector scholarship. Told him about it. Nobody told me. I made grades just as good as his. But they didn't push girls, and my parents couldn't have sent us on." Instead, in 1921, when her mother was well enough, Martha Day moved to the nearest city, worked in the book department of a large department store, and took secretarial courses at night.

Martha Day was part of a major migration of the 1920s — an outflow from the countryside that would help to radically alter the community into which she was born (Danbom, 1995). Nevertheless, many social aspects of a lingering, nineteenth-century agrarian tradition seemed to carry over into the life of the city where she lived, significantly conditioning her opportunities for work and writing.

Chief among these carryovers was the broad overlap of homogeneous social institutions that had organized her childhood and, as we will see below, would subsidize her "love of writing" well into adult life. Early in the interview, Martha Day recalled attending grade school in what she described as "the typical little village of that day." "There was," she said, "a school, a church, and a general store." Education, religion, and commerce were located, literally, at the same intersection of her village, about one mile from the farmhouse that had been in her mother's family for generations. The ethnic homogeneity and close-knit social institutions that characterized rural northern Indiana in Martha Day's childhood were, in fact, an "essential feature of the labor system" of midwestern rural communities at that time (Nelson, 1995, p. 6). Where cash was scarce, barter was common, and transactions depended on trust based on personal acquaintance or local reputation. Social participation in overlapping institutions enhanced trust and knowledge by which people conducted local business and managed local resources. According to Nelson, ethnically homogeneous communities and the value of the informal contract played a role in both the material and social success of community members.

Despite the fact that so many people were on the move at this time — or perhaps because of it — this network was still in place for Martha Day when she relocated to the city, fifty miles away. "I never did have to hunt for jobs," she said. "Somebody from my area always said, 'Call me' or 'We've got a job. Would you be interested in it?' I had a job with the tax commissioners and then, while I was on that job, somebody called me that knew my family and asked if I would be interested in a job as secretary to the vice president of an insurance company." Both the informality and the pervasiveness of these social networks were evident in Martha Day's account of her break into journalism, which occurred shortly after her marriage to a bookkeeper in 1925. She and her husband began attending a Methodist Sunday school class for young married couples that was taught by the managing editor of a local newspaper. Aware of Martha Day's interest in writing, he asked her to put together a monthly newsletter for the Sunday school group. Two years later, this man bought a small regional farm magazine and invited Martha Day to become a part-time "rewrite man," as she called herself. Her job was to recast into short news items the press releases and bulletins that were pouring out of the state agricultural university and experimental stations at that time.

Martha Day worked at home, with a typewriter, desk, and filing cabinet that the editor provided. Each Sunday, she brought her rewrites to church and received a new batch of assignments. Occasionally, the editor asked her to write a feature story, usually about a farm woman. Occasionally, Martha Day's husband would go along on her feature assignments to take photographs that illustrated her published articles. The editor was instrumental in teaching Martha Day classic elements of journalistic style. She recalled:

> He kept building me up, you know, giving me a little more instruction. How the first paragraph had to do this and so forth. He would try to coach me along. He'd say, "Now that might have been better if you'd included a little less in that paragraph," and things like that.

At the same time, the editor encouraged Martha Day to appeal to her farm background as she imagined topics and audiences. "He'd say, 'Imagine you are a farm woman,'" she recalled. "That I grew up on a farm helped me in some respects. It wouldn't today."

When commercial farm publishing entered a bonanza period in the 1940s (Evans & Salcedo, 1974), the newspaperman's local farm journal was bought out by a much larger conglomerate, the *Mid-Plains Farmer*. Martha Day was invited to move to corporate offices and, throughout several more buyouts and mergers, gradually assumed more editorial responsibility. She contributed a bimonthly column on domestic topics, compiled cookbooks that were distributed as complimentary promotions, and traveled regularly to Chicago and other big cities for editorial meetings or conventions of the National Association of Women Farm Editors (whose membership nationwide numbered sixteen). She retired in 1968. At the time of our interview in 1992, she was widowed and residing near her daughter in a residential care facility in Wisconsin, some three hundred miles from her birthplace. She wrote letters to church friends, some from the original adult Sunday school class, and showed me extensive memoirs she had written in several bound journals that her daughter had bought for her. Although her eyesight was deteriorating, she had recently composed a humorous poem about osteoporosis that a nurse helped her to get published in a health magazine for senior citizens.

This account of Martha Day's literacy sponsors illustrates two important connections between literacy development and economic development. It shows, first, how the cultural and social organization of a particular economy creates reservoirs of opportunity and constraint from which individuals take their literacy, and second, how these backgrounds can later become exploited by agents of change. Martha Day's memories of early literacy learning carry the paradoxes and tensions that were alive in rural White societies at the turn of the century, as conservative values of farm and village shaped young people, even while they were heading for lives elsewhere. For Martha Day, these paradoxes registered most painfully for her in the gender inequality that she felt limited her educational and geographical horizons. While both she and her brother left the farm, he went to college and to an eventual science career in the nation's capital. She took her interest in reading and writing fifty miles to her state capital for jobs selling books and taking dictation. Yet staying back left her tethered to the conservative social institutions out of which her subsequent literacy opportunities (and their exploitable value) would come. Although village life was already under radical change, the legacies of the village economy, in which religious, educational, and commercial interests blended so routinely, were still intact in her social sphere. This tradition provided the point of contact for Martha Day's entrance into paid professional writing and sanctioned the informal apprenticeship by which she learned her trade. Local ownership of newspapers and farm journals was part of this social milieu, making Martha Day's local identity part of her qualifications for her first job. Further, in the small, nonspecialized operation of the local farm journal (in which news stories and columns were often contributed by farmers themselves), gender specialization was less pronounced, and Martha Day took on the assignments of a "rewrite man," dealing with technical and agricultural information coming from the land-grant college. Only with her later transfer to the larger corporation would her duties become exclusively that of a "women's" editor.

One more aspect of cultural and social organization is worth noting here. This was a period when print, while becoming more widespread, was nevertheless most readily identified with and experienced through a small set of institutions in society: the church, the school, or the newspaper. These were the basic institutions that had promulgated an initial mass literacy in the latter half of the nineteenth century in the United States (Graff, 1979; Soltow & Stevens, 1981). These institutions and their practices came forward into the twentieth century as dense sites of literate resources. This concentration of resources into a few institutions made it common to find people like the Sunday school teacher-slash-newspaper editor, in whose very figure coalesced the religious and secular print traditions that lie deep within the history of this country. Several other study participants from Martha Day's generation recalled influential teachers who seemed literally to embody these print traditions and make them available in informal apprenticeship relationships. These strong figures were principal forms by which literacy opportunity appeared in the social arrangements of this time and place.

Martha Day's background became an exploitable resource when the farm magazine industry took off in the 1940s. With an infusion of wealth from corporate advertisers and investors, this was a period of favorable growth in agricultural journalism. Farm outputs were up; fertilizers, irrigation, and other commercial products were being sold, principally through print advertising. A rapid rise in education was under way. Agricultural colleges, increasingly geared to the interests of high-tech, capital-intensive agribusiness, continued to pump out information that had to be translated into popular treatments (Hightower, 1973). Farm magazines in this period attempted to appeal to the entire farm family and to uphold feel-good elements of the agrarian tradition, even as they subtly changed habits and practices of farm families toward a new, much more business-oriented mode of farming (Walter, 1996). Women's news was crucial to the commercial success of these magazines, in part because, as Martha Day explained, wives typically were the family members who placed the subscriptions. Although eventually put out of business by full-scale, national women's magazines like *Ladies Home Journal* or *Good Housekeeping*, women's sections in regional farm journals carried features on topics ranging from gardening and canning to dress, diet, faith, and marital advice (Evans & Salcedo, 1974). Martha Day wrote on all of these topics in her column, which was often organized around the seasonal rhythms of the farm life she experienced growing up.

The person of Martha Day, the source of her value in her home community, could be appropriated for its value to farm journalism as it was being practiced at this time. Her conservative farm background, her Methodist mores, and her ideological comfort with print as an agent of improvement all enabled her to voice the values that the *Mid-Plains Farmer* needed for commercial success. These commercial needs became the vehicle for Martha Day's adult literacy development. However, this window of opportunity was brief. By the time Martha Day retired in the late 1960s, general farm magazines were on the wane, women weren't home anymore to be interviewed for her feature stories, more and more of her published recipes came from large food-processing industries, and agribusiness was changing the farm economy from top to bottom. Before these changes, however, Martha Day fulfilled her desire to be a writer and to travel to Chicago and other big cities, where she gathered news, attended conventions, and participated in corporate editorial meetings. All of these opportunities were still immensely satisfying and motivating to Martha Day from the perspective of the 1990s. At the age of eighty-nine, she was still writing and finding her audience in senior citizen magazines.

It was common to find other European American women among Martha Day's cohort whose early opportunities for literacy, education, and work were freighted with similar responsibilities for upholding agrarian traditions. For instance, during the first four decades of the twentieth century, rural farm women were heavily recruited into rural grade school teaching, as they were considered ideal promoters of the Country Life Movement.[6] This curricular program, like the farm journals of the time, upheld a progressive version of agrarian values in an effort to keep rural students "down on the farm" producing the cheap food needed by industrial workers in big cities (Danbom, 1995; see also Tremmel, 1995). Rural schools and farm journals were particularly important organs for reinforcing the values of agriculture and rural society among countryside populations during turbulent economic times. Ultimately, the effort to shore up a fading way of life proved futile, but such ideologically conservative work, much of it poorly paid, frequently fell to women.

In tracing the relationship of Martha Day's literacy development to the economic backdrop in which it occurred, I do not suggest that hers was the only — or even the most typical — experience of the farm people of her generation. Indeed, among other midwestern European Americans of her cohort that I interviewed, extreme physical isolation, poor schooling, instability in farm prices, the catastrophes of the Depression, all could make access to material and institutional supports for literacy difficult and sometimes impossible. For people bearing the burden of racial discrimination, the conditions usually were much more difficult. However, her case illustrates in its particulars how dynamics of economic competition create the context in which literate resources can be pursued, expended, enjoyed, and rewarded. For Martha Day, membership in a cultural majority within a stable and at times expanding economy provided both the means and mentality for her literate interests and skills to pay off. While Martha Day made a successful transition from agricultural to intellectual labor, the transition depended on being well connected to an older order upon whose value she could continue to trade. These social structures provided the forms of sponsorship, invitation, and access for Martha Day to learn and practice literacy. These structures also provided the ideological constraints that determined what Martha Day wrote, for whom, where, and for how long.

"I DID A LOT WITH HOMELESSNESS":
THE CASE OF BARBARA HUNT

If Martha Day's earliest literacy development took place within a local society that was growing together, Barbara Hunt's took place within a local society that was coming apart. Born in 1971, three years after Martha Day retired from the staff of the *Mid-Plains Farmer*, Barbara Hunt was one of three daughters in a family operating a cash-strapped dairy farm during some of the most crisis-ridden years in the history of the dairy industry, as independent farmers continued to lose the struggle with competing conglomerates. Lower commodity prices, lower incomes, decreasing farmland values, and difficulty in servicing debt were putting lots of family farms out of business (Saupe, 1989). Wisconsin saw a 50 percent decline in the number of farms between the 1960s and the 1990s, with the biggest decline between 1987 and 1992, the years that Barbara Hunt was attending high school (*Census of Agriculture*, 1992). In ironic contrast to the confident outlook Martha Day associated with the daily newspaper in her childhood home, Barbara Hunt's keenest memories of the newspaper were the uneasy budget calculations that her father would leave penciled in the margins.

Like Martha Day, Barbara Hunt grew up in a small, ethnically homogeneous community founded in the nineteenth century by German Catholic clerics and dairy-keepers. At the turn of the century, it had been one of the main production areas in the state for butter, grain, and tobacco. Now, still characterized as a place where almost all residents are related to each other, it is anchored by a stone church built in the 1850s, which abides as the main social institution. But at the end of the twentieth century, this unincorporated village had no schools and little commercial base left. Barbara Hunt rode a bus ten miles north across the county line for schooling, and her family drove twenty miles south to find a major shopping district. Passed by when a state highway was built in the 1940s, this community experienced less than a 3 percent economic growth rate between 1980 and 1990, compared to a 14 percent growth rate in the county overall. Per capita income lagged in relation to the rest of the region as well. On the other hand, dairy herds were still thick and competition among the farms was quite keen. In the late 1980s, land in the area was changing hands at a record pace as farmers with deeper capital were buying out their neighbors.

Barbara Hunt's residence in a village that had grown little in ninety years was not "typical for its day," and its homogeneity was no longer relevant to the structure of labor, as many residents scattered each morning in their cars for service jobs that had overtaken the urbanizing county. Farm concerns no longer dominated the regional newspapers to which residents of her community subscribed, and the regional radio, national television networks, and films that infiltrated the Hunt household in the 1970s and 1980s primarily delivered urban-oriented images, information, and perspectives. (Barbara Hunt recalled with a laugh missing her favorite TV sitcoms because of evening milking chores and then having to watch *The Waltons* and *Little House on the Prairie*, which were on at a later hour.) Her school system, answerable to state mandates, typically strained out local culture from its curriculum, so that in high school, for instance, Barbara Hunt and her sister encountered German as a foreign language, not as the language of the founders of their community. The family purchased used books as well as a used typewriter on trips to a Catholic thrift store. "We used to go to [the thrift store] and the books were real cheap. They'd be like three cents," Barbara Hunt recalled. "So a lot of our books at home were like that. Hey, even if you didn't like them, they were cheap." Although, as we will see, the teenaged Barbara Hunt, like Martha Day, was discovering a love of writing and searching for avenues for this love, she was acquiring literacy as part of a demographic minority, as a member of an unincorporated political unit within a county that had undergone the swift economic transformations of the late twentieth century. Compared to Martha Day, her literacy sponsors were more remote and more distributed across geographically and ideologically diverse institutions. Assembling available literacy resources was proving more difficult for Barbara Hunt than it had for Martha Day. So was finding employer-sponsors who could enhance her literacy development in her adult years. Her paying jobs were not related to agriculture, but rather to low-end retail and government-subsidized services common to areas with stagnant economies. Hired as a home health aide after high school, she charted the weight and pulse of elderly clients on Medicare. "If anything happened you had to write," she said, "and I had a lady that everything happened to." But she was laid off when, during major HMO reshuffling in the county, the agency relocated. In the mid-1990s, Barbara Hunt's most steady source of income was in day care and private babysitting, as farm adults sought off-farm employment to stanch the loss of incomes. "Right now I'm baby-sitting and I always read to the kids 'cause I think you should. It sinks in," she said.

To understand how Barbara Hunt undertook literacy development during hard times, it will be useful to look at two major sponsors of her writing during late adolescence and early adulthood: the High School Forensic Association she was a member of for five years and the human resources program of a two-year technical college she attended part-time. Both of these institutions were in some ways helping Barbara Hunt to carry her literacy and literate potential into her local economy.

Barbara Hunt joined the forensic club in eighth grade. "As soon as I heard about it, I knew I wanted to be in it," she said. For one thing, being in the club allowed her to satisfy a lifelong quirk: the love of reading aloud. Early in our interview she described a familiar living room scene from her childhood:

> Ever since I was little, I liked to read aloud, and I'd always bug people. I'd be with [my younger sister] and she'd be on the couch and I'd be on the chair, and we'd be reading out loud. We'd get up to a level and it was, "Stop, stop. Stop reading so loud." We'd get louder and louder. She'd stop and I'd go in my room and read out loud anyway. Maybe it was something where I knew, maybe I knew I would like to do my own thing and write on my own.

As a member of the forensic club, Barbara Hunt first competed in the category of declamation, reciting published dramatic pieces from memory. But by high school, she was performing in the original speech division, composing and delivering four- and eight-minute speeches.

The forensic club in her high school was part of the oldest statewide consortium of speech, debate, and theater clubs in the United States, founded in 1895 by a school superintendent who once administered the district where Barbara Hunt attended high school (Brockhaus, 1949). In later years the consortium was sustained by the state university extension service, and on occasion sponsored joint competitions with Future Farmers of America. By the time Barbara Hunt was a member, the Forensic Association had become an independent organization subsidized by dues from member schools. Headquarters provided handbooks and other instructional guides, trained and certified speech coaches, sponsored regional and statewide competitions, and published a newsletter. This state organization in turn held membership in a national high school forensic association that also sponsored events and provided instructional and promotional print materials.

As a participant in competitions, Barbara Hunt wrote speeches on topics of her choice. She picked topics that in her words "had real emotion," involving issues that "affected me but kind of affected other people." Her preferred topics included abortion, crack use, racism, and homelessness. "I did a lot with homelessness," she explained. "The homeless problem at the time was my sophomore year, 1986–1987. There were three million homeless people in the United States. I wanted to get people to realize what was going on."

To write her speeches, she used the school library as well as notes she took from TV news and magazine shows. She also was influenced by *Hallmark Hall of Fame* specials. Song lyrics that she heard on the radio also helped her to reflect on her life and her speech topics. "Songs to me are like some books or some speeches," she said, "when they seem to be exactly what your life is." Barbara Hunt also sometimes enhanced her presentations with film clips taped on a VCR. She practiced her speeches while doing the chores:

> I'd be going along the front of the cows, feeding them with my shovel, and I'd be doing my speech. Dad probably got so sick of me. He never knew what I was saying because I would never tell him what I was actually saying. I would say it to the cows so he never knew what I was practicing. I could probably give my homeless speech right now, though, if I really thought about it.

Barbara Hunt traveled throughout the region with her speech team, qualifying a couple of times for championships held in the state capital. She also found satisfaction when she developed original introductions that were praised by her coach and sometimes imitated by other students.

Despite its many transformations over a 100-year period, the Forensic Association was carrying forward remnants of an oratorical culture that had traditionally sponsored literacy among rural students.[7] The organization trained extracurricular teachers and subsidized public forums in which Barbara Hunt usually had more freedom to express herself than in school or Sunday school.[8] That her writing could be performed orally was a powerful incentive for her continuous membership in the organization — one of the few to which she belonged in high school. This format also appealed to her ethical sensibilities. "When you give a speech, you have to know the material," she said. "I love it when people [in the competitions] know their speeches and are looking right at you as they give them."

For Barbara Hunt, high school forensics sustained oratorical and ethical values long associated with midwestern agrarian politics and local self-improvement organizations. Through her speeches, Barbara Hunt was able to articulate issues that, as she said, "affected me but kind of affected other people." Like Martha Day, she was voicing the conditions of her time and place, but translated through urban equivalents that dominated national media as well as the prepackaged research materials in her high school library. The expression of rural social problems through dominant urban ones was not a dilemma Martha Day faced as a writer.

At the time of our interview in 1992, the writing that Barbara Hunt did for her forensic club was finding some resonance in a psychology class she was taking in the human services program offered at the urban technical college to which she was commuting. In the class, she wrote short essays on contemporary social problems. The course was part of a two-year degree program that had begun in the early 1980s to prepare people as technical assistants in programs such as drug rehabilitation or family counseling. This vocational program was launched as a response to a growing regional demand for professionalization in social work, which accompanied increased private and public investments in child and family welfare. According to its director, the program, which focuses mainly on problems of urban poverty, racial discrimination, and substance abuse, had become a popular vocational choice for young, first-generation college women from rural areas (personal communication, May 1998). In 1998, six years after our initial interview, Barbara Hunt was still taking courses toward her associate's degree while continuing to work in area day-care centers.

Although it is too soon to predict the full life and literacy trajectory of Barbara Hunt, it is clear that many of the local cultural assets that subsidized Martha Day as she made her way into literacy either are not available to the younger woman, or simply are no longer worth as much in her society. The dairy-farm life that Barbara Hunt was born to will be hard to parlay directly into economic opportunities, except insofar as it has fine-tuned her sensitivity to human distress. But a sensitivity to her rural time and place needs much reinterpretation and transformation to operate in the fields of social service as they are taught and practiced at the end of the twentieth century. To become a writer in her chosen field, Barbara Hunt needs to negotiate formal academic training. She also will need to negotiate complex bureaucratic systems that fund and deliver most social services, as well as the urban locations and orientations of most social service agencies. These are complexities that did not confront Martha Day — at least not so centrally — as she broke into agricultural journalism in the 1920s.

For all of the differences in situation between the two women, it is also worth noticing similarities in their accounts. These include the influence of the division of labor by gender that engaged both of them in forms of women's work designed to stabilize farm families during different periods of farm crisis. If Martha Day as journalist was charged with conserving traditional farm families for the benefit of an industrializing economy, Barbara Hunt as day-care worker was charged with conserving young farm families in transition as women and men were drawn increasingly into wage jobs.[9] Yet it was also conservative cultural supports associated with traditional agrarian societies that provided vital encouragement and validation of the women's aspirations to write. Like the figure of the Sunday school teacher/publisher in Martha Day's young adulthood, the State Forensic Association in Barbara Hunt's life preserved vestiges of older agrarian institutions like the state extension service and self-improvement societies. With its ties to agrarian oratory, speaker integrity, and concern with social issues, the forensic club served as a reservoir of literate practices and values through which Barbara Hunt could use her writing to witness for the economically displaced — even as she encountered a form of schooling and a larger society that did not make that easy.

LITERACY, LEARNING, AND ECONOMIC CHANGE

Literacy learning is conditioned by economic changes and the implications they bring to regions and communities in which students live (Castells, 1989). Economic changes devalue once-accepted standards of literacy achievement but, more seriously, destabilize the social and cultural trade routes along which families and communities once learned to preserve and pass on literate know-how. As new and powerful forms of literacy emerge, they diminish the reach and possibilities of receding ones. Over the last seventy years, a lopsided competition between corporate agribusiness and family farming altered life for millions of people in the rural Midwest. The accounts of Martha Day and Barbara Hunt can aid speculation about where in the processes of literacy learning economic changes like this can have greatest impact. First, we must notice the potential advantages that come with being well connected to dominant economies, whether in periods of stability or change. Dominant economies make their interests visible in social structures and communication systems. Growing up in the heyday of independent agriculture, Martha Day literally could see her way of life reflected everywhere — from the close proximity of the social institutions that sponsored her childhood literacy, to the stories and pictures carried in the print media she encountered. Demographic typicality can enhance literacy development even during periods of stressful transition, because at least for a while the powerful resources and skills built up in well-developed economies are attractive sites for reappropriation by agents of change. But as family farming receded in economic and cultural dominance, its social structures weakened as an objectified presence in the world around Barbara Hunt.[10] With every revolution by which the greater region in which she lived turned to information and service production, the mismatch intensified between the conditions in which her family lived and labored and the conditions in which she was forced to learn and find a living. It is here where economic disadvantage and literacy disadvantage find their relationship.

Barbara Hunt's experience helps to illuminate the effects of late twentieth-century economic life on literacy learning. Even in rural areas, the complexity of social organization, as well as the proliferating reliance on print, means that encounters with literacy are more likely to be spread across ideologically diverse sources and specialized, often remote institutions. Influences on literacy are simply more diffused. The role of multimedia in Barbara Hunt's writing development is perhaps the best illustration of this phenomenon, as she coordinated sources from print, television, radio, and film, and transformed them all into the older rhetorical genre of the timed speech. Especially in contrast to Martha Day, Barbara Hunt's experience also shows how rapid economic change can interrupt or enervate the social mechanisms that traditionally have supported and sustained literacy. As investments in local education, commerce, and social welfare drain away from a community, the process alters if not erases the institutions by which literacy learning — at least until recent times — has been most broadly sponsored. For these reasons, making literacy, like making money, was proving more complicated for Barbara Hunt than for Martha Day, requiring considerable ingenuity, translation, and adaptation. In her early twenties she was learning to write for an economy she aspired to join while enjoying few of the powerful subsidies that the sponsors of that economy contribute to literacy learning. This is a condition faced by millions of literacy learners of all ages at the end of the twentieth century, whose ways of life and labor are undergoing permanent destruction and replacement.

TOWARD IMPLICATIONS FOR LITERACY RESEARCH AND TEACHING

With this chapter I have tried to get beyond the rhetoric that usually surrounds the topic of literacy and the economic needs of the nation. No teacher or policymaker at any level can ignore the power of the country's economic system, its direction of change in the twentieth century, and the implications that brings, especially now, for literacy and literacy learning. However, we do not need to think only in the terms that *Workforce 2000* or similar pronouncements suggest. Our responsibility should not be merely — and perhaps not even mainly — to keep raising standards, revising curricula, and multiplying skills to satisfy the restless pursuers of human capital. We should not think our efforts go only to preparing students for future demands, nor should we define the problems they experience as readers or writers solely in terms of rising expectations versus insufficient skills. Economic changes create immediate needs for students to cope with gradual and sometimes dramatic alterations in systems of access and reward for literacy learning that operate beyond the classroom. Downsizing, migrations, welfare cutbacks, commercial development, transportation, consolidation, or technological innovations do not merely form the background buzz of contemporary life. These changes, where they occur, can wipe out as well as create access to supports for literacy learning. They also can inflate or deflate the value of ex-

isting forms of literacy in the lives of students. Any of these changes can have implications for the status of literacy practices in school and for the ways students might
interact with literacy lessons.

The reverberations of economic transformation form the history of literacy itself.
For these reasons, they deserve a more central stage in developing theories of individual literacy development. How do rapid changes in the means and materials of literacy affect the ways people acquire it or pass it along to others? What enhances or im-
pedes literacy learning under conditions of change? What might we gain by
approaching learning disturbances in reading and writing not as individual cognitive
problems but as the perpetual social condition in which all of us are forced to function? How can we develop approaches to literacy that are more sensitive to the actual
conditions in which people learn to read and write?

The economic conditions of students' lives — although usually the purview of
school social workers or financial aid officers — should also be consulted for guidance
in curricular thinking. Lessons in reading and writing at any level can bring conscious
attention to the origins of texts and their relationships to social context. Learning how
to read and write should include developing knowledge about material and technological conditions involved in these practices, as well as the changes that have occurred in
reading and writing across time. The problems of literacy as a social issue can and
should be incorporated into what counts as basic literacy instruction (for some useful
directions, see, for instance, Giroux & McClaren, 1989; Shor, 1992, 1980).

The concept of sponsorship is a concrete analytical tool that can be used toward
such projects at various levels. Tracing the sponsors who develop and deliver curricular materials to their schools can heighten students' awareness of who is interested
in their reading and writing skills and why. It also can bring attention to the complicated, fast-moving, and far-ranging interrelationships that bear on contemporary
reading and writing, and may give students useful ways to understand the reasons
that school literacy differs from the kinds they engage in elsewhere. Sponsorship is a
tool that can clarify for teachers how students in their classrooms are differentially
subsidized in their literacy learning outside of school by virtue of the economic histories of their regions. Because sponsorship focuses on the many factors that create
and deny literacy opportunity, it moves our sights beyond the SES profiles of individual families toward broad systems of resources for literacy operating in students'
worlds.[11] Those who consider public schools an organ of democracy rather than of
the marketplace can evaluate how well their schools manage the public resources of
literacy under their control in order to extend the broadest benefit to the most people. As public sponsors of literacy — and not merely teachers, testers, or sorters —
schools might include among their measurements of performance how well they re-
distribute their considerable material powers and intellectual resources to equalize
life chances.

I'd like to end with a specific suggestion in this regard. Educators at all levels deal
with curriculum and performance standards that emanate from governments, re-
gents, district offices, or other centralized agencies. These standards, which usually
come in the form of objective aims, goals, requirements, outcome criteria, and so on,
usually mask the struggles among competing parties that have gone into their mak-

ing. They almost always deliver, in unquestioned ways, the prevailing interests of dominant economies. The writing instruction that Barbara Hunt received, the materials she used, the opportunities she was given and not given were all connected, in various ways, to the victories of agents of economic change in her society. New ways of producing wealth invite new forms of social and labor relations, including communicative relations (Gee, Hull, & Lankshear, 1996). These presumed relations work their way into the teaching and learning of writing, both in and out of school. And they are telegraphed in educational standards or policy statements like *Workforce 2000.* Bourdieu (1998) observes:

> What appears to us today as self-evident, as beneath consciousness and choice, has quite often been the stake of struggles and instituted only as the result of dogged confrontations between dominant and dominated groups. The major effect of historical evolution is to abolish history by relegating to the past, that is, to the unconscious, the lateral possibilities that it eliminated. (pp. 56–57)

Yet in Barbara Hunt's writing, in her efforts to "do a lot with homelessness," we see that histories are not abolished, are not yet submerged in full unconsciousness, even as they undergo transformation. Her experiences speak to the importance of rejecting the amnesia invited by the new imperatives for literacy and reanimating standards with historical awareness. In that way, we can better appreciate the positions of students (or entire schools) in receding economies. To be viable, Barbara Hunt, mostly on her own and in the span of a lifetime, must accomplish an abrupt transition from family farm to twenty-first century postindustrialism — a transition that took the country itself several generations and myriad forms of sponsorship to accomplish. And she must rely heavily on the institution of the school to make that leap. For her and many others, literacy learning entails more than attaining the reading and writing abilities implied by ever-rising standards. It also entails an ability — somehow, some way — to make the transformations and amalgamations that have become embedded, across time, in the history of those standards. Teachers, sensitive to the projects of translation and adaptation that underlie students' writing, can listen for those moments when students express them and then recognize their value. But, even further, with the right care and insight, the "lateral possibilities" that Barbara Hunt's writing remembers and imagines may not be eliminated. Barbara Hunt should be able to look to her school for help in articulating the suffering of her community and for realizing her solidarity with those people, urban and rural, who are "kind of affected" by the same issues as she. When we read, write, teach, and learn with historical consciousness, we save from extinction the often inchoate yearnings of voices in change.

NOTES

1. The study involved eighty people ranging in age at the time of the interviews from ninety-eight years old to ten. All of the participants were living in south-central Wisconsin in an area whose population numbered 367,000 at the time of the 1990 census. Fifty-four of the people I interviewed were European American, sixteen African American, four Mexican

American, two Native American, and four of Asian or Middle Eastern descent. Although reading was not ignored in the study, the emphasis was on learning to write. The aim was to redress the neglect of the social history of writing in comparison to reading and to focus on the escalating pressure to write as it emerged with technological and economic developments, especially after World War II. For more on this study, see Brandt (in press).

2. See Brandt (1998) for a fuller treatment of the concept of sponsorship and its use in life history research. For a more positive view of sponsors as legitimizing and authorizing agents, see Goldblatt (1994).

3. These are pseudonyms, as are other specific identity markers relating to participants in the study.

4. See Danbom (1995) and Nelson (1995) for more on this "golden age of agriculture."

5. For descriptions of the buildup of rural schools in the late nineteenth century, as well as political and social organization of the schools, see Fuller (1982).

6. One rural Wisconsin woman I interviewed, who was born in 1896, worked both as a country grade school teacher and as an occasional contributor to the local newspaper in the years before she was married.

7. See Clark and Halloran (1993) for a provocative assessment of how oratorical culture was changing by the end of the nineteenth century because of emerging values stressing individual skill over collective voice. They suggest a direct line between this late oratorical culture and contemporary rhetorics of specialization and professionalization.

8. In several parts of the interview, Barbara Hunt described her distaste for assigned writing, both in school and in catechism class. She was required to keep a journal during a class trip to Germany. "And I didn't really like that because the trip didn't exactly turn out what I wanted it to be," she said. "So there were a few bad things in there and I don't want bad things in my diary so I didn't write everything down." On essay writing in catechism class, she said, "You had to take the First Commandment and say what you believed about it. And I knew I was going to be in trouble if I wrote what I wanted to write. I can either tell the truth, the whole truth, or I can just kind of, I pretty much wrote what he [the priest] wanted to hear." For Barbara Hunt, forensics also was a place to evoke other values that were deeply important to her — eye contact and direct contact with one's audience. "I hate when people don't make eye contact," she said. "I hate it when teachers are continuously at the blackboard or something and never look at you to see if you are learning."

9. See Neth (1995) for the impact of the cash economy and the need for off-farm wage employment in the social lives of farm families. By the time Barbara Hunt reached her teens, most of the residents of her village were involved in at least supplemental cash employment, most of it involving commuting to jobs in more populous areas. Neth observes, "Women and children had to negotiate in a system that increasingly redefined the ways in which they could contribute to the farm economy and threatened the resources of the family and community base" (pp. 11–12).

10. See Jackson (1975) for a pertinent discussion of the effects of literacy and print in objectifying social life.

11. For more on this aspect of sponsorship, see Brandt (1998).

REFERENCES

Bertaux, B. (Ed.). (1981). *Biography and society: The life history approach.* Beverly Hills, CA: Sage.

Bertaux, B., & Thompson, P. (1993). *Between generations: Family models, myths, and memories.* Oxford, Eng.: Oxford University Press.

Bertaux, B., & Thompson, P. (1997). *Pathways to social class: A qualitative approach to social mobility.* Oxford, Eng.: Clarendon Press.

Bourdieu, P. (1990). *The logic of practice* (R. Nice, Trans.). Cambridge, Eng.: Polity Press.

Bourdieu, P. (1998). *Practical reason.* Stanford, CA: Stanford University Press.

Bourdieu, P., & Wacquant, L. (1992). *An invitation to reflexive sociology.* Chicago: University of Chicago Press.

Brandt, D. (1995). Accumulating writing: Writing and learning to write in the twentieth century. *College English, 57,* 649–668.

Brandt, D. (1998). Sponsors of literacy. *College Composition and Communication, 49,* 165–185.

Brandt, D. (in press). *Literacy in American lives.* New York: Cambridge University Press.

Brockhaus, H. H. (1949). *The history of the Wisconsin High School Forensic Association.* Unpublished doctoral dissertation, University of Wisconsin, Madison.

Castells, M. (1989). *The informational city: Information technology, economic restructuring and the urban-regional process.* Cambridge, Eng.: Blackwell.

Census of agriculture. (1992). Washington, DC.: Bureau of the Census.

Clark, G., & Halloran, S. M. (1993). *Oratorical culture in nineteenth-century America.* Carbondale: Southern Illinois University Press.

Conger, R. D., & Elder, G. H., Jr. (1994). *Families in troubled times: Adapting to change in rural America.* New York: de Gruyter.

Danbom, D. B. (1995). *Born in the country: A history of rural America.* Baltimore: Johns Hopkins University Press.

Elder, G. H. (1974). *Children of the Great Depression: Social change in life experience.* Chicago: University of Chicago Press.

Elder, G. H. (1994). Time, human agency, and social change: Perspectives on the life course. *Social Psychology Quarterly, 57,* 4–15.

Elder, G. H., & Liker, J.K. (1982). Hard times in women's lives: Historical influences across forty years. *American Journal of Sociology, 88,* 241–269.

Evans, J. F., & Salcedo, J. F. (1974). *Communications in agriculture: The American farm press.* Ames: Iowa State University Press.

Fuller, W. E. (1982). *The old country school: The story of rural education in the middle west.* Chicago: University of Chicago Press.

Gee, J. P., Hull, G., & Lankshear, C. (1996). *The new work order: Behind the language of the new capitalism.* Boulder, CO: Westview Press.

Giroux, H. A., & McClaren, P. (Eds.). (1989). *Critical pedagogy, the state, and cultural struggle.* Albany: State University of New York Press.

Goldblatt, E. (1994). *'Round my way: Authority and double consciousness in three urban high school writers.* Pittsburgh: University of Pittsburgh Press.

Gowen, S. G. (1992). *The politics of workplace literacy: A case study.* New York: Teachers College Press.

Graff, H. J. (1979). *The literacy myth: Literacy and social structure in the nineteenth-century city.* New York: Academic Press.

Grubb, F. (1990). Growth of literacy in colonial America: Longitudinal patterns, economic models, and the direction of future research. *Social Science History, 14,* 451–482.

Grubb, F. (1992). Educational choice in the era before free public schooling. *Journal of Economic History, 52,* 263–375.

Hightower, J. (1973). *Hard tomatoes, hard times.* Cambridge, MA: Schenkman.

Income, poverty rate reported. (1990, October 5). *Facts on File World News Digest,* p. 744E2.

Jackson, M. D. (1975). Literacy, communication, and social change. In I. H. Kawhauru (Ed.), *Conflict and compromise* (pp. 27–54). Wellington, New Zealand: A. H. & A. W. Reed.

Johnston, W. B., & Packer, A. E. (1987). *Workforce 2000: Work and workers for the 21st century.* Indianapolis: Hudson Institute.

Lummis, T. (1987). *Listening to history: The authenticity of oral evidence.* London: Hutchinson.

Murray, J. E. (1997). Generation(s) of human capital: Literacy in American families, 1830–1875. *Journal of Interdisciplinary History, 27,* 413–435.

Nelson, D. (1995). *Farm and factory: Workers in the Midwest, 1880–1990*. Bloomington: Indiana University Press.

Neth, M. (1995). *Preserving the family farm: Women, community, and the foundations of agribusiness in the Midwest, 1900–1940*. Baltimore: Johns Hopkins University Press.

Purcell-Gates, V. (1995). *Other people's words: The cycle of low literacy.* Cambridge, MA: Harvard University Press.

Reich, R. B. (1992). *The work of nations: Preparing ourselves for twenty-first century capitalism.* New York: Vintage.

Resnick, D. P., & Resnick, L. B. (1977). The nature of literacy: An historical explanation. *Harvard Educational Review, 47,* 370–385.

Ryder, N. B. (1965). The cohort as a concept in the study of social change. *American Sociological Review, 30,* 843–861.

Saupe, W. F. (1989). *How family farms deal with unexpected financial stress* (Agricultural Economics Staff Paper Series). Madison: University of Wisconsin.

Saupe, W. F., & Majchrowicz, A. T. (1996). *Jobs in Wisconsin's farm and farm-related sector* (Community Economics Paper Series No. 234). Madison: University of Wisconsin.

Shor, I. (1980). *Critical teaching and everyday life.* Boston: South End Press.

Shor, I. (1992). *Empowering education.* Chicago: University of Chicago Press.

Soltow, L., & Stevens, E. (1981). *The rise of literacy and the common school in the United States: A socioeconomic analysis to 1870.* Chicago: University of Chicago Press.

Strauss, A. (1987). *Qualitative analysis for the social scientist.* New York: Cambridge University Press.

Strauss, A., & Corbin, J. (1990). *Basics of qualitative research.* Newbury Park, CA: Sage.

Stuckey, J. E. (1991). *The violence of literacy.* Portsmouth, NH: Heinemann.

Taylor, D. (1996). *Toxic literacies: Exposing the injustice of bureaucratic texts.* Portsmouth, NH: Heinemann.

Thompson, P. R. (1975). *The Edwardians: The remaking of British society.* Bloomington: Indiana University Press.

Thompson, P. R. (1988). *The voice of the past: Oral history.* Oxford, Eng.: Oxford University Press.

Thompson, P. R. (1990). *I don't feel old: The experience of later life*. Oxford, Eng.: Oxford University Press.

Tremmel, R. (1995). Country life and the teaching of English. *Research in the Teaching of English, 29,* 5–36.

Walter, G. (1996). The ideology of success in major American farm magazines, 1934–1991. *Journalism and Mass Communication Quarterly, 73,* 594–608.

This research was sponsored by the U.S. Department of Education Office of Educational Research and Improvement under the auspices of the National Center on English Learning and Achievement (Award R305A60005) and the National Institute for Post-Secondary Education, Libraries, and Life-long Learning. The views expressed here are not necessarily shared by the sponsors. The author wishes to thank Nancy Nystrand, Karen Redfield, Barbara Spar-Malamud, Julie Nelson Christoph, Peter Mortensen, and Peter Shaw for their help in preparing the manuscript. Thanks also to Harvey Graff, Victoria Purcell-Gates, Clifford Adelman, and the *Harvard Educational Review* Editorial Board for their useful criticisms on earlier versions of this manuscript.

PART THREE

*Crosslinguistic and Bilingual Issues
in Language and Literacy*

PART THREE

Crosslinguistic and Bilingual Issues in Language and Literacy

T his part of *Perspectives on Language and Literacy* highlights research into bilingualism and into crosslinguistic differences in language and literacy acquisition. The term *bilingualism* refers to the phenomenon of one person's knowledge of two or more languages, whereas *crosslinguistic* refers to the comparison and contrast of language and literacy between (usually monolingual) speakers of different languages. While the *Harvard Educational Review* has published many articles on the subject of bilingualism, the field of crosslinguistic language development is relatively new. Specifically, although the study of bilingualism in the United States began in earnest in the 1960s, it wasn't until 1985, with the publication of Dan Slobin's multivolume compendium, *The Crosslinguistic Study of Language Acquisition*, that this field came into its own.

Part Three begins with an excellent overview of trends in second language acquisition research since the 1940s. Although Kenji Hakuta and Herlinda Cancino's original article, "Trends in Second Language Acquisition Research," was originally published in 1977, it is interesting to note that much of contemporary second language research still falls under their final paradigm, discourse analysis. This chapter provides a highly informative historical synopsis for those just beginning study in this field, and it offers a compact review of major studies in the field for those with some knowledge of second language acquisition research. Hakuta and Cancino end by predicting that the next wave of research in this area will incorporate sociolinguistic factors into analysis in order to "give greater acknowledgment to the complexity of the second language acquisition process" (p. 243). The next chapter in this section demonstrates one way in which this acknowledgment is possible.

"Late Immersion and Language of Instruction in Hong Kong High Schools: Achievement Growth in Language and Nonlanguage Subjects," by Herbert W. Marsh, Kit-Tai Hau, and Chit-Kwong Kong, represents a breakthrough in research on bilingualism. The researchers conducted a longitudinal examination of the effects of English-language instruction on language and content-area scores of 12,784 high school students enrolled in an English-language immersion program in Hong Kong. Because Hong Kong students have a very high motivation to learn English, and because Hong Kong schools have the resources to implement immersion programs, this study examines bilingual education under model conditions, and its findings are not necessarily generalizible to bilingual programs elsewhere. Still, the differing effects concerning nonlanguage subjects as well as the findings concerning effects of language instruction over time should be discussed at length by bilingual education policymakers in any setting.

223

"Challenging Venerable Assumptions: Literacy Instruction for Linguistically Different Students," brings teaching methodology into this discussion of bilingual education. Specifically, María de la Luz Reyes, a Chicana educator, questions the unexamined use of "process instruction" with students whose first language is not English or whose backgrounds differ from White, middle-class children. Such children, she argues, can benefit from native-language instruction, modified forms of process instruction, and (particularly controversial within the debate over the model of writing process instruction) error correction. She buttresses these claims with findings from previous studies and with vignettes from classroom life. Reyes's final message is that "teachers must rise above the euphoria over whole language and writing process and recognize that these programs are not perfect or equally successful for all" (p. 301).

The final chapter in this section, "Writing Development: A Neglected Variable in the Consideration of Phonological Awareness" by Sofía A. Vernon and Emilia Ferreiro, is also a reexamination of previously held beliefs — in this case, those concerning the relationship between phonological awareness, or "the ability to identify the sound structure of words" (p. 309), and writing development. Prior research on this topic has focused on English-speaking children and has used methods and instruments appropriate for evaluating language and literacy development in that language. Vernon and Ferreiro propose that "differences in the internal structure of languages must somehow influence the way children analyze oral stimuli" (p. 313). In order to test this hypothesis, they analyze the results of phoneme identification and word segmentation tasks of native Spanish-speaking five- and six-year-old children and compare their results with previous findings on English-speaking children. The results of this study have research implications for the study of phonological and reading development, as well as powerful implications for those who teach reading to children.

This section draws together many perspectives on bilingualism and crosslinguistic research and pedagogy. From Hakuta and Cancino's historical perspective to Marsh, Hau, and Kong's policy-oriented analysis, from Reyes's classroom-centered writing approach to Vernon and Ferreiro's linguistic and cognitive design, we can appreciate the inherent complexity in studying bilingualism and crosslinguistic differences.

EDITORS' NOTE: CROSSLINGUISTIC AND BILINGUAL ISSUES IN LANGUAGE AND LITERACY

For further reading about crosslinguistic and bilingual issues in language and literacy, we suggest these resources published in the Harvard Educational Review:

Mark W. Lacelle-Peterson and Charlene Rivera, "Is It Real for All Kids? A Framework for Equitable Assessment Policies for English Language Learners," Spring 1994, pp. 55–75.

Sandra Lee McKay and Sau-Ling Cynthia Wong, "Multiple Discourses, Multiple Identities: Investment and Agency in Second-Language Learning among Chinese Adolescent Immigrant Students," Fall 1996, pp. 577–608.

Guadalupe Valdés, "Dual-Language Immersion Programs: A Cautionary Note Concerning the Education of Minority Language-Minority Students," Fall 1997, pp. 391–429.

Trends in
Second Language Acquisition
Research

KENJI HAKUTA

HERLINDA CANCINO

L anguage provides one of the most readily accessible windows into the nature of the human mind. How children acquire this complex system with such apparent ease continues to fascinate the student of human language. The last quarter of a century in particular has witnessed a qualitative leap in our knowledge of the language-acquisition process in young children. In recent years researchers have begun extending their scope of inquiry into the problem of second language acquisition. The motivation underlying this new endeavor is twofold: first, it provides an added perspective on human language, and second, interest in second language teaching and bilingual education has resulted in a greater need to understand the mechanisms underlying second language acquisition. The focus of analysis has undergone distinct shifts in perspective as a function of our changing conceptualizations of what language is and also what the learner brings to the learning situation.

To anticipate the various approaches to be reviewed in this chapter, let us entertain some ways in which one might proceed in analyzing the process of second language acquisition. Assume that we had in our possession a yearlong record of all the conversations of a second language learner since initial exposure to the target language. One way to analyze the data, if we knew the grammars of both the native and the target languages, would be through a *contrastive* analysis of the two language structures. Where the two languages differ we would expect errors, and our predictions could be tested against the acquisition data. Another way to proceed in the analysis would be to catalog all the systematic deviations — the *errors* — in the learner's speech from the target language norm. These deviations, or errors, could be classified into whatever categories our theory might dictate. If we want more specific information than that provided by error data, we could examine *performance* on particular linguistic structures (such as negatives and interrogatives) and look for both the distributional characteristics of errors and correct usage of those structures. Or, we could look not just at linguistic structure but at *discourse* structure as well. For example, we

Harvard Educational Review   Vol. 47   No. 3   August 1977, 294–316

could ask how linguistic forms might be derived from the way in which they are used in conversation.

Over the past thirty years second language acquisition research has passed through the four phases outlined above: *contrastive analysis, error analysis, performance analysis,* and *discourse analysis.* (For a review of earlier studies in this area see McLaughlin, 1977.) In this chapter, we summarize and critically review each of these research traditions. In addition, we discuss reasons for the transition from one form of analysis to the next, particularly that due to the influence of first language acquisition research.

CONTRASTIVE ANALYSIS

From the early 1940s to the 1960s, teachers of foreign languages were optimistic that the problems of language teaching could be approached scientifically, with the use of methods derived from structural linguistics. Essentially, the goal of structural linguistics was to characterize the syntactic structure of sentences in terms of their grammatical categories and surface arrangements. Fries (1945/1972) was explicit about the implications of this approach for foreign language teaching. He claimed that "the most effective materials are those that are based upon a scientific description of the language to be learned, carefully compared with a parallel description of the native language of the learner" (p. 9).

Claims like Fries's were reinforced by informal observations of learners' systematic errors, which seemed to reflect the structure of their native language. Although many of the errors were phonological in nature, as illustrated by the native speaker of Japanese who consistently fails to distinguish between /r/ and /l/, others clearly originated at the syntactic and morphological levels. Consider a native speaker of Spanish who says "Is the house of my mother." The Spanish equivalent would be "Es la casa de mi madre." The English utterance contains two errors, whose sources can be clearly traced back to Spanish. Spanish allows subject pronouns to be deleted. When this rule is transferred to English, "This is" or "It is" simply becomes "Is." Also, Spanish uses the possessed-possessor order: thus we have "the house of my mother" ("la casa de mi madre"). It appeared, then, that the foreign language learner's difficulties could be predicted from the differences in the structures of the two languages. Contrastive analysis was the label given to this comparative approach.

Principles such as imitation, positive and negative transfer, reinforcement, and habit strength were borrowed from the academic psychology of learning and incorporated into the contrastive analysis view of second language acquisition. Presupposing that language development consisted of the acquisition of a set of habits, errors in the second language were seen as the result of the first language habits interfering with the acquisition of the habits of the second. In classroom practice the principles of habit formation and interference led to the use of pattern drills in the audio-lingual method of second language learning. On the basis of contrastive analysis, difficult patterns were predicted and consequently emphasized in the drills. For the interested reader the assumptions underlying the audio-lingual method are carefully examined and evaluated in an important book by Rivers (1964).

The comparison of the structures of languages continues to be a respectable activity within contrastive linguistics (Alatis, 1968) and has come to be conducted within the framework of transformational generative grammar. Its status as a psychological approach to the investigation of the second language acquisition process, however, fell into disrepute for several reasons. One reason was the unfortunate association of contrastive analysis with the behaviorist view of language acquisition, an account whose theoretical adequacy came to be seriously questioned, most notably by Chomsky (1959). In our view a more devastating reason was that contrastive analysis fared quite poorly once researchers, instead of relying on anecdotal impressions from the classroom, began collecting data in more systematic ways (Oller & Richards, 1973). From these data, analyses of learners' errors soon showed that a large proportion were not predictable on the basis of contrastive analysis. In fact, many of these errors, such as rule simplification (as in "Mommy eat tapioca") and overgeneralization (as in "He writed me a letter") exhibited a striking resemblance to those made by children acquiring a first language. Moreover, learners did not in fact make all the errors predicted by contrastive analysis (Nickel, 1971; Stockwell, Bowen, & Martin, 1965). When the inadequacy of contrastive analysis as a predictive model became apparent, Wardhaugh (1970) drew the useful distinction between strong and weak versions of the approach. The strong version claimed to predict errors, while the weak versions simply accounted for errors that occurred. Contrastive analysis survives only in its weak form with an obvious shortcoming; it gives an incomplete representation of the second language acquisition process since it can account only for some, not all, of the errors. Recently it has been incorporated into the more general approach of error analysis (Schumann & Stenson, 1975), which analyzes all systematic deviations of the learner's language from the target language norms.

ERROR ANALYSIS

Chomsky's (1957) formulation of language as a powerful set of transformational rules was received with enthusiasm by many psychologists, and its impact on the study of language acquisition was almost immediate. By the early 1960s researchers began reporting the regularities in the speech of young children and showed that these regularities could be characterized by a set of rules, a grammar (Brown & Bellugi, 1964b). What motivated much of this research was the assumption that the end state of the developmental process is a transformational grammar. Strictly speaking, however, the grammars that were written to describe children's speech were not transformational. Nevertheless, the system of rules reflected in children's utterances was most impressive, particularly some rules for which no adult model seemed to exist. Many of the regularities were morphological in nature, such as "wented" and "hisself," but others were syntactic, for example, "Where he can go?" Although such utterances are errors from the viewpoint of adult grammar, their systematic occurrence in protocols from children gave convincing support to the notion that they were part of each child's developing grammar or linguistic system. The child's errors, rather than being considered products of imperfect learning, came to be regarded as inevitable results of an underlying, rule-governed system that evolved toward the full adult grammar.

From this new perspective the child, in the eyes of researchers, gained the status of an active participant in the acquisition of language.

The influence of early first language acquisition research on second language acquisition research can be found in the error-analysis approach, best represented in collections by Oller and Richards (1973), Schumann and Stenson (1975), and Svartvik (1973). Many investigators noted similarities between the types of errors reported in the first language acquisition literature and the errors made by second language learners. These errors could not be accounted for within the contrastive analysis framework. On the basis of this similarity, researchers speculated that the processes of first- and second language acquisition are essentially the same (Corder, 1967; Dulay & Burt, 1972; Richards, 1973). Like children learning their first language, second language learners were characterized as proceeding through a series of intermediate grammars (Corder, 1971; Nemser, 1971; Selinker, 1972). At any given time the learner was credited with having an "interlanguage," a genuine language in the sense that it consists of a set of systematic rules that can be described in a grammar. An interlanguage incorporates characteristics of both the native and the target language of the learner. Today, the goals of error analysis are twofold: to describe, through the evidence contained in errors, the nature of the interlanguage in its developmental stages and to infer from these descriptions the process of second language acquisition.

The majority of studies in error analysis attempt to classify the errors made by learners. Generally, errors are divided into two categories: interference (or *inter*lingual) and *intra*lingual errors. Interference errors, those errors whose sources can be traced back to the native language of the learner, are the ones that contrastive analysis addressed. An important difference, however, is that within the framework of error analysis these errors are not interpreted as products of the first language habit interfering with the second language habit. Since the language-acquisition process is seen as active hypothesis testing on the part of the learner, interference errors are interpreted as a manifestation of the learner's hypothesis that the new language is just like the native language (Corder, 1967). Unlike interference errors, intralingual errors arise from properties of the target language and can be found among children learning it as their first language. Their errors include errors of simplification as well as overgeneralization.

Several researchers have investigated the extent to which learners make errors of each type. In two widely cited papers Dulay and Burt (1973, 1974b) report a study in which they considered two competing hypotheses about the nature of second language acquisition. The first was that second language acquisition was essentially the same as first language acquisition. The alternative hypothesis was the one embodied in contrastive analysis, which viewed second language acquisition as the acquisition of habits (Lado, 1957). Dulay and Burt's implicit assumptions were that intralingual errors constituted evidence for the first hypothesis, while interference errors were evidence for the alternative hypothesis. Notice that their interpretation of interference errors differed from other workers in error analysis. Using an elicitation device called the Bilingual Syntax Measure (BSM), Dulay and Burt collected speech samples from 179 Spanish-speaking children learning English with varying amounts of English as a Second Language instruction in three different areas in the United States. They tallied errors that could be "unambiguously" classified as being either interference, intralingual (defined as similar to those reported in the first language literature), or unique (neither of the two). The results were dramatic and straightforward: of the 513 unambiguous errors, only about 5 percent were interference, while 87 percent were intralingual, and the remainder were classified as unique. Dulay and Burt interpreted this finding as evidence that "children do not use their 'first language habits' in the process of learning the syntax of their new language" (1974b, p. 134).

Dulay and Burt's results can be interpreted in at least two ways. If we accept their assumption that interference errors constitute evidence for a habit-formation hypothesis, their data make an overwhelming argument against this explanation of second language acquisition. On the other hand, if we take the viewpoint that interference errors are not products of habit formation but rather a form of active hypothesis testing and language transfer (Corder, 1967), a different conclusion emerges. Dulay and Burt's data might be interpreted as evidence that very little language transfer occurs — that is, the learning of the first language has very little influence on the learning of the second.

Whatever theoretical perspective one might take, however, two underlying assumptions in the study make both of the above interpretations questionable: 1) that an error is an appropriate unit of analysis, and 2) that equal weighting should be given to interference and intralingual errors. These assumptions are seriously called into question when one considers that all omissions of grammatical morphemes — including noun and verb inflections and other high-frequency morphemes such as the verb *be* — were classified as intralingual errors. Although Dulay and Burt do not provide the exact figures, there were many instances of these kinds of errors. Since interference errors generally involve either larger constituents or changes in word order, the two types of errors appear to originate from sources whose relative opportunities for occurrence are significantly different. Furthermore, interference errors may appear in the speech of learners only at specific points in development, and a cross-sectional sample might not capture learners at critical developmental levels.

Other studies in error analysis attempt to compare the proportions of interference and intralingual errors in adult learners. Corder (1975), citing Duskova (1969), reports that there is a larger proportion of interference errors for adults than Dulay and Burt (1973, 1974b) found for children. Duskova (1969) analyzed errors made in English composition by adult Czechoslovakians and reported that roughly 30 percent of the 1,007 errors collected were interference and the remainder intralingual. A closer look at the breakdown of her data, however, reveals that many interference errors were omissions of articles, a part of speech for which Czech does not have an equivalent. In the Dulay and Burt analysis, omissions of articles were considered intralingual errors, since children learning English as their first language also omit articles. When one tallies the interference errors according to Dulay and Burt's criteria, the proportion in Duskova's study is reduced to 5 percent. Despite differences both in the ages of the subjects and in the data collection instruments (speech versus composition), this figure is comparable to the Dulay and Burt results.

However, our earlier qualification still holds for the interpretation of the results of these studies of adult learners. The theoretical significance attached to interlingual and intralingual processes should not be considered proportionate to the number of the respective error types found in the learner's speech. An analogy with studies of first language learners serves to illustrate this point. Children overgeneralize rules as in "I go*ed* home," and they simplify their speech into telegraphic form as in "Fraser come Tuesday" (Brown & Bellugi, 1964a). In total speech output there is probably a far greater proportion of oversimplification errors. Yet, no one would argue on this basis that simplification is the more important of the two processes in language acquisition. In fact the errors of overgeneralization in first language learning are fine examples of the child's rule-governed behavior. Similarly, interference errors in second language learning are fine examples of language transfer and should be regarded as such in their own right. Such errors strongly point to areas of dynamic interplay between the two languages.

Other studies of errors are taxonomic, generally classifying errors as interference, overgeneralization, and simplification. Such studies include Politzer and Ramirez's (1973) and Cohen's (1975) analyses of the speech of Mexican American children learning English and a fine paper by Selinker, Swain, and Dumas (1975) analyzing errors in French made by English-speaking children in a language-immersion program (see Swain, 1974). A similar approach in adult studies was used by Jain (1974), Richards (1973), and Taylor (1975).

To summarize thus far, research in error analysis has revealed evidence for three general taxonomic categories of errors: interference, overgeneralization, and simplification. Of these error types, interference errors do not appear with strikingly high frequency. Second language learners make a large number of overgeneralization and simplification errors; they bear a striking resemblance to errors made by first language learners. And finally, there appear to be errors that are unique to second language learners. These findings are of interest because they suggest the reality of distinct processes resulting in the respective types of errors. It is difficult, however, to see how the extent to which these error types occur would be of any empirical value until they are weighted according to their relative opportunities for occurrence. Such attempts, and also attempts at classifying errors with respect to their gravity (James, 1974), should prove informative.

All of the studies cited above used cross-sectional samples; very few studies have followed Corder's (1967) suggestion that errors should be studied longitudinally. Such analyses are needed to tell us whether specific types of errors might be prevalent at specific points in the course of development and whether errors in a learner's speech disappear abruptly or gradually. One of the few studies examining the pattern of interference errors over time was carried out by Cancino (see note 1). Her subject, Marta, a five-year-old Puerto Rican girl, was acquiring English through natural exposure to the speech of English-speaking peers. The data consisted of biweekly, spontaneous speech samples of two hours each, obtained over a period of eight months. In her analysis Cancino classified all instances of possessive (excluding possessive pronouns and adjectives) as being one of the following five types:

1) possessor-possessed order, with 's supplied, e.g., "Freddie's frog,"
2) possessor-possessed with 's omitted, e.g., "Freddie frog,"

3) possessed-possessor order, with preposition *of* supplied, e.g., "Frog of Freddie,"
4) same as (3) except with *of* omitted, e.g., "Frog Freddie," or
5) possessed-possessor order, with Spanish preposition *de* supplied, e.g., "Frog de Freddie."

The distribution for each category, displayed in Table 1, reveals a clear pattern of development.

First, the Spanish word *de* is used in producing English utterances (Type 5). Next, word order indicates the appearance of obligatory contexts for the English form *'s* — that is, contexts in which adult norms clearly require the form (Type 2). After that, *of* replaces *de* (Type 3), and finally *'s* is gradually supplied in obligatory contexts (Type 1). As far as we are aware, this is one of the clearest empirical illustrations of an interplay between the native language and the target language. Two points should be made here. Interference errors, at least for the possessive form, appear primarily in the earliest stages of acquisition. If, for example, Marta's speech had been sampled at a later point in development as part of a cross-sectional study, interference errors might not have been found. In addition, errors do not seem to disappear abruptly. On the contrary, use of the correct forms appears to be quite variable, and development is gradual.

The pattern of gradual acquisition can be illustrated graphically. Figure 1 plots curves for several grammatical forms acquired by Uguisu, a five-year-old Japanese girl learning English in a natural setting, who was observed over a fifteen-month period (Hakuta, 1976). The graph plots over time the percentage of instances when a given form was supplied in obligatory contexts. In terms of errors, each curve represents the complement of errors of omission for a given morpheme. It is clear in this case that for each linguistic item errors disappear slowly and gradually. This pattern, which is

TABLE 1

Distribution of Possessives Used by Marta — Samples Are Biweekly

Sample	's Supplied	's Omitted	of Supplied	of Omitted	de
1					7
2		3			8
3		1			1
4		1			
5		5			
6		7	3		
7		2	6		1
8	2	1			
9	5	1			
10	7				
11	9				
12	8	1	1		
13	7		1		
14	5		1		1
15	5	1			

Source: Cancino; see note 1.

characteristic of first language acquisition (Brown, 1973), may very well hold for second language learners' acquisition of any sort of linguistic item (Cazden, Cancino, Rosansky, & Schumann, 1975; Hakuta, 1975). Such variability in the usage of linguistic forms, even for a single learner at a given point in development, makes it difficult, if not impossible, to write grammars for corpora of utterances.

The above studies examined errors in production, but it is possible that learners might simply avoid certain linguistic structures on which they would be likely to make errors. Perhaps learners avoid particular structures due to differences between their native language and the target language. Error analysis cannot detect this type of language transfer. Schachter (1974) has provided some convincing evidence of such avoidance by looking at relative-clause construction in the English compositions of adult learners. Using contrastive analysis, Schachter predicted positive transfer of such construction interference for one group and negative transfer for the other. Surprisingly, the negative-transfer group made fewer errors than the positive-transfer group, which suggests that there was no interference. This counterintuitive result, however, can be accounted for by the simple fact that the group for which positive transfer was predicted produced twice as many relative-clause constructions as the group for which negative transfer was predicted. The negative-transfer group made fewer errors because they were avoiding such constructions, a fact that the traditional method of error analysis would have obscured. Recently, Kleinmann (1976) found that groups of adult Arabic and Spanish speakers learning English avoided producing a variety of constructions (passives, infinitival complements, direct-object pronouns, and present progressives) for which contrastive analysis predicted difficulties. Hakuta (1976) compared relative-clause constructions in the spontaneous speech of his subject, Uguisu, with those of Cancino's subject, Marta, and found that, as predicted by contrastive analysis, Marta produced more relative clauses. Other writers have also suggested that avoidance may account for some of their data at both the syntactic (see note 2) and the lexical levels (Tarone, Frauenfelder, & Selinker, 1976).

Contrastive analysis was, in effect, consumed by error analysis because the evidence of interference errors it used failed to account for the learner's non-interference errors. Along similar lines, error analysis does not appear to provide a methodology with adequate sensitivity to detect phenomena such as structural avoidance. With increasing sophistication in the methods available to infer knowledge from performance, error analysis is currently in the process of being incorporated within an attempt to describe the learner's overall performance, not necessarily restricting the scope of analysis to errors alone. This line of work, *performance analysis* (Svartvik, 1973), once again bears the marks of work in first language acquisition.

PERFORMANCE ANALYSIS

At the time that researchers of second language acquisition were focusing on error analysis, first language acquisition researchers were beginning to provide rather elegant descriptions of the development of linguistic structures in children. Two studies in particular have had a profound influence in shaping the direction of second language acquisition research: Klima and Bellugi's (1966) study on the acquisition of ne-

FIGURE 1   *Acquisition curves for the three allomorphs of* be (am, is, are) *as the auxiliary to the verb* gonna *(e.g.,* I'm gonna eat this one) *in Uguisu, plotted as percentage applied in obligatory contexts over time. Each sample represents a two-week interval.*

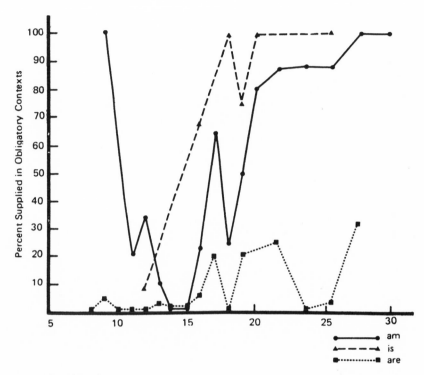

Source: Hakuta (1975).

gation and Brown's (1973) study on the acquisition order of grammatical morphemes. Both studies based their analyses of performance on longitudinal spontaneous-speech samples from three children — Adam, Eve, and Sarah — learning English as their first language. The studies were important in that they were longitudinal, and documented regularities across children in the acquisition of grammatical morphemes and negation. For the first-language-acquisition researcher these findings were appealing because they hinted at universal aspects in first-language-acquisition processes. For the second language acquisition researcher the studies provided norms against which to compare the acquisition of the same structures in second language learners of English. The research also provided the motivation and methodology to search for universal orders of acquisitions of structures across second language learners. This method was a novel way of testing for the role of language transfer.

Within the framework of performance analysis there has been considerable research on the acquisition of negation and grammatical morphemes in second language learners of English. We restrict our review to these two types of structures. Less studied, but equally interesting for analysis are *prefabricated utterances*, utterances that are learned as wholes without knowledge of internal structure but that have high functional value in communications. We will end our discussion of performance analysis with a consideration of such prefabricated utterances.

Negation

Klima and Bellugi (1966) described characteristics of three stages in the development of English negation among first language learners. In Stage 1 children's negation consists of a negative particle — generally, "no" — placed outside the sentence nucleus to produce such utterances as "No Mommy go" and "no eat." In Stage II the negative element moves into the sentence nucleus and takes forms such as "can't," "not," and "don't" (as in "Mommy don't like tapioca"). However, these negative elements are not full auxiliary verbs, since they lack inflection and flexibility. In Stage III the full form with inflection for tense and number is used.

Among studies of the development of negation in second language learners, Milon's (1974) report on Ken, a five-year-old Japanese boy learning English in Hawaii, has attracted considerable attention in the literature. Milon claimed that it was possible to apply Klima and Bellugi's (1966) stages for the development of negation in first language learners in order to summarize Ken's development. He therefore concluded that Ken acquired the English negation system in the same way as first language learners. Milon's application of Klima and Bellugi's stages to his data involved dividing the protocols into three periods roughly corresponding to the first language stages. In his tables he reports the percentage of utterances within each of these periods that are accountable by the rules for each of the first language stages.

In order for Milon's claim to be justified, there must be a majority of utterances within each of Ken's periods to be accounted for by the rules of the corresponding first language stage. Even a cursory examination of Milon's published tables, however, indicates that this is not the case. The Stage I rule, which involves placing the negative particle outside the sentence nucleus, accounts for well over half the utterances not only for Ken's period I, but also for periods II and III as well. In addition, only 9 percent of the utterances within Ken's Stage III are accounted for by Klima and Bellugi's Stage III rules.

Cazden et al. (1975) conducted a rigorous descriptive study of negation in the acquisition of English by six native speakers of Spanish: two adults, two adolescents, and two children. For each sample they calculated the proportion of occurrence for each of four utterance types and their relative frequency over time. Each of these utterances "peaked" in usage at a certain point in acquisition. Although some subjects never attained the more advanced forms, the order in which the forms emerged was the same for all subjects. In the first form of negation to appear, "no" preceded the verb, such as in "Carolina no go to play." Notice that this form corresponds to Klima and Bellugi's Stage II rule in that the negative element is internal to the sentence (*no + verb*). There was no evidence that these second language learners went through anything resembling Klima and Bellugi's Stage I, where the negative element is external to the sentence nucleus. The next acquired form was characterized by utterances in which "don't" preceded the verb, such as "He don't like it." The third form, *aux-neg*, included all negative auxiliaries, such as "can't" and "won't," but not the in-

FIGURE 2 *Development of negation in Marta showing proportion of each negating device to total negatives in each sample.*

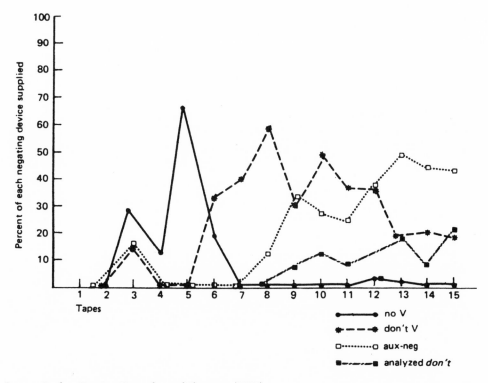

Source: Cazden, Cancino, Rosansky, and Shumann (1975).

flected forms of "don't." The final form, which Cazden and colleagues called *analysed don't*, was essentially the full adult system. For illustrative purposes we include the graph of one of their subjects, Marta, in Figure 2.

Cazden et al. (1975) argue on the basis of their data that the *no + verb* forms represent "the Spanish speakers' first hypothesis . . . that negation in English is like negation in Spanish, hence the learners place *no* in front of the verb" (p. 32). This finding would easily have been obscured had the researchers simply classified learners' utterances according to Klima and Bellugi's stages, since *no + verb, don't + verb,* and *aux-neg* all correspond to their Stage II, and *analysed don't* occurs in Stage III. This might have forced the conclusion that there was no transfer from Spanish. Other studies have also noted *no + verb* utterances in Spanish speakers learning English (Adams, 1974; Butterworth, 1972; Wong-Fillmore, 1976).

There is an alternative explanation for the *no + verb* construction other than as the product of transfer from Spanish. Klima and Bellugi (1966), Bloom (1970), and Lord (1974) have all reported such forms in the speech of first language learners. Perhaps it is not necessary to invoke transfer from Spanish to explain these utterances. Data from Gillis and Weber's (1976) two Japanese children and from Uguisu

(Hakuta, 1976), however, suggest the transfer interpretation to be the correct one. None of the three children produced the *no + verb* construction, thus making this form likely to be unique to speakers of Spanish. Milon (1974) reports the construction of his Japanese subject, Ken, but there is a simple explanation: Ken was exposed to Hawaiian Creole English, which has this form of negation.

Where does this leave us with respect to the development of negation? We now feel confident that *no + verb*, due to language transfer, is a common developmental step in Spanish speakers learning English. It is worth emphasizing once again that if Cazden et al. (1975) had simply tried to categorize their data into Klima and Bellugi's stages for first language learners, this finding would not have been revealed. Their conclusion would have been that the learners went through Klima and Bellugi's Stages II and III. Indeed, this conclusion appears to be consistent with all the studies reported above, but it is too general to be of any value. All it tells us is that at first the auxiliary verb (e.g., "don't," "isn't") is unmarked for person or tense, and later that it becomes fully marked. There is no evidence for Stage I, which is theoretically the most interesting stage.

Before closing this section on negation, it should be pointed out that the universality of Klima and Bellugi's stages has been questioned even in first language learners. Bloom (1970) and Lord (1974), for example, failed to find evidence for Stage I in their subjects. It is easy to overlook the fact that research in first language acquisition is also still in its infancy. Owing to the tentative nature of the first language findings, the second language researcher needs to approach the task of comparing the two processes with extreme caution.

Grammatical Morphemes

With the exception of work by Cazden et al. (1975) the first and second language studies mentioned above were distributional, but not in a rigorously quantitative sense. If we are to obtain more accurate descriptions of learner performance, quantitative studies are particularly important. Grammatical morphemes, which include the articles (*a, the*), the copula and auxiliary *be*, and the noun and verb inflections, lend themselves to quantitative analyses. They afford a particular advantage to the researcher because of their high frequency, which is generally independent of the topic of discourse. Furthermore, contexts where they are obligatory (i.e., clearly required according to adult standards) are easily identifiable. For example, "two book" clearly requires the plural morpheme-*s*.

Brown (1973) analyzed fourteen morphemes in data collected longitudinally from three unacquainted native speakers, Adam, Eve, and Sarah. Defining acquisition as the point at which a given morpheme occurred in more than 90 percent of obligatory contexts for three consecutive samples, he found that they were acquired in a roughly invariant order. De Villiers and de Villiers (1973) substantiated this finding in a larger, cross-sectional first language sample. When Brown (1973) analyzed these morphemes according to semantic complexity and transformational cumulative complexity, he found that both factors predicted the obtained order but that they could not be separated.

Since the findings on first language learners were so dramatic and the method was easily applicable to second language speech samples, a plethora of performance studies on second language learners has been carried out in the last three years. Some have been longitudinal (Hakuta, 1974a, 1976; Gillis, 1975; Rosansky, 1976; see also Cancino, note 1; Mulford, note 3) and others cross-sectional (Bailey, Madden, & Krashen, 1974; Dulay & Burt, 1973, 1974a, 1974c; see also Larsen-Freeman, note 4). Longitudinal second language studies generally have determined the order of acquisition of grammatical morphemes according to Brown's 90 percent criterion described above. In the cross-sectional research the standard procedure is to rank-order the morphemes according to the performance of the entire group. The latter procedure, of course, assumes that all individuals in the sample exhibit the same acquisition order. After obtaining a rank order in either longitudinal or cross-sectional studies, a comparison can be made across learners with different native languages.

Dulay and Burt (1974a) compared the order of acquisition of eleven morphemes for a group of Chinese and Spanish children learning English. They found the order of acquisition to be nearly identical between the two groups, although it was quite different from that established for children learning English as a first language (Brown, 1973; de Villiers & de Villiers, 1973). This similarity in the orders is a striking result in light of the differences between Chinese and Spanish. For example, Chinese, unlike Spanish, has no linguistic marking equivalent to English articles, but both groups performed equally well in supplying these morphemes. A more astonishing result has been obtained from adults receiving formal instruction in English as a second language. The order obtained was again approximately the same as the order found by Dulay and Burt, despite the fact that these adults spoke various native languages (Bailey, Madden, & Krashen, 1974; see also Larsen-Freeman, note 4).

Complicating the results in the above studies is the fact that the speech samples were not spontaneous but were elicited with BSM (Burt, Dulay, & Hernandez-Chavez, 1973). One BSM procedure involves asking the subject in the pretest to point to each object in a set of cartoon pictures with the request, "Show me the ———." Perhaps the reason why articles are easy in this task is that they are modeled for the subjects. Thus, the test itself may have influenced the outcome. A pilot investigation by Porter of children learning English as their first language buttresses this idea (see note 5). Porter administered the BSM with these children and found their order resembled the second language learner's order more than it did the order found by Brown!

Rosansky (1976) questioned whether results obtained from a cross-sectional study would correlate well with a longitudinally derived acquisition order. Using longitudinal data from Jorge, a native Spanish-speaking adolescent, she compared the order of acquisition of the morphemes (longitudinal) with the relative accuracy of the use of the morphemes at a given point in development (cross-sectional). Rosansky found that Jorge's longitudinal order did not correlate with his cross-sectional order, and thus she concluded that cross-sectional orders could not be assumed to be the same as longitudinal orders.

However, there are two problems with Rosansky's results. First, she was able to compare the order of only six morphemes, since Jorge did not attain the 90 percent criterion longitudinally for the other morphemes studied. Second, Jorge was supplying all six morphemes in well over 90 percent of their obligatory contexts by the time of the cross-sectional sample. Since grammatical morphemes in general tend to fluctuate within the range between 90 and 100 percent once they attain the 90 percent criterion, Rosansky's failure to find a correlation with the longitudinal order could have been the result of this random fluctuation.

If we compare the order of acquisition of grammatical morphemes for Rosansky's subject, Jorge, with the order obtained in the Dulay and Burt study, the Spearman rank-order correlation coefficient (rho) is +.91. Cancino (see note 1) found that the longitudinal order for Marta compared favorably with Jorge's (rho = +.88) and correlates highly with that of Dulay and Burt's subjects as well (rho = +.93). Another piece of evidence comes from Mulford (see note 3), who studied the longitudinal-acquisition order for Steinar, an Icelandic boy. The correlation coefficients of Steinar's order with the orders of Jorge, Marta, and Dulay and Burt's subjects respectively are +.90, +.85, and +.82. Thus it might seem that there exists a universal order for acquisition of these morphemes.

The existence of a universal order, however, is not supported by analyses of Uguisu's longitudinal order (Hakuta, 1974a, 1976). Resembling none of the above orders, Uguisu's development indicates some interference from Japanese, which does not have articles and plurals. A comparison of Uguisu's order with those of two Japanese children studied longitudinally by Gillis (1975) reveals that the three children's orders all differ and that none of them correlates with Dulay and Burt's subjects' order either. One reason for this lack of similarity may be that Gillis (1975) only reports on the verb-related morphemes and excludes some morphemes such as articles and plurals. Nevertheless, if there indeed is a universal order, the results should not vary according to the particular items chosen for investigation.

We can probably conclude, though, that among all second language learners of English there may be a tendency to acquire morphemes in a certain order, determined by factors such as their frequency of occurrence (Larsen-Freeman, 1976) and their perceptual salience or distinctiveness (Wagner-Gough & Hatch, 1976). For example, the progressive -ing may be acquired early because of its high salience and high frequency, while the regular third-person indicative -s (as in "she comes") with its low frequency and low salience is acquired relatively late.

Another factor influencing acquisition, semantic complexity of the morphemes (Brown, 1973), may vary depending on the learner's native language. For example, the English articles a and the ("a book" versus "the book"), require rather sophisticated semantic discriminations for their proper use (Brown, 1973; Maratsos, 1971). If a native language makes those contrasts, as Spanish and French do, the learner may already possess the semantic discriminations necessary for using English articles. On the other hand, a native speaker of Japanese or Chinese does not make those discriminations and must learn them in order to make the definite/indefinite contrast. That articles in English have the highest frequency of all grammatical morphemes and appear in a highly predictable position, before nouns, also affects their acquisition. Thus articles may appear early even in Japanese or Chinese learners but with confusions along the definite/indefinite dimension.

Although articles appeared early in her speech, Uguisu had great difficulty with the definite/indefinite contrast, as evidenced by many errors (Hakuta, 1976). Marta and Jorge, on the other hand, acquired articles early and had little difficulty with the definite/indefinite distinction. Their greatest problem appeared to be within the indefinite category, where they initially used *one* rather than *a*, reflecting transfer from the Spanish indefinite articles *un* or *una*. Frauenfelder (1974), who studied the acquisition of gender marking among English-speaking children in a French immersion program, found that although the children made many errors in gender on articles, they never confused the definite/indefinite contrast. That Dulay and Burt found their Chinese learners acquiring articles so early might be attributed to the scoring method: they did not differentiate between *a* and *the*. Finally, Fathman (see note 6), who administered an oral-production task (SLOPE) to Korean- and Spanish-speaking children, found a generally similar ordering on various grammatical forms for these two groups. A close look at her data, however, shows a very large discrepancy in the children's performance on articles: the Korean children, whose language has no article equivalents, performed poorly.

Thus, we conceive the order of acquisition of English grammatical morphemes as resulting from an interplay of at least two factors. One factor, consisting of variables such as frequency and salience, seems to direct the order of acquisition toward a universal order. But a second factor, transfer from the native language, modulates the order so as to produce differences between learners of different language backgrounds.

Routine Formulas and Prefabricated Utterances

Since grammatical rules operate on units or constituents within a sentence, it was only natural for researchers interested in grammatical structure to focus on those utterances that indicated the learner's knowledge of individual constituents. In so doing, they excluded from their analysis utterances that seemed to be routine formulas (such as "What's this?" and "I don't know") learned as wholes through imitation. Huang (1971) related a delightful anecdote about the use of such a routine formula. Paul, a Taiwanese boy, used his first English utterance, "Get out of here," as a formula in roughly appropriate situations for warding off unwanted company. Another example is one of Uguisu's first utterances, "Not in particular!" which was used for the purpose of turning down offers of food. Variants of routine formulas are prefabricated patterns (Hakuta, 1974b), sentences such as "This is ——," where nouns can be inserted into the slots. Most investigators have reported in passing the existence of either routines or prefabricated patterns (Adams, 1974; Butterworth, 1972; Cazden et al., 1975). These patterns have not received close attention, because the central focus of study has been on grammatical structure. This lack of emphasis on prefabricated forms was reinforced by the apparent failure of the process of imitation to account for language acquisition (Chomsky, 1959; Ervin-Tripp, 1964; but see Bloom, Hood, & Lightbown, 1974).

If language were to be viewed from the perspective of communication, however, prefabricated utterances take on an added theoretical significance (Hakuta, 1976). Huang (1971) found a considerable amount of prefabricated utterances in Paul's speech. This led him to postulate imitation as an important process, although it was considered to be less important than, and independent of, the process of rule-formation. Uguisu's speech, particularly in the early stages, also contained many pre-fabricated patterns (Hakuta, 1974b). Such patterns may have value in sustaining second language learners' motivation by enabling them early on to express a variety of meanings. Since the "breakdown" of these forms is gradual and similar to the acquisition of grammatical rules, the use of prefabricated patterns may motivate the learner to search for internal structure (Hakuta, 1976).

In a recent dissertation on English acquisition by five Spanish-speaking children, Wong-Fillmore (1976) found that over half of the children's utterances contained pre-fabricated forms. She argued that through the gradual analysis of such forms, later linguistic structure developed: "All of the constituents of the formula become freed from the original construction, [and] what the learner has left is an abstract structure consisting of a pattern or rule by which he can construct like utterances" (p. 645). For example, Wong-Fillmore's subject, Nora, learned the question, "How do you do dese?" early in development and used only this form. During the next period she attached a noun or prepositional phrase to this form, and created such questions as "How do you do dese flower power?" and "How do you do dese in English?" Later she learned to slot other verbs into the pattern "How do you ———?" and produced such forms as "How do you like to be a cookie cutter?" Nora then began alternating "How do you ———?" with "How did you ———?" In the last period of observation, she was constructing utterances like "How you make it?" and "How will take and paste?" Although Fillmore's examples are provocative, the principles used by the learner to analyze the prefabricated forms need to be specified; the traditional problem of the emergence of syntax remains to be solved.

DISCOURSE ANALYSIS

The focus of research in both first and second language acquisition has shifted only recently to language in the social context. It would be somewhat unfair, however, to claim that earlier researchers did not pay attention to the role of discourse in language acquisition. Brown (1968), for example, succinctly stated:

> It may be as difficult to derive a grammar from unconnected sentences as it would be to derive the invariance of quantity and number from the simple look of liquids in containers and objects in space. The changes produced by pouring back and forth, by gathering together and spreading apart are the data that most strongly suggest the conservation of quantity and number. The changes produced in sentences as they move between persons in discourse may be the richest data for the discovery of grammar. (p. 288)

Current work on discourse analysis can be roughly divided into two approaches (de Villiers & de Villiers, in press). Researchers employing the first approach (Garvey, 1975; Keenan, 1975) investigate rules of discourse, such as turn taking in dialogue. Discourse rules are considered to be another aspect of language that the child must master more or less independently of syntax. The second approach (Antinucci &

Parisi, 1975; Bates, 1976) assumes fundamentally that all language is pragmatic, obeying "rules governing the use of language in context" (Bates, 1976, p. 420). Researchers operating in this vein have investigated the emergence of various pragmatic functions, such as declaratives and imperatives, in very young children. They claim that syntax and semantics can ultimately be seen as derivatives of pragmatics, although it is difficult at this point to envision the specific process of derivation.

In the case of the second language learner, we certainly would not expect to be able to study the emergence of the various pragmatic functions, since they are by definition universal and, presumably, acquired at a very early age. An interesting approach, however, would be to analyze a given pragmatic function over time. Tracing the development of the linguistic forms that the learner uses for the expression of a function might well reveal orderly and lawful patterns. In addition, such an analysis might reveal interesting differences across native speakers whose languages differ in the linguistic forms chosen for the same pragmatic act. In a sense, this approach would be a contrastive analysis of the way different languages map pragmatic functions onto linguistic forms. We believe this would be an extremely fruitful line of investigation, but it has not been pursued. What is sorely lacking before any such inquiry is an explicitly spelled-out theory of pragmatics (see Fraser, note 7). The few studies on discourse reported in the literature have made only preliminary attempts at outlining the structure of discourse and the mechanisms underlying its regulation.

Hatch (1978) found that Huang's (1971) subject, Paul, initiated discourse by first identifying the topic, waiting for the other person to attend or speak, and then making some further comment. Repetition of the other speaker's previous utterance (Hatch, 1978; Keller-Cohen, 1978) has received some attention. We suspect that this is the major way in which prefabricated forms (Hakuta, 1974b; Wong-Fillmore, 1976) enter the learner's speech repertoire. A variant of the process of repetition is incorporation (Wagner-Gough, 1975; Wagner-Gough & Hatch, 1976), as illustrated in the following dialogue with Homer, an Iranian child:

Adult: Where are you going?
Homer: Where are you going is house.
(Wagner-Gough & Hatch, 1976, p. 304)

Hatch (1978) has noted that a topic is broken into parts dictated by the constraints of conversation. The following example taken from a Japanese child, Takahiro, shows the learner taking apart and reassembling these various parts in the course of dialogue (Hatch, 1978).

Takahiro: this
             broken
Adult: broken
Takahiro: broken
             This /iz/ broken.
             broken
Adult: Upside down

Takahiro: upside down
                  this broken
                  upside down
                  broken

Based on such examples, Hatch speculates that "one learns how to do conversation, one learns how to interact verbally, and out of this interaction syntactic structures are developed." This is essentially the same argument made by Wong-Fillmore (1976) for the emergence of syntax, and it is subject to the same criticism: the ultimate question of how exactly this happens has not been addressed. Furthermore, accounting for interference errors remains problematic, since such errors are aspects of the internal organization of language.

Implicit in studies of discourse is the importance of input. Unfortunately, rigorous empirical studies of the characteristics of input to the learner are nowhere to be seen in the second language literature. The pedagogical implications of such studies would be powerful, since classroom instruction is essentially the manipulation of input variables. Although first language learning research has greatly influenced second language research, the numerous studies on mother-to-child speech in first language acquisition (DePaulo & Bonvillian, in press; Snow & Ferguson, in press) have not generated similar studies in second language acquisition. In an exploratory second language learning study, Hatch, Shapira, and Wagner-Gough (see note 8) reinforce the need for future input studies. Anecdotally comparing the input for children with that for adults, they found that the speech addressed to children by native speakers resembled mother-to-child speech reported in the first language literature: it was simple, short, grammatical, and restricted to here-and-now topics. The speech to adults, on the other hand, possessed many of the characteristics of "foreigner talk"; the omission of inflections, an abundance of pauses, and many complex sentence forms (Ferguson, 1977). Furthermore, the topic of conversation often referred to something neither immediate nor present. Whatever the determining sociolinguistic factors, these observations by Hatch and his coworkers should encourage further research in this area. Such investigations may ultimately help explain the difficulty that adults have in acquiring a second language.

THE FUTURE

Each of the four trends covered in this paper can be seen as successive attempts by researchers to create an adequate representation of the second language acquisition process. We began by describing contrastive analysis, which required only a comparison of the linguistic structures of the two languages. We end with the most recent trend, discourse analysis, in which the learner's status as a social being occupies center stage. Although it may take years of hard work before we develop a rigorous and sophisticated methodology for discourse analysis, the rewards will be great. For the results would create a solid link between the observed acquisition of the linguistic structures of the second language and the yet-to-be-determined variables involved in discourse.

Schumann (1975, 1976) has recently argued that there is a correlation between social factors and the degree to which one acquires a second language. These social variables rest at the heart of second language acquisition; they determine the circumstances requiring people to acquire a second language. Along similar lines, Gardner and his colleagues (Gardner & Lambert, 1972; Gardner, 1973) have extensively explored the relationships of attitudes and motivation to degree of proficiency in a second language. While it may be difficult to see a direct relationship between these social factors and their supposed effects on the second language acquisition process, it is not difficult to imagine social factors influencing the types of discourse in which learners engage. This relationship is rigorously definable. Thus, we see discourse analysis as an empirical bridge to our next potential level of analysis, which might be called *sociolinguistic analysis*. Analysis at this level, we believe, would give greater acknowledgment to the complexity of the second language acquisition process.

NOTES

1. H. Cancino, "Grammatical Morphemes in Second Language Acquisition — Marta," Unpublished manuscript, Harvard University, Graduate School of Education, Cambridge, MA, 1976.
2. M. Swain, *Changes in Error: Random or Systematic?* Paper presented at the Fourth International Congress of Applied Linguistics, Stuttgart, August 1975.
3. R. Mulford, Personal communication, December 15, 1976.
4. D. Larsen-Freeman, *The Acquisition of Grammatical Morphemes by Adult ESL Students*, Paper presented at the Ninth Annual TESOL Convention, Los Angeles, April 1975.
5. J. Porter, "A Cross-Sectional Study of Morpheme Acquisition in First Language Learners," Unpublished manuscript, Harvard University, Department of Psychology and Social Relations, Cambridge, MA, 1975.
6. A. Frathman, *Language Background, Age, and the Order of English Structures*, Paper presented at the Ninth Annual TESOL Convention, Los Angeles, April 1975.
7. E. Fraser, *On Requesting: An Essay in Pragmatics*, Book in preparation, 1977.
8. E. Hatch, R. Shapira, & J. Gough, "Foreigner-Talk Discourse," Unpublished paper, University of California at Los Angeles, English Department, Los Angeles, 1975.

REFERENCES

Adams, M. (1974). *Second language acquisition in children: A study in experimental methods: Observations of spontaneous speech and controlled production tests.* Unpublished master's thesis, University of California at Los Angeles.

Alatis, J. (1968). *Nineteenth annual round table meeting on linguistics and language studies: Contrastive linguistics and its pedagogical implications.* Washington, DC: Georgetown University Press.

Antinucci, F., & Parisi, D. (1975). Early semantic development in child language. In E. H. Lenneberg & E. Lenneberg (Eds.), *Foundations of language development: A multidisciplinary approach* (vol. 1). New York: Academic Press.

Bailey, N., Madden, C., & Krashen, S. (1974). Is there a "natural sequence" in adult second language learning? *Language Learning, 24,* 233–243.

Bates, E. (1976). Pragmatics and sociolinguistics in child language. In D. Morehead & A. Morehead (Eds.), *Normal and deficient child language.* Baltimore: University Park Press,.

Bloom, L. (1970). *Language development: Form and function in emerging grammars.* Cambridge, MA: MIT Press.

Bloom, L., Hood, L., & Lightbown, P. (1974). Imitation in language development: If, when and why? *Cognitive Psychology, 6,* 380–420.

Brown, R. (1968). The development of Wh questions in child speech. *Journal of Verbal Learning and Verbal Behavior, 7,* 279–290.

Brown, R. (1973). *A first language: The early stages.* Cambridge, MA: Harvard University Press.

Brown, R., & Bellugi, U. (1964a). Three processes in the acquisition of syntax. *Harvard Educational Review, 34,* 133–151.

Brown, R., & Bellugi, U. (1964b). The acquisition of language. *Monographs of the Society for Research in Child Development, 29*(1).

Burt, M. K., Dulay, H. C., & Hernandez-Chavez, E. (1973). *Bilingual syntax measure.* New York: Harcourt Brace Jovanovich.

Butterworth, G. (1972). *A Spanish-speaking adolescent's acquisition of English syntax.* Unpublished master's thesis, University of California at Los Angeles.

Cazden, C., Cancino, H., Rosansky, E., & Schumann, J. (1975). *Second language acquisition sequences in children, adolescents, and adults.* Cambridge, MA: Harvard University, Graduate School of Education. (ERIC Document Reproduction Service No. ED 123 873)

Chomsky, N. (1957). *Syntactic structures.* The Hague: Mouton.

Chomsky, N. (1959). A review of *Verbal Behavior* by B. F. Skinner. *Language, 35,* 26–59.

Cohen, A. D. (1975). *A sociolinguistic approach to bilingual education: Experiments in the American Southwest.* Rowley, MA: Newbury House.

Corder, S. P. (1967). The significance of learners' errors. *International Review of Applied Linguistics, 5,* 161–170.

Corder, S. P. (1971). Idiosyncratic dialects and error analysis. *International Review of Applied Linguistics, 9,* 147–160.

Corder, S. P. (1975). Error analysis, interlanguage, and second language acquisition. *Language Teaching and Linguistics, 14,* 201–218.

DePaulo, B., & Bonvillian, J. (in press). The effect on language development of the special characterization of speech addressed to children. *Journal of Psycholinguistic Research.*

de Villiers, J., & de Villiers, P. (1973). A cross-sectional study of the acquisition of grammatical morphemes in child speech. *Journal of Psycholinguistic Research, 2,* 267–278.

de Villiers, J., & de Villiers, P. (1978). Syntax and semantics in the first two years: The output of form and function and the form and function of the input. In L. L. Lloyd & F. Minifie (Eds.), *Communicative & cognitive abilities: Early behavioral assessment* (NICHD Mental Retardation Research Series). Baltimore: University Park Press.

Dulay, H., & Burt, M. (1972). Goofing: An indicator of children's second language learning strategies. *Language Learning, 22,* 235–252.

Dulay, H., & Burt, M. (1973). Should we teach children syntax? *Language Learning, 23,* 245–258.

Dulay, H., & Burt, M. (1974a). Natural sequences in child second language acquisition. *Language Learning, 24,* 37–53.

Dulay, H., & Burt, M. (1974b). Errors and strategies in child second language acquisition. *TESOL Quarterly, 8,* 129–136.

Dulay, H., & Burt, M. (1974c). A new perspective on the creative construction process in child second language acquisition. *Language Learning, 24,* 253–278.

Duskova, L. (1969). On sources of errors in foreign languages. *International Review of Applied Linguistics, 7,* 11–36.

Ervin-Tripp, S. (1964). Imitation and structural change in children's language. In E. Lenneberg (Ed.), *New directions in the study of language.* Cambridge, Mass.: MIT Press.

Ferguson, C. A. (1977). Toward a characterization of English foreigner talk. In C. E. Snow & C. A. Ferguson (Eds.), *Talking to children: Language input and acquisition.* Cambridge, Eng.: Cambridge University Press.

Frauenfelder, U. (1974). *The acquisition of French gender in Toronto French immersion school children.* Unpublished senior honors thesis, University of Washington.

Fries, C. (1972). *Teaching and learning English as a foreign language.* Ann Arbor: University of Michigan Press. (Original work published 1945)

Gardner, R. C. (1973). Attitudes and motivation: Their role in second language acquisition. In J. Oller & J. Richards, *Focus on the learner: Pragmatic perspectives for the language teacher.* Rowley, MA: Newbury House.

Gardner, R. C., & Lambert, W. (1972). *Attitudes and motivation in second language learning.* Rowley, MA: Newbury House.

Garvey, C. (1975). Requests and responses in children's speech. *Journal of Child Language, 2,* 41–63.

Gillis, M. (1975). *The acquisition of the English verbal system by two Japanese children in a natural setting.* Unpublished master's thesis, McGill University.

Gillis, M., & Weber, R. (1976). The emergence of sentence modalities in the English of Japanese-speaking children. *Language Learning, 26,* 77–94.

Hakuta, K. (1974a). A preliminary report on the development of grammatical morphemes in a Japanese girl learning English as a second language. *Working Papers on Bilingualism, 3,* 18–43.

Hakuta, K. (1974b). Prefabricated patterns and the emergence of structure in second language acquisition. *Language Learning, 24,* 287–297.

Hakuta, K. (1975). Learning to speak a second language: What exactly does the child learn? In D. P. Dato (Ed.), *Developmental psycholinguistics: Theory and application.* Washington, DC: Georgetown University Press.

Hakuta, K. (1976). Becoming bilingual: A case study of a Japanese child learning English. *Language Learning, 26,* 321–351.

Hatch, E. (1978). Discourse analysis. In E. Hatch (Ed.), *Studies in second language acquisition: A book of readings.* Rowley, MA: Newbury House.

Huang, J. (1971). *A Chinese child's acquisition of English syntax.* Unpublished master's thesis, University of California at Los Angeles.

Jain, M. (1974). Error analysis: source, cause and significance. In J. Richards (Ed.), *Error analysis: Perspectives on second language acquisition.* London: Longman.

James, C. (1974). Linguistic measures for error gravity. *AVLA Journal, 12,* 3–9.

Keenan, E. (1975). Conversational competence in children. *Journal of Child Language, 2,* 163–183.

Keller-Cohen, D. (1978). Repetition in the non-native discourse: Its relation to text unification and conversational structure. In O. Freedle (Ed.), *Discourse processing: A multidisciplinary approach.* Hillsdale, NJ: Ablex.

Kleinmann, H. (1976). *Avoidance behavior in adult second language acquisition.* Unpublished doctoral dissertation, University of Pittsburgh.

Klima, E., & Bellugi, U. (1966). Syntactic regularities in the speech of children. In J. Lyons & R. Wales (Eds.), *Psycholinguistic papers.* Edinburgh: Edinburgh University Press.

Krashen, S., Madden, C., & Baily, N. (1975). Theoretical aspects of grammatical sequencing. In M. Burt & H. Dulay (Eds.), *New directions in second language learning, teaching and bilingual education.* Washington, DC: TESOL.

Lado, R. (1957). *Linguistics across cultures.* Ann Arbor: University of Michigan Press.

Larsen-Freeman, D. (1976). An explanation for the morpheme acquisition order of second language learners. *Language Learning, 26,* 125–134.

Lord, C. (1974). Variations in the acquisition of negation. *Papers and Reports on Child Language Development, 8,* 78–86.

Maratsos, M. (1971). *The use of definite and indefinite reference in young children.* Unpublished doctoral dissertation, Harvard University.

McLaughlin, B. (1977). Second-language learning in children. *Psychological Bulletin, 84,* 438–459.

Milon, J. (1974). The development of negation in English by a second language learner. *TESOL Quarterly, 8,* 137–143.

Nemser, W. (1971). Approximative systems of foreign language learners. *International Review of Applied Linguistics, 9,* 115–123.

Nickel, G. (1971). Problems of learners' difficulties in foreign language acquisition. *International Review of Applied Linguistics, 9,* 219–227.

Olivier, D. (1968). *Stochastic grammars and language acquisition devices.* Unpublished doctoral dissertation, Harvard University.

Oller, J., & Richards, J. (Eds.). (1973). *Focus on the learner: Pragmatic perspectives for the language teacher.* Rowley, MA: Newbury House.

Politzer, R., & Ramirez, A. (1973). An error analysis of the spoken English of Mexican-American pupils in a bilingual school and a monolingual school. *Language Learning, 23,* 39–61.

Richards, J. (1973). A non-contrastive approach to error analysis. In J. Oller & J. Richards (Eds.), *Focus on the learner: Pragmatic perspectives for the language teacher.* Rowley, MA: Newbury House.

Rivers, W. (1964). *The psychologist and the foreign language teacher.* Chicago: University of Chicago Press.

Rosansky, E. (1976). *Second language acquisition research: A question of methods.* Unpublished doctoral dissertation, Harvard University, Graduate School of Education.

Schachter, J. (1974). An error in error analysis. *Language Learning, 24,* 205–214.

Schumann, J. (1975). Affective factors and the problem of age in second language acquisition. *Language Learning, 25,* 209–235.

Schumann, J. (1976). Social distance as a factor in second language acquisition. *Language Learning, 26,* 135–143.

Schumann, J., & Stenson, N. (Eds.). (1975). *New frontiers in second language learning.* Rowley, MA: Newbury House.

Selinker, L. Interlanguage. (1972). *International Review of Applied Linguistics, 10,* 219–231.

Selinker, L., Swain, M., & Dumas, G. (1975). The interlanguage hypothesis extended to children. *Language Learning, 25,* 139–152.

Snow, C. E., & Ferguson, C. A. (Eds.). (1977). *Talking to children: Language input and acquisition.* Cambridge, Eng.: Cambridge University Press.

Stockwell, R., Bowen, J., & Martin, J. (1965). *The grammatical structures of English and Spanish.* Chicago: University of Chicago Press.

Svartvik, J. (1973). *Errata: Papers in error analysis.* Lund, Sweden: Gleerup.

Swain, M. (1974). French immersion programs across Canada. *Canadian Modern Language Review, 31,* 117–130.

Tarone, E. (1976). Some influences on interlanguage phonology. *Working Papers on Bilingualism, 8,* 87–111.

Tarone, E., Frauenfelder, U., & Selinker, L. (1976). Systematicity/variability and stability/instability in interlanguage systems: More data from Toronto French immersion. In H. Brown (Ed.), *Papers in second language acquisition.* Ann Arbor, MI: Research Club in Language Learning.

Taylor, B. (1975). The use of overgeneralization and transfer strategies by elementary and intermediate university students learning ESL. In M. Burt & H. Dulay (Eds.), *New directions in second language learning, teaching and bilingual education.* Washington, DC: TESOL.

Wagner-Gough, J. (1975). Comparative studies in second language learning. *CAL-ERIC/CLL Series on Language and Linguistics, 26.* Arlington, VA: Center for Applied Linguistics.

Wagner-Gough, J., & Hatch, E. (1976). The importance of input data in second language acquisition studies. *Language Learning, 25,* 297–308.

Wardhaugh, R. (1970). The contrastive analysis hypothesis. *TESOL Quarterly, 4,* 123–130.

Whitehurst, G., Ironsmith, E., & Goldfein, M. (1974). Selective imitation of the passive construction through modelling. *Journal of Experimental Child Psychology, 17,* 288–302.

Williams, L. (1974). *Speech perception and production as a function of exposure to a second language.* Unpublished doctoral dissertation, Harvard University.

Wong-Fillmore, L. (1976). *The second time around: Cognitive and social strategies in second language acquisition.* Unpublished doctoral dissertation, Stanford University.

We would like to thank Helen Tager Flusberg, Bella DePaula, Steven Pinker, and Ellen Winner for helpful comments on this paper. We especially thank Roger Brown and Bruce Fraser for extensive written comments. Preparation of this manuscript was supported in part by Grant BNS 73-09150 from the National Science Foundation to Dr. Roger Brown.

Late Immersion and Language of Instruction in Hong Kong High Schools: Achievement Growth in Language and Nonlanguage Subjects

HERBERT W. MARSH

KIT-TAI HAU

CHIT-KWONG KONG

This study examines how instruction in the first language (L1, Chinese) and in the second language (L2, English) affects high school students' achievement in L1, L2, and four content (nonlanguage) school subjects (mathematics, science, geography, and history). This research has important policy implications in Hong Kong, but it also has theoretically and empirically important implications for understanding immersion strategies in other contexts, especially where students are instructed in L2 for all or most school subjects. Although early-immersion programs that begin at the start of formal schooling have a long history of success (e.g., Lambert, 1990, 1992), there has been much less systematic, large-scale research on late-immersion programs that begin in high school, particularly in relation to achievement in nonlanguage school subjects. We begin by reviewing previous empirical and theoretical research that informs our study. Next, we describe the Hong Kong context in which this research was conducted, present results of this large-scale, longitudinal study on second language instruction, and, finally, explore policy implications for the Hong Kong educational system and for immersion programs more generally.

EMPIRICAL AND THEORETICAL BACKGROUND

In the twentieth century, research on second language acquisition and instruction throughout the world has been largely driven by the applied needs of education policy and practice and has been informed by disciplines as diverse as education, linguistics, sociolinguistics, psycholinguistics, cognitive science, psychology, educational psychology, cross-cultural psychology, anthropology, popular culture, sociology, and oth-

Harvard Educational Review Vol. 70 No. 3 Fall 2000, 302–346 ers (e.g., Cummins, 1979, 1986, 1991, 1996; Francis, 1999; Garcia, 1993; Hakuta, 1986; Hakuta & McLaughlin, 1996; Lambert, 1992; Swain & Johnson, 1997; Willig, 1985). Two movements are particularly relevant to our study: the transitional bilingual programs and the Canadian immersion programs.

Transitional Bilingual Programs: Additive Bilingualism v. Submersion

Bilingual and second language studies are often politically controversial, policy-oriented, applied research that is directed at real-world problems. Beginning in the 1980s, particularly in the United States, this research was fueled by political and educational needs arising from large immigrations. It focused on whether minority native languages should be "submerged" (i.e., replaced with the dominant English language), or whether students with limited English proficiency should receive English-language instruction and instruction in other subjects in their own native language until they achieve competence in English (i.e., transitional bilingual programs; see Willig, 1985). Submersion programs have typically focused on the extent and speed of assimilation and the acquisition of the new dominant language; they have typically placed little emphasis on maintenance of the native language. Following the controversial 1974 U.S. Supreme Court *Lau v. Nichols* decision, the critical "Lau question" became whether there was sufficient research evidence to mandate transitional bilingual programs in which non-English-speaking or limited-English-proficient students are taught in their native language until they reach an appropriate level of proficiency in English.[1]

A decade later, Willig (1985) conducted a sophisticated meta-analysis, comparing transitional bilingual education programs in the United States with traditional programs (typically, "submersion" programs in which non-native speakers are taught exclusively in English). In order to juxtapose traditional narrative and meta-analytic reviews, Willig focused on studies from the Baker and de Kanter (1981) review of research, but limited her consideration to U.S. studies. Controlling for prior student differences and methodological inadequacies, students in bilingual programs who were taught in their first language performed better than students taught in L2 on language and nonlanguage achievement tests in both English and L1, and had better attitudes toward self and school. The differences favoring transitional bilingual programs over submersion programs were systematically larger for studies that Willig judged to be methodologically stronger, based on traditional criteria used in meta-analyses. The differences were, however, smaller in methodologically weaker studies in which comparison students were not matched to bilingual students (e.g., non- or limited-English-proficient students in bilingual programs v. English-proficient students in comparison programs). Whereas L1 (non-English) language test scores were substantially higher in the transitional bilingual programs, scores in other school subjects were also higher, as were, to a lesser extent, L2 (English) skills. Although the effects were positive for all language components, they were smaller for oral language than for writing, listening, reading, and vocabulary.

Most research in Willig's 1985 review emphasized language achievement, but the largest effects were for social studies achievement. This finding led Willig to suggest that "bilingual education may be succeeding in preventing academic lag in language-mediated academic subjects, but, unfortunately, these [subjects] are seldom included in evaluation designs" (p. 311). In a similar vein, she emphasized that science comprehension is linked to understanding the language in which it is presented, but lamented that not a single study in her meta-analysis included science achievement. Hence, the failure to evaluate the effects of language of instruction on achievement in both nonlanguage content and language subjects is a critical limitation in this past research.

More recent research (e.g., Collier, 1992; Cummins, 1996; Greene, 1998; Krashen, 1997) provides further support for well-designed transitional bilingual programs. Krashen (1997) argued that good bilingual programs provide students with content knowledge and literacy in L1, which indirectly aids L2 proficiency, because it is easier to learn to read in the L1 language that a child already knows. He concluded that the best bilingual programs provide initial L1 instruction, L2 language classes, sheltered classes in which students with intermediate L2 skills are taught nonlanguage subjects in L2, and a gradual transition to mainstream nonlanguage content classes taught in L2. Focusing on longitudinal studies, Collier (1992) argued that student achievement increases over time with the amount of L1 instruction language-minority students receive in combination with L2 support when compared to matched groups taught entirely in L2. While recognizing that bilingual education per se is no panacea, Cummins (1996) concluded that "both large-scale and small-scale studies consistently show that strong promotion of bilingual students' L1 throughout elementary school contributes significantly to academic success" (p. 121).

Canadian Immersion Programs: Additive Bilingualism

Early History of the Canadian Immersion Program   Lambert (1990, 1992) summarized his research about what has become known as the Canadian immersion program. In Quebec, in the 1950s, French Canadians and English Canadians were distinct groups separated by social status as well as language. Even though French Canadians were a majority in Quebec, they had lower-status jobs than English Canadians and used English to some extent, whereas English Canadians had little need or desire to learn French. Lambert and his colleagues reasoned that learning a foreign language depended not only on general intellect and language aptitude, but also on positive perceptions of the target language group (e.g., the French Canadians in their research). They developed a French language immersion program specifically devised for English Canadian children with little or no exposure to French. In this program, these children spent the first three years of schooling (beginning in kindergarten) learning almost exclusively in French. English was first introduced in second or third grade and gradually increased to about 50 percent of instruction time. The aim of the Canadian immersion program was to achieve additive bilingualism — the acquisition of a new L2 while maintaining or enhancing L1 proficiency and achievement in other school subjects. Based on consistent findings from over twenty-five years, Lambert (1992; also see 1981, 1990) argued that immersion students achieve a remarkably high level of functional bilingualism and biculturalism (a cultural appreciation of

French Canadians; Genesee, 1984). Lambert also contended that bilinguals develop divergent thinking skills. In addition, bilinguals acquire English-language skills by their upper primary school years (even though they have spent much less learning time in English; see Cummins, 1979) and are able to achieve in some content areas at levels comparable to that of non-immersion students. Growing evidence further suggested that the advantages produced by the immersion program generalized for English Canadian students differing in socioeconomic status and IQ (see Genesee, 1987).

Genesee (1985) argued that immersion is not so much a method of L2 acquisition, but a pedagogical approach that promotes L2 acquisition in which L2 instruction in nonlanguage content subjects creates conditions like those in L1 instructional contexts. Genesee also emphasized that immersion programs can be distinguished by two factors of time: the initiation (early, kindergarten; delayed, grade 4 or 5; late, grade 7 or 8) and the extent to which instruction is provided in both L1 and L2 (total, in which all or most instruction is in L2, or partial [mixed]). He then summarized preliminary or formative evaluations of several variations to the traditional immersion program, suggesting that accumulated research evidence demonstrated that gains in L2 proficiency were not at the expense of L1 proficiency. He emphasized, however, that "immersion programs were designed for English-speaking, majority group children, and the evaluation results pertain to this population only" (Genesee, 1985, p. 556). Genesee (1978) also reviewed empirical and theoretical issues having to do with the optimal starting time for immersion programs and concluded that, whereas benefits can result from late-immersion programs, "high levels of second language proficiency are best achieved by an early start and long duration of instruction, provided that effective teaching methods are employed" (p. 1). There are, however, unresolved issues in studies of immersion programs that we now consider.

The Prototypical Immersion Program and Unresolved Issues

Swain and Johnson (1997) focused specifically on how immersion programs differ from other types of bilingual and L2 education programs. This issue is important to our claim that our research is an immersion study. They offered the following defining characteristics of an immersion study: (a) L2 is the medium of instruction; (b) the immersion curriculum parallels the local first language curriculum; (c) overt support exists for L1; (d) the program aims for additive bilingualism; (e) L2 exposure is largely confined to the classroom; (f) students enter with similar and limited levels of L2 proficiency; (g) teachers are bilingual; and (h) the classroom culture is that of the local L1 community. Within this context, Johnson (1997) argued that instruction in English in Hong Kong high schools, the focus of the present investigation, constitutes a late-immersion program.

Swain and Johnson (1997) identified a variety of ongoing, unresolved concerns. For example, a practical problem common to most immersion programs is how to attract and retain the highly committed bilingual teachers who have appropriate expertise in both the language of instruction and the subject content area. The selection of students for participation in immersion programs is also a controversial issue. Swain and Johnson question whether the selection of immersion students is justifiable or an unnecessary form of discrimination. They emphasize that "it seems likely that L1 literacy, general academic achievement, L2 proficiency, and motivation might all become increasingly important the later an immersion program begins" (p. 13). They also recognized that at higher levels of education and in more abstract content areas, L2 instruction might need to be supplemented with L1 instruction, but they also indicated that further research was needed into possible strategies to best meet this apparent need.

Swain and Johnson (1997) are surprisingly silent on the critical issue of the effects of immersion on achievement in content subjects (other than language), particularly in late-immersion programs. The language limitations in what can be presented to students (comprehensible input) and students' inability to grapple with complex and abstract ideas in an L2 they have not yet mastered can place students at a distinct disadvantage relative to what they would have achieved if taught in their L1. Although some researchers claim that immersion students achieve at levels comparable to non-immersion students, such comparisons are often based on performances of an initially elite group of immersion students relative to representative norms and do not control for initial ability differences (e.g., Duff, 1997). Researchers (e.g., Duff, 1997; Met & Lorenz, 1997) have noted that, whereas immersion students may be able to master the concrete objectives required in the primary (K–2) curriculum, their ability to explore more abstract concepts in nonlanguage subjects as required in subsequent levels of education is frustrated by limitations in L2 proficiency.

Swain and Johnson (1997) concluded that under favorable conditions, immersion results in additive bilingualism and provides cognitive, cultural, and psychological advantages as well. They also noted, however, that under less favorable conditions, immersion programs may not be able to achieve their full potential benefits. Although it might be possible merely to dismiss any negative results as not representing true immersion research, Swain and Johnson recognized that a better understanding of why such programs have not resulted in the expected benefits is needed.

Theoretical Models of Bilingual Proficiency

Why are outcomes typically more positive in immersion-type programs like those summarized by Lambert (1992) than in submersion-type programs like those summarized by Willig (1985)? Because of the strong pragmatic and policy orientations of this research, many approaches to this question have not been based on a well-grounded theoretical perspective that is able to generate testable hypotheses. Several models of bilingual proficiency (see reviews by Bourhis, 1990, and Gardner, 1985) have had considerable impact. However, for this study, we focus on two models (Cummins, 1979; Lambert, 1974) that are most relevant to our research.

Lambert's (1974) Social Psychology Model of Second Language Learning   Bourhis (1990; see also Gardner, 1985) argued that Lambert's model is the precursor of the social process models that focus on the social factors that motivate or demotivate students to learn a second language. In Lambert's model, second language learning is a function of (a) prior aptitude (including general cognitive ability and specific language skills) and (b) motivation, which is itself a function of prior attitudes about the language and the people who speak the language and motivational orientations for learning the language. A critical feature of Lambert's model is his emphasis on self-identity. According to Lambert, once bilingualism has developed sufficiently, it will influence self-identity in a manner dependent upon whether or not students feel that they belong to a desired group of people. To the extent that L2 proficiency is not intended to substitute for L1 proficiency (as in the Canadian immersion programs), additive bilingualism is predicted to occur and the effects on self-identity are predicted to be positive. However, when the L2 is intended to replace L1, subtractive bilingualism is predicted to occur that may lead to social alienation.

Cummins's Theory of the Interaction between Student Characteristics and Program Type   Cummins presents an aptitude-treatment-interaction theory in which the effectiveness of the intervention (the type of program) depends on characteristics of the students participating in the program (aptitudes). More specifically, Cummins argues that "a cognitively and academically beneficial form of bilingualism can be achieved only on the basis of adequately developed first language (L1) skills" (1979, p. 222) and posits his interaction model that is based on two theoretical hypotheses (Cummins, 1979, 1986, 1991, 1996; Cummins, Harley, Swain, & Allen, 1990). The *developmental interdependence hypothesis* posits that second language competence is partially a function of actualized L1 competence at the start of second language instruction. Cummins and Swain (1986) more fully articulate this hypothesis, stating that "to the extent that instruction in Lx is effective in promoting proficiency in Lx, transfer of this proficiency to Ly will occur provided there is adequate exposure to Ly (either in school or environment) and adequate motivation to learn Ly" (p. 87). The *threshold hypothesis* posits that students must achieve minimum thresholds of proficiency in both languages before the benefits of bilingualism can be achieved (and to avoid detrimental effects of "semilingualism," or inadequate skills in both languages). Based on these hypotheses, Cummins predicted aptitude-treatment interactions in which outcomes are a function of the interaction between sociocultural background, child input (e.g., language competence and motivation to learn L2 and maintain L1), and educational program factors. Based on this interdependence principal, Cummins (1996) argues against a simple "time-on-task" hypothesis (that more time spent in instruction in English automatically translates into better English proficiency), claiming that development of good L1 proficiency will transfer to L2 proficiency.

Threshold considerations led Cummins (1979) to ask what levels of L2 proficiency are needed at different grade levels for students to benefit from instruction in L2, and whether continued development of L1 skills is important in the development of L2 skills. He proposed that the effects of semilingualism (subthreshold skills in both languages) would be detrimental, whereas the effects of dominant bilingualism (subthreshold skills in one language but high levels in the other) might not be negative. The effects of additive bilingualism (high levels in both languages) would be positive. He also indicated, however, that the required threshold level would vary with stage of schooling. Thus, for example, one of the reasons why no cognitive disadvantages seem to be associated with early-immersion programs is that cognitive development in early school years is less based on formal language than in later school years. In bilingual programs for limited-English-proficient students, maintenance of L1 has benefits compared to students taught entirely in English, who may never achieve competence in either language.

The developmental interdependence hypothesis predicts that L2 acquisition will be better without loss of L1 proficiency when children already have good L1 mastery, as in the Canadian immersion program. Consistent with this hypothesis, Cummins (1979) reports that home and social experiences are sufficient to attain functional L1 proficiency for most middle-class language-majority children, and that the ability to extract language from text is easily transferred from one language to another. Consistent with this hypothesis, he reviewed Swedish research showing that in Swedish schools Finnish students who immigrated to Sweden at age ten quickly achieved competence in Swedish and surpassed migrant children born in Sweden, whereas Finnish students who immigrated to Sweden at age seven or eight had serious problems. The interaction between these two hypotheses explains why native language instruction is important in minority language situations (where it is more difficult to maintain and develop L1), like the bilingual programs reviewed by Willig (1985), but not when L1 is the dominant language (supported in the home and community) as in the Canadian immersion programs. In addition to linguistic and educational program factors, Cummins (1979, 1986; see also Lambert, 1992) argues that motivational factors are important, as students who positively identify with both target language groups are more likely to achieve additive bilingualism, whereas those who identify with neither are more likely to suffer semilingualism.

Critical and Optimal Ages for Learning a Second Language

Second language acquisition, as emphasized in theoretical and empirical research already reviewed, is seen as building substantially on L1 skills already acquired rather than being in conflict with competing habits based on the first language (e.g., Cummins, 1979; Hakuta & McLaughlin, 1996; Lambert, 1992). From this perspective, it is important to ask whether there is an optimal age for L2 learning and whether early- or late-immersion programs are more effective. Singleton (1992; see also Hakuta & McLaughlin, 1996) argues that no clear-cut evidence exists for an optimal age for L2 learning. According to Singleton, on the one hand, students who begin formal instruction in L2 at a later age tend to "catch up" with students who begin at an earlier age. Conversely, for students learning in a naturalistic context, those with an earlier initial exposure gain greater fluency than those with a later initial exposure, even after controlling for overall exposure. Singleton, however, claims that there were other reasons for preferring early-immersion because of the "crowdedness" of the curriculum in later school years. Building on work by Krashen (1981), Singleton also argues that successful L2 learning requires comprehensible input that actively engages the learner's attention.

Cummins, Harley, Swain, and Allen (1990) and d'Anglejan (1990) reviewed research from the Development of Bilingual Proficiency project that focused on age differences and the optimal age for immersion. Based on a large study of Japanese immigrants to Canada, d'Anglejan argued that more information was needed about the ability of Japanese high school students to handle the particularly substantial reading demands in nonlanguage content subjects. She hypothesized that discrepancies in overall school performance between native and non-native speakers of English would be particularly apparent at high school levels. D'Anglejan also offered a particularly candid evaluation of Canadian immersion research comparing the long-term results of early-immersion, late-immersion, and extended French (non-immersion) programs. According to d'Anglejan:

> The discovery a few years ago that the early immersion children's head start in French did not seem to result in the systematic advantages that might have been predicted came as a surprise to many of us. . . . The present study confirms once again the lack of any systematic advantages ascribable to an early start. Indeed, it suggests that some good and some bad things may result from all three types of program. (pp. 152–153)

THE PRESENT INVESTIGATION:
PREDICTIONS IN THE HONG KONG CONTEXT

In this section, we briefly summarize the Hong Kong context and how it relates to research into immersion, bilingualism, and second language acquisition. We then develop research questions and theoretical predictions that are pursued in the present investigation.

In Hong Kong, both Chinese and English are highly valued and important school subjects. Whereas Chinese (Cantonese) is the language of everyday use, English is used mainly for education, government, and business purposes and not usually for social discourse. The Education Commission (1990), the highest government advisory committee on all major educational policy, examined extensively issues related to language of instruction. This commission emphasized that "there is pressure for children to learn English, since this is seen by parents as offering the best prospect for their children's future. Many children, however, have difficulty with learning in English; and conversely, Chinese is undervalued as a medium of instruction and the importance of Chinese-language skills is not sufficiently recognized" (p. 93). Recognizing competing needs, the commission stressed that there was a need for some English-language high schools (i.e., schools that use English as the medium of instruction) in order to maintain Hong Kong's international position as a business, financial, and trading center. On the other hand, "since research has shown that students can study effectively in English only when they have passed a certain threshold of language competence in both their mother tongue and in English, the Working Group proposed that English-medium secondary education should be open only to those who had reached this threshold" (Education Commission, 1990, p. 94), a value suggested to be the top 30 percent of students. The report went on to emphasize that research has shown that "the majority of students will learn more effectively through their mother tongue than through English" (p. 95). From this perspective, policies were pursued to ensure that "each student was educated through a medium likely to lead to maximum cognitive and academic development. English should only be used as a medium of instruction where students could benefit from this" (p. 96). These 1990 policy recommendations were subsequently endorsed in the 1995 Educational

Commission Report No. 6, which formally recommended "embarking on a comprehensive research programme to follow the academic and personal development of groups of students, matched for academic ability and experiencing different medium of instruction models" (p. xvi). On the basis of this recommendation, the present investigation was initiated. This inquiry is a large-scale, quasi-experimental research study following from these recommendations that focuses specifically on student performance in schools that use different languages of instruction.

In contrast to policy recommendations reinforcing Chinese-medium instruction, Hong Kong parents believe that English-medium instruction is most advantageous and that Chinese-medium instruction is potentially disadvantageous (see also Gibbons, 1989). Hence, many of the most prestigious and highly selective schools in Hong Kong use English as the language of instruction. Furthermore, because of parental beliefs, English-language high schools are reluctant to lose any competitive advantage by switching to Chinese, and Chinese-language schools may experience pressure to switch to instruction in English.

Earlier work by Gibbons (1989) demonstrates that these current issues in Hong Kong are not new. Gibbons noted, for example, that initial recommendations by government to provide more instruction in Chinese in the 1960s and again in the 1970s were compromised in the face of strong parental opposition and the commercial value placed on English-language skills. Recognizing limitations in existing research, he nevertheless concluded that the cumulative evidence indicated that instruction in Chinese was more effective than instruction in English because students understood Chinese better and because instruction in English was particularly disadvantageous for lower-ability students. Nevertheless, parental pressure forced some schools to become English-language schools even though the practical realities of the teaching situation forced teachers to use a mixture of English and Chinese. According to Gibbons (1989), there was general agreement among senior administrators in the Hong Kong Department of Education and university academics that more instruction should be in Chinese, but that this was not a politically viable option. This complex interplay between public policy and politics created the paradoxical situation in which a British colonial government pressed for greater emphasis on Chinese instruction but faced strong resistance from the local Chinese community, which wanted more emphasis on instruction in English.

Johnson (1997) discussed specifically the Hong Kong context in relation to immersion programs at approximately the time that the present investigation was initiated. Emphasizing that many students and, perhaps, some teachers were not adequately equipped to deal with a total-immersion into instruction in English, Johnson (1997) argued that much so-called instruction in English actually was based on a "mixing and switching" mode of instruction that is a mix of English and Cantonese language use (see also Gibbons, 1989). Hence, even though many high schools claim to teach in English, there continues to be large variation in the extent to which English is actually used. Although English-language textbooks were designed to meet the requirements of a prescribed syllabus and public examinations, teachers in early high school years tended to simplify the vocabulary and discourse, emphasizing statements of fact and relying on pictures and graphs to convey meaning. Johnson (1997) reviewed

Hong Kong studies evaluating the success of the immersion studies and determined that they were inconclusive. Although Johnson reported some Department of Education research showing that students taught in English and in Chinese did not differ in terms of achievement in content subjects, whereas instruction in English produced better English achievement, it is not clear that the research appropriately controlled for large initial differences in prior academic achievement. Although Johnson noted planned policies to reduce the number of high schools allowed to teach in English or to increase the entrance requirements to enroll in such schools, he also noted that these proposals have been criticized as being "elitist and socially divisive and as relegating Chinese-medium instruction to second-class status" (p. 185).

Johnson (1997) also concluded that immersion education in Hong Kong high schools "fails to produce the high level of second language proficiency that is expected from it and this is the only justification for such a programme, given that the L1 alternative is available and is in all aspects appropriate" (p. 185). He continues by noting, however, that the limited evidence available suggests that no decline in outcomes has occurred in nonlanguage content subjects relative to other developed educational systems and that good Chinese-language skills have been maintained. Given that Johnson cited some research by Gibbons, it is surprising that he did not review Gibbons's earlier conclusion that instruction in English was detrimental to achievement in nonlanguage subjects. Although Johnson seems to reach different conclusions from Gibbons (1989) about the effect of instruction in English on achievement in nonlanguage classes, both agree that there is not adequate research upon which to base firm conclusions. However, Johnson also emphasizes that

> whether it is better, as opposed to easier, to educate students through their native language arguably becomes irrelevant if it is a major requirement of the society the education system serves that it should produce at least some students with high levels of bilingual proficiency that can only be achieved through immersion. (1997, p. 182)

Juxtaposition between the Hong Kong Setting and Previous Research

Although English is taught in Hong Kong primary schools (grades 1–6), the level of English competence for most students is not high (see Gibbons, 1989). At the end of primary school, students are assigned a global achievement score based on their school achievement across academic subjects. All students also take common standardized verbal (Chinese) and mathematics aptitude tests so that the ranking of students from each school can be combined to generate a common basis for ranking all grade-six students (i.e., the school-based achievement is moderated by the standardized tests). In Hong Kong, students can apply to any of a wide variety of high schools where the language of instruction is mainly Chinese (except for English classes), mixed Chinese and English, or mainly English (except for Chinese classes). Using the classification scheme proposed by Genesee (1985), high schools that provide instruction in English represent partial or total late-immersion programs. Using the Swain and Johnson (1997) definition of immersion programs, Johnson (1997) notes that Hong Kong English-language high schools clearly constitute a late-immersion program. In terms of the components of the Cummins model (1979), Chinese students attending high schools taught in English typically have very good L1 (Chinese) proficiency, are highly motivated to learn L2 (English), and are also highly motivated to maintain and develop their L1 skills, which are reinforced in family and community settings. Hence, the Cummins model predicts that these students should be ideally suited for a total-immersion program and that their cognitive and academic performances should be superior to Chinese students attending Chinese-language (nonimmersion) high schools, after controlling for preexisting differences.

A critical, unresolved theoretical issue is whether immersion effects depend on prior academic and language proficiency. Traditional practice in immersion programs includes explicit selection based on student characteristics such as prior achievement levels or implicit selection on the basis of parental (or student) choice. There is, however, a philosophical orientation toward more inclusive selection strategies supported by limited research, suggesting that the benefits of an immersion program are broadly generalizable (e.g., Genesee, 1985; Lambert, 1992). Theoretical models — particularly the Cummins (1979) interaction model — predict that the additive bilingualism needed for students to benefit from an immersion program is more likely when students have appropriate competencies and motivations to participate. Clearly, the Hong Kong Education Commission (1990) accepted the logic of this perspective. They argued that the effects of instruction in English would vary according to initial ability levels and that students who were not particularly able might be disadvantaged by being taught nonlanguage subjects in English. Following from these predictions, we specifically test the hypothesis that the effects of language of instruction vary according to prior student abilities.

Because Hong Kong implemented late immersion rather than early immersion, the present investigation makes an ideal setting for testing the generalizability of findings based on previous research and theoretical predictions from Cummins's 1979 model. Although the predictions are apparently straightforward — even more so, perhaps, than in the original Canadian immersion programs — there are some crucial differences that make the present investigation a particularly important test of the theory. Whereas the predicted advantages of English-language high schools are unproblematic for English-language achievement and, perhaps, even Chinese-language achievement, predictions are more complicated for nonlanguage subjects. As noted earlier, several authors have alluded to potential problems of content mastery in nonlanguage high school subjects, where it may be more difficult to teach complex and abstract concepts in an L2 that has not yet been adequately mastered. Willig (1985) also noted that some of the largest advantages of teaching students in their L1 were observed in the nonlanguage areas, particularly social studies. Although no studies in her review focused on science achievement, Willig also hypothesized that students taught science in their L1 would also be advantaged over students taught science in L2. Also, whereas we interpret Cummins (1979) as predicting that students in English-language schools should also excel in all school subjects, we recognize that he qualified his predictions with the caveat that the level of L2 proficiency needed to achieve additive bilingualism (i.e., his "threshold level") increases at higher levels of schooling.

Specific Research Questions to Be Addressed in the Present Investigation

As emphasized earlier, the overarching research question to be addressed is, What are the effects of language of instruction on achievement during the first three years of high school after controlling for initial differences in student achievement? Based on our review of the theoretical and research literature, and policy issues from the Hong Kong context, we now pose a series of research questions to guide our analyses and presentation of the results:

1. Do the effects of instruction in English vary substantially for different school subjects? Whereas most research has focused on the effects of instruction in L2 on the development of language skills in L1 and L2, it is also important to evaluate the effects of instruction in L2 on nonlanguage content subjects.
2. Do the effects of the language of instruction vary with prior student characteristics, such as prior achievement or prior English skills? For example, are students who initially are brighter in general or have better English skills more advantaged — or less disadvantaged — by being taught in English?
3. Do the effects of instruction in English grow larger or smaller over the first three years of high school? It might be expected, for example, that any negative effects of instruction in English might be larger in the first year of high school when students are first introduced to instruction in English, but that any negative effects might become smaller over time as students became more accustomed to instruction in English and improved their English-language skills.
4. What are the effects of English in English classes and English ethos in nonclassroom activities? In English-language high schools, students are exposed to English in all of their subjects other than Chinese. These students, however, also learn English in English-language classes and are exposed to English in nonclassroom activities (e.g., extracurricular activities, school meetings, and school notice boards). What are the effects of these other sources of exposure to English on achievement in different school subjects and how do these vary with the language of instruction?

METHODS

Sample

In Hong Kong, the highly competitive selection into different high schools at the end of grade six is based on parental choice and on examination results.[2] Schools that attract better students are those with better public examination results, higher admission rates to universities, a longer history of positive results, a good reputation with parents, and other desirable characteristics (e.g., school culture, extracurricular activities, proximity to home). As emphasized earlier, language of instruction is one important consideration in the selection of schools by parents, and schools with instruction in English are highly prestigious. Schools in this study had considerable freedom in choosing the language of instruction. Some schools taught all classes (other than Chinese) primarily in English, some taught all classes (other than English) in Chinese, and some used both Chinese and English. The present study is a large-scale investigation on the effects of language of instruction for secondary schools in Hong Kong. The sample is broadly representative of Hong Kong schools. The schools were selected by the Hong Kong Department of Education, using public documents and their academic subject inspectors' and other officers' knowledge of the schools to provide a large sample of schools that was representative in relation to students' academic ability and the language of instruction used by the school. This local knowledge about language of instruction used by the schools was subsequently validated with a survey completed by students about the language of instruction that was actually used in the school. The original sample consisted of 12,784 Chinese secondary students in grade seven attending one of fifty-six high schools. The schools were selected by the Hong Kong Department of Education to include a diverse sample of schools broadly representative of Hong Kong secondary schools in terms of religious background, mode of government subsidy, gender grouping, and, of particular relevance to the present investigation, language of instruction. For the selected schools, all students entering grade seven were included in the study.

Procedures and Measures

In Hong Kong, all grade-six students are allocated a placement score that represents an internal aggregate of achievement in all school subjects except physical education (although Chinese, English, and mathematics are weighted more heavily) that is moderated by (i.e., adjusted in relation to performance on) external examinations. The external examinations are standardized measures of general ability, with separate mathematics and verbal (Chinese) components, that are administered by the Department of Education. Because these scores are the primary basis for the extremely important selection into high schools, performance on these achievement tests is very important to students and schools. For purposes of the present investigation, prior achievement (performance in grade six at time 0, the year prior to the start of high school) is based on five separate scores: 1) the original placement achievement score (Ach0), 2) the mathematics moderator examination score, 3) the verbal (Chinese) moderator examination score, 4) school-based performance in Chinese, and 5) school-based performance in English.

In each of the three years following entry into high school, the Hong Kong Department of Education administered standardized achievement tests in English, Chinese, mathematics, science, geography, and history in grade seven (T1), grade eight (T2), and grade nine (T3). Achievement tests were administered to all students in the language of instruction in which the student studied the particular subject (i.e., students studying a subject in Chinese completed the test in Chinese, whereas students studying a subject in English completed the test in English), but were otherwise identical. The tests for the six school subjects for each of the first three years of high school were constructed by working parties brought together by the Hong Kong Department of Education with representation from the Advisory Inspectorate Division, the Curriculum Development Institute, and Educational Research Section. In late May or early June of each year, all students who were present on the day that the tests were administered completed achievement tests according to a modified random matrix sampling design in two testing sessions conducted on the same day. In the first testing session, each student was randomly assigned an achievement test in one of three core subjects: Chinese, English, and mathematics.[3] In the second test session that was conducted on the same day, students were randomly assigned to take a test in one of three additional subjects: geography, history, and science.[4]

Language of Instruction

The main independent variable in this study was language of instruction. At the start of the study, the Hong Kong Department of Education broadly classified schools according to their language of instruction (English, Chinese, and mixed Chinese/English) and students' academic ability level. This was done using a combination of public documents and the knowledge of academic subject inspectors and other officers who worked for the Department of Education. For purposes of this study, however, the Hong Kong Department of Education subsequently collected more detailed information about the language of instruction by surveying all students in participating schools at T3, when students were in grade nine. Each student completed a survey about the use of English in the school and in particular school subjects (other than Chinese). For each of the specific school subjects (English, mathematics, science, geography, history, social studies), students responded to four questions: language used in tests and examinations, language used for homework assignments, language used for textbooks, and the actual language used by the teacher. The first three items were measured on a three-point response scale (1 = Chinese only; 2 = mixed; 3 = English only), whereas the final question was answered using a 7-point response scale (1 = all Chinese, not a single sentence in English was spoken; 2 = almost all Chinese, with a few sentences of English explanation; 3 = mainly Chinese, but often supplemented with English; 4 = always switching between Chinese and English explanations and terms; 5 = mainly English, but often supplemented with Chinese; 6 = almost all English, with a few sentences of Chinese explanation; 7 = all English, not a single sentence in Chinese was spoken). There were eight additional items referring to use of English in other (nonclassroom) school activities (e.g., school notice boards, sport events, morning assembly, graduation ceremonies, open day, newsletters), again using a 7-point response scale.

   In order to explore the dimensionality of the responses, separate exploratory factor analyses were conducted, one based on responses by individual students and one based on school-average responses (i.e., each of the 56 cases was the mean response to each item by all students within the particular school). Both analyses demonstrated three distinct language-of-instruction factors: Instruction in English (in all classes other than English, keeping in mind that Chinese was not included in the survey), use of English in English Classes, and English Ethos (use of English in nonclassroom aspects of the school). Based on these preliminary factor analyses and for purposes of this study, we constructed three scores (English Instruction, English in English Classes, and English Ethos) to represent language of instruction for each school. These scores varied along a "primarily Chinese" to a "primarily English" continuum. The three language-of-instruction variables were highly correlated: $r = .66$ ($p < .001$) for English Instruction and English in English Classes; $r = .49$ ($p < .001$) for English Instruction and English Ethos; and $r = .34$ ($p < .001$) for English Instruction in English Classes and English Ethos.

Statistical Analysis

Educational research typically involves hierarchically ordered data in which there are multiple units of analysis. In particular, students are typically nested within classrooms or schools. It is usually inappropriate to treat responses by individual students as if they are a random sample without regard to schools because students within the same school are typically more similar to each other than they are to students from different schools (a violation of the independence of statistical tests that do not take the multiple levels — student and school — into account). Also, if questions of interest involve both individual students and schools, then it is more appropriate to conduct multilevel analyses that allow the researcher to simultaneously evaluate results at both units of analysis than to consider only one of the potential units of analysis. Moreover, relations observed at one level of analysis might not bear any straightforward connection to relations observed at another level. Multilevel analyses allow researchers to simultaneously consider multiple units of analysis within the same analysis. A detailed presentation of the conduct of multilevel modeling (also referred to as hierarchical linear modeling) is available elsewhere (e.g., Bryk & Raudenbush, 1992; Goldstein, 1995; Goldstein et al., 1998; Raudenbush & Bryk, 1988). In the present investigation, statistical analyses consisted of multilevel analyses conducted with the commercially available MLwiN (Goldstein et al., 1998) statistical package.

Multilevel growth modeling (see Bryk & Raudenbush, 1992; Goldstein, 1995) is a statistical approach in which growth in student achievement over time can be compared within and across different school types. In the present investigation, the dependent variable is achievement in each of six school subjects over the T1–T3 period. Pre-test (T0) achievement measures are used as covariates to correct for initial student differences (see Plewis, 1996a, 1996b) and to evaluate how growth in achievement varies as a function of pre-test (T0) achievement, language of instruction, and their interaction (i.e., aptitude-treatment interactions). More specifically, we fit a three-level growth model in which the three levels were time (the occasion of the achievement test score: T1, T2, T3), student ($n = 12,784$), and school ($n = 56$). This model is described in more detail in the appendix.

Multilevel growth modeling offers an attractive approach to the analysis of longitudinal data, as growth trends are allowed to vary for each student. The growth modeling approach does not require all individuals to have the same number of data points over time and provides an efficient approach to the common problem of missing data in longitudinal research. That is, in the same way that the multilevel modeling procedure can handle varying numbers of students in different schools — assuming that the sample of students is a representative sample of the school — such a procedure can incorporate varying numbers of data points for each person, provided that the points are a representative sample of students' achievement. Goldstein (1995) emphasized in particular the appropriateness of this approach for repeated measures of data and, more generally, for multivariate data in studies in which "measurements are missing by design rather than at random" as "in certain kinds of educational assessments, known as matrix sample designs" (p. 7). In the present study, for example, each student completed only two randomly assigned achievement tests from the six achievement tests that were considered so that scores on the other four tests were "missing" in accordance with the matrix sample design of the study. Hence, this multilevel growth modeling approach is ideally suited to the present investigation.[5]

Particularly in multilevel models, data transformations facilitate interpretations. Following Marsh and Rowe (1996; also see Aiken & West, 1991; Bryk & Raudenbush, 1992), we began by standardizing (z-scoring) all variables to have M = 0, SD = 1 across the entire sample.[6] Product terms were the product of individual (z-score) standardized variables (and were not restandardized). Coefficients for the linear growth components were standardized so that the squared coefficients summed to 1.0.

Due to the nature of some of the variables and potential problems associated with multicollinearity, we also "residualized" several of the predictor scores. We used five pre-test variables: pre-test achievement (Ach0), the basis of student selection into high schools, was the primary pre-test variable; we also considered standardized achievement tests scores (verbal and mathematics) and school-based performance measures (in English and Chinese). Each of these additional test scores, however, is substantially correlated with Ach0 and was used in the construction of the variable Ach0. That is, Ach0 was an aggregate of school-based performance measures including the English and Chinese school-based performance measures, and the standardized achievement tests were used to moderate scores from school to school. The four additional achievement pre-test scores were "residualized" by partialling out the effects of Ach0. Thus, for example, the effect of the residualized pre-test English achievement represents the effect of English achievement that is independent of Ach0. This is analogous to a hierarchical approach in which all variance that can be explained by Ach0 is attributed to this variable and only variance that can be explained uniquely by pre-test English is attributed to that variable.

The main language of instruction variable was English Instruction (EInst), but we were also interested in the additional effects of use of English in English Classes (EEng) and English Ethos (EEthos). Because these variables were highly correlated, we partialled out the effects of the English Instruction from English in English Classes and English Ethos. Thus, for example, the effect of English in English Classes represents the effect of this variable independent of English Instruction.

In the present investigation, as in all longitudinal studies, the appropriate handling of missing data was an important issue. Missing values in dependent variables (i.e., achievement scores in different school subjects administered at T1, T2, and T3) due to the matrix sampling design did not pose a problem because of the multilevel approach to growth modeling used in this analysis, as explained earlier. All students in the study had pre-test achievement (Ach0) scores. Missing values for the other pre-test scores were imputed by using scores predicted by Ach0. Since these scores were all completely standardized residuals based on prediction from Ach0, this procedure resulted in assigning all missing values a residual value of 0, indicating no difference from the score predicted by the pre-test achievement score. Because the language-of-instruction variables were all measured at the school level, no missing values existed for any of these variables.

RESULTS

Preliminary Results

The correlations between pre-test achievement, language of instruction, and post-test achievement are presented in Table 1. Although the total sample size was 12,784, the combination of the matrix sampling and missing data meant that the number of achievement scores for a given subject at a particular occasion was much smaller. The residualization strategy is also evident from these correlations in that pre-test achievement (Ach0 in Table 1) is uncorrelated with residual scores for each of the re-maining (residualized) pre-test scores, even though the original (unresidualized) scores for all these variables were highly correlated. Similarly, general English Instruction (EInst in Table 1) was uncorrelated with the remaining two (residualized) English-language scores.

Pre-Test–Post-Test Correlations

The correlations between pre-test and post-test achievements support the construct validity of interpretations of the test scores (Table 1). The unresidualized total pre-test achievement score was substantially and significantly correlated with all post-test achievement scores and the sizes of the correlations were nearly as high at T3 (three years later) as at T1 (due to the very large sample size in this study, almost all correlations are "statistically" significant and so we will focus on whether the size is substantial rather than statistical significance per se). The patterns of correlations between the specific residualized pre-test achievement and post-test achievement scores, however, varied substantially (i.e., varied to an extent that was of practical significance as opposed to statistical significance) depending on the particular school subject. For example, the pre-test Chinese grades and test scores (Chin0 and Verb0) were moderately correlated with subsequent achievement in Chinese (e.g., correlation coefficients of .21and .28 for T1 Chinese achievement; see Table 1), recalling that these correlations represent contributions beyond what was explained by the total pre-test achievement score. Similarly, the residualized pre-test numeric scores were moderately correlated with subsequent achievement in mathematics (e.g., r of .27 for T1 mathematics achievement; see Table 1) and, to a lesser extent, science (e.g., r of .17 for T1 science achievement; see Table 1). Also, the residualized pre-test English scores were moderately correlated with subsequent performance in English (e.g., r of .25 for T1 English achievement; see Table 1). Not surprisingly, there is an overall pattern of slightly stronger relations between pre-test (T0) achievement and T1 achievement than between T0 achievement and T3 achievement, but the differences are small.

Language-of-Instruction Correlations

All three of the language-of-instruction scores (EInst, EEng, EEthos) were empirically derived from student responses to the survey on the use of English collected at T3, whereas one (English language of instruction, ELLOI, in Table 1) is based on an a priori classification provided by the Department of Education at T1. The variable ELLOI correlated .91 with the empirically derived English Instruction scores (EInst) and the pattern of correlations with other variables was very similar for these two general language-of-instruction variables. In particular, the correlation between ELLOI and each of the other variables in Table 1 is nearly the same as the corresponding correlation with EInst [e.g., r (Ach0, ELLOI) = .45, r (Ach0, EInst) = .47]. Hence, the a priori classification of schools made by the Department of Education at T1 based on public records and local knowledge (ELLOI) agreed remarkably well with the empirically derived English Instruction score collected at T3 (EInst). This provides extremely strong support for the construct validity of the language-of-instruction variables. Since the other two empirical language-of-instruction variables were residual scores, they were nearly uncorrelated with both the general scores.

Pre-test achievement was substantially related to language of instruction. For example, pre-test achievement correlates .47 with general English Instruction and .47 with the (residualized) English in English Classes. However, because the pre-test achievement scores were based on achievement before students entered high school, we may attribute some of this correlation to school selection processes: students with higher pre-test scores tend to attend the more prestigious English-language high schools in Hong Kong. Interestingly, language-of-instruction variables (ELLOI, EInst, EEng) were almost uncorrelated with the residualized pre-test English scores (Eng0 Resid, see Table 1). Thus, although students in English-language high schools were much brighter than average, they were not particularly proficient in English, beyond what would be expected in terms of their general achievement. Hence, interpretations must account for these large initial pre-test differences, and relations that do not control for initial differences (i.e., the correlations as presented in Table 1) should be interpreted cautiously.

Correlations between the English Instruction and post-test achievement scores varied widely for different school subjects. For all three time points (see Table 1), the correlations were substantially positive for English, Chinese, and mathematics, but were substantially negative for history, geography, and science. However, these correlations do not control for the higher pre-test achievement of students in English-language high schools. Thus, much of the apparent advantage of attending English-language high schools for English, Chinese, and mathematics was due to preexisting differences and not to language of instruction. For example, the positive correlations between English Instruction (EInst in Table 1) and achievement in English, Chinese, and mathematics were consistently smaller than the strong positive correlation between English Instruction and pre-test achievement (Ach0) science. Even more dramatic, the apparent disadvantage of attending English-language high schools for geography, history, and science was based on uncorrected scores that did not take into account the fact that these students were much brighter than average before entering these high schools. Despite the fact that these students were much brighter than average, their scores in these three subjects were much lower than average. Controlling for preexisting differences significantly increased these negative effects. Additionally, the negative correlations associated with attending English-language schools declined somewhat over time for science and history — suggesting that the negative effects associated with attending English-language schools might become smaller over time. In summary, these results show that students attending English-language high schools score below average in geography, history, and science, even though these students were initially more able and should have performed well above average based on their pre-test achievement levels.

In marked contrast to general English Instruction, the use of English in English Classes (EEng) was consistently positively correlated with achievement in all school subjects (Table 1). Because use of English in English Classes was a residual score (controlling for general English Instruction), these correlations indicate that students in English classes where the emphasis on English was stronger than expected on the basis of the level of English Instruction did better in all school subjects than students in schools where the emphasis on English in English classes was not strong. Two features, however, complicate interpretations of this relation. First, much of this difference was due to preexisting (pre-test achievement) differences. Second, a strong emphasis on English in English Classes would likely be advantageous in learning history, for example, if students were taught history in English, but might not be advantageous if students were taught history in Chinese. The residualized English Ethos of the school (use of English in nonclassroom settings, EEthos) was uncorrelated with each post-test achievement score, suggesting that English Ethos was not an important variable in predicting achievement scores.

In summary, these preliminary analyses provide possible answers to our overarching question and at least some of our more specific research questions. In particular, the effects of instruction in English have negative effects for at least some school subjects (particularly nonlanguage subjects), but these effects seem to vary substantially depending on the particular school subject. Also, the effects of instruction in English appear to be reasonably stable over time. These results are important because they provide preliminary results that are not complicated by adjusting for prior differences in achievement and do not involve complicated statistical analyses. They are also limited, however, for these same reasons. Thus, we now turn to the statistically stronger and more appropriate longitudinal multilevel models of these same data.

Longitudinal Multilevel Analyses

Separate analyses were conducted for each school subject (Table 2; also see Figures 1–6). For each subject, five models were fit. Model 1 (a variance components model) included no predictor variables, but provided a baseline for how much variance in scores could be attributed to differences in school, differences between students, and differences within students over time. In a series of Models (2–5), new variables were added one step at a time according to an a priori sequence to explicate these results. In Model 2, pre-test achievement variables were included to determine how much variation between schools could be explained by preexisting differences. In Model 3, language-of-instruction variables were added to evaluate their effects on subsequent achievement. In Model 4, interactions involving language of instruction were included to see if the effects of language of instruction varied with pre-test levels of achievement. Finally, in Model 5, the growth and stability of the effects over time were evaluated. In addition to the fixed effects associated with these predictor variables, we assessed the extent to which variation from school to school could be explained by controlling for the variables included in each of these models.

Mathematics   Post-test mathematics achievement (see Model 5 for mathematics in Table 2) was substantially related to pre-test achievement (Ach0) and to the mathematics component of the pre-test achievement test (Mth0). Our analysis indicated that English Instruction had a small negative effect on post-test mathematics achievement, but that English in English Classes had a small positive effect (see Model 5 in Table 2 and Figure 1). The small negative effect of time overall was not substantively important because different tests were used on each occasion.[7] Overall, the small negative effect of English Instruction in general did not vary with pre-test achievement, but the small three-way interaction involving time suggests that over time this negative effect became somewhat smaller for initially brighter students. Inspection of the variance components for the five models of post-test mathematics achievement suggests that the substantial school-to-school variation in mathematics achievement was largely explained by the pre-test variables — the variance component (L3VSchl under random effects in Table 1) of .39 in Model 1 dropped to .04 with the addition of pre-test variables in Model 2, and decreased only slightly with the addition of language-of-instruction variables in subsequent models. Thus, it is not surprising that school-type differences in relation to language of instruction were not large.

Chinese   Post-test Chinese achievement was substantially related to pre-test achievement (Ach0) and pre-test Chinese achievement (Verb0 and Chin0). English Instruction had a small positive effect, but interestingly, English in English Classes had a slightly more positive effect on post-test Chinese achievement (see Figure 2). As was the case with mathematics, the small positive effect of English Instruction did not vary with pre-test achievement, but the small three-way interaction involving time suggests that over time this positive effect became somewhat smaller for initially brighter students. Inspection of the variance components for post-test Chinese achievement suggests that the substantial school-to-school variation (.46 in Model 1) was largely explained by the pre-test variables (the variance component was reduced to .04 in Model 2), although the inclusion of language of instruction resulted in a further drop in residual variance due to school-to-school variation (the variance component was .01 in Models 3–5).

English   Post-test English achievement was substantially related to pre-test achievement (Ach0), prior English achievement, and, to a lesser extent, the verbal (Chinese) pre-test achievement. As shown in Figure 3, English Instruction had a substantial positive effect, but not surprisingly, English in English Classes had an even more positive effect on post-test English achievement. Overall, the positive effect of English Instruction was somewhat greater for initially brighter students (the Ach0 x EInst effect in Table 2) and increased slightly with time (the Time x EInst effect in Table 2). Although initially brighter students did substantially better, this advantage declined slightly over time (Time x Ach0 effect in Table 2). The small three-way interaction (Time x EInst x EEng in Table 2) suggests that being in a school that had a strong general emphasis on English Instruction and a strong emphasis on English in English classes had an initial positive effect that declined over time. Inspection of the variance components for post-test English achievement suggests that the substantial school-to-school variation (.60 in Model 1) was explained in large part by the pre-test variables (the variance component was reduced to .11 in Model 2). The inclusion of language-of-instruction variables, however, resulted in a further drop in the school variance component (the variance component was .03 in Models 3–5).

History   Post-test history achievement was substantially related to pre-test achievement (Ach0) and, to a much lesser extent, the pre-test Chinese (Verb0 and Chin0) and English achievement. Because the effects of language of instruction for history were similar to those for geography and science, we describe the history results in somewhat greater detail. Model 5 (Table 2) demonstrates that English Instruction had a very large negative effect on history achievement. Thus, for example, the negative effect of English Instruction (ß = −.67) was more negative than the positive effect of pre-test achievement (ß = .44). Students taught history in English were strongly disadvantaged relative to students who were taught in Chinese. However, our analyses demonstrate that English in English Classes had a substantial positive effect on history achievement and that this positive effect was particularly large in schools with more English Instruction in general. These main and interaction effects are illustrated in Figure 4. For students in schools where the language of instruction was primarily in Chinese (−1.5 SD on English Instruction), the mean post-test history score was about one standard deviation above the mean of history achievement, and English in English Classes had no effect. For students who were taught history primarily in English-language schools (+1.5 SD on English Instruction), the mean history achievement was about one SD below the mean of history achievement. Here, however, the emphasis on English in English Classes made a big difference. Students who were in schools with high scores (+1.5 SD) in both English Instruction and English in English Classes had post-test history achievement scores that were about average, but students in schools with a high score in English Instruction but a low score in English in English Classes did much poorer. Thus, whereas students were strongly disadvantaged by being taught history in English, this effect could be slightly offset by attending schools with a particularly strong emphasis on English in English classes.

The very negative effects of English Instruction on student achievement were balanced somewhat if the student possessed strong prior English skills (the Eng0 x EInst interaction). As shown in Figure 5, the negative effect of being taught history in English was evident for all levels of initial English achievement, but the effects were somewhat smaller for students with initially strong English skills (high [+1.5 SD] English Pre-Test Skills in Figure 5) compared with students with initially weak English skills (low [−1.5 SD] English Pre-Test Skills in Figure 5). Over time, the very negative effects of English Instruction declined somewhat (the Time x EInst interaction). As shown in Figure 6, the very negative effect of English Instruction was slightly larger at T1 (grade seven, the first year of high school) than at T3 (grade

TABLE 1

*Correlations between Pre-Test Achievement, Language of Instruction,
and Post-Test Achievement*

		N	Ach0	Eng0 Resid	Chi0 Resid	Verb0 Resid	Mth0 Resid	ELLOI	EInst	EEng Resid	EEthos Resid
Pre-Test Achievement											
Ach	0	12784	1.00	.00	.00	.00	.00	.45*	.47*	.47*	−.08*
Eng	0	12784	.00	1.00	.10*	−.10*	−.24*	.03*	.05*	.05*	.00
Chi	0	12784	.00	.10*	1.00	.29*	.06*	−.03*	−.00	.02	−.01
Verb	0	12784	.00	−.10*	.29*	1.00	.24*	−.01	−.02	.01	−.00
Mth	0	12784	.00	−.24*	.06*	.24*	1.00	−.04*	−.04*	−.02	.02
English Language of Instruction											
ELLOI		12784	.45*	.03*	−.03*	−.01	−.04*	1.00	.91*	−.01	−.03*
EInst		12784	.47*	.05*	−.00	−.02	−.04*	.91*	1.00	−.02	−.01
EEng		12784	.47*	.04*	.02	.01	−.02	−.01	−.01	1.00	.01
EEthos		12784	−.08*	.00*	.01	.00	−.02	−.03*	−.01	.01	1.00
Post-Test Achievement											
Math	T1	3742	.69*	−.10*	.02	.03	.27*	.25*	.25*	.42*	−.02
	T2	3670	.68*	−.08*	.01	−.00	.24*	.23*	.25*	.42*	−.07*
	T3	3518	.69*	−.08*	−.01	.03	.22*	.20*	.21*	.45*	−.06*
	Tot	7980	.71*	−.09*	−.00	.01	.24*	.24*	.25*	.44*	−.05*
Chin	T1	3943	.75*	.04*	.21*	.28*	.00	.38*	.38*	.46*	−.04
	T2	3668	.69*	.05*	.18*	.24*	−.00	.33*	.33*	.45*	−.02
	T3	3536	.71*	.02	.16*	.22*	.03	.32*	.32*	.45*	−.03
	Tot	8046	.74*	.04*	.19*	.25*	.01	.35*	.36*	.46*	−.03*
Eng	T1	3821	.81*	.25*	.06*	.06*	−.05*	.44*	.46*	.48*	.01
	T2	3665	.78*	.18*	.03	.08*	−.04	.43*	.44*	.49*	.01
	T3	3505	.77*	.17*	.02	.06*	−.04*	.43*	.45*	.47*	−.01
	Tot	7983	.79*	.20*	.04*	.07*	−.04*	.44*	.46*	.48*	.01
Hist	T1	2639	.46*	.05	.08*	.09*	.02	−.40*	−.41*	.67*	.05
	T2	2748	.44*	.05	.06*	.09*	.03	−.39*	−.41*	.64*	.05*
	T3	2622	.49*	.01	.04	.07*	.06*	−.26*	−.27*	.59*	.02
	Tot	5864	.47*	.04*	.06*	.08*	.03	−.35*	−.37*	.64*	.04*
Geog	T1	2862	.52*	.03	.07*	.07*	.09*	−.29*	−.28*	.60*	.01
	T2	2767	.44*	−.04	.04	.08*	.08*	−.22*	−.22*	.51*	−.04
	T3	2668	.50*	.02	.06*	.08*	.05	−.32*	−.33*	.63*	.00
	Tot	6018	.50*	.00	.06*	.07*	.07*	−.28*	−.28*	.60*	−.02
Sci	T1	5991	.30*	−.07*	.11*	.15*	.17*	−.26*	−.25*	.28*	.02
	T2	5519	.36*	−.08*	.05*	.11*	.13*	−.12*	−.12*	.32*	−.01
	T3	5090	.36*	−.03	.10*	.11*	.10*	−.13*	−.14*	.23*	−.00
	Tot	9229	.40*	−.05*	.08*	.12*	.13*	−.19*	−.18*	.36*	−.01

Note. **Pre-Test Scores**: Ach0 = prior school achievement. Eng0 = pre-test English grades; Chin0 = pre-test Chinese grades; Verb0 = pre-test verbal (Chinese) test score; Mth0 = pre-test mathematics test score. **English Language of Instruction**: ELLOI = Language of Instruction (1 = Chinese, 2 = mixed English/Chinese, 3 = English); EInst = English Instruction (in classes other than English and Chinese); EEng = English in English classes; EEthos = English Ethos (in nonclassroom activities). **Post-Test Achievement scores**: Math = mathematics, Chin = Chinese, Eng = English, Hist = history, Geog = geography, Sci = science (T1, T2, T3 refers to Time 1, 2, and 3). **Residualized (Resid) Scores** are supplemental scores in which variance explained by the primary score is partialled. Residual pre-test achievements in specific subjects (Eng0, Chi0, Verb0, Mth0) are controlled for general pre-test achievement (Ach0), and EEng Resid and EEthos Resid are controlled for English Instruction.

*·p < .01

nine). Inspection of the variance components for post-test history achievement suggests that — unlike the models of post-test English, Chinese, and mathematics — the substantial school-to-school variation post-test history achievement (.61 in Model 1) was not substantially eliminated by controlling for pre-test variables (the variance component remained .50 in Model 2). Only with the inclusion of language-of-instruction variables was there a substantial drop in the school variance component (the variance component was reduced to .07 in Model 3). However, the addition of the aptitude-treatment interactions in Model 4 and interactions with time in Model 5 also resulted in further reductions (see Table 2) in school-to-school variation. In marked contrast to mathematics, English, and Chinese, these variance components indicate that language-of-instruction school types did make a substantial difference in school-to-school variation in all subsequent history achievement, although these effects were moderated to some extent by pre-test aptitudes and time.

Geography   Post-test geography achievement was strongly related to pre-test achievement (Ach0) and, to a much lesser extent, the pre-test Chinese (verb0 and Chin0) and mathematics (Mth0) achievement. A general emphasis on English had a very large negative effect on geography achievement, but a strong English emphasis in English classes had a large positive effect — particularly when there was also a strong general emphasis on English. (This was a similar pattern of results to that described for history achievement in Figure 4 and, thus, is not described again in detail). The very negative effect of the general emphasis on English was offset somewhat by having strong prior English skills (the Eng0 x EInst interaction; see also related results for history in Figure 5). The negative effects of the general emphasis on English did not, however, vary with time. Inspection of the variance components for post-test geography achievement suggests that the substantial school-to-school variation (.50 in Model 1) was not substantially eliminated by controlling for pre-test variables (the variance component was .38 in Model 2). Only when language-of-instruction variables were included in Model 3 was there a substantial drop in the school variance component (.04 in Model 3), although the addition of the aptitude-treatment interactions in Model 4 also resulted in a small further reduction in school-level residual variance. As with history, these variance components indicate that language-of-instruction school types did make a substantial difference in all subsequent geography achievement.

Science   Post-test science achievement was strongly related to pre-test achievement (Ach0) and, to much lesser extents, pre-test Chinese (Verb0 and Chin0) and mathematics (Mth0) achievement. A general emphasis on English instruction had a very large negative effect on science achievement, but a strong English emphasis in English classes had a large positive effect. The effect of a strong emphasis on English in English classes was particularly positive in English-language high schools (EInst x EEng). Furthermore, the corresponding three-way interaction (Time x EInst x EEng) indicates that this positive effect increased somewhat over time. The very negative effects of the general emphasis on English were offset somewhat by having strong prior English skills (the Eng0 x EInst interaction). The negative effects of the general emphasis on English also declined somewhat with time (Time x EInst interaction). The substantial school-level variance components for science achievement suggest that school-to-school variation (.34 in Model 1) was not reduced by controlling for pre-test variables (the variance component was .39 in Model 2). Only when the language-of-instruction variables were included in Model 3 did a substantial drop in the school variance component occur (the estimated variance dropped to .07 in Model 3). However, the addition of the aptitude-treatment interactions in Models 4 and 5 also resulted in small further reductions in school-level residual variance. As observed with history achievement, these variance components indicate that language-of-instruction school types did make a substantial difference in all subsequent science achievement.

DISCUSSION

Do Effects of Instruction in English Vary for Different School Subjects?

The results provide a dramatic affirmative response to this first research question. For two subjects, Chinese and, particularly, English, the effects of English Instruction were moderately positive; for one, mathematics, there were small negative effects; and for three subjects, history, geography, and science, the effects were extremely negative. The positive effects of Instruction in English on post-test English achievement were not surprising, which is why public advocates (and parents) argue in favor of English-language high schools. Although the effects for Chinese were small, it is interesting that the effects were positive and not negative. This finding suggests that learning an L2 can benefit L1 achievement and is consistent with earlier results for immersion studies and predictions based on the interdependence hypothesis from Cummins's 1979 model (see also Francis, 1999).

The most important findings, however, were the very strong negative effects of Instruction in English on history, geography, and science. For each of these three subjects, the negative effects of Instruction in English were about as large, or larger, than the positive effects of pre-test achievement. The apparent similarity in these three subjects is that each involves a relatively new content area for students first entering grade seven and requires students to learn new terminology in order to understand the conceptual underpinnings of these subjects. When students are forced to do this in an L2 (English) that is not already well mastered, students must place undue attention on mastering basic terminology that may preclude gaining a deeper conceptual understanding of these subjects, on actively participating in classroom discussion, and even reading the textbook that is also in English. Following this reasoning, because Chinese classes are taught in Chinese and English courses are taught in English, it is not too surprising that the language of instruction for other school subjects in the school did not have any negative effects on Chinese and English achievement. For mathematics, the English Instruction effects were negative, but much smaller than for history, geography, and science. Teaching in mathematics, however, is based largely on a symbolic terminology that may not be so dependent on the language of instruction and may have already been more adequately mastered prior to grade seven relative to the other (nonlanguage) subjects considered here. We suggest that this has to do with the development of mathematics knowledge in general and is not specific to instruction in Hong Kong. This suggestion is supported by the similar pattern of results presented by Willig (1985), based on her review of U.S. research.

Do Effects of Instruction in English Vary with Pre-Test Academic and English Competency?

From both theoretical and policy perspectives, it is important to determine whether the negative effects of Instruction in English on history, geography, and science vary depending on the initial aptitudes of the students (i.e., whether or not there are aptitude-treatment interactions). Fortunately, the quality of our pre-test measures are exceptionally good in that they are comprehensive, reliable, and highly correlated with achievement in subsequent years. Contrary to expectations (based on predictions from Cummins's 1979 model and from the rationale for current policy in Hong Kong about the allocation of students to English-language schools), the disadvantages associated with being taught in English were not smaller for initially brighter students than for initially less-able students (i.e., the EInst x Ach0 interactions were nonsignificant for history, geography, and science, as shown in Table 2). For all three content subjects, however, students who had initially better English skills were somewhat less disadvantaged by instruction in English. The juxtaposition of these two sets of results is important because earlier results (see Table 1) indicated that the allocation into English-language high schools was based primarily on the total pre-test achievement scores and not specifically on prior English skills. The results suggest, perhaps, that more emphasis should be placed on prior English skills when assigning students to English-language high schools in order to minimize the negative effects of Instruction in English. Such an educational policy, however, may contradict the immersion philosophy of starting with students who have limited (or no) L2 proficiency (Swain & Johnson, 1997) and may have undesirable side effects of placing even more emphasis on English, possibly devaluing Chinese, and giving the appearance of a more elitist program in that only students with stronger initial English can study in the prestigious English-language high schools (Gibbons, 1989).

What Are the Effects of English in English Classes and English Ethos?

To the extent that English Ethos accurately reflected the use of English in nonclassroom activities, our results indicated that English Ethos did not contribute significantly to achievement in any of the six school subjects. In contrast, the effects of English in English Classes had positive effects on achievement in all six subjects, even after controlling for pre-test achievement and Instruction in English in general. It is not surprising, of course, that a stronger emphasis on English in English Classes leads to better achievement in English and, perhaps, Chinese (as predicted by the Cummins 1979 model and reflecting the rationale of immersion programs).

More interesting is the question of why a stronger emphasis on English in English Classes has positive effects on achievement in history, geography, science, and, to a lesser extent, mathematics. Apparently, these positive effects of strong English classes extend to other classes taught in English, such that those students are less dis-

TABLE 2

Total Achievement in Six Subjects: Five Models of Relations with Pre-Test Achievement, Language of Instruction, and Time

Variables	Mathematics Models					Chinese Models					English Models				
	1	2	3	4	5	1	2	3	4	5	1	2	3	4	5
FIXED EFFECTS															
Pre-Test															
Ach0		.63*	.62*	.62*	.62*		.65*	.63*	.63*	.63*		.59*	.58*	.58*	.58*
Eng0		-.04*	-.04*	-.04*	-.04*		.04*	.04*	.04*	.04*		.21*	.21*	.21*	.21*
Chin0		.00	.00	-.01	-.01		.13*	.13*	.13*	.13*		.02	.02	.02	.02
Verb0		-.04*	-.04*	-.04*	-.04*		.23*	.23*	.23*	.23*		.09*	.09*	.09*	.09*
Mth0		.24*	.24*	.24*	.24*		-.04*	-.04*	-.04*	-.04*		-.02*	-.02*	-.02*	-.02*
English Language of Instruction															
EInst			-.03	-.06*	-.07*			.05*	.05*	.05*			.20*	.18*	.18*
EEng			.09*	.11*	.11*			.14*	.16*	.16*			.22*	.24*	.24*
EEthos			.02	.01	.01			.02	.01	.01			.05	.04	.04
AchOxEInst				-.04	-.04				-.02	-.02				.07*	.07*
EngOxEInst				.02	.02				.00	.00				.01	.01
EInstxEEng				.03	.04				.03	.03				.05	.05
Time (Linear)															
Time (T)					-.06*					-.01					-.04*
TxEInst					.00					-.03					-.03*
TxAch0					-.01					.01					-.03*
TxAch0xEInst					.05*					-.05*					.02
TxEInstxEEng					.00					.02					-.03*
RANDOM EFFECTS															
L3V Schl	.39*	.04*	.02*	.02*	.02*	.46*	.04*	.01*	.01*	.01*	.60*	.11*	.03*	.03*	.03*
L3V Ach0		.01*	.01*	.01*	.01*		.01*	.01*	.01*	.01*		.02*	.02*	.01*	.01*
L3CV Ach0/Schl		.02*	.01*	.01*	.01*		-.01	.00	.00	.00		.02*	.00	.00	.00
L2V Student	.39*	.19*	.19*	.19*	.19*	.38*	.16*	.16*	.16*	.16*	.34*	.18*	.18*	.18*	.18*
L1V Time	.24*	.24*	.24*	.24*	.24*	.21*	.21*	.21*	.21*	.21*	.10*	.10*	.10*	.10*	.10*
LIKE Ratio	24720	21164	21137	21126	21084	24280	20146	20095	20091	20051	19780	16026	15961	15941	15906

Variables	History Models					Geography Models					Science Models				
	1	2	3	4	5	1	2	3	4	5	1	2	3	4	5
FIXED EFFECTS															
Pre-Test															
Ach0		.44*	.44*	.44*	.44*		.44*	.44*	.43*	.43*		.58*	.59*	.58*	.59*
Eng0		.04*	.04*	.02	.02		.02	.01	-.01	-.01		-.01	-.01	.00	.01
Chin0		.04*	.04*	.04*	.04*		.04*	.03*	.03*	.03*		.03*	.03*	.03*	.03*
Verb0		.08*	.08*	.08*	.08*		.06*	.06*	.06*	.06*		.09*	.09*	.09*	.09*
Mth0		-.02	-.02	-.02	-.02		.03*	.03*	.03*	.03*		.08*	.08*	.08*	.08*
English Language of Instruction															
EInst			-.53*	-.67*	-.66*			-.48*	-.57*	-.57*			-.53*	-.58*	-.58*
EEng			.26*	.36*	.35*			.24*	.28*	.28*			.11*	.19*	.19*
EEthos			.06	.04	.04			.03	.01	.01			.02	-.01	-.01
Ach0xEInst				.01	.00				.01	.01				-.03	-.03
Eng0xEInst				.08*	.08*				.08*	.08*				.06*	.06*
EInstxEEng				.22*	.21*				.14*	.14*				.15*	.15*
Time (Linear)															
Time (T)					-.06*					-.01					-.03*
TxEInst					.13*					-.01					.09*
TxAch0					.00					-.02					.01
TxAchOxEInst					-.01					.02					-.02
TxEInstxEEng					.00					.00					.04*
RANDOM EFFECTS															
L3V Schl	.61*	.50*	.07*	.05*	.05*	.50*	.38*	.04*	.03*	.03*	.34*	.39*	.07*	.05*	.05*
L3V Ach0		.02	.03*	.03*	.03*		.02	.03*	.03*	.03*		.03*	.03*	.03*	.03*
L3CV Ach0/Schl			.02	.00	.00		.03	.01	.00	.00		.04*	.03*	.01	.01
L2V Student	.24*	.16*	.16*	.16*	.16*	.26*	.18*	.18*	.18*	.18*	.42*	.27*	.27*	.26*	.27*
L1V Time	.18*	.18*	.18*	.18*	.17*	.27*	.27*	.27*	.27*	.27*	.33*	.33*	.33*	.33*	.32*
LIKE Ratio	15069	13803	13732	13627	13506	17810	16782	16696	16617	16612	39404	36944	36853	36776	36579

Note: Ach0 = pre-test school achievement. Eng0 = pre-test English grades; Chin0 = pre-test Chinese grades; Verb0 = pre-test verbal (Chinese) test score; Mth0 = pre-test mathematics test score; EInst = English Instruction in general (use of English in classes other than English and Chinese); EEng = English instruction in English classes; EEthos = English Ethos (use of English in nonclassroom activities). For each of six school subjects, five separate multilevel analyses were conducted that included: 1) only random variance components; 2) the pre-test variables; 3) all pre-test variables and the three English language-of-instruction variables; 4) pre-test variables, three language-of-instruction variables, language-of-instruction interactions; 5) all predictor variables including interactions with time. Random effects are variance and covariance components across the multiple levels: level 1 (time, L1V), level 2 (student, L2V), and level 3 (school, L3V, L3CV).

* p < .01

FIGURE 1   *Math achievement (in standard deviation units) as a function of General English Use (extent to which English is the language of instruction in the school, EInst in Table 2) and English in English Classes (extent to which English is used in English Classes, EEng in Table 2).*

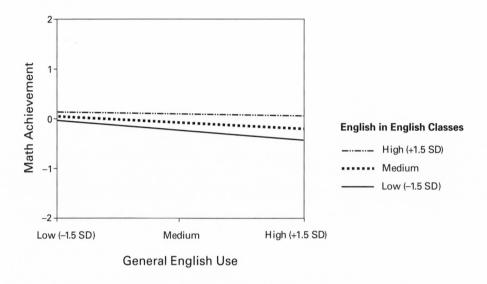

FIGURE 2   *Chinese achievement (in standard deviation units) as a function of General English Use (extent to which English is the language of instruction in the school, EInst in Table 2) and English in English Classes (extent to which English is used in English Classes, EEng in Table 2).*

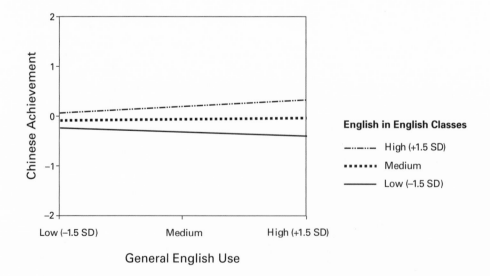

advantaged by Instruction in English. For history, geography, and science, there were interactions between the English in English Classes and the Instruction in English in general. For example, as illustrated in Figure 4 for history, the emphasis on English in English classes had no effect on achievement when the history class was taught primarily in Chinese (i.e., General English Use is low [–1.5 SD] on the left side of the graph) but had a substantial positive effect when history was taught primarily in English (i.e., General English Use is high [+1.5 SD] on the right side of the graph). Even in mathematics, where the effects of language of instruction were much smaller, the direction of this nonsignificant interaction effect (.036, SE = .020) was positive. From a policy perspective, these results are very important, suggesting that having a particularly strong emphasis on English in English Classes can offset some of the negative effects of Instruction in English in nonlanguage subjects.

Do Effects of Language of Instruction Vary over Time?

Contrary to expectations, the effects of language of instruction did not vary substantially over time. In particular, we anticipated that the Instruction in English effects on history, geography, science, and mathematics might be relatively more negative in the first year of high school when students were first introduced to Instruction in English, but might become smaller as students became more accustomed to Instruction in English and acquired better English-language skills. There was weak support for these expectations for history and, to a lesser extent, science, but not for geography or mathematics. Whereas this support was strongest for history, the results (see Figure 6) demonstrate that the reduction in the negative effects over time was not substantial. Whereas the achievement differences between schools taught primarily in English and primarily in Chinese were somewhat smaller at T3 than T1, the differences were not large. Although other interactions involving time existed, these effects were small and not consistent across different school subjects.

In summary, Hong Kong high school students were very disadvantaged by Instruction in English in geography, history, science, and, to a lesser extent, mathematics. The size of this disadvantage was reasonably consistent across the first three years of high school. Although the size of this disadvantage did not vary much with initial achievement levels in general, the disadvantage of Instruction in English was somewhat smaller for students who initially had better English-language skills. Furthermore, these large negative effects of Instruction in English in English-language schools were offset to a limited extent by a strong emphasis on English in English Classes.

IMPLICATIONS FOR THEORY AND GENERALIZATIONS
BASED ON PREVIOUS RESEARCH

The Canadian immersion studies (Lambert, 1992) showed that instruction in L2 (French) for English Canadians with little or no prior L2 proficiency had positive effects on subsequent L2 proficiency, but also on achievement in L1 (English) and some

FIGURE 3   *English achievement (in standard deviation units) as a function of General English Use (extent to which English is the language of instruction in the school, EInst in Table 2) and English in English Classes (extent to which English is used in English Classes, EEng in Table 2).*

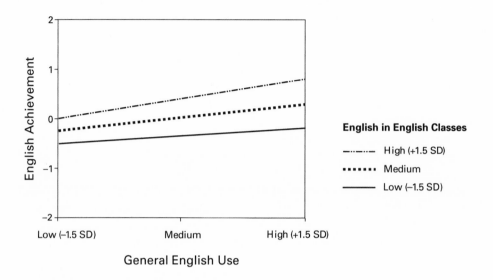

FIGURE 4   *History achievement (in standard deviation units) as a function of General English Use (extent to which English is the language of instruction in the school, EInst in Table 2) and English in English Classes (extent to which English is used in English Classes, EEng in Table 2).*

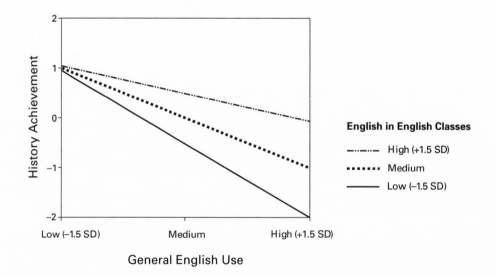

other school subjects. In marked contrast, Willig (1985) concluded that for students with limited L2 (English) proficiency there were consistently positive effects of teaching students in their L1 (in bilingual transition programs) rather than in their L2, but she excluded the Canadian immersion studies. Cummins (1979) provided a theoretical model of L2 acquisition that seemed to be consistent with these seemingly contradictory results. In particular, he argued that students would only realize the benefits of bilingualism if they were sufficiently competent (i.e., above a proficiency threshold) in both languages, when the ongoing development of L1 was reinforced outside of school (e.g., it was the dominant language in the particular society), and, perhaps, if students were motivated to learn and appreciate both languages. Whereas this theoretical position seemed consistent with both the original Canadian immersion studies and the bilingual transition studies, subsequent immersion studies suggested that the benefits of immersion generalized more broadly than might be expected from Cummins's theoretical model. Much of this research, however, was based on early-immersion programs.

Reviews of both immersion and bilingual transitional paradigms have focused almost exclusively on language proficiency, and little attention has been given to achievement in nonlanguage classes. Thus, for example, Willig (1985) reported very few studies that considered social studies achievement and reported no studies that evaluated science achievement. Given the strong applied-policy orientation of most research in this area, this is a shocking omission. Epitomizing this perspective in a discussion of the Hong Kong context from the perspective of immersion research, Johnson (1997) suggested that if the goal of immersion is to create Hong Kong students who are highly proficient in English, then achievement in nonlanguage subjects might be irrelevant. In marked contrast to this apparent disregard for achievement in nonlanguage subjects, the Hong Kong Education Commission (1990) specified that English should only be used if a student's *overall* cognitive and academic development benefited.

We reject Johnson's perspective, which seems to permeate immersion research, and interpret the results of our study — with some qualifications — as largely contradicting the implications of previous immersion studies and, apparently, predictions from Cummins's interaction theory of second language acquisition. Overall, the effects of the immersion program were negative — not positive. These conclusions are important because our study seems to match closely the main characteristics of the prototypical immersion study (e.g., Swain & Johnson, 1997) and seem to satisfy all of the conditions that Cummins indicates are important to achieve the positive benefits of bilingualism. Yet, overall, the results of this study suggest that immersing high school students into L2 instruction has very negative effects. An important qualification, of course, is that the late-immersion program considered here did have small positive effects on language achievement, and this has been the primary criterion used in most other research. From this overly narrow perspective, it may be possible to argue that the effects are consistent with previous immersion studies. When compared to the overwhelmingly negative effects of immersion for the nonlanguage subjects, however, we consider that our large-scale quasi-experimental study — one of the largest late-immersion studies ever conducted — was a failure in terms of provid-

FIGURE 5   *History achievement (in standard deviation units) as a function of English Pre-Test Skills (school grades in English before the start of high school, Eng0 in Table 2) and General English Use (extent to which English is the language of instruction in the school, EInst in Table 2).*

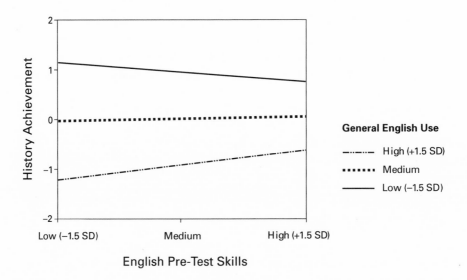

FIGURE 6   *History achievement (in standard deviation units) as a function of Time (Year in school, Time [T] in Table 2) and General English Use (extent to which English is the language of instruction in the school, EInst in Table 2).*

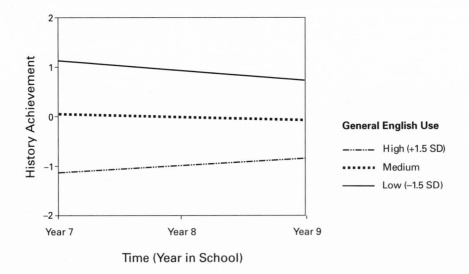

ing academic benefits for Hong Kong students, as well as supporting predictions based on previous immersion research and Cummins's theory.

Why does our research contradict generalizations based on previous immersion studies and theory? The two most likely suggestions seem to be our emphases on (a) achievement in nonlanguage as well as language subjects, and (b) a late- rather than an early-immersion program. In most previous research, there has been a remarkable disregard for achievement in nonlanguage subjects, and research has focused on early-immersion programs. Support exists for both these suggestions based on qualifications that Cummins (1979) offers for his model and implications from Willig's (1985) review. Cummins (1979) emphasized that the threshold of L2 competency needed to achieve benefits from immersion might be much higher at higher levels of schooling and that children may need to experience the immersion early in their schooling, when the language demands are sufficiently low that children can gain L2 fluency:

> Thus, in the early grades the lower threshold may involve only a relatively low level of listening comprehension and expressive skills, but — as the curriculum content becomes more symbolic and requires more abstract formal operational thought processes — the child's "surface" L2 must be translated into deeper levels of "cognitive competence" in the language. (p. 231)

Willig (1985; see also Hakuta & McLaughlin, 1996) offered the related caveat that comprehension of abstract concepts in nonlanguage subjects, such as social studies and science, requires a high level of language fluency in the language of instruction even though the focus of the subjects is not languages per se. This observation, coupled with the dearth of research on nonlanguage achievement, led her to call for more research using achievement in nonlanguage subjects to evaluate better the effects of bilingual and second language programs. Hence, in the context of Cummins's interaction model, it may not be possible for students to gain benefits from a late-immersion program unless they have already achieved a high threshold of functional L2 competency prior to the immersion. On this basis, one might argue that our results were consistent with Cummins's (1979) theory in that many students taught in English may not have reached a critical threshold. This argument, however, becomes circular when L1 and L2 proficiency are used both to evaluate whether students attained the desired threshold and to evaluate the predictions that language achievement will improve. Instead, because the conditions in this study fit so well with those that Cummins says should lead to benefits associated with bilingualism, we interpret our results as an important contradiction to his theory. This conclusion, if supported by subsequent research, requires a substantial rethinking of the generalizability of the benefits of immersion programs and, perhaps, bilingualism and second language acquisition for high school students. The implications of these interpretations argue against the use of a late-immersion strategy in which students with limited L2 proficiency are taught entirely in L2. Some qualifications exist, however, to this overarching conclusion, due to potential limitations in the present investigation and the need for further research.

POTENTIAL LIMITATIONS AND DIRECTIONS
FOR FURTHER RESEARCH

1.   In our quasi-experimental design, large pre-test achievement differences between students existed that were related to language of instruction. Importantly, however, we had a particularly strong set of pre-test covariates to control for these initial differences, and we used particularly powerful statistical tools (the multilevel analyses) to achieve this purpose. Also, even with no correction for the large initial differences, students taught in Chinese (even though their pre-test achievement scores were more than one SD below students taught in English) scored significantly higher than students taught in English for history, geography, and science (see Table 1). Hence, at least the direction of these differences seems robust against alternative explanations due to this potential design limitation.

2.   An implicit assumption is made that the quality of teaching was equivalent in high schools differing in language of instruction. In particular, an immersion program requires teachers to be highly fluent in the language that they are teaching (e.g., Swain & Johnson, 1997), but in Hong Kong there is a shortage of high school teachers in nonlanguage subjects who are fluent in English. Recognizing this problem, the Education Commission (1995) recommended that schools hire more native English-speaking teachers and introduce minimum language-proficiency standards for teachers. A compromise may occur between employing teachers who are highly fluent in English and teachers who have high levels of subject mastery, such that the quality of instruction might be confounded with the language of instruction. If, for example, teachers cannot teach effectively in L2, classes may be less interesting, with more emphasis on rote learning of factual material and less quality discussion and debate. Because we had no measures of the quality of teaching effectiveness, we cannot pursue this conjecture in the present investigation (see related discussion by Johnson, 1997). The particular pattern of results in our study, however, suggests that this potential problem was not the primary reason for the negative effects of Instruction in English. If quality of instruction was the critical variable, it seems unlikely that (a) the negative effects in mathematics should be so much smaller than those in history, geography, and science; and (b) that the emphasis on English in English classes would have been able to offset the negative results.

3.   The strategy of partialling the effect of general Instruction in English from the English in English Classes scores was defensible in terms of determining how additional variance could be explained by the second variable. In effect, all variance in post-test achievement that could be explained either by Instruction in English or by English in English Classes was attributed to Instruction in English. Because Instruction in English and English in English Classes were substantially correlated ($r = .66$), not using this strategy would have resulted in potential problems of multicollinearity. This strategy, however, tended to maximize variance attributable to Instruction in English. For example, when we redid the analyses of English achievement using Instruction in English and English in English Classes without using this partialling

strategy, the Instruction in English effect was not statistically significant, whereas the effect of English in English Classes was, of course, approximately the same. Hence, using this strategy, much of the benefit in English achievement associated with attending English-language schools could be explained by the emphasis on English in English Classes. Similarly, for each of the six school subjects, the effects of Instruction in English became more negative (or less positive in the case of English and Chinese achievement) when the unpartialled English in English Classes score was used. In this respect, our results provide the most positive perspective on instruction in English and, thus, are conservative in relation to our conclusion that teaching nonlanguage subjects in English disadvantages students. Our results may, however, underestimate the relative advantages of English in English Classes compared to Instruction in English.

4.   Because the negative effects of immersion into instruction in English for history, geography, and science were large, it is unlikely that any substantial subgroup of students taught in English were advantaged in these subjects. The Hong Kong Educational Commission (1990) anticipated that the most able students (suggested to be the top 30% in terms of prior achievement) would be advantaged (or, at least, less disadvantaged) by immersion into instruction in English. However, no support existed for this expectation in that interactions with prior achievement and instruction in English were consistently small and mostly nonsignificant (see Ach0 x EInst interactions in Table 2). Nevertheless, a small number of students with extremely good prior mastery of English (e.g., students who were born overseas and migrated back to Hong Kong or had a native English-speaking parent) might not be disadvantaged when taught in English. Furthermore, because our study indicated that the negative effects of immersion declined somewhat over time, and because previous studies (e.g., Cummins, 1979) suggest that the benefits of bilingualism may take more than three years to materialize, the negative effects may lessen as English proficiency improves during the remaining three years of high school (i.e., grades 10–12, not studied in this analysis). Alternatively, students may require a sufficiently long transition period, spent entirely on learning English to an appropriate threshold of proficiency, prior to starting an English-language high school. Consequently, because of the potential social and economic advantages of being fluent in English in Hong Kong, there may be justification for instruction in English in high schools for students with sufficient English-language skills not to be severely disadvantaged by Instruction in English. To explore this possibility, further research is needed that considers a longer period of time (e.g., all six years of high school rather than only the first three) and, perhaps, focuses more specifically on the assessment of English fluency using oral and vernacular measures as well as paper-and-pencil tests. Alternatively, future research in Hong Kong may need to focus on early-immersion programs like those that seem to have been successful in Canada (e.g., Lambert, 1992). However, exploration of the feasibility of such alternatives will require careful consideration because (a) the community language environment may not be conducive to attaining fluency in English because English is rarely used outside the classroom; (b) there are inadequate numbers of teachers with good English proficiency, particularly in primary and kindergarten lev-

els; (c) it would be difficult to determine who would be most benefited by these early-immersion programs or whether such programs should be open to all; and (d) such programs would have the potential of further devaluing Chinese as a language of instruction and creating a preoccupation with English-language skills to the detriment of other school subjects.

POLICY IMPLICATIONS

There should be a consistently strong emphasis on English in English classes. Not surprisingly, the emphasis on English in English Classes was positive for English achievement. This finding is consistent with the guidelines for schools as advocated by the Hong Kong Education Department. A stronger emphasis on English in English Classes will lead to improvement in English proficiency, which subsequently will have a positive effect on students' learning of other academic subjects, particularly when those subjects are taught in English.

Students' prior English-language (L2) skills should be given greater emphasis in allocating students to English-language high schools. Our results show the limited power of using general achievement to predict which students should go to high schools with a strong general emphasis on English. Although brighter students do much better in all school subjects, the negative effect of Instruction in English did not vary with initial ability. Prior English skills (Eng0) appear to be more useful, in that the negative effect of learning through English was somewhat smaller for students who are initially more proficient in English.

With the possible exception of students who are already proficient in English, little justification exists for the current practice of teaching all school subjects, such as history, geography, or science, in English during the first years of high school. Our results suggest that students need to be much more proficient in English before they start high school. This proficiency might be facilitated by (a) starting the immersion much earlier (in primary school or at the very beginning of schooling, as in the Canadian immersion schools); (b) providing a sufficiently long transition period, between the end of primary and the start of high school, that is devoted entirely to learning English to an appropriate threshold of proficiency prior to starting an English-language high school; or (c) giving students stronger support in these content subjects (e.g., extra lessons or bilingual tutors who are able to explain the lesson content in Chinese). Furthermore, although the size of the negative effects of Instruction in English may decline somewhat as students progress through high school, the size of the decline is relatively small, at least for the first three years of high school considered here. Consistent with this recommendation, the Hong Kong Education Department issued strong guidelines to use Chinese as the medium of instruction for subjects other than English in schools where most students do not have the necessary English proficiency to benefit from Instruction in English and emphasized that unless sufficiently strong support and remedial help are offered, the problems of learning various academic subjects through English will not automatically go away, even after several years.

NOTES

1. The *Lau* decision was based on a claim that the needs of Chinese Americans with limited English proficiency had not been met under the Civil Rights Act of 1964. The ruling would have mandated the implementation of transitional bilingual education programs for students with limited English proficiency, but it was subsequently withdrawn. For further discussion, see Hakuta and McLaughlin (1996).

2. A student's examination score (a "secondary school places allocation" score) is placed into five broad bands of equal size (20% of the students per band). For purposes of the present investigation, however, we were given access to the original (continuous) placement scores before they were categorized into the five bands. Students in the higher achievement bands are allocated by their parental choice first. However, students within the same band who apply to the same oversubscribed school are allocated randomly, so that even the most selective schools will have an achievement mix of students within the top 20 percent of all students. In addition, a small number of primary and secondary schools are linked so that some secondary school places are reserved for the linked primary schools if these students can meet minimum placement score standards. Within these constraints, students are free to choose any high school in Hong Kong.

3. For example, the likelihood of a student completing a math exam in any one year was 1/3 and the likelihood of any one student completing math exam in all three years was 1/27 = $1/3 \times 1/3 \times 1/3$.

4. This randomization procedure worked effectively for the three core subjects in the first testing session, in that groups of students taking each test did not differ significantly from each other on the pre-test achievement score (Ach0) common to all students. The randomization procedure was not fully effective for the second set of tests in that some schools did not offer both history and geography so that only two out of the three (geography, history, science) achievement tests were used in the second test session for these schools. Thus, for example, if history was not offered in a particular school, then each student in that school was randomly assigned to complete either the science test or the geography test, but no students were assigned to complete the history test. This strategy resulted in a somewhat higher proportion of science tests in that science was offered by all schools. The group of students taking the science test, however, had significantly lower Ach0 scores than did the groups of students taking the history or geography tests. However, because analyses were conducted for each subject separately, this potential problem is not a critical issue.

5. With multilevel analysis, it is possible to conduct a multivariate analysis that incorporates all school subjects. In the present application this approach was not possible because a particular student on any one occasion completed only one of the three tests administered in the first session (mathematics, English, and Chinese) and only one of the three tests administered in the second session (history, geography, and science), so that correlations among the achievement scores within each set could not be estimated (i.e., no students completed both English and mathematics tests at T1).

6. Goldstein (1995) observes that for educational achievement data on the same individuals over time, it is common to standardize the measures so that they have the same population distribution at each occasion, noting that whereas no trends in the means or variances over time can be estimated, between-individual variation can be estimated and evaluated with multilevel models like those used here. In our study, because the actual items on each achievement test differed from year to year, we could not compare the absolute scores from one year to the next. Thus, for example, we could not say that English or mathematics achievement — averaged across all students — increased over the three years of the study. Instead, as is common in educational research, achievement scores were standardized (mean = 0, SD = 1) separately for each occasion. As emphasized by

Goldstein (1995), however, we could determine relative changes over time for any one student or for students in any particular school. Thus, for example, if students in a particular school had an average mathematics achievement z-score of zero (i.e., were average) for the first year of the study (T1), + .25 (i.e, .25 SD above the mean) at T2, and +.50 at T3, then we could claim that a linear increase occurred in achievement over the three-year period (relative to the scores of the entire sample of students in the study who were broadly representative of the Hong Kong population). Not being able to specify absolute growth was not a limitation in this study because absolute growth without reference to some appropriate standard of comparison is typically not very useful. For example, knowing that students in a particular school on average were able to answer correctly one more mathematics item at T2 than T1 would not be useful unless we knew how this finding compared with performances by other students at other schools (or some normative comparison group). Because of this problem, scores on standardized achievement tests are typically normed separately for students at each grade level (year in school). For example, IQ scores are normed (mean = 100, SD = 15) separately for students of different ages so that changes over time for a given student can only be used to infer growth relative to a normative sample. Hence, the focus of the present investigation was on relative levels of student achievement, relative growth in student achievement, and how this relative achievement varied with different characteristics of individual students and the schools that they attended (see related discussions by Goldstein, 1995; Goldstein et al., 1998; Marsh & Grayson, 1994).

7. The number of students completing achievement tests declined slightly in each year of the study (11,528 in T1, 11,045 at T2, and 10,900 at T3), representing a combination of absence on the particular day the achievement tests were administered and students who withdrew or changed schools. Furthermore, the pre-test achievement scores (Ach0) that were available for all students were slightly higher for students who completed tests at T2 than at T1 (+.047 SD at T2 vs. +.014 SD at T1) and higher still at T3 (+.073 SD). Hence, students who were in the study at T3 tended to be slightly brighter (based on the pre-test achievement score) than those who were not. This explains why there is a slight tendency for achievement tests to decline in the multilevel growth models (the linear effect of time is slightly negative), even though the scores were standardized separately at each occasion. Thus, for example, a student at the mean achievement test score at T1 would tend to be slightly below the mean at T3 (in relation to the slightly brighter cohort of students at T3 compared to those at T1). In contrast, students who completed test scores on all three occasions had scores approximately +.07 SD on the pre-test achievement score and total test score (averaged across the three occasions). Because this small effect of time in the multilevel models is not substantively important, it is not discussed further.

REFERENCES

Aiken, L. S., & West, S. G. (1991). *Multiple regression: Testing and interpreting interactions.* Newbury Park, CA: Sage.

Baker, K. A., & de Kanter, A. A. (1981). *Effectiveness of bilingual education: A review of the literature.* Washington, DC: U.S. Department of Education, Office of Planning, Budget, and Evaluation.

Bourhis, R. Y. (1990). Social and individual factors in the development of language acquisition: Some models of bilingual proficiency. In B. Harley, P. Allen, J. Cummins, & M. Swain (Eds.), *The development of second language proficiency* (pp. 134–145). Cambridge, Eng.: Cambridge University Press.

Bryk, A. S., & Raudenbush, S. W. (1992). *Hierarchical linear models: Applications and data analysis methods.* Newbury Park, CA: Sage.

Collier, V. (1992). A synthesis of studies examining long-term language minority student data on academic achievement. *Bilingual Research Journal, 16,* 187–212.

Cummins, J. (1979). Linguistic interdependence and the educational development of bilingual children. *Review of Educational Research, 49,* 222–251.

Cummins, J. (1986). Empowering minority students: A framework of intervention. *Harvard Educational Review, 56,* 18–36.

Cummins, J. (1991). Conversational and academic language proficiency in bilingual contexts. *Association Internationale de Linguistique Appliquée Review, 8,* 75–89.

Cummins, J. (1996). Bilingual education: What does the research say? In J. Cummins (Ed.), *Negotiating identifies: Education for empowerment in a diverse society* (pp. 97–133). Ontario, CA: California Association for Bilingual Education.

Cummins, J., Harley, B., Swain, M., & Allen, P. (1990). Social and individual factors in the development of bilingual proficiency. In B. Harley, P. Allen, J. Cummins, & M. Swain (Eds.), *The development of second language proficiency* (pp. 119–133). Cambridge, Eng.: Cambridge University Press.

Cummins, J., & Swain, M. (1986). *Bilingualism in education: Aspects of theory, research and practice.* London: Longman.

d'Anglejan, A. (1990). The role of context and age in the development of bilingual proficiency. In B. Harley, P. Allen, J. Cummins, & M. Swain (Eds.), *The development of second language proficiency* (pp. 146–157). Cambridge, Eng.: Cambridge University Press.

Duff, P. A. (1997). Immersion in Hungary: An ELF experiment. In R. K. Johnson & M. Swain (Eds.), *Immersion education: International perspectives* (pp. 19–43). Cambridge, Eng.: Cambridge University Press.

Education Commission. (1990, November). *The curriculum and behavioural problems in schools* (Education Commission Report No. 4). Hong Kong: Government Printer.

Education Commission. (1995, December). *Enhancing language proficiency: A comprehensive strategy* (Education Commission Report No. 6). Hong Kong: Government Printer.

Francis, W. S. (1999). Cognitive integration of language and memory in bilinguals: Semantic representation. *Psychological Bulletin, 125,* 193–222.

Garcia, E. E. (1993). Language, culture and education. In L. Darling-Hammond (Ed.), *Review of research in education 1993, vol. 19* (pp. 51–98). Washington, DC: American Educational Research Association.

Gardner, R. C. (1985). *Social psychology and second language learning.* London: Edward Arnold.

Genesee, F. (1978). Is there an optimal age for starting second language instruction? *McGill Journal of Education, 13,* 145–154.

Genesee, F. (1984). Beyond bilingualism: Social psychological studies of French immersion programs in Canada. *Canadian Journal of Behavioural Science, 16,* 338–352.

Genesee, F. (1985). Second language learning through immersion: A review of U.S. programs. *Review of Educational Research, 55,* 541–561.

Genesee, F. (1987). *Learning through two languages: Studies of immersion and bilingual education.* Cambridge, MA: Newbury House.

Gibbons, J. (1989). The issue of the language of instruction in the lower forms of Hong Kong secondary schools. In C. Kennedy (Ed.), *Language planning and English language teaching* (pp. 124–134). New York: Prentice Hall.

Goldstein, H. (1995). *Multilevel statistical models.* London: Arnold.

Goldstein, H., Rasbash, J., Plewis, I., Draper, D., Browne, W., Yang, M., Woodhouse, G., & Healy, M. (1998). *A user's guide to MLwiN.* London: University of London, Institute of Education.

Greene, J. (1998). *A meta-analysis of the effectiveness of bilingual education.* Clarement, CA: Tomas Rivera Policy Institute.

Hakuta, K. (1986). *Mirror on language: The debate on bilingualism.* New York: Basic Books.

Hakuta, K., & McLaughlin, B. (1996). Bilingualism and second language learning: Seven tensions that define the research. In D. Berliner & R. Calfee (Eds.), *Handbook of educational psychology* (pp. 603–621). New York: Simon & Schuster Macmillan.

Johnson, R. K. (1997). The Hong Kong education system: Late immersion under stress. In R. K. Johnson & M. Swain (Eds.), *Immersion education: International perspectives* (pp. 167–170). Cambridge, Eng.: Cambridge University Press.

Krashen, S. (1981). *Second language acquisition and second language learning.* Oxford, Eng.: Pergamon.

Krashen, S. (1997). *Why bilingual education? ERIC Digest.* ERIC Clearinghouse (ED403101).

Lambert, W. E. (1974). Culture and language as factors in learning and instruction. In F. Aboud & R. Meade (Eds.), *Cultural factors in learning and education* (pp. 91–122). Bellingham, WA: Fifth Western Washington Symposium on Learning.

Lambert, W. E. (1981). Bilingualism and language acquisition. In H. Winitz (Ed.), *Native language and foreign language acquisition* (pp. 9–22). New York: New York Academy of Sciences.

Lambert, W. E. (1990). Persistent issues in bilingualism. In B. Harley, P. Allen, J. Cummins, & M. Swain (Eds.), *The development of second language proficiency* (pp. 201–218). Cambridge, Eng.: Cambridge University Press.

Lambert, W. E. (1992). Challenging established views on social issues: The power and limitations of research. *American Psychologist, 47,* 533–542.

Lau v. Nichols (No. 72-6520) U.S. Supreme Court (1974, January).

Marsh, H. W., & Grayson, D. (1994). Longitudinal stability of latent means and individual differences: A unified approach. *Structural Equation Modeling, 1,* 317–359.

Marsh, H. W., & Rowe, K. J. (1996). The negative effects of school-average ability on academic self-concept — an application of multilevel modeling. *Australian Journal of Education, 40*(1), 65–87.

Met, M., & Lorenz, E. B. (1997). Lessons from U.S. immersion programs: Two decades of experience. In R. K. Johnson & M. Swain (Eds.), *Immersion education: International perspectives* (pp. 243–264). Cambridge, Eng.: Cambridge University Press.

Plewis, I. (1996a). Reading progress. In G. Woodhouse (Ed.), *Multilevel modelling applications: A guide for users of MLN* (pp. 103–129). London: University of London, Institute of Education.

Plewis, I. (1996b). Statistical methods for understanding cognitive growth: A review, a synthesis and an application. *British Journal of Mathematical & Statistical Psychology, 49,* 25–42.

Raudenbush, S. W., & Bryk, A. S. (1988). Methodological advances in analyzing the effects of schools and classrooms on student learning. In E. Z. Rothkopf (Ed.), *Review of research in education 1988–1989, vol. 15* (pp. 423–475). Washington, DC: American Educational Research Association.

Singleton, D. (1992). Second language instruction: The when and how. *Association Internationale de Linguistique Appliquée Review, 9,* 46–54.

Swain, M., & Johnson, R. K. (1997). Immersion education: A category within bilingual education. In R. K. Johnson & M. Swain (Eds.), *Immersion education: International perspectives* (pp. 1–16). Cambridge, Eng.: Cambridge University Press.

Willig, A. C. (1985). A meta-analysis of selected studies on the effectiveness of bilingual education. *Review of Educational Research, 55,* 269–318.

This longitudinal study was part of an ongoing educational policy research project for which the data collection was initiated, designed, and conducted by the Educational Research Section of the Hong Kong Education Department. The data have been graciously provided to the authors for purposes of the present investigation, in part during visits by the first author to the Faculty of Education at The Chinese University of Hong Kong that were partially funded by The Chinese University of Hong Kong. The research was also supported through a Special Investigator Grant to the first author from the Australian Research Council. We would like to thank Denis Burnham, Stuart Campbell, Ray Debus, Bruno Di Biase, John Gibbons, Wijesir Jayasinghe, Ken Rowe, and Alexander Yeung for helpful comments and assistance on earlier versions of this paper, but emphasize that the views expressed here are those of the authors and may not represent those of people whom we have acknowledged. Correspondence in relation to this study should be sent to Professor Herbert W. Marsh, Faculty of Education, University of Western Sydney, Macarthur, PO Box 555, Campbelltown, NSW 2560 Australia (or via email to h.marsh@uws.edu.au), or to Professor Kit-Tai Hau, Faculty of Education, The Chinese University of Hong Kong, Shatin, N.T., Hong Kong (or via email to kthau@cuhk.edu.hk).

APPENDIX

In the present investigation, we used a three-level growth model in which the three levels are time (the occasion of the achievement test score: T1, T2, T3), student (the 12,784 students), and school (the 56 schools). To illustrate the logic, consider the prediction equation in which history achievement, the dependent variable, is related to five independent variables: 1) pre-test achievement (Ach0); 2) English-language use in general (EInst, the extent to which classes are taught in English); 3) Ach0 x EInst interaction (the extent to which the effect of language of instruction varies with pre-test achievement); 4) linear growth in achievement over the T1–T3 period (Linear); and 5) EInst x Linear interaction (the extent to which the effect of language of instruction varies over time). For each of the five independent variables, there is a corresponding effect $(\beta_1 - \beta_5)$.

$$\text{History} = \beta_{0ijk} (\text{cons}) + \beta_{1k} (\text{Ach0}) + \beta_2 (\text{EInst}) + \beta_3 (\text{Ach0} \times \text{EInst}) + \beta_4 (\text{Linear}) + \beta_5 (\text{EInst} \times \text{Linear}) + v_{0k} + \mu_{0jk} + e_{0ijk}$$

where

$$\beta_{0ijk} = \beta_0 + v_{0k} + \mu_{0jk} + e_{0ijk}$$
$$\beta_{1k} = \beta_1 + v_{1k}$$
$$v_{0k} = \text{level 3 (school) residual}$$
$$\mu_{0jk} = \text{level 2 (student) residual}$$
$$e_{0ijk} = \text{level 1 (time) residual}$$

Each of the five effects $(\beta_1 - \beta_5)$ can be fixed (those with no additional subscripts) or can vary (those with additional subscripts). Importantly, the constant term (average history score) is allowed to vary from school to school (v_{0k}), from student to student within each school (μ_{0jk}), and from occasion to occasion for students within each school (e_{0ijk}). In addition, the effect to pre-test achievement is allowed to vary from school to school (i.e., the coefficient β_1 has a subscript k). For each of the residual terms, there is a corresponding variance component $(\sigma^2 v_0, \sigma^2 \mu_0, \sigma^2 e_0$ for the constant term; $\sigma^2 v_1$ for the pre-test achievement effect) and a covariance term whenever there are two or more effects random at the same level (e.g., σv_{10} is the extent to which schools with higher than average achievement after controlling for all other variables in the prediction equation also had high levels of pre-test achievement). As described in the Methods section, we transformed all variables to have M = 0, SD = 1 across the entire sample so as to facilitate comparisons.

Challenging Venerable Assumptions:
Literacy Instruction for
Linguistically Different Students

MARÍA DE LA LUZ REYES

A lmost without exception, teachers throughout the United States are identifying their teaching philosophies with the whole language and writing process movements. Increasingly fewer teachers admit to teaching phonics or skills-based literacy. About three years ago, for example, one of my colleagues attempted to study literacy instruction by comparing a skills-based and a whole language approach, but could find no one in the surrounding school districts who would admit to being a "skills approach" teacher. In my graduate-level literacy classes, composed primarily of teachers, virtually all indicate that they use some form of process instruction — that is, an approach to literacy that focuses on content and process rather than on skills acquisition and form. These teachers report that they "teach whole language," "do the writing process," "use literature as a base for teaching reading and writing," and that they "don't use basal readers" and "don't teach phonics."

Whole language advocates (Goodman, 1986, 1989; Harste, 1989; Newman, 1985; Short & Burke, 1989; Smith, 1986) and classroom-based studies on writing process (Atwell, 1984, 1987; Calkins, 1986; Graves, 1983, 1985; Newman, 1985), conducted primarily with mainstream, native English speakers, claim many positive outcomes from the use of these process approaches. These benefits include exposure to wholistic, authentic literature and improvement in grammar, spelling, sentence structure, and writing fluency. School districts in many states have readily accepted these claims and have responded by either promoting, permitting, endorsing, or mandating whole language approaches (*English Language Arts Framework*, 1987; Gutierrez, 1992). Textbook publishers competing for profits in this lucrative new venture are producing revised versions of basal readers — said to include "literature-based instruction," "whole language," and "writing process" — to keep in step with the process instruction rage. It is not surprising, then, that teachers are eager to implement these programs and associate themselves with the movement.

Harvard Educational Review   Vol. 62   No. 4   Winter 1992, 427–446

ORIGINS OF PROCESS INSTRUCTION

Both whole language and writing process are based on constructivist views of learning and rely on children's literature as a base for literacy instruction (Hiebert & Fisher, 1990). The two have distinct origins — with whole language attributed to Kenneth Goodman and process writing to Donald Graves — but in classroom practice, the distinction between the two blurs. The popularity of whole language in this country is largely attributed to Goodman and his psycholinguistic model of reading (Edelsky, 1990). Although his name is readily associated with the whole language movement, Goodman (1986) himself notes that its practice in English-speaking countries like New Zealand, Britain, Canada, and Australia predates the movement in the United States. He points out that in New Zealand, whole language is a national policy for literacy instruction in all schools.

Many teachers talk about whole language as if it were a method or an approach. Advocates of whole language, however, strongly reject the notion that it is merely a reading approach (Altwerger, Edelsky, & Flores, 1987; Goodman, 1986, 1989; Goodman & Goodman, 1981; Harste & Burke, 1977; Newman, 1985; Watson, 1982, 1989), but at the same time shy away from offering an official definition. They prefer to describe whole language as a "set of beliefs and not methods" (Edelsky, 1990, p. 8) based on and supported by "four humanistic-scientific pillars." These pillars, according to Goodman, are: 1) theories of learning, 2) theories of language, 3) "a basic view of teaching," and 4) "the role of teachers and a language-centered view of curriculum" (Goodman, 1986, p. 26).

Donald Graves, Goodman's writing process counterpart, is credited for reviving interest in writing at the elementary school level. His work began in 1972 with his doctoral dissertation research on the composing processes of seven-year-old children. Later, with funding from the Ford Foundation and the National Institute of Education (NIE), he extended his study to include children aged six through ten in Atkinson, New Hampshire, where he worked with classroom teachers Mary Ellen Giacobbe, Lucy McCormick Calkins, and Susan Sowers — all of whom are now widely known in this field. His work indicates that when children are allowed to choose their topics, they not only write more, but their selections are also broader-ranged. When children are involved in writing, they are in a constant process of "emerging text and thought" (Newman, 1985). However, when they are focused on a new style of writing, or engaged in shaping their ideas more clearly, they seem to lose control over aspects of writing mechanics that they may have previously mastered (Graves, 1983).

In essence, Graves believes that children's writing is an integrated process, an interplay of drawing, talking, writing, and reading. This focus on process, its emphasis on a learner's freedom to select topics, books, and learning activities, are distinguishing characteristics of both whole language and writing process that have been internalized by teachers, and explains why they are treated synonymously. In this article, "process instruction" is used as an inclusive term to refer to whole language, writing process, or literature-based instruction, whether used collectively or individually. The rationale is that all have at their core a focus on meaning (process or "wholeness") rather than on form (product or skills).

GRASSROOTS SUPPORT FOR PROCESS INSTRUCTION

With some exceptions, university- and college-level literacy courses have not kept pace with the widespread implementation of process instruction. Instead, process instruction has been largely a grassroots movement spreading from coast to coast. Organized teacher groups, known as Teachers Applying Whole Language (TAWL), have sprung up everywhere ("Teachers Networking," 1987) and have served as support groups for those implementing whole language. The majority of teachers not involved in these groups, however, has relied primarily on information learned from institutes, workshops, and conferences conducted by whole language and writing process advocates. In many cases, teachers attending these meetings have taught other teachers in their school districts.

While the enthusiasm of teachers teaching teachers is commendable, the short-term nature of such training presents a unique problem: it virtually assures that only the rudimentary elements of these theories can be presented, and that adaptations for linguistically different learners will not be covered. This has led to narrow application of these philosophies — often without reflection and without appropriate modifications to meet the needs of diverse learners (Barrera, 1991, 1992; Delpit, 1986; 1988; Reyes, 1991a, 1991b; Siddle, 1986; Valdes, 1991).

The terms *wholistic, integrated, authentic,* and *relevant* used in reference to process instruction have an instant appeal and a ring of validity, making it difficult to imagine they could be anything but a "perfect fit" for all students. Challenging the effectiveness of process instruction usually incurs immediate and general disapproval from "experts" in the field who define the prevailing teaching paradigms and would have teachers believe that all children benefit equally from the same philosophies and programs. When Lisa Delpit's article "The Silenced Dialogue" (1988) first appeared, advocates of process instruction complained of "her lack of sensitivity to teachers"; some questioned her real understanding of whole language and writing process. On first reading, even today, some of the teachers in my classes feel offended by her challenge to process instruction. Her call for a balance of process and skills instruction needed by African American students was, and still is, almost lost in the rush to defend the philosophies of process instruction.

In a similar vein, in this chapter, I challenge widely accepted assumptions about teaching limited- or non-English speakers and critique current implementation of process instruction that ignores culturally and linguistically supportive adaptations for these students. I also present a discussion of modifications that provide greater opportunities for success. The terms *linguistically diverse students, language minorities,* and *second language learners* refer to students whose first language is not English and whose cultural backgrounds differ from middle-class White children.[1]

ASSUMPTIONS ABOUT LINGUISTICALLY DIFFERENT LEARNERS AND PROCESS INSTRUCTION

As a Chicana university professor who teaches language arts, and social, multicultural foundations of education, I am often asked to comment on the effectiveness of process instruction for limited- or non-English-proficient students.[2] The assumption behind the query is that I will be able to provide examples of programs in which linguistically different students are making significant gains with whole language and writing process. Over the last five years, my inability to cite just such examples has led me to examine why these seemingly successful programs are not producing the same rate of success for linguistically different students as for native English speakers. Delpit's (1986, 1988) seminal writings discussing her dilemma with process instruction for African American students have helped my understanding. My classroom teaching experience with diverse populations, as well as my own research in the literacy development of Spanish/English bilingual students suggests, however, that there are other implicit assumptions specifically related to the delivery of instruction for linguistically different students that play an important role in student outcomes. In various ways, these assumptions contribute to the ineffectiveness of a process approach to literacy for these students. I will discuss four assumptions here, assumptions that through many years of classroom practice are treated as if they were venerable — too sacred to challenge. These are:

1. English is the only legitimate medium for learning and instruction;
2. linguistic minorities must be immersed in English as quickly as possible if they are to succeed in school;
3. a "one size fits all" approach is good for all students;
4. error correction in process instruction hampers learning.

The first two assumptions are related to beliefs that guide common teaching practices in the education of language-minority students. The last two are specifically related to a mismatch between pedagogy and learners. In concert, the four undermine the goals and spirit of process instruction and, as such, must not only be challenged, but abandoned, if linguistic minorities are to derive the potential benefits of process instruction.

THE VENERABLE ASSUMPTIONS

My assertion that process instruction is not working as effectively as might be expected and is not being tailored to the needs of linguistically different students is based on some of my own work with bilingual students in process classrooms (Reyes, 1991a, 1991b) and on the work of Rosalinda Barrera (1991, 1992) and Guadalupe Valdes (1991). These assertions are also consistent with Delpit's (1988) and Emilie Siddle's (1986) work with African American students. I will draw on these data as I discuss and challenge these venerable assumptions.

Assumption One: English is the only legitimate medium for learning and instruction.

School curricula in this country have been developed primarily for native English speakers, thereby according primacy to English as *the* language of instruction. Despite the presence of linguistically diverse learners, other languages have been treated as insignificant in the teaching equation. Challenges to English-only instruction have largely gone unnoticed by mainstream educators, although as early as the 1930s, Chicano psychologist George Sánchez (1932) wrote about the academic disadvantages of treating speakers of other languages as if they were native English speakers, especially in the administration of IQ tests. Throughout his career, Sánchez persisted in pointing out the illogical assumptions that schools make regarding the teaching of Spanish-speaking children (García, 1989) — assumptions that today apply to other language groups as well. In 1951, for example, he noted that

> the first error which such school authorities make is to confuse "English" with "education" — that is, it is evident that they assume that the entire school policy or program should revolve around the question of whether or not a given child or group of children know English. (Sánchez, 1951, p. 23)

Today, despite the existence of bilingual education programs developed for language minorities (Crawford, 1989), and even in the face of widespread linguistic heterogeneity in schools, English continues to be viewed as the *only* valid medium of instruction. An extension of this assumption is the treatment of English and literacy as if they were synonymous (Reyes, 1991a) — a practice that defines literacy in narrow, ethnocentric terms.

Results from a two-year study I conducted with approximately fifty sixth-grade Spanish-speaking students in two bilingual education classes illustrate how the first assumption negatively affected student performance in process classrooms (see Reyes, 1991b). This middle school was situated in the heart of a predominately low- to middle-income Mexican American community in a large city in the Southwest. Student enrollment was approximately six hundred, of whom 73 percent were of Mexican descent; the remainder were primarily White and African American. The teachers' pedagogical backgrounds included ongoing training in whole language methodologies provided by the district, and attendance at institutes and/or conferences presented by prominent individuals in the field of process instruction.

The teachers provided numerous opportunities for integrated reading and writing activities — primarily in English for academic purposes and in Spanish for informal, nongraded activities such as journal writing. Students also kept interactive journals (two-way correspondence between the teacher and the student) and literature logs (notebooks in which students wrote their reflections on the literary books they read). They participated in writing conferences with their teachers and with peers, and took minilessons on writing mechanics. Teachers modeled sustained silent reading and provided good models of conventional writing. Though the teachers were White, they were fluent in Spanish and English.

On the surface, the teachers seemed to be doing everything right, yet the exposure to good models of writing, spelling, and punctuation did not produce correct writing form or growth in the bilingual students' writing fluency. Unlike the success of these models for mainstream students reported in the work of Lucy Calkins (1986), Graves (1983, 1985), and Nancie Atwell (1984, 1987), the bilingual students in my two-year study experienced failure. At the end of two years, most were still making the same spelling and grammatical errors as in the beginning of the study. For example, in a journal entry dated September 9th, a student wrote, "My *ant* is getting married in Saturday." The teacher responded, "How was your *aunt's* wedding?" In a subsequent entry, the student again reported on her *"ant's"* wedding — ignoring the correct form modeled by the teacher. In late February of the same year she wrote, "Her mom my *ant* is a good cook." In the spring of the second year of the study, one of the teachers said of her students, who were then seventh graders, "Students keep making the same errors with spelling, grammar, punctuation, etc. It's frustrating!" (Field notes, April 27, 1990).

Students' journal entries also revealed that many disliked reading and thought the books were boring, difficult, or too long. Students provided many hints that they needed help in completing the literacy assignments, but their pleas went unheeded by their teachers, who seemed to have the impression that, as students became more familiar with the process, they would get the hang of it. A sixth-grade student wrote in her journal, "I really don't like reading I try but I never get the hang of the book or I don't read far anough [enough]" (Journal entry, October 3, 1988). To another student who did not like reading, the same teacher said, "I'm sorry that you don't like reading. Could it be that you just weren't comfortable? Why don't you sit on the floor?" (Journal entry, November 30, 1988). The student wrote back, "Miss . . . I dont like siting in the floor" (Journal entry, December 8, 1988). No explicit guidance in the selection of books was provided in these cases; instead, students were advised to keep trying, in the hope that they would eventually find books they liked.

Although the classes were designated "bilingual," teachers discouraged the use of Spanish for academic tasks, which was in sharp contrast to their informal interaction and communication. For example, there were subtle yet explicit requests that students write in English. Students were also discouraged from writing their literature reflections in Spanish after reading English-language books. In myriad ways, without full awareness of these contradictions, teachers conveyed the message that English was the only acceptable language for academic tasks. In so doing, teachers had no ill intent; they were merely following the school district's policies requiring English as the medium of instruction for language arts — even for limited-English-proficient students.

In their journal writing, where they were permitted to use Spanish, some students did improve their writing fluency and wrote longer, richer entries than they did in their literature logs. The better quality of Spanish writing in the journals suggests that, if students had also been allowed to write in Spanish for academic purposes, they might have experienced success. This was not possible, however, because the local school district's policies, like official policies in the majority of school districts throughout the country, undermined the heart of bilingual education, which permits academic instruction in *two* languages.[3] The message was clear: English is the only legitimate vehicle for learning.

A problem with according legitimacy solely to English is that it offers no compelling reason for teachers to change their teaching strategies to meet the needs of linguistically diverse students, as was the case with the teachers in this study. The veneration of English leads to two popular but erroneous conclusions. First is the notion that the need to adapt is incumbent on the students, *not* on the teachers. Second is the idea that if students are not performing satisfactorily, it is their fault, and not that of the curriculum, the instruction, or the way these are implemented.

Assumption Two: Linguistic minorities must be immersed in English as quickly as possible if they are to succeed in school.

This second assumption, which stems from the first, contains the idea that non-English speakers must be moved to English usage as quickly as possible or they will not achieve academically; or, worse yet, they will refuse to assimilate or to adopt the common language and culture of the larger community (Imhoff, 1990; Hayakawa, 1986 in MacKaye, 1990). Inherent in this assumption is a deep-seated belief that limited English proficiency is equivalent to limited intellectual potential.

The push for English is commonly reflected in school policies regarding instruction for language-minority students (Fishman, 1987; Hornberger, 1990, 1992; McCollum & Walker, 1990, 1992; Saidel, 1991; Wong-Fillmore, 1991). As Crawford (1989) explains, this assumption has recently been injected with new life by proponents of U.S. English, a national organization leading the movement to make English the official language of the United States. One of the six principles promoted by U.S. English, for example, states: "The nation's public schools have a special responsibility to help students who do not speak English to learn the language as quickly as possible" (Imhoff, 1990, p. 49).

This admonition to immerse language minorities in English has been interpreted as implicit permission to police, and even to ban the use of languages other than English in schools. The *El Paso Times* recently reported, for example, that a school principal in Garland, Texas (a Dallas suburb), had imposed a ban on speaking Spanish in hallways and classrooms to prevent students from cursing in Spanish. "Under the ban imposed Friday, students caught speaking Spanish risked detention or possible expulsion" ("School backs off," 1991, p. 1). The imposition of English rules in all aspects of students' lives and an inordinate concern with teaching English even in designated bilingual programs mean that language-minority students cannot take full advantage of innovative instructional programs in their primary languages even where Spanish/English linguistic resources are available (Reyes, 1991b).

Overzealous interest in having children learn English as quickly as possible "for their own good" does not stand up to the body of research conducted over the last twenty years. These studies indicate that bilingual students attain higher achievement levels when allowed to begin literacy instruction in their primary language before transferring to English literacy (Collier, 1989; Cummins, 1979, 1981; Fishman, 1987; Hakuta, 1986; Krashen & Biber, 1988; McCollum & Walker, 1990; Reyes, 1987; Skutnab-Kangas, 1981). Jim Cummins (1979, 1981) suggests that students who learn academic concepts and literacy skills in their native language can more readily and quickly transfer those skills to a second language because knowledge is grounded in the language and schema they comprehend. A recent study conducted for the U.S. Department of Education, which compared the effectiveness of English immersion, early-exit bilingual, and late-exit bilingual programs on Spanish/English limited-English-proficient students, reported the following:

Limited-English-proficient students can be provided with substantial amounts of primary language instruction without impeding their acquisition of English language and reading skills.

Limited-English-proficient students who are provided with substantial instruction in their primary language (≥40%) successfully continue to increase their achievement in content areas such as mathematics, while they are acquiring their skills in English; in contrast, students who are quickly transitioned into English-only instruction tend to grow slower than the norming population. (Ramirez, Yuen, & Ramey, 1991, p. 39)

Support for native-language instruction does not mean that students should not learn to speak, read, and write English well; indeed, they should. Using English to supplant native languages, however, makes very little sense in light of current school demographics. A more reasonable option would be to use native languages to expand the linguistic repertoire of students. In this way, students can maintain their own language while becoming proficient in the common language and in the appropriate forms of discourse of the larger community.

The point here is that when there are linguistic resources to support native languages, it makes more sense to use them to students' academic advantage than to rely on traditional practices and erroneous assumptions. Exclusion of minority voices in the learning process sends the message that non-English languages, dialects, and literatures are obstacles to the acquisition of English literacy, and fails to "affirm and legitimize diverse [cultures], knowledge, and language practices that students bring into the classroom" (McLaren, 1988, p. 215).

Assumption Three: A "one size fits all" approach is good for all students.

This refers to the assumption that instruction that is effective for mainstream students will benefit *all* students, no matter what their backgrounds may be. It is similar to the "one size fits all" marketing concept that would have buyers believe that there is an average or ideal size among men and women. This idea is appealing and lures people into purchasing garments that hang on their torsos, or cry for more room at the seams. Those who market "one size fits all" products suggest that if the article of clothing is not a good fit, the fault is not with the design of the garment, but with those who are too fat, too skinny, too tall, too short, or too high-waisted. Mass production of garments in a generic size is convenient, expeditious, and less expensive for the manufacturer. Furthermore, it makes it easier for the designer and seller to reach the greatest number of buyers *without the need to make adjustments* for differences in body structure, weight, or height.

The widespread use of whole language and writing process has led to a similar "one size fits all" approach to literacy; that is, the implementation of process instruction based on the belief that it is a "good fit" for everybody — as is — *without any modifications*. Well-meaning teachers have lost sight of the fact that mere implementation of these same programs does not necessarily translate into authentic, natural, or wholistic experiences for nonmainstream students (Barrera, 1991, 1992; Delpit, 1986, 1988; Reyes, 1991b; Valdes, 1991).

The fallacy that what works for mainstream students will work for all groups, especially with respect to whole language and writing process, is illustrated by the following lesson I observed in one of the many schools I have visited:

> The teacher and the school principal described this first-grade class as a whole language classroom. Indeed, that seemed to be the case. The room was physically organized into various learning centers. Numerous examples of students' art and writing were prominently displayed on the walls and bulletin boards. There were several bookshelves with children's literature, both commercial-size Big Books and standard-size books. In front of the open carpet space, where the teacher was sitting, was a large easel with a big book written and illustrated by the class. All twenty-some children, mostly from White, middle-class backgrounds (except for three Hmong girls), were sitting on the carpet listening to the teacher's expressive reading of the children's version of "Wishy Washy Washer Woman." The activity was a lively one, with students chiming in on the oral reading wherever they could. The Hmong girls attempted to join in, but their lip movement, like dubbed foreign films, was out of sync with the rest of the native English speakers. The teacher and children showed great enthusiasm reading the book in chorus.
>
> When the oral reading was over (approximately five minutes later), the teacher instructed the students to select a reading book for fifteen minutes of sustained silent reading time. The native English speakers quickly headed to the bookshelves to make their selections. The three Hmong girls followed suit, but the expressions on their faces revealed a great sense of uncertainty and bewilderment about the task. For a full twelve minutes, they superficially browsed through the books, picking them up, whispering in their native language, giving each other blank looks, and putting them back on the shelf, but never selecting one to read.
>
> Meanwhile, all the other students appeared to be engaged in reading their books, either in small groups of two or three, or alone. The teacher also sat in a corner reading her own book, modeling appropriate silent reading behavior. All the while, the Hmong girls continually glanced toward the teacher and circled around the various bookshelves. One or two times, they inched near her chair trying to get her attention, but to no avail.
>
> When the teacher finally looked up from her book, she noticed that the Hmong girls were still "undecided" about their books. She called them by name and asked, "What's the matter, can't you find a book you like?" They smiled and nodded "yes" (which in this case actually meant "no"). The teacher then added, "Would you like me to read to you?" Their little faces lit up as the teacher pulled up a chair and asked them to sit next to her. But while the Hmong girls were getting chairs, two other girls ran and squeezed in on each side of the teacher, leaving the Hmong girls on the outer fringes of the newly formed group. The English-speaking girls joined the teacher in reading aloud. Seeing that they were good readers, the teacher suggested that they (the English-speaking girls) read to the Hmong girls, and so she walked away to help another group. The Hmong girls quietly slipped away and headed once again to the bookshelves.[4]

The experiences of these Hmong children, as well as the Hispanic students described earlier, reveal that even well-meaning teachers assume that the high rate of success with process instruction reported for mainstream students will magically happen for culturally and linguistically diverse learners. As this case illustrates, that is far from the truth. It was obvious that the Hmong students were lost within the free-flowing structure and their lack of familiarity with books. It would have been more beneficial, for example, if the teacher had utilized the sustained silent reading time differently by reading to them and assisting their comprehension or by guiding them in the selection of books.

As a researcher, I have noted that when the focus of instruction is on process, even otherwise good teachers can be unsure about when to allow the process to take its natural course and when to mediate instruction. Teachers are so often caught up in the euphoria and popularity of process instruction that they find it difficult to believe that these programs could possibly need any modifications. As one teacher said to me, "Can so many people be wrong?" Indeed, how many teachers would reject or alter programs that offer so much promise for improvement in reading and writing while using whole and "authentic" literature as a base for literacy instruction? They are, after all, improvements over the old "drill, grill, and kill" reading approaches (Reyes, 1991b). The problem, however, is that carte blanche acceptance of *any* program reduces the likelihood that needed modifications for diverse learners will be made.

An equally important reason why teachers experience difficulties adjusting their teaching techniques for different learners is that the majority of them are members of the dominant culture, implementing programs designed primarily for mainstream students. Teachers implementing these programs tend to treat students of color as exceptions to the norm, as students who should be assimilated into the dominant group, rather than accommodated according to their own needs. Failure to address the needs of nonmainstream students is not due to a conscious omission but to an established tradition of ignoring differences among learners — a practice supported by designing educational programs and school policies primarily for White native-English-speaking students.

In her article about White privilege, Peggy McIntosh (1989) captures aptly and bluntly what, I believe, gets to the heart of this issue regarding failure to recognize the needs of minority students. As a member of the privileged White group, she says, "I can remain oblivious of the language and customs of persons of color who constitute the world's majority without feeling in my culture any penalty for such oblivion" (p. 11). In classrooms and schools, as in larger social structures, educators and policymakers are conditioned to ignore differences or to treat them as deficiencies. They continue to adhere to the misguided assumption that benefits from programs designed for the dominant group will automatically "trickle-down" to minorities, who will also profit from the same treatment (Halcón & Reyes, 1991).

Such disregard for the needs of culturally diverse students can be seen in the selection of literature books in whole language classrooms. In a recent study, Barrera (1992) reports that in an elementary school where Mexican American children make up more than 60 percent of the student population, nothing in the so-called authentic literature-based program is tailored to the needs of these children. On the contrary,

> the program literature is dominated by themes and characters that often do not reflect the faces, experiences, and histories of many of the children at La Vista. The children are more likely to read or hear a story about an elegant tea party among the

aristocratic set or a family who can travel to Africa for its vacation or children and their pets in New Zealand than they are likely to encounter a literature selection that reflects their backgrounds and communities. There is a marked cultural homogeneity to it all that renders the children's lives and experiences invisible. (p. 230)

Spanish-speaking children, as well as other linguistic minorities, are expected to derive the same enjoyment, relevance, and authenticity from stories designed for children from New Zealand where whole language originated. Many teachers, like those in Barrera's (1992) study, strive to remain faithful to the philosophy of whole language as they have learned it, without reflecting on the learners' cultural or linguistic backgrounds. This suggests that they are oblivious to the discrepancies between the "wholistic, authentic approach" they claim to be implementing and their monocultural approach to literacy that continues to rely on traditional canons.

When teachers believe that student success is inherent in adherence to a particular philosophy, rather than dependent on their own teaching expertise, a distrust of self may occur. In this seeming distrust, teachers set aside common sense and behave as if making appropriate adjustments for different learners were a violation of the principles of whole language or writing process. Instead of adapting the program for the learner, the learner is expected to adjust to the program.

Although the philosophies of whole language and writing process do not preclude modifications for diverse learners, failure to include consideration of cultural and linguistic factors as an *integral* part of their training and literature leaves teachers with the impression that these programs are inherently as good as they are. The common practice of taking a "one size fits all" approach to literacy when teaching diverse learners seems to substantiate this assertion and is consistent with conclusions reached by Barrera (1992), Delpit (1988), Siddle (1986), myself (1991b), and others.

Assumption Four: Error correction in process instruction hampers learning.

An important tenet in process instruction, in both whole language and writing process, is that learning is shaped by student input. Instruction is guided by students' "invitations," and the role of the teacher is to facilitate those invitations. Judith Newman (1985) describes it in the following way: "Our role as teachers is best seen as `leading from behind,' supporting the language learning capabilities of students *indirectly* through the activities we offer them" (p. 5, emphasis mine). The rationale is that this allows learners to initiate and participate more actively in their own learning without imposition, and departs from the traditional transmission of information model for instruction (Atwell 1987; Calkins, 1983; Graves, 1983; Hansen, 1987; Newman, 1985; Sowers, 1986). In the writing process, for example, students are free to experiment, make mechanical errors, and use invented spelling without being stifled by teacher correction (Sowers, 1986). Advocates of process instruction often remind teachers that "an overemphasis on accurate spelling, punctuation, and neat handwriting can actually produce a situation in which children come to see the conventions of writing as more important than the meaning they are trying to convey" (Newman, 1985, p. 28). For middle-class, mainstream students, this experimentation may work well. It can, however, be disconcerting for culturally and linguistically different students who expect teachers to provide direct and explicit instruction (Delpit, 1988; Macías, 1989; Reyes, 1991b; Siddle, 1986).

In the study of sixth-grade bilingual students described earlier, for example, students assumed that their writing form was correct because the teachers had not explicitly pointed out their errors — a responsibility they felt was the teachers'. The teachers, on the other hand, truly believed that they were pointing out those errors through the minilessons and that they were also protecting students' self-esteem by presenting the errors anonymously in the lessons. Taking examples of students' errors and embedding them in a lesson seemed to be the sensitive thing to do, but the students saw no direct connection between the topic of the lessons and their own errors. Several minilessons, for example, reviewed subject-verb agreement, including the use of "is not/are not." A sixth-grade girl repeatedly used "ain't" in her journal for several months, until finally the teacher wrote, "Honey, what would happen if you made an effort to say `aren't' every time that you start to say `ain't'?" (Field notes, January 11, 1989). In this case, as in others, unless the teachers explicitly and individually called a student's attention to the incorrect form found in his or her writing (something they rarely did), students ignored the errors.

In attempting to follow the spirit of process instruction, which frowns upon overt attention to form (product) over content (process), teachers generally refrained from pointing out mechanical errors outside of the small-group minilessons for fear that students would be discouraged from developing fluency and voice. This was consistent in my many observations of the classrooms. In the end-of-the-year interviews, students reacted to their spelling and grammatical errors with incredulous comments like, "Por qué no me dijo?" (Why didn't she tell me?); "It was wrong? She never *marked* it wrong" (Reyes, 1991a). One of the teachers countered that even after explicit attention to errors in individual writing drafts, two or three students still ignored them (Teacher interview, June 7, 1989). It was clear that students' expectation of their teachers' responsibility in providing direct instruction and the teachers' version of their role in a process class were at odds.

The high regard that Hispanics hold for teachers as authority figures (Delgado-Gaitan, 1987; Macías, 1989) indicates that they rely on and expect direct instructional intervention from the teacher. Many look for it and may not understand it when it comes masked in indirect requests or disguised in minilessons. In the examples described above, bilingual students sought the teachers' assistance; for example, "Please tell me a little bit about the book" (Reyes, 1991a). Their personal attachment to the teacher and their need for social interaction were often sources of confusion for them, because the rules of engaging in social interaction and written discourse were not made explicit. Similarly, the Hmong girls inched near the teacher for help, yet she failed to assist them in understanding the literacy task, which, no doubt, was culturally foreign to them.

The assumption that error correction hampers student learning rendered the modeling of correct form and the indirect nature of the minilessons ineffective in teaching important literacy skills to linguistically different students. Process instruction often leads to fewer opportunities for "assisted performance" (Vygotsky, 1978); that is, for teacher assistance in helping students learn a specific skill that they cannot yet perform well on their own. Assisted performance is an aspect of teaching much needed by *all* students, but especially by those whose ways of learning require programs tailored to their linguistic and cultural backgrounds.

TAILORING PROCESS INSTRUCTION FOR SUCCESS WITH SECOND LANGUAGE LEARNERS

My misgivings about the implementation of process instruction for linguistically different students do not mean that these programs should be abandoned altogether; rather, I appeal for appropriate adaptations that will increase their likelihood of success with diverse learners.[5] When implemented well, there is little doubt that process instruction offers the potential for more interesting and challenging learning activities than those offered by skills-approach methods. For example, all students are offered increased opportunities to engage in writing activities not commonly available in traditional skills programs. Whole language and writing process offer the potential of exposure to a rich body of authentic, full-length literature as a basis for reading and writing. Nevertheless, teachers must rise above the euphoria over whole language and writing process and recognize that these programs are not perfect or equally successful for all. They are successful only to the extent that teachers understand the theories, assume the role of mediators — not merely facilitators — and create culturally and linguistically sensitive learning environments for *all* learners. What this means is that teachers must do more than "lead from behind." When students are not comprehending a task or performing well, teachers must not water down concepts, but must participate *directly* in providing assistance in understanding those concepts through questions, feedback, and scaffolding; that is, "support that enables a learner to complete a task or achieve a goal that would have been unattainable without assistance" (Gaffney & Anderson, 1991, p. 184; see also Greenfield, 1984; Tharp & Gallimore, 1988; Wood, Bruner, & Ross, 1976).

The following case study is an example of an implementation of process instruction that was successful for mainstream as well as for linguistically different students (see Reyes & Laliberty, 1992). It is also a concrete example of how venerable assumptions about teaching language minorities were challenged by the teacher's validation of students' cultural and linguistic backgrounds, by her understanding of the role of primary language in the acquisition of English, and by her adaptations of whole language and writing process to meet the needs of her learners.

The study was conducted in a fourth-grade bilingual classroom in a Colorado school. Fifty-five percent of the total school enrollment was of Mexican descent. Of the twenty-seven students in the participating classroom, fourteen were Mexican or Mexican American and thirteen were White. The purpose of the study was to examine the development of children's literacy in a process instruction classroom where students were exposed to English and Spanish. The teacher was Mexican American and fluent in both languages. Like many teachers, her background knowledge of whole language and writing process was gained primarily from attendance at whole language institutes and workshops; she had no formal literacy courses in process instruction. At the time of the study, however, she was enrolled in a master's degree program in the social and multicultural foundations of education, to which she attributes her heightened awareness of the needs of linguistically different learners.

Several factors related to her specific teaching style and to the classroom environment she created contributed to her students' success. In examining these ingredients for success, it is important to note that the teacher's organization of instruction was diametrically opposed to the traditional teaching practices and language policies generally accepted in educating language-minority students. The most salient feature of her teaching was that she did not equate English with literacy or with knowledge. Instead of the usual overriding concern for teaching limited-English-proficient (LEP) students the English language per se, she was more interested in developing *literate* students, in nurturing a love for reading and writing, and in tapping her students' full potential. Thus, rather than making English a prerequisite for process instruction, as is usually the case, she allowed students to write in Spanish or English — whichever language was most comfortable for them. She did so with the full conviction that the transfer to English literacy would occur more readily than if writing in English were required immediately.

At the beginning of the year, ten of the fourteen Spanish-speaking students in the classroom were classified as LEP and were writing primarily in Spanish. By the end of the year, three LEP students had written their own full-length stories *in English*, similar in form and style to that of their native English-speaking peers; others had written shorter pieces, and most showed eagerness to write in English. With the assistance of bilingual peers in the class, two native English-speaking students also wrote Spanish translations of their English stories, indicating a strong interest in bilingualism and a recognition of its value. Attention to the development of literacy, rather than to the acquisition of English, not only permitted LEP students opportunities to taste writing success in their own language, it also provided them with the confidence to attempt writing in English. More important, it made them experts on topics derived from their own cultural experiences; for example, a little boy who emigrates from Mexico, leaving his loved ones behind, being raised by his grandparents. There was much enthusiasm and excitement about reading and writing, and no pressure on the students for deadlines or amount of work; yet, the students often requested to be "excused from recess" so they could complete a story, have a draft edited, or have a writing conference (Reyes & Laliberty, 1992).

Other important factors that contributed to the success of these linguistically different students were: (a) the organization of a cooperative learning classroom where assisting others in completing academic tasks was more important than individual competition; (b) the provision of explicit skills instruction within the context of learning activities and, without hesitation, to cite individual errors in a culturally sensitive manner; (c) heterogeneous grouping of students by language and ability so that students could learn both content and a second language from each other; and (d) use of Spanish and English literature books, supported by mediation of LEP students' reading comprehension to help them make relevant connections to universal themes. An additional support system accompanying process instruction included such things as teacher's preselection of books; reading with a partner; oral reading by the teacher; checking for comprehension in Spanish; reading English-language books while permitting discussion and written responses in Spanish; sharing students' Spanish and English written work in the "author's chair"; and providing multiple checkpoints for correcting and learning grammar, spelling, and punctuation from the teacher, peers, and parents.

In essence, the teacher not only set high expectations for all students, without watering down the curriculum, but significantly altered her classroom organization and teaching techniques so that those expectations could be reached by both mainstream and minority students. She also demonstrated the value of cultural and linguistic diversity in concrete and authentic ways. For example, although learning English was acknowledged as one priority, *it was not promoted at the expense of the students' native language*. Each linguistic group was allowed to use its native language for academic and non-academic purposes, but each was also exposed to the second language in a classroom environment that invited respect, sensitivity, and appreciation for diversity.

The inevitable question that arises is, Does a teacher have to be bilingual to be successful with non-English-speaking students? Although I would urge all teachers to become bilingual for their own personal development, for greater marketability in today's teaching work force, for facilitating learning for non-English-speaking students, and for numerous other reasons, my answer here is NO. Bilingualism is not a requirement to create the kind of classroom environment described here, although admittedly, it can be helpful. I have observed a similar case in which success for a Korean girl was made possible by a teacher who could neither speak nor understand Korean, but who encouraged an already literate student to write in her native language during the writing period rather than keep her occupied with "busy work." The teacher found bilingual Korean peers to translate the work for her and the class. This not only boosted the Korean girl's confidence, but accelerated her acquisition of English and her interest in English writing instruction. In turn, it aroused the curiosity of her native English peers for foreign languages (Teacher interview, October 1988). More important than bilingualism is the teacher's conviction about the value of diversity — namely, that differences in language and culture are not deficits — and the teacher's courage to teach out of that conviction, even if it means violating venerable assumptions.

CONCLUSION

When cultural and linguistic factors are treated as if they were incidental to sound pedagogical theories, it implies that they are not a fundamental part of effective instruction. This often leaves the impression that, even without adaptations, process instruction is appropriate for all. Moreover, it implicitly invites teachers to relinquish their role as mediators of knowledge, ignoring the importance of form (i.e., correct reading and writing skills), which, in spite of the widespread use of process instruction, continues to be used as a measure of academic success. Leading from behind, as process instruction suggests, may not always provide teachers with an accurate gauge to monitor the effectiveness of their teaching. As a result, second language learners' lack of success with these programs may be erroneously attributed to insufficient time for the "seeds of process" to germinate, to their need to master the English language first, or to their lack of motivation to learn.

By their failure to address explicitly cultural and linguistic diversity, process approach proponents tacitly promote a narrow, ethnocentric definition of literacy based on strategies designed for mainstream students as the model for *all* learners. To be inclusive of all learners, teaching practices, literacy instruction in particular, must begin with the *explicit* premise that each learner brings a valid language and culture to the instructional context; it is no longer sufficient to infer it. Only then can we ensure that cultural and linguistic modifications will not be *an afterthought*. Without this, we will continue to venerate outdated assumptions about the best ways to educate linguistically different learners and reduce the possibilities that could be derived from whole language and writing process.

NOTES

1. Portions of this chapter are based on a talk presented at an Invited Symposium at the American Educational Research Association (AERA), Chicago, Illinois, April 1991.
2. Chicana refers to a person of Mexican ancestry born in the United States.
3. Although federal and state bilingual education programs are transitional in nature, they allow the use of a student's primary language as a bridge to the acquisition of English (Crawford, 1989). The majority of programs, however, are "bilingual" in name only. At best, they offer minimal English as a Second Language instruction. A report by Catherine Snow and Kenji Hakuta indicates that most "foster monolingualism. . . . The bottom line of these programs has been an almost single-minded interest in the extent and the efficiency of English proficiency development" ("The good common school," 1992, p. 20).
4. This is an actual incident reconstructed from my field notes taken in January 1989.
5. Objection to the implementation of whole language philosophy for White, mainstream students is also emerging. A recent article in the *Denver Post*, with the headline "'Whole-language' program in Poudre angers parents," described that parents were "outraged at the lack of basic reading and writing skills being taught to their children" ("Whole-language program," 1992) and were demanding a change.

   In the same vein, *The Council Chronicle* ("Whole language vs. skills," 1992), a newspaper published by the National Council of Teachers of English, reported that eight of 169 elementary schools in Houston, Texas, decided to adopt DISTAR, a highly structured, skills-oriented reading program.

REFERENCES

Altwerger, B., Edelsky, C., & Flores, B. (1987). Whole language: What's new? *Reading Teacher, 41,* 144–154.

Atwell, N. (1984). Writing and reading literature from the inside out. *Language Arts, 61,* 240–252.

Atwell, N. (1987). *In the middle.* Portsmouth, NH: Heinemann.

Barrera, R. B. (1991, April 7). *What about culture? A look at the literature-based curriculum.* Paper presented at the annual meeting of the American Educational Research Association, Chicago.

Barrera, R. B. (1992). The cultural gap in literature-based literacy instruction. *Education and Urban Society, 24,* 227–243.

Calkins, L. (1983). *Lessons from a child*. Portsmouth, NH: Heinemann.

Calkins, L. (1986). *The art of teaching writing*. Portsmouth, NH: Heinemann.

Collier, V. (1989). How long? A synthesis of research on academic achievement in a second language. *TESOL Quarterly, 23*, 509–531.

Crawford, J. (1989). *Bilingual education: History, politics, theory and practice*. Trenton, NJ: Crane.

Cummins, J. (1979). Linguistic interdependence and the educational development of bilingual children. *Review of Educational Research, 49*, 222–251.

Cummins, J. (1981). The role of primary language development in promoting educational success for language minority students. In California State Department of Education, *Schooling and language minority students: A theoretical framework* (pp. 3–49). Los Angeles: California State University, National Evaluation, Dissemination, and Assessment Center.

Delgado-Gaitan, C. (1987). Mexican adult literacy: New directions for immigrants. In S. R. Goldman & H. T. Trueba (Eds.), *Becoming literate in English as a second language* (pp. 9–32). Norwood, NJ: Ablex.

Delpit, L. (1986). Skills and other dilemmas of a progressive black educator. *Harvard Educational Review, 56*, 379–385.

Delpit, L. (1988). The silenced dialogue: Power and pedagogy in educating other people's children. *Harvard Educational Review, 58*, 280–298.

Edelsky, C. (1990). Whose agenda is this anyway? A response to McKenna, Robinson, and Miller. *Educational Researcher, 19*(8), 7–11.

English language arts framework. (1987). Sacramento: California State Department of Education.

Fishman, J. (1987, January). *English only: Its ghosts, myths, and dangers*. Keynote address at the annual conference of the California Association for Bilingual Education, Anaheim, CA.

Gaffney, J. S., & Anderson, R. C. (1991). Two-tiered scaffolding: Congruent processes of teaching and learning. In E. H. Hiebert (Ed.), *Literacy for a diverse society* (pp. 184–198). New York: Teachers College Press.

García, M. T. (1989). *Mexican Americans: Leadership, ideology, & identity, 1930–1960*. New Haven, CT: Yale University Press.

Goodman, K. (1986). *What's whole in whole language?* Portsmouth, NH: Heinemann.

Goodman, K. (1989). Whole language research: Foundations and development. *Elementary School Journal, 90*, 207–221.

Goodman, K., & Goodman, Y. (1981). *A "whole-language comprehension-centered view of reading development"* (Occasional Paper No. 1). Tucson: University of Arizona, Program in Language and Literacy.

Graves, D. H. (1983). *Writing: Teachers and children at work*. Portsmouth, NH: Heinemann.

Graves, D. H. (1985). The reader's audience. In J. Hansen, T. Newkirk, & D. Graves (Eds.), *Breaking ground: Teachers relate reading and writing in the elementary school* (pp. 193–199). Portsmouth, NH: Heinemann.

Greenfield, P. M. (1984). A theory of the teacher in the learning activities of everyday life. In B. Rogoff & J. Lave (Eds.), *Everyday cognition: Its development in social contexts* (pp. 117–138). Cambridge, MA: Harvard University Press.

Gutierrez, K. D. (1992). A comparison of instructional contexts in writing process classrooms with Latino children. *Education and Urban Society, 24*, 244–262.

Hakuta, K. (1986). *Mirror of language: The debate on bilingualism*. New York: Basic Books.

Halcón, J. J., & Reyes, M. de la Luz. (1991). "Trickle-down" reform: Hispanics, higher education and the excellence movement. *Urban Review, 23*, 117–135.

Hansen, J. (1987). *When writers write*. Portsmouth, NH: Heinemann.

Harste, J. (1989). Commentary: The future of whole language. *Elementary School Journal, 90*, 243–249.

Harste, J., & Burke, C. (1977). A new hypothesis for reading teacher research: Both teaching and learning of reading are theoretically based. In D. Pearson (Ed.), *Reading: Theory, research, and practice, 26th yearbook of the National Reading Conference* (pp. 32–40). St. Paul, MN: Mason.

Hiebert, E. H., & Fisher, C. W. (1990). Whole language: Three themes for the future. *Educational Leadership, 47*(6), 62–63.

Hornberger, N. H. (1990). Bilingual education and English-only: A language-planning framework. In C. B. Cazden & C. E. Snow (Eds.), *The annals. English plus: Issues in bilingual education* (pp. 12–26). Newbury Park, CA: Sage.

Hornberger, N. H. (1992). Bilingual contexts, continua, and contrasts: Policy and curriculum for Cambodian and Puerto Rican students in Philadelphia. *Education and Urban Society, 24,* 196–211.

Imhoff, G. (1990). The position of U.S. English on bilingual education. In C. B. Cazden & C. E. Snow (Eds.), *The annals. English plus: Issues in bilingual education* (pp. 48–61). Newbury Park, CA: Sage.

Krashen, S., & Biber, D. (1988). *On course: Bilingual education's success in California.* Sacramento: California Association for Bilingual Education.

Macías, J. (1989, November). *Transnational educational anthropology: The case of immigrant Mexican students.* Paper presented at the annual meeting of the American Educational Research Association, San Francisco.

MacKaye, S. D. (1990). California Proposition 63: Language attitudes reflected in the public debate. In C. B. Cazden & C. E. Snow (Eds.), *The annals. English plus: Issues in bilingual education* (pp. 135–146). Newbury Park, CA: Sage.

McCollum, P. A., & Walker, C. L. (1990). The assessment of bilingual students: A sorting mechanism. In S. Goldberg (Ed.), *Readings on equal education: Vol. 10. Critical issues for a new administration and Congress* (pp. 293–314). New York: AMS.

McCollum, P. A., & Walker, C. L. (1992). Minorities in America 2000. *Education and Urban Society, 24,* 178–195.

McIntosh, P. (1989). White privilege: Unpacking the invisible knapsack. *Peace and Freedom, 49*(4), 10–12.

McLaren, P. (1988). Culture or canon? Critical pedagogy and the politics of literacy. *Harvard Educational Review, 58,* 213–234.

Newman, J. (1985). Insights from recent reading and writing research and their implications for developing whole language curriculum. In J. Newman (Ed.), *Whole language theory in use* (pp. 7–36). Portsmouth, NH: Heinemann.

Ramirez, J. D., Yuen, S. D., & Ramey, D. R. (1991). *Executive summary. Final report: Longitudinal study of structured English immersion strategy, early-exit and late-exit transitional bilingual education programs for language-minority children* (Contract No. 300-87-0156). San Mateo, CA: Aguirre International. (Submitted to U.S. Department of Education)

Reyes, M. de la Luz. (1987). Comprehension of content area passages: A study of Spanish/English readers in third and fourth grade. In S. R. Goldman & H. T. Trueba (Eds.), *Becoming literate in English as a second language* (pp. 107–126). Norwood, NJ: Ablex.

Reyes, M. de la Luz. (1991a, April 4). The "one size fits all" approach to literacy. *Invited Symposium on Literacy and Cultural Diversity: Voices, visibility, and empowerment.* Paper presented at the annual meeting of the American Educational Research Association, Chicago.

Reyes, M. de la Luz. (1991b). A process approach to literacy using dialogue journals and literature logs with second language learners. *Research in the Teaching of English, 25,* 291–313.

Reyes, M. de la Luz, & Laliberty, E. (1992). A teacher's "Pied Piper" effect on young authors. *Education and Urban Society, 24,* 263–278.

Saidel, P. (1991, April 22-26). *Growing up in linguistic limbo — Immigrant kids lose language and family, study finds.* Pacific News Service.

Sánchez, G. I. (1932). Group differences and Spanish-speaking children: A critical review. *Journal of Applied Psychology, 16,* 549–558.

Sánchez, G. I. (1951). *Concerning segregation of Spanish speaking children in the public schools.* Austin: University of Texas Press.

School backs off Spanish-speaking ban. (1991, October 24). *El Paso Times,* p. 1.

Short, K. G., & Burke, C. L. (1989). New potentials for teacher education: Teaching and learning as inquiry. *The Elementary School Journal, 90*, 193–206.

Siddle, E. V. (1986). *A critical assessment of the natural process approach to teaching writing.* Unpublished qualifying paper, Harvard University, Cambridge, MA.

Skutnab-Kangas, T. (1981). *Bilingualism or not: The education of minorities.* Clevedon, Eng.: Multilingual Matters.

Smith, F. (1986). *Insult to intelligence.* New York: Arbor House.

Sowers, S. (1986). Six questions teachers ask about invented spelling. In T. Newkirk & N. Atwell (Eds.), *Understanding writing: Ways of observing learning and teaching* (pp. 47–54). Portsmouth, NH: Heinemann.

Teachers networking. (1987). *Whole Language Newsletter.*

Tharp, R. G., & Gallimore, R. (1988). *Rousing minds to life.* New York: Cambridge University Press.

The good common school for all students. (1992). *National Council of La Raza, 11*(1), 19–20.

Valdes, G. (1991, April 7). *Background knowledge and minority students: Some implications for literacy-based instruction.* Paper presented at the annual meeting of the American Educational Research Association, Chicago.

Vygotsky, L. S. (1978). *Mind and society: The development of higher psychological process* (M. Cole, V. John-Steiner, S. Scribner, & E. Souberman, Eds.). Cambridge, MA: Harvard University Press.

Watson, D. (1982). What is a whole language reading program? *Missouri Reader, 7*, 8–10.

Watson, D. (1989). Defining and describing whole language. *Elementary School Journal, 90*, 129–141.

"Whole-language" program in Poudre angers parents. (1992, March 31). *The Denver Post*, p. 3B.

Whole language vs. skills: Is it either/or? (1992, April). *The Council Chronicle*, p. 1.

Wong-Fillmore, L. (1991). When learning a second language means losing the first. *Early Childhood Research Quarterly, 6*, 324–346.

Wood, D., Bruner, J. S., & Ross, G. (1976). The role of tutoring in problem solving. *Journal of Child Psychology & Psychiatry, 17*, 89–100.

The author wishes to thank John J. Halcón for his invaluable critique of this manuscript. Partial funding for this research was provided by the Office of the Associate Vice Chancellor for Faculty Affairs, the IMPART Program, of the University of Colorado, Boulder.

Writing Development:
A Neglected Variable in the Consideration
of Phonological Awareness

SOFÍA A. VERNON
EMILIA FERREIRO

The number of publications written on the topic of phonological awareness during the last thirty years has been impressive. These studies have dealt with phonological awareness abilities and their relationship to learning to read and spell, mainly with first language learners. Phonological awareness has been characterized as the ability to identify the sound structure of words, or even pseudo-words. Liberman, Shankweiler, and Liberman (1992) have pointed out that "such awareness is not an automatic consequence of speaking a language, because the biological specialization for speech manages the production and perception of these structures below the level of conciousness" (p. 1).

Children have learned in communicative settings to distinguish between words that differ in only one phoneme[1] (for example: "This is a big pig"). However, this recognition in action between two words very similar in sound but very different in meaning does not imply that the child is able to think about the sound pattern itself, which would make it possible to isolate the elementary sounds.

Discussions around the research findings on phonological awareness are relevant both to a theory of reading and to reading instruction. A considerable debate has taken place around the following issues concerning reading instruction: (a) To what extent is a previous recognition of the phonemes in utterances necessary in order to recognize the same phonemes in a piece of writing? (b) Is phonological awareness a precondition to becoming literate, or is it a consequence of the exposure to written material and reading instruction? Even if it happens not to be a precondition, (c) do children benefit from training in phonological awareness in kindergarten settings? The answers to these questions are undoubtedly connected to the planning of educational activities related to initial literacy.

It is not the purpose of this chapter to summarize all the debates and to present all the data related to phonological awareness. In what follows we only refer briefly to research data and interpretations needed to present our arguments.

Harvard Educational Review Vol. 69 No. 4 Winter 1999, 395–415

Phonological awareness has been studied through a variety of tasks: identifying the presence or absence of a given sound in an utterance (Marsh & Mineo, 1977; Stanovich, Cunningham, & Cramer, 1984); comparing the beginnings or endings of a set of words (Bradley & Bryant, 1983); finding rhyming words in a list (MacLean, Bryant, & Bradley, 1987); isolating the first sound of an utterance (Williams, 1980); segmenting, blending, or counting phonemes (Fox & Routh, 1975; Tunmer & Nesdale, 1985); deleting a given phoneme from a word (Morais, Cary, Alegría, & Bertelson, 1979), and so on.

Children demonstrate varying degrees of sucess at these different tasks because, apparently, the tasks demand different levels of segmenting abilities and place different cognitive demands on children (Defior, 1996; Yopp, 1988). In addition, children's performance at phonological awareness tasks varies with the linguistic level that is tapped by the task — that is, phonemes, syllables, onset and rimes, and so on.

Researchers agree that awareness of syllables is a very early acquisition that appears at about age four or five, or even earlier (Fox & Routh, 1975; Liberman, Shankweiler, Fischer, & Carter, 1974). It is an oversimplification to think that the next level is phonological segmentation.[2] Some linguists assume that the syllable has a hierarchical structure (Kenstowicz, 1993). It can be divided into two main intra-syllabic components: the *onset*, which is constituted by one or more consonants that appear before the syllabic nucleus (or vowel); and the *rime*, which is constituted by the nucleus and the consonants or glides that follow it. These final consonantal elements are called the *coda*. Intra-syllabic units can then be analyzed into phonemes. Of course, an onset may be constituted by a single phoneme (as in *cat*), or by two or more consonantal sounds (as in *smoke*).

Researchers have argued that tasks that draw children's attention to the syllable are easier than those that require attention to phonemes, and that, in turn, tasks that draw attention to onsets and rimes are also easier than tasks that require identifying or "manipulating" phonemes (Treiman & Zukowski, 1991, 1996).

Awareness of intra-syllabic units (onset and rime) seems to develop before children have become literate (Kirtley, Bryant, MacLean, & Bradley, 1989; Treiman & Zukowski, 1991). Awareness of phonemes, on the other hand, develops at an age when children have already begun their reading instruction. Illiterate adults do not succeed on phonological awareness tasks such as deleting the first sound of words or pseudowords (Morais et al., 1979). Literate adults who do not use an alphabetical writing system do not succeed in them either (Read, Zhang, Nie, & Ding, 1986). These findings suggest that phonological awareness is not a consequence of development alone and that it is related to the acquisition of an alphabetical writing system.

It has been well established that there is a strong relationship between phonological awareness and learning to read. In fact, phonological awareness has been considered one of the strongest predictors of reading (Mann, 1991). However, the debate on whether phonological awareness is a precursor or a consequence of learning to read (or both) is still open. As Treiman and Zukowski (1996) point out,

> the answer to this question may depend on the linguistic level under consideration.
> Our data, together with data from illiterate adults and readers of non-alphabetic

scripts, suggest that sensitivity to syllables, onsets, and rimes can develop without knowledge of a writing system that represents speech at these levels. In contrast, phonemic sensitivity may result from experiences connected with the learning of an alphabetic writing system. (p. 211)

That is, even illiterate people can easily segment words into syllables. However, only people who have received some reading instruction in an alphabetic script are able to segment words into phonemes.

Designs of experiments in phonological awareness research show some regular trends. The following research decisions are some that have been taken as "natural."

First, children are usually classified as pre-readers or readers. The readers, in turn, are classified as skilled or less skilled (or "poor") readers, using standardized reading tests (Liberman et al., 1992; Sprenger-Charolles, 1991; Vellutino & Scanlon, 1991). Children's writing is not usually taken into account when classifying children in order to distinguish between various experimental groups. This approach to research design probably reflects the well-known pedagogical tradition of prioritizing reading over writing at the beginning of literacy in English-speaking countries.

In this investigation, we adopted a different starting point. Instead of classifying children according to their reading skills, we took into account their performance as beginning writers. It has been well documented (Ferreiro & Teberosky, 1979/1982) that, when we ask children to write something (i.e., a word or phrase) that they have not yet been taught to write, we can witness a real process of construction. Data collected under such conditions include not only the written product as such, but also all the comments and verbalizations made during the writing process and the interpretation children give once the piece of writing has been completed. These data allow us to infer the ideas children start to create concerning the writing system to which they are exposed, and show that between initial scribbling and invented spellings, which are the two developmental steps that have received most consideration in English-speaking countries (see Read, 1986; Teale & Sulzby, 1986), a whole range of precise conceptualizations take place. We refer to these conceptualizations later.

Second, children's responses to phonological awareness tasks are usually classified in a dichotomous way: correct v. incorrect. However, our assumption, inspired by Piaget's theory, is that differences among incorrect responses are crucial to understanding development. These deviant responses are, in fact, more informative than children's abilities to adjust themselves to a given model — that is, to follow the interviewer's instructions. Previous research on beginning literacy (Ferreiro, 1986, 1991; Vernon, 1993) has shown the importance of an analysis of the so-called deviant or incorrect responses, and we do the same here regarding children's oral and written responses. In oral language acquisition research, a great step forward was taken when the regularities in "deviant" productions were considered in "positive terms" — in other words, as indicators of children's internal processes of organization (Brown, 1973). The same can be said concerning the beginning of reading and writing, which occurs well before school instruction (Ferreiro & Teberosky, 1979/1982). These initial activities can be considered in various ways. Very often, they are analyzed merely as behaviors or performances near or still far away from those expected by society at large and by schools. We, on the other hand, choose to analyze them as indicators of internal conceptualizations constructed by children as they try to understand a piece of sociocultural reality.

Third, in almost all the experimental designs, phonological awareness has been tested in purely oral contexts. That is, written words are presented only when reading is tested but not when phonological awareness is explored. However, when educators or researchers test the possibility of training pre-literate children to acquire proficiency in phonological awareness tasks, the use of letters to show the correspondence between letters or strings of letters and sound units has proven to be beneficial to the children's learning (Bradley & Bryant, 1983, 1985; Hohn & Ehri, 1983). In fact, this debate about the relevance of written stimuli to evaluate phonological awareness is intimately related to the conceptions of the nature of an alphabetical writing system. Traditionally, it has been considered that each letter corresponds to a phoneme (with a few exceptions). Even in languages such as English or French, where this one-to-one correspondence is not obvious, the principles underlying the original Greek alphabet are considered valid. Recent historical, linguistic, and semiotic analyses (Harris, 1986; Olson, 1994; Sampson, 1985) have questioned the traditional view that writing directly maps the phonemes or any other linguistic unit of the language.[3] This is particularly clear in the case of the notion of a "word." The strings of letters separated by blank spaces correspond to the literate conception of what a "word" is. However, the present state of English orthography is the result of a long historical evolution, and the same applies to any historically developed alphabetical writing. (For further details on the difficulty of the definition of "word," see Ferreiro, 1997; for further details on children's definition of "word," see Ferreiro & Vernon, 1992.) Any writing system introduces new dimensions that do not necessarily correspond to oral distinctions. Just to give a trivial example: upper-case letters convey semantic and/or syntactic information to the reader without affecting the reading aloud (upper-case letters do not affect stress, pitch, length, or any other physical parameter of oral speech). In addition to studying the influence of phonological awareness on reading acquisition, some authors have also studied the influence of writing on phonological awareness in adults and primary schoolchildren (Ehri, 1984; Scholes, 1998; Treiman & Cassar, 1997). In our research we explore the influence of writing on phonological awareness with kindergartners who have not had any direct reading instruction.

Fourth, the majority of studies have been conducted with English-speaking subjects since the beginning of research into phonological awareness (Bruce, 1964; Liberman, 1973), though in recent years this research has also been conducted in many other languages (Morais, 1995). However, English-language experimental designs, stimuli, and results continue to be used as the main paradigm for other languages. For instance, the ability to use onset/rime distinction has been tested in Spanish, assuming it would be as important as it is in English (Carrillo, 1994; Defior & Tudela, 1994). Even the construction of the nonsense words used as stimuli sometimes follows the English paradigm instead of the rules of the target language (Jiménez-González & Ortiz, 1993).

HYPOTHESES

In our study, we began with three hypotheses. Our first hypothesis is that there is a strong relationship between phonological awareness and the level of writing development in five- and six-year-old children. In addition, a similar relationship may be found with the awareness of other sound units (see note 3).

Our second hypothesis is that these children may analyze oral words in a different way when provided with purely oral stimuli than when these stimuli are accompanied by a piece of writing. Moreover, we believe that, when presented with written stimuli, children will give more analytical responses. For instance, an analysis into phonemes will be considered more analytical than an analysis into syllables.

Our third hypothesis is that differences in the internal structure of languages must somehow influence the way children analyze oral stimuli. Spanish, the language studied here, has important phonological and orthographic differences from English. For instance, in Spanish, very few content words are monosyllabic (Álvarez, Carreiras, & de Vega, 1992), whereas in English there is a high frequency of monosyllabic content words. In English there is a greater variety of types of syllables (Bradley, Sánchez-Casas, & García-Albea, 1993), and syllabic boundaries are harder to define (Sampson, 1985). In Spanish there is a very strong syllabic rhythm, whereas in English, any syllable can be stressed or unstressed in order to adjust to the rhythmic pattern, based on the unit called "foot" (Halliday, 1985). All Spanish syllables tend to have the same duration,[4] and there are only five vowels. The distinction between long and short vowels that exists in English is not phonological in Spanish. The sensitivity of English-speaking subjects to onset and rime (easily reflected in children's nursery rhymes and language games) may not be as prevalent in speakers of other languages. Taking into account all these differences, we don't expect Spanish-speaking children to follow the same path as English-speaking children to reach phonological awareness.

METHODS

Subjects

Our subjects were fifty-four kindergartners. The mean age of the children was five years, seven months (68.94 months with a standard deviation [SD] of 3.4 months; see Table 1). All of these children were monolingual Spanish-speakers of lower-middle-class background who attended public kindergartens in the city of Querétaro, Mexico. These children had had no previous reading or phonics instruction. Very few reading materials were available in their classrooms, and teachers read aloud to the children infrequently.

We interviewed kindergartners from four different classrooms at the same school. Since our first hypothesis was that children's responses would vary depending on their writing development, we decided to take a stratified sample according to writing levels in Spanish, with an equal number of subjects at each writing level. (These levels will be described later.) The classification of children's written productions was validated by two independent judges. Interrater disagreements were resolved by a third experienced judge.

Additionally, a group of eleven first graders was chosen at random from five different classrooms at a nearby public primary school.[5] These first graders had a mean age of six years, eight months (82.1 months, with an SD of 3.12 months). They were given the same tasks as the kindergartners. These first-grade children were interviewed during the second half of the school year after more than six months of reading instruction,[6] because we wanted them to be able to write alphabetically. In fact, they were able to do so, although their spellings were not always conventional (for example, *benado* instead of *venado*, deer).

Interview Procedure

Children were interviewed twice, on consecutive days. Interviews lasted an average of twenty minutes and were conducted on the premises of each school. During the first interview, children were given a written task, similar to the one used by Ferreiro and Teberosky (1979/1982). The aim of this task was to classify and select children according to their level of writing. During the second interview, children were given two oral segmentation tasks, which will be described in detail later.

In the writing task, used for classification purposes, children were asked to write seven different common nouns in Spanish, one at a time, in the following order: *mariposa* (butterfly), *gusano* (worm), *venado* (deer), *perico* (parrot), *sapo* (toad), *toro* (bull), and *pan* (bread). Three criteria were taken into account in the selection of these nouns:

(a) These words differ in the number of syllables. The task started with the longest word (four syllables), continued with three trisyllabic words, then two bisyllabic words, and ended with a monosyllabic word. This order takes into account previous research concerning the difficulty of the items (Ferreiro & Teberosky, 1979/1982). Contrary to adults' expectations, pre-alphabetic children find it easier to write words that have more than two syllables.

(b) All words present the most common Spanish syllable pattern (CV).[7] The monosyllable also has the most common pattern (CVC) for one-syllable nouns in Spanish.

(c) All words present different syllabic nuclei, which is a vowel in all cases but one (*toro*).

After the children had finished writing each word, they were asked to read it, pointing with their finger to the letters they were reading. Based on their responses, children were classified into six different writing levels. Although the focus of this article is not this classification system, it is necessary to keep in mind the criteria used to characterize each type of writing in order to understand the analysis that follows. We present these categories in reverse developmental order. In our experience, the developmental progression is easier to understand when it begins with writings that are more familiar to adult readers.

TABLE 1

Mean Age of Kindergartners and First Graders at Each Writing Level

Writing Level	Mean Age (Months)	Standard Deviation (Months)
PRE-SYL	67.2	2.7
SYL-1	69.4	1.9
SYL-2	69.6	3.7
SYL-3	69.3	3.4
SYL-ALF	67.8	3.5
ALF-K	70.2	4.5
TOTAL KINDER	68.9	3.4
ALF-F	82.1	3.1

Alphabetic writings (ALF): Children make systematic phoneme-letter correspondences, although their spellings may not be conventional. For example, Mario (5 years, 3 months old) writes *perico* as PERICO and *venado* as BENADO.[8] In Spanish, the letters B and V correspond to the same sound. We refer to children who produce alphabetical writings by ALF-K if they are kindergartners, or ALF-F if they are first graders.

Syllabic-alphabetic writings (SYL-ALF): Children use an apparently mixed system of writing. Sometimes they represent each syllable with a letter, but they also start representing intrasyllabic units when they write. As all items (except the monosyllable) were composed of CV syllables, the result was a mixture of representations of syllables and phonemes. For instance, Karen (5 years, 4 months old) writes MAIOSA for *mariposa*. She writes the first and last syllables with two letters but writes each of the two intermediate syllables with only one letter.

Strict syllabic writings with use of pertinent letters (SYL-3): These children systematically use one letter for each spoken syllable. They also use an appropriate letter for most of the syllables they represent. That is, they write the vowel or (less frequently) the consonant that belongs to the syllable. For instance, Fernando (5 years, 6 months old) writes AIOA for *mariposa*, and reads "ma-ri-po-sa," pointing to one letter for each syllable. Consonants are sometimes used when the name of the letter is the same as the syllable. Fernando uses the letter p, called "pe" (as in the English words "*pe*lican" or "*pay*"), to start the word *perico*, the result being PIO, read as "pe-ri-co," with the same pointing procedure. Children usually plan their writing, either counting the number of syllables before writing or, more frequently, saying aloud each syllable (one by one) while writing a letter for each one of them.

Strict syllabic writings without use of pertinent letters (SYL-2): These children also make a strict one-to-one correspondence between the oral syllables and the letters they write (i.e., they control the number of letters they write). However, the letters they use are still not pertinent, in the sense that any letter can represent any given syllable. For example, Erika (5 years, 3 months old) writes the word *perico* (a three-syllable word) as OIE, reading "pe-ri-co" while pointing to one letter for each syllable.

Initial syllabic (SYL-1): These children begin to make correspondences between letters and syllables. Children write a string of letters and then try to read their own productions, attempting to match them to syllables but without making a one-to-one correspondence between letters and syllables. Sometimes they say one syllable per letter, and sometimes they say a syllable pointing to several letters. There is no evidence that these children actually think about the number or the kind of letters they need to write each word. For example, Omar (5 years, 7 months old) writes *mariposa* (four syllables) as PIOIMOT. The child reads "ma" while pointing to the first letter, "ri" while pointing to the second, "po" while pointing to the three following letters, and "sa" while pointing to the last two.

Pre-syllabic writings (PRE-SYL): These children make no attempts to establish letter-sound correspondences of any kind, either when they write or when they are asked to read their own written productions. They write several letters and then read the written string without analyzing it. An example of this kind of writing is provided by Conchita (5 years, 4 months old), who writes OliEOT for the word *gusano*.

Procedure for the Experimental Tasks

Children were given two separate oral segmentation tasks, which we differentiate according to the kind of stimuli used to elicit responses. Both tasks were audio-recorded.

Pictures: Children were asked to segment orally six CVCV and three CVC common nouns in "little bits." This was done through a guessing game, in which the interviewer gave the child a set of nine cards depicting known animals and objects. The cards did not have printed letters or words. Items were monosyllabic CVC nouns — *gis* (chalk), *pez* (fish), *sol* (sun), *pan* (bread) — and bisyllabic CVCV nouns — *luna* (moon), *foca* (seal), *taco* (taco), *mesa* (table), *sapo* (toad), and *gato* (cat). Children were allowed to choose the order in which they selected the cards.

After naming each of the depicted objects, the interviewer asked the child to say the name of the objects in little bits, so that the interviewer would have a hard time guessing the word. To model the game for the child, the interviewer gave several examples, using the names of objects that could clearly be seen in the room. For instance, the adult chose an object and said, "This is a /kaxa/ (box); if I say /ka-xa/, it is very easy to guess. But if I say /ka-x-a/, it is not so easy to guess. But if I say /k-a-x-a/ it is really hard to guess. You have to say the words in little bits so I have a real hard time guessing." First the interviewer modeled how to segment the word into syllables (/ka-xa/); next, the interviewer modeled how to segment the word into a syllable followed by two phonemes (/ka-x-a/); finally, the interviewer modeled how to segment the word into separate phonemes (/k-a-x-a/). No definition of little bits was provided, and all kinds of segmentations were accepted as little bits, although the interviewer encouraged the child to produce the maximum number of segments, which is achieved only through a complete phonological segmentation.

The children understood these instructions easily. Our goal was to elicit the most analytical responses children could give — that is, to see how far they could go in dividing the word into its smallest phonological components. The interviewer would then start the game, cover her eyes, and then ask the child to choose one card and say the name of the depicted object in little bits. The interviewer would then try to guess which card the child had chosen. For the first two chosen cards, the interviewer would give feedback to the child if she did not produce a complete phonological segmentation. If the child provided syllabic or intra-syllabic (for example, "so-ol" or "so-l") but not complete phonological segmentations, the interviewer would say, "That's very easy. I'm going to guess and win the card. Try making it more difficult. Say it in smaller bits, so I can't guess." If the child could not give an alternative answer, the interviewer would guess the word, and then give information about how the child could make it harder for the interviewer to guess, saying, for example, "That was very easy. It's /mesa/. Next time, make it harder, like this: /m-e-s-a/." Whenever a child hesitated and made more than one attempt, the more analytical response was taken into consideration.

Written words: In this task, children were shown, one by one, different written words, which were printed on white paper in upper-case 28-point Times New Roman font type. Each card measured 5 x 2 centimeters. Items for this task, presented in the following order, included monosyllabic CVC common nouns in Spanish — *pan* (bread), *luz* (light), *gis* (chalk) — and bisyllabic CVCV nouns — *sapo* (toad), *peso* (name of a Mexican coin), *luna* (moon), *taco* (taco), *gato* (cat).

For each card, the interviewer read the word aloud and then asked the child to point to each letter while saying the word in little bits, one bit for each letter. Naming of letters was discouraged. The interviewer gave three examples, showing a strict correspondence between letters and phonemes. The interviewer then read aloud the first card and asked the child to do the task. The same procedure was followed with all the cards. If the child segmented words in a way that suggested that she was not looking at the printed word, the interviewer would draw attention to the card while repeating the instruction. The ability to point to each letter was not taken into account because the main data we are concerned with is the verbal response.

Half the children started with the picture task, while the other half started with the written word task.

RESULTS

For both segmentation tasks, children's responses were classified according to the type of linguistic units they were able to analyze. It is important to note that whenever a child hesitated and produced more than one answer, only the more analytical response was taken into account in data quantification and statistical analysis. Children's responses were divided into six groups. We provide at least one example of each from our data:

1. *No segmentation:* The child said the complete word in spite of the examples and feedback; for example, *pan* for PAN.

2. *Syllabic segmentation:* For example, *ga-to*, or *lu-na*. For monosyllabic words, we considered responses such *so-ol* or *pa-an* in this category because, by repeating the vowel, the child produces two separate, regular Spanish syllables.

3. *Partial isolation of a segment:* Responses included here are syllabically based in that the child produces a syllabic segmentation. However, these responses show the attempt to isolate one of the sounds in the word, because before or after a complete syllable, the child isolates either a vowel or a consonant. For example, for LUNA (a bisyllabic word), children would say *lu-u-na* or *lu-n-na*. For monosyllabic words, children produced segmentations such as *so-o-ol* or *so-l-ol*. Partial vowel isolation was more frequent than consonant isolation. Consonant isolation occurred only in 26.7 percent of the total responses of this kind for both mono- and bisyllabic words.

4. *Phonological segmentation of the second syllable (of the coda, or final consonant, for monosyllabic words):* The first real segmentation seems to take place for the last part of the word. For bisyllabic words, children produce segmentations such as *lu-n-a* or *ga-t-o*, and for monosyllabic words *so-l*, *pa-n*, and the like.

5. *Phonological segmentation of the first syllable (the onset of monosyllabic words):* For example, segmentations such as *l-u-na*, *g-a-to*, or *s-ol* and *p-an*.

6. *Complete phonological segmentation:* Such as *l-u-n-a*, *g-a-t-o*, *s-o-l*, *p-a-n*.

Table 2 shows the percentage of the total number of responses for both tasks according to the level of writing of the children who produced them.

We performed a multiple regression analysis (using a stepwise method) including both kindergarten and first-grade children, with type of segmentation as the dependent variable. A full model, including level of writing, task (pictures v. written word task), age, and type of word (bisyllabic v. monosyllabic) as independent variables (grade was not included as an independent variable) was tested. The final model we chose was the following:

$$Y_i = 06.80 + .72 * X_{1i} + 0.47 * X_{2i} + E_i$$

In this model, Y_i represents the ith subjects' score for *type of segmentation*, X_{1i} is the ith subjects' score for *level of writing*, X_{2i} is the ith subjects' score for *task*, and E_i is an "error term" accounting for the difference between the score derived from the equation and the actual score. R^2 for the first step (level of writing) was 0.70, while it was 0.72 when task was entered. These results show that level of writing explains most of the variance in the child's score for type of segmentation (multiple $R = .83817, R^2 = .70254, F = 2855.3686$, *Signif. F* $= .0000$). The kind of task (pictures v. written words) is also marginally significant (entered on step number 2, multiple $R = .84868, R^2 = .72026, F = 1555.15463$, *Signif. F* $= .0000$). When all of the variables (level of writing, task, type of word, and age) are entered in the linear regression with a stepwise method, SPSS excludes type of word and age from the analysis because in both cases p $\geq$ .10. Thus the only constant predictors left in the model are level of writing and type of task. When each variable is entered separately into a linear regression model with type of segmentation as the dependent variable, $R^2 = .001$ for type of word and $R^2 = .259$ for age. Only in this condition is age marginally significant, probably due to age differences between kindergartners and first graders. When only kindergartners are entered in the linear regression, with age as the only independent variable, $R^2 = .002$.

The boxplot in Figure 1 shows the variability of segmentation responses for both tasks at each level of writing. Darker horizontal lines show the median of responses, and the boxes show values falling between the 25th and the 75th percentiles. The vertical lines that extend from the boxes indicate the lowest and highest values, excluding outliers.

Figure 1 shows that, for children who produce pre-syllabic (PRE-SYL) and initial syllabic writings (SYL-1), the median response is in syllabic segmentations (type 2) for both tasks. However, certain differences have to be noted. First, for the picture task, most pre-syllabic (PRE-SYL) children either do not segment words at all or perform syllabic segmentations (responses of type 1 and 2), with very few type 3 responses. When confronted with the written task, however, these same children almost always at least produce syllabic segmentations (a type 2 response), and many produce type 3 responses as well.

Similarly, children with initial syllabic writings (SYL-1) produce mostly syllabic segmentations in both tasks. Again, there is little variability for the picture task, whereas when they have a written stimulus, partial isolation of a phoneme (a type 3 response) is quite frequent. In fact, these children can produce segmentations up to type 4 (phonological segmentation of the second syllable) only in the written word task.

Children with syllabic writings (SYL-2 and SYL-3) have an identical distribution of responses for the picture task. For both groups, the median of responses is at type 2, although responses range from type 1 to 4. However, for the written word task, there is a difference. SYL-2 children's responses in this latter task included type 2 to type 4, but the median is at type 3 responses. SYL-3 children's responses, on the other hand, range between type 3 and type 5, although the median is also at type 3 responses. Even if these children are unable to read or write conventionally, they can produce more analytical segmentations when they are able to look at a printed word.

SYL-ALF children show the biggest range of variation in response types. For the picture task, most of their responses range between partial isolation and complete phonological segmentation (types 3 to 6), with the median at phonological segmentation of the second syllable (type 4), although responses that show no segmentation and syllabic responses (types 1 and 2) can appear from time to time. However, for the written word task, the median of responses of these children shows phonological segmentation (type 6), and most responses are in the range between type 4 and type 6. The median of responses for children who produce alphabetic writings (ALF-K and ALF-F) is complete phonological segmentation (type 6). For the less experienced kindergartners (ALF-K), there is greater variability in the picture task, whereas there is none for the written word task. With written stimuli, both more and less experienced alphabetic children (ALF-K and ALF-F) have exactly the same performance (phonological segmentations).

TABLE 2

Relationship between Level of Writing and Types of Segmentation (Percentages)
for Written Word Task (W) and Picture Task (P)

Type of Segmentation

Writing Level	1		2		3		4		5		6	
	P	W	P	W	P	W	P	W	P	W	P	W
PRE-SYL	30.7	18.5	68.2	60.5	1.1	19.8		1.2				
SYL-1	9.2	9.9	73.6	58.0	14.9	27.2	2.3	3.7		1.2		
SYL-2	7.1		43.5	25.9	45.9	51.9	3.5	18.5		3.7		
SYL-3	3.5	1.2	58.1	22.2	19.8	34.6	11.6	25.9	7.0	12.3		3.7
SYL-ALF	2.3		13.8		12.6	4.9	29.9	32.1	6.9	7.4	34.5	55.6
ALF-K			3.4		8.0	2.5	18.4	3.7	5.7	4.9	64.4	88.9
ALF-F						1.0	7.5	3.0	9.4	3.0	83.0	92.9

DISCUSSION

We comment on the main results of our research from two perspectives: first, as a contribution to phonological awareness research; second, as a way of rethinking the beginnings of literacy instruction.

Contributions to Phonological Awareness Research

First, the independent variable in this study is the child's level of conceptualization about the writing system described previously in Spanish-speaking children (Ferreiro & Teberosky, 1979/1982). We have shown that the way these children deal with oral segmentation tasks is strongly correlated with this independent variable, regardless of age. To our knowledge, this is the first time that such a strong relationship has been found between writing activities as we defined them and phonological awareness tasks. In evaluating the levels of writing conceptualization, we used oral words that were familiar but whose written representation was unknown to the children. In addition, to evaluate such levels we took into account all aspects of the writing process, including a reading aloud of the written product. Defined this way, this writing task could not be done by simply remembering a visual string. Children put their already acquired knowledge into action. In principle, the task encourages children to adopt an analytical attitude (How many letters? Which ones?) without imposing a particular analysis. In fact, children at pre-syllabic levels do not make a one-to-one correspondence between sound units and letters.

Second, children's answers to oral segmentation tasks seem to be developmentally ordered: they go from the inability to find "pieces" in a word, to syllable-based analysis, then to the ability to make intra-syllabic analysis toward the end of the word, and finally to a full isolation of phonemes.

Third, the preeminence of each one of these types of segmentation depends primarily upon the children's writing levels but is modulated by the type of task given. At every writing level, children perform in a more analytical way when they are asked to take into account each one of the letters on a printed card. Even children at the lowest levels take advantage of the presence of letters to give more analytical answers. This means that, even before being able to read or write at levels that correspond to what in English is called "invented spelling," children are sensitive to quantitative and qualitative properties of printed materials (i.e., the quantity of letters and differences among them).

Fourth, children's responses to the oral segmentation tasks were not dependent upon the interviewer's modeling and instructions. Only children at the most developed level consistently gave the same kind of answers (the complete phonological segmentation). Children were always encouraged to produce more analytical answers in our study, but they did not receive feedback in terms of correct or incorrect matching with a previous model. The few examples we gave them at the beginning of the tasks served as cues to some children but not to others. The children's ability to deal with the task actually seemed to depend on their overall knowledge of the writing system as expressed in their written productions. Based on these results, phonological aware-

FIGURE 1   *Distribution of Responses by Type of Segmentation and Writing Level*

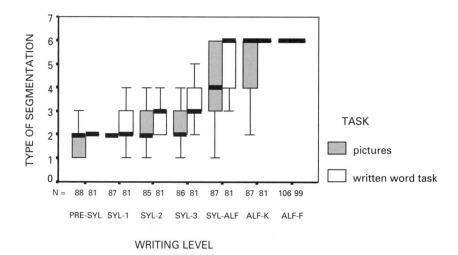

ness does not seem to be an all-or-nothing achievement. Development is not just a substitution of one type of answer (e.g., no segmentation) for another (e.g., complete phonological segmentation). In order to understand development, it is important to allow children to make their own analysis of words without following a fixed model. This allows researchers to avoid, at the same time, a consideration of children's answers in terms of "right" and "wrong."

Fifth, writing and reading activities may help children become aware of the sound structure of language. Oral communication alone does not demand such conscious analysis. In this respect, as Olson (1994) has suggested, writing can act as a model for the analysis of speech. Participation in language games may allow children to learn about rhymes and other linguistic phenomena, but the fact remains that perhaps the only everyday activities that require segmental phonological awareness are writing and reading. Writing seems to be both an end in itself and an instrument to achieve a specific kind of language knowledge. From a developmental point of view, there is no evidence that phonological awareness could arise independently of the efforts to understand an alphabetical writing system. To introduce writing in experimental situations of evaluation of phonological awareness seems to be useful.

Finally, data reported here suggest that generalizations of research results from one language to another may be misguided. Although onset/rime may be natural units for analyzing speech in English, this does not seem to be so in Spanish.

Educational Implications

We now focus on the discussions that prevail in the English-language research literature in order to address the educational implications of our findings. The discussion about phonics instruction has no equivalent in Spanish-speaking countries. Even if our data concern Spanish-speaking children, we believe that this study, as well as previous research, may provide a fruitful frame of discussion about the assumptions underlying the decisions that need to be taken in the educational field. The relationship between phonological awareness and success in reading has been presented as valid in all studied languages (Morais, 1995). That is precisely why it is important to conduct crosslinguistic studies of language development. In our opinion, the folowing implications are most important for beginning literacy. First, since the "Great Debate" concerning the relevance of phonics instruction (Chall, 1967) started, the focus of discussions has been on teaching interventions or methods. (The last issue of 1997 of *Reading Research Quarterly*, as well as a "Commentary" by Chall in the first issue in 1999, shows that the debate is still alive.) Underlying this debate is the equation between "teaching methods" and "learning progression." That is to say, if teachers teach phonics, children will learn phoneme analysis; if they teach "whole language," children will be prevented from making such an analysis. In all our previous research we have shown that teaching instruction is not understood the same way by children at different levels of conceptualization about print. Learning is, no doubt, influenced by teaching, but is not created by it. The insistence on a debate focused on teaching methods seems to reflect the old empiricist ideas about the nature of the learning process.

Second, phonological abilities can be trained in purely oral contexts. This is an attested fact (Lundberg, Frost, & Petersen, 1988). However, direct, systematic phonics instruction, segmental phonological awareness training, and the teaching of letter-sound correspondences may not be useful for all children, regardless of their developmental level. Those children who have already reached advanced levels ("invented spellers," or what we have termed *syllabic-alphabetic* in Spanish) may benefit from it. However, children at less advanced levels of writing development may not be capable of grasping the information about phonemes and letter-sound matching, although they do analyze speech. This analysis leads them to phonological awareness. However, this analytical capability cannot be recognized as such if phonemes are considered the only legitimate way to segment utterances.

In addition, kindergartners participating in the study reported here had not received any phonological training. However, they still demonstrated a capacity and disposition to analyze speech when prompted to do so in oral contexts. They also analyze speech spontaneously while writing meaningful words. In conclusion, children do not need prompting to engage in writing activities. When they write freely, they also analyze their own speech (Quinteros, 1997). If teachers encourage them to write and to reflect on their writing, analysis of speech will take place.

Many factors seem to correlate positively with literacy development. We have witnessed a long period of emphasis on perceptual abilities, short-term visual memory, memory for visual shapes, visual and auditory discrimination, and so on in the field of literacy development and instruction (Vernon, 1977). Nowadays, phonological awareness is considered the most important factor to be taken into consideration (Blachman, 1984; Wagner, 1986). Phonological awareness helped to emphasize the language-related aspects of literacy development, but placed too much emphasis on only one aspect: the phonological component. However, any written language that has developed historically (as opposed to an artificial one, like the ASCII code used for computer programming) is a mixture of phonological, morphological, semantic, derivational, and other "historical accidents" or influences. The mixed character of all existing alphabetical writings prevents us from placing the phonological component as the prevailing linguistic component. One of the great linguists of this century, Vachek, said clearly in 1945: "The phonemic system is only one of the aspects of language considered as a system and, therefore, the phonemic system cannot claim the exclusive right to being reflected in writing. Writing is a system in its own right, adapted to fulfill its own specific functions, which are quite different from the functions proper to a phonetic transcription" (Vachek, 1989, p. 7).

Underlying the importance of phonological awareness is a discussion (less developed in English-speaking countries but well developed in French-speaking countries; see Blanche-Benveniste, 1998; Catach, 1988) about the very nature of an alphabetical writing system. We think that increasing our knowledge of how alphabetical writing systems are related to oral language is crucial to understanding the learner's task. If we retain a naive view that considers an alphabetical writing system as a visual way to represent phonemes, making learners aware of these phonemes seems the only pertinent thing to do. But writing systems are much more complex than that. That is why the task of becoming literate cannot be reduced to the learning of a code.

NOTES

1. A phoneme is "the smallest unit of sound in a language which can distinguish two words" (Richards, Platt, & Platt, 1992, p. 272).
2. Phonological segmentation is the ability to analyze a word into its constituent sounds, or phonemes.
3. Any speech utterance can be divided into many units at various levels of analysis. Phonological units are the smallest ones. Above them are syllabic units, morphological units, syntatic units. We can also distinguish content, pragmatic, and discursive units.
4. Duration is defined as "a term used in phonetics, to refer to the length of time involved in the articulation of a sound or syllable" (Crystal, 1991, p. 115).
5. The last names of boys and girls were separately alphabetically ordered, and every fifteenth child from each list was selected.
6. These first graders had been taught using a syllabic method — that is, the children were taught first the vowels, and then the consonants (one by one) in combination with the vowels, forming what are called "syllabic families," for example, "ma, me, mi, mo, mu." Simple words or short sentences are then created through the combination of known syllables. Writing is introduced through iterative copy of the syllables, words, and sentences.
7. In what follows, C = consonant; V = vowel.
8. Children's writings will be transcribed mostly in upper-case letters because these were the type of letters they used. The words that we asked them to write are presented in italics. Dashes are used to separate syllables or phonemes in the transcription of any oral utterance, whenever the child or the interviewer segmented a word in that way.

REFERENCES

Alegría, J., & Morais, J. (1991). Segmental analysis and reading acquisition. In L. Rieben & C. Perfetti (Eds.), *Learning to read* (pp. 135–148). Hillsdale, NJ: Lawrence Erlbaum.

Álvarez, C., Carreiras, M., & De Vega, M. (1992). Estudio estadístico de la ortografía castellana: (1) La frecuencia silábica. *Cognitiva, 4*(1), 75–105.

Blachman, B. (1984). Language analysis skills and early reading acquisition. In G. Wallach & K. Butler (Eds.), *Language learning disabilities in school-age children* (pp. 271–287). Baltimore: Williams & Wilkins.

Blanche-Benveniste, C. (1998). *Estudios lingüísticos sobre la relación entre oralidad y escritura*. Barcelona: Gedisa.

Bradley, D., Sánchez-Casas, R., & García-Albea, J. (1993). The status of the syllable in the perception of Spanish and English. *Language and Cognitive Processes, 8*, 197–233.

Bradley, L., & Bryant, P. E. (1983). Categorizing sounds and learning to read — a causal connection. *Nature, 301*, 419–421.

Bradley, L., & Bryant, P. E. (1985). *Rhyme and reason in reading and spelling*. Ann Arbor: University of Michigan Press.

Brady, S., & Shankweiler, D. (Eds.). (1991). *Phonological processes in literacy: A tribute to Isabelle Y. Liberman*. Hillsdale, NJ: Lawrence Erlbaum.

Brown, R. (1973). *A first language: The early stages*. Cambridge, MA: Harvard University Press.

Bruce, I. J. (1964). The analysis of sounds by young children. *British Journal of Educational Psychology, 34*, 158–170.

Carrillo, M. (1994). Development of phonological awareness and reading acquisition: A study in Spanish language. *Reading and Writing: An Interdisciplinary Journal, 6*, 279-298.

Catach, N. (1988). *Pour une théorie de la langue écrite*. Paris: Editions du Centre National de la Recherche Scientifique.

Chall, J. (1967). *Learning to read: The great debate*. New York: McGraw-Hill.

Chall, J. (1999). Commentary: Some thoughts on reading research: Revisiting the first-grade studies. *Reading Research Quarterly, 34*, 8–11.

Crystal, D. (1991). *A dictionary of linguistics and phonetics*. Oxford, Eng.: Blackwell.

Defior, S., (1996). Una clasificación de las tareas utilizadas en la evaluación de las habilidades fonológicas y algunas ideas para su mejora. *Infancia y Aprendizaje, 73*, 49–63.

Defior, S., & Tudela, P. (1994). Effect of phonological training on reading and writing acquisition. *Reading and Writing: An Interdisciplinary Journal, 6*, 3, 299–320.

Ehri, L. (1984). How orthography alters spoken language competencies in children learning to read and spell. In J. Downing & R. Valtin (Eds.), *Language awareness and learning to read* (pp. 119–147). New York: Springer Verlag.

Ferreiro, E. (1986). The interplay between information and assimilation in beginning literacy. In W. Teale & E. Sulzby (Eds.), *Emergent literacy: Writing and reading* (pp. 15–49). Norwood, NJ: Ablex.

Ferreiro, E. (1991). Psychological and epistemological problems on written representation of language. In M. Carretero, M. Pope, R. Simons, & J. I. Pozo (Eds.), *Learning and instruction: European research in an international context* (pp. 157–173). Oxford, Eng.: Pergamon Press.

Ferreiro, E. (1997). The word out of (conceptual) context. In C. Pontecorvo (Ed.), *Writing development: An interdisciplinary view* (pp. 47–59). Amsterdam: John Benjamins.

Ferreiro, E., & Teberosky, A. (1982). *Literacy before schooling* (K. Goodman Castro, Trans.). Exeter, NH: Heinemann. (Original work published 1979)

Ferreiro, E., & Vernon, S. (1992). La distinción palabra/nombre en niños de 4 y 5 años. *Infancia y Aprendizaje, 58*, 15–28.

Fox, B., & Routh, D. (1975). Analyzing spoken language into words, syllables, and phonemes: A developmental study. *Journal of Psycholinguistic Research, 4*, 331–342.

Halliday, M. A. K. (1985). *Spoken and written language*. Hong Kong: Oxford University Press.

Harris, R. (1986). *The origin of writing*. London: Gerald Duckworth.

Hohn, W. E., & Ehri, L. C. (1983). Do alphabet letters help prereaders acquire phonemic segmentation skill? *Journal of Educational Psychology, 75,* 752–762.

Jiménez-González, J. E., & Ortiz, M. (1993). Phonological awareness in learning literacy. *Cognitiva, 5,* 153–170.

Kenstowicz, M. (1993). *Phonology in generative grammar.* Cambridge, Eng.: Blackwell.

Kirtley, C., Bryant, P., MacLean, M., & Bradley, L. (1989). Rhyme, rime and the onset of reading. *Journal of Experimental Child Psychology, 48,* 224–245.

Liberman, I. Y. (1973). Segmentation of the spoken word and reading acquisition. *Bulletin of the Orton Society, 23,* 65–67.

Liberman, I. Y., Shankweiler, D., Fischer, F. W., & Carter, B. (1974). Explicit syllable and phoneme segmentation in the young child. *Journal of Experimental Child Psychology, 18,* 201–212.

Liberman, I. Y., Shankweiler, D., & Liberman, A. M. (1992). The alphabetic principle and learning to read. In D. Shankweiler & I. Y. Liberman (Eds.), *Phonology and reading disability* (pp. 1–33). Ann Arbor: University of Michigan Press.

Lundberg, I., Frost, J., & Petersen, O. P. (1988). Effects of an extensive program for stimulating phonological awareness in preschool children. *Reading Research Quarterly, 23,* 263–284.

MacLean, M., Bryant, P. E., & Bradley, L. (1987). Rhymes, nursery rhymes and reading in early childhood. *Merril-Palmer Quarterly, 33,* 255–282.

Mann, V. A. (1991). Phonological abilities: Effective predictors of future reading ability. In L. Rieben & C. A. Perfetti (Eds.), *Learning to read: Basic research and its implications* (pp. 121–133). Hillsdale, NJ: Lawrence Erlbaum.

Marsh, G., & Mineo, R. (1977). Training preschool children to recognize phonemes in words. *Journal of Educational Psychology, 69,* 748–753.

Morais, J. (Ed.). (1995). Literacy onset in romance language. *Reading and Writing: An Interdisciplinary Journal. 7,* 1.

Morais, J., Cary, L., Alegría, J., & Bertelson, P. (1979). Does awareness of speech as a sequence of phones arise spontaneously? *Cognition, 7,* 323–331.

Olson, D. (1994). *The world on paper: The conceptual and cognitive implications of writing and reading.* London: Cambridge University Press.

Quinteros, G. (1997). *El uso y función de las letras en el periodo pre-alfabético.* Mexico City: Centro de Investigación y de Estudios Avanzados.

Read, C. (1986). *Children's creative spelling.* London: Routledge & Kegan Paul.

Read, C., Zhang, Y., Nie, H., & Ding, B. (1986). The ability to manipulate speech sounds depends on knowing alphabetic writing. *Cognition, 24,* 31–44.

Richards, J. C., Platt, J., & Platt, H. (1992). *Dictionary of language teaching and applied linguistics.* Essex, Eng.: Longman.

Sampson, G. (1985). *Writing systems.* London: Hutchinson.

Scholes, R. J. (1998). The case against phonemic awareness. *Journal of Research in Reading, 21,* 177–188.

Sprenger-Charolles, L. (1991). Word identification strategies in a picture context: Comparisons between "good" and "poor" readers. In L. Rieben & C. A. Perfetti (Eds.), *Learning to read* (pp. 175–187). Hillsdale, NJ: Lawrence Erlbaum.

Stanovich, K., Cunningham, A., & Cramer, B. (1984). Assessing phonological awareness in kindergarten children: Issues of task comparability. *Journal of Experimental Child Psychology, 38,* 175–190.

Teale, W., & Sulzby, E. (Eds.). (1986). *Emergent literacy: Writing and reading.* Norwood, NJ: Ablex.

Treiman, R., & Cassar, M. (1997). Can children and adults focus on sound as opposed to spelling in a phoneme counting task? *Developmental Psychology, 33,* 771–780.

Treiman, R., & Zukowski, A. (1991). Levels of phonological awareness. In S. A. Brady & D. P. Shankweiler (Eds.), *Phonological processes in literacy: A tribute to Isabelle Y. Liberman* (pp. 67–83). Hillsdale, NJ: Lawrence Erlbaum.

Treiman, R., & Zukowski, A. (1996). Children's sensitivity to syllables, onsets, rimes and phonemes. *Journal of Experimental Child Psychology 61,* 193–215.

Tunmer, W. E., & Nesdale, A. R. (1985). Phonemic segmentation skill and beginning reading. *Journal of Educational Psychology, 77,* 417–427.

Vachek, J. (1989). *Written language revisited.* Amsterdam: John Benjamins.

Vellutino, F., & Scanlon, D. (1991). The preeminence of phonologically based skills in learning to read. In S. A. Brady & D. P. Shankweiler (Eds.), *Phonological processes in literacy* (pp. 237–252). Hillsdale, NJ: Lawrence Erlbaum.

Vernon, M. D. (1977). Varieties of deficiencies in the reading process. *Harvard Educational Review, 47,* 396–410.

Vernon, S. (1993). Initial sound/letter correspondences in children's early written productions. *Journal of Research in Childhood Education, 8,* 12–22.

Wagner, R. (1986). Phonological processing abilities and reading: Implications for disabled readers. *Journal of Learning Disabilities, 19,* 623–630.

Williams, J. P. (1980). Teaching decoding with an emphasis on phoneme analysis and phoneme blending. *Journal of Educational Psychology, 72,* 1–15.

Yopp, H. K. (1988). The validity and reliability of phonemic awareness tests. *Reading Research Quarterly, 13,* 159–177.

This study was supported by CONACYT (Mexico), grant number 211085-4724H. Correspondence should be addressed to vernon@sunserver.dsi.uaq.mx or ferreiro@data.net. mx

PART FOUR

Critical Perspectives on Language
and Literacy Education

PART FOUR

Critical Perspectives on Language and Literacy Education

Part Four is a new addition since *Language Issues in Literacy and Bilingual/ Multicultural Education* appeared in 1991 — a change that responds to the proliferation of research in this paradigm within the last decade. In the previous volume, Paulo Friere's and Elsa Auerbach's chapters were considered to represent a broadly sociocultural orientation to language. This classification was justifiable, given a certain parallel between sociocultural and critical perspectives on literacy research: both are concerned with the cultural and social dimensions of literacy, and both usually employ the comprehensive term *literacy* rather than the specific terms *reading* and *writing* to refer to activities involving print. In recent years, however, the perspective of critical literacy has taken on a defining identity of its own. Although researchers in this field may not agree on a precise definition of "critical literacy" as a field, we believe that the chapters we present here share a certain orientation to questions about literacy and language use in society. We agree with Arlette Ingram Willis, who argues in "Reading the World of School Literacy: Contextualizing the Experience of a Young African American Male," that critical literacy is unique in its focus on the role of power relations in literacy instruction and literacy practice.

We thought it fitting that Freire's chapter, "The Adult Literacy Process as Cultural Action for Freedom," lead this section. Freire is arguably the grandfather of the critical approach to literacy and one of its most frequently cited scholars. His work also spawned the related field of critical pedagogy, which focuses on power relations in the activity of teaching and learning regardless of subject area. Because his study of literacy is informed by a larger concern with discrepancies of power and opportunity in society, he often uses literacy in a metaphorical way to refer to the perception and interpretation of nonlinguistic symbols. To engage with this aspect of Freire's work and with critical pedagogy, however, is beyond the scope of this volume. For our purposes, we feel that the importance of his essay lies in the radical method of instruction that it proposes. In reporting the findings from his research on teaching agricultural workers in Latin America, Freire contrasts the critical method of teaching individuals to read and write with "nutritional" models of literacy instruction. In a nutritional model, the illiterate person is seen as empty and sick, needing to be filled up or cured by the instructor. In the model that Freire advocates, learners create their own texts to represent their perceptions of the world. This type of literacy instruction constitutes an "effort towards freedom" that leads individuals to "question the very reality which deprives men the right to speak up" (p. 339).

Glynda Hull, in "Hearing Other Voices: A Critical Assessment of Popular Views on Literacy and Work," also discusses ways that official adult literacy curricula disempower workers. In this critical appraisal of popular views about the relationship between literacy and work, she points out that the public alarm about illiteracy rates in the United States is largely driven by economic concerns and by the belief that a more literate work force is a more productive work force. She also notes that the literacy skills deemed necessary for workers are almost never identified through observations of literacy practices in the actual workplace. Furthermore, workers are often assessed on their literacy skills, and these assessments are then used to determine promotion and pay increases, frequently to the neglect of other aspects of job performance such as interpersonal communication or productivity. Hull encourages her readers to rethink the kind of literacy instruction that workers need, and advocates for curricula that are more sensitive to workers' personal goals for using literacy in their lives, and to the actual literacy demands of their jobs.

In "Toward a Social-Contextual Approach to Family Literacy," Elsa Roberts Auerbach transplants a Freirean perspective to the urban United States by critically examining family literacy programs that expect parents to conform to schools' expectations and practices. Auerbach discerns several false assumptions in this approach to family literacy. Some of these assumptions are that language-minority students do not have access to literacy materials in the home; that effective family literacy requires parents to transfer skills to their children; and that the goal of family literacy programs is to replicate school activities in the home context. These and other related assumptions constitute what Auerbach calls a transmission of school practices model. She devotes much of her chapter to discussing research that challenges this model. She then describes a new conception of family literacy that would support the development of the home language and culture, and empower parents to understand and take an active role in addressing school-related issues.

Arlette Ingram Willis documents a similar institutional failure to show sensitivity to learners' individual experiences and attitudes toward literacy in an analysis of her sons' experiences sharing culturally sensitive material at school. Willis, an African American, applies the perspective of critical literacy to questions of cultural diversity in schools, arguing that in our present multicultural society the role of culture in schooling must be precisely addressed and its complexities defined. The examples that she cites from her own sons' experiences illustrate that children from nonmainstream cultures often must adopt a Eurocentric cultural perspective in order to succeed in school. As one example of how educators can work to make schools more culturally responsive, Willis describes her own college-level course for preservice teachers at the University of Illinois, which she designed around literature written by minority authors and cultural autobiographies authored by her own students. This curriculum is evidence of one step taken toward the transformation of literacy curricula for the inclusiveness and humanization of all students, concepts that are central in a critical approach to literacy.

Finally, we include "Why the 'Monkeys Passage' Bombed: Tests, Genres, and Teaching," Bonny Norton and Pippa Stein's study of variations in South African students' response to a passage on a university entrance exam that lent itself to politically charged interpretations. As a result of the controversial and widely discrepant interpretations that it generated during the piloting of the exam, this passage was removed from the exam. While Norton and Stein's chapter makes only brief reference to the work of theorists in the field of critical literacy, it is an appropriate companion to the other chapters in this section because it reveals the power of assessments to inhibit nuanced and diverse responses to texts. Norton and Stein point out that it would have been hypocritical of policymakers and university administrators to expect that students engage in active and critical reading in their university coursework while admitting them based on an ability to accept passively a single interpretation of texts in the context of assessment.

Taken together, the chapters in this section are a helpful introduction to the field of critical literacy. The authors of these chapters embody a stance toward literacy and language research that questions official institutional doctrines about what language and literacy learners need to succeed as productive members of society. Their research generates findings that have real practical import for educators and researchers concerned with making literacy and language instruction more beneficial to students whose interests may not be served by traditional or prescriptive models of instruction.

EDITORS' NOTE:
CRITICAL PERSPECTIVES ON LANGUAGE AND LITERACY

For further reading about critical approaches to language and literacy and critical pedagogy, we suggest these resources by the Harvard Educational Review:

Lilia I. Bartolomé, "Beyond the Methods Fetish: Toward a Humanizing Pedagogy," Summer 1994, pp. 173–194.

Lisa D. Delpit, "The Silenced Dialogue: Power and Pedagogy in Educating Other People's Children," Summer 1988, pp. 280–298.

Paulo Freire and Donaldo P. Macedo, "A Dialogue: Culture, Language and Race," Fall 1995, pp. 377–402.

Henry A. Giroux, "Doing Cultural Studies: Youth and the Challenge of Pedagogy," Fall 1994, pp. 278–308.

Pepi Leistyna, Arlie Woodrum, and Stephen A. Sherblom, Editors, *Breaking Free: The Transformative Power of Critical Pedagogy,* 1996.

Donaldo Macedo, "Literacy for Stupidification: The Pedagogy of Big Lies," Summer 1993, pp. 183–206.

Peter McLaren, "Culture or Canon? Critical Pedagogy and the Politics of Literacy," Essay Review of *Literacy: Reading the Word and the World* by Paulo Freire and Donaldo Macedo, Spring 1988, pp. 213–234.

The Adult Literacy Process as Cultural Action for Freedom

PAULO FREIRE

EVERY EDUCATIONAL PRACTICE IMPLIES A CONCEPT OF MAN AND THE WORLD

Experience teaches us not to assume that the obvious is clearly understood. So it is with the truism with which we begin: All educational practice implies a theoretical stance on the educator's part. This stance in turn implies — sometimes more, sometimes less explicitly — an interpretation of man and the world. It could not be otherwise. The process of men's orientation in the world involves not just the association of sense images, as for animals. It involves, above all, thought-language; that is, the possibility of the act of knowing through his praxis, by which man transforms reality. For man, this process of orientation in the world can be understood neither as a purely subjective event, nor as an objective or mechanistic one, but only as an event in which subjectivity and objectivity are united. Orientation in the world, so understood, places the question of the purposes of action at the level of critical perception of reality.

If, for animals, orientation in the world means adaptation to the world, for man it means humanizing the world by transforming it. For animals there is no historical sense, no options or values in their orientation in the world; for man there is both a historical and a value dimension. Men have the sense of "project," in contrast to the instinctive routines of animals.

The action of men without objectives, whether the objectives are right or wrong, mythical or demythologized, naive or critical, is not praxis, though it may be orientation in the world. And not being praxis, it is action ignorant both of its own process and of its aim. The interrelation of the awareness of aim and of process is the basis for planning action, which implies methods, objectives, and value options.

Teaching adults to read and write must be seen, analyzed, and understood in this way. The critical analyst will discover in the methods and texts used by educators and students practical value options that betray a philosophy of man, well or poorly outlined, coherent or incoherent. Only someone with a mechanistic mentality,

Harvard Educational Review   Vol. 40   No. 2   May 1970, 205–225

which Marx would call "grossly materialistic," could reduce adult literacy learning to a purely technical action. Such a naive approach would be incapable of perceiving that technique itself as an instrument of men in their orientation in the world is not neutral.

We shall try, however, to prove by analysis the self-evidence of our statement. Let us consider the case of primers used as the basic texts for teaching adults to read and write. Let us further propose two distinct types: a poorly done primer and a good one, according to the genre's own criteria. Let us even suppose that the author of the good primer based the selection of its generative words[1] on a prior knowledge of which words have the greatest resonance for the learner (a practice not commonly found, though it does exist).

Doubtlessly, such an author is already far beyond the colleague who composes his primer with words he himself chooses in his own library. Both authors, however, are identical in a fundamental way. In each case they themselves decompose the given generative words and from the syllables create new words. With these words, in turn, the authors form simple sentences and, little by little, small stories, the so-called reading lessons.

Let us say that the author of the second primer, going one step further, suggests that the teachers who use it initiate discussions about one or another word, sentence, or text with their students.

Considering either of these hypothetical cases we may legitimately conclude that there is an implicit concept of man in the primer's method and content, whether it is recognized by the authors or not. This concept can be reconstructed from various angles. We begin with the fact, inherent in the idea and use of the primer, that it is the teacher who chooses the words and proposes them to the learner. Insofar as the primer is the mediating object between the teacher and students, and the students are to be "filled" with words the teachers have chosen, one can easily detect a first important dimension of the image of man that begins to emerge here. It is the profile of a man whose consciousness is "spatialized," and must be "filled" or "fed" in order to know. This same conception led Sartre, criticizing the notion that "to know is to eat," to exclaim: "*O philosophie alimentaire!*"[2]

This "digestive" concept of knowledge, so common in current educational practice, is found very clearly in the primer.[3] Illiterates are considered "undernourished," not in the literal sense in which many of them really are, but because they lack the "bread of the spirit." Consistent with the concept of knowledge as food, illiteracy is conceived of as a "poison herb," intoxicating and debilitating persons who cannot read or write. Thus, much is said about the "eradication" of illiteracy to cure the disease.[4] In this way, deprived of their character as linguistic signs constitutive of man's thought-language, words are transformed into mere "deposits of vocabulary" — the bread of the spirit that the illiterates are to "eat" and "digest."

This "nutritionist" view of knowledge perhaps also explains the humanitarian character of certain Latin American adult literacy campaigns. If millions of men are illiterate, "starving for letters," "thirsty for words," the word must be *brought* to them to save them from "hunger" and "thirst." The word, according to the naturalistic concept of consciousness implicit in the primer, must be "deposited," not born of the creative effort of the learners. As understood in this concept, man is a passive being, the object of the process of learning to read and write, and not its subject. As object his task is to "study" the so-called reading lessons, which in fact are almost completely alienating and alienated, having so little, if anything, to do with the student's socio-cultural reality.[5]

It would be a truly interesting study to analyze the reading texts being used in private or official adult literacy campaigns in rural and urban Latin America. It would not be unusual to find among such texts sentences and readings like the following random samples:[6]

> *A asa é da ave* — "The wing is of the bird."
> *Eva viu a uva* — "Eva saw the grape."
> *O galo canta* — "The cock crows."
> *O cachorro ladra* — "The dog barks."
> *Maria gosta dos animais* — "Mary likes animals."
> *João cuida das arvores* — "John takes care of the trees."
> *O pai de Carlinhos se chama Antonio. Carlinhos é um bom menino, bem comportado e estudioso* — "Charles's father's name is Antonio. Charles is a good, well-behaved, and studious boy."
> *Ada deu o dedo ao urubu? Duvido, Ada deu o dedo a arara. . . .*[7]
> *Se você trabalha com martelo e prego, tenha cuidado para nao furar o dedo.* — "If you hammer a nail, be careful not to smash your finger."[8]

*   *   *   *   *

Peter did not know how to read. Peter was ashamed. One day, Peter went to school and registered for a night course. Peter's teacher was very good. Peter knows how to read now. Look at Peter's face. [These lessons are generally illustrated.] Peter is smiling. He is a happy man. He already has a good job. Everyone ought to follow his example.

In saying that Peter is smiling because he knows how to read, that he is happy because he now has a good job, and that he is an example for all to follow, the authors establish a relationship between knowing how to read and getting good jobs that, in fact, cannot be borne out. This naïveté reveals, at least, a failure to perceive the structure not only of illiteracy, but of social phenomena in general. Such an approach may admit that these phenomena exist, but it cannot perceive their relationship to the structure of the society in which they are found. It is as if these phenomena were mythical, above and beyond concrete situations, or the results of the intrinsic inferiority of a certain class of men. Unable to grasp contemporary illiteracy as a typical manifestation of the "culture of silence," directly related to underdeveloped structures, this approach cannot offer an objective, critical response to the challenge of illiteracy. Merely teaching men to read and write does not work miracles; if there are not enough jobs for men able to work, teaching more men to read and write will not create them.

One of these readers presents among its lessons the following two texts on consecutive pages without relating them. The first is about May 1st, the Labor Day holiday, on which workers commemorate their struggles. It does not say how or where these are commemorated, or what the nature of the historical conflict was. The main theme of the second lesson is *holidays*. It says that "on these days people ought to go to the beach to swim and sunbathe . . ." Therefore, if May 1st is a holiday, and if on holidays people should go to the beach, the conclusion is that the workers should go swimming on Labor Day, instead of meeting with their unions in the public squares to discuss their problems.

Analysis of these texts reveals, then, a simplistic vision of men, of their world, of the relationship between the two, and of the literacy process that unfolds in that world.

A asa é da ave, Eva viu a uva, o galo canta, and *o cachorro late* are linguistic contexts that, when mechanically memorized and repeated, are deprived of their authentic dimension as thought-language in dynamic interplay with reality. Thus impoverished, they are not authentic expressions of the world.

Their authors do not recognize in the poor classes the ability to know and even create the texts that would express their own thought-language at the level of their perception of the world. The authors repeat with the texts what they do with the words, that is, they introduce them into the learners' consciousness as if it were empty space — once more, the "digestive" concept of knowledge.

Still more, the a-structural perception of illiteracy revealed in these texts exposes the other false view of illiterates as marginal men.[9] Those who consider them marginal must, nevertheless, recognize the existence of a reality to which they are marginal — not only physical space, but historical, social, cultural, and economic realities — that is, the structural dimension of reality. In this way, illiterates have to be recognized as beings "outside of," "marginal to" something, since it is impossible to be marginal to nothing. But being "outside of" or "marginal to" necessarily implies a movement of the one said to be marginal from the center, where he was, to the periphery. This movement, which is an action, presupposes in turn not only an agent but also his reasons. Admitting the existence of men "outside of" or "marginal to" structural reality, it seems legitimate to ask: Who is the author of this movement from the center of the structure to its margin? Do so-called marginal men, among them the illiterates, make the decision to move out to the periphery of society? If so, marginality is an option with all that it involves: hunger, sickness, rickets, pain, mental deficiencies, living death, crime, promiscuity, despair, the impossibility of being. In fact, however, it is difficult to accept that 40 percent of Brazil's population, almost 90 percent of Haiti's, 60 percent of Bolivia's, about 40 percent of Peru's, more than 30 percent of Mexico's and Venezuela's, and about 70 percent of Guatemala's would have made the tragic *choice* of their own marginality as illiterates.[10] If, then, marginality is not by choice, marginal man has been expelled from and kept outside of the social system and is therefore the object of violence.

In fact, however, the social structure as a whole does not "expel," nor is marginal man a "being outside of." He is, on the contrary, a "being inside of," within the social structure, and in a dependent relationship to those whom we call falsely autonomous beings, inauthentic beings-for-themselves.

A less rigorous approach, one more simplistic, less critical, more technicist, would say that it was unnecessary to reflect about what it would consider unimportant questions such as illiteracy and teaching adults to read and write. Such an approach might even add that the discussion of the concept of marginality is an unnecessary academic exercise. In fact, however, it is not so. In accepting the illiterate as a person who exists on the fringe of society, we are led to envision him as a sort of "sick man," for whom literacy would be the "medicine" to cure him, enabling him to "return" to the "healthy" structure from which he has become separated. Educators would be benevolent counselors, scouring the outskirts of the city for the stubborn illiterates, runaways from the good life, to restore them to the forsaken bosom of happiness by giving them the gift of the word.

In the light of such a concept — unfortunately, all too widespread — literacy programs can never be efforts toward freedom; they will never question the very reality that deprives men of the right to speak up — not only illiterates, but all those who are treated as objects in a dependent relationship. These men, illiterate or not, are, in fact, not marginal. What we said before bears repeating: They are not "beings outside of"; they are "beings for another." Therefore the solution to their problem is not to become "beings inside of," but men freeing themselves; for in reality they are not marginal to the structure, but oppressed men within it. Alienated men, they cannot overcome their dependency by "incorporation" into the very structure responsible for their dependency. There is no other road to humanization — theirs as well as everyone else's — but authentic transformation of the dehumanizing structure.

From this last point of view, the illiterate is no longer a person living on the fringe of society, a marginal man, but rather a representative of the dominated strata of society, in conscious or unconscious opposition to those who, in the same structure, treat him as a thing. Thus, also, teaching men to read and write is no longer an inconsequential matter of *ba, be, bi, bo, bu,* of memorizing an alienated word, but a difficult apprenticeship in naming the world.[11]

In the first hypothesis, interpreting illiterates as men marginal to society, the literacy process reinforces the mythification of reality by keeping it opaque and by dulling the "empty consciousness" of the learner with innumerable alienating words and phrases. By contrast, in the second hypothesis — interpreting illiterates as men oppressed within the system — the literacy process, as cultural action for freedom, is an act of knowing in which the learner assumes the role of knowing subject in dialogue with the educator. For this very reason, it is a courageous endeavor to demythologize reality, a process through which men who had previously been submerged in reality begin to emerge in order to reinsert themselves into it with critical awareness.

Therefore the educator must strive for ever greater clarity as to what, at times without his conscious knowledge, illuminates the path of his action. Only in this way will he truly be able to assume the role of one of the subjects of this action and remain consistent in the process.

THE ADULT LITERACY PROCESS AS AN ACT OF KNOWING

To be an act of knowing, the adult literacy process demands among teachers and students a relationship of authentic dialogue. True dialogue unites subjects together in the cognition of a knowable object that mediates between them.

If learning to read and write is to constitute an act of knowing, the learners must assume from the beginning the role of creative subjects. It is not a matter of memorizing and repeating given syllables, words, and phrases, but rather of reflecting critically on the process of reading and writing itself, and on the profound significance of language.

Insofar as language is impossible without thought, and language and thought are impossible without the world to which they refer, the human word is more than mere vocabulary — it is word-and-action. The cognitive dimensions of the literacy process must include the relationships of men with their world. These relationships are the source of the dialectic between the products men achieve in transforming the world and the conditioning that these products in turn exercise on men.

Learning to read and write ought to be an opportunity for men to know what *speaking the word* really means: a human act implying reflection and action. As such it is a primordial human right and not the privilege of a few.[12] Speaking the word is not a true act if it is not at the same time associated with the right of self-expression and world-expression, of creating and re-creating, of deciding and choosing and ultimately participating in society's historical process.

In the culture of silence the masses are "mute," that is, they are prohibited from creatively taking part in the transformations of their society and therefore prohibited from being. Even if they can occasionally read and write because they were "taught" in humanitarian — but not humanist — literacy campaigns, they are nevertheless alienated from the power responsible for their silence.

Illiterates know they are concrete men. They know that they do things. What they do not know in the culture of silence — in which they are ambiguous, dual beings — is that men's actions as such are transforming, creative, and re-creative. Overcome by the myths of this culture, including the myth of their own "natural inferiority," they do not know that *their* action upon the world is also transforming. Prevented from having a "structural perception" of the facts involving them, they do not know that they cannot "have a voice," that is, that they cannot exercise the right to participate consciously in the socio-historical transformation of their society, because their work does not belong to them.

It could be said (and we would agree) that it is not possible to recognize all this apart from praxis, that is, apart from reflection and action, and that to attempt it would be pure idealism. But it is also true that action upon an object must be critically analyzed in order to understand both the object itself and the understanding one has of it. The act of knowing involves a dialectical movement that goes from action to reflection and from reflection upon action to a new action. For the learner to know what he did not know before, he must engage in an authentic process of abstraction by means of which he can reflect on the action-object whole, or, more generally, on forms of orientation in the world. In this process of abstraction, situations representative of how the learner orients himself in the world are proposed to him as the objects of his critique.

As an event calling forth the critical reflection of both the learners and educators, the literacy process must relate *speaking the word* to *transforming reality*, and to man's role in this transformation. Perceiving the significance of that relationship is indispensable for those learning to read and write if we are really committed to liberation. Such a perception will lead the learners to recognize a much greater right than that of being literate. They will ultimately recognize that, as men, they have the right to have a voice.

On the other hand, as an act of knowing, learning to read and write presupposes not only a theory of knowing but a method that corresponds to the theory.

We recognize the indisputable unity between subjectivity and objectivity in the act of knowing. Reality is never just simply the objective datum, the concrete fact, but is also men's perception of it. Once again, this is not a subjectivistic or idealistic affirmation, as it might seem. On the contrary, subjectivism and idealism come into play when the subjective-objective unity is broken.[13]

The adult literacy process as an act of knowing implies the existence of two inter-related contexts. One is the context of authentic dialogue between learners and educators as equally knowing subjects. This is what schools should be — the theoretical context of dialogue. The second is the real, concrete context of facts, the social reality in which men exist.[14]

In the theoretical context of dialogue, the facts presented by the real or concrete context are critically analyzed. This analysis involves the exercise of abstraction, through which, by means of representations of concrete reality, we seek knowledge of that reality. The instrument for this abstraction in our methodology is codification,[15] or representation of the existential situations of the learners.

Codification, on the one hand, mediates between the concrete and theoretical contexts (of reality). On the other hand, as knowable object, it mediates between the knowing subjects, educators and learners, who seek in dialogue to unveil the "action-object wholes."

This type of linguistic discourse must be "read" by anyone who tries to interpret it, even when purely pictorial. As such, it presents what Chomsky calls "surface structure" and "deep structure."

The "surface structure" of codification makes the "action-object whole" explicit in a purely taxonomic form. The first stage of decodification[16] — or reading — is descriptive. At this stage, the "readers" — or decodifiers — focus on the relationship between the categories constituting the codification. This preliminary focus on the surface structure is followed by problematizing the codified situation. This leads the learner to the second and fundamental stage of decodification, the comprehension of the codification's "deep structure." By understanding the codification's "deep structure" the learner can then understand the dialectic that exists between the categories presented in the "surface structure," as well as the unity between the "surface" and "deep" structures.

In our method, the codification initially takes the form of a photograph or sketch that represents a real existent, or an existent constructed by the learners. When this representation is projected as a slide, the learners effect an operation basic to the act of knowing: they gain distance from the knowable object. This experience of distance is undergone as well by the educators, so that educators and learners together can reflect critically on the knowable object that mediates between them. The aim of decodification is to arrive at the critical level of knowing, beginning with the learner's experience of the situation in the "real context."

Whereas the codified representation is the knowable object mediating between knowing subjects, decodification — dissolving the codification into its constituent elements — is the operation by which the knowing subjects perceive relationships between the codification's elements and other facts presented by the real context — relationships that were formerly unperceived. Codification represents a given dimension of reality as individuals live it, and this dimension is proposed for their analysis in a context other than that in which they live it. Codification thus transforms what was a way of life in the real context into "objectum" in the theoretical context. The learners, rather than receive information about this or that fact, analyze aspects of their own existential experience represented in the codification.

Existential experience is a whole. In illuminating one of its angles and perceiving the interrelation of that angle with others, the learners tend to replace a fragmented vision of reality with a total vision. From the point of view of a theory of knowledge, this means that the dynamic between codification of existential situations and decodification involves the learners in a constant re-construction of their former "admiration" of reality.

We do not use the concept "ad-miration" here in the usual way, or in its ethical or aesthetic sense, but with a special philosophical connotation.

To "ad-mire" is to objectify the "not-I." It is a dialectical operation that characterizes man as man, differentiating him from the animal. It is directly associated with the creative dimension of his language. To "ad-mire" implies that man stands over against his "not-I" in order to understand it. For this reason, there is no act of knowing without "ad-miration" of the object to be known. If the act of knowing is a dynamic act — and no knowledge is ever complete — then in order to know, man not only "ad-mires" the object, but must always be "re-ad-miring" his former "ad-miration." When we "re-ad-mire" our former "ad-miration" (always an "ad-miration *of* "), we are simultaneously "ad-miring" the act of "ad-miring" and the object "ad-mired," so that we can overcome the errors we made in our former "ad-miration." This "re-ad-miration" leads us to a perception of an anterior perception.

In the process of decodifying representations of their existential situations and perceiving former perceptions, the learners gradually, hesitatingly, and timorously place in doubt the opinion they held of reality and replace it with a more and more critical knowledge thereof.

Let us suppose that we were to present to groups from among the dominated classes codifications that portray their imitation of the dominators' cultural models — a natural tendency of the oppressed consciousness at a given moment.[17] The dominated persons would perhaps, in self-defense, deny the truth of the codification. As they deepened their analysis, however, they would begin to perceive that their apparent imitation of the dominators' models is a result of their interiorization of these models and, above all, of the myths of the "superiority" of the dominant classes that cause the dominated to feel inferior. What in fact is pure interiorization appears in a naive analysis to be imitation. At bottom, when the dominated classes reproduce the dominators' style of life, it is because the dominators live "within" the dominated. The dominated can eject the dominators only by getting distance from them and objectifying them. Only then can they recognize them as their antithesis.[18]

To the extent, however, that interiorization of the dominators' values is not only an individual phenomenon, but a social and cultural one, ejection must be achieved by a type of cultural action in which culture negates culture. That is, culture, as an interiorized product that in turn conditions men's subsequent acts, must become the object of men's knowledge so that they can perceive its conditioning power. Cultural action occurs at the level of superstructure. It can only be understood by what Althusser calls "the dialectic of overdetermination."[19] This analytic tool prevents us from falling into mechanistic explanations or, what is worse, mechanistic action. An understanding of it precludes surprise that cultural myths remain after the infrastructure is transformed, even by revolution.

When the creation of a new culture is appropriate but impeded by interiorized cultural "residue," this residue, these myths, must be expelled by means of culture. Cultural action and cultural revolution, at different stages, constitute the modes of this expulsion.

The learners must discover the reasons behind many of their attitudes toward cultural reality and thus confront cultural reality in a new way. "Re-ad-miration" of their former "ad-miration" is necessary in order to bring this about. The learners' capacity for critical knowing — well beyond mere opinion — is established in the process of unveiling their relationships with the historical-cultural world *in* and *with* which they exist.

We do not mean to suggest that critical knowledge of man-world relationships arises as a verbal knowledge outside of praxis. Praxis is involved in the concrete situations that are codified for critical analysis. To analyze the codification in its "deep structure" is, for this very reason, to reconstruct the former praxis and to become capable of a new and different praxis. The relationship between the *theoretical context*, in which codified representations of objective facts are analyzed, and the *concrete context*, where these facts occur, has to be made real.

Such education must have the character of commitment. It implies a movement from the *concrete context* that provides objective facts, to the *theoretical context* where these facts are analyzed in depth, and back to the *concrete context* where men experiment with new forms of praxis.

It might seem as if some of our statements defend the principle that, whatever the level of the learners, they ought to reconstruct the process of human knowing in absolute terms. In fact, when we consider adult literacy learning or education in general as an act of knowing, we are advocating a synthesis between the educator's maximally systematized knowing and the learners' minimally systematized knowing — a synthesis achieved in dialogue. The educator's role is to propose problems about the codified existential situations in order to help the learners arrive at a more and more critical view of their reality. The educator's responsibility as conceived by this philosophy is thus greater in every way than that of his colleague whose duty is to transmit information that the learners memorize. Such an educator can simply repeat what he has read, and often misunderstood, since education for him does not mean an act of knowing.

The first type of educator, on the contrary, is a knowing subject, face to face with other knowing subjects. He can never be a mere memorizer, but rather a person constantly readjusting his knowledge, who calls forth knowledge from his students. For him, education is a pedagogy of knowing. The educator whose approach is mere memorization is anti-dialogic; his act of transmitting knowledge is inalterable. For the educator who experiences the act of knowing together with his students, in contrast, dialogue is the seal of the act of knowing. He is aware, however, that not all dialogue is in itself the mark of a relationship of true knowledge.

Socratic intellectualism — which mistook the definition of the concept for knowledge of the thing defined and this knowledge as virtue — did not constitute a true pedagogy of knowing, even though it was dialogic. Plato's theory of dialogue failed to go beyond the Socratic theory of the definition as knowledge, even though for Plato one of the necessary conditions for knowing was that man be capable of a *prise de conscience*, and though the passage from *doxa* to *logos* was indispensable for man to achieve truth. For Plato, the prise de conscience did not refer to what man knew or did not know or knew badly about his dialectical relationship with the world; it was concerned rather with what man once knew and forgot at birth. To know was to remember or recollect forgotten knowledge. The apprehension of both doxa and logos, and the overcoming of doxa by logos occurred not in the man-world relationship, but in the effort to remember or rediscover a forgotten logos.

For dialogue to be a method of true knowledge, the knowing subjects must approach reality scientifically in order to seek the dialectical connections that explain the form of reality. Thus, to know is not to remember something previously known and now forgotten. Nor can doxa be overcome by logos apart from the dialectical relationship of man with his world, apart from men's reflective action upon the world.

To be an act of knowing, then, the adult literacy process must engage the learners in the constant problematizing of their existential situations. This problematizing employs "generative words" chosen by specialized educators in a preliminary investigation of what we call the "minimal linguistic universe" of the future learners. The words are chosen (a) for their pragmatic value, that is, as linguistic signs that command a common understanding in a region or area of the same city or country (in the United States, for instance, the word *soul* has a special significance in Black areas that it does not have among Whites), and (b) for their phonetic difficulties that will gradually be presented to those learning to read and write. Finally, it is important that the first generative word be trisyllabic. When it is divided into its syllables, each one constituting a syllabic family, the learners can experiment with various syllabic combinations even at first sight of the word.

Having chosen seventeen generative words,[20] the next step is to codify seventeen existential situations familiar to the learners. The generative words are then worked into the situations one by one in the order of their increasing phonetic difficulty. As we have already emphasized, these codifications are knowable objects that mediate between the knowing subjects, educator-learners, learner-educators. Their act of knowing is elaborated in the *círculo de cultura* (cultural discussion group) that functions as the theoretical context.

In Brazil, before analyzing the learners' existential situations and the generative words contained in them, we proposed the codified theme of man-world relationships in general.[21] In Chile, at the suggestion of Chilean educators, this important dimension was discussed concurrently with learning to read and write. What is important is that the person learning words be concomitantly engaged in a critical analysis of the social framework in which men exist. For example, the word *favela* in Rio de Janeiro, Brazil, and the word *callampa* in Chile, represent, each with its own nuances, the same social, economic, and cultural reality of the vast numbers of slum dwellers in those countries. If favela and callampa are used as generative words for the people of Brazilian and Chilean slums, the codifications will have to represent slum situations.

There are many people who consider slum dwellers marginal, intrinsically wicked, and inferior. To such people we recommend the profitable experience of discussing the slum situation with slum dwellers themselves. As some of these critics are often simply mistaken, it is possible that they may rectify their mythical clichés and assume a more scientific attitude. They may avoid saying that the illiteracy, alcoholism, and crime of the slum, its sickness, infant mortality, learning deficiencies, and poor hygiene reveal the "inferior nature" of its inhabitants. They may even end up realizing that if intrinsic evil exists it is part of the structures, and that it is the structures that need to be transformed.

It should be pointed out that the Third World as a whole, and more in some parts than in others, suffers from the same misunderstanding from certain sectors of the so-called metropolitan societies. They see the Third World as the incarnation of evil, the primitive, the devil, sin, and sloth — in sum, as historically unviable without the director societies. Such a Manichean attitude is at the source of the impulse to "save" the "demon-possessed" Third World, "educating it" and "correcting its thinking" according to the director societies' own criteria.

The expansionist interests of the director societies are implicit in such notions. These societies can never relate to the Third World as partners, since partnership presupposed equals, no matter how different the equal parties may be, and can never be established between parties antagonistic to each other.

Thus, "salvation" of the Third World by the director societies can only mean its domination, whereas in its legitimate aspiration to independence lies its utopian vision: to save the director societies in the very act of freeing itself.

In this sense, the pedagogy that we defend, conceived in a significant area of the Third World, is itself a utopian pedagogy. By this very fact it is full of hope, for to be utopian is not to be merely idealistic or impractical, but rather to engage in denunciation and annunciation. Our pedagogy cannot do without a vision of man and of the world. It formulates a scientific humanist conception that finds its expression in a dialogical praxis in which the teachers and learners together, in the act of analyzing a dehumanizing reality, denounce it while announcing its transformation in the name of the liberation of man.

For this very reason, denunciation and annunciation in this utopian pedagogy are not meant to be empty words, but a historic commitment. Denunciation of a dehumanizing situation today increasingly demands precise scientific understanding of that situation. Likewise, the annunciation of its transformation increasingly requires a theory of transforming action. However, neither act by itself implies the transformation of the denounced reality or the establishment of that which is announced. Rather, as a moment in a historical process, the announced reality is already present in the act of denunciation and annunciation.[22]

That is why the utopian character of our educational theory and practice is as permanent as education itself, which, for us, is cultural action. Its thrust toward denunciation and annunciation cannot be exhausted when the reality denounced today cedes its place tomorrow to the reality previously announced in the denunciation. When education is no longer utopian, that is, when it no longer embodies the dramatic unity of denunciation and annunciation, it is either because the future has no more meaning for men, or because men are afraid to risk living the future as creative overcoming of the present, which has become old.

The more likely explanation is generally the latter. That is why some people today study all the possibilities that the future contains, in order to "domesticate" it and keep it in line with the present, which is what they intend to maintain. If there is any anguish in director societies hidden beneath the cover of their cold technology, it springs from their desperate determination that their metropolitan status be preserved in the future. Among the things that the Third World may learn from the metropolitan societies there is this that is fundamental: not to replicate those societies when its current utopia becomes actual fact.

When we defend such a conception of education — realistic precisely to the extent that it is utopian — that is, to the extent that it denounced what in fact is, and finds therefore between denunciation and its realization the time of its praxis — we are attempting to formulate a type of education that corresponds to the specifically human mode of being, which is historical.

There is no annunciation without denunciation, just as every denunciation generates annunciation. Without the latter, hope is impossible. In an authentic utopian vision, however, hoping does not mean folding one's arms and waiting. Waiting is only possible when one, filled with hope, seeks through reflective action to achieve that announced future that is being born within the denunciation.

That is why there is no genuine hope in those who intend to make the future repeat their present, nor in those who see the future as something predetermined. Both have a "domesticated" notion of history: the former because they want to stop time; the latter because they are certain about a future they already "know." Utopian hope, on the contrary, is engagement full of risk. That is why the dominators, who merely denounce those who denounce them, and who have nothing to announce but the preservation of the status quo, can never be utopian nor, for that matter, prophetic.[23]

A utopian pedagogy of denunciation and annunciation such as ours will have to be an act of knowing the denounced reality at the level of alphabetization and post-alphabetization, which are in each case cultural action. That is why there is such emphasis on the continual problematization of the learners' existential situations as represented in the codified images. The longer the problematization proceeds, and the more the subjects enter into the "essence" of the problematized object, the more they are able to unveil this essence. The more they unveil it, the more their awakening consciousness deepens, thus leading to the "conscientization" of the situation by the poor classes. Their critical self-insertion into reality, that is, their conscientization, makes the transformation of their state of apathy into the utopian state of *denunciation* and *annunciation* a viable project.

One must not think, however, that learning to read and write precedes conscientization, or vice versa. Conscientization occurs simultaneously with the literacy or postliteracy process. It must be so. In our educational method, the word is not something static or disconnected from men's existential experience, but a dimension of their thought-language about the world. That is why, when they participate critically in analyzing the first generative words linked with their existential experience, when they focus on the syllabic families that result from that analysis, when they perceive the mechanism of the syllabic combinations of their language, the learners finally discover, in the various possibilities of combination, their own words. Little by little, as these possibilities multiply, the learners, through mastery of new generative words, expand both their vocabulary and their capacity for expression by the development of their creative imagination.[24]

In some areas in Chile undergoing agrarian reform, the peasants participating in the literacy programs wrote words with their tools on the dirt roads where they were working. They composed the words from the syllabic combinations they were learning. "These men are sowers of the word," said María Edi Ferreira, a sociologist from the Santiago team working at the Institute of Training and Research in Agrarian Reform. Indeed, they were not only sowing words, but discussing ideas, and coming to understand their role in the world better and better.

We asked one of these "sowers of words," finishing the first level of literacy classes, why he hadn't learned to read and write before the agrarian reform.

"Before the agrarian reform, my friend," he said, "I didn't even think. Neither did my friends."

"Why?" we asked.

"Because it wasn't possible. We lived under orders. We only had to carry out orders. We had nothing to say," he replied emphatically.

The simple answer of this peasant is a very clear analysis of "the culture of silence." In the culture of silence, to exist is only to live. The body carries out orders from above. Thinking is difficult, speaking the word, forbidden.

"When all this land belonged to one *latifundio*," said another man in the same conversation, "there was no reason to read and write. We weren't responsible for anything. The boss gave the orders and we obeyed. Why read and write? Now it's a different story. Take me, for example. In the *asentamiento*,[25] I am responsible not only for my work like all the other men, but also for tool repairs. When I started I couldn't read, but I soon realized that I needed to read and write. You can't imagine what it was like to go to Santiago to buy parts. I couldn't get orientated. I was afraid of everything — afraid of the big city, of buying the wrong thing, of being cheated. Now it's all different."

Observe how precisely this peasant described his former experience as an illiterate: his mistrust, his magical (though logical) fear of the world, his timidity. And observe the sense of security with which he repeats, "Now it's all different."

"What did you feel, my friend," we asked another "sower of words" on a different occasion, "when you were able to write and read your first word?"

"I was happy because I discovered I could make words speak," he replied.

Dario Salas reports,[26] "In our conversations with peasants we were struck by the images they used to express their interest and satisfaction about becoming literate. For example, 'Before we were blind, now the veil has fallen from our eyes'; 'I came only to learn how to sign my name. I never believed I would be able to read, too, at my age'; 'Before, letters seemed like little puppets. Today they say something to me, and I can make them talk.'"

"It is touching," continues Salas, "to observe the delight of the peasants as the world of words opens to them. Sometimes they would say, 'We're so tired our heads ache, but we don't want to leave here without learning to read and write.'"[27]

The following words were taped during research on "generative themes."[28] They are an illiterate's decodification of a codified existential situation:

> You see a house there, sad, as if it were abandoned. When you see a house with a child in it, it seems happier. It gives more joy and peace to people passing by. The father of the family arrives home from work exhausted, worried, bitter, and his little boy comes to meet him with a big hug, because a little boy is not stiff like a big person. The father already begins to be happier just from seeing his children. Then he really enjoys himself. He is moved by his son's wanting to please him. The father becomes more peaceful, and forgets his problems.

Note once again the simplicity of expression, both profound and elegant, in the peasant's language. These are the people considered absolutely ignorant by the proponents of the "digestive" concept of literacy.

In 1968, an Uruguayan team published a small book, *You Live as You Can* (*Se Vive como se Puede*), whose contents are taken from the tape recordings of literacy classes for urban dwellers. Its first edition of three thousand copies was sold out in Montevideo in fifteen days, as was the second edition. The following is an excerpt from this book:

THE COLOR OF WATER

> Water? Water? What is water used for?
> "Yes, yes, we saw it (in the picture)"
> "Oh, my native village, so far away . . ."
> "Do you remember that village?"
> "The stream where I grew up, called Dead Friar . . . you know, I grew up there, a childhood moving from one place to another . . . the color of the water brings back good memories, beautiful memories."
> "What is the water used for?"
> "It is used for washing. We used it to wash clothes, and the animals in the fields used to go there to drink, and we washed ourselves there, too."
> "Did you also use the water for drinking?"
> "Yes, when we were at the stream and had no other water to drink, we drank from the stream. I remember once in 1945 a plague of locusts came from some-

where, and we had to fish them out of the water. . . . I was small, but I remember taking out the locusts like this, with my two hands — and I had no others. And I remember how hot the water was when there was a drought and the stream was almost dry . . . the water was dirty, muddy, and hot, with all kinds of things in it. But we had to drink it or die of thirst."

The whole book is like this, pleasant in style, with great strength of expression of the world of its authors, those anonymous people, "sowers of words," seeking to emerge from "the culture of silence."

Yes, these ought to be the reading texts for people learning to read and write, and not "Eva saw the grape," "The bird's wing," "If you hammer a nail, be careful not to hit your fingers." Intellectualist prejudices and above all class prejudices are responsible for the naive and unfounded notions that the people cannot write their own texts, or that a tape of their conversations is valueless since their conversations are impoverished of meaning. Comparing what the "sowers of words" said in the above references with what is generally written by specialist authors of reading lessons, we are convinced that only someone with very pronounced lack of taste or a lamentable scientific incompetency would choose the specialists' texts.

Imagine a book written entirely in this simple, poetic, free, language of the people, a book on which interdisciplinary teams would collaborate in the spirit of true dialogue. The role of the teams would be to elaborate specialized sections of the book in problematic terms. For example, a section on linguistics would deal simply, though not simplistically, with questions fundamental to the learners' critical understanding of language. Let me emphasize again that since one of the important aspects of adult literacy work is the development of the capacity for expression, the section on linguistics would present themes for the learners to discuss, ranging from the increase of vocabulary to questions about communication — including the study of synonyms and antonyms, with its analysis of words in the linguistic context, and the use of metaphor, of which the people are such masters. Another section might provide the tools for a sociological analysis of the content of the texts.

These texts would not, of course, be used for mere mechanical reading, which leaves the readers without any understanding of what is real. Consistent with the nature of this pedagogy, they would become the object of analysis in reading seminars.

Add to all this the great stimulus it would be for those learning to read and write, as well as for students on more advanced levels, to know that they were reading and discussing the work of their own companions.

To undertake such a work, it is necessary to have faith in the people, solidarity with them. It is necessary to be utopian, in the sense in which we have used the word.

NOTES

1. In languages like Portuguese or Spanish, words are composed syllabically. Thus, every non-monosyllabic word is, technically, *generative*, in the sense that other words can be constructed from its de-composed syllables. For a word to be authentically generative, however, certain conditions must be present, which will be discussed in a later section of this article. [At the phonetic level, the term *generative word* is properly applicable only with regard to a sound-syllabic

reading methodology, while the thematic application is universal. See Sylvia Ashton-Warner's *Teacher* (1963; rpt. London: Virago, 1980) for a different treatment of the concept of generative words at the thematic level. — Editor]

2. Jean Paul Sartre, *Situations I* (Paris: Librairie Gallimard, 1974), p. 31.

3. The digestive concept of knowledge is suggested by "controlled readings" by classes that consist only of lectures; by the use of memorized dialogues in language learning; by bibliographical notes that indicate not only which chapter, but which lines and words are to be read; by the methods of evaluating the students' progress in learning.

4. See Paulo Freire, "La alfabetización de adultos, crítica de su visión ingenua; comprensión de su visión crítica," in *Introducción a la Acción Cultural* (Santiago: ICIRA, 1969).

5. There are two noteworthy exceptions among these primers: 1) in Brazil, *Viver e Lutar*, developed by a team of specialists of the Basic Education Movement, sponsored by the National Conference of Bishops. (This reader became the object of controversy after it was banned as subversive by the then governor of Guanabara, Carlos Lacerda, in 1963.) 2) in Chile, the ESPIGA collection, despite some small defects. The collection was organized by Jefatura de Planes Extraordinarios de Educación de Adultos, of the Public Education Ministry.

6. Since at the time this article was written the writer did not have access to the primers, and was, therefore, vulnerable to recording phrases imprecisely or to confusing the author of one or another primer, it was thought best not to identify the authors or the titles of the books.

7. [The English here would be nonsensical, as is the Portuguese, the point being the emphasis on the consonant "d." — Editor]

8. The author may even have added here, "If, however, this should happen, apply a little mercurochrome."

9. [The Portuguese word here translated as *marginal man* is *marginado*. This has a passive sense: he who has been made marginal, or sent outside society, as well as the sense of a state of existence on the fringe of society. — Translator]

10. *La Situación Educativa en América Latina*, Cuadro No. 20 (Paris: UNESCO, 1960), p. 265.

11. [Here Freire stresses that learning to read and write is not just a mechanical acquisition of decoding skills, using the example of a decontextualized "family" of syllables. "Families" of syllables are often used in syllabic languages such as Portuguese and Spanish. — Editor]

12. Freire, "La alfabetización de adultos."

13. "There are two ways to fall into idealism: The one consists of dissolving the real in subjectivity; the other in denying all real subjectivity in the interests of objectivity." Jean Paul Sartre, *Search for a Method*, trans. Hazel E. Barnes (New York: Vintage Books, 1968), p. 33.

14. See Karel Kosik, *Dialéctica de lo Concreto* (Mexico: Grijalbo, 1967).

15. [*Codification* refers alternatively to the imaging, or the image itself, of some significant aspect of the learner's concrete reality (of a slum dwelling, for example). As such, it becomes both the object of the teacher-learner dialogue and the context for the introduction of the generative word. — Editor]

16. [*Decodification* refers to a process of description and interpretation, whether of printed words, pictures, or other *codifications*. As such, decodification and decodifying are distinct from the process of decoding, or word-recognition. — Editor]

17. Re the oppressed consciousness, see: Frantz Fanon, *The Wretched of the Earth* (New York: Grove Press, 1968); Albert Memmi, *Colonizer and the Colonized* (New York: Orion Press, 1965); and Paulo Freire, *Pedagogy of the Oppressed* (New York: Seabury Press, 1970).

18. See Fanon, *The Wretched of the Earth*; Freire, *Pedagogy of the Oppressed*.

19. See Louis Althussser, *Pour Marx* (Paris: Librairie François Maspero, 1965); and Paulo Freire, *Annual Report: Activities for 1968, Agrarian Reform, Training and Research Institute ICIRA, Chile*, trans. John Dewitt (Cambridge, MA: Center for the Study of Development and Social Change, 1969; mimeographed).

20. We observed in Brazil and Spanish America, especially Chile, that no more than seventeen words were necessary for teaching adults to read and write syllabic languages like Portuguese and Spanish.

21. See Paulo Freire, *Educação como Prática da Liberdade* (Rio de Janeiro: Paz e Terra, 1967); Chilean edition (Santiago: ICIRA, 1969).

22. Re the utopian dimension of denunciation and proclamation, see Lescek Kolakowski, *Toward a Marxist Humanism* (New York: Grove Press, 1969).

23. "The right, as a conservative force, needs no utopia; its essence is the affirmation of existing conditions — a fact and not a utopia — or else the desire to revert to a state which was once an accomplished fact. The Right strives to idealize actual conditions, not to change them. What it needs is fraud not utopia." Kolakowksi, *Toward a Marxist Humanism*, pp. 71–72.

24. "We have observed that the study of the creative aspect of language use develops the assumption that linguistic and mental process are virtually identical, language providing the primary means for free expansion of thought and feeling, as well as for the functioning of creative imagination." Noam Chomsky, *Cartesian Linguistics* (New York: Harper & Row, 1966), p. 31.

25. After the disappropriation of lands in the agrarian reform in Chile, the peasants who were salaried workers on the large *latifundia* became "settlers" *(asentados)* during a three-year period in which they received varied assistance from the government through the Agrarian Reform Corporation. This period of "settlement" *(asentamiento)* precedes that of assigning lands to the peasants. This policy is now changing. The phase of settlement of the lands is being abolished, in favor of an immediate distribution of lands to the peasants. The Agrarian Reform Corporation will continue, nevertheless, to aid the peasants.

26. Dario Salas, "Algumas experiencias vividas na Supervisão de Educação básica," in *A alfabetizção funcional no Chile*. Report to UNESCO, November 1968; introduction by Paulo Freire.

27. Salas refers here to one of the best adult education programs organized by the Agrarian Reform Corporation in Chile, in strict collaboration with the Ministry of Education and ICIRA. Fifty peasants receive boarding and instruction scholarships for a month. The courses center on discussions of the local, regional, and national situations.

28. An analysis of the objectives and methodology of the investigation of generative themes lies outside the scope of this chapter, but is dealt with in the author's work, *Pedagogy of the Oppressed*.

The author gratefully acknowledges the contributions of Loretta Slover, who translated this paper, and João da Veiga Coutinho and Robert Riordan, who assisted in the preparation of the manuscript.

Hearing Other Voices:
A Critical Assessment of Popular Views
on Literacy and Work

GLYNDA HULL

Interviewer: What about reading and writing? People are always saying that you need reading and writing for whatever you do. Do you need reading and writing skills in banking?

Jackie: I don't think so, 'cause, say, if you don't know how to spell somebody's name, when they first come up to you, they have to give you their California ID. So you could look on there and put it in the computer like that . . . push it in on those buttons.

Alma: But you still gonna have to look at it and read and write. . . . You've got to read those numbers when you cash their money; that's reading and writing. . . . If you can't read and write, you're not going to get hired no way.

Jackie: That's true.

Jackie and Alma, students in a vocational program on banking and finance, disagree about the nature and extent of the reading and writing actually involved in being a bank teller. They do agree, however, that literacy (or some credential attesting to it) would be a requirement for getting hired in the first place, even if such skills were unimportant in carrying out the job itself. From what I can tell by examining popular literature that is noteworthy for its doomsday tone, Jackie and Alma are right. There is consensus among employers, government officials, and literacy providers that U.S. workers are "illiterate" to a disturbing extent. They agree further that higher levels of literacy are increasingly needed for many types of work, and that literacy tests, "audits," and instruction are, therefore, necessary phenomena in the workplace.

I find most current characterizations of workplace (il)literacy troublesome and harmful, and in this chapter, I hope to show why. To begin, I will illustrate some widely held assumptions about literacy, work, and workers — the debatable though largely uncontested beliefs that turn up again and again in policy statements, program descriptions, and popular articles. Most troubling is the now commonplace assertion, presented as a statement of fact, that because they apparently lack literacy and other

Harvard Educational Review Vol. 63 No. 1 Spring 1993, 20–49

"basic" skills, U.S. workers can be held accountable for our country's lagging economy and the failure of its businesses to compete domestically and internationally. I want to give space to this dominant rhetoric — the call to arms by leaders in business, industry, and government to educate U.S. workers before it is too late — because efforts now well under way to design, implement, and evaluate workplace literacy programs are based largely on these notions.

In the rest of this chapter, I hope to complicate and challenge these views. Drawing on recent sociocognitive and historical research on literacy and work, I suggest that many current characterizations of literacy, of literacy at work, and of workers as illiterate and therefore deficient are inaccurate, incomplete, and misleading. I argue that we have not paid enough attention, as we measure reading rates, design curricula, and construct lists of essential skills, to how people experience instructional programs and to how they accomplish work. Nor have we often or critically examined how literacy can play a role in promoting economic productivity or in facilitating personal empowerment in the context of particular work situations and training for work. Nor is it common, in studies of work or of reading and writing at work, to acknowledge the perspectives of workers — to discover the incentives and disincentives they perceive and experience for acquiring and exercising literate skills.

Alternate points of view and critical reassessments are essential if we are ever to create frameworks for understanding literacy in relation to work; if we are ever to design literacy programs that have any chance of speaking to the needs and aspirations of workers as well as employers; and, most importantly, if we are ever to create structures for participation in education and work that are equitable and democratic. The main point of this article is that we must allow different voices to be heard, voices like those of Alma and Jackie. We must see how different stories and other voices can amend, qualify, and fundamentally challenge the popular, dominant myths of literacy and work.

CURRENT VIEWS ON WORKPLACE LITERACY

In the following sections I present some widespread, popular conceptions of literacy and its relationships to work. To illustrate what I will call the "popular discourse" of workplace literacy — the common values and viewpoints reflected in currently dominant ways of talking and writing about the issue — I quote directly from policy documents, newspapers, magazines, and interviews.[1] In this way, I hope to capture the voices and suggest something of the ideologies that dominate current debates about education and work. I view the arguments and ideologies represented by these quotations as examples of what Giroux and McLaren (1989) have described more generally as "the conservative discourse of schooling" (p. xiv), wherein public schools are defined as "agents of social discipline and economic regulation" (p. xv) that are valued only insofar as they turn out workers with the skills, knowledge, habits, and attitudes thought essential in terms of today's economy. I label the discourse on literacy and work "popular" rather than "conservative" to suggest how persuasive and omnipresent and, well, popular these ways of thinking and talking about workers and literacy have become. Not only do died-in-the-wool conservatives or right-wingers adhere to this discourse, but concerned teachers, committed literacy specialists, well-meaning businesspeople, eager students, interested academics, progressive politicians, worried parents, and a host of others as well — many people who don't necessarily think of themselves as conservers of the status quo.

"Workers Lack Literacy"

The most pervasive and unquestioned belief about literacy in relation to work is simply that workers do not possess the important literacy skills needed in current and future jobs. Here are examples:

> "Millions of Americans are locked out of good jobs, community participation and the democratic process because they lack adequate reading and writing skills," said Dale Johnson, spokesman for the Working Group on Adult Literacy. "Only leadership from the Presidential level can assure that the literacy needs of all Americans will be met." (Fiske, 1988, p. 12)
>
> Anyone who has hired new employees or tried to retrain veteran ones is painfully aware of the problem. As much as a quarter of the American labor force — anywhere from 20 million to 27 million adults — lacks the basic reading, writing and math skills necessary to perform in today's increasingly complex job market. One out of every 4 teenagers drops out of high school, and of those who graduate, 1 out of every 4 has the equivalent of an eighth-grade education. How will they write, or even read, complicated production memos for robotized assembly lines? How will they be able to fill backlogged service orders? (Gorman, 1988, p. 56)
>
> The Department of Education estimates that there are about 27,000,000 adult Americans who can't really read. Almost all of them can sign their names and maybe spell out a headline. Most aren't totally illiterate the way we used to define illiteracy. But they can't read the label on a medicine bottle. Or fill out a job application. Or write a report. Or read the instructions on the operation of a piece of equipment. Or the safety directions in a factory. Or a memo from the boss. Maybe they even have trouble reading addresses in order to work as a messenger or delivery man. Certainly they can't work in an office. (Lacy, 1985, p. 10)

Such accounts are exceedingly common: the shocking illustrations of seemingly basic, taken-for-granted skills that current workers and recent graduates lack; the apparently "hard" evidence that these illustrations apply to large numbers of people; and the frightening implication that, given the severity of the deficits, it is almost too late to solve this enormous problem. Notice the constant emphasis on deficits — what people are unable to do, what they lack, how they fail — and the causal relationship assumed between those deficits and people's performance at work.

Articles reporting worker illiteracy also often specify which groups among the U.S. population will dominate in future work — women, people of color, and immigrants — and then make the point that, since these groups are likely to have the poorest skills, literacy-related problems in the workplace will likely worsen:

> The years of picky hiring are over. Vicious competition for all sorts of workers — entry-level, skilled, seasoned — has begun. Employers must look to the nonmale, the

nonwhite, the nonyoung. There may be a push for non-citizens as well: over the next 10 years . . . only 15% of work force entrants will be native-born white males.

Building a new, more diverse work force and making it tick will be one of corporate America's biggest challenges in the decade ahead. (Ehrlich & Garland, 1988, pp. 107–108)

A growing share of our new workers will come from groups where human resource investments have been historically deficient — minorities, women, and immigrants. Employers will increasingly have to reach into the ranks of the less advantaged to obtain their entry-level work force, frequently those with deficient basic skills. (Former Secretary of Labor Ann McLaughlin, quoted in *The Bottom Line*, 1988, p. ii)

More and more, American employers will no longer enjoy the luxury of selecting from a field of workers with strong basic skills. The demand for labor will create opportunities for those who are less skilled; the disadvantaged will move up the labor queue and be hired in spite of obvious skill deficiencies. (Carnevale, Gainer, & Meltzer, 1988, p. 2)

U.S. employers, such excerpts suggest, feel put upon and without options; they have no choice now but to hire undesirables like the "nonmale, the nonwhite, the nonyoung" — despite their fears that such people are woefully unprepared.[2] And, not surprisingly, fears that new workers are unprepared are accompanied by talk about the competencies that prepared workers ought ideally to exhibit.

"Literacy Means Basic Skills and More"

In the popular discourse, one often hears of deficits in "basic skills." Although what is meant by a basic skill is not always explained, the examples of such skills that are often given — being able to read the address on a letter, fill out a job application, decipher supermarket labels — suggest literate abilities that are basic in the sense of being simple and fundamental, involving the decoding or encoding of brief texts within a structured task or carrying out elementary addition and subtraction calculations. But it is also common to hear claims that the skills gap extends well beyond basic skills. According to this argument, the problem is not basic skills traditionally and narrowly defined, but basic skills amplified, expanded to include those more complex competencies required for an information age and in reorganized workplaces. The alarm is sounded this way:

The jobs created between 1987 and 2000 will be substantially different from those in existence today: a number of jobs in the least-skilled job classes will disappear while high-skilled professions will grow rapidly. Overall, the skill mix of the economy will be moving rapidly upscale, with most new jobs demanding more education and higher levels of language, math, and reasoning skills. (Johnston & Packer, 1987, p. 96)

Qualifications for today's middle- and low-wage jobs are rising even more rapidly than in the past. In 1965, a car mechanic needed to understand 5,000 pages of service manuals to fix any automobile on the road; today, he must be able to decipher 465,000 pages of technical text, the equivalent of 250 big-city telephone books. (Whitman, Shapiro, Taylor, Saltzman, & Auster, 1989, p. 46)

Reading, writing and arithmetic . . . are just the beginning. Today's jobs also require greater judgment on the part of workers. Clerks at Hartford's Travelers insurance company no longer just type endless claim forms and pass them along for approval by someone else. Instead they are expected to settle a growing number of
minor claims on the spot with a few deft punches of the computer keyboard. Now,
says Bob Feen, director of training at Travelers: "Entry-level clerks have to be capable of using information and making decisions." (Gorman, 1988, p. 57)

The U.S. Department of Labor and the American Society for Training and Development have compiled the following much-cited list of the basic skill groups that employers currently believe are important:

- Knowing how to learn
- Reading, writing, and computation
- Listening and oral communication
- Creative thinking and problem-solving
- Self-esteem, goal setting/motivation, and personal/career development
- Interpersonal skills, negotiation, and teamwork
- Organizational effectiveness and leadership
      (Carnevale, Gainer, & Meltzer, 1988, p. 9)

Notice that the traditional idea of basics — reading, writing, and computation —
make up just one skill group of seven. Similarly, the U.S. Labor Secretary's Commission on Achieving Necessary Skills (SCANS, 1991) decided that a broad set of skills
or "workplace know-how" is required if workers are to succeed in the twenty-first century. According to SCANS, solid job performance depends both upon "foundation
skills," such as reading, writing, math, speaking, reasoning, problem-solving, self-
esteem, and integrity, and upon "competencies," such as being able to allocate resources, work in teams, interpret and communicate information, understand social,
organizational, and technological systems, and apply technology to specific tasks.
The burden now placed on our "nonmale," "nonwhite," "nonyoung" work force
seems very high indeed: not only must workers master the traditional basic skills of
reading, writing, and arithmetic, they are also expected to demonstrate facility with
supposedly newer competencies like problem-solving and teamwork, competencies
that often require "nuanced judgement and interpretation" (Lauren Resnick, as summarized in Berryman, 1989, p. 28).

"Illiteracy Costs Businesses and Taxpayers"

In the popular discourse, the bottom line for concern about illiteracy, whether a deficit in basic skills or a lack of nuanced judgement, is economic. Consider the following
claims about the cost of illiteracy:

Millions of employees suffering from varying degrees of illiteracy are costing their
companies daily through low productivity, workplace accidents and absenteeism,
poor product quality, and lost management and supervisory time. (*Functional Illiteracy Hurts Business*, 1988)

In a major manufacturing company, one employee who didn't know how to read a ruler mismeasured yards of steel sheet wasting almost $700 worth of material in one morning. This same company had just invested heavily in equipment to regulate inventories and production schedules. Unfortunately, the workers were unable to enter numbers accurately, which literally destroyed inventory records and resulted in production orders for the wrong products. Correcting the errors cost the company millions of dollars and wiped out any savings projected as a result of the new automation. (*The Bottom Line*, 1988, p. 12)

Already the skills deficit has cost businesses and taxpayers $20 billion in lost wages, profits and productivity. For the first time in American history, employers face a proficiency gap in the work force so great that it threatens the well-being of hundreds of U.S. companies. (Gorman, 1988, p. 56)

Again and again, we hear worker illiteracy being linked directly to big economic losses: due to poor reading and writing skills, workers make costly mistakes, they don't work efficiently, they produce inferior products, and, apparently, they stay at home a lot. A related economic argument is that since many people cannot qualify for jobs, North America is also losing the buying power of a significant segment of the population (see *Functional Illiteracy Hurts Business*, 1988).

"Workers Need 'Functional Context Training'"

Given widespread perceptions that an increasingly illiterate and poorly skilled work force threatens productivity and competitiveness in high-tech, reorganized workplaces, there are calls for business and industry to support and provide literacy-related and basic skills training:[3]

American employers have seen competency in workplace basics as a prerequisite for hiring and viewed the accumulation of such skills as solely the responsibility of the individual. The employer's interest focused on measuring the skills of prospective employees and screening out those who were most suitable for hiring. But times are changing. Employers are beginning to see that they must assist their current and future workers to achieve competency in workplace basics if they are to be competitive. (Carnevale, Gaines, & Meltzer, 1988, p. 1)

Business and industry are going to have to pick up a greater portion of education. It would probably cost between $5 billion and $10 billion over the next few years to establish literacy programs and retool current ones. But the returns of that are going to be tenfold. (Thomas Sticht, quoted in Morelli, 1987, p. 4B)

Right now at Motorola, we're running three or four different approaches, and trying to see which one will meet our employees' needs the best. In a couple of the programs, we actually teach them what they need to know to do their jobs here, so even though their reading levels might be at the sixth grade, they're really being taught to read and comprehend documentation they could use on the job. In other places, we teach them what you would an adult at the fifth-grade level: how to read things in a supermarket, how to read a newspaper. (Wiggenborn, 1989, pp. 21–22)

In the wake of calls for training programs,[4] a whole new market has sprung up for workbook instruction (and its close relative, computer-based instruction) and "how-to-set-up-a-program" guides.[5] Many of these guides give tips on relating literacy training to job tasks, thereby creating programs that provide "functional context training" or instruction that seeks to "integrate literacy training into technical training" (Sticht, Armstrong, Hickey, & Caylor, 1987, p. 107). Indeed, basing instructional materials for literacy training on texts that are used on the job — application forms, brochures, warning signs, manuals, memos — is now almost an axiom for designing workplace literacy programs. One major funder of such projects, the National Workplace Literacy Program of the U.S. Department of Education, recently included as part of its evaluation criteria that a proposal "demonstrates a strong relationship between skills taught and the literacy requirements of actual jobs, especially the increased skill requirements of the changing workplace" ("National Workplace Literacy Program," 1990, p. 14382).[6]

CURRENT VIEWS REVISITED

The popular discourse of workplace literacy is persuasive to a lot of people. It has a logic: workers lack literacy, jobs require more literacy, therefore workers are to blame for trouble at work and employers are faced with remedial training. The goals of workplace literacy appear civic-minded, even laudatory — after all, who would argue against teaching a person to read? I now want to examine this discourse critically, drawing on literacy theory and studies of work. As I question the popular discourse, I will not be claiming that there is no need to worry about literacy, or that people do not need help developing knowledge and skills in order to live up to their potential, or that the nature of work and the literacies associated with it are not in some ways and some situations changing, and changing radically. However, I will be questioning the assumptions that seem to underlie popular beliefs about literacy, work, and learning. In particular, I will object to the tendency in current discussions to place too much faith in the power of literacy and to put too little credence in people's abilities, particularly those of blue-collar and nontraditional workers (those whom Ehrlich & Garland, 1988, p. 107, describe as "the nonmale, the nonwhite, the nonyoung"). I will argue that the popular discourse of workplace literacy tends to underestimate and devalue human potential and to mischaracterize literacy as a curative for problems that literacy alone cannot solve. Such tendencies obscure other social and economic problems and provide a questionable rationale and modus operandi for current efforts to make the U.S. work force literate. They also provide a smokescreen, covering up key societal problems by drawing our attention to other issues that, while important, are only symptomatic of larger ills.[7]

Rethinking the Effects of Literacy and Illiteracy

It is ironic that, at a time when the value of literacy has been rediscovered in public discourse, theorists from many disciplines — history, psychology, anthropology, literary theory, critical theory, feminist theory — are engaged in questioning the grand claims that traditionally have been made for it. At one time, scholars talked of literacy as essential for cognitive development or as transformative in its effect on mental processes (for example, Goody & Watt, 1968; Olson, 1977; Ong, 1982). Others have also put great stock in the social, economic, and political effects of literacy — UNESCO exemplifies such views in its adult literacy campaigns in so-called developing nations (see UNESCO, 1976).

Graff (1979, 1987), however, has called the tendency to associate the value of reading and writing with socioeconomic development and individual growth "the literacy myth." He has pointed out that, contrary to conventional wisdom, societies have at times taken major steps forward in trade, commerce, and industry without high levels of literacy — during, for example, the commercial revolution of the Middle Ages and the eighteenth-century protoindustrialization in rural areas (1987, p. 11). Conversely, higher levels of literacy have not always, in modern times, been the starting place for economic development. Claims about the consequences of literacy for intellectual growth have also been tempered by recent sociocognitive research. For example, in one of the most extensive investigations of the psychology of literacy, Scribner and Cole (1981) scaled down the usual generalizations "about the impact of literacy on history, on philosophy, and on the minds of individual human beings" to the more modest conclusion that "literacy makes some difference to some skills in some contexts" (p. 234).[8]

Contemporary claims about the connection between the economic difficulties of business and industry and the literacy and basic skill deficits of workers thus stand in sharp contrast to current revisionist thinking about literacy. Popular articles repeat stories of individual workers at specific companies who fail to read signs or perform some work-related task involving literacy, and thereby make costly errors; these stories then rapidly become an unquestioned part of the popular discourse on workplace literacy. But there are alternate ways to interpret such events, as Darrah (1990) illustrates in his ethnographic study of a computer manufacturing company where the workplace was temporarily reorganized.

In the company Darrah studied, workers with the same job title had previously labored together, moving around the production floor at the direction of lead workers and supervisors. Under the team concept, new work groups were formed consisting of workers with different specialties, and these groups were ostensibly given total responsibility for producing a line of computers. The management expected that product quality would improve when workers, now with a greater say in decisionmaking, felt a greater commitment to the company's fortunes. In fact, the team concept failed, and when it did, the supervisors blamed the workers. They claimed that these employees, many of them Southeast Asian immigrants, were deficient in oral and written communication skills, and lacked the abilities to self-manage, to "see the big picture," and to analyze the production flow.

Darrah acknowledges that it would have been possible to find instances of workers who did not have the skills the supervisors mentioned. He goes on to demonstrate, however, that the demise of the team concept had little to do with workers' skills, present or absent; rather, it grew from contradictions inherent in how the concept was introduced and experienced. From the beginning, workers were skeptical of management's intentions. For example, the production manager and his supervisors announced the team concept one Thursday, scheduled team discussions for Friday, and instructed workers that beginning on Monday they should "act as if you're the vice-president of your own company" (p. 12). One repair technician commented dubiously to his coworkers after the initial meeting, "They never asked us anything before, but what can we do? We have to do what the company says" (p. 12). Further, workers feared that putting everyone at the same level on a team was a not-so-subtle attempt to eliminate job ladders and hard-won status. They felt shut out from particular kinds of information, even though the team concept was supposed to open communication and encourage workers to understand the totality of production (p. 22). Moreover, they did not believe that they had control over work processes that mattered. For example, they were asked to identify mistakes made by people outside the floor — such as improperly specified cables or faulty work by subcontractors — but when they did so, they were a little too successful: the people at fault complained, and the feedback was stopped.

Historical and sociocognitive studies of the consequences of literacy like Graff's (1979, 1987) and Scribner and Cole's (1981), as well as ethnographic accounts like Darrah's (1990, 1992), should make us question some of the facile claims found in the popular discourse of workplace literacy. They ought to make us think twice, for example, before we assume that increasing the grade level at which someone reads will automatically improve his or her performance on a literacy-related job activity (see Mikulecky, 1982). Further, they ought at least to slow us down when we reason that, if people only were literate, they could get decent jobs. Research on the consequences of literacy tells us that there are myriad complex forces — political, economic, social, personal — that can either foster or hinder literacy's potential to bring about change, as can the variety of literacy that is practiced (Lankshear & Lawler, 1987; Sahni, 1992; Street, 1984). As Graff (1987) concludes in his historical look at the relationship between literacy and economic and social progress, "Literacy is neither the major problem, nor is it the main solution" (p. 82). And in the words of Greene (1989), "The world is not crying out for more literate people to take on jobs, but for job opportunities for the literate and unlettered alike."

It is hardly credible, given the complexities of work, culture, and ideology in this country, that worker illiteracy should bear the blame for a lagging economy and a failure at international competition, or that literacy should be the solution for such grave problems. According to the *World Competitiveness Report* (World Economic Forum, 1989), human resources, including education and training, is only one factor among ten that affect a country's international competitiveness. Others include the dynamism of the economy, industrial efficiency, state interference, and sociopolitical stability. Some have argued (see, for example, Brint & Karabel, 1989; Sarmiento, 1989), in fact, that claims of illiteracy and other deficiencies serve to make workers convenient scapegoats for problems that originate in a larger arena.

Rethinking Workers' Potential

The popular discourse of workplace literacy sets up a we/they dichotomy. It stresses the apparent failures of large numbers of people — disproportionately the poor and people of color — to be competent at what are considered run-of-the-mill daily tasks.

Exaggerated and influenced by race and class prejudice, this dichotomy has the effect of separating the literate readers of magazines, newspaper articles, and scholarly reports on the literacy crisis from the masses who, we unthinkingly assume, are barely getting through the day. As Fingeret (1983) has commented, "It is difficult for us to conceptualize life without reading and writing as anything other than a limited, dull, dependent existence" (p. 133). Thus, in our current accounts of workplace literacy, we are just a step away from associating poor performance on literacy tasks with being lesser and qualitatively different in ability and potential. This association has, of course, been common throughout the history of schooling in this country (Cuban & Tyack, 1989; Fingeret, 1989; Hull, Rose, Fraser, & Castellano, 1991; Zehm, 1973) and is carried into the workplace. We have tended to think of children, adolescents, and adults who have done poorly at English and math as intellectually and morally inferior and have used these labels to justify segregating them in special classes, tracks, programs, schools, and jobs.

When applied to workers, the stigma of illiteracy is doubly punitive, for it attaches further negative connotations to people whose abilities have already been devalued by virtue of their employment. There is a long-standing tendency in our society and throughout history to view skeptically the abilities of people who work at physical labor (see Zuboff, 1988). Shaiken (1984) illustrates the recent history of this tendency in his account of skilled machinists in North America. Before the turn of the century, these accomplished workers had pivotal roles in production and considerable power on the shop floor; they lost their status with the advent of scientific management in the workplace — à la Frederick Taylor and others of a like mind. According to Shaiken, Taylor wanted to ensure that "production workers [were] as interchangeable as the parts they were producing and skilled workers as limited and controlled as the technology would allow" (p. 23). The centerpiece of Taylor's approach was to monopolize knowledge in management, and to justify this strategy he claimed that ordinary machinists were incapable of understanding the "science" underlying the organization of work processes.

The effects of Taylorism are still with us in the workplace and beyond, both in terms of how work is organized and in terms of how we view workers. The trend is still to break complex work into a multitude of simpler, repetitive jobs — 95 percent of U.S. companies organize the workplace this way (Sarmiento, 1991). We still harbor suspicions, even when choosing to introduce new forms of organization, that our workers won't adapt to or thrive in these new work requirements (see Darrah, 1990). Such an orientation provides fertile ground on which any criticism of workers can grow like kudzu, including claims of illiteracy and its effect on productivity.

As demographics shift and workers increasingly are people of color, women, and immigrants — "groups where human resource investments have been historically deficient" (*The Bottom Line*, 1988) — we are more likely to view as deficient, different, and separate those who are not or do not appear to be conventionally literate. However, there is also an increasing research literature that can be used to counter such tendencies. Some of this work documents the uses of literacy in nonmainstream communities and thereby helps to dispel the common myth that certain populations have no contact with or interest in print (for example, Heath, 1983). This kind of scholarship also demonstrates that there are literate traditions other than school-based ones, and that these promote different practices with print. Other work shows how people get along without literacy — through the use of networks of kin and friends, for example (see Fingeret, 1983) — without the feelings of dependency and self-degradation that we sometimes assume are the necessary accompaniment to illiteracy. From the military have come interesting experiments, some unintentional, in which recruits whose test scores fell below the cutoff point were allowed to enter the armed forces; those recruits performed 80 percent to 100 percent as well as "average-aptitude" service members on a variety of indicators (Sticht, Armstrong, Hickey, & Caylor, 1987). Other studies have focused on the reading and writing of under-prepared adults in school settings, showing that literacy performances that appear flawed on the surface do not necessarily imply a lack of intelligence or effort by the writer (see, for example, Bartholomae, 1985; Hull & Rose, 1989, 1990; Shaughnessy, 1977). This work by Shaughnessy and others begins with the assumption that people can acquire whatever literacies they need, given the right circumstances. In Heath's words, "all normal individuals can learn to read and write, provided they have a setting or context in which there is a need to be literate, they are exposed to literacy, and they get some help from those who are already literate" (1986, p. 23).

McDermott and Goldman (1987) provide a work-related example of the benefits of assuming that all people can learn to read and write, given the need and the support. They describe their encounters with a group of New York City workers who needed to pass a licensing exam. These ninety men were pest exterminators for the city's public housing units; half of the group had only a conditional license, which left them with lessened job security, lower pay, and zero access to promotions and extra jobs. To be licensed, the men had to pass what amounted to a literacy test using job-related materials and a test of factual knowledge of exterminating. These tests were rumored to be tough. Some men had been on the job for twenty-five years without even attempting the licensing exam, and others had been thwarted by not being able to fill out complex preliminary forms.

McDermott set about organizing an instructional program based on the belief that "all the men knew more than they needed to know for passing the test, and that we had only to tame their knowledge into a form that would enable them to take and pass the test" (p. 6). He arranged peer teaching situations by pairing a group of ten students with two exterminator/instructors who had already passed the exam, and he also relied on the union's promise to provide whatever instruction was needed until everybody passed. McDermott and Goldman report that most men passed the test on their first try, and the remainder passed the second time around. They go on to raise some important questions: "Why is it that school degrees and literacy tests are the measures of our workers? Whatever happened to job performance?" (1987, p. 5).

When we do look at job performance — when we pay close attention to how people accomplish work — we come away with quite different views of both workers' abilities and the jobs they perform. There is a relevant research tradition growing out of an interest in and respect for everyday phenomena that attempts to understand and study knowledge and skill in work (see Rogoff & Lave, 1984). Instead of assuming that poor performance in school subjects necessarily dictates poor performance on related tasks at work, researchers have used various qualitative strategies to investigate actual work practices (Lave, 1986). This kind of research has tended to show that people carry out much more complex work practices than we generally would expect on the basis of traditional testing instruments and conventional assumptions about the relationship between school learning and work learning.

Kusterer (1978), for example, studied the knowledge that workers acquire and use in jobs pejoratively labeled "unskilled," documenting the "working knowledge" acquired by machine operators in the cone department of a paper container factory and by bank tellers. He illustrated how operators did not just master the procedures for starting and stopping the machines, cleaning them properly, packing the cones, and labeling their cases — routine components of the job that were officially acknowledged. These workers also had to acquire the know-how necessary to accomplish work when obstacles arose that interrupted habitualized routine, such as "how to keep the machine running, overcome `bad' paper, diagnose the cause of defects, keep the inspectors happy, [and] secure the cooperation of mechanics and material handlers" (p. 45). Kusterer points out that although we usually recognize the basic knowledge necessary to do even highly routinized work, we are much less cognizant of how much supplementary knowledge is also necessary. The need for such knowledge, I would add, belies the common perception of much blue-collar work as unskilled and routinized, and of many blue-collar workers as deficient, incapable, and passive.

Research such as Kusterer's recognizes the abilities and potential of human workers. So do the later related studies by Wellman (1986) on the "etiquette" of longshoring, by Wenger (1991) on the "communities of practice" constructed by claims adjustors at an insurance agency, and by Scribner (1985, 1987) and Jacob (1986) on the knowledge and skills of workers at a dairy. The promise of this kind of research is that it will bring to light the literate events — the situated writing, reading, talking, and reasoning activities — that characterize the work that people do in particular job and job-training settings, and that it will cast workers in a different light, one that gives their expertise its due.

Rethinking the Nature of Literacy

The popular discourse of workplace literacy centers on the skills that people lack, sometimes basic literacy skills and sometimes "higher order" thinking skills. These skills that workers need but do not possess are sometimes determined by experts on blue-ribbon panels (for example, SCANS, 1991), and they are sometimes based on opinion surveys of employers and roundtable discussions of business executives and educational experts (for example, Carnevale, Gainer, & Meltzer, 1988). But startlingly, such judgments are almost never informed by observations of work, particularly observations that incorporate the understandings of workers.[9] Instead, skills are listed as abstract competencies and represented as context-free and universal. At best, the skill lists are skimpily customized — for instance, a job requires that a worker "signs forms appropriately," "uses listening skills to identify procedures to follow," or "speaks face to face coherently" (Hull & Sechler, 1987, p. vii).

I am sympathetic to the impulse to understand the knowledge and skills needed in particular jobs. But an uncritical acceptance of the skill metaphor — that is, of the belief that literacy as a skill is a neutral, portable technique — can lead to problems in how we conceptualize literacy and literacy instruction. We think of reading or writing as generic, the intellectual equivalent of all-purpose flour, and we assume that, once mastered, these skills can and will be used in any context for any purpose, and that they are ideologically neutral and culture-free. This view of literacy underlies a great deal of research and teaching, but of late it has begun to be challenged (see de Castell, Luke, & MacLennan, 1986; de Castell & Luke, 1989; Street, 1984). The questioning generally focuses on the ways in which it seems erroneous to think of literacy as a unitary phenomenon. On one level, this could simply mean that literacy might be viewed as a set of skills rather than one skill, that a person can perform differently at reading or writing in different situations; for example, that a person will read well when the material is job-related but less well when it's unconnected to what he or she knows, a point that Sticht makes in his research on the reading performance of military recruits (Sticht, Fox, Hauke, & Zapf, 1977), and that Diehl and Mikulecky (1980) refer to in their work on occupation-specific literacy.

A related implication is that not only will the literacy performances of individuals differ on various tasks, but the uses that people in different communities find for reading and writing will vary too, as Heath (1983) demonstrates in her research on the uses of literacy in three communities in the South. In a later work, she described literacy as having "different meanings for members of different groups, with a corresponding variety of acquisition modes, functions, and uses" (1986, p. 25). A notable instance of these differences occurs among biliterate populations, in which people have a choice of languages in which to speak or write — English and Spanish, for example, or English and Hmong — and choose one or the other based on the social meanings associated with their uses.

But there are other implications of viewing literacy as a multiple construct that offer a different, more sobering critique of the skills metaphor. Consider the following commentary about "what is suppressed in the language of skills":

> Skill in our taken-for-granted sense of the word is something real, an objective set of requirements, an obvious necessity: what's needed to ride a bicycle, for example. It is a technical issue pure and simple. However, what is forgotten when we think about skills this way is that skills are always defined with reference to some socially defined version of what constitutes competence. (Simon, 1983, p. 243)

Simon reminds us that particular activities, characteristics, and performances are labeled "skills," depending on which activities, characteristics, and performances are believed to accomplish particular purposes, to serve certain ends, or to promote special interests — usually the purposes, ends, and interests of those in the position to make such judgments. "Listening" in order to "identify procedures to follow" is a valued skill because employers want workers who will follow directions. "Sign[ing] forms appropriately" is a valued skill because supervisors need to keep records and to hold workers accountable. Conversely, Darrah (1990) discovered that there are skills that supervisors don't acknowledge but that workers recognize and develop — such as learning to represent their decisions in such a way as to "establish their plausibility should they later be challenged" (p. 21; see also Wenger, 1991). "The concept of skill," Simon argues, "is not just a technical question but is also a question of power and interest" (1983, p. 243).

This point is driven home by Gowen (1990), in her study of the effectiveness of a workplace literacy program serving African American entry-level workers at a large urban hospital in the southern United States. Gowen examined, among other things, the program's classroom practices and participant structures, the social relationships among workers and management, and the history of race relations in the region. The program was based on a "functional context approach" in which literacy instruction was linked to job content. Thus, instructors developed a series of lessons based on the memos that one supervisor regularly sent his housekeeping staff. These memos were called "Weekly Tips" and the supervisor thought they were important, although he suspected that employees did not read them. The Tips covered such topics as "Dust Mopping, Daily Vacuuming, Damp Mopping of Corridors and Open Areas, Damp Mopping of Patients' Rooms, and Spray Buffing Corridors" (p. 253), and lessons devised on the basis of this material asked students to discuss, read, and write about the information in the "Weekly Tips."

Gowen found that the employees disliked this instruction. For one thing, they felt they knew a lot more about cleaning than did their supervisors, and they developed "tricks" — Kusterer (1978) would call this "working knowledge" — to get the job done efficiently. One worker commented, "I've been at King Memorial for 23 years, and I feel like if I don't know how to clean now, I will not learn. . . . That's not going to help me get my GED I don't think" (Gowen, 1990, p. 261). Another explained in an evaluation of the curriculum: "I didn't like rewriting things concerning mopping, cleaning, and dish washing. I felt I already knowed that" (p. 262). Workers reacted to the functional context curriculum by resisting: they stopped coming to class, they finished the work as quickly as possible, or they lost their packet of "Weekly Tips." Said one student, "So we off that Weekly Tips junk? I don't want to know nothing about no mopping and dusting" (p. 260). Gowen interpreted such classroom resistance as arising from several factors, including the long-standing African American tradition of resisting control by the dominant class and the use of the functional context approach to literacy training to exercise control. Another factor was the disparity between the workers' goals for taking part in the literacy program and the goals that employers and literacy educators had for employee participation.

Gowen's research throws open the doors of workplace literacy programs, letting us examine reading and writing instruction within one such setting in its many layered complexity. As we plan literacy programs for the North American work force, we would do well to keep her portrait in mind, allowing it to remind us of the ways in which learning to read and write involves something other than acquiring decontextualized decoding, comprehension, and production skills. Literacy can more appropriately be defined as "literacies," as socially constructed and embedded practices based upon cultural symbol systems and organized around beliefs about how reading and writing might be or should be used to serve particular social and personal purposes and ends (see Cook-Gumperz, 1986; Dyson, 1992; Lankshear & Lawler, 1987; Levine, 1986; Scribner & Cole, 1981; Street, 1984). Thus, to understand literacy, to investigate its effect upon people, to construct situations in which it can empower, is to ask what version of literacy is being offered, and to take into account the sociocultural, political, and historical contexts in which that version is taught and practiced.

Rethinking the Literacy Requirements of Work and the Nature of Work-Related Training

There is much worry recently that the changing nature of work — the shift toward high-technology manufacturing and service-oriented industries — will bring changing literacy requirements, both in basic literacy skills and advanced or higher literacy skills for workers previously termed blue-collar (Sum, Harrington, & Goedicke, 1986). There is, of course, some disagreement over just how quickly work is changing and whether such changes will indeed result in jobs that require different, additional, or more complex skills (Bailey, 1990; Barton & Kirsch, 1990; Levin & Rumberger, 1983; Mishel & Teixeira, 1991). But the uncertainties that are sometimes expressed in the research literature rarely make their way into the popular discourse on workplace literacy. The descriptions I have seen of recent workplace literacy projects — I have examined descriptions of and proposals for approximately sixty of them — regularly take as a given that literacy is a requirement for everything and anticipate benefits from a literacy program, both for the worker and the company, that are numerous and wide-ranging, such as productivity, promotions, accuracy, on-time delivery, self-esteem, and job retention. There are almost no attempts at qualifying this rhetoric. The requirements and benefits of literacy, however, are certainly much more complicated than this.

A case in point is a recent *Los Angeles Times* story about the relocation of a large part of one California-based technology firm to Bangkok (Richards, 1990). The chairman of the company reported that there he had access to cheap labor — Thai women who are "conscientious and compliant." "In Thailand," he said, "there is a lot of close work under microscopes," whereas "it is pretty tough to find people in the U.S. to do that kind of work" (p. D3). So his most highly paid and educated employees — about one-fourth of the company — stayed in the United States, while he looked to Asia for the low-cost portion of his work force. The women in the Bangkok factory speak only Thai (no mention is made of whether they read and write it), as do most of the native-born managers. It seems, then, that being able to converse or write in English is not crucial for most of these workers. Nonetheless, the company provides instruction in English as a Second Language (ESL), during which the young women also acquire, according to an account oblivious to stereotyping, "a sense of urgency," being "asked to set aside a typically gentle, easy-going nature that would rather avoid than confront a problem" (p. D3).

We should keep such stories as this in mind. The relocation of the California high-tech firm to Thailand was a move not to seek out a more literate population, but to take advantage of a cheaper one, whether it is literate or not. In light of economic policies favoring "free trade" agreements with countries such as Mexico, we are likely to hear many more such reports. We need to listen with a skeptical ear when blanket pronouncements are made about literacy and its relation to work — when we are told, for example, that high-tech employment necessarily means increased demands for literacy, that foreign workers are illiterate and therefore only too happy to work for peanuts, or that most workers in industries that are non-information-based lack literate competence. We should be skeptical not in order to deny literacy instruction to anyone nor to disparage efforts to create workplace literacy programs, but to appraise more realistically what literacy as it is defined and practiced in a given context can offer, and to assess what else we need to be concerned about if our sights are set on improving the conditions as well as the products of work.

Another case in point is provided by Zuboff (1988), who has studied, among other industries, several pulp and paper mills, where experienced workers are trying to make the transition from older craft know-how to computer-based knowledge. Instead of walking about the vats and rollers, judging and controlling the conditions of production by touching the pulp, smelling the chemicals, and manually adjusting the levers of machines — relying, that is, on "sentient involvement" (p. 60) — workers are now sequestered in glass booths, their work mediated by algorithms and digital symbols, a computer interface, and reams of data. Here is how one worker expressed the sense of displacement he felt as a result of this change in his job:

> With computerization I am further away from my job than I have ever been before. I used to listen to the sounds the boiler makes and know just how it was running. I could look at the fire in the furnace and tell by its color how it was burning. I knew what kinds of adjustments were needed by the shades of color I saw. A lot of the men also said that there were smells that told you different things about how it was running. I feel uncomfortable being away from these sights and smells. Now I only have numbers to go by. I am scared of that boiler, and I feel that I should be closer to it in order to control it. (Zuboff, 1988, p. 63)

Zuboff's research demonstrates in riveting detail how some jobs are changing because of new technologies and how some workers will, as a result, be faced with losing those jobs or retooling by acquiring new work practices and skills. To be sure, finding the best means we can to ease the way for workers in such situations is a worthy goal. I believe it is a mistake, though, as we try to understand what skills are needed, to focus all our attention on technology per se, to assume that once we understand Zuboff's "intellective skills" — those capabilities involved in information-based knowledge — that we are home free. When we think of a worker in front of a computer, we do tend to focus on the individual abilities that a person needs in order to interact with a program. Wenger (1991) points out, however, that if we view intellective skills only as individual abilities, we will overlook important social components in work, such as membership in work-based communities through which particular work practices are generated and sustained (see also Lave & Wenger, 1991).

Wenger (1991) studied the claims-processing center of a large insurance company where workers, mostly women, received claims by mail, "processed" them — determining whether and for what amount a claimant's policy would cover specific medical costs — and entered them into a computer system. He found that there are crucial differences between the institutional setting that an employer provides and the communal setting that workers themselves construct, and he assigns great importance to the latter: "The practice of a community is where the official meets the non-official, where the visible rests on the invisible, where the canonical is negotiated with the non-canonical" (p. 181). If the objectives of the institution are somehow at cross purposes with the ways of functioning that are developed in these communities of practice — as happened in Darrah's (1990) computer company and as was often the case in this insurance company — serious problems occur. For example, Wenger noted an aggravating mismatch between how workers were evaluated and the work their jobs required. Although workers needed to spend time and energy answering telephone calls from irate, puzzled, or misinformed claimants — and this service was a necessary interface with customers — the company evaluated the claims processors only on the basis of their speed and accuracy in production. Such mismatches between community practice and institutional demands resulted in what Wenger called "identities of non-participation" (p. 182). That is, workers thought of themselves as only peripherally involved in the meaning of their work, and this disengagement seriously limited the success of the business. It is worth noting, too, that although the insurance workers were evaluated on literacy-related tasks, much of their work involved interpersonal communication, which did not, in contrast, seem to count.

Wenger's research alerts us to the fact that difficulties will arise when competencies and tools are defined and developed in isolation from workers' "communities of practice," and this holds true as much for Zuboff's mill workers as for the insurance adjusters. As we imagine the training and literacy programs that will greet technological transformations in the workplace, we might question whether the "intellective skills" we teach are in any way anchored in the practice of the workplace community, and if they are not, what difference our instruction will make. This is another reminder that — contrary to the popular discourse — neither all the problems nor all solutions will reside in illiteracy and literacy. Management and workers have a history, and that history more often than not is one of conflicting interests. Among others, Shaiken (1984) argues that the history of machine automation has been the history of deskilling — the effort to reduce reliance on workers' knowledge and thereby to eliminate workers' control. Thus, rather than welcoming advanced technology with enthusiasm, Shaiken wants to see its development proceed in what he views as more socially responsible ways — creating or maintaining jobs and improving the conditions of work.

In like manner, we might be vigilant against uses of literacy in the workplace that are socially irresponsible. Increasingly, businesses and corporations employ literacy-related tests and assessment instruments to determine whether workers are qualified for hiring and promotions; to certify workers (as with the exterminators' exam); and to determine whether workers are proficient at the skills their current or future jobs require. These tests and assessment devices may be administered with good intentions. Literacy audits — tests of workers' reading, writing, math, and reasoning skills — for example, are supposed to result in a customized curriculum. There are several issues worth worrying about, however. Although the courts have ruled that literacy cannot legally be used as a screening device unless the literacy skills required on the test reflect actual job demands (*Griggs et al. v. Duke Power Company*, 1971), such tests may still eliminate qualified job-seekers through literacy-related demands that do not reflect job performance. Others fear a more deliberate discriminatory use of literacy tests and audits (see Carnevale, Gainer, & Meltzer, 1988). "I am concerned that workplace literacy programs will be used to admit a few and eliminate many," writes Añorve (1989, p. 40), a workplace literacy specialist. Añorve goes on to predict that high-tech positions may provide excuses to get rid of employees with low reading skills, and he also worries that new communication criteria such as accentless speech may be used to discriminate against immigrants.[10] For similar reasons, the AFL-CIO's *Union Guide to Workplace Literacy* (Sarmiento & Kay, 1990) also looks on the use of literacy audits in the workplace as potentially abusive, as providing a too-handy rationale to justify decisions that jeopardize workers' earnings and even their jobs.

Understanding the literacy requirements of work is not, then, so simple an issue. Some jobs that are coupled with new technologies may not require much literacy at all (which is not to say they do not require considerable working knowledge). Other, more traditional occupations may involve surprisingly frequent literacy-related activities (see Scribner, 1985). And radically altered jobs may require radically altered literacy capabilities, though the development and exercise of those capabilities will depend on more than literacy alone. Similarly, the complexity that characterizes literacy, literacy learning, and the literacy requirements of work ought to spill over into our conceptions of workplace or work-related literacy programs. It would be needlessly naive to assume, for example, that in order to design a workplace program, one need only collect representative texts used at work and then teach to those documents (one variant of the "functional context approach"), or that whatever is learned in a literacy program will translate directly to promotions or productivity, or even that work-related literacy is something that all workers want to acquire (see Gowen, 1990).

Again, the point is not to argue against work-related literacy projects, but to speak in favor of a serious rethinking of the nature of the instruction we imagine for workers. As we rush headlong to design curricula and programs and to measure reading rates and writing quality, we pay precious little attention to how people experience curricula and programs and for what purposes they choose and need to engage in reading and writing. We steer our ships instead by what corporate and government leaders think they want in a work force and by our own enculturated notions of what teaching is about, even when our students are adults rather than children. Schooling is a bad memory for many adults who are poor performers at literacy, and workplace instruction that is school-based — that relies upon similar participant structures, materials, and assessment techniques — will likely be off-putting by association. I am dismayed, then, to see how frequently proposals for and descriptions of workplace literacy programs rely on school-based notions of teaching and learning. Categories for instruction tend to follow traditional models: ESL, basic skills, GED preparation, or commercially available computer-based programs. Basic skills instruction may be dressed up with occupationally specific materials — hotel workers might practice reading with menus, for example — but the format for this instruction is a teacher in front of a classroom of students with workbooks and readers. Perhaps this approach grows out of the commonplace deficit thinking concerning workers' abilities described earlier. If adult workers lack the literate competencies that we expect children to acquire, then the temptation is to imagine for workers the same instructional practices believed to be appropriate for children.

This is a good time to recall Reder's (1987) research on the comparative aspects of literacy development in three U.S. communities — an Eskimo fishing village, a community of Hmong immigrants, and a partially migrant, partially settled Hispanic community. In these communities, Reder found that adults often acquired literacy spontaneously, without participating in formal literacy education classes, in response to the perceived needs they had for literacy in their lives. They acquired literacy because they needed to, and they did so in collaboration with others. Reder points out that individuals participated in collaborative literacy practices in a variety of ways. Some were "technically engaged"; that is, they were proficient with paper and pencil and other media. Others were "functionally engaged," helping with the literacy practice by providing specialized knowledge and expertise, such as political savvy. Others were "socially engaged," lending background knowledge and approval and thereby certifying the literacy practice.

Perhaps such research can help us rethink traditional conceptions of adult literacy instruction in the workplace.[11] Like Resnick (1990), Reder proposes an "apprenticeship" model for literacy learning:

> Participant structures that provide opportunities for individuals to be functionally engaged in the practice before they have the requisite technological knowledge and skills may be a very successful means of socializing functional knowledge and knowledge of social meanings essential to accomplishment of the practice, stimulating individuals' acquisition of literacy even as they may be just learning basic technological skills. (1987, p. 267)

Instead of (or in addition to) pull-out programs in which workers are sequestered in classrooms, we might imagine apprenticeship arrangements whereby a worker who needs to carry out a complex task involving literacy learns on the job with someone who can already perform that task and, in this way, acquires the requisite technological, functional, and social knowledge. It may be that if we study the workplace to see how such literacy learning occurs "spontaneously," in the absence of formal instruction provided through literacy programs, we may see something similar to this kind of participant structure. We might also find distributed literacy knowledge, where workers typically carry out certain tasks that involve literacy in collaboration with each other, with one person supplying one kind of knowledge and others, different proficiencies. Rather than assuming that structures and practices for learning literacy must be imported from school-based models of teaching and learning, we might do well to study workplaces and communities to see what kinds of indigenous structures and practices might be supported and built upon. What we learn may enrich our school-based versions of literacy and instruction as well.

DIFFERENT VOICES AND OTHER STORIES[12]

At the time I knew Alma and Jackie, the students whose comments on literacy at work provide the headnote for this article, they were both enrolled in a short-term vocational program on banking and finance in a community college. Both of these African American women said that they needed and wanted to work and that they longed to get off public assistance. They dreamed, in fact, of professional, white-collar jobs in banks. Before she enrolled in the banking program, Jackie had been out of high school only two years and had held several short-term jobs, in addition to working at McDonald's: she had been an aspiring rapper, a janitor at an army base, and a food helper at a park and recreation facility. Alma, on the other hand, was in her forties; she had grown up in Arkansas, raised several children, and had worked only at a convalescent home and as a teacher's aide. I don't think either of these women thought of themselves as having a literacy problem, but, rather, as the headnote suggests, they expected to do reading, writing, and calculation at their future bank jobs as a matter of course. I do think, though, that they would be *viewed* both by potential employers and society at large as having a literacy problem, and that this problem would be seen as an impediment to their success at work.

Both women said they expected to do well in the banking and finance program and at work. "All you have to do is try," said Jackie. "I think I can master it, whatever it is," said Alma. And both did do well in the program, coming to class regularly, participating in the "simulated" bank-teller exercises, practicing on the ten-key adding machine, and taking their turn at doing proofs — feeding debit and credit slips through a machine the size and shape of a refrigerator lying on its side. Two months into the semester, representatives of a local bank came to test students' ten-key skills, administer a timed written exam, and carry out interviews. Jackie did just fine and was hired right away, but Alma failed the written exam, which consisted of visual discriminations and problem-solving. To the relief of everyone, Alma passed the test on her second try, though she confided in me that, rather than working the problems, she had memorized the answers to the problem-solving portion during some practice sessions the instructor had arranged and then simply filled them in during the test.

Jackie and Alma were hired part-time at $6.10 an hour at the same proof-operation center. This center takes up an entire floor of a large bank building and is filled with proof machines — a hundred or so are going at the same time when work is in full-swing — most of them operated by women of color. Workers arrive at 4 p.m. and continue until all their bundles are "proved," which is around 11 p.m., except on the busiest day, Friday, when work sometimes continues until after midnight. Jackie worked at this proof-operation center for two months, until she was late three times, the third time by three minutes, and was asked to resign. She blamed her lateness on transportation problems; she had to drop her baby off at a distant, low-cost child-care center, she said, and then take the bus back to the subway stop, and sometimes she was late or the trains did not arrive right on time. Jackie added, though, that she liked working at the proof center: "I would have stayed. . . . I liked the environment and everything . . . you have to even have a card just to get on the elevator." And she believed that if she could have held on to this job, and if her hours had been increased, she might have been able to make enough money to support herself.

Being late was not a problem for Alma, but being left-handed was. To make production in the proof-operation center, workers have to process twelve hundred items an hour — that is, they have to feed twelve hundred credit and debit slips into a machine with one hand and enter calculations on a ten-key pad with the other. The machines all have the keypad on the right, so if you are left-handed you are at a distinct disadvantage. When I talked to Alma a few months after she, too, had lost her job, she said she felt good about having worked at the bank. "I was doing the work," she said. "I had no problem opening the machine and closing the machine. I was doing that work." She was adamant, though, about the lack of relationship between the test she had failed and the job she had performed.

Right now, both Alma and Jackie are at home taking care of their children. They are presently receiving Aid for Families with Dependent Children, but they both look forward to getting another bank job. The vocational program in banking and finance is thriving, and so, for that matter, is the bank. The program had thirty new students last semester, some of whom will be offered the jobs that Jackie, Alma, and others have vacated.

Certainly there are literacy practices that Jackie and Alma are not acquainted with; perhaps they even could have benefited from a workplace literacy program or from "academic" training integrated into their vocational program. But there are many other complex factors in their situations that push literacy from a central concern to the periphery. These factors include short-term, narrowly focused vocational training; the lack of child care at work; part-time employment with no benefits, stressful tasks, few rights, and low pay; and workplaces where women of color inherit the most tedious jobs an industry can offer. To blame the problem on illiteracy in this instance, and I believe in many others, is simply to miss the mark.

We need to look from other perspectives, to hear other voices and the different stories they can tell. Many people from a variety of disciplines and perspectives are beginning to talk these days about honoring difference. Part of the impetus for these conversations comes simply from the increasing diversity of our country, where different cultures, languages, and orientations by virtue of their numbers and presence are forcing a recognition of North America's plurality. Part of it comes from educators who are pressed daily to find ways to teach in classrooms that are nothing if not richly diverse. Part of it comes, too, from a sense among many in academic communities that times are changing intellectually, that a "postmodern" age is now upon us, an age in which there is no widespread belief in a common rationality or a shared knowledge, but, rather, a growing conception of the world as "continuously changing, irreducibly various, and multiply configurable" (Greene, 1989).

In this age of difference, diversity, otherness, and change, we are lost if we do not learn to admit other views, to hear other voices, other stories. This means, for those workers whose situations have been represented univocally in the popular discourse of workplace illiteracy, looking anew at training programs and workplaces, not simply by measuring reading rates, collecting work-based literacy materials, or charting productivity — the customary focuses of much previous research and even teaching (see Grubb, Kalman, Castellano, Brown, & Bradby, 1991; Sticht, 1988). We need, rather, to seek out the personal stories of workers like Jackie and Alma, and to learn what it is like to take part in a vocational program or a literacy class and what effect such an experience has, really, on work and living. We need to look with a critical eye at how work gets accomplished and to examine what roles literacy has within work and what relationships exist between skills at work and the rights of workers. We must ask what is meant by literacy, and in what contexts and under what circumstances this literacy will be empowering. We need to ask, then, with Maxine Greene (1989), "How much, after all, depends on literacy itself?" What else must we be concerned with, besides literacy, if we want to improve the conditions and products of work?

In the popular discourse of workplace literacy, we seem to tell just a few stories. We are able to tell sad tales of people who live impoverished lives and cause others to suffer because they don't know how to read and write. Or we are able to tell happy, Horatio Alger–type stories of people who prosper and contribute to the common good because they have persevered and become literate. We have our dominant myths — our story grammars, if you will — of success and work, from which it is hard to break free. Other stories, with their alternate viewpoints, different voices, and other realities, can help us amend, qualify, and fundamentally challenge the popular discourse of literacy and work.

NOTES

1. In addition to the articles and interviews mentioned in this chapter, other recent examples of the popular discourse of workplace literacy can be found in *Basic Skills in the U.S. Work Force* (1982); Bernstein (1988); Cole (1977); Holmes and Green (1988); *Investing in People: A Strategy to Address America's Workforce Crisis* (1989); *Job-Related Basic Skills* (1987); Lee (1984); *Literacy in the Workplace: The Executive Perspective* (1989); Oinonen (1984); Rush, Moe, and Storlie (1986); *The School-to-Work Connection* (1990); Stone (1991); "Workplace Literacy" (1990); and *Workplace Literacy: Reshaping the American Workforce* (1992).

2. The popular view that unskilled minorities and women will increasingly dominate the work force while future jobs will require more highly skilled workers (see the next section) is largely based on a widely disseminated report prepared by the Hudson Institute for the Department of Labor, *Workforce 2000* (Johnston & Packer, 1987). For a counterargument, see Mishel and Teixeira's *The Myth of the Coming Labor Shortage* (1991).

3. See *Business Council for Effective Literacy: A Newsletter for the Business and Literacy Community*, published especially for the business community to keep employers apprised of developments in adult literacy and to encourage them to provide support in the field.

4. Given worries about workers' skills and the relationship assumed between those skills and a company's ability to compete, one might expect to see a great deal of corporate investment in the training and retraining of workers, similar to the efforts at Motorola. However, this has not been the case. Although various politicians, policymakers, and literacy specialists are applying pressure (see, e.g., SCANS, 1991), the percentage of companies that currently invest in the training and retraining of their work force remains very low. See *America's Choice: High Skills or Low Wages!* (Commission on the Skills of the American Workforce, 1990), Sarmiento (1991), and Mishel and Teixeira (1991).

5. For example, *The Bottom Line: Basic Skills in the Workplace* (1988); *Workplace Basics: The Skills Employers Want* (Carnevale, Gaines, & Meltzer, 1988); *Upgrading Basic Skills for the Workplace* (1989); and *Literacy at Work: The Workbook for Program Developers* (Philippi, 1991). Publishers are even beginning to produce customized materials for particular industries, for example, *Strategic Skill Builders for Banking* (Mikulecky & Philippi, 1990).

6. The U.S. Department of Education has published a description of the National Workplace Literacy Program as it has been implemented in its first three funding cycles — *Workplace Literacy:*

Reshaping the American Workforce (1992). For an argument that we should guard against a "new orthodoxy" in designing such programs, including a reliance on a functional context approach, see Schultz (1992).

7. See, for example, Apple (1987), who writes, "It is possible to claim that by shifting the public's attention to problems of education, the real sources of the current crises are left unanalyzed. That is, the crisis of the political economy of capitalism is exported from the economy onto the State. The State then in turn exports the crisis downward onto the school. Thus, when there is severe unemployment, a disintegration of traditional patterns of authority, and so on, the blame is placed on students' lack of skills, on their attitudes, on their 'functional illiteracy.' The structural problems of poverty, of the de-skilling and elimination of jobs, of capital flight, of systemic racism and sexism, problems that are `naturally' generated out of our current economic and political arrangements, are distanced from our discussions" (p. viii; see also Apple, 1985).

8. This extensive literature has been reviewed by Street (1984), Bizzell (1987), Salvatori and Hull (1990), and Walters (1990). Even those scholars who support claims for the value of literacy at one time have more recently qualified their endorsements (see Goody, 1987; Olson, in press; Ong, 1988).

9. Despite the many and frequent claims concerning the skills, including the literacies, required in reorganized, technologically sophisticated workplaces, as well as what skills workers lack, little is known about the actual skill demands of these workplaces or the kinds of training new jobs might require. There have been studies of the "reading difficulty level" of job-related materials through the application of readability formulas (see Diehl & Mikulecky, 1980; Duffy, 1985; Mikulecky, 1982; Rush, Moe, & Storlie, 1986), as well as attempts to differentiate reading at school from reading at work (see Diehl & Mikulecky, 1980; Sticht, 1979; Sticht, Armstrong, Hickey, & Caylor, 1987; Sticht & Hickey, 1987). And there have been a handful of projects that examined literacy at work within larger ethnographic studies of knowledge acquisition in real-world settings (e.g., Jacob, 1986; Martin & Scribner, 1988; Scribner, 1985, 1987; Scribner & Sachs, 1991). However, for the most part, complaints about worker "illiteracy" arise, as Darrah (1990, 1992) points out, not from detailed observations of work, but from surveys and anecdotal reports (see also Baba, 1991).

10. His worries are realistic. In Massachusetts, parents recently objected to the transfer of a teacher who spoke English with a Spanish accent from a bilingual class to a "regular" one and drew up a petition to prevent anyone not demonstrating "the accepted and standardized use of pronunciation" from taking teaching jobs in elementary school. The petitioners claimed that they were attempting through their proposed ban to protect the quality of public education during a current period of budget cuts (Canellos, 1992, p. 27).

11. For other attempts to rethink adult literacy instruction in the workplace, see Soifer et al. (1990) and Jurmo (1989).

12. The stories of Alma and Jackie, reported below, come from a larger ethnographic study (Hull, 1992). I am aware that in presenting their stories so briefly here I increase the risk of oversimplifying the complexities of their situations and views. Interested readers are urged, then, to examine the longer report. See also Fine (1992), who provides some helpful cautionary comments on the use of personal stories and voices in qualitative research.

REFERENCES

Añorve, R. L. (1989). Community-based literacy educators: Experts and catalysts for change. In A. Fingeret & P. Jurmo (Eds.), *Participatory literacy education* (pp. 35–42). San Francisco: Jossey-Bass.

Apple, M. (1985). *Education and power*. Boston: Routledge & Kegan Paul.

Apple, M. (1987). Foreword. In Lankshear, C., & Lawler, M. (Eds.), *Literacy, schooling and revolution* (pp. vii–xii). New York: Falmer Press.

Baba, M. L. (1991). The skill requirements of work activity: An ethnographic perspective. *Anthropology of Work Review, 12*(3), 2–11.

Bailey, T. (1990). *Changes in the nature and structure of work: Implications for skill requirements and skills formation*. Berkeley: University of California at Berkeley, National Center for Research in Vocational Education.

Bartholomae, D. (1985). Inventing the university. In M. Rose (Ed.), *When a writer can't write* (pp. 134–165). New York: Guilford Press.

Barton, P. E., & Kirsch, I. S. (1990). *Workplace competencies: The need to improve literacy and employment readiness*. Washington, DC: Office of Educational Research and Improvement.

Basic skills in the U.S. work force: The contrasting perceptions of business, labor, and public education. (1982). New York: Center for Public Resources.

Bernstein, A. (1988, September 19). Where the jobs are is where the skills aren't. *Business Week*, pp. 104–106.

Berryman, S. (1989). The economy, literacy requirements, and at-risk adults. In *Literacy and the marketplace: Improving the literacy of low-income single mothers* (pp. 22–33). New York: Rockefeller Foundation.

Bizzell, P. (1987). Literacy in culture and cognition. In T. Enos (Ed.), *A sourcebook for basic writing teachers* (pp. 125–137). New York: Random House.

The bottom line: Basic skills in the workplace. (1988). Washington, DC: U.S. Department of Education and U.S. Department of Labor.

Brint, S., & Karabel, J. (1989). *The diverted dream: Community colleges and the promise of educational opportunity, 1900–1985*. New York: Oxford University Press.

Business Council for Effective Literacy: A Newsletter for the Business and Literacy Community. (Available from the Business Council for Effective Literacy, 1221 Avenue of the Americas, 35th Floor, New York, NY 10020)

Canellos, P. S. (1992, July 4). Attorney general says accent ban is illegal. *Boston Globe*, pp. 1, 27.

Carnevale, A. P., Gainer, L. J., & Meltzer, A. S. (1988). *Workplace basics: The skills employers want*. Washington, DC: U.S. Department of Labor and the American Society for Training and Development.

Cole, G. (1977). The chains of functional illiteracy. *The AFL-CIO American Federationist, 84*(6), 1–6.

Commission on the Skills of the American Workforce. (1990). *America's choice: High skills or low wages!* Rochester, NY: National Center on Education and the Economy.

Cook-Gumperz, J. (Ed.). (1986). *The social construction of literacy*. Cambridge, Eng.: Cambridge University Press.

Cuban, L., & Tyack, D. (1989). *Mismatch: Historical perspectives on schools and students who don't fit them*. Unpublished manuscript, Stanford University, School of Education, Stanford, CA.

Darrah, C. N. (1990). *An ethnographic approach to workplace skills*. Unpublished manuscript.

Darrah, C. N. (1992). Workplace skills in context. *Human Organization, 51*, 264–273.

de Castell, S., & Luke, A. (1989). Literacy instruction: Technology and technique. In S. de Castell, A. Luke, & C. Luke (Eds.), *Language, authority, and criticism: Readings on the school textbook* (pp. 77–95). London: Falmer Press.

de Castell, S., Luke, A., & MacLennan, D. (1986). On defining literacy. In S. de Castell, A. Luke, & K. Egan (Eds.), *Literacy, society, and schooling: A reader* (pp. 3–14). Cambridge, Eng.: Cambridge University Press.

Diehl, W., & Mikulecky, L. (1980). The nature of reading at work. *Journal of Reading, 24*, 221–227.

Duffy, T. M. (1985). *Literacy instruction in the Armed Forces* (CDC Tech. Rep. No. 22). Pittsburgh: Carnegie Mellon University, Communications Design Center.

Dyson, A. H. (1992). The case of the singing scientist: A performance perspective on the "stages" of school literacy. *Written Communication, 9*, 3–47.

Ehrlich, E., & Garland, S. B. (1988, September 19). For American business, a new world of workers. *Business Week*, pp. 107–111.

Fine, M. (1992). *Disruptive voices: The possibilities of feminist research*. Ann Arbor: University of Michigan Press.

Fingeret, A. (1983). Social network: A new perspective on independence and illiterate adults. *Adult Education Quarterly, 33*, 133–146.

Fingeret, A. (1989). The social and historical context of participatory literacy education. In A. Fingeret & P. Jurmo (Eds.), *Participatory literacy education* (pp. 5–16). San Francisco: Jossey-Bass.

Fiske, E. B. (1988, September 9). Policy to fight adult illiteracy urged. *New York Times*, p. 12.

Functional illiteracy hurts business (rev. ed.). (1988, March). New York: Business Council for Effective Literacy.

Giroux, H. A., & McLaren, P. (1989). Introduction: Schooling, cultural politics, and the struggle for democracy. In H. A. Giroux & P. McLaren (Eds.), *Critical pedagogy, the state, and cultural struggle* (pp. xi–xxxv). Albany: State University of New York Press.

Goody, J. (1987). *The interface between the oral and the written*. Cambridge, Eng.: Cambridge University Press.

Goody, J., & Watt, I. (1968). The consequences of literacy. In J. Goody (Ed.), *Literacy in traditional societies* (pp. 27–68). Cambridge, Eng.: Cambridge University Press.

Gorman, C. (1988, December 19). The literacy gap. *Time*, pp. 56–57.

Gowen, S. (1990). *"Eyes on a different prize": A critical ethnography of a workplace literacy program*. Unpublished doctoral dissertation, Georgia State University, Atlanta.

Graff, H. J. (1979). *The literacy myth: Literacy and social structure in the nineteenth-century city*. New York: Academic Press.

Graff, H. J. (1987). *The legacies of literacy: Continuities and contradictions in western culture and society*. Bloomington: Indiana University Press.

Greene, M. (1989, March). *The literacy debate and the public school: Going beyond the functional*. Talk given at the annual meeting of the American Educational Research Association, San Francisco.

Griggs et al. v. Duke Power Co. 401 U.S. 424 (1971).

Grubb, W. N., Kalman, J., Castellano, M., Brown, C., & Bradby, D. (1991). *Coordination, effectiveness, pedagogy, and purpose: The role of remediation in vocational education and job training programs*. Berkeley: University of California at Berkeley, National Center for Research in Vocational Education.

Heath, S. B. (1983). *Ways with words: Language, life, and work in communities and classrooms*. Cambridge, Eng.: Cambridge University Press.

Heath, S. B. (1986). The functions and uses of literacy. In S. de Castell, A. Luke, & K. Egan (Eds.), *Literacy, society, and schooling: A reader* (pp. 15–26). Cambridge, Eng.: Cambridge University Press.

Holmes, B. J., & Green, J. (1988). *A quality work force: America's key to the next century*. Denver: Education Commission of the States.

Hull, G. (1992). *"Their chances? Slim and none": An ethnographic account of the experiences of low-income people of color in a vocational program and at work*. Berkeley: National Center for Research in Vocational Education.

Hull, G., & Rose, M. (1989). Rethinking remediation: Toward a social-cognitive understanding of problematic reading and writing. *Written Communication, 62*, 139–154.

Hull, G., & Rose, M. (1990). "This wooden shack place": The logic of an unconventional reading. *College Composition and Communication, 41*, 287–298.

Hull, G., Rose, M., Fraser, K. L., & Castellano, M. (1991). Remediation as social construct: Perspectives from an analysis of classroom discourse. *College Composition and Communication, 42*, 299–329.

Hull, W. L., & Sechler, J. A. (1987). *Adult literacy: Skills for the American work force* (Research and Development Series No. 265B). Columbus: Ohio State University, Center on Education and Training for Employment.

Investing in people: A strategy to address America's work force crisis. (1989). Washington, DC: U.S. Department of Labor, Commission on Workforce Quality and Labor Market Efficiency.

Jacob, E. (1986). Literacy skills and production line work. In K. M. Borman & J. Reisman (Eds.), *Becoming a worker* (pp. 176–200). Norwood, NJ: Ablex.

Job-related basic skills. (1987). New York: Business Council for Effective Literacy.

Johnston, W. B., & Packer, A. B. (1987). *Workforce 2000: Work and workers for the 21st century.* Indianapolis: Hudson Institute.

Jurmo, P. (1989). The case for participatory literacy education. In A. Fingeret & P. Jurmo (Eds.), *Participatory literacy education.* San Francisco: Jossey-Bass.

Kusterer, K. C. (1978). *Know-how on the job: The important working knowledge of "unskilled" workers.* Boulder, CO: Westview Press.

Lacy, D. (1985, November). American business and the literacy effort. *PIA Communicator,* pp. 10–12.

Lankshear, C., & Lawler, M. (1987). *Literacy, schooling and revolution.* New York: Falmer Press.

Lave, J. (1986). Experiments, tests, jobs and chores: How we learn what we do. In K. M. Borman & J. Reisman (Eds.), *Becoming a worker* (pp. 140–155). Norwood, NJ: Ablex.

Lave, J., & Wenger, E. (1991). *Situated learning: Legitimate peripheral participation.* Cambridge, Eng.: Cambridge University Press.

Lee, C. (1984). Who, what, and where? *Training, 2*(10), 39–47.

Levin, H., & Rumberger, R. (1983). The low-skill future of high-tech. *Technology Review, 86*(6), 18–21.

Levine, K. (1986). *The social context of literacy.* London: Routledge & Kegan Paul.

Literacy in the workplace: The executive perspective. (1989). Bryn Mawr, PA: Omega Group.

Martin, L. M. W., & Scribner, S. (1988). *An introduction to CNC systems: Background for learning and training research.* New York: Graduate School and University Center of the City University of New York, Laboratory for Cognitive Studies of Work.

McDermott, R., & Goldman, S. (1987). Exterminating illiteracy. *Information Update: A Quarterly Newsletter of the Literacy Assistance Center, 4*(1), 5–6.

Mikulecky, K., & Philippi, J. (1990). *Strategic skill builders for banking.* New York: Simon & Schuster.

Mikulecky, L. (1982). Job literacy: The relationship between school preparation and workplace actuality. *Reading Research Quarterly, 17,* 400–419.

Mishel, L., & Teixeira, R. A. (1991). *The myth of the coming labor shortage: Jobs, skills, and incomes of America's work force 2000.* Washington, DC: Economic Policy Institute.

Morelli, M. (1987, October 29). Reading up on literacy: What USA businesses can do to educate workers. *USA Today,* p. 4B.

National workplace literacy program: Notice inviting applications for new awards for fiscal year. (1990, April 17). *Federal Register, 55*(74), 14382.

Oinonen, C. M. (1984). *Business and education survey: Employer and employee perceptions of school to work preparation* (Parker Project No. 3, Bulletin No. 4372). Madison: Parker Pen Company and Wisconsin Department of Public Instruction. (ERIC Document Reproduction Service No. ED 244 122)

Olson, D. R. (1977). From utterance to text: The bias of language in speech and writing. *Harvard Educational Review, 47,* 257–281.

Olson, D. R. (in press). *The world on paper.* Cambridge, Eng.: Cambridge University Press.

Ong, W. J. (1982). *Orality and literacy: The technologizing of the word.* London: Methuen.

Ong, W. J. (1988). A comment about "Arguing about Literacy." *College English, 50,* 700–701.

Philippi, J. (1991). *Literacy at work: The workbook for program developers.* Westwood, NJ: Simon & Schuster.

Reder, S. M. (1987). Comparative aspects of functional literacy development: Three ethnic communities. In D. Wagner (Ed.), *The future of literacy in a changing world, Vol. 1* (pp. 250–270). Oxford, Eng.: Pergamon Press.

Resnick, L. B. (1990). Literacy in school and out. *Daedalus, 119*(2), 169–185.

Richards, E. (1990, June 25). Why an American high-tech firm recruits in Asian rice fields. *Los Angeles Times,* pp. D3–D4.

Rogoff, B., & Lave, J. (1984). *Everyday cognition: Its development in social context.* Cambridge, MA: Harvard University Press.

Rush, R. T., Moe, A. J., & Storlie, R. L. (1986). *Occupational literacy education.* Newark, DE: International Reading Association.

Sahni, U. (1992, September). *Literacy for empowerment*. Paper presented at the First Conference for Socio-Cultural Research, The Society for Socio-Cultural Studies, Madrid.

Salvatori, M., & Hull, G. (1990). Literacy theory and basic writing. In M. G. Moran & M. J. Jacobi (Eds.), *Research in basic writing* (pp. 49–74). Westport, CT: Greenwood Press.

Sarmiento, A. R. (1989, September). *A labor perspective on basic skills*. Talk presented at Conference on Workplace Basic Skills, sponsored by Columbus Area Labor Management Committee, Columbus, OH.

Sarmiento, A. R., & Kay, A. (1990). *Worker-centered learning: A union guide to workplace literacy*. Washington, DC: AFL-CIO Human Resources Development Institute.

Sarmiento, T. (1991, July). Do workplace literacy programs promote high skills or low wages? Suggestions for future evaluations of workplace literacy programs. *National Governors' Association Labor Notes, 64*, 7–11.

The school-to-work connection. (1990). Report on the Proceedings of "The Quality Connection: Linking Education and Work," a conference sponsored by the Secretary of Labor and the Secretary of Education, Washington, DC.

Schultz, K. (1992). *Training for basic skills or educating workers? Changing conceptions of workplace education programs*. Berkeley: National Center for Research in Vocational Education.

Scribner, S. (1985). Knowledge at work. *Anthropology and Education Quarterly, 16*(3), 199–206.

Scribner, S. (1987). Literacy in the workplace. *Information Update: A Quarterly Newsletter of the Literacy Assistance Center, 4*(1), 3–5.

Scribner, S., & Cole, M. (1981). *The psychology of literacy*. Cambridge, MA: Harvard University Press.

Scribner, S., & Sachs, P., with DiBello, L., & Kindred, J. (1991). *Knowledge acquisition at work* (Technical Paper No. 22). New York: The Graduate School and University Center of the City University of New York, Laboratory for Cognitive Studies of Work.

Secretary's Commission on Achieving Necessary Skills (SCANS). (1991, June). *What work requires of schools: A SCANS report for American 2000*. Washington, DC: U.S. Department of Education.

Shaiken, H. (1984). *Work transformed: Automation and labor in the computer age*. New York: Holt, Rinehart, & Winston.

Shaughnessy, M. (1977). *Errors and expectations*. New York: Oxford University Press.

Simon, R. I. (1983). But who will let you do it? Counter-hegemonic possibilities for work education. *Journal of Education, 165*, 235–255.

Soifer, R., Irwin, M. E., Crumrine, B. M., Honzaki, E., Simmons, B. K., & Young, D. L. (1990). *The complete theory-to-practice handbook of adult literacy: Curriculum design and teaching approaches*. New York: Teachers College Press.

Sticht, T. G. (1979). Developing literacy and learning strategies in organizational settings. In H. F. O'Neil & C. D. Spielberger (Eds.), *Cognitive and affective learning strategies*. New York: Academic Press.

Sticht, T. G. (1988). Adult literacy education. *Review of Research in Education, 15*(1), 59–96.

Sticht, T. G., Armstrong, W., Hickey, D., & Caylor, J. (1987). *Cast-off youth*. New York: Praeger.

Sticht, T. G., Fox, L., Hauke, R., & Zapf, D. (1977). *The role of reading in the Navy* (Tech. Rep. NPRDC TR 77-40). San Diego: Navy Personnel Research and Development Center.

Sticht, T. G., & Hickey, D. T. (1987). Technical training for "mid-level" literate adults. In C. Klevenn (Ed.), *Materials and methods in adult and continuing education*. Los Angeles: Klevenn.

Stone, N. (1991). Does business have any business in education? *Harvard Business Review, 69*(2), 46–62.

Street, B. (1984). *Literacy in theory and practice*. Cambridge, Eng.: Cambridge University Press.

Sum, A., Harrington, P., & Goedicke, W. (1986). *Skills of America's teens and young adults: Findings of the 1980 National ASVAB Testing and their implications for education, employment and training policies and programs*. Unpublished report prepared for the Ford Foundation, New York.

UNESCO. (1976). *The experimental world literacy programme: A critical assessment.* Paris: UNESCO Press.

Upgrading basic skills for the workplace. (1989). University Park: Pennsylvania State University, Institute for the Study of Adult Literacy.

Walters, K. (1990). Language, logic, and literacy. In A. A. Lunsford, H. Moglen, & J. Slevin (Eds.), *The right to literacy* (pp. 173–188). New York: Modern Language Association.

Wellman, D. (1986). Learning at work: The etiquette of longshoring. In K. M. Borman & J. Reisman (Eds.), *Becoming a worker* (pp. 159–175). Norwood, NJ: Ablex.

Wenger, E. (1991). *Toward a theory of cultural transparency: Element of a social discourse of the visible and the invisible.* Palo Alto, CA: Institute for Research on Learning.

Whitman, D., Shapiro, J. P., Taylor, R., Saltzman, A., & Auster, B. B. (1989, June 26). The forgotten half. *U.S. News & World Report*, pp. 45–53.

Wiggenborn, B. (1989, January). How can businesses fight workplace illiteracy? *Training and Development Journal, 41*(1), 20–22.

Workplace literacy [Special issue]. (1990, October). *Vocational Education Journal, 65*(6).

Workplace literacy: Reshaping the American work force. (1992, May). Washington, DC: U.S. Department of Education, Office of Vocational and Adult Education, Division of Adult Education and Literacy.

World Economic Forum and the IMEDE. (1989, July). *World competitiveness report.* Lausanne, Switz.: Author.

Zehm, S. J. (1973). *Educational misfits: A study of poor performers in the English class, 1825–1925.* Unpublished doctoral dissertation, Stanford University, Stanford, CA.

Zuboff, S. (1988). *In the age of the smart machine: The future of work and power.* New York: Basic Books.

The preparation of this paper was supported by funding from the Office of Vocational and Adult Education, U.S. Department of Education, to the National Center for Research in Vocational Education for Project 3.2, "Preparing a Literate Workforce," codirected by Glynda Hull and Jenny Cook-Gumperz. Points of view or opinions do not necessarily represent official U.S. Department of Education position or policy. Special thanks to Kay Losey Fraser, whose help with research and analysis was essential throughout the project; to Margaret Easter, Norton Grubb, Judy Kalman, Mike Rose, Kathy Shultz, Wendy Waymen, Gloria Zarabozo, and Oren Ziv for insightful discussion and helpful commentary; to Sandy Larimer for expert editorial assistance; and to Ed Warshauer, whose perspectives on work were important for conceptualizing the paper and shaping its arguments.

Toward a Social-Contextual Approach to Family Literacy

ELSA ROBERTS AUERBACH

Why I didn't do the homework

Because the phone is ringing
the door is noking
the kid is yumping
the food is burning
time runs fast.

Rosa

R osa's writing is a window on her world. It reflects the tensions she faces as a young mother pursuing educational dreams in a new country. Given Rosa's strong motivation, her teacher was curious about why she hadn't done the homework. As Rosa explains, she is more than a student: she is also a parent, wife, cook, neighbor, member of an extended family and community, and someone who is trying to balance the demands of these many roles. Although she sees the importance of learning and has made the effort to enroll in English classes, she is asking her teacher to look at schoolwork in the context of her life and to understand the complex set of demands that sometimes takes priority over assignments.

Rosa's voice is both her own and the voice of many immigrant and refugee students. Her dilemma is their dilemma: how can parents with low proficiency in English and literacy find ways to integrate learning into their busy lives and, at the same time, provide a context for literacy development in their children's lives?

This dilemma is a challenge to educators: how should we view Rosa's situation, and what can we do to support her efforts? Rosa's class, part of the University of Massachusetts (UMass) at Boston English Family Literacy Program, is one of many set up around the country in recent years to provide English literacy instruction to parents of bilingual students so that they, in turn, can support the literacy development of their children.[1] In the UMass/Boston Program my colleagues and I have found that the way family literacy is defined has critical implications for addressing Rosa's dilemma. If it is defined narrowly to mean performing school-like literacy activities within the fam-

Harvard Educational Review   Vol. 59   No. 2   May 1989, 165–181

ily setting, the social-contextual demands on family life become obstacles that must be overcome so that learning can take place. In this view, successful literacy and language acquisition are closely linked to the culture of schooling and to mainstream literacy practices; life demands are seen as taking parents away from literacy development and as conflicting with the demands of schooling (such as doing homework). This view implies that it is the teacher's job to make work on academic skills manageable and the parents' job to set aside time to work on these skills (see, for example, Simich-Dudgeon, 1987).

If, on the other hand, educators define family literacy more broadly to include a range of activities and practices that are integrated into the fabric of daily life, the social context becomes a rich resource that can inform rather than impede learning. In this more inclusive view, doing formal schoolwork and developing literacy are not necessarily synonymous. The acquisition of literacy skills is seen in relation to its context and uses (Heath, 1983; Street, 1984): literacy is meaningful to students to the extent that it relates to daily realities and helps them to act on them (Freire, 1970); divorced from such contexts and purposes, however, it can become one more burden. In this view, the teacher's role is to connect what happens inside the classroom to what happens outside so that literacy can become a meaningful tool for addressing the issues in students' lives.

The difference between these two perspectives on Rosa's dilemma is important because of its potential effect on policy and practice, as well as on students' learning. As the national focus on family contributions to literacy acquisition intensifies with, for example, the establishment of the Barbara Bush Foundation for Family Literacy and the passage of Even Start legislation (see Business Council for Effective Literacy (BCEL), 1989), it will become increasingly important to ground program development in a sound conceptual framework, informed by research, theory, and practice.

The UMass/Boston English Family Literacy Project staff has developed its own conceptual framework by examining not only current models for family literacy programs, but also the ethnographic literature on family contributions to literacy development as well as the evidence provided by the program's own students.[2] What we learned from students came not from formal "research" but from observing what they said, did, and showed in the course of day-to-day classroom interaction. The project staff did not go into students' homes or communities to examine literacy uses and practices or to collect data; instead, we listened, read, and talked with students about literacy in their lives.

We found, as a result of this investigation, a gap between research and implementation: existing models for family literacy programs seemed not to be informed by ethnographic research or substantiated by what we learned from the students themselves. This chapter will discuss the results of this preliminary investigation and the assumptions behind current models for family literacy programs in light of recent research, both inside and outside the classroom; it will also suggest alternatives. While the perspective represented here focuses specifically on work with immigrant and refugee families, our sense is that the analysis and pedagogical implications may well be valid for other populations too (such as low literate native speakers of English), because it is informed by a broad base of research in a variety of cultural and economic contexts (Chall & Snow, 1982; Goldenberg, 1984; Heath, 1983; Taylor, 1983; Taylor & Dorsey-Gaines, 1988; Tizard, Schofield, & Hewison, 1982).

THE CONTEXT FOR THE FAMILY LITERACY TREND

The attention now being paid to parental roles in literacy development must be seen in the context of the current alarmist concern about the "literacy crisis," the dropout rate, and declining academic achievement. This concern is often embedded in an analysis that links illiteracy and unemployment, claiming that inadequate literacy skills inhibit both personal and national economic advancement (see Shor, 1986, for an analysis of the context of this crisis). The makers of national educational policy argue that we must look beyond the school systems to the family in order to locate the cause of the problem. Former secretary of education Terrell Bell (1988) characterized this position with the comment: "Not even the best classroom can make up for failure in the family." The contention is that illiteracy breeds illiteracy: in an "intergenerational cycle of illiteracy," the "plague" passes from one generation to the next, creating a permanent, self-perpetuating "underclass" (see BCEL, 1989).

This analysis, in turn, is often justified by a series of studies on family literacy (although the authors of these studies may not agree with those who cite them); most of these focus on English-speaking families. One group of studies (Chall & Snow, 1982; Heath, 1983) examines a wide range of family literacy practices within and across social classes, showing that children whose home literacy practices most closely resemble those of the school are more successful in school. Other research (for example, Epstein, 1986; Topping & Wolfendale, 1985) indicates that parental involvement in children's schooling has a positive impact on school achievement. Taken together, these studies suggest that one explanation for the relative success in school of middle-class Anglo students is that their home environments provide them with the kinds of literacy skills and practices needed to do well in school. The fact that their parents use and transmit literacy in the specific ways that schools expect gives these children an advantage.

But what about those children from homes that do not promote middle-class "ways with words," whose parents are not involved with their children's schooling or do not speak English? Despite some of the researchers' intentions, these studies are often interpreted to mean that nonmainstream families may lack appropriate environments for fostering literacy development because of inadequate parental skills, practices, and materials (Bell, 1988).

Furthermore, research indicates that until recently little systematic institutional support existed to help parents develop specific skills or take an active role in education (Moles, 1982). Traditional forms of parent involvement — such as creating a home atmosphere conducive to learning, responding to school communications, helping at school, performing academic tasks with children, and working in parent advisory groups — have been limited in scope and often have not included low-income or language-minority families (Epstein, 1986). Many policymakers (Home and School Institute, for example, and The Academic Development Institute) and program designers use this body of research to recommend a systematic, school-based attempt to structure parental participation in children's education. According to this formulation, parents are responsible for helping teachers do their jobs, and schools are responsible for showing parents how to do so (Epstein, 1986).

THE "TRANSMISSION OF SCHOOL PRACTICES" MODEL

The source of the problem is widely formulated as a lack of appropriate literacy practices in the home, and, further, in the case of bilingual families, lack of understanding of the language and culture of American schooling (see BCEL, 1989), compounded by a lack of institutional support for developing them. As a result, the solution is often formulated in terms of intervention programs that give parents specific guidelines, materials, and training to carry out school-like activities in the home. Simich-Dudgeon argues that parents with limited English proficiency must become their children's tutors, performing "structured academic activities that reinforce school-work" (1987, p. 3). Programs for these parents (see those described in *Issues of Parent Involvement and Literacy*, 1986) often focus on such practices as:

- Teaching parents about the American educational system and philosophy of schooling
- Providing parents with concrete methods and materials to use at home with children
- Assisting parents to promote "good reading habits"
- Training parents for home tutoring in basic skills (often extending a subskills approach to literacy with phonics, word-attack worksheets, and so on)
- Giving parents guidelines and techniques for helping with homework
- Training parents in how to read to children or listen to children read
- Training in "effective parenting"
- Giving parents a calendar or recipe book of ideas for shared literacy activities
- Teaching parents to make and play games to reinforce skills
- Teaching parents how to communicate with school authorities

While these programs take many forms (from competency-based behavior to behavior modification methods), what they have in common is their shared goal: to strengthen the ties between the home and the school by transmitting the culture of school literacy through the vehicle of the family. Parents are taught about mainstream ways of relating to print and about specific school literacy tasks that they can engage in with their children. The model starts with the needs, problems, and practices that educators identify, and then transfers skills or practices to parents in order to inform their interactions with children; its direction moves from the school/educator to the parents, and then to the children.

EXAMINING THE ASSUMPTIONS

As our project staff reviewed the ethnographic literature on family literacy, as well as evidence from our own students, it became clear that a number of the assumptions

implicit in this "transmission of school practices" model do not correspond to the realities of participants' lives. The first assumption is that language-minority students
come from literacy-impoverished homes where education is not valued or supported.
The second assumption is that family literacy involves a one-way transfer of skills
from parents *to* children. Third, this model assumes that success is determined by
the parents' ability to support and extend school-like activities in the home. The
fourth assumption is that school practices are adequate and that it is home factors
that will determine who succeeds. And fifth, the model assumes that parents' own
problems get in the way of creating positive family literacy contexts.

Taken together, these assumptions contribute to a new version of the deficit hypothesis, placing the locus of responsibility for literacy problems with the family. The
danger is that, left unexamined, these assumptions will justify a model that blames
the victim by attributing literacy problems largely to family inadequacies.

Assumption 1: Home Environments

The first assumption concerns the home literacy environments of language-minority
students. The "transmission" model presents the homes of low-income and minority
students and of students who speak English as a second language (ESL) as "literacy
impoverished," with limited reading materials and with parents who neither read
themselves nor read to their children, who do not provide models of literacy use and
do not value or support literacy development (see, for example, BCEL, 1989).

A growing body of research, however, indicates that this does not reflect the reality
of many low-income, minority, and immigrant families. Taylor and Dorsey-Gaines
(1988) studied the literacy contexts of families living below the poverty level, in conditions where neither housing nor food could be taken for granted, where the parents
often had not completed high school, and where families had been separated. They
found that even in these homes where day-to-day survival was a struggle, "families
use literacy for a wide variety of purposes (social, technical, and aesthetic purposes),
for a wide variety of audiences, and in a wide variety of situations" (1988, p. 202).
Homes were filled with print, and literacy was an integral part of daily life.

The Harvard Families and Literacy Study (Chall & Snow, 1982; Snow, 1987) investigated the home literacy practices of successful and unsuccessful low-income elementary school students in order to identify those factors and patterns of interaction
that contributed to the acquisition of literacy. This study also found a range of literacy practices and materials in the homes of working-class, minority, and ESL students:

> Perhaps the most surprising finding was the generally high level of literacy skill and
> literacy use among the parents of the children. For example, only twenty percent of
> the parents said they did not like to read and never read books. Thirty percent read
> factual books . . . and could name at least one favorite author. Fifty percent read a
> major newspaper on a regular basis and thirty percent could remember books from
> their childhoods. These low-income children also demonstrated considerable famil-
> iarity with literacy. The vast majority owned some books of their own and half
> owned more than 20 books. . . . *It seems then that explanations implicating the ab-*

sence of literacy in low-income homes as the source of children's reading failure are simply wrong. (Snow, 1987, p. 127, emphasis added)

In a study of the functions and meaning of literacy for Mexican immigrants, Delgado-Gaitan (1987) also found that each of the four families she investigated used a range of text types in a variety of ways that went beyond school-related reading. Despite the fact that parents had little prior schooling and did not perceive themselves as readers, they regularly used texts in English and Spanish (including letters from family members, newspapers, and their children's schoolbooks) as an integral part of daily life. Further, they wanted to develop their own English literacy as a way to support their children.

Study after study (for example, Chall & Snow, 1982; Delgado-Gaitan, 1987; Diaz, Moll, & Mehan, 1986; Goldenberg, 1984) has refuted the notion that poor, minority, and immigrant families don't value or support literacy development. In fact, often, quite the opposite seems to be the case for immigrants: those families most marginalized frequently see literacy and schooling as the key to mobility, to changing their status and preventing their children from suffering as they did. For some, the desire to get a better education for their children may even be the central reason for coming to the United States (Delgado-Gaitan, 1987).

Beyond a general recognition of the importance of literacy, parents support it in specific ways. Each family in the Delgado-Gaitan study, for example, systematically rewarded children for work well done, completed homework, and good grades. Moreover, these "illiterate" parents recognized that their support could extend beyond helping with skills:

> Some parents assisted their children in school work by sitting with them to do homework and working out the problem, showing them examples for solving their problems, encouraging them to do their homework before playing, reading to them, taking them to the community library and providing them with a space at the kitchen table to do their homework. (Delgado-Gaitan, 1987, p. 28)

Parents in each of these studies understood that supporting children academically went beyond helping with skills to include emotional and physical support. Our own students have repeatedly confirmed these findings. For example, one parent wrote:

> I help my kids by staying together with them, by talking to them. I help them by confronting them and telling them what's wrong or right just as they do me. I help them when they need a favor or money, just as they do me. It's just like you scratch my back, I scratch your back with my family.

Assumption 2: Directionality of Literacy Interactions

The phrase "you scratch my back, I scratch your back" points to a second false assumption of the predominant model — namely, that the "natural" direction of literacy learning is from parent to child, and, more narrowly, that the parent's role is to transmit literacy skills to the child. Interestingly, the example just cited was written through a collaborative mother-daughter writing process: the woman who wrote it was at a very beginning literacy level, and could only produce this text with the help of her daughter — it became a language-experience exercise for them.

This two-way support system characterizes the literacy interactions of many immigrant families. In fact, one study of parental involvement with very promising findings is based on a model of children reading to parents (Tizard, Schofield, & Hewison, 1982). This study found that children who read to their parents on a regular basis made significant gains, in fact greater gains than did children receiving an equivalent amount of extra reading instruction by reading specialists at school. Particularly significant was the fact that low parental English literacy skills did not detract from the results. This study suggests that the context provided by parents and their consistent support may be more important than any transfer of skills.

University of Massachusetts English Family Literacy Project work with immigrants and refugees indicates that the distribution and sharing of language and literacy practices in families is complex and by no means unidirectional from parents to children. Family members each contribute in the areas where they are strongest: instead of the parents assisting children with literacy tasks, the children help their parents with homework, act as interpreters for them, and deal with the outside world for them. Parents, in turn, often foster their children's first language development and help in areas where they feel competent. One of the parents in our program wrote about how this works in her family:

> When I say some words wrong she corrects me. And sometimes I ask her how to say the word and she tells me. And I help her with her Spanish homework because she takes a class in Spanish in her school. I feel very happy that she helps me, and that she knows good English. Sometimes she laughs at me and I laugh too.

This uneven distribution of language and literacy skills in immigrant families often leads to highly charged, emotionally loaded family dynamics. The fact that the children's English and literacy proficiency may be more developed than the parents' can lead to complicated role reversals in which parents feel that respect for them is undermined and children feel burdened by having to negotiate with the outside world for their parents. Diaz et al. found that since children often took responsibility for conducting transactions with important social institutions (banks, schools, and so forth), "they assumed control and power usually reserved for adults" (1986, p. 210).

A further example from one of our classes serves to illustrate the complexity of this parent-child role reversal. A teacher noticed that the handwriting in the dialogue journal of one of her students was not the student's own and, upon investigation, she learned that the student's daughter had written the journal for her mother. The teacher wrote back, inviting the daughter to keep a separate journal while letting the mother do her own work. The daughter responded with an entry about her own language use, ending with this:

> I'm glad my mother is going to school so she could speak English. It finally mean that I don't have to translate for her every time she watches a movie that she don't understand. I usually have to explain it to her. It must be hard for you to teach the students. You've also got to be patient. If one of your students don't understand

what you mean then you have to explain it in a different way. I'll never be a good teacher because I'm not good at teaching.

Here the daughter is describing her own discomfort at being placed in the role of translator and teacher, a role she doesn't feel ready for. These comments suggest that in some families the power of the parents' learning may be that it reduces this parent-child literacy dependency, and frees the children to attend to their own development, including schoolwork.

What emerges from the composite of these studies and student writings is not at all a picture of deficit or literacy impoverishment, but instead a picture of mutual support — of family members working together to help each other in a variety of ways. Clearly a model that rests on the assumption of unilateral parent-to-child literacy assistance, with a neutral transfer of skills, misses important aspects of this dynamic and may in fact exacerbate already stressful family interactions.

Assumption 3: Family Contexts of Successful Readers

A third assumption concerns the nature of family contributions to literacy development. The recognition that certain ways of using literacy in the home may better prepare students for success in school is often accompanied by the assumption that children succeed because their families do specific school-like tasks with them — that home learning activities are the key to success for literate children and that literacy programs must provide support for this kind of interaction.

An examination, however, of the actual family contexts for the acquisition of literacy provides compelling counterevidence. Studies that examine the home literacy environments of successful readers (both lower and middle class) reveal a range of factors that contribute to literacy development. The Harvard study, for example, found no simple correlation between parents' literacy level, educational background, amount of time spent on literacy work with children, and overall achievement (Chall & Snow, 1982). Rather, the acquisition of literacy was found to be affected differentially by such factors. Indirect factors including frequency of children's outings with adults, number of maternal outings, emotional climate of the home, amount of time spent interacting with adults, level of financial stress, enrichment activities, and parental involvement with the schools had a stronger effect on many aspects of reading and writing than did direct literacy activities, such as help with homework.

Taylor's (1981, 1983) three-year study of six families of proficient readers provides further evidence that a wide range of home experiences and interaction patterns (rather than narrow, school-like reading and writing activities) characterizes homes of successful readers. Parents in this study often intentionally avoided "doing literacy" with their children in the ways they had been taught in school in order to avoid replicating what they remembered as negative experiences. The interactions around print varied from family to family and were, within each family, "situationally diffuse, occurring at the very margins of awareness . . ." (1981, p. 100). Specific types of interactions did not emerge as significant across families; rather, Taylor found that these interactions were *not* activities "which were added to the family agendas, but that they had evolved as part of everyday life" (1981, p. 100). She concludes:

The approach that has been taken in recent years has been to develop parent education programmes, which very often provide parents with a battery of specific activities which are designed to teach reading, and yet very little available information
suggests that parents with children who read without difficulty actually undertake
such "teaching" on any kind of regular basis. The present study suggests that there
are great variations in approaches the parents have evolved in working with their
children and that the thread that unites the families is the recognition that learning
to read takes place on a daily basis as part of everyday life. (Taylor, 1981, p. 101)

A second study by Taylor and Dorsey-Gaines (1988) among poor urban families
confirmed these findings, indicating that similar dynamics are at work across social
classes. These studies indicate that successful readers' homes provide a variety of
contexts for using literacy, and that literacy is integrated in a socially significant way
into many segments of family life, and is not isolated as a separate, autonomous, add-
on instructional activity. The more diverse the contexts for using literacy, the wider
the range of literacy achievement factors affected.

Assumption 4: School Contributions to the Acquisition of Literacy

A further danger with the "transmission of school practices" model is that the focus
may be shifted away from school roles and their interaction with home factors in literacy development. This view perceives what happens at home to be the key to school
success, often assuming a direct correlation, even a cause-and-effect relationship, between home factors and school achievement. The flip side of this assumption is the
claim that what happens at school is either less important or already adequate and
need only be reinforced at home. Again, there is counterevidence from a variety of
sources.

For instance, Heath's (1983) ethnographic investigations of three rural communities in the Piedmont Carolinas found not a lack of literacy practices in the two poorer,
working-class communities, but a difference in the ways that literacy was used and
perceived. In each community, there was a wide and different range of uses of literacy
at home. The relationship between home and school literacy practices was significant: the ways of using print in middle-class homes were similar to those of the
school. Since authority is vested in those belonging to the mainstream culture, the literacy practices of the mainstream become the norm and have higher status in school
contexts. Heath's analysis suggests that the problem is not one of deficit in the family
environment, but one of differential usage and power.

In case studies that examined both home and school contexts, Urzua (1986) contends that it is *school* rather than *home* factors that shape differences in attitudes and
abilities relating to literacy. She reports that two refugee children who had homes
seemingly less conducive to literacy acquisition were more successful in school. Although their mothers were illiterate in their first language, did not speak or read English, and provided no reading materials in the home, these children progressed greatly
in reading and writing. In contrast, another child whose home was filled with reading
materials (books, maps, newspapers, dictionaries, and so forth), who had his own
study space and school supplies, and whose parents overtly supported his literacy de-

velopment, had enormous difficulties with reading and writing. Urzua asks, "What makes children like Vuong, loved and encouraged by parents who have offered many possibilities for literacy events in their home, face school with rigidity and approach literacy with fear?" (1986, p. 108).

She suggests that the answer to this question may be found in the classroom experiences. Both of the children who came from less literate home environments were in classes where the teacher valued writing. In these classes writing took place nearly every day, a variety of writing genres (such as autobiographies, fables, journals) was offered, and subskills work (spelling, phonics) was subordinated to the expression of meaning. In the class of the child who came from a home providing more support for literacy acquisition, however, students never wrote more than one sentence at a time, filled in the blanks in workbooks, copied dictionary definitions, and so forth. Urzua then asks, "How powerful are the influences of curriculum and instructional techniques . . . which either teach children to find their own voices, or discourage them from doing so?" (1986, p. 108).

The Harvard study (Chall & Snow, 1982) offers further support for the view that school factors account as much as home factors for the acquisition of literacy. Classroom factors that affected literacy included the availability of a wide variety of reading materials, the amount and nature of writing, the use of the library, and the quality of instruction. The researchers found that in the early grades, "either literate, stimulating homes or demanding, enriching classrooms can make good readers" (Snow, 1987, p. 128). However, while strong parental factors could compensate for weak schooling up to grade three, even those children with positive home literacy environments fell back after this point if school practices were deficient. While positive home factors were sufficient to carry a child in the lower grades, both positive home and school factors were necessary for literacy development in the upper grades.

One particularly interesting finding of the Harvard study (Chall & Snow, 1982) is that even with such family-based factors as parental aspirations, the interaction with school factors is critical. When the researchers investigated the validity of the commonly held view that parents' hopes for their children affect their children's school success, they found that although these aspirations per se did not influence achievement, parental willingness to advocate for their children (talking to teachers about academics, and so on) did. The authors link this finding to teachers' expectations: parental involvement in an advocacy role is important because it shapes teachers' perceptions, which in turn influence student achievement. One of our students expressed this understanding succinctly:

> The parents should go to all of the meetings of the parent-teacher organization at the school one afternoon each month because you help your son's or daughter's progress in class. If you help the teacher, the teacher help your children.

The need to take on an advocacy role presents a particular challenge for low-income language-minority parents. They may, for cultural reasons, defer to the authority of the teacher and the school, assume that the teacher is always right, or feel unable to intervene on behalf of their children because of the power differential between themselves and school authorities. Further, the time pressures from working several jobs and dealing with the survival demands of poverty-level existence may impede advocacy. The studies suggest, however, that for less literate parents it is precisely this attitude of advocacy and critical examination of school practices that may be their most powerful tool in shaping their children's school achievement.

How can parents with limited language and literacy skills provide input into schooling? Some of our own students have suggested that this dilemma can be approached through "critical support" — that being an advocate can range from helping the teacher so "the teacher help [the] children," to monitoring children's progress and letting teachers know of parental concerns, to participating in parent advocacy groups. Taking this perspective, the family literacy class can become a context for critical and reflective thinking about education, as well as for modeling ways of shaping children's education.

Assumption 5: The Social Context for Family Literacy

A final problem with the "transmission of school practices" model rests with the focus on parents' inadequacies, which obscures scrutiny of the real conditions giving rise to literacy problems. The social context for parents' own needs and strengths is often ignored or seen as an inherently negative factor that ultimately undermines the possibilities for learning. This social context may include, as Rosa suggests, family obligations, as well as housing, health care, and employment needs. In one study, parents identify "family health problems, work schedules, having small children, receiving only 'bad news' from school, and fears for safety" (Moles, 1982, p. 46) as factors inhibiting participation. Taylor and Dorsey-Gaines (1988) argue that it is the lack of social, political, and economic support for parents in dealing with these contextual concerns that puts children at risk (as opposed to lack of support by parents for children's literacy development).

Cultural differences may also be perceived as impediments to participation. Some parents, for example, come from cultures that view education as the exclusive domain of schools (Oliva, 1986). The solution is then framed in terms of "overcoming" cultural differences and "molding" parents to conform to school-determined expectations: parents must reorder their priorities so that they can become involved in school-determined activities. In one case, for example, programs were advised to send home notes in the imperative, telling parents they *must* attend meetings (Tran, 1986). But in order to make parental involvement possible, programs must provide support services (such as child care and translators for meetings).

Certainly these are important ways to encourage involvement; nevertheless, the underlying formulation remains: social-contextual and cultural factors are considered external factors that need to be dealt with outside the classroom, through program structures. Inside the classroom, the assumptions, goals, processes, and content of parental involvement still follow a "from the school to the parent" model. The expectation that "obstacles" should (or can) be taken care of as a precondition to participation may result in reinforcing the advantage of students who come from the least complicated social contexts.

On the other hand, if we believe that the social context is not a negative external force and recognize that the conditions that shape family literacy are central to the learning dynamic itself, we can begin to make literacy work relevant for parents (Collier, 1986). Although being expected to conform to culturally unfamiliar school expectations and practices may intimidate parents and drive them away, being encouraged to explore their own concerns and to advocate for their own expectations may free parents to become more involved with their own and their children's literacy development. In this alternative formulation, housing, education, work, and health issues are acknowledged and explored in the classroom, with literacy becoming a tool for addressing these issues, and cultural differences are perceived as strengths and resources that can bridge the gap between home and school. As these issues become part of the curriculum content, literacy will become more socially significant for families, which, as Taylor and others so often remind us, is what characterizes the families of successful readers.

Again, this alternative perspective is supported by both researchers and parents. The study of Mexican families in San Diego (Diaz et al., 1986) confirms the importance of situating literacy in its social context. Rather than starting with mainstream ways of using literacy and transmitting them to families, researchers looked at community practices as the basis for informing and modifying school practices. Local residents were trained as ethnographers to collect data on community writing practices; they then worked with teachers to use this data in developing classroom instructional modules. The function of writing to address community issues proved to be important.

> Parents, students, and others all impressed us with their concern for social issues that permeate community life. Virtually every conversation that began as a discussion of writing eventually turned to the problems of youth gangs, unemployment, immigration, the need to learn English and the like. It became clear to us that writing, schooling and social issues are complexly related phenomena in the community. (Diaz et al., 1986, p. 211)

Thus, by investigating community uses of writing, the researchers discovered essential social issues, which, when introduced into the classroom, became the vehicle for improving writing instruction. Student writing focused on the content of students' and families' interactions, life histories, conditions within the families, and parents' educational values. The underlying direction of curriculum development here is from the community to the classroom, rather than from the classroom to the community.

In Pajaro Valley, parents and children are involved in a project in which they read, discuss, and write children's stories together (Ada, 1988). Critical for this project is the positive value placed on the use of the home language both as a vehicle for communication within the family and as the foundation for children's academic success. Also important is the linking of readings to students' lives through a process of dialogue: readers share personal reactions and feelings, relate the story to their own experiences, critically analyze the events and ideas in the stories, and discuss real-life applications of this understanding. The process of sharing Spanish children's literature becomes the foundation for then asking children and parents to write their own stories about significant events in their lives. This kind of family literacy work draws on parents' cultural strengths and encourages critical thinking about key issues in family life.

Another project designed to build home and school links is the Chinle Navajo Parent-Child Reading Program (Viola, Gray, & Murphy, 1986). In this project, children bring books home and share them with their parents, either by reading or telling the stories. Children also write their own books based on Navajo stories they have heard from their parents and grandparents. In the process, the home culture is validated and promoted through literacy work; the parents' cultural knowledge contributes to rather than conflicts with school learning.

Work with parents in the UMass Project confirms the power of instruction centered around community and family issues. Through a process of co-investigation with students, our teachers have identified concerns about the new immigration law (the Immigration Reform and Control Act), housing, AIDS, language use at work, and bilingualism as relevant for their students. Students have developed their own language and literacy proficiency in the process of exploring these concerns through the use of collaboratively generated texts, thematic readings, language experience stories, Freirean problem-posing (Auerbach & Wallerstein, 1987; Wallerstein, 1983), dialogue journals, process writing, and photo stories. They have written letters to the editor about community problems, written and presented testimony for state funding hearings, and written about concerns for their children's schooling and their own language and literacy use in the community. One teacher reported that the quantity of her students' writings doubled when they wrote about immediate community issues such as day care. Not surprisingly, we have found that the quality of the work improves when the content is most closely linked with students' real concerns.

IMPLICATIONS FOR FAMILY LITERACY PROGRAM DESIGN

The analysis in this chapter points to a social-contextual model of family literacy that asks, How can we draw on parents' knowledge and experience to inform instruction? rather than, How can we transfer school practices into home contexts? The goal then is to increase the social significance of literacy in family life by incorporating community cultural forms and social issues into the content of literacy activities. This model is built on the particular conditions, concerns, and cultural expertise of specific communities, and, as such, does not involve a predetermined curriculum or set of practices or activities. Instead, the curriculum development process is participatory and is based on a collaborative investigation of critical issues in family or community life. As these issues emerge, they are explored and transformed into content-based literacy work, so that literacy can in turn become a tool for shaping this social context.[3]

This approach fosters a new formulation of what counts as family literacy. This broadened definition includes, but is not limited to, direct parent-child interactions around literacy tasks: reading with and/or listening to children; talking about and giving and receiving support for homework and school concerns; engaging in other activities with children that involve literacy (such as cooking, writing notes, and so on).

Equally important, however, are the following, often neglected, aspects of family literacy work:

1. *Parents working independently on reading and writing.* On the most basic level, just by developing their own literacy parents contribute to family literacy; as parents become less dependent on children, the burden shifts and children are freer to develop in their own ways.
2. *Using literacy to address family and community problems.* Dealing with issues such as immigration, employment, or housing through literacy work makes it possible for literacy to become socially significant in parents' lives; by extension it models the use of literacy as an integral part of daily life for children.
3. *Parents addressing child-rearing concerns through family literacy class.* By providing mutual support and a safe forum for dialogue, parents can share and develop their own strategies for dealing with issues such as teenage sex, drugs, discipline, and children's attitudes toward language choice.
4. *Supporting the development of the home language and culture.* As parents contribute to the development of the home language and culture, they build the foundation for their children's academic achievement, positive self-concept, and appreciation for their multicultural heritage. By valuing and building on parents' strengths, the status of those strengths is enhanced.
5. *Interacting with the school system.* The classroom becomes a place where parents can bring school-related issues and develop the ability to understand and respond to them. They can explore their attitudes toward their own and their children's school experiences. They can assess what they see and determine their responses, rehearse interactions with school personnel, and develop support networks for individuals and group advocacy.

The function of family literacy programs becomes the promotion of activities, events, and practices that correspond to this broadened definition. Our own attempts to implement this approach with bilingual parents include using reading and writing in a variety of ways:

1. To investigate home language use (for example, documenting who uses what language, to whom and when)
2. To explore family literacy practices (for example, evaluating critically a "how to help your children with homework" guide sent home by the school, which includes questions like these: Which of these things do you already do? Which would you like to do? Which do you think are not possible? What do you do that's not already included here?)
3. To explore cultural issues (for example, writing about children's positive and negative attitudes toward the home language, participating in a community Spanish literacy day, writing about faith healing)
4. To model whole-language activities that parents might do with children (for example, telling stories, making books)
5. To validate culture-specific literacy forms (for example, reading, writing, and telling folktales and proverbs)

6. To explore parenting issues (for example, exchanging letters with American parents in an Adult Basic Education program, writing letters of advice to pregnant teenagers in a high school program)
7. To use literacy to explore issues of learning and teaching (for example, responding to pictures of different educational settings in terms of their own educational experiences and expectations for children's education)
8. To address community, workplace, and health-care issues (for example, writing a class letter about police discrimination to a local newspaper, writing testimony for funding hearings on adult education and community services)
9. To practice advocacy in dealing with schools (for example, writing letters about concerns to children's teachers)
10. To explore political issues (for example, writing language-experience stories about the elections in Haiti)

We began this chapter by offering a window on Rosa's home context for literacy learning and by showing that schools need to take this context into account. This broader perspective on family literacy reflects our approach to addressing Rosa's challenge. We would like to end with another piece of Rosa's writing that illustrates how her writing has developed following this approach. It also illuminates the complexity of this challenge and her strengths in taking it on. Rosa paints here a picture of the richness of family interactions as she reflects on language and literacy use in her life:

> At Home
>
> I talk to my kids about school.
> I ask . . . ¿Como se portaron?
> They say very good.
> I continue to ask
> about the food . . . and the homework.
> they speak to me in english . . .
> I say I am sorry . . .
> Yo no entendi nada; por favor hablame
> en Español. . . . The older boy says OK . . . OK
> You study english you are supposed to
> understand. They repeat again to me
> slowly and more clearly. Yo les digo . . .
> Muchas gracias. . . . I love you.

NOTES

1. Students in our classes reflect the diversity found in many immigrant and refugee communities: at any given time, there may be up to 25 language groups represented in the program. Students' first language (L1) and educational backgrounds range from no L1 literacy or ESL proficiency to strong L1 literacy and intermediate ESL proficiency — from students who sign their names with an X to students with teaching degrees in their homelands.
2. Our annotated bibliography of English family literacy (Nash, 1987) lists sources used in addressing the following questions: What are the ways that families contribute to literacy develop-

ment? How do their contributions vary according to class and culture? What models are now being used to involve families in children's literacy development? What assumptions are these models based on? What are the particular issues that must be addressed in programs for non-English-speaking families and how is this being done? What alternatives are there to the predominant models?

3. Participants in the University of Massachusetts Family Literacy Project are documenting how this curriculum development process has been implemented in our classes. This curriculum development report will include a discussion of how students' concerns are identified, a range of themes that have emerged in our classes, how language and literacy have been extended around these themes, and issues that have arisen in the process of putting this participatory, social-contextual approach into practice.

REFERENCES

Ada, A. F. (1988). The Pajaro Valley experience: Working with Spanish-speaking parents to develop children's reading and writing skills in the home through the use of children's literature. In T. Skutnabb-Kangas and J. Cummins (Eds.), *Minority education: From shame to struggle* (pp. 224–238). Philadelphia: Multilingual Matters.

Auerbach, E., & Wallerstein, N. (1987). *ESL for action: Problem-posing at work*. Reading, MA: Addison-Wesley.

Bell, T. M. (1988, October). Keynote address at *Adult Learners: Arizona's Future* conference, Phoenix, AZ.

Business Council for Effective Literacy. (1989, April). Newsletter.

Cazden, F. (1986). ESL teachers as language advocates for children. In P. Rigg & D. S. Enright (Eds.), *Children and ESL: Integrating perspectives* (pp. 9–21). Washington, DC: TESOL.

Chall, J. S., & Snow, C. (1982*). Families and literacy: The contributions of out of school experiences to children's acquisition of literacy*. A final report to the National Institute of Education.

Collier, V. P. (1986). Cross-cultural policy issues in minority and majority parent involvement. In *Issues of parent involvement and literacy. Proceedings of the symposium at Trinity College* (pp. 73–78). Washington, DC: Trinity College, Department of Education and Counseling.

Delgado-Gaitan, C. (1987). Mexican adult literacy: New directions for immigrants. In S. R. Goldman & K. Trueba (Eds.), *Becoming literate in English as a second language* (pp. 9–32). Norwood, NJ: Ablex.

Diaz, S., Moll, L., & Mehan, K. (1986). Socio-cultural resources in instruction: A context-specific approach. In *Beyond language: Social and cultural factors in schooling language minority children* (pp. 87–229). Los Angeles: California State Department of Education and California State University.

Epstein, J. (1986). Parent involvement: Implications for LEP parents. In *Issues of parent involvement in literacy. Proceedings of the symposium at Trinity College* (pp. 6–16). Washington, DC: Trinity College, Department of Education and Counseling.

Freire, P. (1970). *Pedagogy of the oppressed*. New York: Seabury Press.

Goldenberg, C. N. (1984, October 10–13). *Low-income parents' contributions to the reading achievement of their first-grade children*. Paper presented at the meeting of the Evaluation Network/Evaluation Research Society, San Francisco.

Heath, S. B. (1983). *Ways with words*. Cambridge, Eng.: Cambridge University Press.

Issues of parent involvement and literacy. (1986). Proceedings of the symposium at Trinity College, June 6–7. Washington, DC: Trinity College, Department of Education and Counseling.

Moles, O. C. (1982, November). Synthesis of recent research on parent participation in children's education. *Educational Leadership, 40,* 44–47.

Nash, A. (1987). *English family literacy: An annotated bibliography*. Boston: University of Massachusetts/Boston, English Family Literacy Project.

Olivia, J. (1986). Why parent tutors? Cultural reasons. In *Issues of parent involvement and literacy. Proceedings of the symposium at Trinity College* (pp. 79–81). Washington, DC: Trinity College, Department of Education and Counseling.

Shor, I. (1986). *Culture wars: School and society in the conservative restoration, 1969–1984.* New York: Routledge & Kegan Paul/Methuen.

Simich-Dudgeon, C. (1987, March). Involving limited English proficient parents as tutors in their children's education. *ERIC/CLL News Bulletin, 10*(2).

Snow, C. (1987). Factors influencing vocabulary and reading achievement in low income children. In R. Apple (Ed.), *Toegepaste Taalwetenschap in Artikelen*, Special 2 (pp. 124–128). Amsterdam: ANELA.

Street, B. V. (1984). *Literacy in theory and practice.* Cambridge, Eng.: Cambridge University Press.

Taylor, D. (1981). The family and the development of literacy skills and values. *Journal of Research in Reading, 4*(2), 92–103.

Taylor, D. (1983). *Family literacy: Young children learning to read and write.* Exeter, NH: Heinemann.

Taylor, D., & Dorsey-Gaines, C. (1988). *Growing up literate: Learning from inner city families.* Portsmouth, NH: Heinemann.

Tizard, J., Schofield, W. N., & Hewison, J. (1982). Symposium: Reading collaboration between teachers and parents in assisting children's reading. *British Journal of Educational Psychology, 52*, 1–15.

Topping, K., & Wolfendale, S. (Eds.). (1985). *Parental involvement in children's reading.* New York: Nichols.

Tran, B. T. (1986). Cultural issues in Indochinese parent involvement. In *Issues of parent involvement and literacy. Proceedings of the symposium at Trinity College* (pp. 65–66). Washington, DC: Trinity College, Department of Education and Counseling.

Urzua, C. (1986). A children's story. In P. Rigg & D. S. Enright (Eds.), *Children and ESL: Integrating perspectives* (pp. 93–112). Washington, DC: TESOL.

Viola, M., Gray, A., & Murphy, B. (1986, May). *Report on the Navajo Parent Child Reading Program at the Chinle Primary School.* Chinle School District, AZ.

Wallerstein, N. (1983). *Language and culture in conflict: Problem-posing in the ESL classroom.* Reading, MA: Addison-Wesley.

The work reported on in this paper was funded by Title VII Office of Bilingual Education and Minority Language Affairs, grant number G008635277, procurement number 003JH60021. The views, opinions, and findings contained in this chapter are not to be construed as OBEMLA's position or policy, unless so designated.

The work reported on here is the result of collaboration with UMass/Boston English Family Literacy Project staff: Ann Cason, Rosario Gomez-Sanford, Loren McGrail, Andrea Nash, and Madeline Rhum. We owe a special debt of gratitude to the students whose work appears in the paper and the many others who taught us about their ways of learning and teaching. We would also like to thank Candace Mitchell for her insightful critique of earlier drafts of this paper.

Reading the World of School Literacy: Contextualizing the Experience of a Young African American Male

ARLETTE INGRAM WILLIS

L et me share a conversation that I had with my nine-year-old son, and the context in which it occurred:

It's a cold, frosty winter morning, and everyone has left for work or school except my youngest son Jake and me. I am busy applying last-minute touches to my makeup and encouraging Jake, in the next room, to "step it up." I wonder why he is dragging around; school starts in ten minutes and we haven't yet left the house. Jake knows the routine; I wonder if something is troubling him. So, I peek around the corner and find him looking forlorn — you know, a scowl on his face, a look of growing despair and sadness. I forget about the clock and attend to him.

"Jake, what's wrong? Why are you so unhappy?" I ask.

"We have the Young Authors [writing] Contest today, and I don't have anything to write about."

"Sure you do. There are lots of things you can write about," I encourage him. (I believe people write best about those subjects they know and care about.) "Why don't you write about baseball or soccer?"

"No," he replies. "A kid at our school wrote about cancer last year, and the story went all the way to the next state [regionals]."

"Well," I answer, "maybe you should write about something funny — like when you go to the barbershop. You and your brothers are always talking about your trips there."[1]

"Oh no, Mom, they wouldn't understand. When I just get my haircut, they always ask me, 'Why do you have that line in your hair?' 'It's not a line, it's a part,*' I try to tell them. I can't write about the barbershop. They won't understand."*

"Well," I say, trying to clarify what I really mean, "I don't mean write about getting a haircut. I mean writing about all the funny people that come in and the things that happen while you are at the barbershop. You and your brothers always come

Harvard Educational Review Vol. 65 No. 1 Spring 1995, 30–49

home tellin' a funny story and laugh about it for the rest of the week. That's what I mean by writing about the barbershop."

"No, Mom. They won't understand," he insists.

"What do you mean, `they won't understand?' Who is this `they'?" I ask.

"The people in my class," he replies, somewhat frustrated.

Jake continues, "You should read this story that M. wrote. It is a mystery story and it's really good. I can't beat that story. I'll bring you a copy of it if I can. I know it will win." (Sadder now that he has had time to consider his competition, Jake turns and walks toward his room.)

Wanting him to participate in the contest, I ask, "How do you know M.'s story is good?"

"She read it in class. Everybody said it's really good," he responds.

"Well, I still think you should try. You are a really good writer. Look at all the `good stuff' you wrote in Mrs. S.'s room. You could rewrite some of it and turn it in."

Finally he answers, "I'll think about it," and we go off to school.

As I remember the conversation, Jake's tone of voice hinted at both frustration and defensiveness. I interpreted his use of phrases like "they always ask" and "I try to tell them" to mean that since he gets his hair cut every two weeks, it gets pretty tiresome answering the same questions from his classmates so frequently.[2] Furthermore, I interpreted his intonation to mean that he has had to stand his ground with other children who either do not agree with his definition of a "part," or who try to define its meaning for him.

I believe that Jake cannot bring this aspect of his life and culture into the classroom because he doesn't feel that it will be understood by his classmates and teacher. When Jake says "They won't understand," I interpret his words to mean that if his classmates cannot understand the simplest action in getting a haircut — the barber taking less than ten seconds to place a part in his hair — how can he expect them to understand the context and culture that surround the entire event. Also, I see Jake's reluctance to share something as commonplace in his home and community life as a haircut as a way of distancing this portion of his life from the life he leads at school. It seems that he has come to understand that as an African American he must constantly make a mediating effort to help others understand events that appear to be commonplace on the surface, but are in fact culturally defined.

Several interwoven incidents have helped me to understand the conversation with Jake. I will briefly describe them to provide the context for my understanding of the subtle, yet ever-present and unquestioned role of cultural accommodation that occurs in the school literacy experiences of children from diverse backgrounds. I have been teaching courses in multicultural literature at my university for several years. After my fall 1993 course, I reflected, using journal writing, on my growing experience teaching multicultural literature courses.[3] Teaching these courses has led me to a more informed understanding of how, in the practice of school literacy, there are many culturally defined moments of conflict that call daily for cultural understanding, knowledge, and sensitivity from teachers. These "moments" also challenge non-mainstream students to choose between cultural assimilation and accommodation, or resistance. My journal entries centered on my readings, research, and, most importantly, my daily conversations about school life with my three sons, who range in age from nine to seventeen. In my classes, I have often shared my sons' school experiences and my reactions to them in an effort to help my students understand how teachers' daily subtle and seemingly inconsequential decisions can affect the learning of the children they teach.

A striking example of a teacher's unintentional disregard for the cultural history, understanding, experiences, and voice of a student occurred when my oldest son struggled to meet the requirements of a national essay contest entitled, "What it means to be an American." One of the contest's restrictions was that students should not mention the concept of race. My son thought this was an unfair and impossible task to complete, since his African American identity is synonymous with his being American. Yet, his efforts to articulate the difficulty of the task to his English teacher were frustrated by her response that, although she was empathic, she did not have the authority to change the rules. I intervened and spoke with the teacher at length about my son's values, beliefs, and his unwillingness to compromise himself in order to compete in an essay contest in which he had little or no interest other than a grade.

My second son also had a similar experience involving unintentional cultural insensitivity. He is a member of the school band, which was having its fall concert. While attending, I noticed that all the music the band played was composed by Europeans or European Americans. I spoke with one of the band directors, and asked rhetorically if there were any songs that the band members could perform that were composed by people of color. She responded that she had never considered the choices she made as nonrepresentative of all the students who had to learn them, while I could see little else than the absence of cultural diversity. I was pleased when the winter concert included some Hanukkah tunes. It was a start.

REFLECTIONS

Though my conversation with Jake is now months old, it has continued to haunt me. I have been deeply concerned about a noticeable shift in my son's attitude toward writing. Jake's early writing experiences in kindergarten and first grade revealed that he found writing to be a natural outlet for self-expression. He often wrote for pleasure and has kept all of his drafts. Jake learned the process approach to writing in first grade and treasures his portfolio, which he had originally developed in that class. I have found him in his room revisiting a piece he had written earlier. However, this past year I have noticed a change in his level of production. Jake no longer writes detailed accounts. Instead, he spends a great deal of time thinking about what to write and how to say it. While I believe these are laudatory traits of a good writer, his teachers often accuse him of being underproductive.

Reflecting on our conversation, I sense that Jake believes (understands?) that his perceived audience will neither value nor understand the cultural images and nuances he wishes to share in his writing. Jake is a child wrestling with an internal conflict that is framed by the sociohistorical and sociocultural inequities of U.S. society. He is trying to come to grips with how he can express himself in a manner that is true to his "real self," and yet please his teacher and audience of readers who are, in effect, evaluating his culture, thinking, language, and reality.

Jake's perception of an unaccepting audience is not unique. Several researchers have expressed similar concerns about the narrowly defined culture of acceptable school literacy and the growing literateness of culturally and linguistically diverse children (Delpit, 1986, 1991, 1993; Gutierrez, 1992; Heath, 1983; Labov, 1972; Ovando & Collier, 1985; Reyes & Molner, 1991; Sawyer & Rodriguez, 1992).[4] Why is it clearer to children than to adults that there are systematic, institutional inequalities in the decisions teachers make about the "appropriate" methods and materials used to enhance their students' literacy development?

Like millions of culturally and linguistically diverse people, Jake understands the unstated reality of schooling in U.S. society: It is built upon a narrow understanding of school knowledge and literacy, which are defined and defended as what one needs to know and how one needs to know it in order to be successful in school and society. As Barrera (1992) explains:

> The school culture can be seen to reflect the dominant class and, so too, the cultures of literacy and literature embedded within the school culture. For this reason, the teaching of literacy and literature are considered to be neither acultural nor neutral, but cultural and political. (p. 236)

The real question is, why do we as educators continue this "sin of omission" — that is, allowing the cultural knowledge of culturally and linguistically diverse children to be ignored, devalued, and unnurtured as valid sources of literacy acquisition? Excerpts from the writings of five noted African Americans help to illustrate my point.

The Past Revisited

The problem of defining one's literary self is not a new one. As noted scholar W. E. B. Du Bois argued in 1903:

> After the Egyptian and Indian, the Greek and Roman, the Teuton and Mongolian, the Negro is a sort of seventh son, born with a veil, and gifted with second-sight in this American world, — a world which yields him no true self-consciousness, but only lets him see himself through the revelation of the other world. It is a peculiar sensation this double-consciousness, this sense of always looking at one's self through the eyes of others. . . . One ever feels his twoness, an American, a Negro; two souls, two thoughts, two unreconciled strivings; two warring ideals in one dark body, whose dogged strength alone keeps it from being torn asunder. The history of the American Negro is the history of this strife, — this longing to attain self conscious manhood, to merge his double self into a better and truer self. (1903/1965, pp. 214–215)

Similarly, historian Carter G. Woodson (1933/1990) stated:

> In this effort to imitate, however, those "educated people" are sincere. They hope to make the Negro conform quickly to the standard of the whites and thus remove the

pretext for the barriers between the races. They do not realize, however, that if the Negroes do successfully imitate the whites, nothing new has thereby been accomplished. You simply have a larger number of persons doing what others have been doing. The unusual gifts of the race have not thereby been developed. (p. 4)

Poet Langston Hughes (1951) expressed a similar notion:

> I guess being colored doesn't make me not like
> the same things other folks like who are other races.
> So will my page be colored that I write?
> Being me, it will not be white.
> But it will be
> a part of you, instructor.
> You are white —
> yet a part of me, as I am a part of you.
> That's American.
> Sometimes perhaps you don't want to be a part of me.
> Nor do I often want to be a part of you.
> But we are, that's true!
> As I learn from you,
> I guess you learn from me —
> although you're older — and white —
> and somewhat more free. (pp. 39–40)

Novelist Ralph Ellison (1952) writes:

> I am invisible, understand, simply because people refuse to see me. Like the bodiless heads you see sometimes in circus sideshows, it is as though I have been surrounded by mirrors of hard, distorting glass. When they approach me they see only my surroundings, themselves, or figments of their imagination — indeed, everything and anything except me. (p. 3)

And, finally, Toni Morrison (1992) refers to the phenomenon of double consciousness as "writing for a white audience" (p. xii). She asks:

> What happens to the writerly imagination of a black author who is at some level *always* conscious of representing one's own race to, or in spite of, a race of readers that understands itself to be "universal" or race-free? In other words, how are "literary whiteness" and "literary blackness" made, and what is the consequence of these constructions? (p. xii)

Like other culturally and linguistically diverse people before him (including myself and every other person of color with whom I have shared this incident), Jake has encountered the struggle of literary personhood.

Questions and concerns flood my mind: Where, I wonder, has he gotten the idea of a "White" audience — that is, the sense that his classmates and others who read his writing will not appreciate what he has to share? When did his concept of a "White" audience arise? My questions persist: How long has Jake known, intuitively perhaps, that his school literacy experiences have been tempered through a mainstream lens?

Will Jake continue to resist "writing for a white audience?" When do culturally and linguistically diverse children learn that they must choose between selfhood and accommodation?[5] When do they learn that "the best way, then, to succeed — that is, to receive rewards, recognition . . . is to learn and reproduce the ways of the dominant group?" (Scheurich, 1992, p. 7). Must there be only one acceptable culture reflected in current school literacy programs? What thoughts, words, and language is Jake replacing with those of the dominant culture in order to please his audience? Will he ever be able to recapture his true literate self after years of accommodation?

As a third grader, Jake is writing, but not for pleasure. Whereas once he wrote as a way of expressing himself or as a hobby, now he does not. He only writes to complete assignments. Much of the "joy" he experienced in writing for pleasure seems to have waned. I recently read some of his writings and noted that he concentrated on topics that do not reflect African American culture. For example, his most recent entries are about his spoon collection, running track, rocks, and football — pretty generic stuff.

My fears are like those of all parents who believe they have prepared their child, having done all that they have read and know a parent should do, yet see their child struggling with a history, a tradition, that is much larger than they can battle.[6] What can I do to help my son and children like him enjoy the freedom of writing and reading? How can I help them value the culturally relevant events in their lives? How can school literacy programs begin to acknowledge, respect, and encourage the diverse cultural knowledge and experiences that children bring to school?

In this article, I am speaking as a teacher educator and parent. This article is an attempt to begin conversations with my colleagues that will address cultural complexities so often ignored in literacy research and practice. For too long, the only perspective published was European Americans' understanding of literacy events. Over the past few years, other cultural perspectives have been published and, more recently, a few have questioned the connection between the theoretical notions of literacy and the historical, and daily, reality of institutionalized inequalities.

As a scholar, I can begin conversations with my colleagues about reexamining theories of literacy to include the role of culture and linguistic diversity. Moreover, teachers and teacher educators like myself can then extend these conversations to reinterpret literacy development, school literacy programs, and teacher education methods and materials to include the experiences of nonmainstream cultures. Finally, I can further extend these conversations into rethinking how we teach and practice school literacy.

BROADENING THE SCOPE

Several contemporary positions on literacy serve to enlighten our understanding of how literacy is defined in the field and how it is defined in practice. In this section, I will offer a brief look at several definitions. First, Cook-Gumperz (1986) describes two competing definitions of school literacy that are useful in framing this discussion. She states that "inherent in our contemporary attitude to literacy and schooling is a confusion between a prescriptive view of literacy, as a statement about the values and uses of knowledge, and a descriptive view of literacy, as cognitive abilities which are promoted and assessed through schooling" (p. 14). Second, a more expansive definition of how literacy is conceptualized is offered by Freire and Macedo (1987). They suggest that "literacy becomes a meaningful construct to the degree that it is viewed as a set of practices that functions to either empower or disempower people. In the larger sense, literacy is analyzed according to whether it serves a set of cultural practices that promotes democratic and emancipatory change" (p. 141). Further, they clarify their position on literacy by noting that "for the notion of literacy to become meaningful it has to be situated within a theory of cultural production and viewed as an integral part of the way in which people produce, transform, and reproduce meaning" (p. 142). Third, more general discussions of literacy define literacy as functional, cultural, or critical. Each of these concepts also refers to very different ways of thinking about literacy. *Functional literacy* refers to mastery of the skills needed to read and write as measured by standardized forms of assessment. This view of literacy is similar to Cook-Gumperz's (1986) notion of a descriptive view of literacy. The functional view promotes literacy as a cognitive set of skills that are universal, culturally neutral, and equally accessible through schooling, and is based on a positivistic ideology of learning. Further, this view is heavily dependent on the use of standardized testing measures as a proving ground for literacy acquisition. Most basal reading series and programmed reading approaches embrace the functional/descriptive view of literacy.

Cultural literacy is a term that is most often associated with E. D. Hirsch's 1987 book, *Cultural Literacy: What Every American Needs to Know.* Hirsch defines cultural literacy as "the network of information that all competent readers possess. It is the background information, stored in their minds, that enables them to take up a newspaper and read it with an adequate level of comprehension, getting the point, grasping the implications, relating what they read to the unstated context which alone gives meaning to what they read" (p. 2). Cook-Gumperz (1986) has labeled this form of literacy "prescriptive." In effect, this form of cultural literacy validates language forms, experiences, literature, and histories of some and marginalizes or ignores the language forms, experiences, literature, and histories of others. In the United States, the prescriptive view can be seen in the use of standard English, Eurocentric ways of knowing and learning, a Eurocentric literary canon, and a conventional unproblematic rendering of U.S. history. This form of the cultural/prescriptive view marginalizes the pluralistic composition of U.S. society by devaluing the language, contributions, and histories of some groups. Traditional or conventional approaches to school-based literacy take this form. McLaren (1987) argues that there is a second form of cultural literacy. He writes that this form of cultural literacy "advocates using the language standards and cultural information students bring into the classroom as legitimate and important constituents of learning" (p. 214). Cultural literacy, thus described, suggests that the language and experiences of each student who enters the classroom should be respected and nurtured. This form of cultural literacy recognizes that there are differences in language forms, experiences, literature, and histories of students that will affect literacy learning. Social constructivist theories fall into this prescriptive/cultural literacy category. These approaches to literacy emphasize the active engagement of learners in making meaning from print, the social context of literacy learning, and the importance of recognizing individual and cultural differences.

Critical literacy refers to the ideologies that underlie the relationship between power and knowledge in society. The work of Brazilian educator Paulo Freire has been influential to U.S. efforts to adopt a critical literacy position. Freire, among others, suggests that literacy is more than the construction of meaning from print: Literacy must also include the ability to understand oneself and one's relationship to the world. Giroux's (1987) discussion is worth quoting here at length:

> As Paulo Freire and others have pointed out, schools are not merely instructional sites designed to transmit knowledge; they are also cultural sites. As sites, they generate and embody support for particular forms of culture as is evident in the school's support for specific ways of speaking, the legitimating of distinct forms of knowledge, the privileging of certain histories and patterns of authority, and the confirmation of particular ways of experiencing and seeing the world. Schools often give the appearance of transmitting a common culture, but they, in fact, more often than not, legitimate what can be called a dominant culture. (p. 176)

Giroux goes on to state:

> At issue here is understanding that student experience has to be understood as part of an interlocking web of power relations in which some groups of students are often privileged over others. But if we are to view this insight in an important way, we must understand that it is imperative for teachers to critically examine the cultural backgrounds and social formations out of which their students produce the categories they use to give meaning to the world. For teachers are not merely dealing with students who have individual interests, they are dealing primarily with individuals whose stories, memories, narratives, and readings of the world are inextricably related to wider social and cultural formations and categories. This issue here is not merely one of relevance but one of power. (p. 177)

Similarly, Apple (1992) has argued for nearly a decade that "it is naive to think of the school curriculum as neutral knowledge. . . . Rather, what counts as legitimate knowledge is the result of complex power relations and struggles among identifiable class, race, gender, and religious groups" (p. 4). Critical literacy draws attention to the historical, political, cultural, and social dimensions of literacy. Most importantly, this form of literacy focuses on power relations in society and how knowledge and power are interrelated. Educationalists, practitioners in particular, have not yet fully grasped this position on literacy. The other forms of literacy, functional/descriptive and cultural/prescriptive, do not include, among other things, the notion of power relations in literacy instruction.

Philosophically, social constructivist notions (a form of prescriptive/cultural literacy) may be seen as comparable to those espoused by critical literacy. From the schema theorists of the early 1980s to the social constructivist theories of the 1990s, literacy development is understood to be a "meaning making process" — that is, socially mediated (Meek, 1982). Drawing primarily on the work of Halliday (1975),

Vygotsky (1978), and Goodman (1989), a number of literacy researchers have stressed the universality of language learning. For example, Goodman's (1989) discussion of the philosophical stance of whole language is that:

> At the same time that whole language sees common strengths and universals in human learning, it expects and recognizes differences among learners in culture, value systems, experience, needs, interests and language. Some of these differences are personal, reflecting the ethnic, cultural, and belief systems of the social groups pupils represent. Thus teachers in whole-language programs value differences among learners as they come to school and differences in objectives and outcomes as students progress through school. (p. 209)

However, I argue that the role of culture in the social constructivist theories is not as well defined as it needs to be in a pluralistic or multicultural society. While it is fair to say that unidimensional views of culture would not be supported by social constructivists, it is also fair to say that the multilayered complexity of culture, especially the cultures of historically oppressed groups, is not explicitly addressed by them either. By way of example, I will examine the prescriptive/cultural literacy foundation of whole language. Goodman (1986) argues that "language begins as means of communication between members of the group. Through it, however, each developing child acquires the life view, the cultural perspective, the ways of meaning particular to its own culture" (p. 11). But this definition fails to acknowledge that in addition to acquiring culturally "neutral" knowledge, some children must also acquire a Eurocentric cultural perspective to be successful in school. It is not sufficient to suggest that the language and culture of every student is welcomed, supported, and nurtured in school without explicitly addressing the power relations in institutions, social practice, and literature that advantage some and hinder others (Delpit, 1988; Reyes, 1992). School-based literacy, in its varying forms, fails to acknowledge explicitly the richness of the cultural ways of knowing, forms of language other than standard English, and the interwoven relationship among power, language, and literacy that silences kids like Jake.[7] To fail to attend to the plurality and diversity within the United States — and to fail to take seriously the historic past and the social and political contexts that have sustained it — is to dismiss the cultural ways of knowing, language, experiences, and voices of children from diverse linguistic and cultural backgrounds. This is not to imply that programs based on such theories need to be scrapped. It does mean that social constructivist theories need to be reworked to include the complexities of culture that are currently absent. It will also mean that teacher education will need to: 1) make explicit the relationship among culture, language, literacy and power; and 2) train teachers to use cultural information to support and nurture the literacy development of all the students who enter their classrooms.

When taken at face value, social constructivist theory would lead one to assume that new holistic approaches to literacy are culturally validating for all students. An examination of Jake's home and school contexts for his developing understanding of literacy illustrates that this is not always true. That is, we need to understand where he acquired language and his understanding of culture, as well as his history of literacy instruction, to understand how he is "reading the world" of school literacy and how his experiences with a variety of school literacy forms, including holistic approaches, have not addressed his cultural ways of knowing, experiences, language, and voice.

LITERACY CONTEXTS

Home Context

Literacy acquisition does not evolve in one context or through one type of event; rather, it is a complex endeavor that is mediated through culture. Jake's home literacy environment began with our preparations for him as a new baby. He was brought into a loving two-parent home in which two older brothers were awaiting his arrival. Jake also entered a print- and language-rich environment. He was read to when only a few months old, and continues to share reading (and now writing) with family members. Like the homes of many other middle-class children, Jake's is filled with language, and a range of standard and vernacular languages is used. Our talk centers around family issues, but also includes conversations about world events, neighborhood and school concerns, and personal interests. There are stories, prayers, niceties (manners), verbal games, family jokes, homework assignments, daily Bible reading and discussion, as well as family vacations and excursions to museums, zoos, concerts, and ball parks. Daily routines include reading and responding to mail, making schedules, appointments, grocery and chore lists, and taking telephone messages, all of which include opportunities for shared conversations. There is also a family library that consists of adult fiction, nonfiction, and reference materials. Conversations flow constantly and with ease as we enjoy sharing with each other.

Prior to Jake's entering school, we enjoyed music, games, songs, fingerplay, writing notes on unlined paper with lots of different writing tools, long nature walks, as well as trips to the store, library, barbershop, and church.[8] All these activities were accompanied by lots of talk to expand understanding and draw connections. In addition, Jake and his brothers all have their own bedroom library in which they keep their favorite books, collected since early childhood. Jake's written communications include telephone messages, calendar events, schedules, notes, recipes, invitations, thank-you notes, game brackets (Sega or Nintendo), and occasionally letters and poems.

Jake has a special interest in his collections of stickers, stamps, coins, puzzles, board games, maps, newspaper clippings, and baseball, football, and basketball cards. He also enjoys reading his bedtime story books, magazines (especially *Sports Illustrated for Kids*), and the newspaper (his favorite parts are the sports page, the comics, and the weather map).

What makes Jake's understanding of language and literacy so culturally different from his school's, although both are apparently based on middle-class standards, is that his home literacy events have been culturally defined and are mediated through his cultural understanding. Jake's world is African American; that is, his growing understanding of who and what he is has consciously and unconsciously been mediated through an African American perspective. We select our artwork, magazines, novels, television programs, music, videos, and movies to reflect interests in African American life and society.

School Context

Like most parents, I inquired about the kindergarten's literacy program before enrolling Jake in school.[9] I wanted to have some idea of how his teachers viewed literacy development and how they planned to conduct literacy instruction. My primary question was, "What approach to literacy will you use?" Jake's private, full-day kindergarten was founded by three Jewish women, two of whom taught the kindergarten class, while the third served as school administrator. The teachers informed me that they had taught for many years and were aware of the modern trends. They had therefore designed a program that included what they considered to be the strong points of several programs. Jake's classmates included twelve European Americans (eight were Jewish) and two African American children. His teachers tried to provide all the children with what they thought the children would need to know in order to be successful readers and writers in grade one. As a result, the classroom was colorful and full of print. Labels were placed on cubbyholes, activity centers, children's table chairs, and charts.[10] The reading material was an eclectic mix of basals, trade books, and a small library of children's classics.

In first grade, Jake attended a public elementary school. This classroom was a mixed-age group (grades one and two) of twenty-three children, including seventeen European Americans, four African Americans, and two Asian Americans. His teacher described her literacy program as literature-based, and she stressed reading and writing. This teacher read to the children, who also read individually or in small groups. The reading materials included recipients of the Caldecott award and other award-winning books, stories, and poems by children's favorite authors, classics of children's literature, and writing "published" by the students. The children especially liked to read folk tales. As they gained reading and writing skills, the children coauthored, published, and shared their own work. Students were also encouraged to read and write for pleasure. In all these works, I recall that very few were written about or authored by people of color, except for a few on the Caldecott list.

Jake attended a different elementary school for second grade. I eagerly met his new teacher and asked my standard question about literacy. She informed me that she used the basal approach, which she believed ensured that all the "skills" needed to be a successful reader would be covered. The particular basal series she used included "universal" themes and contained illustrations of various racial/ethnic groups but made little reference to the culture of the people. There were several "ethnic" stories, but I consider their authorship suspect, at best.[11] The series also included isolated skill development, vocabulary regulated text, several thematically organized stories, informational selections, and limited writing opportunities. This class of twenty-eight children included twenty European Americans, five African Americans, and three Asian Americans.

Not wishing Jake to repeat this basal approach in grade three, I spoke with other mothers in the neighborhood, soliciting information about the "good" third-grade teachers. After much prayer, I informed the principal of my choice. Now in third grade, Jake is experiencing what his teacher refers to as a whole language approach to literacy, which includes lots of reading and writing for meaning, working in cooperative groups, process writing, and having sustained time for reading and writing. Writing is a daily activity, and Thursday mornings are designated as Writing Workshop mornings with parent volunteers who assist students in a variety of ways, from brainstorming topics to editing their writing. The teacher allows time for individual and small group readings of trade books on a daily basis. Since my conversation with Jake, I have learned his teacher had selected the books she planned to use during the school year, ahead of time, and the children were allowed only to choose which of these books to read. All of the books were written by European American authors. Even the folk tales from other countries were rewritten by European Americans. Very few books by or about U.S. minorities have been read to students by the teacher, student teachers, or in the reading groups.

I cannot account for the moment-by-moment decisions Jake's teachers have had to make each day. However, I can review the philosophies behind the programs they use. Theoretically, each literacy program purports to be culturally neutral and not mediated by any dominant view of language, when, in fact, a Eurocentric, mainstream cultural view dominates. Darder (1991) argues that it is important to understand the historicity of knowledge:

> The dominant school culture functions not only to support the interests and values of the dominant society, but also to marginalize and invalidate knowledge forms and experiences that are significant to subordinate and oppressed groups. This function is best illustrated in the ways that curriculum often blatantly ignores the histories of women, people of color, and the working class. (p. 79)

Having held a conference with each of Jake's teachers and observed each class setting on several occasions, I can say without hesitation that each teacher believed that she was doing her best to meet the needs of each child in her classroom. That is, she was trying to foster a growing sense of literacy competence in each child. Yet, I don't believe that any of Jake's teachers were aware that they were also narrowly defining the cultural lens through which all children in the classroom were expected to understand literacy.

Thus, in four short years Jake has experienced a wide range of philosophies, approaches, and instruction in literacy, and, at the same time, a narrow ethnocentric view of school literacy. All of his teachers have meant to encourage his growth and development as a literate person. Why, then, have they failed to acknowledge an important part of who he is and what he *culturally* brings to the school literacy program? Reyes (1992) argues that teachers often fail to make adjustments in their approaches to literacy for culturally and linguistically diverse learners because

> the majority of [teachers] are members of the dominant culture, implementing programs designed primarily for mainstream students. Teachers implementing these programs tend to treat students of color as exceptions to the norm, as students who should be assimilated into the dominant group, rather than accommodated according to their own needs. (p. 437)

Some theorists, researchers, and teachers may suggest the counterargument; that is, that elements of the mainstream culture are apparent in all "parallel cultures" and that it is easiest to teach to the mainstream (Hamilton, 1989).[12] I would argue that to ignore, consciously or not, the culture and language that each child brings to the literacy table is to miseducate him or her. As the research by Au (1993), Morrow (1992), and Reyes and Laliberty (1992), among others, has shown, when cultural and linguistic adjustments are made to school literacy programs, all children benefit.

You may wonder if I have tried to inform Jake's teachers of the narrowness of the literacy lens through which they seem to be defining literacy development and instruction. I admit that I have failed miserably to take a strong stand. Rather than confront them about the lack of culturally responsive literacy instruction, I have expressed my concerns for Jake's personal literacy growth. For example, I have shared multicultural book lists with Jake's teachers and offered to serve as a resource. I have honestly wanted to inform Jake's teachers of two things: one, the need to be more sensitive in their approach to the language and cultural experiences that children bring to the classroom; and two, the need to incorporate more books written by people of color to legitimize the contributions of all literate people. Yet I have also believed that expressing my thoughts might jeopardize Jake's educational future with some kind of backlash.

A STATUS REPORT

While literacy theorists, researchers, and practitioners continue to suggest that school literacy is culturally neutral, Jake's literacy experiences offer an intimate and compelling argument that, as currently practiced, school literacy has been and still is narrowly defined in terms of culture. Only the packaging is new.

Descriptions of my conversation with Jake have met with lots of head nodding and similar stories from many of my non-White students. Delpit (1988) has shared similar insights into what she correctly describes as the "silenced dialogue." The commonsense response among some people of color to school literacy (and schooling in general) has been to take a "way things are" attitude. Many people of color understand that there are inequalities in the educational system; however, we also understand that little can be done without massive school reform. So, to be educated in our current system requires accepting that "this is the way things are. If you want to advance you must learn to play the game." That is, institutionalized racism is something we all know, but see as an unavoidable part of education in U.S. society.

In sharing my analysis with my graduate students, several European Americans have questioned why I refer to Jake's school literacy experiences as being narrowly defined and inquired what is so "acultural" about his literacy education. They ask, "Aren't literature-based and whole language programs built upon notions of constructivist theory that embrace notions of culture?" Of course, my students' understanding is correct: Current holistic school literacy programs support constructivist theory. I guess that's what is so frightening.

While the rhetoric of school literacy programs suggests that culture is part of the theoretical framework, "culture" has been narrowly defined to mean middle-class European American culture. The tacit assumption is, then, that all children are being well served by the new literacy programs that are built on the "natural" language acquisition of middle-class European American children. However, natural language acquisition is mediated through the particular culture in which the child lives. The reality, then, as shared in this article, is that theoreticians, researchers, teacher educators, practitioners, and publishers of literacy approaches and programs are frequently unaware of their assumptions.

Some may truly believe that they are delivering on their promise to build on the culture and language of the child, but what they have been unable, or unwilling, to acknowledge is that school literacy, as it exists, is not universal or reflective of the language and culture of many children. They claim that current school literacy programs and practices are acultural. These programs, however, clearly put some children at a disadvantage, while giving an advantage to others. It is clear, even to a nine-year-old, that school literacy is narrowly defined.

DISCUSSION

In order to meet the needs of our U.S. society, which is rapidly becoming more culturally diverse, our literacy programs should offer more than sensitivity training, human relations, or attitudinal shifts to issues of culture and linguistic diversity. Programs are needed that will also help teachers transform their thinking about the role of language and culture in literacy development. It is simply not enough to inform teachers of what they do not know. Teachers need to question "cultural bumps," or mismatches in expectations of performance in literacy development (Garcia, 1994, personal communication). As Barnitz (1994) states, "Teachers must recognize difference as manifestations of cultural discourse which can be expanded rather than interrupted or suppressed" (p. 587).

What I see is an institutionalized racism that is grounded in the theories used to discuss literacy and to inform and educate teachers and teacher educators. I believe that we need to enhance preservice teacher curricula and education. The current method of dispersing concepts of diversity, inclusivity, or multiculturalism across several courses, hoping students will synthesize these issues into a workable whole, has been ineffective. Preservice teachers also need intensive education in understanding the dynamic role that culture plays in language and literacy development and in defining school literacy.

In a preservice teacher education course I teach, I use literature authored by domestic minority men and women as a starting point for preservice teachers to begin to reflect on their cultural assumptions about how they "read the word and the world" (Freire, 1985). The method has been effective in helping many students face their own, heretofore unvoiced, assumptions of their own culture and the cultures of other groups.

Most of my students are in their early twenties and have never really concerned themselves with issues of race. Even the students who are members of U.S. minority groups prefer not to discuss race, ethnicity, or culture openly. At the opening of class, for example, many of my students think that their cultural understanding will not affect the students they teach. They believe that their most important concern should be the subject matter and how to transmit effectively a love for their subject to their students. Some of my students also have difficulty understanding the notion of institutionalized racism in U.S. public education. It is at this point in the course that I begin to share the daily occurrences in the lives of my children. Further, some of my European American students see themselves only as "American" and do not wish to deal with their heritage. They want to minimize any tie to Europe and only concentrate on their "Americanness." Some students believe that most U.S. minority group members are poor people, and that most poor people (from all racial groups, but especially those seen most frequently in the media — African Americans and Latinos) really don't care about their children's education. Some also think that children from minority groups don't care about their own education. Most of my students have not even considered how to prepare to teach in multicultural or multilingual classrooms. They tend to live under the false assumption that they can get jobs in homogeneous, suburban school districts.

As in most preservice teacher education courses nationwide, my students are predominantly European American women. However, in each of my classes, I have had at least one U.S. minority group member. The presence of members from these groups has helped give voice to the concerns of their various communities. My courses are elective, which I believe is important, because it means that the students in my class are interested in issues of diversity. In the best of all worlds, all students would be so inclined, but they are not.

One of the first things I do to help my students become aware of their own cultural understandings is to have them write an autobiographical essay. The essay requires them to trace their ancestry over four or five generations, and to explain their families' use of language, food traditions, and other interesting cultural habits. The essays are shared first in small groups and then with the whole class. In this way, students can readily understand that everyone is a product of their culture, knowingly or not. I too share my cultural and ethnic background. As a person of African, Native, and European American descent, yet who looks only African American, I use my background and life as a springboard for discussions of students' cultural diversity and the limited conception of "culture" in most schools. Since this is a semester-long course, we have the time to engage in many activities, such as community and faculty presentations, videos, and readings by U.S. minority members. However, I believe that some of the most productive work occurs in the small group discussions my students have with each other as they respond to literature written by U.S. minority group members. For example, recently we read a number of novels written by Asian Americans. Many of my students had not heard of the internment of Japanese Americans during World War II.

After my students and I have reflected upon the cultural assumptions from which we perceive our world (and those worlds that might differ from our own), we begin to address teachers' roles and how their cultural assumptions affect the decisions they make, their interactions with students, and their selection of teaching materials. I then give the students opportunities to use their growing understanding of cultural knowledge in lessons they design and teach. My students are all required to teach two literacy lessons during the semester. Many of them choose activities that require participants to work together in cooperative learning groups. Four examples come to

mind. One student asked each of us to recall an event using the Native American concept of a "skin story" — drawing on animal pelts — to create pictograph symbols to
relate that event. Another student separated class members by attributes they could
not control (gender, hair color, size of feet). The "minority" group members (men in
this case) were seated in the front of the classroom and were the only students the
leader of the exercise asked to respond to her questions. In a third example, a student
distributed a series of photographs to small groups and had each group classify the
people in the photos, rating them on attributes such as who appeared most intelligent, most successful, and nicest. Finally, a student asked us to read current newspaper articles about war-torn countries and write a diary entry or letter to a government
official from the perspective of someone in the country. Through such exercises and
activities, my students have learned that culture is a complex issue, one that cannot
be taken lightly. They learn to think and act reflectively and become predisposed to
considering issues of race, class, gender, age, and sexual preference. Moreover, they
understand that their decisions must be based on more than theory; they must also
consider the interrelationship of power and knowledge.

I also design in-class lessons around students' responses to the authentic texts
they have read. Throughout their field experiences, I have been impressed by the culturally responsive approach to literacy and literature that many of my students have
taken with them into the field. For example, one of my students invited recent Asian
immigrants to her eighth-grade class to be interviewed by her students. She believed
that the face-to-face interactions her students had during the interviews allowed
them to understand better the hardships endured by the new U.S. citizens. Another
student taught *Huckleberry Finn*. She began the lesson by sharing the historical context in which the novel was written, a model I insist each student use in my class.
When confronted by an African American student about the use of the word "nigger"
in the novel, she was able to facilitate a group discussion on the use of derogatory
terms. She believed that membership in my class enabled her to deal openly with the
student and the offensive term. Her experience demonstrates that it is possible to create multicultural learning communities within classrooms that are based on critical
literacy theory that validates and legitimizes all learners.

CONCLUSION

In this chapter, I have argued that for school literacy to begin to move beyond its
"neutral" conception of culture, educators at all levels must acknowledge the role and
importance of more than one culture in defining school literacy. Educators have not
effectively built upon the culture and language of every child, and have set arbitrary
standards of acceptance and defined them as normative. I have also argued for the
reconceptualization and program development of school literacy, not to dismantle,
but to strengthen, literacy frameworks. We can and must do a better job of inviting all
students to the literacy table and including them in conversations on school literacy.

I had initial misgivings about sharing my conversation with Jake, as I feared that
my thinking would be misinterpreted. My fears lay with the "predictable inability"

(West, 1993) of some European Americans to consider honestly the shortcomings of programs they espouse as universal. In addition, I was concerned that my colleagues would view the conversation as one isolated event, ignoring the fact that there are countless instances of narrow cultural constructions of literacy in the daily lives of culturally and linguistically diverse children. I was also reluctant to give such an intimate look into my private world. Therefore, I hope that sharing the incident opens conversations about reconceptualizing and reforming school literacy. When I wonder if I've done the right thing, I recall Jake saying to his older brothers, "I want to share a picture of my real self."

NOTES

1. Going to the barbershop and getting a haircut is a bimonthly occurrence for many African American males. A number of Jake's classmates differed in their definition of what constituted a "part"; however, the other African American children in his class have a similar cultural understanding of the term.

2. As a Writing Workshop parent volunteer in his class, I know that Jake's class consists of ten European American boys, nine European American girls, four African American boys, two African American girls, and one Asian American girl. The class is taught by a European American woman with over twenty years of experience. Also, during this school year, there have been three student teachers (all European American women) and several other parent volunteers (also European American women).

3. In the fall of 1993 I taught a pilot course, which included multicultural education, reading methods for grades six–twelve, and literature for grades six–twelve with special emphasis on multicultural literature.

4. To me, "growing literateness" means an understanding of how language, reading, and writing fit into the communication patterns of home and school life. It can also mean the development of literate behaviors, the adoption of literate attitudes, and the confidence that allows one to define oneself as a reader and a writer.

5. Selfhood, as used in this article, means the awareness of oneself as a person, in particular as a person who belongs to a specific culturally and linguistically distinct group.

6. Cose's (1993) book, *The Rage of a Privileged Class*, gives examples of the frustration experienced by other middle-class African Americans who believed that by doing everything according to plan they would reap just rewards. For example, Cose quotes Darwin Davis, senior vice president of Equitable Life Assurance Society: "They [young Black managers] have an even worse problem [than I did] because they've got M.B.A.'s from Harvard. They did all the things that you're supposed to do . . . and things are supposed to happen" (p. 76).

    By *history*, I mean how the inequalities that exist in schools reflect a much greater history of institutionalized inequalities. By *tradition*, I mean teachers' tendency to teach how they were taught. Whether history or tradition is the overriding factor in this instance, I am not sure.

7. Silencing, as used by Michelle Fine (1987), "constitutes a process of institutionalized policies and practices which obscure the very social, economic and therefore experiential conditions of students' daily lives, and which expel from written, oral, and nonverbal expression substantive and critical `talk' about these conditions. . . . Silencing constitutes the process by which contradictory evidence, ideologies, and experiences find themselves buried, camouflaged, and discredited" (p. 157).

8. *Fingerplay* is a term often used to describe actions made with the fingers as children sing a song. For example, the motions used with the song "The Itsy Bitsy Spider" are fingerplay.

9. During my years as a classroom teacher, many parents asked what type of reading program I planned to use. While most parents do not use the term *literacy programs* or inquire about writ-

ing programs per se, they do inquire about reading. I have also found that parents are interested in the methods used to teach spelling and vocabulary.

10. Activity centers are areas set aside for special activities. For example, the science center, math center, etc., all have activities specifically designed for children interested in learning more about a selected topic.

11. Many stories contained in basals, like the one Jake used in second grade, are written by teams of authors seeking to control vocabulary or teach specific skills. Basal stories are often abridged or edited versions of original works, and in some instances, such as folk tales, legends, and fairy tales, are translations or a retelling of the original.

12. Recently, Hamilton (1989) used the term *parallel cultures* to refer to the historical experiences of domestic minorities in the United States. *Parallel* conveys a sense of coexistence with the more dominant European American culture so loosely referred to as American culture. The term *domestic minorities* is used to refer to minority groups that have a long history in this country (African Americans, Asian Americans, etc.) but whose forefathers and foremothers lived elsewhere — except in the case of Native Americans.

REFERENCES

Apple, M. (1992). The text and cultural politics. *Educational Researcher, 21*(7), 4–11, 19.

Au, K. (1993). *Literacy instruction in multicultural settings*. Fort Worth, TX: Harcourt Brace Jovanovich.

Barnitz, J. (1994). Discourse diversity: Principles for authentic talk and literacy instruction. *Journal of Reading, 37*, 586–591.

Barrera, R. (1992). The cultural gap in literature-based literacy instruction. *Education and Urban Society, 24*, 227–243.

Cook-Gumperz, J. (Ed). (1986). *The social construction of literacy*. Cambridge, Eng.: Cambridge University Press.

Cose, E. (1993). *The rage of a privileged class*. New York: Harper Collins.

Darder, A. (1991). *Culture and power in the classroom: A critical foundation for bicultural education*. New York: Bergin & Garvey.

Delpit, L. (1986). Skills and other dilemmas of a progressive Black educator. *Harvard Educational Review, 56*, 379–385.

Delpit, L. (1988). The silenced dialogue: Power and pedagogy in educating other people's children. *Harvard Educational Review, 58*, 280–298.

Delpit, L. (1991). A conversation with Lisa Delpit. *Language Arts, 68*, 541–547.

Delpit, L. (1993). The politics of teaching literate discourse. In T. Perry & J. Fraser (Eds.), *Freedom's plow: Teaching in the multicultural classroom* (pp. 285–295). New York: Routledge.

Du Bois, W. E. B. (1965). *The souls of Black folks*. New York: Bantam. (Original work published in 1903)

Ellison, R. (1952). *Invisible man*. New York: Random House.

Fine, M. (1987). Silencing in public schools. *Language Arts, 64*, 157–174.

Freire, P. (1985). Reading the world and the word: An interview with Paulo Freire. *Language Arts, 62*, 15–21.

Freire, P., & Macedo, D. (1987). *Literacy: Reading the world and the word*. South Hadley, MA: Bergin & Garvey.

Giroux, H. (1987). Critical literacy and student experience: Donald Graves' approach to literacy. *Language Arts, 64*, 175–181.

Goodman, K. (1986). *What's whole in whole language?* Portsmouth, NH: Heinemann.

Goodman, K. (1989). Whole-language research: Foundations and development. *Elementary School Journal, 90*, 207–221.

Gutierrez, K. (1992). A comparison of instructional contexts in writing process classrooms with Latino children. *Education and Urban Society, 24*, 244–262.

Halliday, M. (1975). *Learn how to mean*. London: Edward Arnold.

Hamilton, V. (1989). Acceptance speech, Boston Globe–Horn Book Award, 1988. *Horn Book, 65*(2), 183.

Heath, S. (1983). *Ways with words: Language, life and work in the communities and classrooms*. Cambridge, Eng.: Cambridge University Press.

Hirsch, E. (1987). *Cultural literacy: What every American needs to know*. Boston: Houghton Mifflin.

Hughes, L. (1951). Theme for English B. In L. Hughes, *Montage of a dream deferred* (pp. 39–40). New York: Henry Holt.

Labov, W. (1972). The logic of nonstandard English. In R. D. Abrahams & R. C. Troike (Eds.), *Language and cultural diversity in American education* (pp. 225–261). Englewood Cliffs, NJ: Prentice Hall.

McLaren, P. (1988). Culture or canon? Critical pedagogy and the politics of literacy. *Harvard Educational Review, 58*, 213–234.

Meek, M. (1982). *Learning to read*. Portsmouth, NH: Heinemann.

Morrison, T. (1992). *Playing in the dark: Whiteness and the literary imagination*. Cambridge, MA: Harvard University Press.

Morrow, L. (1992). The impact of a literature-based program on literacy achievement, use of literature, and attitudes of children from minority backgrounds. *Reading Research Quarterly, 27*, 251–275.

Ovando, C., & Collier, V. (1985). *Bilingual and ESL classrooms: Teaching in multicultural contexts*. New York: McGraw-Hill.

Reyes, M. de la Luz. (1992). Challenging venerable assumptions: Literacy instruction for linguistically different students. *Harvard Educational Review, 62*, 427–446.

Reyes, M. de la Luz, & Laliberty, E. (1992). A teacher's "Pied Piper" effect on young authors. *Education and Urban Society, 24*, 263–278.

Reyes, M. de la Luz, & Molner, L. (1991). Instructional strategies for second-language learners in content areas. *Journal of Reading, 35*, 96–103.

Sawyer, D., & Rodriguez, C. (1992). How native Canadians view literacy: A summary of findings. *Journal of Reading, 36*, 284–293.

Scheurich, J. (1992). Toward a White discourse on White racism. *Educational Researcher, 22*(8), 5–10.

Vygotsky, L. (1978). *Mind in society*. Cambridge, MA: Harvard University Press.

West, C. (1993). *Race matters*. Boston: Beacon Press.

Woodson, C. (1990). *The mis-education of the Negro*. Nashville, TN: Winston-Derek. (Original work published 1933)

Why the "Monkeys Passage" Bombed: Tests, Genres, and Teaching

BONNY NORTON*

PIPPA STEIN

Insurgent readings are not simply struggles over the sign — what a text means — but actually struggles over forms of life, struggles over how people's identities will be constituted and history lived. (Simon, 1992, p. 116)

We wish to relate a cautionary tale of an experience in a high school graduation class in Johannesburg, South Africa, in which we piloted a passage from a reading test to be used for admissions purposes at the University of the Witwatersrand (Wits), Johannesburg. The piloting of a reading passage about an encounter between monkeys and humans, what we call the "monkeys passage," began as a routine procedure and turned into a classroom experience that disrupted our assumptions about tests, texts, and teaching. We believe that the process we underwent provides a window onto a number of important issues in assessment, reading, and pedagogy that are of importance not only in the South African context, but also for many teachers in the wider educational community who are concerned about issues of educational equity.

ADMISSIONS TESTING IN POST-APARTHEID SOUTH AFRICA

Educational assessment is a growing industry in post-apartheid South Africa. Institutions across the country, from schools and universities to businesses and corporations, are attempting to identify students of color who have the potential to succeed academically and professionally, despite the debilitating effects of an apartheid legacy (Yeld & Haeck, 1993).

At the end of secondary school in South Africa, all students write a national matriculation examination based on the courses they have taken for graduation purposes. In the apartheid era, different racial groups had different matriculation examinations, a practice that is in the process of being dismantled. All students who pass

---

*This article was originally published under the name Bonny Norton Peirce.

Harvard Educational Review   Vol. 65   No. 1   Spring 1995, 50–65

these examinations receive a secondary school certificate. Some of these students will also qualify for a university entrance certificate. Because of high demand in some universities, such as Wits, some faculties and departments impose additional cutoff points for entry, over and above the government-stipulated criteria for university admission.

An additional barrier for Black students is the status of the English language, notwithstanding the fact that there are now eleven official languages in South Africa. Although English is the first language of less than 10 percent of the population, and only one of the official languages, it is de facto the most dominant language in the society. Black South Africans, who constitute the majority of the South African population, frequently speak two or three languages, but do not speak English as their first language. Of particular relevance to this article is the fact that English is the medium of instruction in the majority of universities in the country. Thus, the Wits University requirement (as stated in the General Information for Applicants, 1994) that students in all faculties must be proficient in English is a particularly onerous requirement for Black students.

The matriculation examination that most students write has been an unreliable predictor of Black student success, and has often served as a barrier to their admission to universities. Since 1985, the Faculty of Arts of Wits University has been administering an alternative admissions procedure to identify students who have fulfilled the requirements for university entrance, but who nevertheless fall below the cutoff point for automatic entry into the Faculty of Arts (Stack, 1994). Currently the three main components of the alternative admissions procedure are a test of English-language usage, a test of reasoning and table reading, and a biographical questionnaire. Students within the Black community who have been particularly disadvantaged by apartheid education are the main target group for the Faculty of Arts Admissions Committee.

The Faculty of Arts English test seeks to determine the extent to which applicants, most of whom are English Language Learners (ELLs), can cope with the language demands of an English-medium university.[1] The purpose of the test is to facilitate the admission of students into the Faculty of Arts who would otherwise be denied admission, based on their matriculation examination results.

In our respective capacities as teacher educator (Stein) and language testing specialist (Norton), we have participated in the development of this English proficiency test, currently referred to as the "Exercise in English Language Usage."[2] Pippa Stein is a White South African woman who has worked in English-language teacher education at the preservice and in-service level since 1980. She is based at Wits University, working at a preservice level with secondary school teachers who intend to teach in multicultural, multilingual secondary school classrooms. Bonny Norton is a White woman who has worked in language education in South Africa, Canada, and the United States. She received her training in language test development at the Educational Testing Service in Princeton, New Jersey, from 1984 to 1987, and was invited by the Faculty of Arts of Wits University in 1991 to help revise their English admissions test. At the time the research was conducted, Norton was a postdoctoral fellow in the Modern Language Centre, Ontario Institute for Studies in Education, Toronto, Canada. She spent several months in 1991, and again in 1993–1994, as a visiting scholar at Wits University. Norton and Stein have mutual interests in assessment, literacy, and educational equity, and were both members of the Faculty of Arts Admissions Committee in 1991.

The English proficiency test has undergone many revisions since it was first developed in 1985. Although the university is now in a post-apartheid era, it still needs to set criteria for admission because of high student demand for admission. The 1992 version of the English test had three components: a short, multiple-choice reading test, a longer comprehension test with short answer questions, and an essay question. The monkeys passage, based on a local Johannesburg newspaper article, and a set of multiple-choice questions on the text were to be included in the first component of the short, multiple-choice reading test. The purpose of the first component of the test was to serve as an initial screening device to identify the applicants who did not perform well on the monkeys passage test and exclude them from further consideration for alternative admission.

Below is the text of the monkeys passage, followed by the multiple-choice questions:

MONKEYS ON RAMPAGE*

A troop of about 80 monkeys, enraged after a mother monkey and her baby were caught in a trap, went on the rampage at a Durban home at the weekend attacking two policemen who were forced to flee and call for help. A 14-year-old boy also had to run for his life and reached the safety of a home split seconds before a full-grown monkey hurled itself against the door. The troop also attacked a house, banging windows and doors.

Mrs Kittie Lambrechts, 59, of Firdale Road, Sea View, told reporters how the monkeys' behaviour was sparked off by events on Saturday. She said her family had been pestered by monkeys for over a year.

"They come nearly every day, and they steal all the fruit from our fruit trees before it's ripe enough to pick," she complained. "We didn't know what to do, so we wrote a letter to the Durban Corporation. They said that it would be unsafe to use guns in the neighborhood, and that we should not poison the monkeys because sometimes dogs and cats eat the poison; rather, we should set traps. On Saturday we bought a trap and put it in our garden. Shortly afterwards, the monkeys arrived and a mother and her baby were caught in the trap. The whole troop went into a raging fury and attacked us. Edwin Schultz, a young visitor from the Transvaal, had to run for his life and slammed the door closed just before a full-grown monkey could get hold of him. It jumped against the door. The troop attacked our home and hit against the doors and windows. It was terrifying."

Mrs Lambrechts telephoned the police and Const N M Moodley and Const E Coetzer of the Bellair police station went to investigate. But when they arrived, the troop turned on them and they had to run for cover as well. "The men ran to their van and called for help while monkeys surrounded them and jumped against the vehicle," Mrs. Lambrechts said. Police armed with shotguns arrived on the scene and four monkeys were shot dead. The troop then fled into the bushes, apparently because their leader had been among the monkeys shot dead.

*This material has been adapted from *The Star*, a Johannesburg-based newspaper within the Independent News & Media group.

1. This newspaper article is about
   (a) Edwin Schultz's visit to Durban from the Transvaal;
   (b) how Mrs Lambrechts runs her fruit business;
   (c) monkeys that attacked people;
   (d) the accidental poisoning of dogs and cats.

2. A "troop" of monkeys is
   (a) monkeys that live near people;
   (b) any group of monkeys living together;
   (c) any group of animals living together;
   (d) monkeys having the same mother.

3. Why were the monkeys considered pests?
   (a) The monkeys were dangerous and attacked people.
   (b) The monkeys made a lot of noise and disturbed the family.
   (c) The monkeys took unripe fruit from the garden.
   (d) The monkeys made a mess in the garden.

4. The Durban Corporation advised Mrs Lambrechts
   (a) to shoot dead the leader of the troop;
   (b) to set traps in her garden;
   (c) to poison the fruit in her trees;
   (d) to telephone the police.

5. When the monkeys went on their rampage,
   (a) Mrs Lambrechts was enraged;
   (b) Mrs Lambrechts' husband called the police;
   (c) Mrs Lambrechts' son was chased by a full-grown monkey;
   (d) Mrs Lambrechts was terrified.

6. Edwin Schultz, at the time of the story,
   (a) was visiting the Transvaal;
   (b) was 14 years old;
   (c) lived on Firdale Road in Sea View;
   (d) was caught by a full-grown monkey.

7. Const Moodley and Const Coetzer
   (a) shot dead the leader of the troop;
   (b) called for help;
   (c) never left their van;
   (d) interviewed Mrs Lambrechts.

8. Why did the monkeys flee into the bushes?
   (a) Police arrived with shotguns.
   (b) The monkeys had already chased the people inside.
   (c) Their leader had been shot dead.
   (d) Their leader led them into the bushes.

9. How many monkeys were shot dead by the police?
   (a) 1 (the leader)
   (b) 4
   (c) 5
   (d) all of them

10. This article was written by
   (a) Const E Coetzer;
   (b) a witness;
   (c) Kittie Lambrechts;
   (d) a journalist.

At a Faculty of Arts test development meeting in August 1991, Norton raised questions about the suitability of the monkeys passage text for Black students. She was concerned that in the prevailing political climate of violence and instability, the young adults whose communities had been most affected by violence might become distressed by the passage. Her primary concern was that if test takers became unduly disturbed by the content of the test, their performance might be compromised. This, in turn, would weaken the validity of the test and undermine the credibility of the alternative admissions procedure in the Faculty of Arts. Norton suggested that the text be piloted on a sample of the target population to determine whether the passage might be disturbing to test-takers. Stein volunteered to administer the test to a graduation class of Black students in a Johannesburg secondary school. The following section is Stein's personal narrative describing the testing event.

STEIN: PILOTING THE TEST

In August and September of 1991, I piloted the first section of the proposed 1992 English Proficiency Test with Black high school students whose first language was not English. I had been involved in preservice teacher development work in local Black high schools since 1986. Part of my job was to visit teacher-trainees who were completing their practicum in English-language teaching in local schools. Through this work, I had established connections with a large network of schools, particularly in downtown Johannesburg. It was in one of these schools that I wished to pilot this section of the test.

This secondary school had been recently established by a group of private individuals for students from the surrounding segregated townships whose schooling had been interrupted by the chronic instability and violence of the apartheid era. This was not a state-run school and it had no state subsidy. As a privately run enterprise, it was financially dependent on private funds from the commercial sector and tuition paid by students.

The school of four hundred students was housed in a building on a run-down office block. On the day I visited, a nearby building was being demolished. There was constant traffic outside the main classrooms. Material resources were scarce: there were no photocopying or reproduction facilities, few textbooks or exercise books, and no overhead projectors. During my visit, I learned that a group of students had been suspended from classes for not having paid their fees. In my view, the school environment, administratively and educationally, was not conducive to sustained and focused learning.

The principal allowed me to conduct the piloting procedure with the graduation class who, one month later, would be writing their matriculation examinations. I was introduced to the students' English teacher. I told her that I was evaluating the suitability of a reading comprehension passage that was possibly going to be used for examination. She introduced me to her nineteen students as a "lecturer from Wits" and asked if they would be prepared to take a short reading comprehension test for me. Even though the students' lunch break was about to begin, they agreed to take the test. From the expressions on students' faces, I was concerned that many were apprehensive. I assured them that I was in no way assessing their individual abilities, but rather the suitability of the test. I indicated that the results of the test would not affect their grades or be used against them in any way. This statement appeared to put them at ease. I also introduced the students to Jean Ure, a visiting colleague from Edinburgh, Scotland. A colleague of mine had asked me if Ure could accompany me on my school visits that day, and I asked Ure if she would help me to administer the test. Later, after the class, she commented on how interesting she had found the experience, and I asked her to record what she had observed. My main purpose for this was to have a written record from a different perspective to present at the Admissions Committee meeting the next day. The majority of the class took between nine and twelve minutes to complete the test.

After the students had completed the test, I wanted to initiate an informal discussion with them on their responses to the text. I have enough experience as a teacher to know that in order to do this successfully, I had to try to change the atmosphere in the classroom from the formality of the testing event to a more informal context that would facilitate open discussion. I had to shift my position from a subjective "tester" to that of a "conversational partner." For me, this shift is deeply connected to the spatial and body relationships in the classroom, so I knew I had to change my physical position in relationship to the students. I had to shift from the position of being the "surveillant" in the testing event, where I had stood and walked around the classroom, to one of conversational partner, where I sat informally on one of the desks. In retrospect, it is interesting to note that I was not ready to relinquish complete control — I was still sitting on the desks "above" the general sightline of the class.

I asked the students, "What did you think of the passage?"[3] The first student to answer said that it was "funny." "What do you mean, 'funny'?" I asked. At this point, other students started to participate in the discussion, which rapidly became centered on the topic of monkeys. It became clear to me as the discussion progressed that the use of the word "funny" specifically meant "strange" or "threatening." One woman explained the cultural significance of monkeys for her:

> I was offended by the passage because monkeys have a special significance in our culture. . . . They are associated with witchcraft.

Other students pointed out the racist associations:

> Black people are often thought of as monkeys.

Building on their readings of the monkeys as "Black people" in this text, several students interpreted the text as an extended metaphor for Black and White social relations:

> It's about Black people, who are the "monkeys" "on the rampage" in White people's homes.

This discussion led to an animated debate among the students on the issue of land ownership:

> It's about who owns the land — the monkeys think the land belongs to them but the Whites think they own the land.

> How are the monkeys supposed to know about private ownership of property?

Many students expressed sympathy for the monkeys and deep rejection of their violent treatment at the hands of the police:

> Why did they need to shoot the monkeys? The monkeys were hungry. Why don't they have the right to pick the fruit?

> I don't like the violence in this passage. We live with violence . . . why do we need to read about it?

> It was unnecessary to shoot the monkeys. They should have found other ways of dealing with the problem.

However, a few students rejected these alternative readings of the text:

> I think it's just a story about monkeys. It was nice and easy. I hope we get something like this in the final exam.

The atmosphere in the classroom became more and more charged as the students became increasingly interested in debating the moral issues raised in this text: Who owns the land? Why should the monkeys go hungry? Which parties have the right to the fruit? Why not seek nonviolent solutions to the problem? Most of the students entering the discussion read the monkeys passage as an example of racist discourse and appeared to identify with the plight of the dispossessed monkeys. Jean Ure described the atmosphere in the classroom in a written account:

> This test, which the students appeared to do quite carefully but without enthusiasm, led to an increasingly richer and more impressive discussion following questions pressed on them consistently and persistently by PS [Pippa Stein], which gradually broke down an initial reserve and which by the end, most of them seemed to find exciting. . . . The questions brought out a deeply felt rejection of the text, on a variety of grounds. . . . Two men, older than the rest, objected on the grounds both

of the violence extended to the animals and to the reporting of violence in these terms. . . . I had the impression that, although this test proved excellent for discussion, and the discussion was cathartic, not only would it have been disastrous as a test, but that it worked as well as it did because of the shared, communal nature of the discussion.

My own response to what was emerging from the discussion was complex. I was completely taken by surprise at the students' reading of the text as racist. My reading of this text as a simple factual report about monkeys in Durban shot by the police was fundamentally challenged by the students. I was embarrassed that I had not been more sensitive to a possible reading of this text as racist.

I left the class feeling confused and disoriented. I had entered the classroom with what I assumed to be a "universal" understanding of the monkeys passage as a factual account of monkeys who are a nuisance to a Durban family and who are shot by the police. My assumptions about the meanings of a text were seriously challenged. Where does the meaning of a text lie? Is this text about monkeys or is it about the dispossessed? What discursive histories did each individual student bring to bear on that text in that particular place at that particular moment?

Another assumption was challenged as well: my assumption that high school students are relatively naive about the ways in which they might use the different readings of text to their advantage. In this classroom, students were extremely adept at juggling a series of different readings in their heads, which they used appropriately, according to the demands of the social occasion.

I reported back to the Faculty of Arts Admissions Committee on how the students had responded to the test. The monkeys passage was rejected by the committee on the grounds that it might be interpreted by test takers as a racist text.

ANALYSIS: TEXTS AND GENRES

From such an impassioned discussion of the offensiveness of the passage, we were concerned that the students' performance on the test might be compromised. We were surprised that so many (63 percent of the students) scored high (80 percent correct). In order to address this paradox, we turned to recent developments in genre analysis. While genre analysis has been used in a wide variety of fields, such as literary studies, linguistics, and rhetoric (Swales, 1990), it has only recently been applied to the field of language testing, where the standardized reading test has been framed as a particular genre (Norton Peirce, 1992).

Our conception of "genre" is not the more conventional notion of "text type" as, for example, a sonnet, term paper, interview, or prayer. Drawing on Kress (1989, 1991, 1993), we conceive of a genre as a social process in which different texts — either oral or written — are socially constructed:

> Language always happens as text; and as text, it inevitably occurs in a particular generic form. That generic form arises out of the action of social subjects in particular social situations. (Kress, 1993, p. 27)

In Kress's terms, a genre is constituted within and by a particular social occasion that has a conventionalized structure, and that functions within the context of larger institutional and social processes. In this formulation, the social occasions that constitute a genre may be formulaic and ritualized, such as a wedding or committee meeting, or less ritualized, such as a casual conversation. The important point is that the conventionalized forms of these occasions, along with the organization, purpose, and intention of the participants within the occasion, give rise to the meanings associated with the specific genre.

A central aspect of Kress's formulation of genre concerns the differences between spoken language and written language:

> A social theory of genre will need to be closely attentive to the constantly shifting relations between the language in the spoken and in the written mode, and its relations to shifts in power. (1993, p. 37)

The immediate presence of an audience in speech makes it potentially interactional and spontaneous. Both speakers and listeners jointly construct a world of shared meanings, constantly modifying and elaborating according to the responses of the moment. Turn-taking patterns shift according to the power relations between the interlocutors. In a conversation, for example, where the power relations may be relatively equitable, turn-taking may be subject to negotiation. In a typical classroom lesson, on the other hand, the interaction between teacher and students may be controlled to a greater extent by the teacher.

Kress (1989) argues that the power relations between participants in an interaction have a particular effect on the social meanings of the texts constructed within a given genre. In essence, the *mechanism* of interaction — the conventionalized form of the genre — is of primary importance in genres where a greater power difference exists between the participants, while the *substance* of the interaction — the content — is of secondary importance. The power differences also affect the relative "closedness" or "openness" of an interaction — in other words, the extent to which the social meaning of an interaction is open to negotiation. In a lesson — a genre in which the power differentials are great — the interaction is more closed, whereas in a conversation — a genre in which power differentials are reduced — interaction is more open.

Norton Peirce (1992) argues that the standardized reading test is a genre. The value ascribed to texts within the standardized reading test genre is associated with a ritualized social occasion in which participants (test makers and test takers) share a common purpose and set of expectations, but whose relationship is constituted on inequitable terms. The social occasion is characterized by strict time limits in which test takers have little control over the rate at which information is transmitted or needs to be processed. The test takers are expected to be silent at all times, observe rigorous proctoring procedures, and read the text in solitude. Both test makers and test takers recognize that the purpose of the test is to discriminate among readers with reference to an arbitrary criterion established by the test makers. The shared expectations are that the personal experience of the test takers has little relevance to the items being tested, and that the test makers decide what an acceptable reading of the text should be. The relationship between test makers and test takers, a manifestly unequal one, has a direct bearing on the social meaning ascribed to texts in the standardized reading test.

Kress's conception of genre and Norton's conception of the standardized reading test help to make sense of the contrasting readings of the monkeys passage that occurred on September 19, 1991. The intended reading, which occurred during the written test-taking event, positioned the text as a story about monkeys who were a nuisance to a Durban family, and who were accordingly disciplined by the authorities. This intended reading — or what we call the "dominant reading" — was, in fact, partly an artifact of the test maker, as evidenced in the framing of multiple-choice questions and the optional answers provided. The very first question, for example, is phrased as follows: "This newspaper article is about . . ." The test-takers are provided with four options, including the intended answer, "monkeys that attacked people." Question three reinforces the view that the monkeys were "pests," while question five depicts the monkeys' actions as destructive and undisciplined. Although the students were presented with multiple choices, they were not given the option of considering whether the text had multiple meanings. This problem is inherent in the structure of multiple-choice tests.

The divergent reading, or "insurgent reading" (taken from Simon, 1992), which arose out of the discussions following the test-taking event, positioned the text as a metaphor for inequitable social relations between Blacks and Whites in South Africa. Simon's conception of an insurgent reading is a reading produced at a particular point in time and space that contests sets of meanings that hegemonically frame text interpretation. These "sets of meaning" are the taken-for-granted assumptions shared by the writer and the intended audience.

In the case of the monkeys passage, the newspaper reporter who wrote the story takes for granted that the rights of the powerless are secondary to the rights of the powerful, and uses language in such a way that it obscures the manner in which the powerful abuse power. For example, the author positions the actions of the monkeys who were defending a trapped mother and baby as violent and extreme through words such as "rampage," "attacking," and "hurled." Later, the writer does not use the active voice to state that the police "killed" the monkeys. Instead the writer uses the agentless passive voice to indicate that the monkeys were "shot dead." In the insurgent reading of the text, it is precisely such sets of meaning that are called into question.

Our central argument is that these two contrasting readings of the text were revealed within the context of two very different social occasions, albeit on the same day and in the same place. The first social occasion was the test-taking event, with its ritualized procedures and time constraints. Key features of the first occasion included the emphasis on the written mode, the individual nature of the reading event, the reductive characteristics of the multiple-choice format, and the imposition of direct control by a White adult "expert." The second social occasion was the subsequent class discussion about the text, which began as a typical teacher-initiated discussion but rapidly developed into a conversational interaction. The mode of communication was oral rather than written.

We argue that the difference in the power relations between the teacher (Stein) and the students on the two different social occasions is implicated in the production of two different readings of the monkeys passage. To support our argument, we will explore this dynamic in greater detail.

On the first social occasion, when Stein was introduced and administered the test, she was the "test maker" — a White, English-speaking professional from prestigious Wits University. The students were the "test takers" — Black, secondary school English Language Learners from a city school with scarce resources. Despite Stein's attempts to put students at ease, we believe that her race, class, and institutional position at that point in time put her in a position of power relative to the students. We assert that not one of the students was, in fact, in a position to refuse the request to give up their lunch break in order to take the test. In this context, the mechanism of the interaction — the conventionalized form of the test event — determined to a great extent how the students "read" the text. They understood that they were expected to comply with the dictates of the genre, and to reproduce the test maker's reading of the text. When Stein asked students, "What did you think of the passage?" it is significant that some students responded to her question by highlighting the *level of difficulty* of the passage and not its interest value. Those who said, "It was nice and easy. I hope we get something like this on the final exam," were responding to the text as test. In other words, their interest in the text was structured largely by the *mechanism* of the interaction and not the *substance* of the interaction. Many students voiced less of a concern about a critical analysis of the text than with how easy it was to ascertain a "legitimate" reading of the text — a reading that a lecturer from Wits University would validate.

On the second social occasion, after the tests had been duly collected, we believe that the power relations between Stein and the students altered dramatically. Stein was no longer the test maker nor the students the test takers. Stein sat informally on the desk, inviting comment and criticism. Although she may have positioned herself at the beginning of the discussion as the controller of knowledge and power, her subject position seems to have shifted in the course of the interaction. In Stein's view, the students were no longer apprehensive, and they appeared to become more confident as they verbalized their critical reading of the text. On this social occasion, the substance of the interaction — the content of the text — became more important than the mechanism of the interaction, and there was no longer a single, legitimate reading of the text voiced by the students. Students could draw on their background knowledge and experience to analyze the social meaning of the text, and there was space for multiple readings. Students no longer appeared isolated, silent, and unenthusiastic. They interacted with one another animatedly; they debated, argued, and laughed together. The predominantly *social* context in which this discussion took place allowed for the further development of an insurgent reading that gained widespread support in the class as the discussion deepened.

Given this social occasion, the value ascribed to the monkeys passage was complex and contested. For most students, the text reflected race and class interests at the expense of less powerful communities: "It's about Black people, who are the monkeys 'on the rampage' in White people's homes." "It's about who owns the land." "It's about violence in our society." For other students, the story remained simply a story about monkeys disturbing a family.

In sum, the piloting of the monkeys passage illustrates that the social meaning of a text is not fixed, but is a product of the social occasion in which it is read. This social occasion, in turn, is a complex tapestry in which the status of the participants, their use of body language, their race (among other characteristics), the time and place of interaction, and the purpose of interaction have a direct bearing on the social meaning of texts apprehended within the occasion. Our analysis of the two contrasting readings of the monkeys passage is, however, incomplete. We do not know what power relations existed among the students themselves — whose voices were taken up and whose were ignored. We do not know whether the women were silent, or whether the speakers of minority African language were marginalized, because such differences were not attended to by Stein during the test event.

IMPLICATIONS FOR TESTING AND PEDAGOGY

We have argued thus far that the shifting power relations between Stein and the students on the two different social occasions was an important factor in the construction of the two contrasting readings of the monkeys passage. However, the debate raises two important questions that we wish to address. First, did the monkeys passage test really "bomb"? Second, what are the implications of the test event for pedagogy? The question of whether the monkeys passage really failed to achieve its objectives of measuring English reading comprehension is complex. It is difficult to determine from such a small sample whether the psychometric qualities of the test were satisfactory. The Admissions Committee rejected the text because committee members were concerned that the students had read the text as racist. The committee did not want Wits University, with its stated ideals of nonracialism, implicated in the use of a racist test.

While this issue is clearly an important one that should not be underestimated, there is another issue about the suitability of the text-as-test that should be addressed: the "washback" effect of a test. The washback effect of a test, sometimes referred to as the systemic validity of a test (Alderson & Wall, 1993), refers to the impact of a test on classroom pedagogy, curriculum development, and educational policy. If test developers are accountable only to administrators, then a test such as the monkeys passage, with more trials, might well have proved to be a successful instrument as an initial screening device. If, on the other hand, test developers are concerned about how texts and testing impact learning and teaching in the classroom, a more complex picture emerges (see, for example, Lacelle-Peterson & Rivera, 1994).

It would be paradoxical for a university to promote a student's passive and uncritical reading of a text in an admissions test, and then expect these same "successful" students to display an active and critical approach to learning and testing once they have passed through the university gates. If a student's academic potential is defined as the ability to recognize the assumptions and worldview of test makers, then the monkeys passage did not fail; if, on the other hand, a student's potential is defined as the ability to draw on experience and knowledge to understand and critique existing knowledge, then the monkeys passage has little utility as a testing instrument. In our view, the monkeys passage failed, not because of its psychometric qualities, but because it could not be justified on pedagogical grounds.

Furthermore, even if the ability to recognize the assumptions of test makers is considered acceptable for testing purposes, equity issues become a central concern. In essence, if test makers are drawn from a particular class, a particular race, and a particular gender, then test takers who share these characteristics will be at an advantage relative to other test takers. Clearly, such inequities are not restricted to the testing of English proficiency or language testing in South Africa (see, for example, Hanson, 1993). To promote equity in educational assessment, different stakeholders, such as testers, teachers, administrators, parents, and students should be able to contribute to the test development process.

This does not address our second question, however: What are the implications of the test event for pedagogy? More specifically, how does the teacher create the conditions that will enable students to draw on their experience and understanding of the world to engage with texts and become active, critical readers? We have found Simon's (1992) work on textual interpretation particularly helpful in addressing this question. Drawing on the work of Said (1982), Simon argues that all texts are apprehended within socially regulated discourses, and that there is an "inherent instability" of textual meaning. The very fact that the same students provided at least two different readings of the monkeys passage on the same day and in the same place testifies on behalf of this position. Simon believes, however, that although a text can be read in multiple ways, such a possibility does not mean that we are "adrift in a relativism that challenges nothing and takes us nowhere" (1992, p. 113). He argues that what is pedagogically productive is to ask ourselves what makes insurgent readings possible.

With reference to the monkeys passage, a wide range of social and pedagogical conditions enabled the students to construct an insurgent reading of the text. At one level, the inequitable social and economic conditions that regulated the students' day-to-day lives in South Africa led them to identify with the dispossessed protagonists in the monkeys passage. We question whether White, middle-class students would have been likely to construct a similar reading of this text because the White, middle-class Admissions Committee had not anticipated that the text might be read as racist. As Simon argues:

> [An insurgent reading] ruptures the taken-for-granted grounds of our own understanding and teaches us that the scars and wounds of history cannot be erased within our search for universal truths. (1992, p. 24)

At another level, the pedagogical conditions that made this insurgent reading possible were significant. From the learner's point of view, the context for reading had shifted from a focus on an individual, highly ritualized, and controlled reading event (in the case of the test) to an interactive, collective oral discussion.

Drawing on Simon, we suggest that the challenge for the teacher is to *reframe* the focus of classroom discourse from a consideration of what the text "really" means to a consideration of how multiple readings of the text are socially constructed:

> The question to be asked from an educator's point of view is what discourse is regulating an insurgent reading and whether it would be desirable and possible to support that as a counterdiscursive position. (1992, p. 115)

What this means in practice is that the teacher can use the range of readings produced to explore critically with the students what investments they have in the readings and how these investments intersect with the students' histories, their relationship to the social world, and their desires for the future.[4] It is not possible for a teacher to predict the many readings students may produce from a single text, nor is it easy to predict which text will ignite insurgent readings in which context (Janks, 1993). Clearly, however, when readers' investments and identities are at stake, they may go to great lengths to seek validation for their claims to knowledge and power. What becomes important, then, is that the teacher not uncritically privilege different readings, but instead create possibilities for discussion and analysis of the social construction of these readings.

CONCLUSION

In post-apartheid South Africa, both the National Educational and Policy Initiative reports (NEPI, 1993) and the African National Congress (ANC) draft framework on education and training (1994) promote fundamental principles of nonracism, nonsexism, democracy, and redress. In the wider educational community, both in South Africa and internationally, such principles are inseparable from the promotion of equity in assessment and pedagogical practices. In striving for educational equity, teachers, testers, parents, students, and politicians will be inextricably enmeshed in debates and struggles over the meaning of texts and the purposes of tests.

The struggle over the meaning of the monkeys passage and its place in a university admissions test is part of larger, related questions that have relevance in many international contexts. For example, if students from historically disadvantaged communities seek access to schools, universities, and workplaces, what forms of assessment would give them the best opportunity to demonstrate their talents and abilities? Are students being excluded from certain institutions because they do not share the worldview of test makers, or because they do not have the potential to succeed? Indeed, who determines criteria for "success?" Related questions concern the meaning of texts and the validity of insurgent readings. Who determines what an acceptable reading of a text should be? Which texts are considered works of art and which are relegated to the margins of social life? Such questions, in turn, are inseparable from struggles over the ownership of tests: to whom should test makers be accountable? How should test makers address the diverse interests of stakeholders such as administrators, teachers, students, parents? Who are the test makers?

Our chapter may have raised more questions than it has successfully addressed. However, drawing on our experience with the monkeys passage, we have demonstrated that consideration must be given to the way both tests and textual meanings are socially constructed, and whether these social constructions serve the interests of justice and equality. In addition, we have highlighted a fundamental validity paradox in some language tests that are used for university admissions purposes: While admissions officers may desire language tests that identify critical, independent learners, the testing instruments they use may not give test takers the opportunity to demonstrate such abilities. Furthermore, students of color may feel particularly constrained to draw on their background experience to engage with texts used in tests. We have suggested that both test developers and teachers should use their talents to validate the histories and identities of test takers and students, encouraging them to deconstruct their insurgent readings of texts. In this way, test takers from diverse backgrounds may have the opportunity to demonstrate the richness of their experience, and students may learn not only about their past, but also construct a hopeful vision for their future.

NOTES

1. The term *English Language Learners* is taken from Lacelle-Peterson and Rivera (1994) and refers to students whose first language is not English. The term includes those who are beginning to learn English, as well as those who have considerable proficiency.
2. Many members of the academic staff at Wits have participated in the development of the test, including Norman Blight, Qedusizi Buthelezi, Lorraine Chaskalson, Hilary Janks, Tom Lodge, Debra Nails, Esther Ramani, and Louise Stack.
3. The following quotations are taken from the field notes that I wrote the evening after the testing event.
4. See Norton Peirce (1995) for a discussion of the relationship between investment and social identity.

REFERENCES

African National Congress (ANC). (1994). *A policy framework for education and training.* Johannesburg: National ANC Office.

Alderson, C., & Wall, D. (1993). Does washback exist? *Applied Linguistics, 14,* 115–129.

Hanson, F. A. (1993). *Testing testing: Social consequences of the examined life.* Berkeley: University of California Press.

Janks, H. (1993). *Closed meanings in open schools.* Proceedings of the Australian Reading Association First International Conference, Melbourne, Australia.

Kress, G. (1989). *Linguistic processes in sociocultural practice.* Oxford, Eng.: Oxford University Press.

Kress, G. (1991). Critical discourse analysis. *Annual Review of Applied Linguistics, 11,* 84–89.

Kress, G. (1993). Genre as social process. In B. Cope & M. Kalantzis (Eds.), *The powers of literacy* (pp. 22–37). London: Falmer Press.

Lacelle-Peterson, W., & Rivera, C. (1994). Is it real for all kids? A framework for equitable assessment policies for English Language Learners. *Harvard Educational Review, 64,* 55–75.

National Educational and Policy Initiative. (1993). *Framework report.* Cape Town: Oxford University Press.

Norton Peirce, B. (1992). Demystifying the TOEFL reading test. *TESOL Quarterly, 26,* 665–691.

Norton Peirce, B. (1995). Social identity, investment and language learning. *TESOL Quarterly, 29*(1), 9–31.

Said, E. (1982). *The world, the text and the critic.* Cambridge, MA: Harvard University Press.

Simon, R. (1992). *Teaching against the grain: Texts for a pedagogy of possibility.* New York: Bergin & Garvey.

Stack, L. (1994). *Report to the Arts Faculty Admissions Committee.* Johannesburg: University of the Witwatersrand.

Swales, J. (1990). *Genre analysis: English in academic and research settings.* Cambridge, Eng.: Cambridge University Press.

Yeld, N., & Haeck, W. (1993). Educational histories and academic potential: Can tests deliver? In S. Angeli-Carter (Ed.), *Language in academic development at U.C.T.* Unpublished manuscript.

We would like to thank Heather Brookes, Hilary Janks, Gunther Kress, Nomsa Ngqakayi, Roger Simon, and Sue Starfield for their valuable comments on an earlier draft of this paper. In addition, the support of the Social Sciences and Humanities Research Council of Canada and the Academic Support Programme, University of the Witwatersrand, is gratefully acknowledged.

ABOUT THE AUTHORS

Elsa Roberts Auerbach is Associate Professor of English and Applied Linguistics at the University of Massachusetts Boston. Her work focuses primarily on critical perspectives on adult ESL/literacy, participatory curriculum development, and family literacy. She is coauthor, with B. Barahona, J. Midy, F. Vaquerano, A. Zambrano, and J. Arnaud, of *From the Community to the Community: A Guidebook for Participatory Literacy Training* (1996), and, with N. Wallerstein, of *ESL for Action: Problem Posing at Work* (1987).

Ursula Bellugi is Professor and Director of the Laboratory for Cognitive Neuroscience at the Salk Institute for Biological Studies, located in La Jolla, California. Her research centers around the biological foundations of language and other cognitive functions and their genetic basis. Her most recent publications include *Connecting Cognition, Brain, and Gene: Constraints on Williams Syndrome*, coedited with M. St. George (in press), and, with G. Hickok and E. S. Klima, "Sign Language Aphasia: A Window on the Neural Basis of Language" in *Scientific American* (in press).

Roger Brown, who died in 1997, founded the modern field of developmental psycholinguistics in the 1960s. He was John Lindsley Professor of Psychology at Harvard University, where his research interests included sociolinguistics and politeness theory. He was a recipient of the Fyssen International Prize in Cognitive Sciences. His published works include *Social Psychology: The Second Edition* (1987) and *A First Language* (1973).

Deborah Brandt is Professor of English at the University of Wisconsin–Madison, and a researcher with the National Research Center on English Learning and Achievement. Her professional interests include literacy learning and writing theory. She is author of *Literacy in American Lives* (forthcoming) and *Literacy as Involvement: The Acts of Writers, Readers, and Texts* (1993).

Herlinda Cancino is Professor of Education at San Francisco State University. Her research interests center around second language acquisition and the influence of language on cognition and self-concept. Her publications include *First Language Transfer in the Acquisition of English Locative Prepositions and Genitives by Four Spanish Speakers* (1980) and *Grammatical Morphemes in Second Language Acquisition: Marta* (1976).

Carol Chomsky, a linguist who works in the fields of child language development, psycholinguistics, and reading, is a consultant and a former Lecturer at the Harvard Graduate School of Education. She is also interested in applications of technology in the classroom and develops educational software in the areas of language and reading. She is author of "Reading, Writing, and Phonology" in *Harvard Educational Review* (1970) and *The Acquisition of Syntax in Children from 5 to 10* (1969).

Michael Cole is University Professor of Communication and Psychology at the University of California at San Diego. His current research focuses on cultural theories of mind and human development, which involves a longitudinal study of specially organized after-school educational activity systems. His most recent books are *The Development of Children*, with S. Cole (4th ed., 2000), and *Cultural Psychology: A Once and Future Discipline* (1996). He is also editor of *The Journal of Russian and East European Psychology* and *Mind, Culture, and Activity*.

Emilia Ferreiro is a researcher with the Centro de Investigación y de Estudios Avanzados del Instituto Politécnico Nacional, located in Mexico City. Her primary area of research is literacy development. She is coauthor, with C. Pontecorvo, of "Managing the Written Text: The Beginning of Punctuation in Children's Writing" in *Learning and Instruction* (1999), and author of "The Acquisition of Cultural Objects: The Case of Written Language" in *Prospects* (1996).

Paulo Freire, who died in 1997, was a pioneer in promoting the universal right to education and literacy. He served as Brazil's Secretary of Education, as a Special Advisor in Education to the World Council of Churches in Geneva, Switzerland, and was Professor of Philosophy of Education at the Catholic University of São Paulo and the State University of Campinas, Brazil. His published works include *Literacy: Reading the Word and the World*, coauthored with D. P. Macedo (1987), and his best-known work, *Pedagogy of the Oppressed* (1971).

Kenji Hakuta is the Vida Jacks Professor of Education at Stanford University. His research interests are in the areas of language acquisition and bilingualism, and policy development for the education of language-minority students. He is author of *In Other Words: The Science and Psychology of Second Language Acquisition* (1994) and *Mirror of Language: The Debate on Bilingualism* (1986).

Kit-Tai Hau, Professor and Chair of the Faculty of Education at The Chinese University of Hong Kong, is interested in structural equation modeling, motivation, and educational policy. His publications include "Confirmatory Factor Analysis: Strategies for Small Sample Size" in *Statistical Strategies for Small Sample Research* (edited by R. H. Hoyle, 1999).

Glynda Hull is Associate Professor of Education at the Graduate School of Education, University of California at Berkeley. Her research interests include literacy, work and learning, and community-based education. She is editor of *Changing Work, Changing Workers: Critical Perspectives on Language, Literacy, and Skills* (1997) and coauthor, with J. P. Gee and C. Lankshear, of *The New Work Order: Behind the Language of the New Capitalism* (1996).

Chit-Kwong Kong is a part-time Lecturer in the Faculty of Education at The Chinese University of Hong Kong. His research interests include self-concept, structural education modeling, and multilevel analysis. He is coauthor, with H. W. Marsh and K.-T. Hau, of "Longitudinal Multilevel Modeling of the 'Big Fish Little Pond Effect' on Academic Self-Concept: Counterbalancing Social Comparison and Reflected Glory Effects in Hong Kong High Schools" in *Journal of Personality and Social Psychology* (in press).

Penny Lee is Lecturer and Coordinator in the Master of Education in Applied Linguistics program and the TESOL curriculum course at the Graduate School of Education, The University of Western Australia, Nedlands. She is interested in the role of language in thinking and learning, multilingualism, and linguistic relativity principle. Her publications include "When Is 'Linguistic Relativity' Whorf's Linguistic Relativity?" in *Explorations in*

Linguistic Relativity (edited by M. Putz and M. Verspoor, 2000), and *The Whorf Theory Complex: A Critical Reconstruction* (1996).

Herbert W. Marsh is Professor of Education and Director of the SELF Research Centre at the University of Western Sydney, Macarthur, located in Campbelltown, Australia. His professional interests center around self-concept research, student evaluations of teaching, confirmatory factor analysis, and research design. His recent publications include "Separation of Competency and Affect Components of Multiple Dimensions of Academic Self-Concept: A Developmental Perspective," with R. G. Craven and R. Debus, in *Merill-Palmer Quarterly* (2000), and "Effects of Grading Leniency and Low Workloads on Students' Evaluations of Teaching: Popular Myth, Bias, Validity or Innocent Bystanders?" in *Journal of Educational Psychology* (2000).

Bonny Norton is Associate Professor in the Department of Language and Literacy Education at the University of British Columbia in Vancouver. Her professional interests center around the social and political context of language learning, teaching, and assessment. She is author of *Identity and Language Learning: Gender, Ethnicity and Educational Change* (2000).

David R. Olson is Professor of Applied Psychology at the Ontario Institute for Studies in Education, and University Professor at the University of Toronto. His research focuses on issues of cognition, literacy, and schooling. He is author of *The Study of Education: Mind, School, Society* (forthcoming) and coeditor, with P. Zelazo and J. Astington, of *Developing Theories of Intention* (1999).

Charles Read is Dean of the School of Education and Professor of Linguistics at the University of Wisconsin–Madison. His major teaching and research interests are in linguistics and education, including the phonetic and phonological foundations of reading and writing. He is the coauthor, with R. D. Kent, of *The Acoustic Analysis of Speech* (1992) and author of *Children's Creative Spelling* (1986).

Daniel P. Resnick, Professor of History at Carnegie Mellon University in Pittsburgh, is interested in literacy studies, historical perspectives on public policy, and the history of postsecondary education. His published works include, with J. L. Gordon, "Literacy in Social History" in *Literacy: An International Handbook* (edited by D. A. Wagner, R. L. Venezky, and B. V. Street, 1999), and *Social History and Issues in Human Consciousness: Some Interdisciplinary Connections*, coauthored with L. B. Resnick (1989).

Lauren B. Resnick is Director of the Learning Research and Development Center in the Department of Psychology at the University of Pittsburgh. Her research focuses on assessment, the nature and development of thinking abilities, and the relationship between school learning and everyday competence. She is author of "Literacy in School and Out" in *Daedalus* (1990) and *Education and Learning to Think* (1987).

María de la luz Reyes is Professor Emerita at the University of Colorado in Boulder. She is interested in literacy for students learning English and the education of Mexicano/Latino students. Her current research examines Mexicano/Latino children's development of biliteracy. Her publications include *The Best for Our Children: Critical Perspectives in Literacy for Latinos* (2000) and "Racism in Academia: The Old Wolf Revisited" in *Harvard Educational Review* (1988), both coauthored with J. J. Halcón.

Sylvia Scribner, who died in 1991, was Professor of Psychology in the Developmental Psychology Program of the Graduate Center of the City University of New York, as well as Director of the Laboratory for Cognitive Studies of Work. Her publications include *Psychology of Literacy* (1981) and *Culture and Thought* (1974), both coauthored with M. Cole.

Catherine E. Snow is Henry Lee Shattuck Professor of Education and Chair of Human Development and Psychology at the Harvard Graduate School of Education. Her major research interest is children's language development, including the role of the family and cultural differences in familial roles. Her books on language and literacy development include *Pragmatic Development*, coauthored with A. Ninio (1996), and *Unfulfilled Expectations: Home and School Influences on Literacy*, with W. Barnes, J. Chandler, I. Goodman, and L. Hemphill (1991).

Pippa Stein is a Senior Lecturer in the Department of Applied English Language Studies at the University of Witwatersrand in Johannesburg, South Africa. Her professional interests include social semiotics, multimodal pedagogies, and multiliteracies. She is author of "Rethinking Resources: Multimodal Pedagogies in the ESL Classroom" in *TESOL Quarterly* (2000) and "Multimodal Critical Pedagogies: Finding a More Representative Base for Representation" in *Critical Pedagogies and Language Learning* (edited by B. Norton and K. Tooney, forthcoming).

Sofía A. Vernon is a Professor in the Faculty of Psychology at the Universidad Autónoma de Querétaro in Querétaro, Mexico. Her major professional interests include phonological awareness, teaching of reading and writing in elementary and middle school, and reading comprehension.

Arlette Ingram Willis is Associate Professor at the University of Illinois at Urbana-Champaign. Her research interests include the history of reading research in the United States, sociohistorical foundations of literacy, and teaching/learning multicultural literature for grades 6–12. She is author of "Cultivating Understandings through Reader Response: Dawn's Responses to *The Things They Carried* and *When Heaven and Earth Changed Places*" in *Reader Response in the Classroom* (edited by N. Karolides, 1999) and editor of *Teaching and Using Multicultural Literature in Grades 9–12: Moving beyond the Canon* (1998).

ABOUT THE EDITORS

Sarah W. Beck is a doctoral student in Language and Literacy at the Harvard Graduate School of Education. Her research centers on secondary school writing instruction and assessment; her other professional interests include reading comprehension, discourse analysis, and the relationships among writing, reading, and critical thinking. She has taught English and writing at the high school and college level, and has also worked as a writing consultant to school districts and educational programs.

Leslie Nabors Oláh is a doctoral student in Human Development and Psychology at the Harvard Graduate School of Education. Her current research involves crosslinguistic comparisons of early language acquisition. She has taught ESL at the University of Pennsylvania and the University of California at Berkeley, as well as EFL at the Eötvös Lórand University in Budapest, Hungary. She also served as editor-in-chief of the *Working Papers in Educational Linguistics* at the University of Pennsylvania.

NAME INDEX

Ellul, J., 148
Epstein, J., 383, 384
Ervin, S., 18
Ervin-Tripp, S., 239
Evans, J. F., 207, 209

Farnham, G., 129
Farr, M., 161
Farr, R., 184
Farrell, T., 188
Fathman, A., 239
Ferguson, C. A., 242
Ferreira, M. E., 347
Ferreiro, E., x, xii, 224; *Writing Development: A Neglected Variable in the Consideration of Phonological Awareness*, 309–327
Filby, N., 155, 189
Fine, M., 415
Fingeret, A., 362, 363
Fischer, F., 310
Fisher, C. W., 290
Fishman, J., 295
Fiske, E. B., 355
Flavell, J., 193
Flood, J., 161
Flores, B., 290
Fodor, J. A., 139
Ford, W. G., 153
Fox, B., 310
Fox, L., 197, 365
Francis, W. S., 248, 270
Franks, J. J., 139, 152
Fraser, E., 241
Fraser, K. L., 362
Frauenfelder, U., 232, 239
Freire, P., ix, xi, xii, 47, 331, 382, 405, 406, 412; *The Adult Literacy Process as Cultural Action for Freedom*, 335–351
Fries, C., 226
Frost, J., 323
Fry, C., 193
Frye, N., 143, 156
Functional Illiteracy Hurts Business, 357, 358

Gadamer, H. G., 138
Gaffney, J. S., 301
Gaines, L. J., 356, 357, 358, 364, 370
Gallimore, R., 301
Ganambarr, M., 87, 104
Garcia, E. E., 248
Garcia-Albea, J., 313
Gardner, R. C., 243, 251
Garland, S. B., 356, 359

Garrett, M. F., 139
Garvey, C., 239
Gay, J. P., 137, 152
Gee, J. P., 217
Geisel, T.. *See* Seuss, Dr.
Gelb, I. J., 144
Genesee, F., 250, 256, 257
Giacobbe, M. E., 180
Gibbons, J., 255, 256, 271
Gibson, E. J., 141
Gillis, M., 235, 237, 238
Giroux, H. A., 216, 354, 406
Gleason, J., 180
Gleick, J., 81
Gleitman, H., 180
Gleitman, L., 179
Glick, J., 137, 152
Goedicke, W., 367
Goldenberg, C. N., 383, 386
Goldfield, B., 172, 173
Goldman, S., 363
Goldstein, H., 261, 283, 284
Gombrich, E., 144
Goodman, K. S., 141, 289, 290, 407
Goodman, N., 149
Goodman, P., *Gestalt Therapy: Excitement and Growth in the Human Personality*, 96
Goodman, Y., 290
Goodnow, J., 137
Goody, J., 137, 143, 144, 146, 147, 192, 193, 360
Gorman, C., 355, 357, 358
Gowen, S. G., 202, 366
Graff, H. J., 208, 360, 361
Graves, D. H., 289, 290, 293, 299
Gray, A., 393
Gray, M., 143
Grayson, D., 284
Greene, J., 249
Greene, M., 361, 373, 374
Greenfield, P. M., 137, 150, 188, 189, 190, 192, 196, 301
Greif, E., 180
Grice, H. P., 139
Grubb, F., 203
Grubb, W. N., 373
Gutierrez, K. D., 402; *English Language Arts Framework*, 289

Haeck, W., 419
Hakuta, K., x, xii, 223, 248, 253, 279, 283, 295, 304; *Trends in Second Language Acquisition Research*, 225–246

SUBJECT INDEX

Abstractive processes in cognition, 87–88, 102–108, 340–341

Academic achievement and language of instruction, 256–280

Accountability procedures, language and literacy development, 163, 171

Additive bilingualism, 248–250, 252–253, 257

Adjective and adverb forms, 11

Admissions testing. *See* "Monkeys passage" admissions test

Adult literacy, xii, 331, 335–351. *See also* Workplace literacy

Affrication in phonology, 32–34

African American literacy and culture. *See* School-based literacy and cultural insensitivity

Age(s): critical and optimal for learning a second language, 253–254; linguistic stages, 70–74; maturation, preschooler literacy and language acquisition, 163. *See also* Syntax acquisition

Agreement, calibration of, 90–92, 106, 107–108

Alphabet: ABC books and routinized context, 173–177; development and meaning of, 143–145, 149; phonemes for English, 24; and Western culture, 142; words and phonological awareness, 312. *See also* Bias of language in speech and writing; Writing

Alveolar flaps in phonology, 34–35

American education model of literacy, 122–124, 131

Analytics (Aristotle), 146

An Essay Concerning Human Understanding (Locke), 148

Annunciation and denunciation, utopian pedagogy of, 345–347, 351n23

Assessment issues: Army, historical view of literacy, 129–130; Hong Kong bilingual instruction, 254–255, 259–260, 264–270, 280, 281; workplace literacy, 362–363, 368–370. *See also* "Monkeys passage" admissions test

Autonomous text, 140, 142, 147–148

Basic skills deficits and workplace literacy assessment, 354, 356–357

Bias in language use, 118, 137–160; comprehension and literacy effects, 151–152; essayist technique, 147–150; meaning as explicit in alphabetic writing, 143–145, 146, 149; meaning in oral tradition, 142–143; meaning in text, 138–142; overview, 118, 137–138, 155–157; reading and literacy effects, 155; reasoning and literacy effects, 152–154; written text as exploratory device, 145–147

Bilingual, multilingual, and crosslinguistic issues, x, xii, 223–327; instructional language and immersion in Hong Kong, 223, 247–287; linguistic relativity principle, 77–78; linguistic thinking, 86, 108–109; literacy instruction assumptions, 224, 289–307; overview, x, xii, 223–224; role of practice in acquisition, 180, 195; second language acquisition research trends, 223, 225–246; writing development and phonological awareness, 224, 309–327

Black literacy and culture. *See* "Monkeys passage" admissions test; School-based literacy and cultural insensitivity

Blue-collar worker literacy. *See* Workplace literacy

Calibration of agreement, 90–92, 106, 107–108

Canadian immersion programs, 249–250

Cartesian Linguistics (Chomsky), 351

The Cat in the Hat (Seuss), 172

Chall's five stages of reading, 132

Children, language development in. *See* Cognitive and developmental approach; Syntax acquisition

Children of Promise (Heath and Mangiola), 109

Civic-national schooling model of literacy, 125–128, 131

Coda, intra-syllable components, 310, 311, 312, 313